THE CONSTITUTION
OF THE POST-ECONOMIC STATE

To Victoria,
for the good of all,
for the love of one.

THE CONSTITUTION OF THE POST-ECONOMIC STATE

POST-INDUSTRIAL THEORIES AND POST-ECONOMIC TRENDS IN THE CONTEMPORARY WORLD

VLADISLAV L. INOZEMTSEV

Ashgate

Aldershot • Brookfield USA • Singapore • Sydney

Published by
Ashgate Publishing Limited
Gower House
Croft Road
Aldershot
Hants GU11 3HR
England

Ashgate Publishing Company
Old Post Road
Brookfield
Vermont 05036
USA

British Library Cataloguing in Publication Data
Inozemtsev, Vladislav L.
 The constitution of the post-economic state :
 post-industrial theories and post economic trends in the
 contemporary world
 1. Social indicators 2. Economic indicators 3. Social change
 4. Social prediction
 I. Title
 303.4'9

Library of Congress Cataloging-in-Publication Data
Inozemtsev, Vladislav L. (Vladislav Leonidovich)
 The constitution of the post-economic state : post-industrial
theories and post-economic trends in the contemporary world /
Vladislav L. Inozemtsev.
   p.   cm.
 Includes bibliographical references.
 ISBN 1–84014–481–5 (hb). — ISBN 1–84014–706–7 (pbk.)
 1. Social evolution. 2. Civilization. Modern—Philosophy.
3. Postmodernism—Social aspects. I. Title.
HM106.I559   1998
303.4—dc21
                                                                98–35236
                                                                CIP

Ashgate ISBN 1 84014 481 5 Hbk
Ashgate ISBN 1 84014 706 7 Pbk

Printed and bound in Great Britain by MPG Books Ltd, Bodmin, Cornwall

Contents

Foreword by Mikhael S. Gorbachev　　　　　　　　　xi
Preface　　　　　　　　　　　　　　　　　　　　xiii

Introduction　　　　　　　　　　　　　　　　　　1

PART I　CREATING A CONCEPT

Introduction to Part I　　　　　　　　　　　　　　13

1　Inadequate Theories　　　　　　　　　　　　　17
　　The Traditions of Antiquity　　　　　　　　　　17
　　In the Name of Christ　　　　　　　　　　　　22
　　A 'New Version' of the Social Contract　　　　　28
　　Utopia　　　　　　　　　　　　　　　　　　32

2　Establishing a Coherence　　　　　　　　　　　41
　　The First Steps　　　　　　　　　　　　　　　41
　　The Liberalism of the Modern Age　　　　　　　44
　　The First Attempts at an Economic View of History　47
　　The Making of Positivism　　　　　　　　　　　52

3　Coherent Theories　　　　　　　　　　　　　　63
　　Marxist Conception　　　　　　　　　　　　　63
　　　　General View of History　　　　　　　　　　64
　　　　The Periodization of History　　　　　　　　70
　　　　The Revolutionary Doctrine　　　　　　　　77
　　　　The Marxist Theory's Contradiction and Demise　84
　　Theory of Post-industrial Society　　　　　　　88
　　　　A General Picture of Historical Progress and its
　　　　　　Periodization　　　　　　　　　　　　91
　　　　The Characteristics of Contemporary Post-industrial
　　　　　　Society　　　　　　　　　　　　　　95
　　　　The Prospects for Civilization in the Light of
　　　　　　Post-industrial Theory　　　　　　　　104
　　　　The Evolution of the Theory of Post-industrial Society　107

Two Coherent Theories: The Basic Elements of Similarity
and Mutual Supplementation   109

PART II   POST-ECONOMIC SOCIETY

Introduction to Part II   123

4   The Meaning of Post-economic Society   125
    The Current State of Theory   126
    The Post-economic Condition as Idea and Reality   132

5   Creativity: The Global Challenge to the Economic Order   147
    The Notion of Work and Creativity: Terminology   148
    The Prerequisites for the Formation of Creative Activity   158
        The Development of Material Production and
            Economic Structures: The Objective Component of the
            Prerequisites for Creativity   159
        The Growth of Human Opportunities: The Subjective
            Component of the Prerequisites for Creativity   168
    How Creativity is Manifested in Modern Society   175
        Elements of Creativity and Individual Behaviour   176
        Creativity and the Modern Corporation   184
        The Non-profit Sector: Too Much or Too Little
            Creativity?   195

6   The Main Aspects of Post-economic Revolution   211
    The Destruction of the Market Economy   213
        The Factors of Contemporary Production   217
        Reproduction Processes and the Destruction of Value
            Relations   225
        The Diffusion of Value and the Future of the Market
            Economy   233
    The Displacement of Private Property   245
        Private versus Private: Palliative Solutions   249
        Personal versus Private: a Radical Challenge   257
        State Property: Between Private and Personal   267
    The Elimination of Exploitation and the New Social Conflict   272
        Exploitation: Objective or Perceived?   277
        Class Conflict in the Post-economic Society   286
        Post-economic Causes and Economic Effects   295
    Conclusion   305

7   The Post-economic Transformation and the Modern World   319
    The Roots of Sustainability in the Post-economic Society   323
    The Inner Contradictions of Post-economic Society   343

The Post-industrial World and the External Environment:
    The likely scenario for the interaction   359
    The Economic Aspects of Confrontation   360
    The Ecology and the Making of a Post-economic System   372
    The Problems and Outlook for the World's Poorest
        Regions   381

Conclusion   403

Subject Index   419

Name Index   433

'Nobody can know or hold the secret of the future. . . . . Anyone claiming to have in their pocket a detailed map of that *terra incognita* is insane.'

Auguste Blanqui, *Critique Sociale*

Foreword

Vladislav Inozemtsev is a young academic, a researcher in the Faculty of Economics of Moscow State University. On perusal I have found his new book to be extremely interesting and I draw the attention of Western readers to it.

Inozemtsev has made an interesting attempt to conceptualize the historical place and prospects of modern developed societies as sociological entities of a non-capitalist kind. He detects features in them that show them to have gone far beyond the framework of the abstract model that was accepted as an aim by Russian reformers. One of his conclusions that merits particular attention is that the success of economic development will henceforward be dependent first and foremost on human aptitudes, on the ability to produce information and knowledge, and on the system of guidelines and values that gives point and meaning to human existence. The idea of a 'post-economic' society is one possible explanation for the evolution of modern society and one that, in my opinion, is certainly not the most improbable.

The book is crammed with interesting facts, comparisons and new theoretical arguments and hypotheses. The author reveals a detailed knowledge of the most diverse social theories. He bases the historical section of the work on an analysis of the way views on social progress came into being, starting with the philosophical and economic thought of Classical Antiquity, and he makes use of the most up-to-date information and quotes from the latest publications of Western sociologists and economists. There are undoubtedly points in Inozemtsev's study that are open to dispute. However, although it is possible to disagree with some arguments that he advances as axiomatic, one is bound to note the logicality and structured nature of the author's overall concept.

The author advances his vision of the present stage of social progress, a view conditioned in equal measure by the spirit of Russian social thought in which he is steeped and by a deep study of the works of Western researchers. When we proclaimed the policy of openness (*glasnost*) and *perestroika* as a 'new way of thinking for the country and for the world', it was precisely in order to establish a meaningful dialogue on equal terms with the Western world and its intellectual community. If this book attracts the interest of readers and initiates an academic debate, the author may be considered to have achieved his aim.

MIKHAEL S. GORBACHEV

Preface

As a Russian author and sociologist it is very important to have this work published in the English language. Throughout the past year, as I wrote and rewrote the text, I caught myself wondering where my work would be received with greater scepticism and distrust – in my own country, which has been constrained by decades in ideological blinkers, or in the West, where free theoretical inquiry has always been cultivated?

For a Russian reader this book would undoubtedly seem too 'Western' since it is not 'inscribed' in the context of the sociological debate going on in Russia today. I deliberately elected to take such an approach. I am firmly convinced that Russian social science, whose old ideals (or dogma) lie in ruins while new ones have not yet emerged, and whose practitioners relate to the West with a combination of respect, as a source of scarce financial infusions, and hostility, as a society of internal emancipation of a sort that has not increased in Russia itself under the current political regime, is in its present-day form primarily characterized by an unprecedented moral unease, which has never yet helped the search for Truth. However, Russian sociologists are today more than ever before prepared for any new scientific paradigm which does not entirely copy the principles of 'mathematicized' economics and claim to be the kind of sweeping generalization the Soviet academic community, formerly one of the most credible successors to the great research tradition of the nineteenth century, used to welcome in its rather naïve attachment to global theories.

It is somewhat different in the West. The turmoil in sociological theory, which mostly occurred in the 1960s and 1970s, is now giving way to relative conservatism and to the transition from general concepts to the development of relatively private issues and problems. The concept of the post-industrial society, which has evolved as a theory capable of changing (and which has significantly changed) representations of humanity at the end of this century, has not, in our opinion, fully utilized the genuinely revolutionary potential inherent in its every position. If a quarter of a century ago researchers were paying particular attention to the search for new features which distinguished contemporary society from the preceding one, then today the focus has shifted to the search for signs of historical continuity. It is completely understandable: any organized concept acquires an element of conservatism, any mature society wants to think of itself as strengthened by the march of history leading up to it. In such a situation, a book constructed according to a few outdated canons and aiming to advance broad (maybe even too broad) generalizations will inevitably meet with some mistrust. Meanwhile, I consider that the generalizations and forecasts, which may well be unnecessarily radical, might be understood more readily where realistic social conditions for doing so exist, than where only the previous academic tradition will have paved the way for them. And that is why I think that regardless of the range of conceptual challenges contained in this work, it will be more satisfactorily greeted by Western readers.

This is the situation that led me to write the introductory remarks below. This work is devoted not to the logic of the establishment of the post-industrial order, but rather to the problems of transcending the *economic* society. For most sociologists, this way of posing the question will sound challenging and strange. Reading the books that signalled a turning point in the development of Western social theory in the latter half of the twentieth century, I often noted that the authors stopped at the outer approaches to the problem; meeting the academics whose authority in sociology seems unquestionable, I was told that my hypothesis was not so much premature as not entirely correct. The sheer self-confidence of these researchers was such that for some time I tried to find arguments that refuted rather than justified my ideas. I was sincere in seeking them; it might be that my own inadequacy did not permit me to find them.

That is why this work opens with three preliminary observations.

As the philosophers of antiquity said, *ex determinatio negatio est*. In presuming the emergence of a *post-economic* society to be impossible, contemporary philosophers and sociologists mostly do not think about the meaning they themselves invest in the concept of 'the economy'. If it is in that limited space of freedom which came out of humankind's dependence on nature, has it not consigned to the past the last explosion of apocalyptic ecological ideas at the end of the 1980s? If this understanding is linked to *Homo economicus* in the traditional sense of the bearer of the values of the Protestant ethic, then do not the events of the past 30 years testify to the emergence of a new kind of consciousness and new paradigms of behaviour by the contemporary individual? If the present economic order cannot be replaced while there is still the factor of the scarcity of goods, commensurate with their marginal utility, then the arrival of the information society may be the clearest sign that the 'economic' approach may not last for ever. I believe that opposition to the idea of the post-economic society comes from too broad an understanding of the very concept of 'economy'. In English, unlike in German (or Russian), this term originally meant in fact the entire sphere of human productive activity. However, in the past, that productive activity was inseparable from the features I have just mentioned – the narrow space of freedom, the work ethic and the constant comparison of outlay and results. Humans have known no other system than the economic, but that still does not mean that an alternative to it cannot exist. Therefore, by post-economic society I mean a social system which is not run according to the logic of *Homo economicus*, a system which undoubtedly supposes *Wirtschaft* but not *Oekonomie*, a system which cannot be understood without reconsidering two other equally fundamental and well-grounded concepts.

The most important of them is the concept of work. 'Cursed is the ground because of you; through painful toil you will eat of it all the days of your life [...] By the sweat of your brow you will eat your food ...' said the Lord God to Adam (Genesis, III, 17-19). At the same time as the Christian tradition introduced the concept of endless progress into the historic world-view, it generated and implanted that idea – absolutely static by nature – deep in the human mind. In this case though I am not trying to depict post-economic society as being based on leisure, as opposed to productive activity. On the contrary, regardless of the marked increase in material comfort for most citizens in Western countries, recent decades do not appear to have lead to an inevitable decline in their participation in public life. There is more. It is precisely at the basis of this unprecedented prosperity that elements of the new system of motives and values of contemporary individuals are appearing. That is why I consider it possible to assert that greater attention must be devoted to the changes taking place today in the internal structure of human activity. In English terminology the most satisfactory method of analysing this problem is, I believe, to contrast the concepts of *labour* and *creativity*. Both of them are related to instrumental conscious productive activity which might on the whole be interpreted as *work*, although the first includes the concept of that internal lack of freedom which is inherent in economic society, whilst the second can be used to mean any new kind of activity leading it to change. However, in that case, as when we considered the concept of 'the economy', we come up against a certain conservatism in the conceptual apparatus of science. It is very complicated to explain that creativity differs from labour not in its outward manifestation, but in its internal structure, that the changes bringing about the establishment of post-economic society are to a greater degree changes of consciousness than transformations of the material world. Therefore, post-economic society will come about not when the information sector begins to dominate in the structure of production, nor when the free time of individuals exceeds time worked; it will come about as and when people stop relating mentally to their own activity as if it were the product of external circumstances. The line between the economic and the post-economic society lies in the human mind in the same way that the border between the earthly and heavenly cities in the theory of St. Augustine existed primarily 'not indeed evidently, but in God's foreknowledge' (St. Augustine, De civ. Dei, xii, 27).

It follows then that post-economic society is not a society in which *scarcity of goods* has been removed or overcome. The idea of scarcity is now firmly rooted in economics, occupying, quite rightly, an important place. Such a position is the result of the long development of the academic tradition, and the entire history of the evolution of utopian and socialist ideas which linked all the basic defects of society since its very emergence to property inequality and the unfair distribution of wealth. Meanwhile, the preponderant role of this notion does not mean that the impossibility of transcending the economy is entailed by the impossibility of overcoming scarcity. It is well known that a whole range of leading Western sociologists of recent decades, including the most famous representatives of post-industrialism, have devoted considerable efforts to debunking primitive utopian (and partly Marxist) interpretations in which the ideal society was one where 'material wealth flowed like honey'. However, at the same time some researchers forget that the real opposite of scarcity is not abundance, just as the opposite of love is not hate. Again the eighteenth century moralists quite rightly showed that the real opposite of love can be simply indifference. Therefore, it is neither the spread of the production of material wealth, nor the expansion of the flow of information, but the relative decline in peoples' attention to the objects of their external environment, together with the simultaneous shift of stress onto the personal development of the individual which is the process that is overcoming what had seemed to be the everlasting role of scarcity as a component in the economic construction of human society.

Having noted all this, I would like to stress that the interpretation I am proposing of the post-economic society is not one of the approaches in the framework of the theories of post-industrialism (as could be considered, for instance, the concept of the information society). The establishment of the post-economic order of course presupposes the development of a post-industrial trend, but presupposes it as its material foundation and not as a preliminary step in its historical evolution. Daniel Bell once showed that 'the concept of post-industrial society is an analytical construct, ... a paradigm or social framework that identifies new axes of social organization and new axes of social stratification in advanced Western society' (D. Bell, *The Coming of Post-Industrial Society*, p. 483). The concept of the post-economic society has another aim and another task. It considers the value system and nature of human behaviour as the most important tool in changing the contemporary world order, and endeavours to look into social reality of the day as those superficial forms generated by the evolution of an individual's self-awareness. In it, individual perception of the world is placed above social stratification, and the self-improvement of the individual higher than the advance of material production. The theory of the post-economic society is thus constructed around research into how, and in what forms, the development of the human individual determines contemporary social progress, taking it beyond the framework of human relations with nature and with the world they themselves have transformed. That which has historically changed this kind of mutual relation is, in my opinion, not even a 'game between persons' but growing reflection by people within themselves. Its development and forms of expression will determine the basic features of society in the twenty-first century.

The concept set out is not aiming for truthfulness, but assumes that there is a rational element in each of the existing opinions on social processes. It reflects the author's striving for self-improvement, for the study of the issues contained in the book has been the very stuff of my intellectual growth in recent years. If, as a result of reading this book, the faintest shadow of a doubt in the perfection of contemporary ideological paradigms occurs to even a few people, I will consider that it has done what it set out to do.

In conclusion, I would like to thank everybody who has helped me with this book. First of all, I would like to address my sincere thanks to Mr Aleksei I. Antipov, who over the past few years has become not so much the editor of my texts as a wise and gracious academic mentor. To a great extent it is indeed to his credit that a small work on the problems of the post-economic society, published in Russian in Moscow in 1995, has today taken the form of this book. I am also most grateful to Ms Olga Antipina who, throughout the long months of work on the book, made a series of valuable comments and did a vast amount of editorial work preceding its Russian publication. A great impression was made on me by discussions on the problems raised in this book with Professors Peter F. Draker, Francis Fukuyama and Marshall I. Goldman. Long talks with Professor Daniel Bell were for me more valuable sources of reflection than the hundreds of books I had read beforehand, and I am grateful to him for that. The group of translators under the guidance of Ms Yelena Khrulyova deserve special thanks; over many months David Leask and Philip Read did all that was asked of them so that those thoughts which were not always clearly and correctly expressed in the text could be worded as accurately as possible in this edition, and their Russian colleagues Alla Varavitskaya, Natalia Nekrassova and Tatiana Gromova did the editorial checking. I would also like to thank many other friends who, with help, advice and just by being there, assisted me in the work embodied in this book.

Vladislav L. Inozemtsev
June 1998

Introduction

Humanity throughout its history has never lost its interest in its own future. Yet that interest has been heightened over recent decades. It is no exaggeration to say that humanity has never before been so absorbed with futurology, with the desire to understand the prospects of civilization and the directions and forms of its development. Never before has such an impressive corps of academics, recognized authorities in history, philosophy and economics, devoted so much space in their works to the social trends leading us into the future. Never before has futurology been seen as a separate discipline among the social sciences.

Such an enlivened interest in social evolution could not but lead to the application of some of the methods of less widely defined disciplines to futurology. However, for a range of reasons it was not so much the past and the future that came to be compared and contrasted, as required by the logic of historical and philosophical research, but the present and the future. As a result the majority of concepts proposed suffer from, at best, one-sidedness. Some of the interpretations of social transformation on offer are extremely narrow. Others attempt to contrast modern phenomena with trends that have only manifested themselves clearly over recent decades rather than with global historical tendencies.

Thus the majority of futurological doctrines of recent years are incomprehensive and logically inadequate. Their followers mostly try to apply the sharpest possible contrasts; incorporate phenomena that mark the very latest advances in technology, particularly information technology, into their concepts; achieve the greatest possible recognition for their new ideas by inventing new terms that are far from always reflecting the essence of profound economic processes; and provide extremely specific descriptions of what they believe to be the most undoubted elements of the future social structure, regardless of whether they are of interest or not.

It is now almost 30 years since the very notion of a new phase in progress was introduced en masse in most of the developed nations simultaneously. Now two fundamental flaws can be pointed out in modern research into the prospects of the development of

1

civilization. The first flaw was caused by focusing too much on individual technological, economic or even social processes. Such an approach has not given and could not provide a comprehensive picture of the development of the social structure. Even the most salient and radical change in modern society relating to the development of information technology and the growth of the production of knowledge as a share of overall economic output in our view may not form the basis, not only for a new periodization of history, but even for a conceptualization of our own century, without being supplemented by an analysis of a mass of other issues, which, moreover, should not be regarded as accompanying such a process or being of secondary importance to such a process. It has, after all, never occurred to anybody to regard the development of commodity exchange, private property or the formation of financial capital as being phenomena that merely accompanied or supplemented the proliferation of the steam or internal combustion engines. The second flaw is in that emphasis on such changes already shows that scholars wittingly or unwittingly want to place such changes at the root of social evolution. However, it can seldom be proved that trends traced over several decades are really enduring and that the new social whole under formation will not undergo radical change, alter into a whole new state or take on a whole new course of development. And here we see one more grave contradiction typical of the majority of contemporary futurological theories.

It seems that all are agreed that the current epoch is revolutionary and marks a breakthrough. Thus it must be recognized that the majority of traditional trends are either to undergo radical transformation or to come to nothing. At the same time, as we have noted, sometimes it is impossible to provide convincing evidence that trends begun merely a few decades ago really mark the boundary in history between 'pre' and 'post'. In our view neither comprehending the real importance of the changes affecting humanity today nor appraising the prospects of its progress are possible outside the framework of a global concept capable of placing any period under study without contradiction into a general scheme of the main phases of the development of society. Thus in this book we intend to offer our vision of such a global concept and a scientific methodology for the analysis of contemporary life.

We believe the most important key to the understanding of the nature of social dynamics is the study not only of the historical facts and laws themselves but the study of humanity's perception of those facts and laws. People have been conceptualizing the societies in which it is their fate to live for millennia. This process of conceptualization runs parallel with historical development. But at the same time human thought is constantly returning to the past in search of the answers to questions about the present and the future, and the further the thinker is from the start of history the richer his perception of it is. An analysis of the dynamics of these perceptions allows us to see history in such a way that many apparently chance events and changes prove to be a smooth progression. We are not afraid to assert that the study of the history of the way society regards itself could prove to be a no less effective instrument for the comprehension of real progress for humanity than traditional historical research itself.

The history of the theory of progress shows that, at each higher level of the comprehension of the laws of civilization, philosophers grow further from two extremes: the belief that history can be divided into periods of 'pre' and 'post', 'before' and 'after', or into an indeterminate number of periods based on the domination of one or another group of factors of social development. Most recognition is given to those concepts that in one way or another divide history into three epochs, each of which is a complete whole. Historians then divide each epoch into periods using criteria typical of the epoch itself. Each such epoch in its own development paves the way for the next and the whole process is of profoundly evolutionary character. This means that the radical jumps that occur in social development cannot seriously alter the course of history set by the consistent substitution of the social forms.

Thus the transition humanity is undergoing today is not the first of its scale in the history of civilization. On the contrary, today's transition marks the completion of a lengthy period that was in its turn born of the fall of the bases of the primitive societies that existed in the archaic period. Today the contradictions and relations typical of that period are being surmounted. New contradictions and relations are being formed in their place that are not merely the opposite of the trends of the last one or two hundred years but a kind of complex synthesis of the entire historical experience accumulated by civilization starting from its primitive forms and ending with the flowering of bourgeois society.

We have found two extreme approaches to periodization to be unacceptable within our study. Firstly, we believe that the laws of technological progress should not be regarded, as they often are, as fundamental for periodization because they do not directly determine the laws of the development of modern social relations and because there is no precedent of their having done so in the history of the material factors of production. The progress of productive forces provides the basic foundation for evolution of human society and is, overall, irreversible. Humanity never reverted to hunting after it had developed settled agriculture and it never reverted to craftwork after it developed manufacturing. Individual cases of regress usually took place when higher civilizations were dissolved into lower ones. Such periods, however, never lasted and after a time economic progress resumed, already over a greater area, and achieved incomparably greater successes. The advancement of the technological bases of social production may not therefore serve as the basis for the periodization of historical progress because progress as a single-tracked process provides for the consequential successes of the human species and the constant growth of the power of man over nature.

Secondly, we also cannot accept the approach under which the development of civilization is regarded as the replacement of one separate social form by another, each regarded as a complete and self-contained whole. It should be stressed that here we are talking about the types of society in their generally accepted sense, about the stages of social progress, and not about phenomena observed in the history of one nation or another, not about individual political regimes, which have changed during the course of historical progress with kaleidoscopic speed. Today the majority of social scientists accept the division of European history into ancient, feudal and bourgeois. Each of these types of society was based on completely distinct principles, which were not only not accepted by the previous type of society, but which were not even reflected in any single trend, except the obvious growth of productive forces and the degree of man's freedom from natural forces that this growth provided. In the framework of such an approach the society currently under formation can be defined as the fourth period of European history. However, such a definition will not help the study of its main principles, its principal relations and the basis of its internal structure.

The modern transformation is too global to define the coming society as post-capitalist. Changes are occurring not only in the industrial form of production but in the very nature of human activity. Non-material interests and desires are taking on a dominant significance in the system of preferences and values of individuals. It is quite obvious that the differences between the ancient and the feudal and the feudal and the bourgeois were of a different scale. All previous economic structures were based on the dominance of material interests that determined the main laws of behaviour of economic agents and formed the main sources of social conflict and contradictions.

Two clear global epochs of progress can be traced in the civilization that preceded the current period. The first was the epoch of the formation of human society when human behaviour was directly determined by material interests. People withstood the forces of nature as a single organism. They did not perceive common material interests or the need for common activity: they were driven by primitive instincts of self-preservation and survival. Such an archaic community did not know the basic relations characteristic of more developed forms of a social whole. During the second epoch humans recognized themselves as members of a society, representatives of a certain class or social group, occupying a specific place in the social hierarchy or in social production. The division of labour and exchange of its products, the establishment in various forms of the principle of private property, the class division of society and the exploitation of one part of society by another were the principal characteristics of this society. Thus the boundary between these two epochs lies where the system of individual material interests was formed.

So we intend to regard historical process as divided into three epochs, the boundaries between which will be determined by an analysis of the corresponding systems of material interests. In the framework of the first such epoch, which corresponds to primitive society, the material interests of humans amounted to the direct appropriation of natural goods and did not entail any kind of complete social determination. The interests of any given individual were identical to the interests of his fellow-tribesmen and could only differ quantitatively within the limits of the physical requirement of each individual. The material desires of individuals, in no way differing from those of the social whole, could not form the basis for a system of social connections and contradictions as a result of which the human community retained the form of a primitive association formed exclusively in order to directly oppose the forces of nature.

The second epoch was marked by the formation of the material interests of individuals different from those of other people and the social whole. The process was begun by the division of labour and exchange, which provided a multitude of options for the achievement of personal well-being. Individualized appropriation could not but prompt the development of private ownership. There were many forms of contradiction and conflict between individuals and classes struggling to provide for their own material interests at the expense of others. The scarcity of goods made such conflicts arise again and again and this, in its turn, served as the basis for the constant recreation of this type of social structure.

Found in many forms – from the ancient polis to the modern capitalist order – such an organization of production corresponded to the requirements of social development. It reaches its natural ceiling when society achieves a certain level of satisfaction of its basic requirements. It appears that, when this level is reached, the desire to achieve ever greater material wealth is no longer capable of providing the necessary dynamism for economic progress. Today the pro-duction of information and knowledge dominates all spheres of social production. Under such conditions neither the desire for material wealth nor the thirst for social recognition can take the place of the requirement for self-development and the augmentation of one's knowledge and abilities. This factor, which affects an increasing number of people with each new generation, stimulates the formation of a system of non-material interests and the new dominant factors in social development.

The following ought to illustrate what has been said above. In the archaic society the interests of people, who formed a single common organism, had a common aim and differed only in the urgency of their material requirements. These corresponded totally to the vector of social interest. The second epoch of social development looks different: now the interests of individual members of society are still on the same plane, set by their material interests, but they no longer have a common aim. Indeed, their aims are often contradictory. As a result the vector of social interest became a certain sum of these desires, clearly contradicting several individual interests in the most radical way. Today, when the transition to the third epoch of social organization is taking shape, a significant proportion of individual and social interests are leaving the plane which they previously occupied, are losing their material aims. The result is the emergence of a multidimensional picture.

The comparable scale of the transition from the first to the second epoch and from the second to the third epoch can be seen in the following circumstance, which has never before been noted by sociologists. It is accepted practice to say that the forms of human cohabitation, relations of production and, less directly, political processes are determined by the technological level of production and the degree to which the social economy is developed. The founders of Marxism formulated this thesis as the law of the correspondence of relations of production to the nature and level of development of the productive forces. In one form or another this law is acknowledged by the majority of sociological schools. However, outside the realm of this thesis there remains the fact that radical changes in the relations of production and in the whole organization of social production came about as the direct result not so much of a revolution in productive forces as a sharp transformation of human psychology.

In this context the transition from archaic social forms to the second epoch is a reflection of the emergent understanding of man's personal material interests and the recognition of the conflict between one's own aims and those of other individuals and society. The second transition takes place when the individual realizes that his main requirements and desires are not connected with the augmentation of his material wealth. Hence, non-material interests become the main factor responsible for the further development of humanity.

Undoubtedly, both in the first and the second case, it was the development of production that provided the opportunity for these changes in human consciousness to take place. However, we wish to stress that it was the latter that was the direct reason for the modernization of the system of the relations of production.

We believe it is possible to identify three main epochs in the progress of civilization by the main types of human activity in each of these epochs. The most common activity during the second epoch was called 'labour' in its most exact sense. Its main stimulus was material interest. It was also characterized by the reproducible nature both of the conditions and the results of activity and the possibility for the free appropriation and alienation of these. The preceding form of human activity was not of a fully conscious nature. It was only carried out within the framework of the community as a single whole and embodied characteristics of man as a natural element of nature rather than a subject contradicting nature. We call this kind of activity instinctive pre-labour activity. The new type of activity, motivated in a superutilitarian way and not determined by material interests and creating material goods not as the aim of the production process but merely as its by-product, is regarded as creativity. It is not embodied in reproduced goods. Its source is the intellectual potential of the creator and it leads to the appearance of inalienable qualities for the individual and inexhaustible resources for society that cannot be consumed in the same way as material goods. In the corresponding sections of this book we plan to consider all these forms of activity in more detail. Here we shall merely underline the qualitative difference of the three main epochs of social evolution.

Thus we see the significance of the current social transition. However, our task is not merely to declare its epochality but to understand which new phenomena accompany this transition and which new forms the social structure will acquire. We shall do this on the basis of trends and processes characteristic of all history of that second phase of social evolution that is currently being replaced by the new order. Such an approach is practically never applied in modern Western sociology, which limits itself to comparing today's society with the capitalist and industrial types of economies. In these economies contradictions and relations characteristic of the second epoch as a whole have their fullest manifestation. However, an analysis of the established social whole cannot be as informative for futurologists as an analysis of those contradictions and relations in the process of their formation and development.

The main characteristics of the second epoch are, in our view, market exchange, private property and exploitation. The division of labour and the commodity production based on it cannot only be attributed to the capitalist order. As soon as the division of labour was established it was the contradictions that emerged in the process of exchange that became the main source of social progress. The first elements of commodity production were seen in early antiquity and remained the main factor of social transformations throughout the whole epoch. The development of social production itself – from the ancient polis city state, an odd mixture of a commodity sector dominated by a natural economy, through the Middle Ages, when commodity relations started to penetrate the entire economy, to the bourgeois mode of production, when the sphere of commodity circulation incorporated all the factors and results of production – was probably more a reflection of the development of commodity economy from its most primitive to its most advanced forms than a mere history of the progress of political forms and the replacement of one class society by another. The history of the second epoch shows that the development of the commodity economy was a very difficult and lengthy process and that means that it will be just as difficult to overcome market relations.

Property relations provide a fine illustration of the functioning of a society founded on the contradictions of the material interests of the individuals and corporations which it comprises. Private property, which is characteristic of bourgeois society, is very different from the kinds of property which existed throughout the pre-capitalist periods of the second epoch. The history of property relations begins with personal property in its many forms: from ownership of part of the common land, agricultural tools and the products of labour which the farmer was able to exchange with his neighbours through to ownership of whole states, including subjects, as characteristic of Asiatic monarchies. Private property in its most common sense did not emerge until much later, when the atomized nature of production became a social norm and forces reflecting the economic aims and guidelines of the new order took political power. Private ownership over the means of production, which provides its holder with economic power over other members of society, may not be quickly overcome, however passionately revolutionaries have called for this in different times and places. The overcoming of private property entailed in the framework of the current social transformation is a natural and inevitable process and will be the matter of a very long period of social progress.

Finally, exploitation has determined most social problems throughout the second epoch. Those who regard the new epoch as the rejection of the capitalist order believe that the only way to overcome this evil is to reform distributive relations, redistributing that part of the social product appropriated by the idle classes to the real producers of social wealth. This, however, will only lead to an impasse, if only because, on the one hand, it is impossible to appraise the real input of the owners of the means of production into the development of the production process and, on the other, society cannot exist without the alienation of part of the product of labour from its direct producer. If we accept that the society that has come to replace the current order is the rejection of the entire second epoch, we must overcome exploitation not just in its quality as an economic phenomenon but, primarily, in its quality as a phenomenon of the human consciousness. Exploitation is the fellow-traveller of a society in which each producer regards material interest as basic and its violation as exploitation. Exploitation ceases to exist as a significant element of social relations where interests are no longer tightly tied to material aims. And once again we have to note that the overcoming of this characteristic attribute of the second epoch will take a lot longer than was earlier envisaged since human consciousness is much more inert than social institutions.

Thus even such a superficial review shows how our understanding of the future epoch is changing, both in contrast to capitalism and the industrial order and in contrast to the whole period of class societies. Today it is hardly possible to fully and properly characterize the stage of social progress that is being opened by the global changes that we have seen over the last few decades. This should not prompt feelings of vexation or a desire to accuse humanity of a dearth of knowledge. After all, it is only now, when it is coming to its end, that we are beginning to understand the unity of the entire second epoch. And we regard a clear terminological definition of this very epoch as now not only possible, but necessary in order to advance modern sociology. We believe that the current stage of development, characterized by the conflict of individuals and classes for material goods, commodity relations, private property and exploitation, and labour as the main form of human activity, may be described as the economic epoch in the history of humanity. The German term *oekonomische* is probably the best, since the English language lacks the necessary contrast of *Oekonomie* and *Wirtschaft*, which have significant connotations. We describe the period that preceded the *oekonomische Gesellschaft* as the *pre-oekonomische Gemeinschaft* and the coming epoch as the *post-oekonomische Gesellschaft*. In our view any attempt to define the future society in its positive aspect, by discovering its fundamental relations and laws, is unlikely to be successful. Contemporary social science is limited to a study of only the most complex prerequisites for future society and the identification of those trends that, judging by their development, will be of extreme importance in the process of its formation.

All this determines the structure of our book. In its first part we will try, as far as it is possible in such a limited framework, to reflect the process of the formation of the theories of historical progress, to show the laws of their formation which, in the end, reflect the real laws of the movement of the society itself. We believe it is necessary to consider several theories that in one way or another divide historical progress into three stages as undoubted advances on the path to understanding our future, and to discuss their pluses and minuses.

In the second part of our book we shall try to present a comprehensive and consistent notion of the society that is under formation today as a post-economic society. This will require substantial attention to terminological problems which, along with methodological issues, number among the biggest barriers to an adequate understanding of the nature of the modern epoch and the future society. We are convinced that the theory of social development designed to explain the formation of the basis of the social structure of the future should be founded on a profound and comprehensive analysis of the system of human interests as the motive force of progress. It is for that very reason that we regard the transition from labour to creative activity as the main issue of modern social transformation and why we have devoted the central, fifth, chapter of our book to it. We believe the most important issue of the current transitional stage, as has already been noted, is the transformation of the relations of commodity exchange, property and exploitation which determined the most characteristic features of the economic epoch. Considering the unfolding of the corresponding processes, we have the opportunity to convince ourselves of the scale of the changes taking place today and, equally, of the fact that the post-economic condition will not arrive within the next few years or even the next few decades. In conclusion we will look at the issue of the relations and interaction of the new post-economic structures with their economic milieu and the problem of the system and environment under the conditions of today's transformations.

This is the plan of our study. Bringing this study to life we are trying to traverse a very narrow corridor restricted on the one side by the famous view of Oscar Wilde that a thought that is not dangerous does not deserve to be called a thought and, on the other side, by an understanding that modern social theories, which in one way or another affect the development of society, could become a dangerous weapon if they fall into the hands of zealots. It will be up to the reader to decide whether we have succeeded in our desire to study the changes under way without in any way accelerating them.

PART I
CREATING A CONCEPT

Introduction to Part I

A study of the theories of history is not only a necessary condition for analysing current views on the historical process, but also an important source from which to understand the very laws of human civilization. Although the development of philosophical views on history and society is a phenomenon undoubtedly more complex and many-sided than history itself and stands apart from the fundamental laws governing social change, it nonetheless contains in some senses even more information about the directions and tendencies of progress than historical materials themselves.

History knows many examples of social change taking a most unexpected turn, so that in some cases it seems that progress comes to an end and society regresses. Civilization certainly does not move in a straight line: social systems that seem ideal to the contemporary observer have been destroyed by more backward societies, great cultural centres crushed under the heel of barbarians. But throughout the ages a process has continued that suffered the effects of such incidental factors in far lesser measure. This was and remains the process of understanding what has happened. While war can lead to the defeat and decay of one of two conflicting states, a struggle between different schools of philosophy can never end with the outright victory of one over the other; war brings destruction and loss to all of its participants, but any serious discussion between philosophers of different persuasions only strengthens both sides.

Given that an ideology can become obsolete only when all the material and spiritual conditions that originally spawned it have receded far into the past and been totally erased from humanity's collective memory, changes in the dominant historical viewpoint take place much more slowly than those in the object of their attention. Thus the value in studying the development of social thought lies in the fact that it can allow us to grasp the true nature of social change even better than the analysis of specific historical events.

The aims of our research, which concerns the genesis of the post-economic society and an identification of those features differentiating it from the pre-economic and economic epochs, demand that particular attention be paid to an accurate *periodization* of the

13

historical process. We believe that *those principles upon which separate stages in historical progress are defined are fundamental to a theory of history*; the inner coherence of these principles and the correspondence with reality of schemes based upon them are measures of its *adequacy*. However, it is obvious that the criteria for a periodization of history, like the periodization itself, depend in large measure on the researcher's subjective approach. How else can one explain the great variety of theories of history when there is but a single common object of research? An understanding of the reasons why a particular theoretician chooses one or other criterion for his or her periodization of history must start from his or her contemporary intellectual milieu and the level of development of philosophical and historical thought attained in that epoch. When the question is posed in this way and the subjective peculiarities of an author are taken into account, there can be no doubt that a strictly scientific result in the study of the evolution of principles of historical periodization is impossible. We can, however, identify certain general patterns that facilitate our understanding of the nature of these principles and ways in which they were developed.

From the moment that the idea of progress took hold in philosophy, a naive mistake came into being and took root in philosophers' consciousness, a mistake shared by supporters of such widely differing views on historical development that it would seem they could have nothing in common whatsoever. This prejudice consists in the conviction, direct or indirect, that it is the epoch contemporary to the author that is witnessing the greatest revolution ever known to civilization. Authors sharing this view boldly draw a line through their immediate historical period, dividing human history into 'before' and 'after'.

This behaviour is easily explained. Any thinking person is inclined to exaggerate the significance of the historical period contemporary to him or her, at the very least because it is the only fleeting moment during which he or she is destined to exist. Thus the objective border between past and future that runs through each of us at any moment in our own lives obviously seems of greater significance to us than the greatest revolution separating previous historical events. The researcher, in consequence, while often exaggerating the significance of the present, tends to play down as far as possible the importance of earlier changes and to turn insignificant events into historical milestones. In other words, the approach is what Francis Bacon termed 'nos nihil magni fecisse, sed tantum ea, quae pro magnis habentur, minoris fecisse'. Focusing attention on the heterogeneity of the past, philosophers have thus devoted their theories to proving the *indivisibility and perfection of the future in relation to all previous historical epochs*.

The development of historical thought, however, has inevitably meant that approaches of this kind have found fewer and fewer adherents. The indications of a second gigantic epoch in world history have become weaker and weaker; an understanding has grown that the historical changes so often proclaimed have turned out to be but a prelude to new and transient periods which, far from being indivisible, themselves consisted of a series of fleeting moments. Thus, with the passage of time, the scrupulous division of human history into separate periods, together with an acceptance of the sufficiency of an immanent 'tomorrow' have gradually given way to a new methodological approach. This method divides the historical process into three major epochs, with further additional divisions within each. This approach, or at least its methodological foundations, has almost as long a history as the other, but differs in that it can appear only when the philosophy of history begins to base itself firmly on a recognition of the progressive nature of social development.

Moving on to a brief assessment of theories of periodization, we shall structure our account in accordance with the principles discussed above. Those theories of history that we have mentioned we shall call, albeit provisionally, *inadequate*. There are various shades of meaning to this concept. Firstly, inadequate theories bear the stamp of an exaggeration of the significance of the historical period contemporary to their authors, which leads to a shift of focus in their periodization of social progress from fundamental to more superficial aspects that are more easily observed. Secondly, the periodization itself is, as a rule, performed in accordance with criteria that are essentially of different orders, making the overall scheme insufficiently logical, vulnerable to criticism and, moreover, in conflict with concrete reality. Thirdly, schemes of this sort either employ a criterion of progress that is external to the social organism or reject any criteria of progress altogether; the goals of social development are thereby imposed from without, which makes any periodization inapplicable to the analysis of social development and complicates its verification according to the facts of social progress.

Apart from these inadequate theories, there are also theories of development that lie partway *along the road to an adequate conception*. To varying degrees, the authors of these theories criticize those who absolutize the significance of their own historical period, there being some who deny it altogether. They seek to provide a periodization of history based on criteria inherent to the social organism itself and, moreover, they gradually move away from the division of history into 'before' and 'after' the period in which the 'observation' is taking place. An important feature of conceptions of this sort is the researchers' strict approach to criteria of periodization and thus the sufficiently coherent nature of these criteria.

Finally, there are theories that we shall call *coherent*. They clearly reveal a dialectical triad in their divisions of the historical process, while the formulation of their criteria for periodization takes place on a single substantive level, which allows these theories to achieve a high degree of internal rigour and correspondence with the real historical process, not merely describing but also partly predicting it. At the present time there are dozens of such theories. As a rule, the methodological maturity of these conceptions, none of which claims to describe human history in its entirety (either in its temporal or qualitative aspects), permits them to coexist, supplementing and enriching each other.

Having made these preliminary remarks, we can now go directly to a discussion of the theories of social progress developed by the great philosophers of the past. The aims and nature of this research permit us, however, to examine only the general directions in which social theory has evolved, since the tendencies present in this immensely complex process interest us more than a particular author's views.

1   Inadequate Theories

Those conceptions of history that we consign to the category 'inadequate' are extremely varied and are to be found throughout the history of European social philosophy. Common to these theories are postulates which to a greater or lesser extent make them incapable of describing human history in terms of an internal motive force of social progress.

Depending on the epoch in which their authors lived, these theories either denied the progressive nature of social change altogether, judged its development in terms of factors external to society or rejected any serious periodization of historical progress, preferring to counterpose the impending future to all preceding history. We shall try to illustrate this with a brief review of inadequate theories of history, beginning with Ancient Greece and ending with the utopian communism of the 19th century.

The Traditions of Antiquity

The philosophy of history in the ancient world cannot be separated from the general foundations of the Ancient Greek world view. Two factors heavily influenced its emergence: the mythologized perception of the world shared by the ancients, and the attempt by most Greek authors to apply basic philosophical principles taken from the natural sciences to theories of social development.

The ahistorical nature of the principal features of Ancient Greek mythology is obvious. In contrast to religious doctrines of later times, ancient belief did not posit some major historical event connected with supernatural phenomena or the appearance of religious sentiment which could have become a milestone on the road to social development. Preaching the immortality of the gods of Olympus and effectively identifying them with natural phenomena, the ancients came to the inevitable conclusion that repeated cyclical processes brought about by the will of the gods were the standard form of development. Linear development thus seemed an exception from the general course of history, an anomaly that was negative by definition.

Only in this way can one explain the first attempt to describe human history made by Hesiod in the 8th century BC. Hesiod portrayed a 'golden age' of humanity in which people 'worked when they liked and calmly gathered their bounties'.[1] He drew a picture of suffering and calamity for the human race growing from century to century, and concluded that for the modern man 'there is no respite or salvation from labour, from grief, and from unhappiness'.[2] One must bear in mind, however, that Hesiod was also the author of another theory: that of the emergence of organized nature from an elementary Chaos, which proposed a gradual growth in the complexity and coherence of natural phenomena, whose peak was the attainment of a state of cyclic motion which alone could be considered the perfect form of movement.

But Hesiod's ideas could not provide a basis for a theory of history: they explained neither the origins of human society nor the processes at work within it. The real emergence of a tradition took place three centuries later when Democritus and Antiphon undertook a highly abstract description of the origins of man as a form of animal that gradually ascended to its present condition. Nevertheless, these ideas, just like those of Hesiod (although in terms of the meaning of development that they preached these theories were entirely opposite), were not in total agreement with the methodological fundamentals of the ancient world, which absolutized the significance of cyclical motion.

Thus the task of the best known philosophers of antiquity was to remove the contradiction between the relatively purposeful development of man in the period of his emergence as a social being and the cyclical character of social development that followed from general methodological principles. Plato, one of the outstanding philosophers of the ancient world, also assumed that humanity began its history in a 'golden age',[3] from which it was driven by the gods, who sent a flood, the central catastrophe in the history of the human species. Plato tried as far as possible to ignore the period in which humanity developed towards its social condition, and analysed only that piece of history in which the cyclical character of social development was most clearly seen.

Plato's approach to the emergence of society (or the state, which in his view was effectively one and the same thing) represents a major achievement for the social theory of that time. Noting that movement towards the creation of a state could be initiated not only by representatives of the 'mighty', that is the ruling class, but also by the 'weak', united in the face of oppression, Plato sees the appearance of the state as an objective necessity for the human community: 'the state arises ... when we each of us cannot satisfy ourselves and require a great deal more'.[4] Its creation is described as a process, in the course of which 'an ever greater number of people enter into contact, creating ever larger communities'.[5]

Plato assumes, however, that the creation of the state is nonetheless an act of will that lays down the laws of a new community and its form of government.[6] It is the latter that Plato considers the basic feature of state formation and thus he concentrates his attention on different forms of state organization, of which he identifies four: timocracy, oligarchy, democracy and tyranny.[7] Examining the history of their rise and fall, he discovers that they follow one another in this very order, reappearing again in due course. However, he notes no major changes to the economy, and the class structure of society and its division into freemen and slaves is taken for granted.

Plato's theses allow us to understand the views of the Ancient Greeks on the relationship between cycles and progress. He states that 'motion taking place around a central point ... is as far as possible and in all aspects similar to and ever closer to the cyclical motion of the Mind'. He continues: 'Given that the soul produces circularity in everything we have, one must recognise that the responsibility for the cyclical motion of the sky ... belongs to the soul.'[8] Thus the appearance of elements of cyclical motion in social life is possible only when reason begins to dominate society with the creation of the state; and on the contrary, for that period of history when humanity was not the responsibility of the gods and had not yet risen to the level of self-organization, its development was purposeful and directed.

Aristotle, the second genius of antiquity, began his researches from the same assumptions. In his social philosophy the methods of natural philosophy are more actively applied to the philosophy of history. The main idea of Aristotle's doctrine is to substantiate his total refusal to examine that progressive period in the history of civilization, the existence of which was assumed by his predecessors. Stagirite argues that humans are 'social animals' as follows: 'It is obvious,' he writes, 'that the existence of the state is natural and naturally precedes each individual; insofar as the latter is not a self-sufficient entity and is isolated, his relationship to the state is the same as the relationship of any part to its whole ... and it is necessary that the whole should precede the parts.'[9]

In accordance with this postulate, Aristotle accepts as given the existence of 'state-forming' principles in the organization of any human community. The family and the settlement – the two forms of community in his theory, sometimes treated by commentators as historical stages in the genesis of the state – are no more than logical categories. Stagirite identifies forms of subordination common to any state (the absolute subordination of women to men and slaves to freemen, and the relative subordination of young to old) and also defines three forms of relationship (manorial, marital and paternal).[10]

A similar and largely ahistorical approach is also the cause of Aristotle's neglect, in comparison with Antiphon and Plato, of the problem of the social contract. Aristotle does not judge the artificial creation of the state to be of epochal significance, while Stagirite merely mentions in passing that 'nature has instilled in all of us an urge to statehood, and the first to organise this form of intercourse did a supreme service to humanity'.[11]

As in Plato, the bulk of Aristotle's political theory concerns the evolution of forms of state organisation. Distinguishing three basic forms of government – monarchy, aristocracy and polity[12] – Aristotle also examines the distorted forms derived from them: tyranny, oligarchy and democracy.[13] Stagirite describes in detail the process of transition from one state form to another, but the causes of these changes and their overall direction are barely analysed. Determinacy in the development of state forms (as Aristotle writes: 'in general, whichever way the state structure inclines, this is the direction of change … polity, for example, is transformed into democracy, aristocracy into oligarchy'[14] is limited in Aristotle's theory by a single principle: any hitherto existing social form must in one way or another be restored, since the most perfect form of motion is, Aristotle believes (in full agreement with other authors of his time), the circle.[15]

Thus in Aristotle's works a static approach to qualitative features of human society had already taken shape, an approach according to which nothing apart from the external forms of statelike communities can ever change. Followers of the Greek tradition, in particular the Roman philosophers, only strengthened this perception. In his *History*, Polybius, the eminent Greek historian and social philosopher, gives a clear picture of the world as the Romans saw it. By this time the principle of the autocratic state was axiomatic, and it was accepted that 'autocracy arises of itself and without a plan'.[16] The concept of cyclical motion, again limited to changes in the political structure, also seemed incontestable, for no one doubted that 'the cyclical motion of the community of the state … is the natural order of things, according to which forms of government change from one to another and back again'.[17] The principle of cyclical motion received powerful empirical confirmation in the historical experience of the late Hellenic states as they collapsed into civil war. A more global cycle was associated with the rise of Rome, which turned the Mediterranean into its own private sea. Thus the cyclical theory became, not just a means for describing history, but also a method of social extrapolation. 'In relation to the Hellenic states,' wrote

Polybius, 'which rise and fall repeatedly, it is simple both to explain their past history and predict their future, since it is not difficult to communicate what one already knows, and easy to foresee the future on the basis of the past.'[18]

The final step towards a theory of absolute cycles was made in the twilight of antiquity, its formal basis being provided by the well-known Roman materialist Lucretius. In developing the views of the atomists Democritus and Epicurus, Lucretius argued that all movement is the result of atomic motion, and the latter's vibrations are constantly destroying old forms or creating new ones and revealing them to humanity, but only in order to return to their original starting point in the course of time. With respect to society, Lucretius believed that it had already achieved the highest point of its ascent and soon would begin to fall, marking a new twist in the cycle. Tacitus also supported the idea of total cyclical motion, noting that all existence exhibits a circular movement, and just as the seasons come around once more, so is it with morals.

By the 3rd century AD, the cyclical theory had been stated in its fullest and most self-sufficient form in the works of the neo-Platonic school. Plotinus, the founder of this school, wrote: 'The whole is everything and nothing, since the beginning of everything is not everything, but everything is of it, since everything returns to it, or rather, has not yet, but will.'[19] Another neo-Platonist, Proclus, developed Plotinus' thought, believing that all the essential aspects of existence were in a state of cyclical motion. He wrote: 'All that is initially in motion can return to itself',[20] and concretized this statement with respect to essences of a lower order: 'All that emanates in essence returns to that from which it emanates.'[21] Proclus provided an explanation of the course of the cycle: 'All that emanates from a certain number of causes returns through the same number of causes through which it emanates. Moreover, any return takes place through those causes, through which it emanates.'[22]

In these formulations, the idea of cycles is taken to an extreme and is applied equally to the analysis of both society and the natural world. The philosophers of antiquity ignored the obvious fact that the development of their cyclical theory of history was itself purposeful, that the contradictions existing in the theory from the outset were gradually resolved and it acquired a significant degree of direction (at the same time as the Christian approach, assuming the progressive nature of social development, on the contrary, revealed through its own development a certain element of circularity). Essential changes in the social structure remained outside the limits of their thought, and obviously their theories cannot be included in the list of coherent historical theories.

A major reason for the inadequacy of the historical theories of antiquity was their dependence on the specifics of religious doctrine in their epoch. While in subsequent religions such as Christianity or Islam religious events took place in the context of human society, as it were, and their central problems were those of a moral nature (that is, belief was from the outset socialized), religion in antiquity was thought to explain not the origins of the world so much as each separate element in the order of things. As a result, nature itself was the real divinity and the divine order was that of an orderly procession of natural conditions, while social relations, which were more multifarious and complex, could not be adequately described on the basis of the corresponding methodological foundations.

Typical of the conceptions of history prevalent in the ancient world is their ahistorical approach both to society and to human beings: no other theories of *history* so stubbornly refuse to examine the *historical* origins of human society. The easily observable changes in state forms contemporary with the ancient Greek philosophers were the only sphere in which they applied their methodological principles, as a result of which their theories were largely worthless and they were unable to reveal the more significant changes under way in society.

The Christian theorists who followed them exceeded their predecessors in many respects. And if the words of St Thomas Aquinas, whose theories led him to the conclusion that future relations between husband and wife would be based on full equality and that society would cease to be divided into classes, cannot serve as an adequate comparison with Aristotle, for whom 'the modern family should definitely include slaves and freemen',[23] since they were written 1500 years after Stagirite's philosophy was at its peak, then one can nonetheless grasp the insufficiency of the ancients' world view by comparing Tacitus on the circularity of moral principles with the words of St Paul: 'Do not be deceived: Evil company corrupts good habits!'[24]

In the Name of Christ

While incorporating certain features of the Greek tradition, the doctrine of Christianity, appearing over seven centuries after the founding of Rome, nevertheless seriously undermined existing ideas about humanity and its place in the world. Despite the fact that the Old Testament has plenty of references to cyclical concepts ('The sun also ariseth, and the sun goeth down, and hasteth to his place where he arose. The wind goeth toward the south, and turneth about unto the north, it whirleth about continually, and the wind returneth again according to his circuit. All the rivers run into the sea, yet the sea is not full: unto the place from whence the rivers come, thirther they return again... And that which is done is that which shall be done: and there is no new thing under the sun',[25] these elements are not central to the Christian tradition.

Their place is filled by notions of God as the creator (*causa sui*) and saviour of the world. What is more, the Son of God – the first believer to attain eternal bliss – passes through all the main stages of man's earthly life, and this, Christ's mortal journey, gives Christianity a highly historical character. The central idea of Christ's resurrection and ascension means the possibility for man, having attained moral perfection through belief in an almighty and all-merciful God, to achieve unity with Him and eternal life in a heavenly paradise. Thus in the Gospel according to St Matthew, Jesus says: 'Great is your faith! Let it be to you as you desire.'[26]

The idea of salvation turned this new theory face to face with man, enabled it to go beyond principles of natural science applied to society and, having identified a single objective worthy of pursuit by each individual, made an important contribution to morality. Moreover, since this objective was the same for all (there is no distinction between Jew and Greek), it naturally enabled the new world view to preach the doctrine of equality. The Christian principle of equality stems from the idea of creation, which contains an element of evolution: the world is made in seven days. Indeed, while 'in the beginning God created the heaven and the earth. And the earth was without form and void and darkness was upon the face of the deep. And the Spirit of God moved upon the face of the waters',[27] it was only at the end of the creation, on the seventh day, that 'the Lord God formed man of the dust of the ground, and breathed into his nostrils the breath of life; and man became a living soul'.[28]

The Christian concept of creation contains two important elements: the thesis of the social existence of man as a condition of enforced activity ('In sorrow shalt thou eat of it all the days of thy life; thorns also and thistles shalt it bring forth to thee; in the sweat of thy face shalt thou eat bread, till thou return unto the ground; for out of it wast thou taken: for dust thou art, and unto dust shalt thou return'[29] and the idea of the brotherhood of man (the one and only God created man to show how 'unity amid the multitude' pleased Him.[30] The idea of the unity of the human race assumes a gradual emergence and formation of society and, since it is this process that is the object of historical research, history was an organic element of the general outline of this new world view. Apart from this, the predetermined destiny of the world resulting from the creation suggests that humanity also has a certain goal, which in principle excludes any notions of cyclical development.

Thus Christianity developed a theory of history based on the idea that God was the source of social development, not in the sense of the immediate motive cause, but as an entity to which 'man relates as to its objective'.[31] Thus the first social division made by one of the early fathers of the Christian church, Tertullian, concerned his discovery of a community of the righteous who preached the word of Christ and represented the camp of God (*castra Dei*), while the mass of pagans living in sin were united in the camp of the Devil (*castra diaboli*). Tertullian saw history as the progress of the first camp, which would be joined by an ever-growing number of followers. Man's movement towards God he understood to be a manifestation of a divine will 'that is the inspiration both of the world, which is ruled, and of the people who rule it'.[32] The goal set by this divine will suggests the progressive character of human development.

Tertullian's theory of history is based on the moral perfection of the individual. Social forms, however, such as the Greek polities, the kingdom of Judah or the Roman empire, he saw as stages of material progress, which he identified far more precisely than the Greeks. He took no account of cyclical patterns in the development of state forms, since he considered various social organizations to represent qualitatively new conditions, and not something 'which hath been already of old times, which was before it'.[33]

The works of Lactantius, a Christian philosopher of the mid-4th century, provide a fuller description of history. According to his approach, human beings are also inclined towards equality, and state power seems to be unnatural, arising when man himself chooses a confrontation with God and rejects His commandments. According to Lactantius, only if we 'expel from our hearts all foolish thoughts and desires ... will the golden age swiftly be returned, for we cannot achieve it except by honouring the true God'.[34] In consequence, Lactantius makes two positive proposals: on the one hand, he posits (in full agreement with the doctrine of original sin) the existence of a pre-state condition for humanity and sharply criticizes the Epicurean idea of 'natural' existence as a ceaseless battle of man against man; on the other hand, he sees the state as a foreign and unnatural growth on the body of society, with the help of which 'the rulers, obsessed with greed, defend what they have acquired by robbing the majority'.[35]

We can see Lactantius' theory as the first example in the history of philosophy of an inspired conjecture as to the triad formed by the historical process, moreover a triad expressed in the recognition of pre-state, state and post-state conditions attained side-by-side with moral improvements made by man. Lactantius' theory and the epistemologically related social doctrine of St Thomas Aquinas will be further examined below. A more balanced theory of social development appeared in the 5th century in *De civitate Dei*, the enormous work of St Augustine, one of the foremost Christian theologians, and in which a philosophy of history was formulated for the first time ever. According to St Augustine, Tertullian had oversimplified the problem, since the border between the *castra Dei* and the *castra diaboli* is a border, not between people, but within each individual. This approach assumes that 'at his creation there were two societies within man, two communities as it were within the human species, apparent to God's vision but yet to make themselves known'.[36] The border between them, says St Augustine, is determined in accordance with the ruling form of love, since 'the earthly community results of love for oneself that has become contempt for God, while the heavenly community is formed of love for God grown into contempt for oneself'.[37]

St Augustine's description of the earthly community is somewhat contradictory, but his approach abounds with ideas that demand our attention. One should note that the break with notions of cycles takes place at this stage: history, according to St Augustine, is not a closed cycle but is open to the future,[38] since God has set the goal which humanity is approaching and will achieve when its history is complete. As the natural form of human existence and the natural means of moral improvement, human society is defined by St Augustine principally on the basis of theological notions such as 'the multitude of people gathered together'[39] and 'united by agreement over the things that they love'.[40]

St Augustine consequently proposes a duality in his periodization of the development of the earthly community (*civitas terrestris*); moreover, in neither case is progress defined by stages on the road to moral perfection. On the one hand, St Augustine identifies these stages as the family, the city and the world.[41] This represents a step forward in comparison with antiquity, since his concept of the world includes a rejection of the state, which in St Augustine's work is identical with the concept of 'community'. On the other hand, St Augustine suggests a periodization found in embryonic form in the works of Eusebius Caesarienus and partly reproducing the periods of history identified in the Gospel according to Matthew. The first epoch identified by St Augustine spans the period between the creation of Adam and the flood, the second from the flood to Abraham, the third from Abraham to David, the fourth from David to the exodus to Babylon, and the fifth from captivity in Babylon to the birth of Christ.

The two subsequent periods completing human history are a source of disagreement between commentators on St Augustine, but in any case the latter considers the only significant event after the birth of Christ to be the Judgement Day, and thus admits that 'the earthly community will not last for ever'.[42] St Augustine's theory reflects the basic problem with the Christian doctrine of history: the assertion of the finite nature of humanity's existence on Earth and the borrowing of criteria for periodization from outside the historical process itself. It is of course entirely inadequate to equate the subsequent history of humanity (from the birth of Christ to the Judgement Day) with insignificant periods in the earthly sufferings of the Jewish people, as St Augustine does. At the same time, however, certain ideas contained within the theories of this outstanding philosopher were of enormous importance to the development of a theory of history and were adopted not so much by the Catholic tradition as by later European philosophy.

The development of Christian social doctrine after St Augustine took two different directions. On the one hand, in the 13th century St Thomas Aquinas, whose ideas prompted attempts at a coherent conception of history and so will be further examined below, adopted several of St Augustine's views and successfully developed a theory of periodization of social life independent of biblical events. Agreeing with St Augustine that 'it is natural for man to be a social and political animal and live in a community',[43] St Thomas considered that this community is defined, not by adherence of its members to certain ideals, but by the material needs that follow from their social nature.[44] Moreover, society is seen, not as a unity of ideas and faith, but as a unity of action: unity not in *esse*, but in *agere*. Developments in St Thomas' theory of social progress opened up the epoch in which humanity was to achieve a true understanding of its place in history. On the other hand, certain authors have tried to dogmatize St Augustine's teachings on the two communities. The basis for a theory of progress and an outstanding intellectual achievement in the 4th century, this theory could not satisfy the thinkers of the 15th–16th centuries, when neo-Augustinism was at its peak.

Dogmatization was linked to the development of Christian thought and practice. The transformation of the Church from a traditional religious institution into an important factor in European political and social life provoked an understandable reaction: an urge to return it to its original positions and purge it of its accretions, the result first and foremost of political considerations. According to its ideologues, the European Reformation was to fulfil these tasks. The best known representative of the Reformation in Germany, Luther, was not a philosopher of history as such, though his views have left a significant mark on the history of political and social doctrines and allow us to assess the direction in which Christian sociological theory was developing in the late mediaeval period.

Luther attempted to resurrect St Augustine's idea of the two communities, suggesting that the moral perfection of man is determined not so much by his actions and behaviour as by his belief in God, without which no observance of the Commandments could bring salvation. However, this revival of the theory took place alongside its radicalization, as a result of which Luther remained, in our opinion, not so much a follower of St Augustine as an obvious plagiarist of Tertullian. Just as Tertullian had denounced the Roman rulers for rejecting wise methods of governing the state, so Luther writes: 'No kingdom has ever maintained itself by force; it must always secure itself by wisdom.' Just as Tertullian announced the necessity of differentiating civil from religious authority, so Luther says: 'Given that civil government is established by God to punish the evil and defend the righteous, it shall be obliged to spread freely and unrestrictedly throughout the body of Christianity.'[45] And as Tertullian did not call for war against the pagans, so Luther believes that 'we must conquer the heretics by the Word, not with fire'.[46]

However, Luther's work was not a total reversal to Tertullian. In contrast to the early Christian authors, Luther did not examine the emergence of the state, nor did he consider it to be a retreat from Christian principles, thereby absolutizing the biblical thesis concerning the divine origins of authority. Christian authors thus accepted the natural origins of social life, and Luther transferred this acceptance to the origins of state power. Therefore his theory of history was static and was not subsequently developed in any significant way.

The decline of Christian theories of history is even more marked in the famous *Reflectionas theologicae* of the Spanish Dominican monk Francis Victoria, written in the first half of the 16th century. This work demonstrates a retreat from all the fundamental postulates of Christian social doctrine: the origins of society through the social contract are effectively given an Aristotelian treatment; the author states that all people are naturally independent of each other and come together only when conscious of the benefits of communal living; and finally, he argues that state authority arises when it is granted to a ruler who as been chosen and when the social contract is made.

Thus for over a thousand years Christian social thought has seen periods of both rise and fall. Having introduced to the philosophy of history the idea of progress, albeit understood in a deeply theological way, at the same time, and with the exception of its most outstanding figures, it failed to create a theory of *social progress*, reducing positive changes in human society to the moral development of the individual as the source of progressive movement. In its orthodox form, the Catholic doctrine offered no scientific conception of the periodization of history, limiting itself to a very crude division into epochs in which family, state and religious relations were predominant. Meanwhile the majority of Christian theorists, believing social progress to be generated by the goal which the human species was approaching, accepted that this goal was an attainable one and linked it to the end of human history – hardly a positive contribution to historical theory.

In addition to this, the development of Christian theory has shown that, while preaching the progressive character of human development, the theory itself became trapped in its own evolution. By the 16th century it had arrived at the very dogma from which it had set out a thousand years before, and was unable to integrate itself with the theories of the best known philosophers of the Middle Ages, whose ideas became the basis for further fruitful research. In our view, this circumstance was a result of the fact that the Christian tradition, like that of the ancient world, remained mainly a *political philosophy*, and never became a *philosophy of history* in the true sense of this concept. Its dependence on the immediate political conjuncture clashed with the high ideals of Christian teaching and we must therefore conclude that in this case also a coherent approach to history was doomed not to be developed.

A 'New Version' of the Social Contract

The Modern Age, as we are accustomed to call this period, began in the 17th century and introduced several new directions to the philosophy of history. A characteristic feature of the majority of these was their attempt to synthesize the social teachings of Christianity with the ideas of antiquity. One cannot help noting that the dubious nature of such attempts doomed their authors to the creation of eclectic systems similar, as a rule, to their ancient and Christian counterparts only in form, but in essence representing contradictory and often far from humanistic theories.

The failure of attempts to construct theories of history in the 17th century was to a considerable extent determined by the nature of the epoch itself. The criticism of Christianity in which the philosophers of the Modern Age were frequently engaged required a methodological foundation, which they believed could be found in the theories of antiquity. From the ancient world the philosophers of the 17th century borrowed the idea of the social contract, while from the Middle Ages they took the idea of the progressive direction of social development. However, attempts to improve on these ideas ended in failure because of their extremely simplified approach to the assessment of man's place in nature and society. In contrast to antiquity, whose thinkers considered man to be a likeness of the gods and separated him clearly from nature, and in equal contrast to Christian theorists, who believed human beings to be distant both from nature and from God, the Modern Age philosophers posited a unity of the laws governing both nature and society, and placed man among the natural phenomena, ignoring the features that undoubtedly differentiate us from the natural world. Having brought humanity close to nature, these philosophers continued the developments begun by both ancient and Christian thinkers, but without adjusting their new theoretical platform to take account of even the most obvious notions of social development. In other words, ancient and Christian doctrines were united on a foundation that was foreign to each, which resulted in significant contradictions and logical inconsistencies.

The best known advocates in their day of the theory of the 'social contract', Nicholas Machiavelli, Hugo Grotius and Thomas Hobbes, based their theories on ideas that seem today to be impossible to combine in a non-contradictory manner. In the first place, these theories stood out with their inclusion of materialist themes. By bringing man close to nature and explaining social phenomena with the laws of physics, they undoubtedly distanced themselves from the moralist methodology of Christianity. This, however, did not prevent them from claiming that the social organism is governed by reason (which allowed them to posit the rational establishment of society by means of a social contract). Reason 'is a natural law granted by God to each with which to judge his own actions', while 'the rules of everyday behaviour were proclaimed by our Lord Jesus Christ, the holy prophets and the apostles to be the Divine Will and the laws of the heavenly kingdom'.[47] Moreover, Hobbes went so far as to state: 'I am the atheists' enemy in such degree that I have most diligently sought some indication on the basis of which I might accuse them of infringing the law.'[48]

Secondly, there was an obvious contradiction between these authors' theories of the emergence of the state and their thoughts on natural law. According to Machiavelli, Grotius and Hobbes, the constant war of man against man was a natural condition, the basic motive for which was personal material gain. Machiavelli sees the transition to society not as a radical change so much as a more regulated version of the same thing; on the one hand, the role of force remains just as important as before while, on the other, irreconcilable animosity is transferred from the level of isolated individuals to that of peoples and states. This idea is also to be found in Grotius.[49] The transferral to inter-state relationships of principles taken from pre-social life raises doubts regarding both the stability of the state system and its advantages relative to pre-state society.

Thirdly, the practical impossibility of encompassing the progressive character of social development within the framework of such theories led Machiavelli and Grotius to limit their research to purely political processes, while their adoration of absolute monarchy together with their treatment of cyclical forms of state organization is nothing but a simple repetition of Polybius.

Thus no significant progress was achieved. Although he resolved some of the more obvious contradictions in the doctrine, Hobbes was nonetheless unable to present a finished theory in any form: both his assumptions and conclusions are highly dubious. Hobbes' theory of the social contract is constructed on the basis of his claim that the primitive human was a being hostile to all others. The justification for this thesis, which seems to place evil at the very heart of existence, seems entirely sensible: 'The clearest reason why people wish to harm one another' writes Hobbes, 'is that many simultaneously desire the same thing, which they can neither use together nor divide amongst themselves, from which it follows that this thing must be given to the strongest; the strongest is decided in struggle.'[50] According to Hobbes, while the human species continues to exist this struggle is to all intents and purposes unavoidable. The urge for material wealth determines the thirst for power, which is as natural to each individual as his urge for prosperity. 'In the first place,' says Hobbes, 'I put for a general inclination of all mankind, a perpetual and restlesse desire of Power, that ceaseth only in Death. And the cause of this is not always that a man hopes for a more intensive delight than he was already attained to; or that he cannot be content with a moderate power: but because he cannot assure the power and means to live well which he hath present, without the acquisition of more.'[51]

Hobbes' underlying assumptions, however, clearly prevent him from constructing a non-contradictory theory of the social contract. If in the ancient world the reason for such a contract was the urge to regulate one's life in order to combat nature, and people combined their efforts as it were in one direction and with one aim, the same towards which they had lived their lives before, then Hobbes depicts the social contract as an urge to radically alter the features earlier characteristic of humankind, which, while not impossible, can at best be achieved only in small measure.

Hobbes believes that, at the moment at which the social contract is concluded, each person 'be willing, when others are so too, as farre-forth, as for Peace, and defence of himselfe he shall think it necessary, to lay down this right to all things; and be contented with so much liberty against other men as he would allow other men against himselfe'.[52] However, this thesis is obviously contradicted by his understanding of the state. In the first place, man is not free to measure the extent of his own liberty in relation to that of others: if each individual enjoyed such a right then it would be logical to strive for a certain degree of equality within the social (state) unit. But Hobbes is so firmly opposed to any notion of equality that he raises inequality to the level of a fundamental principle, writing that animals 'do not live in societies and cannot be called social; their existence depends on the *consensus of many wills* directed towards one end, and *not on one will*' as in human society (emphasis added).[53]

This shows that, from the moment at which the social unit is formed, Hobbes considers man, not as a rational being who limits his actions according to the principle of correlating the extent of his own liberty with that of other members of society, but exclusively as an element of the state system and subordinate to the sovereign's will. 'If I am ordered to do something which is a sin for the person giving the order,' he writes, 'and I obey the order, I do not thereby commit a sin as long as the person giving the order is my rightful master. For example, if I go to war by order of the state, whilst believing the war to be unjust, I will not be in the wrong; on the contrary, I will be guilty if I refuse to fight, usurping the state's right to define the difference between what is just and unjust.'[54] But even this is not strict enough for Hobbes, who remarks that, in the course of implementing the social contract, relations of slavery arise (a situation in which, it seems to us, almost every member of society must find himself in relation to the state) and writes that a citizen may say of a slave 'he is mine', 'from which it follows that everything belonging to the slave before his enslavement subsequently belongs to his master ... because he who owns another owns all that the other may own'.[55]

Such is the extent of liberty in Hobbes' social system. It is entirely obvious that there can be only one version of history in this context: apart from the fact constituting the conclusion of the social contract, any positive history is impossible. And while Machiavelli was critical of any social development that disturbed society from its absolute subordination to the supreme ruler, at the same time he accepted the cycles in state forms. Hobbes, on the other hand, rejects out of hand the legitimacy of any changes to the social structure. According to him, where a given form of rule has already been established there is no need to speculate over which form is the better, and one must give preference and support to the existing form as the best of all forms, for to do something that might lead to the overthrow of the existing government contradicts both the natural law and the positive law of God.

Hobbes rejected the basic assumptions adopted by other theorists of the social contract. As a result his doctrine could explain neither the advantages of society, the reasons why it arose, nor the evolution of human society and its driving forces. Hobbes gave pride of place to man's asocial features, his destructive instincts, his hostility to others like him, features that were warned against by many well-known philosophers, the followers of whom were the theorists of the Modern Age. It was Aristotle who wrote that it is a mistake to base one's analysis on evil or some other vice, since 'vice destroys itself, and upon maturity becomes unendurable'.[56] Sharing this opinion, Proclus remarked that 'the origin and primary cause of all existence is good',[57] and, according to St Thomas Aquinas, 'the essence of evil is to depart from good',[58] while 'with the destruction of all good, which is necessary for the existence of evil, so evil, the substrate of which is good, itself would be destroyed'.[59]

It was from this position that Hobbes' contemporaries began their critique. In a book published four years after Hobbes' death, Cumberland announced that evil cannot be a fundamental concept in social theory: peace cannot be defined as the absence of war, 'since peace must be primary in relation to war, just as life is primary in relation to death'.[60] Cumberland correctly identified a number of logical contradictions in Hobbes' theory: in particular, he accused the latter of basing war and law on one and the same substance, since reason is the source both of natural right and state law.[61] In this case the transition from the natural condition of society to the state becomes entirely meaningless.

Cumberland makes a detailed examination of the logical contradictions in Hobbes and is correct to say that the latter's theory contradicts not only his own initial assumptions but also the facts of social life. Drawing attention to Hobbes' thoroughly argued proposal that subjects cannot judge their rulers' actions, Cumberland notes that the very course of history consists of events that obviously imply judgements of this sort; the people participating in the historical process act according to these judgements.[62] Thus the static nature of Hobbes' system contradicts the dynamic of social life, and it cannot therefore be considered a successful theory.

Relentless criticism of Hobbes, Grotius and Machiavelli based on a primitively materialist concept of society and its historical development led to modifications of these philosophers' theories of the social contract. Once the weakness of its sudden transition from the 'natural' to the 'social' had been revealed, the idea of the social contract was applied to the analysis of genuinely evolutionary processes, while the concept itself came increasingly to be used as a logical formula rather than a term describing radical changes in human development.

Notions of a rigid state system, however, as the only possible means of improving human nature remained popular among those 17th-century thinkers who had turned their attention to possible future forms of human society. Running ahead a little, one should note that such factors featured only in the works of the founders of this new direction in social thought, while the majority of their followers in the main adopted humanistic principles.

Utopia

Observing the strict morals of the late Middle Ages, social thinkers of the 16th and 17th centuries applied their efforts not only to justifying the sovereign's absolute power, but also to the search for an improved form of social organization 'that has any right to call itself a republic'.[63] The first such attempt is traditionally linked to the names of More and Campanella. However, they can scarcely be considered the harbingers of a humanistic approach to future society. Although their ideas have a highly tenuous relation to *theoretical* thought, More and Campanella adopt as their basic postulate the possibility of building a perfect society using, not only existing implements and productive forms, but also the existing social relations – an idea rejected by many thinkers long before the utopians.

Whether consciously or not, their ideas reflect a desire to preserve the current stage of social development, and they propose but minor and superficial changes to certain social relations. Thus More believes that the economic basis of the perfect society will be semi-artisan, semi-agricultural communes consisting of 2000–3000 people using tools hardly considered advanced even in More's time. An end to the division of labour is seen only in terms of moving large numbers of people from the city to the country and vice versa: technical progress is ruled out.

Correspondingly, social life can rise scarcely any higher than the everyday reality that More himself observed. One should also note that in certain important aspects More even regressed in relation to his period. Thus he divided the inhabitants of Utopia rigidly into freemen and slaves and saw nothing wrong in such a degree of inequality. His famous thesis that 'any real justice or prosperity is impossible so long as there is private property'[64] loses much of its attraction in the context of his vision of statehood.

In More's *Utopia* and Campanella's *City of the Sun* it is state power that plays the role of the main motive force of social progress. To an extent one can speak of the regulation of social life in these illusory societies as a function of the social organisms themselves, since in one form or another they include the election and accountability of government. However, the very form of such 'democracy' – which assumes, on the one hand, the exclusion of slaves, women and minors from decision making and, on the other, bases itself on multi-stage elections that restrict the expression of the people's will to the barest minimum – prevents the masses from influencing government to any serious extent. Under such a grim totalitarian regime, the absence of property is not the means of liberation that More thought it to be so much as a method of subordinating the people to the state.

In the social utopias of More and Campanella the state has almost unlimited rights. Its prerogatives include the moving of inhabitants from town to countryside and vice versa, the use of collective slave labour for tasks unworthy of free citizens (the slaves belonging in equal measure to all citizens and therefore being an object of ownership), control of the often humiliating marriage procedure and so on, even going as far as the propagation of religious beliefs. In Utopia the latter have a very significant function and practically underpin the excessive role that More assigns the state in his work. He writes: 'They feel so sure that there must be rewards and punishments after death. Anyone who thinks differently has, in their view, *forfeited the right to be classed as a human being*' (emphasis added).[65] This formulation illustrates the extent of freedom of thought in a society that More considered to be ideal.

The ideas of More and Campanella are examples of a most primitive approach to the historical dynamic: their schematic method is also apparent, however, in later versions of utopian thinking and achieves its zenith in the works of Charles Fourier. Despite Fourier's original periodization of history, his picture of social progress is an unprecedented mix of realism and fantasy. On the one hand, Fourier begins his research in Eden, which takes the place of the 'golden age' depicted by the thinkers of antiquity. Humanity's own development brought this condition to an end, and it was followed by rather more gloomy times. 'The excessive propagation of the tribes,' writes Fourier, 'led to poverty; at the same time the spread of predators prompted the invention of lethal weapons, and the growing taste for robbery was further stimulated by the fact that the embryonic state of agriculture and the difficulty of cultivating the land meant that superabundance of food could not be maintained.'[66] As a result, humanity found itself in a historical dead-end: the period of barbarism. In this regard Fourier proposes the original notion that it was in this epoch that people developed large-scale production, which is the lever of social harmony. Until then the social world retreated in the face of happiness, rather like the man who, when faced with a ditch, takes a few steps back in order to jump it more easily. However, the coming era of civilization, in which society is divided into rich and poor and in which 'poverty is born of abundance itself',[67] is also far from ideal to Fourier, who saw the goal of social progress as '*sociantisme*', a future just society, the forerunner of which is a transitional order which he called '*garantisme*'.

Fourier's description of the future society repeats all the errors of the earlier utopians, which is surprising given that their theories are separated by over two centuries that changed the face of Europe and the whole world beyond all recognition. The basis of the future society is again a small community, this time called the 'phalanx'. In this case, however, the complete abolition of property is denied: individual property of the phalanstery's inhabitants exists side-by-side with the property that they own in common. Owing to the different contributions made by each individual to the phalanstery, Fourier justifies a division into classes, though he derives it formally from the proposition that people are by their nature unequal and differ in their characters, abilities and desires. Certain of Fourier's views, however, belong firmly to the utopian tradition: the need to accelerate the development of agriculture (as the more 'natural' form of production) in comparison with industry, the use of primitive technology, rotation of tasks as a means of overcoming the division of labour and, most important of all, the detailed regimentation of life in the phalanstery, in which labour occupies its members from morning until night and prevents them from engaging in any other activities.

In sum, Fourier contributed certain advances to utopian thought regarding the future society, but the foundations of his historical theory remained primitive in the extreme. Thus he decided that human evolution had begun a mere 80 000 years ago; considered that all the modest achievements of social progress are the result not of political or moral science but of pure chance; linked social development to quite fantastic changes in the natural environment;[68] stated without bothering to provide the slightest proof that 'the properties of friendship are precisely generated by the laws of the circle ... love by the laws of the ellipse ... and ambition according to the hyperbola';[69] and declared that it is not the world that regulates social development but society that regulates the world, since it is more advanced, 'and this means that the properties of animals, plants, minerals and even the stars are a consequence of human passions in the social world, and everything from atoms to heavenly bodies obey the patterns of human desire'.[70]

Only in the mid-19th century did researchers seeking a vision of the future society recognize the impossibility of ever constructing such a scheme, and that no single description of a future social order could be completely satisfactory. 'No one knows and no one keeps the secret of the future,' wrote Blanqui. 'The most far-sighted person can have but a premonition, see only a glimmer and catch but a vague and fleeting glance of the future ... Those who believe they have a detailed map of this unknown land are out of their minds.'[71] 'Whoever believes in progress,' echoed Weitling, 'should not consider any doctrine to be complete',[72] though at the same time they should not doubt that such a doctrine was a real possibility.

Blanqui and Weitling developed ideas that were similar in many respects and differed favourably from the early utopians. Certain aspects of their theories indicate that they were close to a partially coherent understanding of the historical process. In their works we find an analysis of the economic epoch, an explanation of the role of exchange in the development of human society, an understanding of the origins of exchange, the limitations of barter and an explanation of the nature of money.[73] Advanced commodity production is seen as a necessary stage of progress, though both authors are of the opinion that 'exchange by means of ... money has in sufficient measure revealed its inability to create a social order based on justice'.[74]

Blanqui and Weitling considered the negation of a society of inequality and injustice to be communism, noting, however, that despite the necessity of revolutionary change the new society must come about in a natural and evolutionary manner. While Fourier, for example, insisted on a rapid change in property relations and proposed that by the end of spring 1808 the first phalanx would start, and across the world the chaos of civilization, barbarism and savagery would instantly dissolve, taking with it the unanimous damnation of the entire human species, when, according to Blanqui, 'attacking the principle of private property would be just as futile as it would be dangerous. Communism cannot be announced by decree, and its arrival must be heralded by the free decision of the nation'.[75] Social development following this 'decision' is seen in terms of an evolutionary, organic transformation of the economic system.

Blanqui treated the social and economic progress of his time as a process identical to the arrival of communist society, an organic element of the historical path travelled by humanity. In his opinion, 'all progress is the victory of communism, all regress is its defeat. Its development is fused with that of civilisation, and both these ideas are identical. All problems posed throughout history and induced by human needs are resolved communistically'.[76]

In comparison with their predecessors, Blanqui and Weitling made a significant change of emphasis in their descriptions of the future society. Thus they proposed that communism is 'the only possible form of society for highly educated people'[77] and is based on the achievements of technical progress. They treat labour as an inherent requirement of each person who recognizes his duty to society, and thus full equality is possible in its remuneration. In the future community all the governing bodies must inevitably be elected so as to ensure citizens' basic freedoms.

Thus in the first half of the 19th century the theorists of communist society had made major advances in relation to the utopians of the 16th–18th centuries. Their ideas, however, did not constitute a coherent theory. Before we begin to examine the development of historical thought towards a coherent theory of history, however, let us briefly repeat the main conclusions that follow from the historical approaches discussed above.

Firstly, inadequate historical theories have existed in various forms throughout human history. Our decision to end this overview with the utopian socialists is a provisional one: theories that are inadequate according to our classification have continued to appear and still do so today. Thus it would be wrong to assume that the authors of such schemes simply 'didn't rise to an understanding' (as Soviet researchers were fond of putting it) of certain historical laws. It should be noted that the thinkers whose opinions we have discussed began by applying methodological approaches very different from those that seem most suitable today. *De principiis non est disputandum*, and thus one must not conclude that theories of this kind are less likely to persist than those that we shall examine below.

Secondly, and without contradicting the previous paragraph, the methodological principles adopted by the authors of inadequate historical doctrines contained a number of internal contradictions that seriously reduced their explanatory value. For this reason, while identifying many historical laws and generalizing an enormous quantity of facts, these authors were unable to combine them into a total system enabling them to make successful social prognoses. The latter is particularly obvious with regard to the utopians.

Thirdly, and this requires particular attention, these thinkers were unable to incorporate into their theories *in any natural manner* a concept of social progress. Either they denied any progressive social development (as in the theories of antiquity, which taught the cyclical rotation of social life) or the latter was included as an accidental factor (Fourier) or directly linked to human will (as was the case to various degrees with theorists of the social contract). The exceptions are the theories developed by Christian philosophers, though here the place of social progress is largely taken by the progress of the individual, which of course has enormous importance but does not determine the development of society as a whole.

Consequently, until the concept of social progress becomes fundamental to historical theory and until it is examined in terms of processes internal to the social organism itself, the construction of coherent theories is highly unlikely. An analysis of the development of historical theory towards coherence is thus an analysis of the idea of progress.

Notes

1 Hesiod, *Work and Days*, 119–20.
2 Ibid., 176–7.
3 See Plato, *Laws*, 679d.
4 Plato, *Republic*, 369b.
5 Plato, *Laws*, 680e.
6 Ibid., 681c–d.
7 Plato, *Republic*, 544c.
8 Plato, *Laws*, 898a, 898c.
9 Aristotle, *Politics*, 1253a25–8, a20.
10 Ibid., 1252b22–1253b14.
11 Ibid., 1253a30–31.
12 See ibid., 1279a33–7.

13   See ibid., 1279b4–10.
14   Ibid., 1307a21–3.
15   See Aristotle, *Physics*, VIII, 9.
16   Polybius, *History*, VI, 4(7).
17   Ibid., VII, 9(10–11).
18   Ibid., VI, 3(1–3).
19   Plotinus, *Enneades*, V, 2, 1.
20   Proclus, *The Elements of Theology*, 17.
21   Ibid., 31.
22   Ibid., 38.
23   Aristotle, *Politics*, 1253b5.
24   The First Epistle of Paul the Apostle to the Corinthians, 15: 33.
25   Ecclesiastes, 1: 5–7, 9.
26   The Gospel According to Matthew, 15: 28.
27   Genesis, I: 1–2.
28   Genesis, III: 17–19.
29   Genesis, II: 7.
30   St Augustinus, *De civitate Dei*, XII, 21.
31   St Thomas Aquinas, *Summa theologiae*, Prima parte, Qu. 1, Art. 1.
32   Tertullianus Q.S.F, *Apologiae*, 26.
33   Ecclesiastes, 1: 10.
34   Lactantius, *Divine institutes*, V, 8.
35   Ibid., V, 7.
36   St Augustinus, *De civitate Dei*, XII, 27.
37   Ibid., XIV, 28.
38   See ibid., XII, 13, 17.
39   St Augustinus, *Epistulae*, 155, 3.
40   St Augustinus, *De civitate Dei*, XIX, 24.
41   See ibid., XI, 16.
42   Ibid., XV, 4.
43   St Thomas Aquinas, *De regimine principum*, I, 1.
44   See St Thomas Aquinas, *Summa contra gentiles*, III, 85, 102; *De rege et regno*, I, 1; *Contra impugnantes Dei cultum et religionem*, VIII.
45   M. Luther, *Address to the German Nobility*, III. One should note that, after criticism of his views in 1521 by the diet of Worms, Luther made major changes to his opinions, remarking, for example: 'And what if a prince is wrong; are the people obliged to follow him? No, because no one must go against the truth; it is more fitting to obey God than to obey a man' (M. Luther, *On Civil Power*, III).
46   M. Luther, *Address to the German Nobility*, II.
47   T. Hobbes, *De cive*, IV, i.
48   Ibid., XIV, XIX, note.
49   See H. Grotius, *De jure belli ac pacis*, II, xxiii.
50   T. Hobbes, *De cive*, I, VI. Despite its apparent justification, this thesis is inadequate precisely when applied to primitive society, from which Hobbes begins his theory of history. Ferguson's thesis that the aquisitive urge is unnatural to primitive society is better grounded in fact (see A. Ferguson, *Essay in History of Civil Society*, Basle, 1789, p.125).
51   T. Hobbes, *Leviathan*, London, 1980, p.161.
52   Ibid., p.190.
53   T. Hobbes, *De cive*, V, v.
54   Ibid., XII, II. In this case Hobbes goes too far with his analogy of the state and its rulers. As we have already noted, even Luther, far from being the most progressive of social thinkers in the late Middle Ages, wrote: 'And what if a prince is wrong; are the people obliged to follow him? No, because no one must

go against the truth; it is more fitting to obey God that to obey a man' (M. Luther, *On Civil Power*, III). Hobbes contradicts his professed desire to construct his theory within the Christian tradition and ends up as one of the very atheists he is attempting to fight.

55   Ibid., VIII, v.
56   Aristotle, *Nicomochean Ethics*, IV, 5, 1126a13–14.
57   Proclus, *The Elements of Theology*, 12.
58   St Thomas Aquinas, *Summa theologiae*, Prima parte, Qu. 48, Art. 2.
59   Ibid., Prima parte, Qu. 49, Art. 3.
60   R. Cumberland, *De legibus naturae...*, Lubeca et Francofurti, 1683, p.277.
61   See ibid., p.87.
62   See ibid., pp.403–9.
63   T. More, *Utopia*, London, 1977, p.128.
64   Ibid., p.65.
65   Ibid., p.120.
66   C. Fourier, *Oeuvres complètes*, Vol. I, Paris, 1845, p.81.
67   Ibid., Vol. VI, Paris, 1845, p.35.
68   Thus, for example, Fourier argues that 'the leap from chaos to harmony' takes place in accordance with the 'appearance of a northern corona' and 'the disinfection and fragrance of the seas owing to the northern fluid', while the reverse 'leap from the harmony to chaos' is linked to 'the second infection of the seas by the southern fluid' and the 'changing of magnetized iron at the south pole' (see C. Fourier, *Oeuvres complètes*, Vol. VI, Paris, 1845, pp.140–41, 'Tableau du cours du mouvement social').
69   C. Fourier, *Oeuvres complètes*, Vol. I, p.47, notes.
70   Ibid.
71   A. Blanqui, *Critique sociale*, Vol. I, Paris, 1885, pp. 195–6.
72   W. Weitling, *Garantien der Harmonie und Freiheit*, Berlin, 1908, S.162.
73   See A. Blanqui, *Textes choisis*, Paris, 1955, pp.143–4; W. Weitling, *Garantien der Harmonie und Freiheit*, S.74.
74   A. Blanqui, *Critique sociale*, Vol. I, p.208.
75   A. Blanqui, *Textes choisis*, p.167.
76   Ibid., p.146.
77   Ibid., p.169.

2 Establishing a Coherence

The development of coherent theories of human history has essentially been a lengthy process: the attempt below to distinguish it from the general progress of human thought is inevitably provisional, and the principles on which it is based are open to criticism. Since, however, we have shown that those historical theories are coherent that (a) *reject an artificial beginning to human history*, (b) *place no limits on social development*, and (c) *conduct their periodization of the historical process based on an analysis of the inner mechanisms driving human society*, we shall discuss the development of coherent historical theories spanning the entire history of theories concerning the inner nature and basic directions of social systems.

The First Steps

Elements of coherent historical theories can sometimes be found where it seems that an inadequate conception of the world is totally dominant. Theoretical propositions indicative of attempts to develop a coherent set of views are barely visible within the general intellectual context, and can be classified as rudiments of a new theory only very conditionally.

Thus in the ancient world Democritus, that outstanding protagonist of materialism, counterposed an evolutionary development of humanity from the animal world and a gradual development of the foundations of social life to the doctrine of divine creation and the contractual nature of the state. He proposed that, while coexisting with the animals, the first people gradually 'began to seek refuge in caves' and 'learnt how to use fire'.[1] According to Democritus, the emergence of the first human communities was characterized by the fact that, 'in communicating with one another, [people] began to assign verbal symbols to objects and themselves created a habitual language of description'.[2] It was need, Democritus proposed, rather than divine intervention, that forced people to

41

improve their skills and abilities, and finally, as a result of a long evolutionary process, 'art was invented along with everything else of use to social life'.[3] Today these ideas seem naive, but in Democritus' day they were practically the only evidence that elements of an evolutionary doctrine of progressive social development were occupying thinkers' minds.

The same can be said with regard to Lactantius, who in the first centuries AD attempted in full correspondence with the new religious teaching to examine the pre-state (taken to be the period before Adam's original sin, and therefore an epistemological rather than historical category), the state and post-state stages of humanity. The latter concept of course remained hypothetical, and was derived from the possibility of a society all the members of which would be suffused with Christian morality, excluding any need for violence of man against man.

The first real step towards the creation of a coherent vision of the historical process, however, was made in the 13th century by St Thomas Aquinas, one of the greatest theologians of the Middle Ages. In terms of symmetry and lack of contradiction, his theory of social progress, in our opinion, was to be bettered only in the 18th century. St Thomas was one of the first figures in history to recognize that human society is at one and the same time part of and separate from the natural environment. In his opinion, human beings were the result of all the preceding phases of progressive development in the material world,[4] and they 'represent the greatest perfection in nature'.[5] St Thomas distinguished four types of law: *lex divina, lex aeterna, lex naturalis* and *lex humana* – a list that is astonishingly similar to the list of sciences later proposed by Comte.[6] And just as Comte did in the 19th century, St Thomas in the 13th century pointed out that, with the transition from one type of law to another, so the level at which it can be considered absolute is lowered, while the variety of possible developmental routes increases. St Thomas' formulation of the difference between social and natural philosophical laws seems particularly apposite: 'Each human law,' he wrote, 'is a law to the extent to which it is distanced from the laws of nature. But if it is completely incompatible with the laws of nature, then it is not a law, but a travesty of the law.'[7]

St Thomas in many respects followed Aristotle and St Augustine in considering social features of human life to be natural. His formulations, however, are far less categorical than those of his predecessors. Regarding the human desire for social existence, for example, St Thomas notes that 'this is far more inherent to human beings than to animals',[8] and thus he places no insurmountable barrier between humans and their natural environment.[9]

Starting from his concept of man as the highest form of natural phenomenon, St Thomas develops his thesis concerning society's relative independence from the natural world, the possibility of human intervention to change the environment, and the natural exploitation by man of the external world's potential to satisfy his daily needs. In contrast to Aristotle, however, St Thomas does not transfer to society the former's understanding of the interrelation of advanced and backward principles, of the 'weak' and the 'strong'. On the contrary, basing himself on his idea of *lex humana*, St. Thomas argues that the subordination of the weak to the strong, which may indeed have influenced the emergence of society, should not be made the basis of the social system and will inevitably be eliminated;[10] moreover (and here St Thomas sticks to the teachings of his mentor) the efforts of the holy Church should facilitate this process.[11]

All these positive aspects of St Thomas' work are but a prelude to his main achievement: his theory of social progress. He depicted history mainly as a reflection of the Christian world view, which was to be incorporated into several other sciences so as to enrich its theological doctrine, which 'can take something from philosophical disciplines ... to make its teachings more easily understood'.[12]

St Thomas' theory of development is constructed on two planes, as it were. On the one hand, its hierarchy of societies is built up in accordance with the objectives of their inhabitants. These objectives he divides into direct, intermediate (or mediated) and maximal. This aspect of his theory is to a certain extent borrowed from earlier Christian authors and bears a meaningful theological nuance. The second part of the theory, which could be seen as a consequence of Aristotle's ideas, in fact introduces a major innovation: the identification of three epochs, the distinguishing features of which is the essence of their social relations.

The *first* Aquinas calls the commune stage, and indeed he adopts Aristotle's idea that individual humans at this time are like parts of a body subordinate to the whole. The main feature of this society is the dependence of all its members on their ruler (council of elders, tsar and so on). The *second* stage St Thomas considers to be a society which he calls *civilis conversatio*, which is governed by laws guaranteeing the basis of citizens' legal independence, while the ruling authority ceases to suppress its subjects as forcefully as before. Underlying this type of society is the equal cooperation of citizens who are legally independent of each other. Finally, the *third* stage he calls an association or society of universal brotherhood, in which people cease to oppress and humiliate each other. Along with major changes in the dominant social and economic relations, during the third stage there is also a crystallization of individuals' supreme (maximal) goals in connection with their urge for moral perfection.

It is to this third stage of social development that St Thomas devotes his most penetrating observations concerning a just and fair state system. His rather trivial argument that 'if a group of free people is led by its rulers in the name of the common good of the entire group, then such a government is just and right because it suits people's needs; if the government is formed not for the good of all but merely in the ruler's personal interest, then it will be an unjust and perverted government',[13] is augmented by his statement in the same work that, at the stage of association, 'in the course of carrying out his functions the ruler must satisfy needs that correspond to a good life',[14] though 'not for certain individuals, but a good life for all'.[15]

Commentators on St Thomas Aquinas today are inclined to see more originality in his views on the future society than there actually is. His thesis that the future might see a world confederation of states in which a central authority would maintain peace and guarantee the economic, social and cultural progress of humanity through collective institutions can hardly be considered anything more than evidence of his support for the leading role of the Church, while his opinion that the basic functions of society would in the future consist of providing its members with the necessities of life can certainly not be treated as an embryonic communism.

All the same, it is worth noting that St Thomas' work contains the basis for a coherent understanding of social progress as a complex phenomenon, the periodization of which can only be conducted on the principles of society's own inner development, without the application of various external factors. When concerned with social progress, the inevitably theological character of his theory recedes into the background, since, as we mentioned above, he considers social progress to be, not a unity of existence, but a unity of action: unity not in *esse*, but in *agere*.

In our view, the theories of St Thomas Aquinas are practically the only example in the Middle Ages of an intellectual breakthrough towards an understanding of the true nature of history and the principles of its periodization. Only the most realistic philosophers of the 17th–18th centuries were able to continue this development, and with their researches they paved the way for a coherent understanding of history.

The Liberalism of the Modern Age

St Thomas' intellectual achievement acquired the features of a theory five centuries later, assisted by works of the early European materialists. To varying degrees Grotius, Cumberland, Bacon and Locke all accepted the main methodological postulates of Christianity, though interpreting them partly in the spirit of the 'social contract'. Thus, for example, Locke, defending the natural origins of human social life, explained the latter as St Augustine had before him: God created man to be such that, by His divine decision, man suffered when alone, and since all people are created by one almighty and infinitely wise creator, they are thus all the servants of one supreme sovereign and are sent to Earth at His command. Their existence must continue while it pleases not them, but Him.

St. Thomas' doctrine of the laws of nature and society looks very different in the works of 17th-century authors. In contrast to Spinoza and Descartes, who transferred the laws of nature to society, Francis Bacon and his followers proposed an attractive combination of *historia naturalis* and *historia civilis*. Bacon considered the material progress of society, which he understood partly as the progress of natural science, partly as technical improvement, to represent a mutual interpenetration of these two types of history. Seeing the science of man and civil society as part of the science of nature, Bacon discovered gradual evolutionary changes both in nature and society, which served as the object of historical research. Thus the relationship between the laws of nature and society was still being treated in the same way as by St Thomas Aquinas six centuries later, when Montesquieu wrote: 'The world of rational beings is not governed ... to such perfection as the physical world because, although it has laws that are by their nature immutable, it does not follow them with the same constancy with which the physical world obeys its own laws.'[16]

The central question for the philosophy of history in the 16th–18th centuries was the problem of social relations, their origins and prospects. Theories of history became formally inclined to the 'social contract' concept, but a major difference was concealed by this formal devotion to an old doctrine, a difference which undermined the very basis of such notions. In contrast with Hobbes, Locke and the philosophers of the Enlightenment interpreted the natural condition as a condition of peace, of good will, mutual assistance and security, which was 'least subject to change and by far the most blissful for man'.[17]

The interpretation of the social contract itself evolved rapidly during this period from its relative acknowledgement as a political phenomenon – as with Locke, who believed that all people remained in the natural condition until they joined some political society of their own free will – until it came to be viewed in the logical, rather than the historical sense. Rousseau, who believed that 'a man's first perception was the perception of his existence, and his first consideration – consideration for himself',[18] remarked that the affirmation of one's own interest, one which differed from the interest of others, was evidence of the formation of society. 'The first to think about sectioning off land and saying "this is mine!",' wrote Rousseau, 'the first to come across people sufficiently unsophisticated to believe this, was the true founder of civil society'.[19]

Thus the social condition ceased to be an artificial one, and blended organically with the overall picture of history. Rousseau thought that natural law applied also to the social condition. Here he distinguished the *droit naturel proprement dit* and *droit naturel raisonné* as being based on instinct in the first place and on reason in the second.

The French philosophers of the 18th century also fairly categorically linked the making of the social condition, not to the relationship of power and subordination (although this remained important),[20] but to the formation of private ownership. The interpretation of the emergence of ownership was closely interwoven with the study (albeit very primitive) of economic relations. 'As long as people performed only labours that could have been performed by one person alone,' wrote Rousseau, 'they continued to enjoy the benefits of independent relations to the full. But the moment one man started to require the help of another ... then the equality disappeared, and ownership emerged.'[21] However, the concept of ownership, according to Rousseau, was not given to man from above: 'There was much journeying to be done on the path of progress; many skills and knowledge had to be acquired; and these had to be passed down and accumulated from age to age in order to arrive at this final boundary of the natural condition.'[22]

It was through this analysis of ownership and the emerging exploitation based on ownership, the subjugation of one man by another, that the philosophers of the 18th century approached the central idea in their system of equality and freedom. Rousseau made the latter the basis of his theory of the future society, a return on a new footing to a condition characterized by the absence of ownership and inequality.[23] Meanwhile the problem of the future society was for Rousseau a matter of equating the features of the natural condition with some of the positive aspects of the social order. This formula, involving synthesis of the aspects of two conditions of mankind that apparently disclaimed each other fully, was something totally new for that time.

The main points of Rousseau's conception found sympathy and support among the European philosophers. The transition from the natural (primitive) condition, devoid of ownership and organized production, to the civil society had been considered, and the analysis of the emergence of labour and its division, and of the forming of ownership and inequality, had been traced in more detail by Johann Gottfried Herder in his *Ideas on the Philosophy of History of Mankind*;[24] and Anthony Ashley Cooper Shaftesbury gives a fine description of the future society as one that removes all of the positive aspects of the past conditions of mankind, in which the nature of man is manifested more completely and has fully matured.[25]

The notions of 18th-century philosophers on the higher stages of the development of civilization contain a forthright recognition of the objectivity of all the changes that had hitherto taken place in society, even those changes that most contradicted the aspects of human nature as declared by the philosophers. The theory of history becomes, as a result, the conception of the development of individual and social interests and how they equate with each other. This gives rise to the definition of the purpose of the future association as the free development of each person provided by the material progress of society.

In fact an interpretation methodically reminiscent of the Thomistic teachings on the progress of society again became widespread towards the middle of the 18th century, but it differed from Catholic doctrines mainly through the introduction, by the vulgar materialism of the 16th–17th centuries, of an understanding of the meaning of the natural, technical and, ultimately, economic factors that influenced social progress. So a synthesis of the economic approach to social progress with the idea of the triadic nature of that progress itself ought to have been the last stage leading up to the emergence of coherent theories of social progress.

The First Attempts at an Economic View of History

The emergence at the end of the 18th century of the capitalist type of society with its inherent fast industrial growth potential prompted philosophers and historians to take a closer look at the economic processes in society. One way or another, the whole history of civilization came to be viewed, not through the prism of the moral betterment of man, but from the viewpoint of the economic possibilities and expediency of selected phenomena of social life. There was a simultaneous sharp growth of interest in the study of the making and development of society as the world's horizons were expanding as a result of geographical discoveries, and the representatives of European civilization came into contact with communities about which they could previously only fantasize.

The most prominent writers on the influence of economic factors on social progress at the end of the 18th century were J. Turgot in France and A. Ferguson and A. Smith in Britain. They were avid critics of the concept of the 'social contract' in its extreme manifestations, and supported the interpretation of the natural and historical character of the formation of social ties. These and philosophers like them studied the historical events of the past in close association with the economic processes of different periods. This produced a deeper comprehension of the principles of the functioning of their own society. In all their aspects the views of the aforementioned 18th-century thinkers inevitably ushered in the appearance of acceptable historical theories. The generalization of their conceptual principles became a task for another of their great contemporaries.

The primitive view of the period preceding the 'social contract' as wildness had been virtually overcome at the end of the 18th century. The coupling of the thesis of the social essence of man with the real facts of the relative isolation of primeval communities was achieved by appealing to the nature of the activity of those times when the main sources of subsistence were hunting and gathering, and the hunter's way of life inevitably presupposed 'families or small tribes, very isolated from each other, for each one of them needed a lot of space to obtain their means of subsistence'.[26] In these conditions only a small number of people could live together, as a large number could soon have exterminated all the game in a certain locality and thereby have exhausted the basic means of survival.[27]

Turgot and Smith stressed that there was no place for social inequality in such a condition of society, for general poverty establishes the general equality of people. Ferguson, for his part, pointed out that there can be no ownership in a place where the accumulation of wealth is impossible or undesirable owing to the forms that it assumes. In a tribe existing by hunting and fishing, wrote the philosopher, the weapons, small utensils and animal skins which every hunter used were his only possessions, while the food that would be consumed in the future could not be appropriated until it had been caught.[28] So there was no need for the appropriation of a larger quantity of the tools of labour as property than that which could effectively be utilized, nor was it possible to appropriate consumer goods.

Correspondingly, ownership arose only at a time and place in which the first opportunities for the retention and accumulation of socially significant goods arose. Ferguson viewed the transition to private ownership in the classical sense of the concept and associated it with the spread of agriculture and the individualization of the consumption of retainable goods.[29] Smith in his *The Theory of Moral Sentiments* emphasized that the economic nature of ties between separate families weakened with the transition from the appropriating to the productive economy, although the need for some collective actions remained. Turgot, however, analysed the formation of ownership relations among communities of herdsmen, pointing out that it was then that slavery was conceived as having been conditioned by force: 'Nations were sometimes unable to avoid struggle with a band of determined people ... These, after winning their struggle, became the masters of their herds ... The fear of death by hunger restrained the vanquished from flight ... and [they remained] the slaves of their masters.'[30] Here it was pointed out that both the emergence of surplus goods and the situation which forced some people to reconcile themselves to their wretched existence resulted in the formation of classes. Smith thought that it was precisely this initial economic period, that of the herdsmen, that permitted the great inequality of conditions, and that there was no other period in which wealth would have given greater power to those who owned it.

The economists and historians of the late 18th century thought that the emergence of ownership and property inequality had led to the emergence of power and rule as a necessary cause. They showed that the making of ownership relations was a totally natural process, divorced from considerations about whether or not this was needed, considerations which consequently furthered and supported the strengthening of power and subordination.[31] They showed that the most respected members of a tribe (in terms of strength or know-how) became its rulers. This esteem subsequently passed to their sons and their families, making power hereditary.[32] All of the aforementioned writers noticed that the state was established to defend ownership, to defend those who possess any kind of property from those who do not, to ensure the security of property and to protect the wealthy from the poor.[33]

Turgot and Smith stressed the objective character of the emergence of property inequality and class structure and said that the division of labour that had resulted in these phenomena, while unquestionably adverse from the moral point of view, at the same time played an enormously positive role in the history of mankind, ensuring economic progress and enabling society to achieve its present level. The singling out of intellectual labour, when 'a genius, freed from the burden imposed by needs of the first order, departs from the narrow sphere in which those requirements held him, and channels all his strength into scientific design ... [gives birth to] the powerful ascent of human reason, which draws away with it all sections of society and derives the new strength from improving them'.[34] But Ferguson and Smith stressed that people engaged in productive activity turn into machines, and the capabilities of a master of his field develop in parallel with the stupefaction from which an unskilled labourer suffers.[35]

The analysis of the division of labour as presented in the works of the aforementioned authors is to us far more important than all the directly historical studies which they, especially Smith, carried out.[36] It was this circumstance that became central to the philosophy of history, the conception of which, based on the viewpoints cited here, was created by the leading British thinker, historian and economist, David Hume.

Hume thought that social organization was not so much a natural thing for man as such as something that naturally emerged from the requirements of communal life. Only with society's help, he wrote in *A Treatise of Human Nature*, can man compensate his own shortcomings and acquire a superiority over other living beings; our capacity for labour increases thanks to the unification of forces, our ability to work develops thanks to the division of labour, and we are less vulnerable to the whim of fate and chance thanks to mutual assistance. Hume viewed the emergence of social institutions as a process of deepening and improving the ties that are forged between people during the course of their activity. Moreover, he believed that the making of such ties and their specific forms suggested the existence of specific agreements between people: from assigning a specific meaning to language to the recognition of the steadfast relations of the possession of goods.

Hume gathered the views of many researchers who commented on the serious influence of economic processes on social life; he argued in favour of the emergence of inequality among the farming tribes and analysed the significance of the division of labour and trade not only for the progress of production but also for the development of society, the stability of which he linked with the formation of a strong middle class of independent industrialists and merchants.

However, his analysis of the stages in the development of human civilization is of the utmost significance. It stands to reason that Hume, like all theorists of his time, should begin his analysis in the pre-state epoch, but it is also highly noteworthy that he described its main feature not as the absence of the state or of civil society but as the absence of ownership relations. Then followed the epoch of ownership; moreover, Hume was one of the first to use consequential methodology to analyse it.

In contrast with his contemporaries, Hume dismissed the view of the history of class societies as a rigidly progressive or singularly regressive phenomenon. Assessing the economic foundations of the ancient societies, he became the first and one of few European philosophers to show that small-scale agriculture performed by independent property-owning farmers, by its very nature, was the basis of the ancient economies. The influence of slavery was insignificant, and this did not define the basis of the ancient economies.[37] Hume went on to regard the next social order, feudalism, as an unquestionably progressive one from the point of view of the development of industry and the means of industry, but noted that feudal society meant the masses were far more dependent on the suzerain than the ancients, and he viewed the oppression of the masses under feudalism as being far tighter and more universal.

Hume linked the improvement of the social order with his own society, but in a very specific way. While thinking that the achievement of political freedoms accelerates social progress, and showing that the latter is accompanied by the achievements of industry, science and the arts, Hume nevertheless did not regard the capitalist society to be the ideal one and did not associate any historical perspective with it. He believed that this social order, although it eased the burdens of inequality and oppression as it developed, could not directly be described as the 'society of the future'. From his point of view the betterment of people and social institutions would inevitably make people more humane as a consequence of becoming accustomed to intercourse, which has something in common with the thesis of Smith.[38] But it is worth pointing out that Hume links the appearance of a new society with a certain type of person aware of the nature of personal and social well-being and who takes these as the point of subordination. If every man, he wrote, was quick-witted enough to understand this great interest which makes him uphold justice, and possessed enough inner strength to follow rigidly and undeviatingly general and distant interests, and to resist the temptations of the pleasures and benefits that he enjoys, there would be nothing resembling a government or a political society, and every man, guided by his own freedom, would live in full peace and harmony with all others.

This passage from Hume, distantly reminiscent of Marxian notions of the making of the 'new type of individual', is based on a profound understanding of the conditions under which this sort of change in mankind could become possible. Hume clearly links this change with overcoming ownership, which he sees as the basis of all social cataclysms (although it is not a major driving force of progress). Ownership can be disclaimed only when the need for the struggle between people for the satisfaction of their daily needs disappears, when production is virtually in a position to provide humanity with all it needs. Hume wrote, in *A Treatise of Human Nature*, that the concept of ownership is no longer present when there is an abundance of things of all kinds, and all the desires of people are satisfied; in this event the concept of ownership becomes lost entirely and everything remains common. Society distinguished by the absence of ownership and separation, society with a high degree of morality, becomes the third great stage in social evolution as the leading humanists of the Age of Enlightenment saw it.

The Making of Positivism

There were many premises for the establishment of coherent historical constructions towards the end of the 18th century. The notion of the progressive nature of social development, of the possible identification of a triad in the course of that progress, of the naturalness of social evolution as such and as caused by economic changes that took place as the productive forces developed, was firmly established in the minds of the researchers. Most of these principles were adopted by Karl Marx and Frederick Engels in the middle of the 19th century. It is with these names that the first adequate representation of history emerged, one, inevitably, aggravated by some contradictions, but no less grandiose for this. However, before embarking on an analysis of this picture, we will consider another movement, one which also had its beginnings in this period and which led to one more trend of the historical theory which was very close to the acceptable notions of social development: the conception of positivism, or 'positive philosophy', as its authors called it.

The positivist school was the leading one of the first half of the 19th century, although the work of its leading exponents was not confined purely to this period. Positivism was a natural successor to the theories of the Age of Enlightenment and rejected philosophy which was not based on knowledge and facts. The beginnings of positivism can be seen in the works of Turgot and Condorcet, and elements can be traced clearly in the works of the British late 18th-century social thinkers. But positivism flourished as a movement of its own in the first half of the 19th century and is associated mainly with the names of Saint-Simon and Comte. Saint-Simon and Comte held largely similar views, but we will look at them in relative isolation from each other.

Saint-Simon's thoughts on the social order were not concentrated in a single fundamental work, as with Comte, therefore a large number of works have to be consulted. The philosopher created a very realistic and unswerving idea of social progress, despite a number of contradictions and some inconsistencies.[39] The crux of his philosophy was the assertion that mankind was progressing towards a state or condition distinguished by the ideal organization of communal life, which to a degree falls under the heading of the 'realm of reason', to use a term from the Age of Enlightenment. But Saint-Simon closely links the onset of this condition with social and economic progress, making his conception an integral and rounded one.

Saint-Simon underlined the progressive character of development when he wrote that the future takes its shape from the last members of a row in which the first members constitute the past. This, according to him, indicates that social organization is characterized by secure relations which do not change fundamentally with the transition from one historical epoch to another and which ensure succession of development. One of these relations is ownership: he wrote that 'the existence of society depends on the retention of the right of ownership'.[40] Another is religion, which he believes cannot be disclaimed even in the industrial period.

The philosopher in his theory successfully combines the ideas of social and moral progress. On the one hand, he repeats the principles of the 18th-century thinkers on the role of the division of labour in social development, rightly concluding that 'the division of labour develops both in the religious and secular areas in the very broadest sense' and therefore 'people depend less on each other individually, but each of them depends on the whole mass'.[41] It was this, he wrote, that was important to understand the development of morality, for the 'most general moment in the advancing movement of societies, the fact implicitly containing all others, is the progress of moral conception, which makes man aware of his social significance'.[42] So, he noted, production progresses in the same direction as the moral idea, dominant in society.

Social progress itself could still be subdivided into separate phases which largely corresponded with the moral, intellectual and religious character of an epoch. On the one hand, the works of Saint-Simon divided history into three epochs: the theological, dominated by religion; the metaphysical, when religious doctrines began to give way to the embryonic scientific approach to nature and society; and the positive, meaning mainly the social order of the future. On the other hand, there was another classification, based entirely on religious and intellectual criteria: idol worship corresponded to the epoch of the primitive economy; polytheism to the epoch of fine arts; deism to the epoch of political and moral knowledge; and physicism to the epoch of mathematical and physical sciences.

One of Saint-Simon's main achievements is that he addressed the nature of social progress and discovered that it contained periods which could be split into two groups: the critical and organic epochs. He wrote that 'the objective of social activity has been clearly defined during organic epochs, and all efforts are geared towards that objective ... Critical epochs are a diametrically opposed spectacle ... The objective of social activity becomes something unknown, there is a lack of certainty in common relations, a transition to the area of private relations ... the legitimacy of power the people wield is questioned, and the governors and the governed are in a state of war with each other'.[43] The author noted within these epochs destructive periods, during which the bases of the organization that preceded them were destroyed and constructive periods, during which a new type of public order came into being.

Saint-Simon noted a number of important features of European history. It was he who justified milder forms of exploitation with the development of economic management, as a result of which 'the lot of the overwhelming majority of people who constituted society in the theological and feudal system was far less wretched than in the social order of the Greeks and Romans'.[44] He rightly suggested that the distinctive features of the political order were caused by the distinctive features of the economic organization of society, and that the progress of that economic organization brought about the need for adequate changes to the political system. Saint-Simon demonstrated the struggle between economic progress and political inertness in the French Revolution, which he depicted as a war between industrialists (a word he used to describe both proletarians and entrepreneurs, since all were, to the same degree, *travailleurs* and *collaborateurs*) and the representatives of the idle classes.[45] Here he commented that the 'pretensions of the bourgeoisie sully the idea of equality less than the claims of the gentry',[46] because only the industrial class was able to provide the progress society needed so much.

Saint-Simon in his works represented the future society as a society of a mature industrial order with his own typical methodology. He saw the development of industry as a means of providing social prosperity and not, like the utopians, as an evil. He believed the progress of industry might not only eliminate the causes of class conflict, but also help end interethnic conflicts and wars. Saint-Simon formulated his concept of the future society entirely from the point of view of industrial progress, saying that all of our thoughts and efforts must be directed towards the one and only goal of organizing industry in its broadest sense, one which embraces all types of useful labour. He regarded industry as democratic; its development depended on increased consumption and social well-being:

> In the new political order our only concern – our constant concern – should be how best to apply the knowledge found in the sciences, the arts and trades to satisfy the needs of man; and the broadening of this knowledge, its betterment and greatest possible accumulation, in short to find the fullest combination of all separate works of the sciences, the arts and the trades.[47]

Industrialists would head society and, as a result, 'the prosperity of the state will grow as quickly as ever possible, and society will possess all the individual and social fortune that human nature can bestow on it'.[48]

Saint-Simon would appear to be suggesting the presence of a social contract in his future society. The society would be based on that contract, although commentators have barely touched on this element of the philosopher's theory. On the one hand, the lower classes of industrial society had to acknowledge before *les chefs industriels*: 'You are rich, and we are poor; you work with your head, and we with our hands; from that fundamental difference it follows that we must obey you.' But this must be a two-way process: 'Since the minority no longer has to resort to violence to keep the proletarian class in obeyance, it ought to do the following: firstly, take action which will give the proletariat more interest in a peaceful society ... and, thirdly, action designed to give the workers a higher degree of political influence.'[49] Is this not a vision of what in fact happened in the Western world a century and a half after the philosopher's death?

And so the founder of positivism viewed the historical process primarily through the development of the industrial system. August Comte, a pupil of Saint-Simon, refined his mentor's methodological and theoretical elements of historical construction. Comte's conception was accepted as a sign of the times, largely because the fundamentals of his philosophy were not his alone – they were the common property of the century, said John Stuart Mill when writing about his predecessor, in his *Auguste Comte and Positivism*.

Comte offered to arrange the sciences according to their degree of complexity, and he put sociology in the top category (which he later supplemented with psychology). He saw the main virtue of positive sociology in the fact that it always regards the current state as the inevitable result of the whole of evolution before it. It always assigns, in the study of modern events, a dominant place to the rational assessment of the past, which eliminates there and then the critical trends which are incompatible with any healthy historical conception. The point of creating this theory, wrote Comte, was that teaching which satisfactorily explains the totality of the past will receive, on this merit, a leading role in the direction of future thought.

It follows that a task like this needs a specific method of study. Comte wrote that historical science had already acquired a sufficient amount of factual material to alter the course of research into mankind's progress in a big way: 'In the search for social laws, reason must necessarily go from the common to the private, that is begin by understanding the entire development of the human race in unity, distinguishing in it only a very few consistent phases, and then gradually, increasing the number of intermediate links, achieve more and more precision.'[50]

Comte's social philosophy began, on the face of it, with the definition of society formulated by Thomas Aquinas. Agreeing with the fact that 'mankind is a continuous aggregate of beings with a common aim',[51] the philosopher stressed that society exists only where common and combined activity is performed. In any other hypothesis we obtain only a conglomeration of a certain number of individuals on one and the same ground. It is in this that human society differs from that of animals living in herds. Comte's theory of social progress was marked, firstly, by its realistic nature and, secondly, by the form inherited from his predecessors Turgot, Condorcet and Saint-Simon.

On the one hand, Comte showed that the progress of society was an objective process which manifested itself during the evolutionary movement of the social organism from one stage to another. 'The order of nature,' he wrote, 'must consist of the beginnings and premises of all possible kinds of progress. The positive view of human relations consists of a consideration of all of their changes not as new acts of creation, but as new stages of evolution. This principle is manifested in its entirety in history.'[52] Comte believed that 'the progress of mankind is a continuation of the advancement of the animal kingdom and is its highest level' at the initial stages of the development of society.

Comte's conception of progress involved three stages of evolution, which followed on historically one from the other. They were the theological, the metaphysical and the positive. They corresponded to the war, the transitional and the scientific and industrial organization of society. He used the European states to illustrate the objectiveness of the historical process, claiming that feudalism was inevitable ('the feudal order would have arisen even if it had not been for the [barbarian] invasions ... they simply influenced the timing of the new regime')[53] and that its character was progressive (the mediaeval order resulted in 'the labour of man beginning to be replaced more and more by the forces of nature, which the ancients had made so little use of').[54] Comte said, importantly, that technological progress had been conditioned not only by the development of reason but also by the progress of social relations, particularly overcoming slavery, which eliminated the possibility of the use of man as a silent tool of labour. But the transition to the industrial stage became possible only when servitude had been eliminated, when city communities had gained a greater degree of freedom and when the use of money became more widespread.[55]

On the other hand, Comte stressed the immense role of human knowledge (and the sphere of the ideal in general) in the making of social development. He warned his contemporaries against underestimating the intellectual level of one era or another and said that society always progressed alongside the progression of knowledge. 'The positive features of the Medieval order,' he wrote, 'reveal how unjust was that superficial philosophy which described the wonderful era when Thomas Aquinas, Albert the Great, Roger Bacon and Dante were in their eminence as a barbarian and dark age'.[56]

Borrowing from his predecessors, Comte attached great meaning to the intellectual development of man characteristic of late 18th-century thought. He believed that 'ideas govern the world and cause violent shocks in it; after all the social mechanism is supported ultimately by the opinions of people',[57] and he was convinced that 'intellectual evolution should always be considered first as the basis of the development of mankind … the history of the human mind stands at the head of the history of mankind. We must acknowledge, rather *continue* to acknowledge the common history of the human mind as the leader of our historical studies'.[58]

So Comte's sociology, in our view, was the limit to the improvement of conceptions which one way or another had their roots in the ideological principles of the Age of Enlightenment. Correspondingly, Comte's notions about the future of mankind did not differ greatly from those of Saint-Simon. Claiming that 'wealth, which has social origins, should be [social] in its purpose, retaining the personal attribution necessary for it to retain its independence when serving society',[59] Comte believed that 'it is unimportant for a nation who controls capital as long as it is used in a way that benefits it'.[60]

John Stuart Mill's contribution to positivism and a few of his achievements should also be mentioned. This inventive thinker greatly improved a whole range of principles advanced by the founders of positivism. Mill offered the highly justified formula of equating ideas like the factor of social development with the evolution of the social basis itself, a formula which disclaimed that of Saint-Simon and, to some extent, that of Comte on the domineering role of ideal factors in social progress. He wrote that ideas in general, if they are not helped by external influences, do not have a fast or direct bearing on human relations; but the most favourable external circumstances may pass by without exerting any influence if there are no ideas capable of facilitating their direct influence; however, if favourable external circumstances do encounter ideas already existing in society, then fast and good results can certainly be expected. It was this approach that led Mill to think that there was no strict law of social progress; Comte also indirectly stressed this principle in his thesis that 'precision' played a less important role in the social sciences than other scientific disciplines. Mill wrote that the continuity of the conditions of the human mind and human society is not governed by its own special and independent law; it must depend on psychological and ethological laws which govern how circumstances affect people and how people affect circumstances; until this law is no longer associated with the psychological and ethological laws on which it should depend, it cannot be turned from an empirical law into a scientific law, and it is generally early to predict the future paths of progress.

Mill saw the source of social development in the struggle between opposites existing in society, the main ones being immobility and the drive towards progress. The struggle between these principles, between progress and immobility, is what makes the history of mankind so interesting, he wrote in his work, *On Liberty*, going on to say that, if the permanent antagonism which fired the human spirit were to give way to the prevalence of only one element, be it the most 'salutary', then it would transpire that we are putting too much faith in the progression so often talked about as an 'inherent property of our species',[61] since further progress is impossible outside the struggle between opposing historical principles.

Mill quite rightly pointed out that the struggle between progress and immobility not only conditioned the course of history but was itself conditioned by the course of history. Regarding the feudal order, he wrote that at a certain stage it embodied the dynamic nature of development, and then, when it ceased to comply with the requirements of the age, it became a static formation, doomed to destruction. There was substantial progress in society 'under the domination and auspices of feudality', and the reason for the demise of that system lay not in its faults but in its positive aspects, namely progress under its auspices, which made mankind 'desirous of obtaining and capable of realising' a better social form than that which feudality gave it.[62]

Mill, like his predecessors, believed in the improvement of the industrial society, the main principles of which he thought were adequate for human nature. The shortcomings, which the philosopher had neither the desire nor the grounds to disclaim in his own society, could,[63] in his opinion, be overcome by an increased degree of freedom for all members of society. Mill thought this was a key condition for social progress (*On Liberty*). Meanwhile the latter process culminated automatically as economic progress was achieved, so the industrial order was able to evolve in its own way, gradually overcoming its inherent negative aspects. The flaws and injustices of the present system are significant, wrote Mill, but are not inclined to increase; on the contrary, the tendency is for them to subside.[64] Mill, like Saint-Simon and Comte, denied that it was necessary to radically alter the industrial system with a view to forming relations of the communist type. This complied fully with the sociological doctrine of positivism.

There we round off our short survey of the development of historical thought, the essence of which was progress in the making of coherent historical theories. The theorists of this movement belonged to all manner of sociological schools, but were all linked by a number of circumstances which deserved special mention.

Firstly, there was a bond between the Ancient Greek atomists, the ideas of St Augustine and St Thomas Aquinas and the scholars of the Modern Age and positivism in which all of these thinkers acknowledged *social progress*. The idea of social progression was presented in the texts we have discussed with varying degrees of justification and from various points of view, but the very fact that it existed as a key methodological principle displays the clear compatibility of the positions of the authors described and makes their concepts applicable, in varying degrees, to a description of the true history of mankind.

Secondly, the theories discussed contain attempts (not always uniformly successful) to assess social progress from the point of view of internal processes in the social organization. The fact that society was self-propelled was central to these theories. Of course the approaches themselves were very varied (Thomas Aquinas one way or another adhered to the thesis of the determining role of the moral perfection of selected persons in the modernization of society as a whole; the scholars of the Age of Enlightenment viewed the progress of human reason and the enrichment of knowledge as the basis of social improvement; authors who concentrated on research into economic life found the source of social progress in the development of modes of production; and so on), but social development was neither reduced to biological or even mechanistic processes, nor was it attributable to defined external (or even supernatural) circumstances.

Thirdly, all of the authors in this section undertook to divide social progress *in accordance with the main methodological principles of their teaching*. If, for example, the biblical events which formed the basis of the historical periodization of St Augustine had nothing in common with the struggle between 'the two communities of mankind' which he used as a source to illustrate progress, the eras distinguished by Thomas Aquinas, Locke, Smith and Hume, Saint-Simon and Comte reflected modifications of notions about the basic motive forces of history. In this respect the theories analysed here were without doubt more secure than those discussed in the previous section.

So the conceptions which became landmarks on the way to achieving acceptable historical constructions took a very long time to perfect. And there was some philosophical succession to their development, in contrast with the inadequate theories. The writers we have discussed were able to knot the thread which seemed to have been broken by the adherents of primitive materialism in the 16th and 17th centuries,[65] and to ensure the movement of European philosophical tradition.

But all of these conceptions were just a prelude to more improved theories which clearly divided history into three phases and which were backed by terminology and methodology well adapted to those objectives. The first of these coherent theories was that of Marx, subjected to some undeserved criticism today.

Notes

1   Here and below, Democritus is in the words of Diodorus. See Diodorus, I, 8 (7).
2   See ibid., I, 8 (3).
3   See ibid., I, 8 (7).
4   See St Thomas Aquinas, *Summa theologiae*, Prima secundae, Qu. 75, Art. 4.
5   Ibid., Prima secundae, Qu. 75, Art. 4.
6   See A. Comte, *Cours de philosophie positive*, Vol. I, Paris, 1864, p.79.
7   St Thomas Aquinas, *Summa theologiae*, Prima secundae, Qu. 95, Art. 2.
8   St Thomas Aquinas, *De regimine principum*, I, 1.
9   Clashing as it does with the rest of his doctrine, St Thomas' idea that the individual is not the product of society (see St Thomas Aquinas, *De rege et regno*, I, 10) is most likely a tribute to Catholic dogma rather than a major element of his theory.
10 See St Thomas Aquinas, *Summa theologiae*, Secunda secundae, Qu. 61, Art. 4.
11 See St Albertus Magnus, *Politica*, I, 1.
12 St Thomas Aquinas, *Summa theologiae*, Prima parte, Qu. 1, Art. 5.
13 St Thomas Aquinas, *De regimine principum*, I, 1.
14 Ibid., I, 15.
15 Ibid., I, 1.
16 C. Montesquieu, *L'esprit des Lois*, I, 1.
17 J.-J. Rousseau, *De l'inégalité parmi les hommes*, Paris, 1965, p.117.
18 Ibid., p.109.
19 Ibid., p.108.
20 See C. Montesquieu, *L'esprit des Lois*, I, 2.
21 J.-J. Rousseau, *De l'inégalité parmi les hommes*, pp.118–19.
22 Ibid., p.109.
23 Voltaire did not understand this other quality of the new economic condition in Rousseau's theory. He described Rousseau's *Le contrat social* as 'a book against the human race', and considered that 'nobody has ever made such mental effort to instil among all of us the desire to become animals' (Voltaire, *Oeuvres complètes*, Vol. XVIII, Paris, 1879, p.475).
24 See J.G.Herder, *Ideen zur der Philosophie der Geschichte der Menschheit*, IV, I–III; VIII, iv; IX, i–iv.
25 See A.A.C. Shaftesbury, *Moralists*, London, 1876, pp.56–72.
26 A.-R.J. Turgot, 'Sur l'histoire universelle', *Oeuvres*, Vol. 2, Paris, 1808, p.216.
27 Adam Smith, *Lectures on Justice, Police, Revenue and Arms*, Oxford, 1896, p.20.
28 See A. Ferguson, *Essay on the History of Civil Society*, Basle, 1789, p.125.
29 See ibid., pp.125–6.
30 A.-R.J. Turgot, *Sur l'histoire universelle*, pp.218–19.
31 See Adam Smith, *An Inquiry into the Nature and Causes of the Wealth of Nations*, London, 1894.
32 See A. Ferguson, *Essay on the History of Civil Society*, pp.152–3.
33 Adam Smith, *Lectures on Justice, Police, Revenue and Arms*, p.15.
34 A.-R.J. Turgot, 'Sur les progrès successifs de l'esprit humain (Discours prononcé le 11 décembre 1750 à la Sorbonne)', *Oeuvres*, Vol. 2, Paris, 1808, p.57

35 See A. Ferguson, *Essay on the History of Civil Society*, p.277.

36 Smith's contribution to the true scientific panorama of history was very substantial. His *Lectures* were an attempt to analyse the progress of mankind, beginning with the ancient times. Moreover, from predominantly economic positions he explained such fundamental circumstances as the city structure of the state in Ancient Greece, the nature of the republican regime in Greece, forms of the degeneration of this regime and the coming of the monarchy. To his great merit, Smith analysed the inner limitation of the slave-holding economy, in the course of which he offered the thesis that the Roman Empire was not so much a higher form of the prosperity of ancient times but a military monarchy, with the aim of suppressing contradictions within that order. Moreover, Smith defied universal notions of the time to prove the progressive nature of the barbarian invasions of Rome, noting that these only accelerated the process which had its beginnings in the natural decomposition of the inner structure of the ancient society (see Adam Smith, *Lectures on Justice, Police, Revenue and Arms*, pp.23–37). The philosopher's merits can be demonstrated more in his analysis of the economic and political systems of feudal society, but this does not fall under the present study.

37 See D. Hume, *Essays Moral, Political and Literary*, Vol. 1, London, 1912, pp.419–22. This is also worth mentioning because not only Hume's contemporaries (for example E. Gibbon) talked about an equal number of slaves and free men in Rome, but later authors, for example Engels, blindly followed Gibbons in his assertions that 'when Athens was in its heyday ... for every adult male citizen there were at least eighteen slaves and more than two wards' (K. Marx and F. Engels, *Collected Works*, Vol. 26, Moscow, 1978, p.222).

38 See Adam Smith, *An Inquiry into the Nature and Causes of the Wealth of Nations*, pp.129, 419.

39 It must be noted that Condorcet's conception, for all its sketchiness, was highly consistent when speaking of the progress of human reason, implying the development of its material embodiment. In Saint-Simon this sort of terminology is used directly to denote the achievements of reason.

40 C.H. de Saint-Simon, *Vues sur la propriété et la legislation*, Paris, 1824, p.265.

41 C.H. de Saint-Simon, *Du système industriel*, Paris, 1821, p.xiii, notes.

42 *Doctrine de Saint-Simon. Exposition. Première année, 1829*, Paris, 1924, p.161.

43 Ibid., pp.196–8.

44 C.H. de Saint-Simon, *Opinions littéraires, philosophiques et industrielles*, Paris, 1825, p.33.

45 See C.H. de Saint-Simon, *Du système industriel*, p.viii.

46 C.H. de Saint-Simon, *Cathéchisme des industriels*, Paris, 1824, p.11.

47 C.H. de Saint-Simon, *Opinions littéraires, philosophiques et industrielles*, p.90.

48 C.H. de Saint-Simon, *Cathéchisme des industriels*, p.36.

49 C.H. de Saint-Simon, *Opinions littéraires, philosophiques et industrielles*, pp.109–10.

50 A. Comte, *Opuscules de philosophie sociale. 1819–1828*, Paris, 1883, p.200.

51 *La philosophie positive. Auguste Comte par le Dr Robinet*, Paris, 1889, p.125.

52 A. Comte, *A General View on Positivism*, London, 1898, p.77.

53 *La Sociologie par Auguste Comte. Résumé par Emile Rigolage*, Paris, 1897, p.211.

54 Ibid., p.224.

55 See ibid., p.224.

56 Ibid., p.224.

57 A. Comte, *Cours de philosophie positive*, Vol. I, Paris, 1830, p.48.

58 *La Sociologie par Auguste Comte. Résumé par Emile Rigolage*, pp. 116–17.

59 *La philosophie positive. Auguste Comte par le Dr Robinet*, p.125.

60 *La Sociologie par Auguste Comte. Résumé par Emile Rigolage*, p.399.

61 See J.S. Mill, 'M. Guizot's "Essays and Lectures in History"', *The Edinburgh Review*, October 1845, 166, p.393.

62   Ibid., p.414.
63   He writes that, if there exist people who endure physical deprivations or who are degrading morally, or whose vital necessities are not satisfied or, if they are satisfied, then in a manner fit only for animals, that is an indication of the imperfection of their social environment. (See J.S. Mill, 'Chapters on Socialism', *The Fortnightly Review*, New Series, XXV, February–April 1879, p.225).
64   See J.S. Mill, 'Chapters on Socialism', p.382.
65   This tradition of European philosophy received a fine commentary from Gilbert Keith Chesterton, who quite rightly showed that the hiatus in philosophy came neither before Thomas, nor at the beginning of the Middle Ages, but after Thomas, at the beginning of the Modern Age. The great philosophical continuity between Pythagoras and Plato was not broken by the fall of Rome, or the triumph of Attila or the barbarians. It was broken by the printing of books, the discovery of America, by the Renaissance. It was then that the long, fine thread which stretched from the most ancient times, a thread drawn peculiarly towards thought, broke or was broken (*The Everlasting Man*).

3 Coherent Theories

Having come to the conclusion that social progress is connected with changes in the economic structure of civilization, philosophical thought reached the level that allowed it to build conceptions of history that could be categorized as coherent. It is worth repeating that we understand the coherence of a historical doctrine as its correspondence to a number of principles, most importantly an appeal to the economic basis of society as the material foundation for its development and the distinction of three main phases of the development of civilization on a dialectic basis. Different researchers may regard different aspects of social evolution as being of primary importance to enable the construction of theories that do not coincide with each other on most parameters but which nevertheless satisfy the basis criteria of coherence. We believe that such theoretical constructions include such formally diverse (if not diametrically opposed) theories as the conception of social development shaped by Marx in the middle of the 19th century and the notion of a post-industrial society that formed in the 1960s and 1970s. A comparison of the methodological bases of both theories reveals substantial similarities and determines their potential significance in the formation of approaches to the study of the post-economic society.

Marxist Conception

The theory of historical development established in the middle of the 19th century by Marx and Engels was the first coherent conception of history that accepted most of the main trends in philosophical thought of its time and seriously modernized the theory of social progress. Many researchers, following Lenin's interpretation, often claim that there are just three sources for the Marxist theory: British political economy, classical German philosophy and French utopian communism. This is an erroneous view. Marxism incorporated not merely selected teachings and schools but the basic tenets of 18th-

century European humanist philosophy: the universally acknowledged approach of the Enlightenment, the division of history
into an epoch characterized by the absence of the division of labour
and private property, an epoch characterized by their presence and an
epoch that opens after their passing.

The founders of Marxism to a great extent used Hegelian dialectics
as a more profound method of arguing the principles on offer rather
than as a method of research. The materialist elements of the new
theory could be found in the works of Turgot, Rousseau, Condillac,
Condorcet, Ferguson, Shaftesbury, Hume and Smith to a much
greater degree than in Feuerbach. The very idea of socialism as set
down by the founders of Marxism could have been borrowed from
Saint-Simon, Fourier and Owen, only with a high degree of relativity.

On the whole the theory created by the founders of Marxism
followed a number of historical developments at the end of the 18th
and the start of the 19th centuries, but it was distinguished by its all-
embracing nature and rigorous methodological consistency. At the
same time the theoretical work of Marx and Engels is entangled with
and often contradicted by their topical political programmes of the
day. This circumstance is particularly important because it is the very
reason for the crisis in Marxism as a scientific theory after it was
established as the leading political doctrine in a number of nations.

General View of History

The materialistic approach to the understanding of history is one of
the determining principles of Marxist theory. An excerpt from the
Preface to *A Contribution to the Critique of Political Economy* serves as
an illustration of historical materialism. Here Marx says:

> In the social production of their existence, men inevitably enter into
> definite relations, which are independent of their will, namely relations
> of production appropriate to a given stage in the development of their
> material forces of production. The totality of these relations of
> production constitutes the economic structure of society, the real
> foundation, on which arises a legal and political superstructure and to
> which correspond definite forms of social consciousness. The mode of
> production of material life conditions the general process of social,
> political and intellectual life. It is not the consciousness of men that
> determines their existence, but their social existence that determines
> their consciousness.[1]

On the basis of Marx's postulate of the primacy of production over
other aspects of social life, the founders of Marxism attempted to
interpret the very first stages of history. The main issues they
analysed were firstly, labour as production; secondly, the study of the

division of labour and property relations; thirdly, the interchange of activity and its results; and fourthly, exploitation and inequality. Today, 150 years later, we can say that Marx and Engels viewed the emergence and role of labour in social society as the most simplified of the four problems. Marx gave a famous definition in *Capital* which related to labour as an established phenomenon: 'Labour is ... a process in which both man and Nature participate, and in which man of his own accord starts, regulates, and controls the material re-actions between himself and Nature.'[2]

This was a direct statement of the use of this definition to describe mature forms of human activity, accounting for the abstraction from 'those primitive instinctive forms of labour',[3] that is from those stages in the development of the active nature of human beings, of that primitive activity which 'was not yet labour in the proper sense of the word'.[4] This activity can begin to be described as labour only when the tools of labour are first made as witness to a fully conceived type of activity.

It is important to note that Marx and Engels gave a high evaluation of the role of labour. They thought that it was the emergence of the labour process that formulated the main human qualities: 'First labour, after it and therewith speech – these were the two most essential stimuli under the influence of which the brain of the ape gradually changed into that of man.'[5] In this case it looks as if Marx and Engels viewed the development of labour and the making of man as identical *processes*, since one cannot state with complete certainty that the emergence of man (definable in Marxist tradition through *ability to work*) was conditioned exactly by the development of *labour* itself. Yet theses on the development of the skills of using tools and these skills assuming a conscious nature were vital contributors to the theory of making the individual. But it is necessary once more to stress that there were very substantial contradictions in the Marxist interpretation of the emergence of labour and its role in the making of the social organization. It was those contradictions that presented one of the main reasons for the interpretation of the role and historical limits of labour discussed below, and which we regard as the methodological foundation for the formulation of the conception of post-economic formation of society.

The second set of problems concerns necessities, the division of labour and ownership. Explaining why private appropriation was impossible at the communal stage in much the same way as Ferguson and Smith, the classic Marxist thinkers, however, quite justly pointed out the fact that the source for private appropriation was the progress of man's necessities, which specified his activity, which in turn formed the basis of the division of labour. Giving the division of labour as prominent a role in his theory as 18th-century social philosophers did in theirs, Marx believed that at the early stages of social evolution it played a great part in undermining 'the communality of production and appropriation' and 'made appropriation by individuals the predominant rule'.[6] The latter circumstance suggested the making of material interests of selected individuals and transpired to be the main reason for the destruction of the communal order.

This process manifested itself in the process of exchange, to which the founders of Marxism attach huge importance. They viewed exchange primarily as the exchange of activity and the exchange of the products of activity, the latter performing many functions, depending on who was the subject of exchange. Marx and Engels said that initially the exchange of products was caused by natural factors such as differences in the environment in which selected groups of people existed,[7] and bore the traits of intercourse between groups and not between selected individuals. 'The evolution of products into commodities,' Marx wrote, 'arises through exchange between different communities, not between the members of the same community'.[8] In these conditions the commercial organization of an economy did not exist as such, although Engels noted that 'the production and circulation of commodities may take place, while the overwhelming mass of products – produced for immediate domestic self-use – is never changed into commodities'.[9]

The last question vital to address in the analysis of the approach by Marx and Engels to the making of society was that of the emergence of inequality and exploitation. The founders of Marxism believed that all of these processes began 'on the day when the labour of the family created more products than were necessary for its maintenance... A surplus of the product of labour over and above the costs of maintenance of the labour, and the formation and enlargement, out of this surplus, of a social production and reserve fund, was and is the basis of all social, political and intellectual progress'.[10]

It was progress in the division of labour that resulted, ultimately, in the formation of a new type of relations within a community, the dependence of all of its members on certain workers who possessed specific skills. This became the basis for the formation of various levels of consumption, as a result of which the practice of redistribution of some of a product in favour of higher levels of society gradually became consolidated, and it was here that social inequality had its roots.

The formation of the class society took different forms, each of which, however, led to the creation of a state, a force, capable of keeping the lower classes in obedience. The way the class society was formed hinged on the natural, economic and social and cultural peculiarities of peoples. Engels showed that there were two main paths to the making of class structure, described by him as the Asiatic path and the ancient path. In the first type, influenced by the need for collective management, the tribal and later the neighbourly communities became tightly consolidated, and power arose primarily from the need to control such collective production. The tight state system of Asiatic communities was founded on the total domination by the higher levels of society over the lower ones. Any surplus product and part of the necessary product was appropriated for the state's benefit and then redistributed to satisfy the economic and political interests of the communities. To a certain extent this system was akin to the planned economy. It was historically the first form of class society, which existed in huge expanses from Egypt to China. Elements of this system could be seen also in the Aztec and Inca empires on the American continent. This was *the Asiatic mode of production.*

The second type bore elements of ownership and social inequality within communities, which happened when the individual activity of members of a community brought them (depending on the skill of a worker or other factors) different results. The community became layered as some of its members became dependent on others. Wars between communities brought, in the form of trophies, not only property but also prisoners, who became the slaves of various masters. Barter progressed alongside the division of labour. This kind of progress caused a community to disintegrate from within, and gave birth to a privileged and wealthy class of citizens, the spread of slave labour and a split between wealthy citizens and plebeians. It culminated in what was described as *the ancient mode of production.*

A comparison of the Asiatic and ancient modes shows us clearly that the latter provided more room for the improvement both of the productive forces and of production relations. The domination of the state over society in the Eastern despotic regimes stimulated economic progress largely artificially, while in the West the improvement of the economy was a condition for the survival not only of forms of production but also of the individual himself. Therefore Engels' assessment of the role of slavery in a famous excerpt from the *Anti-Dühring* ought to be considered totally justified:

> The introduction of slavery under the conditions prevailing at that time was a great step forward. For it is a fact that man sprang from the beasts, and had consequently to use barbaric and almost bestial means to extricate himself from barbarism. Where the ancient communities have continued to exist, they have for thousands of years formed the basis of the cruellest form of state ... It was only where these communities dissolved that the peoples made progress of themselves, and their next economic advance consisted in the increase and

development of production by means of slave labour ... So long as human labour was still so little productive that it provided but a small surplus over and above the necessary means of subsistence, any increase of the productive forces ... was possible only by means of a greater division of labour. And the necessary basis for this was the great division of labour between the masses discharging simple manual labour and the few privileged persons ... The simplest and most natural form of this division of labour was in fact slavery.[11]

Marxism, overall, however, does not exaggerate the role that the division between slaves and freemen played in ancient society.

It is well known that, in the *Communist Manifesto*, Marx stressed that the basis of ancient history was the struggle between the patricians and the plebeians, or between different classes of free citizens, and later demonstrated directly that the internal history of Rome could plainly be reduced to a struggle between small and large landowners, introducing, obviously, those modifications that were conditioned by the existence of slavery.

The founders of Marxism viewed the emergence of European feudalism primarily in connection with the seizure of peasants' land in the barbarian states and its redistribution among representatives of the domineering classes. This process was largely the result of sovereign gifts to military leaders, high officials and the upper clergy that quickly proved to be ineffective. Under Pippinus Brevis and Charles the Great there occurred a decisive transformation in agricultural relations to which the founders of Marxism attached great importance. Analysing it Engels wrote:

This transformation depended basically on two new institutions. First, in order to keep the barons of the empire tied to the Crown, the Crown lands they received were now as a rule no longer a gift, but only a 'beneficium', granted for life, and moreover on certain conditions nonfulfilment of which entailed the forfeiture of the land. Thus they became themselves tenants of the Crown. And secondly, in order to ensure that the free tenants of the barons turned up for military service, the latter were granted some of the district count's official powers over the free men living on their estates and appointed their 'seniors'.[12]

In the future, in the 9th and 10th centuries, the beneficiary system grew into a feudatory one, and the fragmentary nature of feudalism was born.

It is worth pointing out that the economic order of European feudalism was characterized mainly by the overcoming of the dominant forms of large-scale production of ancient times; small production in farming and the trades made mediaeval society in the economic sense far more homogeneous than ancient society, which enabled progressive commodity relations to apply to society as a whole. This gave rise to both hired labour and elements of active trade in the products of urban craftsmen and farmers alike.

A new wealthy class emerged from trade and the beginning of financial speculation and was able to concentrate the means of production. As Engels wrote:

> The first capitalists found ... wage-labour ready-made for them on the market. But it was exceptional, complementary, accessory, transitory wage-labour. The agricultural labourer, though, upon occasion, he hired himself out by the day, had a few acres of his own land on which he could at all events live at a pinch. The guilds were so organised that the journeyman of to-day became the master of to-morrow. But all this changed, as soon as the means of production became socialised and concentrated in the hands of capitalists. The means of production, as well as the product, of the individual producer became more and more worthless; there was nothing left for him but to turn wage-worker under the capitalist. Wage-labour, aforetime the exception and accessory, now became the rule and basis of all production; aforetime complementary, it now became the sole remaining function of the worker.[13]

However, this transformation was unlikely to have been possible if the Middle Ages had not created, albeit in limited amounts, both hired labour and domestic and external markets to sell the products of that labour. The significance of exchange and market relations which arose as early as in feudal times was underlined many times by Marx and Engels. Engels wrote on this theme:

> In the Middle Ages ... the peasant, e.g., sold to the artisan agricultural products and bought from him the products of handicraft. Into this society of individual producers, of commodity-producers, the new mode of production thrust itself. In the midst of the old division of labour, grown up spontaneously and upon no definite plan, which had governed the whole of society, now arose division of labour upon a definite plan, as organised in the factory; side by side with individual production appeared social production.[14]

The results of this process had a swift impact. Using the advantages of cooperation and machine production, which increased the productivity of labour, the new economic structure created a destructive competition for the small production of goods in the late feudal era. The artisans were quickly ruined and joined the ranks of the hired labourers. Another source of labour was the countryside, which had also seen better days. The growth of industrial output required the constant formation of new markets – both national and foreign markets. In the leading European countries even the rural dwellers, inclined to the natural form of economy, turned more and more to the market. The capitalist form of production was busy establishing itself.

Thus, towards the middle of the 19th century, the period when the founders of Marxism were creatively active, the development of both the European and the Asian nations presented a wealth of material for historical generalization and periodization. The consecutive changeability of economic systems became obvious; just as clear was the dependence of the political development on the evolution of the economic basis. All preceding historical forms, excepting only the period of the tribal community, laid bare the domineering role of economic life, so these historical forms could be considered to be historical conditions of a single order.

The other side to the problem of periodization was the explanation of the reasons for and course of the social changes which accompanied the movement from one form of social production to the next. These changes were not afterwards similar in cause or form of progress, and required the formulation of a special conception within the general theory of social progress. Both of these tasks were solved by the development of a theory of social formations (*Gesellschaftsformationen*) and modes of production (*Produktionsweisen*): issues connected with the transition from one social formation to another and from one mode of production to another were reflected in the concepts of social and political revolutions. It was thanks to such elements that the picture of historical progress began to look more like consistent scientific theory with a considerable prognostic and futurological potential.

The Periodization of History

Marx's periodization of social formations was not set down in any one work or cycle of works. The comments vital for an understanding of the subject were spread over a great many works. Terminology is of particular importance for the interpretation of this part of Marxian theory. It was neglect of terminology by Soviet Marxists that led to a simplification of the theory and the loss of its prognostic significance.[15]

Gesellschaftsformation (social formation), a key term in Marx, was first introduced in 1851 in *The Eighteenth Brumaire of Louis Bonaparte*. In a discussion of the French Revolution, Marx wrote that the transition of the ideologues of the bourgeoisie from revolutionary to counter-revolutionary positions took place when the new orders became dominant, when a new *Gesellschaftsformation* had taken shape.[16] Seven years later, in 1858, Marx in his Preface to *A Contribution to the Critique of Political Economy* introduced the term *oekonomische Gesellschaftsformation*, thereby concretizing the term

Gesellschaftsformation and limiting the sphere of application of either concept. 'In broad outline,' Marx wrote, 'the Asiatic, ancient, feudal and modern bourgeois modes of production may be designated as epochs marking progress in the economic development of society. ... The prehistory of human society ... closes with this social formation.'[17] The author makes it clear that there is a historical epoch that is 'social formation' (*Gesellschaftsformation*) and that the main characteristics of this epoch are economic (*oekonomische*). It follows beyond question from the text that it is 'with this' (*mit dieser*), that is with *economic* formation of society, that the prehistory of human society culminates.

Meanwhile, as research into other texts shows, Marx preferred when using the term *Gesellschaftsformation* not to give a clear definition either to the term itself or to the historical states, or conditions, which it signified. One gets the impression that the term is used to signify global historical epochs and could virtually never have been applied in direct economic analysis.

It should be stressed that Marx did not apply the adjective 'bourgeois' to the term *Gesellschaftsformation*. He preferred to use other concepts to describe capitalist society. A classic example of this was a thesis in the *Theories of Surplus-Value*, when Marx wrote, concerning the laws of capitalist society: 'This is the tendency in the form of society in which the capitalist mode of production predominates.'[18] This excerpt very clearly testifies to the fact that the term *Gesellschaftsformation* in its chronological aspect is broader than the concept of the *Produktionsweise*: Marx used the term *Gesellschaftsformation* to describe a historic reality that was not exhausted by the capitalist mode of production alone.

The most convincing confirmation of this sort of assumption was contained by a work which in our view has given more substance for an understanding of the theory of social formation than any other: that is, drafts of the reply by Marx to a letter from Vera Zasulich in 1881. If earlier the term *Gesellschaftsformation* was not coupled with any adjective other than *oekonomische*, then we see three such instances here in just a few pages. Marx wrote that 'the "agricultural commune" occurs everywhere as the *most recent type* of the archaic form of societies, and ... in the historical development of Western Europe, ancient and modern, the period of the agricultural commune appears as a period of transition from communal property to private property, as a period of transition from the primary form to the secondary one' (emphasis added).[19] He continued: 'As the last phase of the primitive formation of society, the agricultural commune is, at the same time, a transitional stage leading to the secondary formation, and hence marks the transition from a society founded on communal property to a society founded on private property. The secondary formation, of course, includes the series of societies resting on slavery and serfdom.'[20]

It is fairly obvious from the examples given that Marx understood society without exploitation as the 'archaic formation of society'. This definition also covers the commune, including that in the Asiatic societies. However, as the Asiatic society and the agricultural commune were not only the last phases of primary (primitive) formation of society but also the first elements of the secondary formation, it can be stated that exploitation was the beginning of the transitional period from the primary to the secondary formation, not the exploitation of man by man, but of caste by caste. This period finally ended when the exploitation of man by man crystallized; that is, when the commune was broken down, and industry, oriented towards exchange, spread. Goods came into circulation, there appeared a law of value and other economic laws. So there is every reason to treat the period which replaced the era of the supremacy of personal forms of dependence as an economic formation (*oekonomische Gesellschaftsformation, formation économique de la société*).

Marx made direct reference to the identical nature of the concepts 'primary' and 'archaic' formation of society. In the same drafts he wrote: 'The archaic or primary formation of our globe itself contains a series of layers of differing ages, one superimposed on the other; in the same way, the archaic form of society reveals to us a series of different type, marking progressive epochs.'[21] If one follows this analogy and accepts it to the extent to which it is given, one could contend that both terms are used to signify that period of history which preceded the formation of classes. Marx proffered a number of theses from which it follows that an understanding of communism as a tertiary formation of society is a totally natural concept for him. He wrote that the improvement of the productive forces of bourgeois society gives birth to the possibility of replacing 'capitalist property with a higher form of the archaic type of property, i.e. communist property'.[22]

But the most important circumstance stemming from an analysis of the given formulae is that Marx viewed the primitive formation (*formation primitive*) as a social, not an economic formation. Given that economic relations played no noticeable role for some time, the archaic formation of society (*formation archaïque de la société*) can be described as social, with the supremacy of the primitive communist relations of the tribal order. However, if we accept that *formation primitive* cannot be termed economic on the basis of the given circumstances, we must also recognize that communist society as a tertiary formation (*formation tertiaire*) cannot be described as economic either. Marx himself never described communism as an *oekonomische Gesellschaftsformation*.

Thus the term *Gesellschaftsformation* is used in two senses: firstly, in the broader sense of the meaning to describe any essential phase in social evolution as a whole; in this case *Gesellschaftsformation* (*formation de la société*) can be understood to mean a phase of social development regardless of the period under analysis; and secondly, when the term is qualified by an adjective ('archaic', 'primary', 'secondary' and so on), to describe qualitatively defined episodes in social evolution. Going by the above, we can suppose that the most correct interpretation would be that of *Gesellschaftsformation* as a collective concept which reflects a stage in the development of society, separated on the basis of a sign of the presence or absence of antagonistic classes, exploitation and private ownership.

The final notion of the meaning of the term *Gesellschaftsformation* can be obtained only from a thorough analysis of instances in which Marx and Engels used their more widespread derivative of the concept – that of *oekonomische Gesellschaftsformation* and one of the most discussed elements of Marxian theory. The term *oekonomische Gesellschaftsformation* was first used by Marx in his Preface to *A Contribution to the Critique of Political Economy*, in 1858. This work, together with the draft reply to the letter of Vera Zasulich, is extremely important in the understanding of the Marxian theory.

Marx, as we have already noted, writes in the Preface: 'In broad outline, the Asiatic, ancient, feudal and modern bourgeois modes of production may be designated as epochs marking progress in the economic development of society. ... The prehistory of human society ... closes with this social formation.'[23] It is here, in this excerpt, that Marx claims that civilization may have had an epoch (which he calls *oekonomische Gesellschaftsformation*) which combines a number of modes of production on the basis of universal features.

The concept *oekonomische Gesellschaftsformation* testifies to the fact that the main feature of all periods incorporated was viewed by Marx as the economic nature of all kinds of social activity, that is a means of interaction between members of the social organization, which is defined not by religious, moral or political factors, but primarily by economic factors. The term applies only to the period of the supremacy in social life of relations based on private ownership, individual exchange and the consequent emergence of exploitation.

Just as with the use of the concept *Gesellschaftsformation* (which once again underlines the systematic nature of Marxian methodology), Marx and Engels use the term *oekonomische Gesellschaftsformation* both to signify a selected historical period characterized by the above features and to describe a number of historical states, or conditions, each of which possesses the same basic characteristics. For example, when guarding against the notion that phases of social evolution are stages between which there are no transitory periods or transitional forms of social relations, Marx wrote: 'Just as one should not think of sudden changes and sharply delineated periods in considering the succession of the different geological formations, so also in the case of the creation of the different economic formations of society.'[24]

A careful analysis of Marxian texts gives us a fairly profound understanding of how Marx defined the notions of *oekonomische Gesellschaftsformation* and *Produktionsweise*. Analysing productive capital and signifying this by the term 'capital-relation' (*Capitalverhaeltniss*), he wrote: 'In any case, the capital-relation develops at a historical stage of the economic formation of society which is already the result of a long series of previous developments.'[25] This principle partially duplicates, although in a slightly different way, the thesis that different modes of production (*Produktionsweisen*) based on exploitation are progressive epochs of *oekonomische Gesellschaftsformation*. The concept here clearly means more than the capitalist mode of production. The quotation implies that exploitation, based on the application of hired labour, becomes possible only when, on the one hand, exploitation itself develops and, on the other, when commodity relations penetrate society deeply enough for the workforce to become a commodity. But we have shown that the development of exchange, which resulted ultimately in the emergence of the exploitation of the workforce as a commodity, is the essence of secondary social formation and lies behind its development. So we come by yet another confirmation that the secondary and economic formations of society (*formation secondaire* and *oekonomische Gesellschaftsformation*) are one and the same thing in Marxist terminology.

We will cite yet another formulation that sheds light on the content of the notion of *oekonomische Gesellschaftsformation*: 'From the standpoint of a higher economic form of society, private ownership of the globe by single individuals will appear quite as absurd as private ownership of one man by another.'[26] This makes two things clear: on the one hand, the founders of Marxism did not think the communist social system had anything to do with *Gesellschaftsformation*; and on the other, the private ownership of land cannot be defeated in the capitalist mode of production, which the quotation is about. It turns out that the capitalist mode of production is not the ultimate phase of *Gesellschaftsformation*.

This is supported by the following passage from Volume Three of *Capital*:

> The actual wealth of society, and the possibility of constantly expanding its reproduction process ... do not depend upon the duration of surplus-labour, but upon its productivity and the more or

less copious conditions of production under which it is performed. In fact, the realm of freedom actually begins only where labour which is determined by necessity and mundane considerations ceases; thus in the very nature of things it lies beyond the sphere of actual material production. Just as the savage must wrestle with Nature to satisfy his wants, to maintain and reproduce life, so must civilised man, and he must do so in all social formations and under all possible modes of production. With his development this realm of physical necessity expands as a result of his wants; but, at the same time, the forces of production which satisfy these wants also increase. Freedom in this field can only consist in socialised man, the associated producers, rationally regulating their interchange with Nature, bringing it under their common control, instead of being ruled by it as by the blind forces of Nature; and achieving this with the least expenditure of energy and under conditions most favourable to, and worthy of, their human nature. But it nonetheless still remains a realm of necessity. Beyond it begins that development of human energy which is an end in itself, the true realm of freedom, which, however, can blossom forth only with this realm of necessity as its basis.[27]

Marx clearly did not and could not have had the capitalist mode of production in mind when talking about a social production advanced and oriented one way or the other towards satisfying the needs of man, where exchange does not rule people like a blind force, where there is an organized, systematic exchange between man and Nature, and where production is carried out on terms acceptable to human nature. On the contrary, the passage depicts what the post-Marxists described as the socialist type of society, but at a more advanced stage. Marx showed that this state is not yet the realm of freedom, as it is merely the highest and ultimate level of the realm of necessity. Therefore the given state, which is not a communist formation of society, is the conclusive phase of economic formation, and its stage of descent, during which the contradictions which have arisen during the making of this social formation, are resolved and overcome. At this stage ownership is no longer private, as it would have been in the Asiatic mode of production, there is no direct exploitation of man by man, and the anarchy of production which undermined the capitalist order has been overcome. It is to a society like this, to the closing stage of economic formation of society, that Marx's statement about the common ownership of land as the main condition for the productive process relates.

The two latter principles are of immense methodological significance, as they make it possible to define more precisely the chronological frameworks of the phenomenon characterized as *oekonomische Gesellschaftsformation*, as an epoch beginning with the decomposition of the primitive order under the influence of the exchange of goods and division of labour and characterized by exploitation, the class division of society and relations of a commodity and monetary nature, and culminating in the negation of the latter of these. Societies which succeeded each other in the framework of *oekonomische Gesellschaftsformation* were based on relations of an economic nature, their development was conditioned by the evolution of an economic basis, and social progress in that period was defined by progress in the division of labour and the subsequent expansion of relations of a commodity and monetary nature. Society in obedience to economic laws and developing together with commodity relations had an evolutionary path definable by economic laws. Marx in this connection wrote that his standpoint is that 'from which the evolution of the economic formation of society is viewed as a process of natural history'.[28]

So Marx's theory was a rounded scientific conception, based on a thorough study of the internal laws of social development and guided by the acknowledgement of the existence of a dialectic triad as a form of progress of anything that had become a whole. A profound understanding of that theory may be acquired by analysing the Marxian terminological system, particularly the coordination of the terms *Gesellschaftsformation* and *oekonomische Gesellschaftsformation*. Marx and Engels used both of these in a dual sense: in the narrow, exclusively terminological sense and in a broader sense which allows some interpretation. In this case they did not differ from each other too much and denoted a certain stage in social evolution. Moreover, the concept *oekonomische Gesellschaftsformation* relates mainly to selected phases of development solely within secondary social formation. The term *Gesellschaftsformation*, though, synonymous with *oekonomische Gesellschaftsformation* when denoting the era of the development of class society, has a much broader application and is used for the periodization of both pre-class and classless society.

Any analysis of the Marxian theory of the periodization of social progress requires the consideration of another aspect of the conception, the transitions from one formation to another. We said above that Marx called the historical periods inside *oekonomische Gesellschaftsformation* modes of production. He referred to the Asiatic, ancient, feudal and bourgeois modes of production, but did not call them *Gesellschaftsformationen*. If, following the Marxian example, we divide social development into three *Gesellschaftsformationen*, noting modes of production in the central one (that was what Marx had in mind when he wrote that 'the capital-relation develops at a historical stage of the economic formation of society which is already the result of a long series of previous developments',[29] at the stage 'in which the capitalist mode of production predominates',[30] then we have to acknowledge that the transition from one mode of production to another within an *oekonomische Gesellschaftsformation* was not a single process with respect to the change of the *Gesellschaftsformationen* themselves. There has to be a marked difference, both in sense and in terminology, between these two types of historical change, between the revolutionary transitions from one mode of production to another within an *oekonomische Gesellschaftsformation* and the revolutions which signify its historical limits. So a discussion of the conception of revolutionary changes which explain the justice of the three divisions of history should round off our study of Marxian historical theory.

The Revolutionary Doctrine

The conception of revolution as a form of transition from one state of society to another was one indicator of the high degree of perfection of the Marxian system of the periodization of social progress. The first reference to the two types of revolution can be found in Marx's articles in the *Deutsch–Franzosische Jahrbucher*. He wrote with respect to the bourgeois revolution and its historical role:

> The character of the old civil society was *directly political*, that is to say, the elements of civil life, for example, property, or the family, or the mode of labour, were raised to the level of elements of political life ... The political revolution which overthrew this sovereign power and raised state affairs to become affairs of the people, which constructed the political state as a matter of *general* concern, that is, as a real state, necessarily smashed all estates, corporations, guilds, and privileges, since they were all manifestations of the separation of the people from the community. The political revolution thereby *abolished* the *political character of civil society*.[31]

But there was another revolutionary change, namely the social revolution, understood to mean the annihilation of the whole order of things based on private ownership and exploitation. Only this revolution, staged by the proletariat, would give mankind the opportunity to organize its '"forces propre" as social forces'.[32]

Engels formulated similar, even more distinct principles. Take his so-called *Speeches in Elberfeld* of the winter of 1845, possibly the first Marxian work entirely devoted to the problems of communist transformations. In a speech of 15 February 1845, the orator says: 'But one day the proletariat will attain a level of power and of insight at which it will no longer tolerate the pressure of the entire social structure always bearing down on its shoulders, when it will demand a more even distribution of social burdens and rights; and then – unless human nature has changed by that time – a social revolution will be inevitable.' And further: 'the unavoidable result of our existing social relations, under all circumstances, and in all cases, will be a social revolution. With the same certainty with which we can develop from given mathematical principles a new mathematical proposition, with the same certainty we can deduce from the existing economic relations and the principles of political economy the imminence of social revolution'.[33]

But not even these quotations carry the ultimate notion of the views of Engels. Besides what he said about social revolution, resulting in the liberation of the proletariat, Engels said the following about the distinction between the social and political revolutions:

> A social revolution, gentlemen, is something quite different from the political revolutions which have taken place so far. It is not directed, as these have been, against the property of monopoly, but against the monopoly of property; a social revolution, gentlemen, is *the open war of the poor against the rich*. And such a struggle, in which all the mainsprings and causes, which in previous historical conflicts lay dark and hidden at the bottom, operate openly and without concealment, such a struggle, to be sure, threatens to be far fiercer and bloodier than all those that preceded it.[34]

We believe that these theses are very important. Engels said feudal society was a predominantly political establishment. He quite rightly said that the cause of the bourgeois revolutions in England and France was the struggle of the bourgeoisie against the political establishment of the old society for the realization of its ideals. And it was precisely because the main struggle was directed against the political obstacles to the development of the new order that this type of revolution was qualified as political. We find confirmation of this in various works of Marx and Engels relating to various periods.

One of the most vivid definitions is given in *The German Ideology*, in which, analysing the roots of political revolution, Marx and Engels pointed out that 'an earlier interest, the peculiar form of intercourse of which has already been ousted by that belonging to a later interest, remains for a long time afterwards in possession of a traditional power in the illusory community (state, law), which has won an existence independent of the individuals; a power which in the last resort can only be broken by a revolution'.[35] It follows from this premise that the fathers of Marxism regarded bourgeois revolution as a coup resulting from a contradiction between the basic relations of production, which go far ahead at a fast pace, and the ossified political and legal systems: that is, that which Marxists usually call 'superstructure'. This understanding is unquestionably of great importance in interpreting the position of Marx, as it demonstrates the difference in principle that, according to Marx, exists between the bourgeois and communist revolutions: in contrast to the latter, a bourgeois revolution is a banal political coup rather than a vehicle of substantive change in the foundations of society.

History bears out quite fully the particular idea of Marx and Engels that political revolution stems from a contradiction between the foundation of society (the sum total of the productive forces and the relations of production) and the political superstructure. Taking a close look at the situation that took shape in France on the eve of the Revolution of 1789, we will find that the relations of production, which were largely capitalist in character, were quite consistent with the existing productive forces that had outgrown the feudal system. That is why we do not believe it possible to identify in this case any considerable contradiction other than contradiction between the economic realities and political superstructure. Marx believed that both the productive forces and relations of production underwent evolutionary change within the *oekonomische Gesellschaftsformation* (with the exception of the period immediately preceding a communist revolution) that ruled out antagonistic contradictions between them. 'A change in men's productive forces,' he wrote, 'necessarily brings about a change in their relations of production.'[36]

Thus it will be seen that 'political revolution' and 'social revolution' are entirely different terms used by the founders of Marxism to identify disparate forms of historical change. The conception of social revolution that is central to the revolutionary teaching of the classics of Marxism was the focus of their attention throughout their work. This had to do with the need to substantiate the prospects for a communist future for the continued development of modern civilization. As early as in *The German Ideology*, in which Marx and Engels introduced the concepts of productive forces and relations of production, they pointed to the emergence of a contradiction between them. It was precisely that contradiction that they made the basis for their theory of social revolution. At that period, and afterwards, that conception referred only to the communist-type revolution.

In the view of the fathers of Marxism, the contradiction between productive forces and relations of production as a factor in social revolutions came about at the turn of the 19th century, when there still was a relative correspondence between the productive forces and relations of production of the continuously developing and expanding capitalist system. As Marx and Engels noted, 'For many a decade past the history of industry and commerce is but the history of modern productive forces against modern conditions of production.'[37] Thus they asserted that capitalist organization of production, which by its very emergence eliminated the contradiction between the basis and the superstructure that gave rise to the bourgeois revolution, completely changed the content of the contradiction between the productive forces and relations of production.

Karl Marx emphasized this idea throughout his active work, refining it to perfection in the famous passage from Volume Three of *Capital*:

> The *real barrier* of capitalist production is *capital itself*. It is that capital and its self-expansion appear as the starting and the closing point, the motive and the purpose of production; that production is only production for *capital* and not vice versa, the means of production are not mere means for a constant expansion of the living process of the *society* of producers … The means – unconditional development of the productive forces of society – comes continually into conflict with the limited purpose, the self-expansion of the existing capital. The capitalist mode of production is, for this reason, a historical means of developing the material forces of production, … is, at the same time, a continual conflict between this historical task and its own corresponding relations of social production.[38]

With the passage of time the productive forces reach a stage in their development at which, given existing production relations, they cause little but trouble, acting as destructive rather than productive forces.

These points indicating that the contradiction between productive forces and the relations of production are inherent in the capitalist mode of production (*buergerlische Produktionsweise*) should not be seen as proof that it is unique to capitalism alone and only emerged when it came on the scene. The contradiction between the productive forces and the relations of production is an inevitable feature of the history of mankind; that said, it should be noted that, within the *oekonomische Gesellschaftsformation* prior to the establishment of the *buergerlische Produktionsweise*, it did not have an antagonistic character that might lead to a revolutionary change in the whole social system. The contradiction had an immense impact on the previous history of human society, thereby lending a largely evolutionary character to historical progress. As Marx and Engels commented in this connection, 'the contradiction between the productive forces and the form of intercourse [relations of production] has occurred several times in past history, without, however, endangering its basis'.[39]

Marx and Engels made many comments in their writings from which it follows that it was precisely a communist-type revolution that they meant by 'social revolution'. They used the term 'social revolution' in a way that makes it impossible to confuse its implication with anything else or to assume that it might refer to a revolution indirectly effecting a change in the *Produktionsweisen* within the *oekonomische Gesellschaftsformation,* much less any other revolutionary changes. Therefore, in our view, the position of Marx and Engels concerning the social revolution may be interpreted exclusively as their treatment of the type of revolution that replaces the capitalist mode of production with the communist one and, consequently, the *oekonomische Gesellschaftsformation* with communist *Gesellschaftsformation,* as a social revolution. Accordingly, the founders of Marxism regarded revolutionary transformations that brought about a change of any individual mode of production within the *oekonomische Gesellschaftsformation* as political revolutions.

However, such an interpretation necessarily requires answers to be found to two key questions regarding Marx's timeline of social progress, as it were, and how he identified the various periods in social progress. We shall be looking into this in subsequent pages. The first question is how social revolution correlates with the time boundaries of a given *oekonomische Gesellschaftsformation.* As long as it is assumed that the transition from the *oekonomische Gesellschaftsformation* to communist *Gesellschaftsformation* is made through a social revolution, it would be logical also to assume that a different social revolution may exist – a revolution which is the vehicle for a transition from the primary *Gesellschaftsformation* to the secondary one and the establishment of an *oekonomische Gesellschaftsformation.*

Marx and Engels devoted far less attention to the problem of the transition from the primary *Gesellschaftsformation* to the secondary one than to the communist transformation of society; they did, however, deal closely with the transition to the *oekonomische Gesellschaftsformation* precisely as a social revolution, and that in full accordance with the terminology and method of the theory of social formations. According to Marx, the main feature of that revolution was the demolition of the patriarchal forms of the organization of social life, in particular the communal structures, and the transition to a system based on one form of private property or another. For example, Marx noted that in India, during the colonization period, British involvement led to the destruction of the small, semi-barbarian and semi-civilized communities as a result of the destruction of their economic basis, thereby bringing about the greatest and the only truly social revolution ever to occur in Asia. Engels made a similar point with regard to ancient Roman history, specifically the period of the downfall of the patriarchal relations that formed the core of the social system of the Etruscan communities which existed in Italia during the first centuries of the history of Rome. In his view, the destruction of the communal order and the establishment of a class state also constituted a social revolution.[40] It speaks volumes that this term was no longer used for the history of the East and ancient European history; for instance, the founders of Marxism stopped short of describing the events bearing on Europe's transition from antiquity to the feudal system. That is why the premise that social revolution was a phenomenon signifying a change in *Gesellschaftsformationen* to Marx and Engels appeared to be factually incontrovertible.

The second question has to do with the sequential order of transformations brought about by the social revolution, and the way in which it occurs. Marx wrote in his Preface to *A Contribution to the Critique of Political Economy*, 'At a certain stage of development, the material productive forces of society come into conflict with the existing relations of production or – this merely expresses the same thing in legal terms – with the property relations within the framework of which they have operated hitherto. From forms of development of the productive forces these relations turn into their fetters. Then begins an era of social revolution.[41] Almost in the same breath Marx says, however, that as a result of the revolutionary process 'the changes in the economic foundation lead sooner or later to the transformation of the whole immense superstructure'.[42]

These statements by Marx raise the issue of the relationship between changes in the economic foundation and the superstructure at the time of a social revolution. He virtually admitted that transformations in the superstructure follow changes in relations of production. Marx treated the era of social revolution as a period of change determining the emergence and evolution of the new *Gesellschaftsformation* while, in contrast to political revolution, social revolution transformed the very foundations of the social system and was not a one-off phenomenon; in his view, it was an extended process whose time boundaries were to a large extent relative, and identifying them was largely a matter of convention. His words in regard to the transition to the *oekonomische Gesellschaftsformation* are well known to researchers; he argued that 'in the historical development of Western Europe, ancient and modern, the period of the agricultural commune appears as a period of transition from communal property to private property, as a period of transition from the primary form to the secondary one'.[43] Thus the founders of Marxism did not suggest any geographic or chronological boundaries of the phase of the social revolution that is the vehicle for the establishment of the *oekonomische Gesellschaftsformation*.

This is also applicable in part to analysis of social revolution in which the *oekonomische Gesellschaftsformation* culminates. In this case, the whole problem is far more complicated, and Marx and Engels defined the boundaries of this process in more definite terms. However, Engels, in particular, denied the possibility of proletarian revolution as a one-off act. For instance, he wrote in his letter to Karl Kautsky of 12 September 1882:

A reorganised Europe and North America will have such colossal power and provide such an example that the semi-civilised countries will automatically follow in their wake; they will be pushed in that direction even by economic needs alone. It seems to me that we can only make rather futile hypotheses about the social and political phases that these countries will then have to pass through before they likewise arrive at socialist organisation.[44]

Therefore transformations in the superstructure follow precisely economic changes even in the event of transition to a tertiary *Gesellschaftsformation*; this is of considerable importance, as this testifies to Marx's and Engels' recognition, albeit insufficiently well formulated and diluted by numerous directly opposite statements, of the fact that a proletarian uprising was the beginning but by no means the whole content of the sweeping social revolution which marked the transition from the *oekonomische Gesellschaftsformation* to the communist one.

Marx's conception of revolution is totally subordinate to the key element of Marxist social theory: the teaching about changes in and historical succession of *Gesellschaftsformationen* and *Produktionsweisen*. In accordance with the subdivision of social evolution into three distinct *Gesellschaftsformationen* they suggested, Marx and Engels pointed to two global changes in the history of mankind and described them as social revolutions. The realistic approach to studying human history manifests itself in this case in that there is a recognition of the fact that the period in which one *Gesellschaftsformation* replaces another is a lengthy one; this is emphasized by the use of the term 'an epoch of social revolution'. According to Marx's conception, the period of social revolution continues from the beginning of changes in the fundamental relations of production to the time when all relations of production and the type of means used for regulating production that are characteristic of the preceding *Gesellschaftsformation* are overcome and a new *Gesellschaftsformation* takes shape which is fully self-regulating and self-adjusting.

The excerpt from the draft letter we quoted above, which Marx wrote in response to Vera Zasulich's letter, serves to illustrate this approach. Marx pointed out in it that the commune could only be overcome in full by the capitalist mode of production. It is therefore reasonable to suggest that social revolution leading to the establishment of the *oekonomische Gesellschaftsformation* does not exhaust its potential and lose momentum until that *Gesellschaftsformation* reaches its peak and takes on its most mature form; throughout the corresponding changes, the whole social structure undergoes transformations. The same is true of communist revolution. As with the epoch of social revolution that demolished the archaic *Gesellschaftsformation,* the communist revolution begins at a point when the existence of private property (as well as its absence, as is the case with the archaic *Gesellschaftsformation*) turns into an insurmountable obstacle to economic and social progress. In that case, the contradiction between the productive forces and the relations of production loses its 'positive' character as the motive force behind the evolutionary movement ahead and engenders social clashes from which the new society emerges. Beginning with a proletarian uprising against the oppressors, this revolution ushers in the long era of the replacement of the relations of the *oekonomische Gesellschaftsformation* by essentially non-economic relations.

As distinct from social revolutions, there is another kind of revolution: the one that the founders of Marxism called political revolution. The revolutionary changes these revolutions stand for are more superficial than in the case of social revolutions and can be traced within the *oekonomische Gesellschaftsformation,* in effect proving to be the means whereby transition is made from one mode of production to another. Political revolutions stemming from the contradiction between the developing economic relations and the political structure of society carry out the task of freeing that society from outdated forms of organization. Thus we are able to establish a high degree of consonance between the theory of revolution and the concept of periodization, as well as congruence of the major tenets of both theories and their mutually complementary nature.

The Marxist Theory's Contradiction and Demise

Marx's theoretical constructs were riddled with inner contradictions between theory proper and theory as a means of changing life. At the beginning of the 20th century, when Marxism evolved into one of the most influential political movements and the places of Marx and Engels were taken by their successors – the European Social Democrats – theoretical problems again came to the fore. It turned out that most revolutionaries who called themselves Marxists did not fully comprehend the evolutionary content of the social doctrine of their great teachers; instead they focused most of their attention on its revolutionary form.

The understanding of Marxist theory was especially one-sided in Russia, where the revolutionary movement was least prepared for grasping its essence. Vladimir Lenin, the motive force behind the Russian Revolution of 1917, was practically the first to try to lend a specific Russian flavour to Marxism. He started off with a major simplification of the major methodological principles of the Marxist doctrine that was not overcome in the Soviet Union until the collapse of the communist regime.

The principle of the development of society by stages, which Lenin borrowed from the theory formulated by Marx, came to be the central tenet of his teaching. As it was precisely that principle that was the cornerstone of the theory of revolutionary transformations, Russian Marxists understandably attached paramount importance to it. Wholly preoccupied with dividing history into separate periods easily lending themselves to analysis, Lenin made some serious mistakes in translating, to give rise to the irrational notion of socioeconomic formation that later became the main term applied in Soviet social science. The term eliminated from Marxism for more than eight decades one of the cornerstone ideas of Karl Marx – that of two cycles of the development of society: the first one being consecutive succession of three *Gesellschaftsformationen* and, the second, succession of modes of production within the *oekonomische Gesellschaftsformation*. By presenting pre-class society, ancient society, the feudal system, capitalist order and the society of the future as conceptual equals, this term became the basis for virtually every sociological misconception and biased view existing in Soviet times.

Moreover, Lenin, emphasizing the role of class struggle in the development of society, and the role of the proletariat at his time, formulated his own doctrine of revolutions, transforming the conception of political revolution into a term denoting exclusively a semi-military coup in which the proletariat seized power and presenting the political coup d'état as one of the aspects of the social revolution. It follows that not only the communist but also, for example, the bourgeois revolution, which has some social and political aspects, is a 'social' revolution. As a result, the fundamental difference between the social and political revolutions, on which Marx's theory of revolution was based, was eliminated.

The unification of all the revolutionary changes begun by Lenin was completed by Stalin, who stated that any revolution represented a clash between the major classes of a given society, be it ancient, feudal or capitalist society. Believing that in ancient society these classes were the slaves and slave-owners, Stalin said, 'the revolution carried out by slaves eliminated the slave-owners and abolished the mode of production based on slavery',[45] and made a similar point with regard to the collapse of the feudal and capitalist systems. Stalin said that all previous revolutionary changes differed from a socialist revolution in that 'all these were one-sided revolutions. One form of exploitation of the working people was replaced by another, but exploitation remained. Exploiters and oppressors replaced others, but the exploiters and oppressors remained. Only the October Revolution set itself the goal of abolishing all exploitation and eliminating each and every exploiter and oppressor'.[46]

Although the idea about the difference between the bourgeois and communist revolutions connected with the problem of state structure is very consonant with those of Lenin, and the thesis that there is a fundamental difference between the proletarian revolution and all previous revolutionary changes in many respects echoes Friedrich Engels' statements to the same effect, the general direction in which Stalin's own brand of theory points certainly has nothing to do with Marx's understanding of the course of the development of the *oekonomische Gesellschaftsformation*.

Having grasped and evaluated the nuances of the discussions between Soviet Marxists in the 1920s and 1930s, Stalin came to the conclusion that it was necessary to limit the number of formations of society to five: the primitive, slave-owning, feudal, capitalist and communist. This conception, which hopelessly mangled the Marxist theoretical schema, was reasonably close to Lenin's views, also based on a recognition of five socioeconomic formations.

In 1938, in his work, *On Dialectical and Historical Materialism*, Stalin gave a synopsis of his point of view on the problems of historical progress. It contained a concise description of the distinguishing features of each of the five major modes of production, starting with the primitive mode of production:

> Under the primitive communal system, the relations of production are based on socialised ownership of the means of production. This largely corresponds to the character of the productive forces in that period ... the tools ... made it impossible to take on the forces of nature ... on one's own ... Common labour leads to communal ownership of the means of production, as well as the product. Here the notion of private ownership of the means of production is still non-existent, except for personal ownership of some tools which doubled as weapons for protecting oneself from predators. There is no exploitation here, and no classes.[47]

Stalin goes on to describe, in respective sequence, 'the five basic types of relations of production, known in history: the primitive communal, slave-owning, feudal, capitalist and socialist relations of production'.[48] And no mention whatsoever of communism as a formation of society or mode of production.

A little later on, Stalin turned to the interaction and correlation between the basis and superstructure of society, the two structural elements of social relations. Although he did not directly give a definition of the basis of society, a number of his statements warrant the conclusion that by the basis he meant the relations of production of the corresponding society. As for the superstructure, which is a complex of political and other relations, he pointed out that it 'is not directly related to production and man's productive activity. It is only indirectly related to production, via the basis. That is why the superstructure does not immediately and directly reflect changes in the level of the development of the productive forces, but following changes in the basis, through the prism of changes in production reflected in changes in the basis'.[49] In analysing the interaction between the basis and the superstructure, Stalin gave the latter a largely passive role. Despite his previous statements about the role of the break-up of the old machinery of state during the transition to socialism, inevitably bringing about preventive (with respect to the basis) transformations in the superstructure, he wrote: 'The superstructure is a product of one epoch, during which a given economic basis exists. For this reason, the superstructure ... is eliminated when the given basis is eliminated and ceases to exist.'[50] This point of view is at variance with Marx's ideas about the active role of the superstructure, and runs counter to the Marxist tenet that it can and does become an important aspect of a key contradiction, determining political-type revolutions.

We have named, point by point, the most important ideas which Stalin put forward in social philosophy. His last significant work, entitled *Economic Problems of Socialism in the USSR*, published in 1952, was largely devoted to economic, rather than philosophical, problems. Over several decades, social thought was restricted in the USSR by the boundaries set by Stalin's theoretical constructs, which were essentially very primitive and sketchy outlines of the fundamental tenets of Marxism, as interpreted by Lenin. From the 1960s on, the first signs began to appear of a revival of the original and truly Marxist tradition; however, this movement gained little ground. As a consequence, Soviet theoretical constructs and models were totally incompatible with the actual course of the development of civilization. Coupled with abysmally low efficiency of the socialist mode of production, they finally brought about the collapse of the communist regimes in the late 1980s and early 1990s.

Marxist theory in Russia has followed a long path that is both tragic and farcical, from its rise as a social doctrine adopted by liberal intellectuals and Social Democrats, to an ideology dominating a vast territory and determining global processes for seven decades. At the same time, this doctrine, in common with any teaching coalescing into an ideology, lost the features of a science and became something else.

The Russian brand of Marxism went through two stages of degradation. In the first stage, associated with Lenin, the key question was whether this theory would attract a sufficient following, and whether a force capable of shaking the foundations of the existing social order could be marshalled on its basis. It is obvious that any modifications of the doctrine, which were called upon to inculcate its tenets in the minds of the masses, were limited to a certain extent, because a 'thinned-out' and primitive conception was less suited to explaining social processes than those advanced by its opponents. That is why it was widely believed that in that stage the conception put forward by Marx, for all the simplifications it had suffered, could still be fine-tuned and developed; attempts were being made to interpret on its basis such new phenomena as imperialism, and to predict the course of social progress, as was the case with Lenin's approach to the issue of whether or not socialist revolution could win in one country.

It emerged after the victory of the Russian revolution, when attempts were made to cast the tenets, under whose banners the Bolsheviks had come to power, into systematized theory, that the masses had failed to assimilate them in their entirety and, worse still, the Bolshevik ideologues themselves did not have any adequate notion about the basics of the very sociological conception they upheld. The next stage was Stalin's decisive intervention against the backdrop of party in-fighting. As a consequence, the doctrine of the victorious proletariat had finally given up its claim to being a living and developing teaching. It metamorphosed into a set of easily digestible, cut-and-dried formulae, guarded closely against any attempts to renovate the sacrosanct dogmas.

Despite the sweeping changes that had taken place in the 20th century, the potential of Marxist theory proper was far from having been exhausted. The methodology proposed by Marx and Engels for singling out three major periods in the history of civilization, and their dialectical and essentially evolutionary approach to evaluating social change and its root causes, went largely unrequired and underrated, despite their great usefulness for understanding new social phenomena.

Theory of Post-industrial Society

Parallel to the Marxist theory of historical periodization, several positivist philosophers and sociologists in the second half of the 19th century began to develop a new concept that better served, they believed, the requirements of the new century than that of the positivist classics. Sharing the notion of Claude Henri de Saint-Simon, Auguste Comte and John Stuart Mill that late 19th-century bourgeois society was a society of *industriels*,[51] they focused on determining individual historical phases on the basis of a study of the technological elements of production, the exchange and the distribution of the goods created in society. Representatives of the 'historical school of political economy', developing the notions of Adam Smith, Jean-Antoine de Condorcet and Johann Gottfried Herder,[52] divided history into stages of primitive, animal herding, agricultural, agricultural–manufacturing, agricultural–manufacturing–commercial[53] and, under several other criteria, of household economy, municipal economy and national economy.[54] By analysing the processes of distribution and exchange of goods they also determined periods of natural, money and credit economy[55] and, slightly later, of individual, transitional, craft and social economy.[56] This concept of periodization based on a study of the principles of the organization of production and the exchange of goods appeared in a relatively complete form in the works of the 'new historical school' at the beginning of the 20th century.[57]

At that time Thorstein Veblen made a successful attempt to create a global doctrine of socioeconomic progress on the basis of an analysis of the development of the industrial system,[58] supplemented by a study of the institutional structure of society. The latter element imparted his concept with a much more prognostic nature than the works of his predecessors. Even today many advocates of post-industrial theory describe Veblen as their spiritual mentor. His concept, considering also many other factors, including the organization of exchange and the interaction between social groups and classes and the formation of individual motivation, was, without doubt, one of the fullest and most comprehensive theories of social progress developed in the first half of the 20th century.

The advances in manufacturing technology and the rapid pace of technological progress that characterized the postwar era brought radical change to Western societies and inspired much-increased intellectual enquiry into the structure of social production and its development. The 1940s brought the works of Britain's Colin Clark[59] and France's Jean Fourastié[60] which, albeit slightly differently, formulated the main methodological principles of a theory of post-industrial society, the division of all social production into the primary (extractive), secondary (industrial) and tertiary (service) sectors and the notion of the coming redistribution of the labour force and the national product from the primary and secondary sectors into the tertiary sector. Fourastié in many ways anticipated the post-industrial classics of the 1970s by showing that up to 90 per cent of the labour force would be concentrated in the service and information sector; that the human race would be able to devote itself to more advanced activities than direct production; that elements of technocrat supremacy would emerge; that the state would start to wield real control over the economy; and that the means of production would cease to be the object of class struggle.[61]

The theory of a post-industrial society emerged fully formulated in the 1950s and 1960s. The notion that industrial society could be contrasted with all previous history had become so commonplace by then that Raymond Aron in the late 1950s disputed the view that

Europe was split into two profoundly different worlds, the Soviet and Western blocs. There was, he said, only one reality: industrial civilization.[62] It was in those years that David Riesman used the expression 'post-industrial' in the title of his famous essay[63] and Daniel Bell used the expression during his lectures in Salzburg. Some elements of the concept can be found in Walt Rostow's *The Stages of Economic Growth. A Non-Communist Manifesto* and *Politics and the Stages of Growth.*[64] Rostow in the latter publication, moreover, alongside the periodization of economic history, contended that the stage to follow industrial civilization would be characterized by the focus of economics on the development of the human personality.[65]

Bell's seminal work, *The Coming of Post-industrial Society. A Venture in Social Forecasting*, appeared in 1973 to generate a boom of interest in the issue and pave the way for the prevalence of futurological concepts in Western sociology in the 1970s. Many works were to appear in the 1970s and 1980s that tried to conceptualize the historical borderline before which humanity found itself. Characteristically, most scholars view the coming social phase primarily as a negation of previous institutions of the socium and therefore practically always use the prefix 'post': the future society is called post-industrial capitalism by R. Heilbroner, post-bourgeois by J. Lichteim, post-capitalist by R. Dahrendorf and P. Drucker, post-consumer by D. Riesman, post-market by J. Rifkin, post-economic by H. Kahn and even post-historic by R. Seidenberg. Attempts to provide a positive definition were far from comprehensive and focused on mere details of social and economic life: the coming phase was described as superindustrial by A. Toffler, technetronic by Z. Brzezinski, a society of professionals by H. Perkin, a society of services by J. Fourastié, a telematic society by M. Ponyatovski. But notions of a future society based on information began to prevail in the 1980s: the society of information and high technology of J. Naisbitt, the informed society of J.-J. Servan-Schreiber and, finally, the information society of Y. Masuda, J. Naisbitt and T. Stonier.

Reviewing the works of the 1970s and 1980s as component parts of a theory of post-industrial society, we ought not to be distracted by the differences in the works of one group of authors or another and concentrate, on the one hand, on the basic principles for appraising historical progress contained in all the works and, on the other hand, on the possibilities they discovered for studying the prospects for social and economic development.

The theory of post-industrial society is the result of the interaction and development of a considerable number of concepts from economics, social science and political science. Its relatively close predecessors include the division of the economy into primary, secondary and tertiary sectors on the basis of the work of the new historical school of the 1940s and 1950s; the theory of the stages of economic growth developed in the 1950s and early 1960s, often identified with the stages of the development of human civilization itself; the theory of a 'single industrial society' that was extremely popular among the technocrats of the 1960s; and the theory of the positive and negative convergence of methodological principles that enabled the then opposing Western and Eastern blocs to be viewed from a relatively unified position.

Born of a natural development of the highly profound and multifaceted positivist tradition, the theory of post-industrial society cannot be clearly attributed to economics, sociology or political science. The relatively isolated position that it occupies in a number of other social doctrines is determined, we believe, by the fact that any theory that is global by its methodological principles and the extent of the issues that it covers cannot but occupy a special place in the line-up of applied theories that are limited by their very pragmatic nature.

Viewing the theory of post-industrial society as an example of a coherent historical construction, we will dwell on those of its elements that are capable of providing a fairly full representation of the methodology used and enable us to compare the theory with the Marxian historical doctrine.

A General Picture of Historical Progress and its Periodization

Advocates of a theory of post-industrial society share a materialist approach to the study of social phenomena with the Marxians. The main problem of this theory is the problem of production and its organization. But advocates of a post-industrial theory give particular emphasis to the technological aspects of production, distribution and exchange, leaving their class nature and the issues of exploitation and political power to the side, which is particularly salient in studies of the first periods of the development of human society.

Advocates of the post-industrial society contrast industrial society with the agrarian society as its predecessor and post-industrial society as its successor. Recently the expression 'agrarian society' has come to be replaced by 'pre-industrial society' with increasing regularity. This has been brought about by a modification in the terminology used by Western sociologists that believe industrial society emerged in Europe at the beginning of the 19th century. Braudel writes: 'The word "industry", before the eighteenth century – or rather, before the nineteenth – risks evoking a false picture... Pre-industry, even in the eighteenth century, had only medieval sources and forms of energy... Such industry as there was found itself hemmed in by an archaic economic system: derisory agricultural productivity, costly and primitive transportation, and inadequate markets';[66] Soboul attributes the emergence of industrialism in France to the events of the first quarter of the 19th century.[67] Scholars of the economic development of European nations in the 16th–18th centuries prefer to use what they regard as the more advanced notion of manufacturing economy rather than industrial economy to identify the pre-industrial phase.[68] Then, starting in the early 1970s, following the appearance of Mendels' famous essay[69] the term 'proto-industrialization' increasingly became synonymous with the transitional process from the agrarian to the industrial system.[70] Thus the triad of pre-industrial society, industrial society and post-industrial society is completed from the methodological and terminological points of view.

The main sign of the pre-industrial stage of the development in society is considered to be the organization of production in which almost all the labour force is occupied directly in the production of consumer goods, mostly foodstuffs; in which the mechanisms of exchange are undeveloped; in which there is practically no urbanization; and in which the political elite rules society without any kind of real economic basis. Bell said:

> Life in pre-industrial societies – still the condition of most of the world today – is primarily *a game against nature*. The labor force is overwhelmingly in the extractive industries: agriculture, mining, fishing, forestry. One works with raw muscle power, in inherited ways, and one's sense of the world is conditioned by the vicissitudes of the elements – the seasons, the storms, the fertility of the soil, the amount of water, the depth of the mine seams, the droughts and the floods. The rhythms of life are shaped by these contingencies.[71]

Toffler reiterated, 'First Wave societies drew their energy from "living batteries" – human and animal muscle-power – or from sun, wind and water ... goods were normally made by handcrafts methods. Products were created one at a time on a custom basis. The same was largely true of distribution.'[72]

It should be stressed that the post-industrialists did not contrast the stage of pre-industrial society with all the other stages of social evolution as something that ought to be destroyed and rejected by the emerging industrial civilization. Bell underlined that the agrarian society differed from the industrial society in that it used raw materials and not energy as its main resource; that it involved the extraction of products from natural materials rather than their fabrication; and that it used labour more intensively than capital. Bell, moreover, said 'a post-industrial society does not "displace" an industrial society, or even an agrarian society... A post-industrial society adds a new dimension, particularly in the management of data and information as necessary facilities in a complex society'.[73]

Advocates of post-industrial theory have often noted the methodological difficulty of finely defining the individual stages of society, never mind determining their chronological boundaries. Neither the first nor the second difficulty, however, is regarded as a potential deficiency in their theoretical system because the system was primarily conceived to study and affirm the evolutionary and not revolutionary nature of history. For example, Aron, showing that the industrial structure that replaced the traditional society consists of a type of socium that opens a new era in historical development, admitted that it was easy to give an abstract definition of every type of society but hard to identify each type of society's boundaries and clarify whether one society or another is archaic or industrial.[74] Bell, considering the process of the formation of post-industrial society, noted that it was coming to replace industrial society in the same way that industrial society came to replace agrarian society. Yet that does not mean the curtailment of the production of material goods. Post-industrial trends, he continued, do not replace the previous social forms as 'stages' of social evolution. They often coexist, deepening the complexity of society and the nature of the social structure.[75]

Such notions of the pre-industrial and industrial societies assume that post-industrial society is unlikely to receive a clear definition grounded on just one or a few of its basic characteristics within the framework of the given doctrine. The detailed definition of post-industrial society given by Bell fails to define clearly such a society's fundamental characteristic. He wrote:

> Post-industrial society was defined as one in which the economy had moved from being predominantly engaged in the production of goods to being preoccupied with services, research, education and amenities; in which the professional–technical class had become the major occupational group; and – most importantly – in which innovation in the society, as reflected in the changing relationship of science to technology, and economics to the polity, was increasingly dependent on advances in *theoretical* knowledge … The post-industrial society … presupposes the rise of a new class who, on the political level, serve as advisors, experts or technocrats.[76]

Naturally it is fairly difficult to determine the chronological framework of such a socium and, as a rule, that is not what post-industrialists are setting out to do. Usually it is asserted that post-industrial trends began to develop after the Second World War, although sometimes they developed in such a way as to give the appearance of the expansion of industrialism.[77] If we use the state of the tertiary sector as our criterion, the critical point in the shift to post-industrialism can be considered to have taken place in the middle of the 1950s in the United States, when the number of Americans employed in the service sector outweighed the number employed in the manufacturing and extractive sectors of the economy.[78] However, the real changes that promoted the vast majority of Western futurologists to describe modern developed societies as post-industrial took place in the mid-to-late 1970s. Here we are talking about a radical acceleration in technological progress, rapid changes in the structure of employment and the formation of a new mentality among much of the population. There also emerged a whole range of situations that could not be explained by traditional economic theory.

When post-industrialists strive to stress the increasingly radical nature of technical innovation they more and more frequently cite the development of information technology. Analysing the 1940s–1970s, the post-industrialists note that generations of computers and new technological solutions are being replaced with ever-growing frequency. The pace of information revolution is not only three to six times faster than the development of, say, motion energy, but it is constantly accelerating.[79] Another sign of the acceleration of technological progress is the shortening of the period between the invention of some process and its introduction in mass-production: it took humanity 112 years to absorb the technology of photography and 56 years to absorb telephony but just 15, 12, five and three to absorb, respectively, radar, television, transistors and integrated microcircuits.[80] Swift changes in the structure of employment also came in the 1970s and 1980s. For example, in the US the share of employees engaged directly in manufacturing operations fell to 12 per cent by the beginning of the 1980s,[81] and the entire factory proletariat numbered no more than 17 per cent of the able-bodied population.[82]

An equally clear sign of the emergence of the post-industrial epoch has manifested itself in a crisis of traditional economic concepts generated by the rise in the production and consumption of information. The fact is that the main resource determining progress in a post-industrial society is knowledge, both theoretical and applied. The consumption of knowledge, unlike the consumption of material goods, firstly, does not amount to the destruction of material goods and, secondly, may be carried out simultaneously by a practically unlimited number of active and managing subjects.[83] These factors make it impossible to apply a whole range of fundamental principles of political economy, starting with the fact that the costs of producing goods calculated in the labour theory of value are no longer commensurable and ending with the removal of the factor of the scarcity of goods, on which many postulates of modern macroeconomic analysis are based. Clearly, it is fair to say that the challenge of post-industrial changes is the greatest to face economics as a science since it was established.[84]

Thus it is the period from the beginning of the 1970s to the end of the 1980s that is presented by the advocates of post-industrialism as the very historical stage that conditioned the formation of the new society. The significance of the social changes that took place at that time is underlined by the fact that many classics of post-industrialism talked of the overcoming of industrial trends as a global revolution, despite their cool attitude to 'revolutionary' rhetoric. Moreover, they talked of a revolution that was not limited to technical innovations, but provided a means for a transition to a qualitatively new state of society,[85] and even stressed that this revolution was the most significant of all those that humanity had undergone.[86]

In completion of our short review of the picture of social progress, presented in the framework of post-industrial theory, we will denote the basic methodological principles for the definition of the three stages of social evolution. The advocates of post-industrial theory distinguish the periods by revolutionary transitions. Moreover, such a periodization is made on the basis of several criteria, each of which is relatively logical, methodologically strict and consistent. The post-industrial society is contrasted with the pre-industrial and industrial societies by the following criteria: by the main production resource, which is information and not raw materials and energy, respectively; by the nature of productive activity, which is processing as opposed to extraction and fabrication; and by technology, which is knowledge-intensive, rather than labour-intensive or capital-intensive. Thus we arrive at the famous formula of the three societies, which have been described as a game against nature, a game against fabricated nature and a game between persons for the pre-industrial, industrial and post-industrial societies, respectively.[87]

The Characteristics of Contemporary Post-industrial Society

Most advocates of post-industrial theory in describing the contemporary socium stress, first, the processes that led to its emergence; second, the advances in the productive sphere; third, the changes in the character of human activity; fourth, the improvement of basic social relations; and fifth, the establishment of new political and social elites. Naturally, these elements do not exhaust all the problems considered by post-industrial theorists. But their illumination gives a fair understanding of the new kind of society that has emerged in what many scholars regard as the main event of the late 20th century.

The formation of the post-industrial society is usually viewed in the context of the formation of a relatively homogenic society, free from class differences in their Marxist sense. Bell quite fairly criticizes Marx for his simplified approach to the class structure of society that concentrates on the contradictions between the two main classes of any given society, regardless of the role either of them could play in the further evolution of the corresponding social organism. Meanwhile, European history provides philosophers with an extremely interesting fact. *No polar class was able to become dominant after any transition at any time, not from ancient to feudal, not from feudal to bourgeois and not in the current transformation.* As the ruling and oppressed classes of antiquity dissolved in the new European society so feudal masters and serfs made way for bourgeoisie and the proletariat, which have now too been thrust to the side by the meritocracy (a term first introduced by M.Young in his *The Rise of Meritocracy*, published in London in 1958,[88] and now increasingly widely used in modern sociology) and the information class, sometimes known as the 'cognitariat'.[89] Thus the emergence of the post-industrial society better reflects the logic of historical progress than the introduction of socialism, which envisages an illusory victory of the industrial proletariat, which then 'acquires a dominating position' in society. The formative process of the post-industrial society takes place wherever there is social mobility that brings most employees from the proletariat to the tertiary sector, wherever the role of information is heightened and wherever class differences are ironed out and a social state run by a meritocracy emerges.

Despite significant differences of approach to an appraisal of post-industrial society and its characteristics, the vast majority of post-industrialists believe that the most fundamental exterior sign of the new society is the shift in focus from the production of material goods to the production of services and information. The gross product of human services outweighed the gross product of material production by the early 1980s in the United States and slightly later in the nations of Western Europe. The growth in human services in the first half of the 1980s was much faster than the growth in material production, by factors of two in France, six in Germany and the United States and 30 in Britain.[90]

The service sector, traditionally called the tertiary sector, is heterogeneous and can itself be divided into the true tertiary (material services like transport, communications and warehousing), the quaternary (trade, finance, insurance and real estate) and the quintary (personal, professional and business services and government administration) sectors. The social product is growing fastest in those industries which entail human interaction to the greatest extent and whose product is the least reproducible. That can be traced in the structure of employment by industry. In the United

States between 1950 and 1993, the share of the total labour force fell by a factor of 5.2 in agriculture and forestry, by a factor of four in extractive industries and halved in manufacturing. Yet there was no contraction of employment in the highly individualized industries of the secondary sector, like construction, and in the primitive industries of the tertiary sector (transport, communications and warehousing). There was a rise from 19 per cent to 21 per cent for employment in trade. That makes the increase in the personal, professional and business service industry look even more impressive. Its share of the overall structure of employment rose from 20 per cent to 35 per cent. The share of people occupied in finance, insurance and real estate went up from 3 per cent to 12 per cent in the same period.[91] Of the American working population, 63 per cent was engaged in the information sector by the middle of the 1980s, accounting for 67 per cent of the total aggregate payroll.[92]

Brzezinski said that 'the post-industrial society is becoming a "technetronic" society: a society that is shaped culturally, psychologically, socially and economically by the impact of technology and electronics – particularly in the area of computers and communications. The industrial process is no longer the principal determinant of social change, altering the mores, the social structure, and the values of society'.[93] The result of that global historical transition is the supplanting of humans from direct material production. Most of the labour force is transferred into the service sector.[94] Machines are programmed to carry out a complete production process.[95] As a result, 'the fact that individuals now talk to other individuals, rather than interact with a machine, is the fundamental fact about work in the post-industrial society'.[96]

Advocates of post-industrial theory underline the importance of the restructuring of the labour force and the growth of employment in the service sector, noting that the largest growth has taken place, not in those industries that provide traditional services, like household, transport and commercial services, but in those industries that deal with human beings as individuals, where the production and consumption of a service are indissolubly linked. Bell said, 'the word "services" conjures up images of fast-food, low-wage employments. This is misleading. The major services are financial services; professional and design services; human services (health, education and social services); and, at the low end of the scale, personal services. The core of the postindustrial society is its professional and technical services'.[97]

Such is the attention given by the post-industrialists to the problems of the development of information technology that sometimes the theory of an information society is viewed as a concept that can stand on its own. We shall not follow that approach.

Information, its production and consumption are closely associated with the service sector and it is practically impossible to make a clear distinction between the service and information sectors. Some authors define a post-industrial society as one based on the consumption of high-tech information services.[98] Bell stresses the growth in the role of codified theoretical knowledge for technical innovation and asserts that the new intellectual technologies have become the main element in decision making.[99]

The unfolding of the above processes cannot but bring substantial changes in the system of human activity, its objective characteristics and motivations. A radical shift has been seen in the organizational forms of human activity from the corporate industrial type to the so-called 'adaptive corporations'. They reject the priority of maximizing profits and not only focus on traditional economic values but stimulate the search for the new and form creative work styles.[100] That shift can also be seen in research centres and universities, which now group together ever greater numbers of people and where an increasing share of the national product is being generated.[101] It can also be seen in other mostly voluntary non-profit organizations, which are becoming important centres for decision making and influence on other social institutions.[102] All this is generating serious changes in the system of social institutions that reflect the transition from an economy based on the arbitrary laws of the market to an economy that is 'coordinated' rather than planned and the transition from the 'economized' model of society seen in industrial civilization to the 'sociologized' model of society.[103]

But another change of even more importance is the change in the structure of internal activity. This is because the game between persons[104] of the post-industrial society decisively supplants the game with fabricated nature typical of industrial society. As a result of alienation of people from the means of production in industrial society, human beings do not perceive themselves as active bearers of their own power and wealth and feel like an improved physical entity, dependent on outside forces that determine the meaning of their lives.[105] Moreover, the formation and growth of such alienation is the direct result of the expansion of the industrial society.[106] There are real opportunities to overcome alienation under the conditions of a post-industrial society. The first step on the way to doing so will be to pull down the walls that separate education, labour and leisure.[107]

The are two main directions for surmounting alienation. Firstly, the division between the producer and the means of production must be eliminated. Moreover, to a certain extent the bourgeois class must lose its monopoly over the means of production that provides its dominant role in the capitalist society. Secondly, a modification of social values and a change in the motivation of human activity will come to make relations with the means of production irrelevant.

The overcoming of the monopoly of means of production by one social group or class is associated primarily with such changes, as a result of which 'in post-industrial economies the limiting factors tend not to be land, labour or capital. The limiting factor in modern productive systems is information … hence it is the information producers to whom economic and political power accrues'.[108] But the consumption and production of information differ greatly from the consumption and production of material goods. Where large-scale production, which required thousands of people and the use of huge, complex mechanisms, dominated, the division of labour and class boundaries were natural and insurmountable; but where all that was required to create new information products was a computer, linked up to global information networks, and other standard equipment, fully accessible to the individual who uses it, labour and means of production are able to blend harmoniously in a way unknown to former social organizations.[109] Some researchers go even further and claim that the proliferation of information networks and computer data bases, together with the transformation of information into a core subject and product of labour, leads to the replacement of the very concept of 'means of production' with that of 'models of communication'.[110]

The modification of social values, which made the problem of alienation less acute, was also closely linked with the expansion of the information-based economy. Automation and information which, as P. Drucker so successfully notes, represent nothing other than the swift replacement of labour by knowledge,[111] bring mind-workers in to replace industrial workers alienated from labour. These mind-workers possess qualifications and information which are the essential tools of intellectual labour, tools which unqualified factory workers could never have possessed.[112] The production and consumption of information expand the circle of processes based on subject-to-subject interactions, and this circle may in the very near future extend to the limits of the whole of social production. 'If the dominant figures of the last hundred years have been the entrepreneur, the businessman and the industrial executive, the "new men" are the scientists, the mathematicians, the economists and the new engineers of the new intellectual technology';[113] as a result of the expansion of the new system of production, where the proportion of mass industrial production constantly decreases, the 'proletariat', now the minority, is constantly being forced aside by the 'cognitariat'.[114]

The technological achievements of recent decades which guaranteed high standards of consumption, and high demand made of those engaged in the production process, also caused the modification of the stimuli and motives of activity. On the one hand, workers prefer to be paid less if they can accomplish something at their place of work and not have to perform routine tasks, are able to make decisions themselves, and can expect cultural and professional growth and, as a consequence, career growth. This gives many sociologists grounds to speak of the possible replacement of labour as an activity by a new type of activity which contains many elements of creativity and which is characteristic of post-industrial civilization.[115] On the other hand, an ever-increasing number of people are striving to devote as much time as possible to their families, involvement in various public organizations, self-education, sport and so on. Surveys carried out in the mid-1990s show that even the prospect of fast professional and career growth – the main motive of the activity of the 1970s and 1980s – no longer appeals to 55 per cent of all workers, if in order to achieve this they would have to devote less time to their families and give up their usual pastimes.[116]

The creative style of activity emerges even in those areas of the economy in which activities not identified with creativity as such are widespread. Sociologists are becoming more and more inclined to the view that 'creative citizenry will be central to success in the post-industrial era … a few Einsteins and Picassos will not be enough. The entire population must be transformed so that everyone, or at least most people, exercise more creativity than they do at present'.[117] In turn, the management of creative personnel requires another style of leadership, one which is heterogeneous, individual, anti-bureaucratic, intellectual and creative.[118] The amalgamation of the aims of the individual, society and corporation makes it possible to speak of the latter not only as an economic but also as a 'sociological' institution. Bell is convincing when he claims:

> Even so, if we set up a continuum, with *economizing* at one end of the scale (in which all aspects of organization are single-mindedly reduced to become means to the goals of production and profit) and *sociologizing* at the other (in which all workers are guaranteed life-time jobs, and the satisfaction of the work becomes the primary levy on resources), then in the last thirty years the corporation has been moving steadily, for almost all its employees, towards the *sociologizing* end of the scale.[119]

The institutional structure of contemporary society consists of six elements: economic enterprises, the social sector, scientific institutions, enterprises which manufacture consumer goods, voluntary organizations and the domestic economy. The first four elements constitute the formal economy, and the latter two the complementary economy. In the formal economy, universities, research centres and academic institutes 'where theoretical knowledge is sought, tested, and codified ... become the primary institutions of the new society',[120] in contrast to industrial society, where the key factor was the firm, on account of its leading role in the organization of the mass-production of material benefits.

The assertion that the main institutions of the new era will be intellectual ones serves not so much to signify that the majority of representatives of post-industrial society will consist of scholars, engineers, specialists in technology or intellectuals (although already 'the majority of individuals in contemporary society are not businessmen'[121]) as to draw attention to the constructive role fulfilled by science as an essentially non-commercial undertaking during the transition to the post-industrial society. The social sector, which implies non-profit-making production, today progresses quickly thanks both to the scientific sector and to the production of consumer goods and the service sector as a whole. The existence of this sort of tendency indicates that the characteristic goal of the industrial society to generate income on the overall economic scale is being 'eroded' by the goals of achieving common well-being and improving the 'quality of life'. It is precisely these goals and the opportunities that can be opened by technological progress for those whose labour is not needed any longer in a market-type sector that condition the development of an alternative occupation or the so-called 'complementary economy'. Its components are 'community-based organizations', 'voluntary organizations' and the domestic sector.

Information and knowledge, or 'symbolic capital', are of a principally different nature compared to the earlier symbols of economic power; they are more democratic than land or capital. If land and capital are finite, knowledge can be generated and accumulated infinitely; if land and capital have a limited number of users, knowledge is accessible to an infinite number of people. And, finally, if land and capital belong only to the rich and powerful, the revolutionary trait of knowledge is its accessibility to the weak and poor. Amid swift scientific and technological progress occurs the 'erosion' of ownership, expressed in the loss of the monopoly of knowledge and the proliferation of intellectual know-how which presuppose a high level of education and qualification on the part of the worker.

However, these characteristics of information and knowledge as a strategic and essential subject of ownership do not eliminate the problem of class conflicts even in the post-industrial society. As this advances there emerges a technocratic class,[122] which includes not only those who possess information and knowledge but also those who succeed in manipulating them on three levels: the national level of governmental bureaucracy; the sectoral, or industrial level of professionals and academic experts; and the level of the economic organization, or technostructure. The latter, the brain of the contemporary corporation, embraces a large number of people, from enterprise bosses to the working masses, or all who possess the necessary abilities and knowledge.

The transformation of information into a limiting factor of production leaves the corresponding imprint on the nature of economic power. 'Visible things' like land and capital, possessed by specific individuals, cease to be objects of ownership or to bring economic power; these become information and knowledge possessed by specific people.[123] It is by the strength of this that the technocrats constitute the ruling class of post-industrial society, confronted by an oppressed and particularly alienated class.[124] The ruling class is the governmental bureaucracy, professional and academic experts and technostructure, that is, people one way or another involved in governing and managing and who stand next to the very sources of information. The oppressed class is diverse. It includes those led by government, including the technicians and maintenance personnel who guarantee the flow of information, not to mention the operators and blue-collar workers in material production. Another position is occupied by a particularly alienated class – the members of local communities as distinct from central institutions, labourers unable to jump on the high-tech bandwagon and, finally, workers in obsolete professions – all the elements of society which, from the point of view of the political set-up, confront post-industrial tendencies. This class division is based on criteria such as the scope of controllable information or knowledge man possesses.

Professional and academic experts are the ruling group with respect to technical and maintenance personnel, even more so with respect to labourers. The priority of professionals working in education and health care is reinforced by the important role of these sectors in post-industrial development. Academic experts, who also form part of an elite, are, as a rule, to be found in universities and research centres, that is in autonomous organizations where different theoretical trends coexist, including also trends alternative to the ruling ones, on the strength of which 'professionals are defined much less by their hierarchical authority than by their scientific competence'.[125] However, by proclaiming its adherence to progress, the ruling class acts in accordance with its own ideas, not always remaining sensitive to the interests of specific groups, local communities and selected individuals.

If the governmental bureaucracy controls and manipulates information, defining the political, economic and social aims of society, then at the level of economic organization the ruling class is represented by the technostructure, which incorporates those who possess the necessary abilities and knowledge, and which consequently performs decisive production-related functions. A subordinate position with respect to the technostructure is occupied by the operators and blue-collar workers, representatives of dying professions being particularly alienated. The relations of dominance and subordination have been preserved in post-industrial society because, firstly, despite the increasing opportunities to obtain the necessary knowledge and education, people if only by the strength of their natural capabilities are unable to be equal; and secondly, although the contemporary worker is better educated and trained and possesses better skills, he has still not been able to assume a position equal to that of his opponent, the employer.[126] 'This is the reason why the idea of alienation is so widespread. We are leaving a society of exploitation and entering the society of alienation',[127] in which new forms of conflict, information wars, manifesting themselves in the 'battle for standards', 'information rivalry' and 'computer espionage' arise; moreover, technological advances are making it easier and easier to gain access to information and may make the total information war infinite.

The emergence of the fundamentals of post-industrial society brings about a new understanding of the essence of the class conflict arising between the ruling and oppressed classes primarily on account of non-economic values: the desire to engage in creative activity, receive or improve education, have a flexible working schedule, contribute to the life of the organizations, city and community life, and so on. Change in values denotes neither the elimination of conflict nor denial of the need for its resolution. Workers from the oppressed class can try to improve their position in two ways: first, individually, by acquiring uncommon skills for which there are no easily accessible substitutes; that is, by becoming members of the technostructure; and, second, collectively, by creating unions, guilds and associations at the place of work or on the scale of cities and whole countries.[128] Thus labour parties[129] and trade unions which 'have over the past 100 years transformed themselves from craft-centered organizations with guild-like characteristics to powerful enterprises for organizing mass-production and semiskilled workers into huge industrial unions'[130] are being deindustrialized in the post-industrial society rather than disappearing alongside the deindustrialization of production and employment. This kind of evolution corresponds to the requirements of the post-industrial worker, who gains the opportunity together with more or less qualified colleagues to participate in the advancement of essential (from the collective's point of view) demands.

The Prospects for Civilization in the Light of Post-industrial Theory

The theory of post-industrial society was created primarily as an instrument for interpreting the specific nature of the day and the course of the development of civilization. However, generally accepted forecasts are limited in the number of courses available. For example, in the future-established post-industrial society there will prevail a quaternary and a quintary sector of the economy which will employ between three-quarters and four-fifths of the whole able-bodied labour force. The activity of the overwhelming majority of the people employed in social production will abandon the characteristics of the labour process for the intrinsic elements of creative activity.[131] There will emerge a society characterized by the virtual absence of the sort of class contradictions capable of serving as a serious destructive element, a society in which the system of values is able 'to establish, however roughly, the "right" distribution of income in the society, the minimum income available to all citizens, etc.'.[132] The state, represented by a meritocracy and by scientific sector workers, will be responsible for the rational programming of social production and preserve the necessary control over the social sphere. As a result, the spirit of the information-based society will become the spirit of globalism, of a symbiosis in which man and nature may coexist in a harmony consisting in strict self-discipline and social collaboration.[133]

However, there are many questions which have not been answered to this day. Moreover, it ought to be pointed out that present-day societies are encountering not only 'external' problems with respect to post-industrial structures but also problems arising directly from post-industrial development.

When contemplating the emergence of post-industrial theory, one should not forget that this occurred at a very difficult time for Western civilization, when the tension caused by the wave of social movements at the end of the 1960s had only just subsided; a time when the world had still to enter the biggest economic crisis in postwar history, when decolonization was increasing, when the defeat of communism was still a long way off and when the possibility of armed clashes between the superpowers sometimes looked very real indeed. Therefore it was only natural that the authors of post-industrial conceptions should have paid attention to the global processes unfolding in the contemporary world.

When describing the 'environment' in which post-industrial societies are developing, researchers have commented not only on purely economic contradictions which gave rise to cyclic and structural crises (which is set out most boldly by A. Toffler in his famous work on the 'eco-spasm',[134] but also on problems of an ecological nature. Moreover, one of the key characteristics of the 'environment' has been considered to be the contradictions which constantly arise in relations between East and West and between North and South. It is worth mentioning that most of the classic post-industrial theorists, while not overtly hostile to the communist regimes, and pointing to the inefficiency of the economic models they created, were confident of the prevalence of the Western system of production and the Western system of values. It was precisely the principles of a free society, democracy and the possibility of free economic choice as the object of man's natural desire in the 20th century, but inaccessible to the majority of the population dominated by communist regimes, that undermined political stability in the East European countries and destroyed the communist system.[135]

Meanwhile the problem of the widening gap and mounting confrontation along the North–South line has attracted and continues to attract the attention of absolutely all futurologists. Despite the swift progress of technology, only a few of the developing countries have been in a position to reap its fruits; for most countries the dawning of the technetronic era resulted in nothing more than access to information and the acutest awareness that Western standards of life and the Western level of consumption were unattainable. The consequence is an increasing feeling of deprivation, which has become widespread in the Third World and is capable of sparking off an explosion of indiscriminate hatred.[136] Contradictions of this type become more and more relevant in view of the increasing migration from Third World countries to Western Europe and the United States, where the population and governments are often unable to find adequate measures to cope with the acceleration of this process. The activization of Islamic ideology and politics, and the possible economic and political consolidation of Japan and China in the next century, will create new world centres of power, capable, in unforeseen circumstances, of undermining the fragile stability of the 1990s.

However, far more interesting for our study is the analysis by the post-industrial theorists of the social changes born directly of the very process of the emergence of this new form of social organization. We have been noticing more often the fact that the development of the non-commercial sector, the increase in the number of voluntary organizations and similar processes testify not so much to the triumph of progressive post-industrial tendencies as to a final bid by people to make at least some sort of reply to their accelerating displacement from the sphere of material production itself and from the services sphere. The number of jobs is declining not only in industry but also in the tertiary sector and even in the financial sector, where banks in 1983–93 had to lay off 37 per cent of their staff as a result of computerizing more and more services; meanwhile, according to statistics, 'in the United States a one percent rise in unemployment results in a 6.7 percent increase in homicides, a 3.4 percent increase in violent crimes, and a 2.4 percent increase in property crime'.[137] In today's conditions,

> the death of the global labor force is being internalized by millions of workers who experience their own individual death, daily, at the hands of profit-driven employers and a disinterested government. They are the ones who are waiting for pink slips, being forced to work part-time at reduced pay, or being pushed onto the welfare rolls. With each new indignity, their confidence and self-esteem suffer another blow. They become expendable, then irrelevant, and finally invisible in the new high-tech world.[138]

The whole danger of this phenomenon can be adequately assessed only if account is taken of the following two circumstances. On the one hand, the majority of people made redundant in this way cannot be utilized in the quickly developing sphere of the information-based economy – which requires a high level of education and creative potential – and, consequently, cross over into the ranks of citizens who have virtually no chance of finding a worthy occupation at any time in the future. On the other hand, these people, as most members of the free society, have been brought up according to the principles of the Western 'permissive cornucopia' which, in terms of action, can be reduced entirely to permissiveness, if greed is artificially instilled as the only motive for this action.[139] The speed of technological progress is such that it caused power at the one pole to arise over the gigantic information mountains and the ascent of creative activity among a large section of the population and, at the same time, created at the other pole a no less considerable number of people who had also left the sphere of material production but had crossed over, not into the information sector, but to a 'nowhere' from which there is no return to the fast-changing world.

Moreover, one other fairly dangerous tendency is at play. Besides the development of creative activity both at work and in free time, the technological breakthrough of the last few decades gives rise also to a completely non-productive activity which draws in more and more people. This slows down the rate of economic growth,[140] while creating more and more selectivity in choice of activity and so on. The result is increasing idleness among a public which would rather get a wage considered to be adequate and earned with the minimum amount of commitment; and orientation to working only in sectors it likes. This situation for post-industrial societies is fraught not only with potential internal instability but also with a lack of preparedness to deflect increasing economic aggression on the part of the Asian and Third World countries.

Thus, in the framework of the theory of post-industrial society, we find pointers to a whole range of contratendencies which must at all costs be taken into account, either when studying contemporary Western realities or when assessing the outlook for the development of civilization. However, on the whole in the 1980s and 1990s, the general tone of the post-industrial theorists has become quieter than in the 1970s. The overcoming of economic crisis, indisputable progress in resolving ecological problems, the collapse of East European communism, examples of successful confrontation with aggressive regimes, demonstrated vividly in the Gulf War, the united Europe – all this has made the outlook for the technological and social progress of Western societies less murky.

The Evolution of the Theory of Post-industrial Society

And so we come to problems related to the development of the conception of post-industrialism and the prospects for the theory itself. Originating in the 1960s, the conception of post-industrial society may be viewed as the embodiment of the principles of positivism in the light of the 20th century. It is symptomatic and natural that it was formulated at a time when Western societies were in the middle of a turbulent technological growth and utilized the latest technological achievements both in industry and in everyday life. This era was strongly reminiscent of the period of the triumph of science and technology in the last third of the 19th century, when the spirit of discovery prevailed in the natural sciences, and the austere principles of positivism, which cast dialectical doctrinarianism aside, flourished in the social sciences.

It was during the early phase in its development, in the latter half of the 1960s and early 1970s, that post-industrial theory, grounded on technological optimism, became very widespread and won over many academic circles. The works of Bell, Toffler, Touraine and Etzioni in the 1970s developed first and foremost ideas that had become very common by that time. Theory was as open as possible to the future, and Bell reflected its essence well when he wrote that it represented 'a fiction, a logical construction of what could be, against which the future social reality can be compared in order to see what intervened to change society in the direction it did take'.[141] It was this that distinguished the theory from a number of sociological and philosophical theories which, as a rule, were profoundly pessimistic studies, and became an important contributor to its success.

The theory flourished in the 1970s: the serious economic difficulties of those years did not render the theory worthless but even confirmed a whole number of its conclusions. The history of the 1970s, despite the several elements of alarmism that then existed, demonstrated the correctness of the conception, uncovering a far more decisive turn than in previous years towards the expansion of the service-oriented economy; granting the Western world the opportunity to taste the full might of the information revolution; opening major possibilities for the harmonization of relations between man and nature; and making production more ecologically acceptable. It was in the mid-to-late 1970s that interest in futurological conceptions became thoroughly obvious, and the theory soared in popularity. Many assume that the theory of post-industrial society 'declined' somewhat in the 1980s and 1990s, but this is hardly the case. Like any doctrine which has conquered minds with its main methodological canons, post-industrial theory had already attained scientific maturity.

The main areas in which the theory of post-industrial society can be developed today are associated, on the one hand, with the interpretation of nature and the consequences of the information revolution (the conceptions of an 'information society' formed in the 1980s should be regarded as an integral part and form of the development of the post-industrial theory) and, on the other hand, with the advancement in specific directions of theory, which preserve its main methodological parameters, but which are of a predominantly applied nature. This advancement in applied directions is extremely important, and we shall deal with questions relevant in future to post-industrial theory on a relatively applied level, questions to which answers have still to be found, more than once in this book. Research has been stepped up into problems associated with the change in the character of human activity, the regularities of exchange in contemporary society, social justice and unemployment; and scientific interest has increased in new types of public organization and in the social structure of post-industrial society as a whole, and in the cultural changes that have been so significant during the last few decades.

Against this background the relative indifference of the post-industrial theorists to the neo-institutional theories of the early 1990s looks strange, the more so given that the roots of post-industrial doctrine can be traced back to the institutionalism of the first half of the century. The only explanation for this is that post-industrial theorists consider they are fully able to develop a course which they have introduced within the framework of methodological principles formulated earlier, without following the changing fashion for economic theory.

Nor have the crisis of communism and collapse of the Eastern bloc been particularly subject to scrutiny by the researchers of post-industrialism. In fact the early works of post-industrialists, from Aron to Bell, dwelled more on Eastern Europe than did their more recent works. The notion that the USSR was an industrial superpower lay at the foundation of many original and bold conclusions of the 1950s and 1960s; the observation of the remains of an empire, cast to the upper limit of proto-industrialism, could hardly present today's sociologists with any interesting facts.

So it can be said that contemporary post-industrial theory is going through a phase of internal development before embarking on a new ascent. In fact, this theory to this day remains virtually the only example of coherent historical construction with a major futurological potential.

The conception has not undergone any serious changes of course since it first emerged. It would be untrue to say, for example, that there was more historical optimism in the works of the 1970s that in those of today, or that alarmist sentiments have declined sharply. Each of the post-industrial theorists is forging his own spiritual evolution: either, as in Bell's case, without altering his main assessment of contemporary society or, as a comparison of Toffler's *Future Shock* and *Eco-Spasm* with *The Third Wave* and *Previews and Premises* shows, softening his assessment and reviewing some of his conclusions in a more serene light; or, as can be seen from a comparison of Brzezinski's *Between Two Ages* and *Out of Control*, actually insisting that crisis manifestations are on the increase and must be countered.

All of this convinces us even more that the scientific quest begun in the 1970s continues today with the same momentum and it seems that a new wave of theoretical generalizations is not too far away. If one remembers the many works published in the 1960s and 1970s with reference to the year 2000 in their titles, it can be assumed that during the first decade of the next century most of the classic post-industrial theorists and their followers will produce conceptual works which offer many new insights into the contemporary state of affairs and into the outlook for the development of civilization.

Two Coherent Theories: The Basic Elements of Similarity and Mutual Supplementation

Completing the first part of our work, we wish to consider the similarity of two coherent concepts of history, to note their common achievements and faults, to name the main problems in which the methodological principles of Marxism and post-industrial theory might enrich each other and to give impulse to further investigations. Moreover, we will briefly formulate several objectives of the analysis that we plan to carry out later.

The Marxian and post-industrial theories share several characteristics that allow us not only to consider the two doctrines as coherent historical constructions but to assert that perhaps not a synthesis but some form of mutual interaction may bring a series of radical breakthroughs in the understanding of history and the place of contemporary society within it.

Firstly, the two theories are based on the recognition that *the advancement in the forms and methods of material production serve as the source and measure for the progress of civilization*. Whatever method of appraisal of whatever society we take in Marxism or post-industrialism, it will be connected with an understanding of the stage of advancement of material (or non-material in the corresponding historical stage) production. Moreover, it should be stressed that neither the Marxists nor the advocates of post-industrial theory consider the development of production for its own sake. They are both interested in two fundamental changes prompted by that process: the growth in productivity as an economic indicator and the growth in individual freedom as a social indicator. Marxists believe one society to be superior to another if it has higher productivity. Post-industrialists judge the same thing according to the energy resource and form of the production process. One of the best-known Marxian divisions of the historical process, the periods of personal dependence, material dependence and free individuality, are chronologically little different from the divisions of pre-industrial, industrial and post-industrial societies.

Secondly, and this we regard as being most significant, *both theoretical trends divide history into three main phases*: moreover, on the basis of a similarity of methodological principles that reveals itself simultaneously in several directions. Both the Marxists and the post-industrialists define archaic, economic and communist *Gesellschaftsformationen*, and, on the basis of an appraisal of the forms and methods of social production of the corresponding social organizations, categorize them as agrarian, industrial and post-industrial societies. Both Marxists and post-industrialists recognize that each of the above divisions is relatively abstract and the notion of Marx and Engels that communism is a movement destroying the current state fully corresponds to Bell's notion of a post-industrial society as an abstraction created to impose order on our knowledge of the future progress of civilization. Neither the founders of Marxism nor the theorists of post-industrialism believe it is possible to talk on clear terminological boundaries between *Gesellschaftsformationen* and industrial society. Marx, in a letter to Vera Zasulich, clearly says that the change of *Gesellschaftsformationen* is a separate historical epoch. Aron admits the difficulty of determining the chronological boundaries of one society or another and even says that it is far from always clear whether a society is agrarian or industrial. The doubts of both thinkers are addressed to past historical changes. Marxists and the advocates of post-industrial theory respectively believe that every new *Gesellschaftsformation* and every new phase of history does not contradict and does not replace the former formation or phase but rests on it as on its basis (Marx) or adds a new measure (Bell). A whole series of comparisons can be made along these lines. *This astonishing methodological similarity in the creation of a historical triad is the main sign that the two theories can be coherently combined.*

Thirdly, the founders of Marxism and the classics of post-industrial theory agree that the transition between *Gesellschaftsformationen* and the borders of industrial society are marked by revolutionary changes. Moreover, both recognize that the transition from a primary *Gesellschaftsformation* to a secondary formation or from a pre-industrial to an industrial society is a lengthy process, more revolutionary in essence than in character. The truly revolutionary nature of the transition that replaces *oekonomische Gesellschaftsformation* with communism and industrial civilization with post-industrial civilization was understood by the founders of Marxism and by post-industrialists. Engels wrote that the proletarian revolution will differ from all previous revolutions as a social rather than a political revolution. Servan-Schreiber called it the most significant social revolution in human history.

Fourthly, there is a *great similarity in the way the communist Gesellschaftsformation and post-industrial society are portrayed*. That similarity, of course, should be viewed bearing in mind the historical context in which Marxian theory was developed. It was impossible in the middle of the 19th century to know what technological breakthroughs would be made by the end of the 20th century. Nevertheless, the founders of Marxism often talked of technological progress as the basis for social change. Post-industrial theorists, forming their theory in the heat of the information revolution, also define the post-industrial society as a socium based on high technology, moreover, that definition is made not as a forecast but as an affirmation of a change that has already taken place in real life. Marx and Engels were quite right to call the coming historical condition a society of free individuals. But it is the development of human abilities and the replacement of labour by creative activity that the classics of post-industrialism believe to be the basic characteristic of the new condition of society. Their ideal is also a society based on social justice, although post-industrialism, quite rightly, does not allow for the possibility of the class-based approach preached by the founders of Marxism. The general direction of both theories remains humanistic and their ideals are a worthy objective of historical progress that reflects human nature.

Fifthly, the *terminological similarities* between the Marxian and post-industrial doctrines are also very interesting. They could, of course, be coincidental. They could also indicate something more than a coincidence. Both the founders of Marxism and famous post-industrialist authors like Kahn and Bell call the third phase of social evolution *post-economic*. True, the term 'post-economic' has to be deduced from the works of Marx: he did not directly call the communist *Gesellschaftsformation* post-economic. But both Kahn and Bell use the term in their works.

It is also symptomatic that a number of post-industrialists, notably Horowitz, point out when discussing modern economics that the concept of the factors of production may be replaced by the term 'models of communication'; the term 'form of communication' was used heavily by Marx in his early works, when his theory was not as subordinated to the aims of justifying the necessity for class struggle and the revolutionary transformation of society as in later Marx.

The list of elements common to the Marxian model and the theory of post-industrial society could go on. But it would make sense to assess the strengths and weaknesses of both models in order to consider the possibility of such interaction that could be useful for either of them.

The strengths of Marxism lie mainly in the logical and methodological rigidity of Marxian theory. The founders of Marxism were able to depict the historical process as an alternating three-phase process in which each phase could be acknowledged as being an autonomous and integral stage in history. The archaic society existed for tens of thousands of years and was a regular social organism. The economic society also has a long history: it laid down a specific path of evolution, and accommodated most of the documented history of the human race. Economic society incorporated four modes of production, each of which was a relatively complete historical whole. The society of the future – communism – contrasted radically with the economic epoch, but was at the same time depicted as a dialectic synthesis of the first two periods. All of this endows Marxian theory with a significant inner wholeness and formulates its strikingly futurological potential.

The stronger aspects of post-industrial theory are associated primarily with the fact that its authors were able to more or less overcome the principle of assessing society from the point of view of its class structure, a principle that had prevailed in historical science since the 19th century and in philosophy since far earlier times. Without denying the presence of class conflicts and their role in social evolution, the post-industrialists focused on those processes which influenced society as an integral whole, even if they did not eliminate class differences. From these angles they address a whole range of issues – technological progress, information and changes in the character of labour as such and of production as a whole – and assess the state of the global problems of their times. But it must not categorically be claimed that this approach was necessarily more perfect than the class approach made absolute by the followers of Marxist teaching; nevertheless, it can in modern circumstances bear the sort of fruit the traditional method is incapable of bearing. Another important aspect is that the theory of post-industrial society, born in a highly utilitarian world, began to develop mainly with the evaluation of the real phenomena which altered the countenance of Western society. It was based on concrete facts that can be presented by contemporary civilization, and that is its main advantage: in this theory general methodological schemes occupy a fittingly subordinate position and do not rule over the whole scientific construction.

The weaker aspects of both theories are a kind of mirror-image of their stronger aspects. The main shortcoming of Marxism was the radical reappraisal by Marx and Engels of the significance and role of class struggle in the history of mankind. The founders of Marxism, consistent followers of the materialist outlook on the historical process, held their own unique conclusions in such disdain to please the principles of the 'emancipation' of the oppressed proletariat that their own 'theory' of the socialist transformation of society was, paradoxically, no longer materialistic. Materialism taught that the *oekonomische Gesellschaftsformation*, which in the capitalist *Produktionsweise* gained its fullest expression after centuries of formation, cannot be destroyed in its most established form; materialism also taught that the opposing classes who determined the development of a certain *Produktionsweise* leave the proscenium when another is formed; and, finally, materialism taught that a society in radical terms differing from the existing one, just as one *Gesellschaftsformation* differs from another, cannot be built on the same technological basis as the preceding one. Marx and Engels at least three times had to overstep the principles of their own historical doctrine in order to proclaim the theory of the forcible introduction of communism by means of the revolutionary overthrow of the bourgeoisie. *Planomernost'* (planned development) – a fetish thrown up by the Marxists against commodity chaos – proved to be a natural result of economics, which was going through the primitive stage of mass-production, a result caused objectively and which did not require the radical intervention termed voluntarism. Today, as a result of the ruinous 70-year experiment, only the citizens of the former communist states are compelled, by developing primitive forms of market relations, to move along a path which directly contrasts with the one along which the whole world is moving.

The main shortcoming of post-industrial theory, for its part, is its insufficient 'theory saturation'. Standing on the firm soil of reality, and building their theory on the basis of real facts presented by the very course of social development, the post-industrialists reflected in this theory the whole internal self-contentment of the industrial order, which considered itself to be the reason for the successes of human civilization. Having rejected the principle of viewing the 'class-based' or 'economic' world as a single whole, and having scornfully neglected the 'agrarian' societies, these theorists broke the single thread of history which had stretched from the Roman *ergasterions* and mediaeval trade alliances to the industrial world. If one follows through the idea of the post-industrial society as a society based on the supremacy of the tertiary sector, not forgetting that the supremacy of the primary sector is identified with the pre-industrial society, one can make the totally firm deduction that the industrial era, say in France or, more manifestly, in Germany, continued for not more than 60 or 70 years from the 1880s to the end of the Second World War. If, moreover, the post-industrialists believe the post-industrial era to be as prolonged, is it worth trying so hard to interpret a historical period, half of which has already passed in the theoretical discussions of the last decades? If post-industrial society is regarded as the global perspective of humanity, is it right to portray both of the main historical dramas played out in the last two centuries alone? It is the incoherent theoretical character of post-industrial doctrine that is in discord with the analysis of contemporary reality undertaken by its authors and makes one doubt the actual worth of such a relatively superficial view.

So with the situation as it stands today it is not only possible but also vital to synthesize the Marxist methodology of historical development with many of the important elements of the post-industrial conception. It is necessary to abandon the paranoid idea of class enmity and to consider the development of *oekonomische Gesellschaftsformation* not as a mechanical sum of the four *Produktionsweisen* but as a gigantic epoch, united by the process of the development of market relations and the ripening of industrial civilization. It is necessary from materialistic positions to view the overcoming of industrialism as a departure from the confines of those flaws and shortcomings characteristic also of the eras of social production, which gave birth to and coaxed into life the industrial system. It is necessary finally to interpret the laws of the development of modern society as essentially post-economic, a society based not only on high technology, unknown in the 19th century, but also on non-market relations, on the absence of exploitation, on the transition from labour to creative activity – on phenomena unknown throughout the whole history of mankind. All of these tasks, however, are too broad in scale to be considered and resolved in this book. But even if the book is successful in raising the vital and burning issues in such a way as to prompt a fresh theoretical reaction, we will consider our work completed.

Notes

1   K. Marx and F. Engels, *Collected Works*, Moscow, Vol. 29, p.263.
2   K. Marx, *Capital*, Vol. I, Moscow, 1986, p.173.
3   Ibid., Vol. I, p.173.
4   F. Engels, *Dialectics of Nature*, Moscow, p.176.
5   Ibid., p.174.
6   K. Marx and F. Engels, *Collected Works*, Vol. 26, p.273.
7   See K. Marx, *Capital*, Vol. I, p.332.
8   Ibid., Vol. III, p.177.
9   K. Marx and F. Engels, *Collected Works*, Vol. 20, p.245.
10 Ibid., Vol. 25, p.180.
11 Ibid., Vol. 25, pp.168–9.
12 Ibid., Vol. 26, p.66.
13 Ibid., Vol. 24, pp.310–11.
14 Ibid., Vol. 24, pp.308–9.
15 See V. Inozemtsev, *Contribution à la théorie de la formation post-économique de la société*, Paris, 1996, pp.159–92.
16 See K. Marx, *The Eighteenth Brumaire of Louis Bonaparte*, Moscow, 1983, p.13.
17 K. Marx and F. Engels, *Collected Works*, Vol. 29, pp.263, 264. In the original: 'In grossen Umrissen koennen asiatische, antike, feudale und modern buergerliche Produktionsweisen als progressive Epochen der oekonomischen Gesellschaftsformation bezeichnet werden … mit dieser Gesellschaftsformation schliesst daher die Vorgeschichte der menschlichen Gesellschaft ab' (Marx and Engels, *Werke*, Bd. 13, S.9).
18 K. Marx, *Theories of Surplus-Value*, Part I, Moscow, 1969, p.409.
19 K. Marx and F. Engels, *Collected Works*, Vol. 24, p.352.
20 Ibid., Vol. 24, p.367. In the original: 'Comme dernière phase de la formation primitive de la société, la commune agricole est en même temps phase de transition à la formation secondaire, donc transition de la société, fondée sur la propriété commune, à la société, fondée sur la propriété privée. La formation secondaire, bien entendu, embrasse le série des sociétés reposant sur l'esclavage et le servage' (Marx and Engels, *Gesamtausgabe*, Abt. 1, Bd. 25, S.238).
21 K. Marx and F. Engels, *Collected Works*, Vol. 24, p.363.
22 Ibid., Vol. 24, p.362. In the original: 'en remplaçant la … propriété capitaliste par une forme supérieure du type archaïque de la propriété, c.a.d. la propriété communiste' (Marx and Engels, *Gesamtausgabe*, Abt. 1, Bd. 25, S.232).
23 K. Marx and F. Engels, *Collected Works*, Vol. 29, pp.263–4.
24 Ibid., Vol. 33, p.42.
25 Ibid., Vol. 30, p.252.
26 K. Marx, *Capital*, Vol. III, p.776. In the original: 'Vom Standpunkt einer hoehern oekonomischen Gesellschaftsformation wird das Privateigentum einzelner Individuen am Erdball ganz so abgeschmackt erscheinen wie das Privateigentum eines Menschen an einem andern Menschen' (Marx and Engels, *Werke*, Bd. 25, S.784).
27. K. Marx, *Capital*, Vol. III, p.820.

28   Ibid., Vol. I, p.21. In the original: 'mein Standpunkt ... auffasst ... die Entwicklung der oekonomischen Gesellschaftsformation als einen naturgeschichtlichen Prozess' (Marx and Engels, *Gesamtausgabe*, Abt. 2, Bd. 5, S.14).
29   K. Marx and F. Engels, *Collected Works*, Vol. 30, p.252.
30   K. Marx, *Theories of Surplus-Value*, Part I, p.409.
31   K. Marx and F. Engels, *Collected Works*, Vol. 3, pp.165–6.
32   Ibid., Vol. 3, p.168.
33   Ibid., Vol. 4, pp.257, 262.
34   Ibid., Vol. 4, p.262.
35   Ibid., Vol. 5, p.83. In the original: 'ein frueheres Interesse, dessen eigentuemliche Verkehrsform schon durch die einem spaeteren angehoerige verdraengt ist, noch lange im Besitz einer traditionellen Macht, in der den Individuen gegenueber verselbstaendigten scheinbaren Gemeinschaft (Staat, Recht) bleibt, einer Macht, die in letzter Instanz nur durch eine Revolution zu brechen ist' (Marx and Engels, *Werke*, Bd. 3, S.72–73).
36   K. Marx and F. Engels, *Collected Works*, Vol. 6, p.175. In the original: 'Changement survenu dans les forces productives des hommes amène nécessairement un changement dans leurs rapports de production' (K. Marx, *Misère de la philosophie*, Paris, 1961, p.131).
37   K. Marx and F. Engels, *Collected Works*, Vol. 6, p.489.
38   K. Marx, *Capital*, Vol. III, p.250.
39   K. Marx and F. Engels, *Collected Works*, Vol. 5, p.74.
40   Ibid., Vol. 26, p.230.
41   Ibid., Vol. 29, p.263.
42   Ibid., Vol. 29, p.263.
43   Ibid., Vol. 24, p.352.
44   K. Marx and F. Engels, *Selected Correspondence*, Moscow, 1975, p.331.
45   J.V. Stalin, *Works*, Vol. 13, p.239 (in Russian).
46   Ibid., Vol. 13, p.239 (in Russian).
47   *A Short History of the All-Union Communist Party (Bolsheviks)*, Moscow, 1938, p.119 (in Russian).
48   J.V. Stalin, *On Dialectical and Historical Materialism*, Moscow, 1954, p.25 (in Russian).
49   J.V. Stalin, *Marxism and Problems of Linguistics*, Moscow, 1950, p.21 (in Russian).
50.   Ibid., p.17.
51   See: C.H. de. Saint-Simon, *Cathéchisme des industriels*, Paris, 1832, pp.24–36; *La Sociologie par Auguste Comte. Résumé par Emile Rigolage*, Paris, 1897, p.399; J.S. Mill, 'Chapters on Socialism', *On Liberty and Other Writings*, Cambridge, 1995, pp.228–34.
52   See Adam Smith, *Lectures on Justice, Police, Revenue and Arms*, Oxford, 1896, pp.23–37; J.-A. de Condorcet, *Esquisse d'un tableau historique des progrès de l'esprit humain*, Paris, 1969, chs 1–5; J.G. Herder, *Ideen zur der Philosophie der Geschichte der Menschheit*, Berlin, 1972, IV, i–iii; VIII, iv; IX, i–iv.
53   See F. List, *Das nationale System der politischen Oekonomie*, Berlin, 1982, S.13.
54   See K. Bucher, *Die Entstehung der Volkswirtschaft*, Tübingen, 1911, S. 39–150.
55   See B. Hildebrand, *Die Nationaloekonomie der Gegenwart und Zukunft*, Frankfurt am Main, 1848.
56   See W. Sombart, *Der moderne Kapitalismus*, Munich and Leipzig, 1924, S.23, 40, 91, 180, 319.
57   See, for example, A. Dopsch, *Naturalwirtschaft und Geldwirtschaft in der Weltgeschichte*, Vienna, 1930, S.1–23.
58   See T. Veblen, *The Theory of Business Enterprise*, New York, 1904, pp.302–400; *The Absentee Ownership and Business Enterprise in Recent Times*, New York, 1923, pp.69–118, 205–50.

59 See C. Clark, *The Economics of 1960*, London, 1944.
60 See J. Fourastié, *Le grand espoir du XXe siècle*, Paris, 1949.
61 Ibid., pp.42, 80–83, 319.
62 See R. Aron, *28 Lectures on Industrial Society*, London, 1968, p.42.
63 See D. Riesman, 'Leisure and Work in Post-Industrial Society', in E. Larrabee and R. Meyersohn (eds), *Mass Leisure*, Glencoe, Ill., 1958, pp.363–85.
64 See W.W. Rostow, *The Stages of Economic Growth. A Non-Communist Manifesto*, Cambridge, 1960; *Politics and the Stages of Growth*, Cambridge, 1971.
65 See W.W. Rostow, *Politics and the Stages of Growth*, p.230.
66 F. Braudel, *A History of Civilisations*, London, 1995, p.374.
67 See A. Soboul, 'La reprise économique et la stabilisation sociale, 1797–1815' in F. Braudel and E. Labrousse (eds), *Histoire économique et sociale de la France*, Vol. III, Paris, 1993, pp.105–12.
68 See, for example, J. Rule, *The Vital Century. England's Developing Economy, 1714–1815*, London, New York, 1992, pp.93–134.
69 See F.F. Mendels, 'Proto-Industrialisation: The First Phase of the Industrialisation Process', *Journal of Economic History*, 1972, **32**, pp.241–61.
70 See S.C. Ogilvie and M. Cerman, 'The Theories of Proto-Industrialisation', in: S.C. Ogilvie and M. Cerman (eds), *European Proto-Industrialisation*, Cambridge, 1996, pp.1–11.
71 D. Bell, *The Cultural Contradictions of Capitalism*, New York, 1996, p.147.
72 A. Toffler, *The Third Wave*, New York, 1990, pp.25, 26.
73 D. Bell, *Cultural Contradictions*, p.198, note.
74 See: R. Aron, *The Industrial Society. Three Lectures on Ideology and Development*, New York, Washington, 1967, p. 97.
75 See D. Bell, 'The Third Technological Revolution and Its Possible Socio-Economic Consequences', *Dissent*, Spring 1989, XXXVI (2), p.167.
76 D. Bell, 'Notes on the Post-Industrial Society', *The Public Interest*, 1967, 7, p.102.
77 See A. Toffler, *The Third Wave*, p.17.
78 See D. Bell, 'Notes on the Post-Industrial Society', *The Public Interest*, 1967, 6, p.28.
79 See Y. Masuda, *The Information Society as Post-Industrial Society*, Washington, 1983, p.45.
80 See J. Clark, *Post-Industrial America: A Geographical Perspective*, New York, London, 1985, p.27.
81 See J. Naisbitt, *Megatrends. The New Directions, Transforming Our Lives*, New York, 1984, p.5.
82 See D. Bell, 'The Third Technological Revolution' …, p.168.
83 See P. Sadler, *Managerial Leadership in Post-Industrial Society*, Aldershot, 1988.
84 See T. Stonier, *The Wealth of Information. A Profile of the Post-Industrial Economy*, London, 1983.
85 See H. Kahn, W. Brown and L. Martell, *The Next 200 Years. A Scenario for America and the World*, New York, 1971, p.22.
86 See J.-J. Servan-Schreiber, *Le défi mondial*, Paris, 1980, p.374.
87 See D. Bell, *Cultural Contradictions*, p.198, note.
88 See M.Young, *The Rise of Meritocracy 1870–2033*, London, 1958.
89 See A. Toffler, *The Third Wave*, p.75.
90 See E. Wohlers and W. Weinert, *Employment Trends in the United States, Japan and European Community*, Oxford, 1988, p.69.
91 See J. Clark, *Post-Industrial America: a Geographical Perspective*, p.220; *Statistical Abstract of the United States 1995*, Washington, 1995, p.416.
92 See E.M. Rojers, *Communication Technology: The New Media in Society*, New York, 1986, p.112.
93 Z. Brzezinski, *Between Two Ages*, New York, 1970, p. 9.

94 See J. Naisbitt, *Megatrends*, pp.7–9.
95 See Z. Brzezinski, *Between Two Ages*, pp.9–10.
96 D. Bell, *The Coming of Post-Industrial Society. A Venture in Social Forecasting*, New York, 1976, p.163.
97 D. Bell, *The World and the United States in 2013*, New York, 1987, p.8.
98 See W. Dizard, *The Coming of the Information Age. An Overview of Technology, Economics and Politics*, New York, 1982, p.305.
99 D. Bell, *The Social Framework of the Information Society*, Oxford, 1980, p.130.
100 See D. Bell, *The Social Framework of the Information Society*, Oxford, 1980, p.130.
101 See A. Toffler, *Previews and Premises: An Interview with the Author of 'Future Shock' and 'The Third Wave'*, New York, 1983, p.34.
102 See D. Bell, *Sociological Journeys. Essays 1960–1980*, London, 1980, pp.56–7.
103 See H. Kahn and A. Wiener, *The Year 2000. A Framework for Speculation on the Next 33 Years*, London, 1967, pp. 25, 186.
104 See D. Bell, *Cultural Contradictions*, p.198, note.
105 See E. Fromm, *The Sane Society*, London, 1991, p.124.
106 See A. Etzioni, *A Responsive Society: Collected Essays on Building Deliberate Social Change*, San Francisco, 1991, p.177.
107 See R. Dahrendorf, *The New Liberty: Survival and Justice in a Changing World*, London, 1975, p.74.
108 T. Stonier, *Wealth of Information*, p.23.
109 See T. Sakaiya, *The Knowledge-Value Revolution or A History of the Future*, Tokyo, New York, 1991, pp.267–71.
110 See I.L. Horowitz, *Communicating Ideas: The Crisis of Publishing in a Post-Industrial Society*, New York, 1986, p.141.
111 See P.F. Drucker, 'The Educational Revolution', in E. Etzioni-Halevy and A. Etzioni (eds), *Social Change: Sources, Patterns and Consequences*, New York, 1973, p.236.
112 See A. Toffler, *Previews and Premises*, p.35.
113 D. Bell, *The Coming of Post-Industrial Society*, p.344.
114 See A. Toffler, *The Third Wave*, p.75.
115 See H. Glaser, *Das Verschwinden der Arbeit. Die Chancen der neuen Taetigkeitsgesellschaft*, Düsseldorf, 1988, S.176; S. Bailin, *Achieving Extraordinary Ends. An Essay on Creativity*, Dordrecht, 1988, pp.3–7.
116 See J. Rifkin, *The End of Work*, p.233.
117 J. Hage and C.H. Powers, *Post-Industrial Lives: Roles and Relationships in the 21st Century*, Newbury Park, Cal., 1992, p.72.
118 See A. Toffler, *Powershift: Knowledge, Wealth and Violence at the Edge of the 21st Century*, New York, 1990, p.199.
119 D. Bell, *The Coming of Post-Industrial Society*, p.288.
120 D. Bell, 'Notes on the Post-Industrial Society', *The Public Interest*, 1967, 6, p.30.
121 Ibid.
122 See B.S. Kleinberg, *American Society in the Postindustrial Age: Technocracy, Power and the End of Ideology*, Columbus, Oh., 1973, pp.51–2.
123 See A. Toffler, *Powershift*, p.12.
124 See A. Touraine, *The Post-Industrial Society. Tomorrow's Social History: Classes, Conflicts and Culture in the Programmed Society*, London, 1974, p.70.
125 Ibid., p.65.
126 See K.W. Wedderburn *et al.*, *Labour Law in the Post-Industrial Era*, Aldershot, 1994, p.89.
127 A. Touraine, *The Post-Industrial Society*, p.61.
128 See W. Clement and J. Myles, *Relations of Ruling: Class and Gender in Postindustrial Societies*, Montreal, 1994, p.33.
129 See F.F. Piven, *Labour Parties in Postindustrial Societies*, Oxford, 1991, p.6.

130 A. Kessler-Harris and B. Silverman, 'Beyond Industrial Unionism', in B. Silverman, R. Vogt and M. Yanovitch (eds), *Double Shift: Transforming Work in Postsocialist and Postindustrial Societies: a US–Post-Soviet Dialogue*, Armonk, 1993, p.261.
131 See S. Bailin, *Achieving Extraordinary Ends*, p.6.
132 D. Bell, *The Coming of Post-Industrial Society*, p.283.
133 See Y. Masuda, *The Information Society*, p.33.
134 See A. Toffler, *The Eco-Spasm*, Toronto, 1975, pp.3–7.
135 See Z. Brzezinski, *Out of Control: Global Turmoil on the Eve of the 21st Century*, New York, 1993, pp.58–60.
136 See ibid., p.52.
137 J. Rifkin, *The End of Work*, p.208.
138 Ibid., p.197.
139 See Z. Brzezinski, *Out of Control*, p.66.
140 See H. Kahn, W. Brown and L. Martell, *The Next 200 Years*, p.54.
141 D. Bell, *The Coming of Post-Industrial Society*, p.14.

PART II
POST-ECONOMIC SOCIETY

Introduction to Part II

Treatment of the society that has formed in the developed countries of the West during the last few decades as post-economic requires, before passing to the analysis of modern economic, social and political processes, a few preliminary comments on the aims of this part of the book.

The first set of problems is related to the definition of post-economic society. The concept, the application of which is capable of substantially facilitating the deeper understanding both of the main features and character of modern society and of the global transformation that society is living through is hardly used by Western sociologists, economists and philosophers. Therefore we will begin with an analysis of those objective and subjective factors which for the last few decades have obscured the broader understanding of the changes in progress today as post-economic transformation. Then we will assess the present-day state of the terminology applicable to the studies and methodology, and mark out the key positions which can be used to distinguish post-economic society as the third of the main historical phases of social evolution. The most important task at this stage of research is to define the relation or complex of relations which incorporate in a certain form the main characteristics of the post-economic condition or state. By defining them, we obtain a 'theoretical fulcrum' which enables us to lay the foundations, in a way that befits our task, of the theory both of modern and of future society.

The second set of problems is concerned with the assessment of the main changes taking place in the economic basis of modern society, in its economic and social relations and its political system. These problems also include the important question of how the system of motivation of modern activity changes, what new phenomena occur in the sociopsychological rather than the social sphere, and how not only society as a whole but also the individuals who make up society alter. Such an analysis enables us to assess how and to what degree all of these transformations affect the formation of the new system of ties and relations which cement the coming state of civilization. This analysis reveals the element of succession present in the development of human society and it demonstrates the dependence of the future historical state on the nature and tendencies of contemporary social processes.

Finally, the third set of problems, one of the most interesting and complex sets, is related to the consideration of the reverse effect of the social system of the future forming in the depths of contemporary civilization on the various aspects of social life, and their modification. This effect is especially important with respect to the laws of commodity production as a whole and the value nature of exchange in particular; the forms and methods of the contemporary organization of production in the industrial and information sectors of the economy; the principles of private ownership and its role in the social structure; the phenomenon of the exploitation of man by man, which some researchers used to consider to be just about the main characteristic of modern society; and also with respect to a whole number of other, minor social relations and laws.

This study's significance lies mainly in that, by determining the main characteristic of the global transformation of humanity, we gain the opportunity to view the modern social revolution not as one bringing certain new features to modern society but as one mediating the transition from one global and complete social order to another; and to view these historical conditions themselves as complex systems, organized around a single base principle and developing according to single laws. We think it is this that is most lacking both in Marxist social theory and in the sociological conceptions created by Western researchers during the past few decades. Therefore, despite the fact that the given doctrines have received the highest praise in this book as examples of coherent historical constructs, we must still and frequently subject selected aspects of those conceptions to criticism and disagree with the opinions of some authors.

4 The Meaning of Post-economic Society

The development of the theories of history discussed in the first part of the book testify to the considerable advantages of the doctrines that distinguished in the evolution of humanity three qualitatively different epochs. However, since most such existing conceptions interpret the contemporary period as the embodiment of one of the most significant transformations ever experienced by humanity, questions about what this transition represents, what features of society have been left in the past and what features arising before our very eyes become the main ones, and whether, as a result of the changes today, a new society is emerging or whether we are presented with a modification – albeit a serious one – of the former social and economic relations become exclusively relevant.

In today's conditions it is more important than ever to try and build a conception of the social order under formation, but in doing so to avoid two extremes. On the one hand, we must not try too unswervingly to think up some kind of determining characteristic of future society, because the state of emergence in which society currently finds itself rules out the possibility of defining those relations and laws which will occupy the central position when the formation of the future social structure nears completion. On the other hand, we must be wary of empirical research, of giving priority consideration to those phenomena and processes which are today most prominent but which, firstly, may turn out to be far from decisive for the future appearance of society and, secondly, may create the illusion of historical succession, diminishing to a considerable extent the significance of the unfolding social change.

The scale of the tasks before today's social sciences affects the state that has arisen in industrial and post-industrial sociology. In all countries of the world for the last few decades researchers in their quest for an answer to the question about the directions and patterns of social change have been looking intently into the mechanism of the development of their own society. However, the debate that began back in the 1960s is far from completion; on the contrary, it has given

125

rise to conceptions, the authors of which are less united today than at any time in the past.

The Current State of Theory

We will begin by surveying the views that had formed by the middle of the 1990s of the character and scale of the changes in progress and of the nature and main features of the society under formation. Most worthy of our attention is the assessment of different approaches to the definition of the new social order and to the interpretation of the importance of the transition from the current state of humanity to the civilization of the 21st century.

There are two distinct approaches in terms of the terminology used for the assessment of the new society. One of them dwells on the openness of modern society to the future, on the unfolding process of the active surmounting of many of the features of previous forms of the social order. The advocates of this approach prefer, proceeding from the characteristics of today's society, to speak of the future as of its negation. In this case definitions of the new society are built according to the feature of the old society which is viewed by an author as the main one; however, a constant feature of the emerging concept becomes the very widespread prefix 'post'.

The given approach may be regarded as a relatively new one from the terminological, rather than the essential, point of view. If we turn, for example, to the social theory of Marxism, created more than a century ago, we see that the main features of the future communist condition were not defined by that theory in a positive aspect. Far more attention has been paid to the characteristic of the new order as one in which the antagonistic classes have been eliminated, the exploitation of some social groups by others has been removed, the spontaneity of the capitalist economy has been surmounted and man has departed from the confines of purely material production. But the real characteristics of communist society remain hidden from the followers of Marx. It must be said in this connection that during the past century a huge number of processes and features have been uncovered that were surmountable in the course of the new social revolution experienced by humanity, but the theoretical image of the new society as represented by researchers has not as a result become much more structured.

In the Western tradition these definitions were first formalized in the works of Penty on post-industrial society, published back at the beginning of the 20th century.[1] Used for the first time after the Second World War by Riesman,[2] the concept then became the basis of a theory that won wide recognition[3] and became generally accepted. The latter circumstance inevitably resulted in the term coming to be used also within conceptions which differed greatly from the original, well-known position of Bell. For example, post-industrial capitalism is today spoken of as 'a stage of capitalism and not as a decisive step beyond capitalism',[4] as post-industrial socialism;[5] and as ecological post-industrialism[6] and conventional post-industrialism.[7]

All of these definitions[8] are grounded on an understanding of the elements of post-industrial society, defined by Daniel Bell, who noted that this society is characterized by transition from primarily material production to the production mainly of services and information,[9] the proliferation of knowledge and its confirmation as a key production resource,[10] the reduction of the role of market principles in regulating economies, the development of the non-profit sector and the formation of non-market welfare economics;[11] and by marked changes in social structure, namely the annihilation of the working class in the traditional sense, the heightened role of state regulation of the economy and the emergence as a main wielder of power of the technical and intellectual elite, known as the meritocracy.[12] As a result there arise qualitatively new types of resources, new production processes, a new social structure and new principles of interrelation between individuals.[13]

But the theory of post-industrial society, having become the first of the complex conceptions the authors of which prefer to describe new society as the embodiment of the negation of a number of features of the preceding one, proved not to be the first in the series. In the 1980s it was subjected to fairly radical criticism by the advocates of the theory of postmodernity, the principles of which are today beginning to prevail in research into the future society.[14] The theory of postmodernity is based on a whole series of concepts which reflect the movement of today's society beyond the realms not only of the traditional (that is, pre-industrial) but also the modern (industrial) principles. They include overcoming mass-production and con-sumption and replacing this with, on the one hand, individualized production and, on the other, a consumption which is a continuation of the production process; transition from adherence to market principles to the prevalence of post-material values and the active use of social regulation; departure from former modes of organizing labour and the maximum use of the creative potential of workers; and also a whole host of particularly sociological phenomena, including the formation of a new type of family and new forms of social partnership, the heightened role of knowledge, changes in the system of education, and national, ethnic and other problems.

The theory of postmodernity, within which it is possible to assess not only technological and economic progress but also the sociocultural and sociopsychological realignments, is somewhat more complex than the doctrine of post-industrialism. It gives rise to a situation characteristic of the social science theories which developed up to the middle of the 19th century: economic conceptions, if we take their basic elements, are finding themselves included organically in the system of social sciences and becoming inseparable from it to the same degree as modern society itself is inseparable from the real forms of social life. Besides the theory of postmodernity, ideas that modern society can be described as post-bourgeois,[15] post-capitalist,[16] post-business,[17] post-market,[18] post-traditional[19] and even post-civilized and post-historic[20] were born in the 1960s and 1970s and are developing today.

The other approach to the definition of the new social order is linked with attempts to define the society under formation from the point of view of uncovering certain fundamental characteristics. The first and most successful of these attempts was linked with the introduction at the beginning of the 1960s, almost simultaneously in the United States and Japan, by Machlup and Umesao[21] of the term 'information society', which gave birth to the theory of information society, developed by such famous authors as Porat, Masuda, Stonier, Katz and others.[22] According to this position, 'through all of human history from its earliest beginnings until now, there have been only three basic stages of economic life: hunting-and-gathering societies; agricultural societies; and industrial societies. Now, looming over the horizon, is something entirely new, the fourth stage of social organisation: information societies'.[23] Putting information and knowledge in a central position in the definition of the future state of society fully complies with the main trends of Western philosophical tradition, starting with Condorcet and Saint-Simon,[24] and continued by other 19th-century thinkers;[25] nor can one fail to agree with the opinion of Kumar that 'the concept of information society fits in well with the liberal, progressivist tradition in western thought; it maintains the Enlightenment faith in rationality and progress ... this view, despite its pronouncement of a radical shift in social arrangements, continues the line of thought inaugurated by the positivists'.[26]

Among the doctrines that described the new society with the help of the 'positive' term, the theory of information society plays the same central role as the theories of post-industrialism and postmodernity play among conceptions that define society through the 'negative' term. But of relevance here too are other conceptions, which when defining modern society draw attention to its other features. Closest of all to the theory of information society is the conception of the technetronic society by Zbigniew Brzezinski[27] and the doctrines which underscored the role of knowledge and described modern society as 'the knowledgeable society',[28] the 'knowledge society'[29] and the 'knowledge-value society'.[30]

A number of researchers point to new principles in the social and economic organization of society, creating the theory of 'organized society'[31] and 'conventional society'.[32] This tendency gained its fullest expression in the theory of Alain Touraine of a programmed society (la société programmée).[33] Some researchers are inclined to use terms which do not characterize today's state of society with as much definition, a tendency that has become widespread in recent years. The best known attempts of this nature are associated with the introduction of the concepts 'active society'[34] and 'good society'.[35] The list of terms used to describe the contemporary state of the development of society could go on. But the aforementioned are enough for us to realize that all of the definitions on offer are incomplete. This was acknowledged most clearly in 1980 by Alvin Toffler, who wrote that not only all previous definitions of the future society but also his own term, 'the super-industrial society' were inadequate.[36] This inadequacy can be linked to two circumstances.

On the one hand, some of the authors who offered one definition or the other designed to focus attention on certain technological, economic and social processes artificially make absolute only one of the aspects of social life; these authors to a certain degree abstract themselves from other aspects. This gives rise, for example, to contradiction in the interpretation of the modern society as simultaneously a post-industrial and an information society. Most of the post-industrial theorists share the understanding of society as the information society, and vice versa. But the development of the service sector, which is considered one of the characteristics of post-industrial society, is not at all identical to the expansion of information and knowledge; and information and technological progress has, for its part, become manifest in the last decades in the industrial sector no less visibly than in the tertiary sector. This yet again underlines the fact that each of the definitions which draws the attention of the researcher to one particular feature of society distracts him from the study of other and quite possibly no less important ones.

On the other hand, all of the definitions offered, even the most general ones, remain relatively superficial. Nobody to date has succeeded in defining the new social stage as a social whole, presented as a single global characteristic or the emergence of some principal relation; nor has anybody explained how all the other obviously important processes and phenomena were conditioned by such a fundamental transformation. In other words, the conceptions designed to explain and describe the new society cannot identify a central element or relation within that society as a means of explaining all other changes. For now society is being described on different levels of abstraction simultaneously, and the main elements of changes are being considered in parallel, with no interdependence.

Bell distinguished four main areas of pre-industrial, industrial and post-industrial society: resources, mode, technology and design.[37] Toffler distinguished five analysing the First, Second and Third Waves in history: energy base, resources, work, the info-sphere and political system.[38] In both cases the processes in action at completely different levels of the economic and social structure are treated as relatively uniform; moreover, their interdependence is traced in an unacceptably formal way or is not analysed at all. As a result, the picture of the future society appears like a mosaic, and the main principles of its organization appear to be indefinite.

Therefore we assume that the conception of the new society must satisfy two fundamental requirements: first, it must entail the definition of fundamental social change which, being prepared by progress in all spheres of social life, would be capable of affecting all of its manifestations, bringing far more substantial changes and shifts; second, the new conception must be presented in the form of a finished analytical construct which explains the course of social change proceeding from the internal logic of the development of that main contradiction and that main process which serve as the main factor of social progress.

It is worth once again stressing a factor that we have already mentioned. We are today able only to uncover the place of the unknown fundamental relation of the future society in the structure of social relations which will be occupied by it, and not to define it sufficiently accurately. Therefore it is premature at the current stage of the development of the theory to attempt to formulate a 'positive' definition of the new social state. When speaking of post-economic society, we acknowledge the use of the prefix 'post' as the most appropriate one, but we strive to depart from both the robotic nature of the concept 'post-industrialism' and from the too universal term 'postmodernity'.

Moving on, to the significance of the transition to the civilization of the 21st century, we must concentrate on the general methodological approach to modern social changes and decide whether it is worth treating their consequences as the emergence of a new type of society or as a substantial modification of the previous one. Current social transformations are perceived as the emergence of the new type of society by the authors of the conceptions of post-industrialism in its most diverse forms,[39] of postmodernism,[40] the theory of flexible specialization,[41] and the doctrine of the informational mode of development.[42] The advocates of the assessment of modern changes as a certain modification of the preceding form of society include neo-

Marxists,[43] the advocates of regulation theory,[44] the public-sphere theorists,[45] and representatives of some other areas.[46]

However, there is absolutely no unity among those who view modern changes as the emergence of a new society. For example Bell, the most consistent advocate of the theory of post-industrial society, notes that this society 'does not "displace" an industrial society, or even an agrarian society… A post-industrial society adds a new dimension, particularly in the management of data and information as necessary facilities in a complex society',[47] that 'post-industrial developments do not replace previous social forms as "stages" of social development. They often coexist, as a palimpsest, on top of the others, thickening the complexity of society and the nature of social structure'.[48] He writes:

> The concept of a post-industrial society is not a picture of complete social order. It is a paradigm or social framework that identifies new axes of social organisation and new axes of social stratification in advanced Western society. Social structures do not change overnight, and it may often take a century for a complete revolution to take place … As a social system, post-industrial society does not 'succeed' capitalism or socialism, but … cuts across both. It is a specification of new dimensions in the social structure.[49]

Bell holds to the view about the degree of succession in social evolution and the evolutionary character of social modernization to this day.[50]

Toffler, though, is far more radical. His discourse on the Third Wave was born partly of the desire to erase from the reader's mind any doubts about the scale and importance of the transformation in progress. As we noted above, the sociologist considers unacceptable and as not very productive all previous terms used to describe the new society, and the desire to render the conception safe from the voluntary or involuntary disparagement of the innovation that characterizes modern society is not the latest factor to determine such a position. Toffler believes:

> this Third Wave of historical change represents not a straight-line extension of an industrial society but a radical shift of direction, often of negation, of what went before. It adds up as nothing else than a global transformation at least as revolutionary in our day as industrial revolution was three hundred years ago;[51] 'we are creating a new society… . Not a changed society. Not an extended, larger-than-life version of our present society. But a new society.'[52]

Both of the aforementioned points of view are fully grounded and do not contradict each other as much as they would appear to at first sight. We think that Bell, in his approach, grasps perfectly that the fundamental principles which define the emergence and development of post-industrial society cannot arise from anywhere but the depths of industrial civilization; these principles must run through all stages of social evolution, guaranteeing the historical succession of social progress. But Toffler's position is more refined in the sense that it underlines the importance of modern changes which, we believe, are those that make it possible to speak, not of a new quality of society, but of a new society coming to replace its previous form. Assessing this area of the modern debate, we would like to back Toffler's position, and within our hypothesis of the post-economic state stress the qualitative difference possessed by the society that is emerging, as it is this methodological technique that enables us to depict adequately the historical changes taking place today before our very eyes.

By dwelling on the positions of the modification of the previous social structure, the researcher is deprived of the opportunity not only to analyse that basic relation around which the new society should be built, but even to study its possible place among other social ties, since in this case he must assume that the main relation for the new social order is one of the relations that characterize contemporary society, and that the main problem of research consists merely of identifying the areas of its modernization. This approach contradicts the understanding of the modern epoch as the epoch of social revolution and treats the formation of the third main stage of social progress as an indefinite period in the future.

To illustrate further our position with regard to the main characteristics of the post-economic condition, and even to run ahead a little, we shall note that the importance of the modern transformation is defined by not entirely obvious deep-rooted changes in the fundamental bases of the social organism to a much greater extent than by the more obvious but still superficial modifications in the character of the resources to be used by humanity, by the changes in the technology of production processes or by the improvement of the political system.

The Post-economic Condition as Idea and Reality

By discussing the departure of civilization beyond the economic epoch we are attempting a terminological definition and a theoretical grasp of the most global change that humanity has ever experienced. Therefore the distinct formulation of the basic concepts assumes a special importance. The task is complicated further by the fact that not one of the modern sociological doctrines contains a terminological system capable of coherently setting down the principles and features of post-economic transformation.

The idea of distinguishing the economic epoch as a key stage of social progress belongs to Marx. Marx introduced the concept of 'social formation' (*Gesellschaftsformation*) in 1851,[53] and, seven years later, wrote that all class societies, namely the Asiatic, ancient, feudal and modern bourgeois modes of production, may be designated as 'epochs marking progress in the economic development of society (*oekonomische Gesellschaftsformation*)'; moreover, 'the prehistory of human society ... closes with this social formation'.[54] Subsequently the theory of a single economic social formation did not gain the sort of development in Marxist sociology that it should have and this methodological approach was virtually consigned to oblivion.

In Western sociological science, and particularly in the conceptions of post-industrial society, the term 'post-economic society' has been encountered only a few times, and then only in the period when the tendency was in its stage of emergence. In one of his speeches for the Hudson Institute at the end of the 1960s, Kahn spoke of the coming state as the negation of the economic principles of the preceding society.[55] Later he and Bell, analysing the corresponding position, used this concept, but its application remained highly episodic.[56]

But these authors on a far more radical scale indicated that any form of human community was based on economic laws, and these could not be eliminated. To quote Bell, the

> ineluctable fact about any society ... is that there is no escape from 'economics'. Men constantly redefine needs so that former wants become necessities. The constraints of resources are tangible, and while the amounts needed may not become physically exhausted, the costs of using these rise, and relative costs, not physical quantities, become the measures of scarcity.[57]

This approach to the idea of post-economic transformation may be explained by two circumstances. On the one hand, the fathers of post-industrialism created their conception primarily with the purpose of explaining the concrete changes taking place in their own society. The fact that the works of the 1960s and 1970s drew attention to the service sector and the change in the nature of production resources and technological processes demonstrates first of all the empirical character of the approach being formed. And it was in this period that the main terminological postulates of the theory were formulated, those which to a large extent are defining the face of today's conception, 30 years later. Therefore the lack of due attention to post-economic problematics is fully understandable.

On the other hand, the term 'post-economic' in English has a very different connotation from that, for example, in German, in which most of the works of Marx were written. If in the latter there exist two complementary concepts – *Oekonomie* and *Wirtschaft* – which generally correspond to the Russian *ekonomika* and *khozyaistvo*, in English we only encounter the term 'economy'. This gives the term total supremacy, and any doubts about the eternal nature and unchangeability of this foundation of the social system evoke the sort of stark misunderstanding we would encounter by expounding the idea of *Verschwinden der Wirtschaft* in a German auditorium.

However, despite all of these difficulties, we consider the formation of a new terminological system of research into modern processes to be not only desirable but also essential. The character of the changes taking place in the world simply demands such an approach, without which the emergence of the methodological foundations of coherent theory is impossible.

But before proposing the concept of post-economic society, we ought first to define the limits of the concept 'economy'. Taking into account both the deep-rooted traditions of *Wirtschaftstheorie* in Germany and the importance that German researchers have given to the comprehension of the methodological problems of *politischen Oekonomie*, we will take the liberty of applying German terminology – at least while we examine the purely methodological issues. As we have mentioned, the broadest concept to describe the system of social production is *Wirtschaft*. The term *Oekonomie* is usually applied to denote the stage in the development of *Wirtschaft* when *wirtschaftliche Verhaeltnisse* are not reduced to relations of direct production, but exist as a whole entity, supplemented by the relations of exchange, money economy and other attributes of modern society. But even in this case German terminology can differentiate the social production system as an aggregate of economic relations, and the national economy as an integral organism, from the rest of the world, as *Volkswirtschaft* and *Nationaloekonomie*. Moreover, it must be pointed out that the term *Wirtschaft* as a more general term undoubtedly incorporates the concept *Oekonomie* and enables 'oekonomische' relations to be regarded as 'wirtschaftliche', but not the other way round.

In this connection two small remarks that illustrate the relation to the given approach in different countries are relevant. Firstly, within German terminology, it is quite natural to describe the money economy as *Geldwirtschaft*, but absolutely unacceptable to describe the primitive stages of economic development as *Naturaloekonomie*. But Dopsch's book, *Naturalwirtschaft und Geldwirtschaft in der Weltgeschichte*,[58] gained in its French translation a title perfectly acceptable to the French researcher, but unacceptable to the German methodologist: *Economie-nature et économie-argent dans l'histoire mondiale*.[59] However, even the French sociologists attempted by their own means to describe the differences between *Wirtschaft* and *Oekonomie*: it was not by chance, in our view, that Braudel, a leading researcher into the bourgeois type of economy in mediaeval Europe, entitled one of his main works *Civilisation matérielle, économie et capitalisme*,[60] thereby distinguishing the 'vie matérielle', which he used to describe the phenomenon he called *économie très elementaire*, from 'économie' in the sense the French reader had been accustomed to.[61] However, the English translation of his work bore the simple and comprehensible title: *Civilisation and Capitalism, 15th-18th Centuries*.[62] This example splendidly demonstrates the willingness of the English-speaking community to comprehend the theory of post-economic society.

So we consider it necessary once more to point out that in this work, every time the concept of 'post-economic society' is used, it will denote *post-oekonomische Gesellschaft*, although strictly speaking they are not one and the same thing; however, we hope that the introductory remarks in this chapter will enable the reader to get a fully coherent grasp of the interpretation we are offering. And so the conception of *post-oekonomische Gesellschaft* is based on the understanding that the period in which *oekonomische Verhaeltnisse* are prevalent in the system of relations which constitute *Volkswirtschaft* has its limits; the period has frontiers in history both in the past and in the future. Humanity left the first of these frontiers behind long ago, and the attainment of the second is one of the nearest landmarks of the progress of civilization.

The *oekonomische System* in our understanding is built on two fundamental principles. The first is the absolute supremacy in the system of motivating forces behind human activity of material interest, which expresses the desire to satisfy one's vital necessities. The isolation of human material interests was present at the early stages of human evolution, as amid the catastrophic lack of material well-being any tangible interest had to be a material interest, and any material interest that was realized had to constitute man's departure from the *Gemeinschaft* and, as a consequence, the transformation of this *Gemeinschaft* into *Gesellschaft*. In this respect Rousseau was right when he wrote that 'Le premier qui ayant enclos un terrain s'avisa de dire: Ceci est à moi, et trouva des gens assez simples pour le croire ... fut le vrai fondateur de la société civile'.[63]

The second mandatory condition for the formation of the *oekonomische System* is the existence of opportunities for the adequate realization of the tangible material interest. The vital factor in such realization is economic and political freedom as one of the basic rights of economic man. Circumstantial confirmation of this may be considered to be the fact that economic science began to realize itself as such only when the object of its analysis became the actions of free economic subjects; it must be recognized that the areas researched by ancient authors and the theorists of modern times differed to a far lesser extent than the title of Varro's work, *De agricultura*, differed from the *Traité d'économie politique* by Montchrestien.

The coupling of material motivation with economic freedom does not signify that 'Oekonomie' is replacing 'Wirtschaft'. It would be more correct to say that in this case Wirtschaft gains economic dimension. Moreover, *oekonomische Verhaeltnisse* do not cease to be simultaneously *wirtschaftliche Verhaeltnisse*. What is in fact happening is that more and more relations which have always been wholly 'wirtschaftlich', are becoming simultaneously 'oekonomisch'.

The aforementioned methodological techniques can be used to describe the frontiers of *oekonomische Gesellschaft*. The first of its elements arose during the disintegration of the rural communities, when selected producers had only just begun to conduct an economy of their own that was relatively independent of the other members of the *Gemeinschaft*. However, the economic nature of such a society remained obscure for two reasons: on the one hand, interaction between individuals as economic subjects was limited to the bare minimum amount of transactions; on the other hand, there were many 'wirtschaftliche', but not 'oekonomische' factors, beginning with the influence of traditions and ending with the authority of the tribal chiefs. The preservation of the communal structures in the despotic states of the Orient presents a classical example of the *Volkswirtschaft* in which all embryos of *oekonomische Verhaeltnisse* were completely stifled.

In contrast, in Europe the emergence of the ancient and the mediaeval economic systems placed a significant number of economic subjects in conditions favourable for the appearance of the first shoots of economic progress. In the societies of the period of antiquity we already encounter some sectors of the economy within which people acted not as the executors of the will of others but as independent economic subjects, performing their productive activity on the basis of an understanding of the objectives before them, of the selection of the best modes of achieving them, and of opposition to other members of society who were also free and independent agents. Progress was frequently achieved by direct and brutal coercion (the best example of which is the market-oriented and fully economic production at the Roman villa, where most of the workforce consisted of prisoners of war and slaves), but elements of economic organization gradually spread, nevertheless, to the whole range of economic relations.

Economic relations arise where and when the material interests of the individual begin to be satisfied as the result of activity in which the individual acts as an equal agent to other members of society. The superficial embodiment of this situation is the exchange of activity or its products, which can be termed commodity exchange; the product of the development of this system becomes market economy and the political form the nation state of the modern world. Thus the concept of the economic epoch on the one hand is close to the concept of the industrial epoch and, on the other hand, differs radically from it. The chronological framework of the economic epoch has hardly been subject to clear definition; the industrial revolution which is so often described as the forerunner of the industrial society was not so much the beginning as the end of the process of the formation of *oekonomische Gesellschaft*.

In Marx we find an interesting extract in which the author analyses the emergence of *oekonomische Gesellschaftsformation*. Writing in French, Marx abandons the use of the term 'formation économique de la société' or anything similar to this, preferring to treat *oekonomische Gesellschaftsformation* simply as the second great phase of social evolution, as 'formation secondaire'. Marx writes:

> Comme dernière phase de la formation primitive de la société, la commune agricole est en même temps phase de transition à la formation secondaire, donc transition de la société, fondée sur la propriété commune, à la société, fondée sur la propriété privée. La formation secondaire, bien entendu, embrasse la série des sociétés reposant sur l'esclavage et le servage.[64]

Here Marx, in our view, attaches far too much importance to private ownership as a factor of economic development, since private ownership does not point unequivocally to the economic nature of society; its use can be directed quite fully and has on several occasions been directed, on the contrary, towards the suppression of economic relations themselves. Marx was more accurate when he wrote that 'dans le mouvement historique de l'Europe occidentale, ancienne et moderne, la période de la commune agricole apparaît comme période de transition de la propriété commune à la propriété privée, comme période de transition de la formation primaire à la formation secondaire'.[65] In this case Marx wrote about the transition throughout the centuries, the ground for which was 'l'Europe occidentale, ancienne et moderne'. Thus the emergence of economic relations is a process of many centuries' duration; its beginning was associated with the disintegration of the rural communities ('les communes agricoles') and its culmination can be observed when economic freedom for the first time manifests itself as being as all-embracing as the supremacy of material interests over all other desires of man – in the period of the consolidation of the bourgeois mode of production ('buergerliche Produktionsweise').

And so, for a very long period, *wirtschaftliche Verhaeltnisse* have assumed more and more the features of *oekonomische Verhaeltnisse*. By the time *buergerliche Gesellschaft* had finally been formed and when commodity production had become the overall phenomenon that has remained for the past three centuries, it became possible to speak of two epochs in the development of human society and of a gigantic transition period which divided them. On the one hand, the exclusively 'non-economic' epoch was left in the past and, on the other hand, humanity entered the 'economic' epoch. The latter was accompanied by both the strengthening of rationalism, the optimization of the ways and methods of satisfying material needs (Weber rightly defined the 'Protestant ethic' as a component of the 'spirit of capitalism'[66]) and by an enormous growth in the feeling of equality and freedom (we recall that Saint-Simon described all representatives of the class of 'industriels' as 'travailleurs' and 'collaborateurs'[67]).

Man's inherent desire to satisfy his material needs with the least possible effort resulted in the triumph of rationalism, which proved to be the basis of the formation of economic society. And man's political freedom became a condition for this society's supremacy. These factors have changed places today. Now social freedom is becoming the basis of modernization of the social whole on a large scale, while transition from the supremacy of material needs to the prevalence of non-material needs is a condition for the departure of humanity from the realms of the economic epoch.

But as the mature forms of *oekonomische Gesellschaft* were achieved and economic relations began to prevail more clearly over all others, all *wirtschaftliche Verhaeltnisse* came to be viewed as economic, and the concepts of 'Oekonomie' and 'Wirtschaft' as identical. During the centuries that have passed humanity has become so rooted in this delusion that today even those who decisively declare that the downfall of industrial civilization is approaching find it difficult to perceive this as the forerunner of post-economic revolution.

After discussing some of the more general concepts of the theory of *post-oekonomische Gesellschaft*, we will now look once more at the questions raised in this chapter. We have shown that, both in the chronological and in the theoretical aspects, *oekonomische Gesellschaft* is a mightier social phenomenon than industrial society. Therefore it can confidently be stated that the emergence of *post-oekonomische Gesellschaft* should be considered not as a certain change in the existing social structure but as the emergence of a new society which displaces the economic order. Moreover, such a displacement must not be viewed as the destruction of the former 'wirtschaftliche' structure; after all, industrial civilization did not eliminate the agrarian civilization. Yet the emerging social organism is not defined by the laws and relations that it will naturally inherit from the economic epoch.

For several millennia 'Wirtschaft' appears to have absorbed elements of the 'Oekonomie', assimilating and using them to ensure technological and social progress. Today it is pushing them aside, as in the new line of social development this driving force is already unable to sustain the rate of progress achieved by the very changes it gave rise to in centuries past. Moreover, both the assimilation and the rejection of economic principles is embodied in two gigantic social revolutions, one of which we are witnessing; the results of these two revolutions are new societies, which are carrying the baton of material progress from the preceding ones, but which are developing according to their own laws and principles.

However much it may hurt the pride of the researcher, it must be acknowledged today that we are unable to define the main characteristics of the coming new condition or state. As demonstrated above, the changes anticipated by humanity are comparable not so much with transition from the feudal society to the bourgeois one, mediated by industrial revolution, the meaning of which has been examined in such detail by the post-industrial theorists, as with a leap from the period of the primitive society to the state of relatively advanced market economy. And just as the brilliant philosophers of antiquity were unable to rise in their social visions above hypotheses about the constant rotation of forms of state authority, today's researchers are unable to look into the future far enough to fully comprehend the principles of the functioning of society in the next millennium. Therefore it would be most consistent to define the coming social state as precisely *post-oekonomische Gesellschaft*, thereby underlining, on the one hand, the main direction of social evolution and, on the other, mentioning that humanity within this new period is departing from the realms of the 'Oekonomie', but remains within the confines of 'Gesellschaft', preserving its own social structure and the main principles of social interaction. Thus, when speaking of *post-oekonomische Gesellschaft*, we fix in this definition both the changeability of society and the elements of succession inevitably present in the development of civilization.

Now we can attempt to define the characteristic of society which, when it alters, becomes the essence of global transformation, changing *oekonomische Gesellschaft* into its antithesis. We assume that modern changes are more fully focused on the phenomenon – human activity – that unites all aspects of life in society and which makes society what it is. Human activity has assumed two main forms throughout history. The pre-economic forms of primitive production were characterized by activity definable by instincts and primitive traditions; the economic epoch was one of rational activity, defined by material interests, an activity intended to overcome the forces preventing man from achieving his mainly material aims. The latter activity, which embodied the contradictory nature of the material interests of individuals characteristic of *oekonomische Gesellschaft*, is labour in the pure sense of the word. Labour has been most successfully defined by Alfred Marshall, who understood the word to mean 'any exertion of mind or body undergone partly or wholly with a view to some good other than the pleasure derived directly from the work'.[68] In the next chapter we will examine the definition and boundaries of labour as a philosophical and economic category; for now it is important to make a few remarks to complete the construction of the methodology that will then be applied to analyse modern society.

Labour emerged before the economic epoch; as the embodiment of the principles which achieved their fullest development within the framework of *oekonomische Gesellschaft*, labour became the basic precondition and the most important foundation for this type of social order. The opening up of the system of relations in *oekonomische Gesellschaft* may be presented as the opening up of contradictions concealed by labour as an economic phenomenon. Each step in the forward movement of *oekonomische Gesellschaft* was in a specific way interpreted in the content and forms of labour; however, these changes themselves to a considerable extent defined the course and direction of the further development of *oekonomische Gesellschaft*.

Labour is the element inevitably shadowing the romantic perception of the economic epoch as an epoch of freedom and equality. The central position it occupies in the system of categories and relations of this historical period emphasizes that the freedom of man within an economic epoch is only political and not social freedom. Man is free to choose the ways and methods he may use to attain certain material aims, but the very existence of these aims and their supremacy over the system of values and preferences show that man has still not become totally free, that his life is still, as Bell wrote, a game against fabricated nature, and has not yet become the game between persons that the author described.

Confronting nature as an external force (be this the direct struggle between primitive man and the elements, the struggle of the oppressed classes in ancient societies for their rights or the usual modern-day activity of hired labourers), man perceives his activity, his labour, as one that is not free, as one that is alienated and gives rise to and heightens the confrontation between the individual and society. In order to eliminate these contradictions and open a way for society to a post-economic condition, it is necessary to overcome labour as the main form of human activity. In order to overcome labour, it is necessary to overcome material interests as the main constituent of the system of values and preferences of the modern individual. All of the preconditions for this exist today and they will be analysed in the following chapters. But right now it ought to be mentioned that labour, being the central historical form of human activity, is an element of a complex dialectical triad, constituted by forms of human activity in their progression.

Primitive forms of activity were characterized by the fact that its motives – instincts and traditions – were of an internal nature with respect to the individual. Activity itself, performed in conditions when man hardly distinguished himself from the 'Gemeinschaft', was irrational. Labour became as distinct from this form of activity as the economic society from primitive forms of communication. Its driving motive was material interest, material interest which testifies to the dependence of this activity on the external circumstances of human existence; its main feature became rationality, suggesting abstract thought and purposefulness. Following the Hegelian principle, we are able to depict the primitive instinctual activity of man and labour as a thesis and antithesis. The synthetic result of the development of forms of human activity in this case becomes activity which, on the one hand, possesses rational nature, inherited from labour, and, on the other hand, is driven by an inner motive, which was characteristic of its earlier forms. Such activity is conditioned by the desire for inner betterment and possesses features which differ radically from the labour which is widespread today. We define this form of human activity as creativity. This is not the only possible definition, nor is it necessarily the most successful one, but we believe that it is capable of fulfilling two key tasks: to underline the difference between creativity and labour and, with relative lack of contradiction, to fit in with the terminological ideas of modern sociologists and psychologists who have long been interested in the problems of social creativity.

Creativity represents the global challenge to the economic order. This phenomenon can be viewed as a system-formational element of the new type of social order which is replacing the economic order. This does not mean making creativity absolute or that it immediately negates labour and that all characteristics of the new post-economic society can be explained directly by appeals to this new entity. We want merely to note that, with the advancement of the hypothesis that treats creativity as the most fundamental characteristic of the new social order, it becomes possible to stress three important circumstances which are frequently not taken into account when formulating conceptions of coming historical changes.

Firstly, the distinction between creativity and labour highlights the scale of the transition in progress and sufficiently clearly demonstrates precisely which epoch in the development of human society the new social order emerging today is displacing. Moreover, understanding is formed by the link between the new society and the preceding historical state as human activity is selected as the most important characteristic – always the base phenomenon for any social structure.

Secondly, a structural element is defined, one that, if altered, becomes the basic element for assessing the transformation in progress: leaving aside for the time being the full definition of relative progress and pattern of such change, we note that the decisive importance the form of activity has for any society can hardly be disputed.

Thirdly, when discussing the new form of human activity as the main characteristic of the future society, we avoid having to negate or radically review the methodology of contemporary social science, a methodology which to some degree is based on the analysis of human activity, be it instinctive, irrational activity or labour. In this respect, for all the importance of the progress being made, its consequences may be analysed as the result of the natural development of the social structure which has been under formation for thousands of years.

Closing the chapter devoted to terminological and methodological problems, we note that research into the future society from the point of view of the emergence and development of the alternative form of human activity for all the methodological austerity and justification of such an approach is a palliative decision, conditioned primarily by the fact that researchers today are capable of assessing, not so much the new social state itself, as the period of its emergence. Identifying the dichotomy of labour and creativity as the key aspect of the modern transition, and assuming that creative activity will become the main characteristic of the future society, we do not strive to prove that it is the contradictions of creativity that determine all elements of tomorrow's social structure; we are merely stressing that today a whole series of important social changes can be viewed as comprehensively and productively as possible, presuming them to be either factors of the formation of the creative activity of man or the forms of its manifestation.

This approach also determines the plan of the second part of the book. From the start we believe it essential to consider the modern economic, social and political processes taking place in the more developed countries of the West from the point of view of forming the material, social and psychological conditions for the emergence and development of creative activity. This includes the problem of assessing the modern state of creativity, the proliferation of creative activity in various spheres of human activity and, to a slightly lesser degree, assessing the general effect of creativity on the perception of the world and system of motives governing the modern individual.

The first part of the analysis may be described as 'introvert'. We attempt to show how modern man and modern society, resolving what would appear to be problems fully characteristic of the economic epoch develop and cultivate in the depths of the social whole a new type of activity which may in the near future radically alter forms of civilization. Then we want to show that creative activity today, despite not yet having become the main type of the human activity which has already formed, is capable of affecting and affects all aspects of social life. We will assess the degree of this influence on the laws of commodity production, the modification of relations of the value exchange and the prospects for the development of market economy as a whole; we will discuss the changes that creative activity may bring to the process of organizing social production, its influence on the role of ownership as an economic category; we will study how acceptable for the assessment of creative activity and its results is the conception of the exploitation of man by man, so widespread in the social theories of this century. And we will analyse those social and interpersonal problems which inevitably stand before society, in which creativity is the main type of activity.

The second part of the analysis is 'extrovert'; in it we try to comment on the influence of creativity itself, even in its immature forms, on social life and its main characteristics. This approach concurs with our previously declared aim of identifying the fundamental feature of the new social organization. Without claiming that creativity is that feature to the full extent, we will try to demonstrate that the many important social transformations for today's age can be considered as phenomena which stimulate the emergence of creative activity; at the same time many of the phenomena of modern life can be treated as the manifestations of creative activity. In creativity the fundamental problems of the contemporary world are focused and gain new interpretations, problems which sociology is accustomed to regard as relatively isolated from each other. It is this circumstance that determines our attitude to creativity as the main subject of research in a work which nevertheless aims to analyse the laws of post-economic society.

Notes

1 See A. Penty, *Old Worlds for New: A Study of the Post-Industrial State*, London, 1917; *Post-Industrialism*, London, 1922.

2   See D. Riesman, 'Leisure and Work in Post-Industrial Society', in E. Larrabee and R. Meyersohn (eds), *Mass Leisure*, Glencoe, Ill., 1958.
3   See D. Bell, *The Coming of Post-Industrial Society. A Venture in Social Forecasting*, (1st edn), New York, 1973.
4   R.L. Heilbroner, *Business Civilization in Decline*, New York, London, 1976, p.73.
5   See A. Gorz, *Farewell to the Working Class: An Essay on Post-Industrial Socialism*, London, 1982.
6   See T. Roszak, *Where the Wasteland Ends: Politics and Transcendence in Postindustrial Society*, New York, 1972; R. Bahro, *From Red to Green*, London, 1984.
7   See I. Illich, *The Tools for Conviviality*, London, 1985.
8   For more detail, see B. Smart, *Modern Conditions, Postmodern Controversies*, London, New York, 1992, pp.28–9.
9   See D. Bell, *The Coming of Post-Industrial Society*, New York, 1976, pp.14–15, 127–9.
10   See ibid., pp.212, 216–21, 274–8.
11   See ibid., pp.118–19, 269.
12   See ibid., pp.148–54, 404–10, 471–2.
13   See D. Bell, *The Cultural Contradictions of Capitalism*, New York, 1978, p.198, note.
14   See, for example, S. Crook, J. Pakulski and M. Waters, *Postmodernization. Change in Advanced Society*, Newbury Park, London, 1993; E. Gellner, *Postmodernism, Reason and Religion*, London, 1992; A. Giddens, *Modernity and Self-Identity*, Cambridge, 1991; F. Jameson, *Post-Modernism, or, The Cultural Logic of Late Capitalism*, London, 1992; S. Lash, *Sociology of Postmodernism*, London, New York, 1990; S. Lash and J. Friedman (eds), *Modernity and Identity*, Oxford, 1992; M.A. Rose, *The Post-Modern and the Post-Industrial*, Cambridge, 1991.
15   See G. Lichtheim, *The New Europe: Today and Tomorrow*, New York, 1963, p.194.
16   See R. Dahrendorf, *Class and Class Conflict in Industrial Society*, Stanford, 1959, pp.51–9, 98–105, 274; P.F. Drucker, *Post-Capitalist Society*, New York, 1993, pp.4–6, 14–15.
17   See P.F. Drucker, *The New Realities*, Oxford, 1996, p.168.
18   See T. Burns, *The Rationale of the Corporate System*, p.50, quoted in D. Bell, *The Coming of the Post-Industrial Society*, 1976, p.54, note.
19   The term was introduced by S.N. Eisenstadt in 1970 and is today widely used in the framework of the theory of postmodernity (see A. Giddens, *Modernity and Self-Identity*, pp.2–3).
20   See K. Boulding, *The Meaning of the 20th Century: The Great Transition*, New York, 1964; R. Seidenberg, *Post-Historic Man*, Chapel Hill, 1950.
21   See F. Machlup, *The Production and Distribution of Knowledge in the United States*, Princeton, 1962; H.S. Dordick and G. Wang, *The Information Society: A Retrospective View*, Newbury Park, London, 1993, p.1.
22   See, for example, M. Porat and M. Rubin, *The Information Economy: Development and Measurement*, Washington, DC, 1978; Y. Masuda, *The Information Society as Post-Industrial Society*, Washington, DC, 1981; T. Stonier, *The Wealth of Information*, London, 1983; R.L. Katz, *The Information Society: An International Perspective*, New York, 1988.
23   J.D. Davidson and Lord William Rees-Mogg, *The Sovereign Individual. How to Survive and Thrive During the Collapse of the Welfare State*, New York, 1997, p.12.
24   See J.-A. de Condorcet, *Esquisse d'un tableau historique des progrès de l'esprit humain*, Paris, 1794; C.H. de Saint-Simon, *Catéchisme des industriels*, Paris, 1832.
25   For more detail, see B. Smart, *Modern Conditions*, pp.24–5.
26   K. Kumar, *From Post-Industrial to Post-Modern Society. New Theories of the Contemporary World*, Oxford (UK), Cambridge (USA), 1995, p.3.
27   See Z. Brzezinski, *Between Two Ages*, New York, 1970, p.9.
28   See R.E. Lane, 'The Decline of Politics and Ideology in the Knowledgeable Society', *American Sociological Review*, 1966, **31**, pp.649–62.

29   See D. Dickson, *The New Politics of Science*, New York, 1984, pp.163–216; N. Stehr, *Knowledge Societies*, Thousand Oaks, London, 1994, pp.5–18.
30   See T. Sakaiya, *The Knowledge-Value Revolution or A History of the Future*, Tokyo, New York, 1991, pp.57–8, 267–87.
31   See S. Crook *et al.*, *Postmodernization*, pp.15–16.
32   See J. Pakulski and M. Waters, *The Death of Class*, Thousand Oaks, London, 1996, p.154.
33   See A. Touraine, *Critique de la modernité*, Paris, 1992, pp.312–22.
34   See A. Etzioni, *The Active Society*, New York, 1968.
35   See R. Bellah, R. Madsen, W.M. Sullivan, A. Swidler and S.M. Tiptom, *et al.*, *Good Society*, New York, 1985; J.K. Galbraith, *The Good Society: The Human Agenda*, Boston, New York, 1996; A. Etzioni, *The New Golden Rule*, New York, 1997, pp.25–8.
36   See A. Toffler, *The Third Wave*, New York, 1980, p.9.
37   See D. Bell, *The Cultural Contradictions of Capitalism*, p.198, note.
38   See A. Toffler, *The Third Wave*, pp.132–8; 85–8, 96–7; 180; 155–78; 50–78, 437–8.
39   See D. Bell, *The Coming of the Post-Industrial Society; The Cultural Contradictions of Capitalism*.
40   See J. Baudrillard, *The Mirror of Production*, St. Louis, 1975; *For a Critique of the Political Economy of the Sign*, St. Louis, 1981; *The Transparency of Evil: Essays on Extreme Phenomena*, London, 1993; J.-F. Lyotard, *The Post-Modern Condition: A Report on Knowledge*, Manchester, 1984; M. Poster, *The Mode of Information: Poststructuralism and Social Context*, Cambridge, 1990.
41   See M. Piome and C. Sabel, *The Second Industrial Divide*, New York, 1984; L. Hirschhorn, *Beyond Mechanization: Work and Technology in the Post-Industrial Age*, Cambridge, Mass., 1984.
42   See M. Castels, *The Informational City*, Oxford, 1989; M. Castels and P. Hall, *Technopoles of the World: The Making of Twenty-First Century Industrial Complexes*, London, New York, 1994.
43   See H.I. Schiller, *Who Knows: Information in the Age of the Fortune 500*, Norwood, NJ, 1981; *Information and the Crisis Economy*, Norwood, NJ, 1984; *Culture, Inc. The Corporate Takeover of Public Expression*, New York, 1989.
44   See M. Aglietta, *The Theory of Capitalist Regulation*, London, 1979; A. Lipietz, *Mirages and Miracles: The Crisis of Global Fordism*, London, 1987; *Towards a New Economic Order: Postfordism, Ecology and Democracy*, Cambridge, 1993.
45   See J. Habermas, *The Philosophical Discourse of Modernity*, Cambridge, 1987; *The Structural Transformation of the Public Sphere: An Inquiry into a Category of Bourgeois Society*, Cambridge, 1989; N. Garnham, *Capitalism and Communication: The Global Culture and the Economics of Information*, Thousand Oaks, London, 1990.
46   For more detail, see F. Webster, *Theories of the Information Society*, London, New York, 1995, pp.1–5.
47   D. Bell, *The Cultural Contradictions of Capitalism*, p.198, note.
48   D. Bell, 'The Third Technological Revolution and Its Possible Socio-Economic Consequences', *Dissent*, Spring 1989, **XXXVI** (2), p.167.
49   D. Bell, *The Coming of the Post-Industrial Society*, 1976, pp.119, 483.
50   See D. Bell, 'Afterword: 1996', *The Cultural Contradictions of Capitalism. Twentieth Anniversary Edition*, New York, 1996, pp.299, note; 306.
51   A. Toffler, *The Third Wave*, p.349.
52   A. Toffler, *Future Shock*, New York, 1971, p.185.
53   See Karl Marx, *The Eighteenth Brumaire of Louis Bonaparte*, Moscow, 1983, p.13.
54   Karl Marx and Frederick Engels, *Collected Works*, Vol. 29, pp.263, 264.
55   See H. Kahn, *Forces for Change in the Final Third of the Twentieth Century*, New York, 1970.

56   See H. Kahn and A.J. Wiener, *The Year 2000. A Framework for Speculations on the Next Thirty-Three Years*, New York, 1967, p.186; D. Bell, *The Coming of Post-Industrial Society*, 1976, p.38.

57   D. Bell, *The Cultural Contradictions of Capitalism. Twentieth Anniversary Edition*, p.254.

58   See A. Dopsch, *Naturalwirtschaft und Geldwirtschaft in der Weltgeschichte*, Vienna, 1930.

59   See A. Dopsch, *Economie-nature et économie-argent dans l'histoire mondiale*, Paris, 1932.

60   See F. Braudel, *Civilisation matérielle, économie et capitalisme, XVe–XVIIIe siècles*, Vols 1–3, Paris, 1979.

61   Ibid., T.2, *Les jeux de l'échange*, p.7.

62   See F. Braudel, *Civilisation and Capitalism, 15th–18th Centuries*, Vols 1–3, London, 1985.

63   J.-J. Rousseau, *L'inégalité parmi les hommes*, Paris, 1965, p.108. ('The first man who, having enclosed a piece of ground, bethought himself of saying *This is mine*, and found people simple enough to believe him, was the real founder of civil society' (J.-J. Rousseau, 'On the Origin of Inequality', *Great Books of the Western World*, Vol. 35, Encyclopaedia Britannica Publishers, 1994, p.348).) In this context, however, we consider the French term, 'la société civile' to be associated not with its direct German equivalent of 'buergerliche Gesellschaft', but directly with the concept 'Gesellschaft', which may be used to describe any society. The term 'la société civile', in our opinion, was used by Rousseau in view of the exclusive variety of meanings the term 'société' as such possesses in the French language.

64   K. Marx, 'Troisième projet de la lettre à Vera Zassoulitsch', in K. Marx and F. Engels, *Gesamtausgabe* (MEGA), Erste Abteilung, Bd. 25, Berlin, 1985, S. 238. ('As the last phase of the primitive formation of society, the agricultural commune is, at the same time, a transitional stage leading to the secondary formation, and hence marks the transition from a society founded on communal property to a society founded on private property. The secondary formation, of course, includes the series of societies resting on slavery and serfdom' (Karl Marx and Frederick Engels, *Collected Works*, Vol. 24, p.367).)

65   K. Marx, 'Premier projet de la lettre à Vera Zassoulitsch', in K. Marx and F. Engels, *Gesamtausgabe* (MEGA), Erste Abteilung, Bd. 25, Berlin, 1985, S. 224. ('in the historical development of Western Europe, ancient and modern, the period of the agricultural commune appears as a period of transition from communal property to private property, as a period of transition from the primary form to the secondary one' (Karl Marx and Frederick Engels, *Collected Works*, Vol. 24, p.352).)

66   See M. Weber, *The Protestant Ethic and the Spirit of Capitalism*, London, 1992.

67   See C.H. de Saint-Simon, *Du système industriel*, Paris, 1821, p.viii.

68   A. Marshall, *Principles of Economics*, Vol. I, London, 1961, p.65.

5 Creativity: The Global Challenge to the Economic Order

Like our analysis of the post-economic transformation, our study of the characteristics of contemporary activity, the directions of the development of its forms and the prospects of its progress in the future must begin by settling a number of terminological and methodological issues. The transition from labour to creativity has been much more thoroughly researched than the relation between the economic and non-economic forms of society since the modification of activity is undoubtedly regarded as being of more importance than a general methodological discussion on the post-economic condition. The theme is to a greater or lesser extent present in every work on the formation of the post-industrial society. Most sociologists do not regard the condition that society is now entering to be post-economic. Equally, the forms of activity that characterize the post-economic condition are not defined as creativity.

This can be explained by two analogous factors. Firstly, the notion of the disappearance of work (although found in some works[1]) is unlikely to be accepted by those who understand 'work' to mean all rational human activity. Secondly, while the notion 'work' may have a broad definition, 'creativity' acquires the connotation of a sociopsychological process that is mostly studied by a narrow circle of psychologists and behaviour theorists rather than sociologists or economists.

The notion of creativity is practically never applied in modern economic theory. We are not trying to put the term and the phenomena that it defines at the centre of any study of today's economy, but the significance that we believe that creativity will acquire in the future requires a contemplation of the terminological and methodological relation of work and creativity.

147

The Notion of Work and Creativity: Terminology

The relation of work and creativity is coming to the forefront today as the role of the individual becomes in many respects more important than the relations between classes and social groups, to which most economists have traditionally devoted their work. The whole issue of new forms of human activity has become one of the most topical as an individual's behaviour is determined more by his actions as a subject of interpersonal relations than by his actions as the subject of a market for material goods geared only to utility and preferences.

Works written at various times in English, French, German and Russian have failed to provide a strict definition of what they respectively call 'work', 'travail', 'Arbeit' and 'trud', primarily thanks to the wide range of phenomena traditionally ascribed to the terms. J.K. Galbraith formulated the problem best:

> The controlling fact, which has been rarely remarked in economic literature, must be made clear at the outset: there is a problem with the word 'work'. It is used to characterise two radically different, indeed sharply contrasting, commitments of human time. Work can be something that one greatly enjoys, that accords a sense of fulfillment and accomplishment and without which there would be a feeling of displacement, social rejection, depression, or, at best, boredom. It is such work that defines social position – that of the corporate executive, financier, poet, scholar, television commentator, even journalist. But work also consigns men and women to the anonymity of the toiling masses. Here it consists of repetitive, tiring, muscular effort replete with tedium. It has often been held that the good workman enjoys his work; this is said most frequently, most thoughtfully, by those with no experience of hard, physical, economically enforced toil. The word 'work' denotes sharply contrasting situations; it is doubtful whether any other term in any language is quite so at odds with itself in what it describes.[2]

There is a real chance to escape this difficulty in English-language terminology. But it will be very difficult indeed to do so in French, German and Russian.

The English notion of work, as we have already noted, is very wide indeed. Elliott Jaques, a renowned researcher of work and creativity, wrote: 'I shall define [work] as the exercise of judgment (discretion) in order to reach a goal, always within limits and always with a maximum targeted completion time.'[3] He particularly emphasized his rejection of the 'common or vulgar definition of work'. He wrote: 'I do not hold with the common or vulgar definition of work as being something we do because we have to do it, or do just for money. Work thus includes not only the work we do for a living, but also "creative" work, recreational work (goal-directed play activities), house- and homework, parental work and so on.'[4] The same can be said of 'Arbeit' and 'travail'. Karl Marx in the German edition of his *Capital* defined the 'Arbeitsprozess' as 'ein Prozess zwischen dem Menschen und der Natur, ein Prozess, worin er seinen Stoffwechsel mit der Natur durch seine eigne That vermittelt, regelt und kontroliert'.[5] In the authorized French edition of 1875, he said the same thing of 'travail': 'Le travail est de prime abord un acte qui se passe entre l'homme et la nature. L'homme y joue lui-même vis-à-vis de la nature le rôle d'une puissance naturelle.'[6]

The English language, meanwhile, includes an important word, 'labour', that complements 'work'. The difference between these words is obvious, although many writers fail to distinguish their different connotations. We fully agree with Jaques that work is not just 'something we do because we have to do it', but we believe that that is exactly what labour is. Labour is the 'economically enforced' activity that Galbraith talked about.[7] 'Labour' replaces 'work' by habit, almost subconsciously, when major English-language theorists write about economic issues. The greatest economist of the 18th century wrote: 'The annual *labour* of every nation is the fund which originally supplies it with all the necessaries and conveniences of life which it annually consumes, and which consist always either in the immediate produce of that *labour*, or in what is purchased with that produce from other nations'[8] (emphasis added). One of the best known scholars of the beginning of this century wrote: 'Labour is any exertion of mind or body undergone partly or wholly with a view to some good other than the pleasure derived directly from the work.'[9] Yet there is no such complementary notion for 'Arbeit' or 'travail' in German and French.

However, as we have already noted, several scholars, some of them trying to provide a more radical formulation of certain issues, have clearly confused the notions of work and labour. Hannah Arendt, as early as the 1950s, persistently used both terms when contrasting productive and unproductive, skilled and unskilled and manual and mental activities.[10] In our times Francis Fukuyama allowed an even clearer contradiction when he wrote that 'traditional economic theory, beginning with Adam Smith, maintains that *work* is an essentially unpleasant activity, undertaken for the sake of the utility of the things created by *work*'[11] and that 'this view would also be supported by Locke, who sees *labor* only as a means of producing things useful for consumption'[12] (all emphasis added). What Locke's interpretation of 'labour' has to do with Fukuyama's notion of 'work' remains a mystery. Often superficial and conspicuous characteristics of human activity may give the impression that 'the distinction between work and labor, although the words are often used synonymously in modern English, lies in the connotations of labor with pain and trouble, and work with effort and product',[13] but such a formulation could hardly be regarded as meeting the requirements of scientific analysis.

Yet in both the Marxian approach and Western economic theory there is some understanding of the dual nature of work, 'Arbeit' and 'travail', of work as internally unfree activity and of work as any kind of productive activity. Marx in *Capital* may have defined 'Arbeit' as 'the everlasting condition of human existence ... independent of every social phase of that existence, or rather, common to every such phase',[14] but in his earlier works, when his views were still forming and the new concept was of a largely philosophical nature and yet to be directed exclusively to justify the inevitability of the victory of the proletariat over the bourgeoisie, he clearly talked of 'Arbeit' as an alienated activity carried out under external necessity and therefore unfree. 'It is one of the greatest misapprehensions,' he wrote, 'to speak of free, human, social labour, of labour without private property.'[15]

The consequence of this approach was a rejection of the need to 'liberate' labour because labour was already 'free' in bourgeois society, and the elaboration of the theses of eliminating labour,[16] theses that 'the communist revolution is directed against the preceding mode of activity [and] does away with labour',[17] and other similar tenets. We believe that Marx was right to note the global nature of the new social revolution and correctly linked the transition to the communist society – which for Marx served as a transition to the non-economic condition – with the destruction of 'Arbeit', which he understood here as labour.

The dual nature of work is also gradually gaining recognition in Western economic theory. The basic trend is relatively salient, although often such notions involve identifying labour with all the negative characteristics of activity and work with all the positive. Starting with the Marshall definition there developed a definition of labour as internally unfree activity determined by material necessity. Using Marshall's definition of labour as 'economic work of man, whether with the hand or the head',[18] John Naisbitt said it was an economic activity that entailed, first, the production of material goods and services, second, the exchange of goods, and, third, consumption. The material side of life depends on these phenomena. Its conditions are dictated by external factors. Labour, thus, is the process of the creation of economic goods that requires, according to the concept of alternative cost, sacrifices of scarce resources, money, physical energy and intellectual capabilities.

Both neoclassicism and Marxism regard labour as an activity dictated by external necessity and defined within the boundaries of material production. The profound differences in meaning between work as labour and work as any other form of activity is shown in the works of Western futurologists and historians of work. The notion 'work' and, much less frequently, 'job', is often used to distinguish several basic forms of human activity. Daniel Bell, for example, talks of pre-industrial, industrial and post-industrial work.[19] Several other scholars use 'work' and 'job' interchangeably: Best talks of the 'work activities of today' and 'today's jobs'.[20]

Meanwhile, most researchers of human activity point out that neither labour nor even work were always indisputable attributes of human society. Jacques Ellul, analysing the differences between pre-industrial and industrial societies, wrote:

> I shall not write about the difference between conditions of work today and in the past – how today's work is less fatiguing and of shorter duration, on the one hand, but, on the other, is an aimless, useless, and callous business, tied to a clock, an absurdity profoundly felt and resented by the worker ... whose labor no longer has anything in common with what was traditionally called work.[21]

Robert Heilbroner went even further to reach an understanding that 'the picture is astonishing because it is blank: there is no work in primitive societies', clarifying his statement thus:

> what can it mean to say that primitive man does no work? I mean that the tasks associated with the physical sustenance of the group are not distinguished by organization or esteem from other tasks and activities also required to maintain collective life, such as the rearing of children, the participation in various social decisions, the transmission of culture, and the like. In this skein of activities, the performance of those that we would call work carry no special identifying characteristic that sets them apart.[22]

A no less contradictory attempt was made by André Gorz, who said that modern workers should do all they could 'to free themselves from work by rejecting its nature, content, necessity and modalities'.[23] All these notions, despite their internal contradictions, deserve attention as examples of a desire to break out of the methodological framework dominated by the notion of work as a single term.

It was Heilbroner, in our view, who got closest to an understanding of the relationship between the main forms of human activity without actually departing from the framework of work as a term. He quite correctly said that work cannot be overcome as the result of the development of technological processes and the coming of automated production. The global transformation of work will only be achieved as a consequence of changes in its internal structure and social characteristics, when work will be 'conducted under the aegis of ambition, not duress, so that subordination and submission would simply disappear'.[24] This formulation is very close to the one we use when contrasting labour and creativity. Heilbroner, underlining the significance of the self-expression and self-development of the individual in future society, said: 'the vision of a world without work is not to be interpreted as a world without effort, perhaps exhausting effort, or a world without personal achievement'.[25] His final conclusion that 'a world without work is a fantasy, and a dangerous fantasy at that'[26] is quite right, given all his provisos. This example proves that the ground has already been prepared for the idea of contrasting labour with the phenomenon that we call creativity within the framework of the notion 'work' and that such an idea could well set the agenda for reassessing contemporary notions of the prospects of the development of human activity.

The rejection of labour as the main type of human activity in studies of future society is even more salient. It is now established practice not to use the term 'labour' in a theoretical analysis of the formation of a new type of activity. This is demonstrated, firstly, by Jaques, who contrasted creative work with employment work (Jaques said that the product of creative work was of a purely symbolic character and that the activity itself is driven only by internal desire, whereas employment work presupposed coercion and was not based on the possibility of the inclusion of subconscious processes[27] and this is as correct as Bell's distinction of pre-industrial, industrial and post-industrial work; and, secondly, by the categorical rejection of the notion 'creative labour', which cannot be used in scientific analysis because of its irrationality.[28] We can trace a similar situation in German-language terminology. The German word 'Arbeit' is less coloured by connotations of servility than the English word 'labour'. Germans, however, find it improper to talk of 'kreative Arbeit'. Two terms have come into usage since German sociologists began exploring the theory of creativity in the 1950s. They are *Kreativitaet* and *kreative Taetigkeit*, creativity itself and creative activity, or creative work. The notions 'Arbeit' and 'Kreativitaet' not only do not overlap but are often considered to be opposites. Hermann Glaser, for example, talks of a significant process of change in human activity that he terms 'the disappearance of labour' in society or 'Verschwinden der Arbeit' and is constantly comparing a society based on labour, 'Arbeitsgesellschaft', and a society based on creative activity, 'Taetigkeitsgesellschaft'.[29]

In our view the concept of the transformation of human activity must be constructed as a concept of the overcoming of labour and not work, 'Arbeit' and not 'Taetigkeit'. The overwhelming majority of philosophers and economists would reject the notion of the end of work as we know it. Take, for example, the response of French sociologists to the French edition of Jeremy Rifkin's work, which was translated literally as *La fin du travail*.[30] Many French scholars responded with works that criticized Rifkin for his terminological radicalism rather than for his position itself. Given the specific nature of French terminology, Rifkin's work could not have received the understanding it deserved.[31]

Thus we believe that the understanding of the evolution of work in modern Western sociology and philosophy allows us to carry out a systemization that, not contradicting any one of the above-mentioned positions, nevertheless will help align various viewpoints in the framework of a fairly well-balanced methodological scheme. Several conditions must be observed within the framework of this scheme.

Firstly, the term work ('Arbeit', 'travail', 'trud') should unequivocally be understood as meaning all the main forms of rational human activity, regardless of which historical period in the development of civilization is the subject of analysis. In English, as in French, German and Russian, rejecting this interpretation of work would amount to an unjustifiably radical change in the terminological scheme and, especially given the established scientific stereotypes, would be inexpedient.

Secondly, the English notion of labour should be contrasted to the notion of work and designate economically enforced activity; that is, in the widest sense of the word, activity designed to satisfy the material interests of individuals through interaction with nature, either directly or with nature that has already been fabricated by man. We believe that it would be useful to propose new definitions for 'Arbeit', 'travail' and 'trud' that would limit their meanings to the narrowest sense rather than productive activity as a whole.

Thirdly, there needs to be some theoretical clarity over what types of human activity are contrasted with labour within the framework of the notion of work. What we mean here is a clear terminological definition of those phenomena that precede labour and those phenomena that replace labour. Here there is much room for terminological and methodological study: a whole range of terms could be proposed to fill this gap. Here we are not talking about the term itself, but of its ability to play the role of a universally recognized notion contrasted with labour.

On the basis of this approach, we believe it is possible to distinguish three types of human activity: instinctive work during the early stages of human development, labour itself and creativity or creative work as the negation of labour. It should be stressed that each of these three forms of activity represents the three forms of rational activity with tools, the latter of which, as is accepted in traditional terminology, can be sufficiently well designated by the established notion of work.

The central element of this dialectical triad, labour, we believe can be defined as rational and goal-directed physical or mental activity that is an individual's response to the external environment and serves to satisfy his physiological or social requirements rather than to meet the need for self-development.

As we have already pointed out, the principal differences between instinctive work, labour and creativity are determined not so much by their material characteristics as by their inner structure. That is why it is so hard to study the transition from one type of activity to another. Moreover, whereas there are several signs to be found of the transition from instinctive work to labour, signs which can be clearly seen on the surface of social relations, the shift from labour to creative work takes place at a much deeper level and is not easily identified. In this respect it can be accepted that the transition from instinctive work to labour was very important for the progress of society while the transition from labour to creativity is a no less fundamental means to provide the progress of the individual. In so far as the individual is a more complex subject than society, it is harder to achieve an understanding of creativity than labour.

The fundamental distinction between instinctive work and labour and between labour and creativity is to be found in the motive that determines the structure and main characteristics of each of those types of activity. Instinctive work was a primitive activity, prompted by instincts and traditions within the individual and to a large degree unperceived. But the emergence of labour brought cardinal change. Labour, prompted by material requirements as a means for their satisfaction, is distinguished from instinctive work, firstly, by the motive for activity that becomes a material of nature that has to be used to satisfy the individual's needs and thus is profoundly external; by the fact that such an activity requires the individual to perceive himself as a being distinct from the rest of the world and not as a component part of that world and that from that time the development of nature becomes not a manifestation of the life of a biological being but perceived tooled activity carried out under the influence of material necessity, that is labour itself.

Creativity, which replaces labour, continues this characteristic of rational activity since the individual cannot escape the framework of nature and his activity will always be limited by several factors of the balance between civilization and the environment. This alone ensures the continued conscious nature of creativity, which has the same material basis as the conscious nature of labour. Yet creativity is not so much aimed to modify nature as to modify the individual himself. Such a change, we can call it self-development, could apply to the individual as a subject of production or of leisure. The result of such a process may be a form of activity where production and leisure are divided in neither time nor space but have a single goal and are carried out under the influence of and to the degree that they facilitate the self-development of the individual. It is important to point out that it is not just the degree of such progress and the means of its achievement but the very understanding of one or another direction of the development of the individual as corresponding to his requirements that can only be determined by the individual himself. Therefore, having understood creativity as self-motivated rational activity, we assert that only the individual carrying out a given activity can determine whether the activity is creativity or labour. The elimination of labour, however paradoxical it may be, is carried out, first and foremost, at the sociopsychological level; since the process of labour gives rise to a whole range of fundamental economic phenomena and laws (we will discuss this in the following chapters) it appears that the economic bases of society can be overcome, not by the transformation of social structures, but as a result of the internal evolution of individuals that such social structures are composed of. It is this conclusion, impossible under any of the theories of post-industrialism, that is the essence of our notion of post-economic transformation.

Instinctive work, labour and creativity can be contrasted in another way too. Instinctive work can be defined as a process of a primarily biological nature, the reproduction of nature by its very self. Labour is the matter of the social condition of man; inherently being the creation of material goods, it amounts to a form of the reproduction of social structures. Creativity is identical to the process of self-realization and as such acts as a form of the reproduction of the personality. Thus the material product of instinctive work is inalienable from the producer since the process of production frequently coincides with the process of consumption. The material product of instinctive work is also irreproducible since it resulted from an activity that was much more accidental and circumstantial than constant, repetitive and established. Labour from its very outset was an alienated activity that gave rise to a whole range of forms of alienation, from the alienation of the product to the alienation of the individual; the result of labour is alienable and reproducible. Creativity in this respect includes characteristics of both instinctive work and labour: its product, which in its material form may be completely identical to the result of labour, is alienable. Yet it is as irreproducible as the forms, motives and the internal structure of the creative activity of which it is a result. Such relations determine the place of any individual in worlds dominated respectively by instinctive work, labour and creativity. Individuals where instinctive work dominates are an inherent part of nature, the forces of which determine the main forms of the manifestation of instinctive work.

Labour, as the complete antipode of instinctive work, marks man's opposition to his environment and his desire to subjugate his environment, perceived as an alien force, to his own needs. Creativity is activity in which man becomes the embodiment of nature, which is manifested at its highest level in the creative personality.

Figure 5.1 and Table 5.1 show the relation of instinctive work, labour and creativity and the characteristics considered above.[32] Contrasting creativity to labour, we ought to focus on specific forms of human interaction that are coincident to creativity as a form of activity. As has already been noted, creativity is born of the desire of an individual for self-development and its object is the creator himself. To quote Nuernberger, the creative individual sets out to create 'something more of what he already is'.[33] The means for such a process is not in the first place the transformation of material nature, but the interaction between persons that Daniel Bell correctly calls the games between persons. The interpersonal characteristics of creativity are the most fundamental. Alain Touraine wrote:

> Aucune expérience n'est plus centrale que ce rapport à l'autre par lequel l'un et l'autre se constituent comme sujets. Mais il serait artificiel d'opposer cette relation privée à la vie publique. Tous les individus sont pris dans un réseau de roles, existent pour autrui, et la rencontre de l'autre ne s'opère jamais en terrain découvert, comme dans une image de film où deux personnages surgissent, l'un face à l'autre, dans un décor vide.[34]

This transformation is of enormous importance for understanding the modern world, in respect of which for the first time it may be said that 'I is not Ego' or 'je n'est pas moi'. Subjectivation takes on an important meaning for the construction of a picture of modern civilization. It is defined by Touraine as 'le contraire de la soumission de l'individu à des valeurs transcendantes: l'homme se projetait en Dieu; désormais, dans le monde moderne, c'est lui qui devient le

Figure 5.1   **The relationship between instinctive work, labour and creativity**

instinctive work	labour	creativity
instinktive Taetigkeit	Arbeit (?)	Kreativitaet
(?)	travail (?)	creativité
instinktivniy troud	troud (?)	tvorchestvo

Table 5.1   The characteristics of work[32]

	Work (Arbeit, travail, troud)		
	Instinctive work	Labour	Creativity
Motive of activity	internal	external	internal
Character of activity	irrational	rational	rational
Type of activity	biological process	processing of goods	self-realization
Meaning of activity	reproduction of Nature	reproduction of the social structure	reproduction of the creative self
Type of resulting material product	inalienable and irreproducible	alienable and reproducible	alienable and and irreproducible
Relationship between man and Nature	man as a simple part of Nature	man directly opposes Nature	man as an embodiment of Nature

fondement des valeurs, puisque le principe central de la moralité devient la liberté, une créativité qui est sa propre fin et s'oppose à toutes les formes de dépendance'.[35]

'The new society ... now beginning to take form, will encourage a crazy-quilt pattern of evanescent life-styles ... [It] requires ... people richly different from one another'[36] and this requirement becomes the most fundamental for the modern world.

Considering these problems, we will note that in Marxian theory it was also often underlined that, on the one hand, creative activity was primarily directed at the creator himself and that its basis was 'not a limited material result but a manifestation and development of man's ability for self-production'.[37] On the other hand, creativity is in essence interpersonal and 'creative essential forces are totally permeated by interpersonal logic' and 'it is this interpersonal nature that is the key to creativity'.[38]

We believe this brief terminological study provides a clear picture of the terminological and methodological approach we have adopted and allows us to move forward to a study of creative activity itself, its prerequisites and its forms and content in the modern world. However, first we would like to make one or two comments.

Unlike the issue of the post-economic transformation, issues regarding the theory of labour and creativity can be adequately analysed using English-language terminology. Moreover, the fairly blunt contrast of labour and creativity within the framework of the notion of work not only does not contradict the methodological approaches established in modern sociology, but, on the contrary, enables us, without entering into contradiction with the main theoretical provisions suggested by Western scholars, to give these theories a more whole and more coherent nature. In our view this aim fully reflects the main trends in the development of modern sociology.

Meanwhile, underlining the need to define labour and creativity (even on the totally subjective level), we are not attempting to study labour and creativity as exclusively sociopsychological phenomena; our main aim was and remains to analyse their role in humanity's transition to the post-economic condition. Thus from now on we will be discussing the place and role of creativity in the modern economy.

In that connection first arises the question of the conditionality of the expansion of creativity by modern material production, considered, on the one hand, as the goal of man's creative abilities and, on the other hand, as the material basis without which the formation and development of creative activity would be impossible. It is on the basis of this very analysis of material production, its dynamics, structure and development trends and the nature of the resources utilized, the requirements made of the workforce and the organization of the production processes that we can make our conclusions on the formation of the creative nature of work, one of the clearest signs of the current epoch. The second and no less important question concerns the influence of knowledge and information on social values and people's system of motivation. It is also a question about how on the basis of the headlong proliferation of knowledge and information a radical expansion of the potential of man is taking place and creativity is becoming the very activity that realistically determines the nature of the coming epoch.

The Prerequisites for the Formation of Creative Activity

Appraising the prerequisites for the formation of creativity, it should be noted that practically all the changes taking place in society today are to a greater or lesser degree having an influence on this profoundly global process. Therefore the division of prerequisites into largely material or objective and largely intellectual or subjective is fairly conditional. Considering them as two groups of factors, we were not trying to stress their relative independence in the real world, but to give our study the most structured nature possible.

The prerequisites that we call largely material are made up of phenomena that mark the achievement by the economic forms inherent to the industrial society of a certain boundary, after which a major transformation will come. Meanwhile, these processes – the tertiarization of the economy, the expansion of the output of unique and irreproducible goods and the formation of production structures that reflect the new conditions – are regarded primarily as the development of economic systems that originated in their previous forms but have a significant social component, since they cannot be considered without an appraisal of modern man as a subject of both production and consumption.

The prerequisites that we regard as primarily subjective, despite being largely connected with the process of the formation of new personal characteristics, are also to a large degree dependent on the development of material production and the evolution of the economic structure of society. The growing well-being that is facilitating the formation of a system of post-materialist values, new opportunities for the manifestation of economic and individual freedom and the swift proliferation of knowledge and information in society are all to a greater or lesser degree based on the progress of social production and therefore, in this respect, even the primarily subjective prerequisites for creative activity presuppose a close association with the economic development.

Therefore the study of objective and subjective prerequisites for creativity will be interrelated and mutually supplementary. However, it must be most categorically stated that the objective and subjective prerequisites alike facilitate the formation of creativity, not as an activity that contradicts the *gesellschaftliche Charakter* or social nature of modern society, but as an activity that facilitates the transition from *oekonomische* to *post-oekonomische Gesellschaft*.

The Development of Material Production and Economic Structures: The Objective Component of the Prerequisites for Creativity

The progress of the secondary and tertiary sectors of the economy is today marked by a multitude of new phenomena that can be sorted into three main groups. The first group shows the shift away from the secondary sector to the service economy in terms of both employment and output. The second group indicates changes in the very nature of goods and their increasing irreproducibility. The third group shows the development of organizational structures of production under the influence of both social and economic factors. The expansion of the internal world and the development of abilities of man as the subject of production are both the basis and the consequence of such processes both in the secondary and tertiary sectors. However, this issue will be given more attention later.

The essence of the phenomena currently to be observed in modern production is the formation of social rather than economic regulation of the world. These changes are of an enormous scale and very difficult to conceptualize. Alvin Toffler wrote: 'What is happening, therefore, is a thoroughgoing reconceptualization of the meaning of production and of the institution that, until now, has been charged with organizing it.'[39] Regarding economic organizations, it might be said: 'If we set up a continuum, with economizing at one end of the scale ... and sociologizing at another, then in the last thirty years the corporation has been moving steadily ... towards the sociologizing end of the scale.'[40] However, this phenomenon represents just one side of 'sociologizing', which includes a whole range of the most diverse processes, some of them 'of the economizing mode of thought', as Bell said.[41] And although the progress of production, being the unchanging background against which the new man is emerging, has at least until recently been to a greater degree the cause rather than the consequence of social transformation, the economy, previously determined by the technical abilities of productive capacity and the economic abilities of the consumer, is now increasingly developing under the influence of the needs of man to realize himself both in consumption and in production.

In our view, even a quick consideration of the problems as they are stated is enough to be convinced of the scale of the changes that are taking place and their significance in the formation of conditions that facilitate the unfolding of creativity as the main form of human activity in the framework of the emerging post-industrial society. The first significant transformation – the shift in production towards the tertiary sector – has already been noted in the works of classical post-industrialism. When Bell stressed the importance of the fact that 'a post-industrial society is based on services'[42] he was talking about one of the basic changes that was already and obviously manifesting itself in the late 1960s.

The expansion of the service economy, which is of great importance for the understanding of the nature and direction of the change in modern society, takes two different and specific forms. One of those forms is the change in the structure of employment, of which much has been said and much is still being said. The other is the change in the share of material production and services in the economy and is much less frequently studied. Only a comprehensive approach that takes account of both these manifestations of the expanding service economy can give us an adequate understanding of the structure of modern social production. It should, however, be borne in mind that each of these well-observed trends has its own no less weighty countertrend and that the arguments of those who deny that today's economy can be described as a service economy are highly convincing.

The restructuring of employment is salient: masses of people are lured from primitive manual and monotonous labour into the production of technically complex goods and services. In 1850, '60 per cent of the working population of the United States were employed in agriculture. Today, less than 2.7 per cent of the workforce is engaged directly in farming'.[43] The number of people employed in the production of goods and services, respectively, in the United States was about 13 million and not more than five million in 1900. By the end of the 1980s, the figures were 35 million and 65 million, respectively.[44] These and similar examples could be continued infinitely.

Statistical studies show that two radical breakthroughs were made over the last few decades, in the late 1970s and late 1980s, respectively, in the United States. The first breakthrough marked the end of the growth in the absolute number of people employed in the processing industries. The second marked the end of the growth in the absolute number of people engaged in construction and transport. In the early 1990s, US material-sector employment started to decline in absolute terms. Employment in extractive and manufacturing industries, respectively, fell by more than 41 per cent and 11 per cent between 1980 and 1994. The drop in employment in construction was 4 per cent between 1990 and 1994 alone. Figures for employment in transport were unchanged.[45] Absolute numbers for those employed in manufacturing industries began to fall in European nations even earlier: in 1972 in Germany and in 1975 in France. This may be explained by the fact that the share of employees in manufacturing industries was higher in France and Germany than in the United States. But that has been compensated for by the fact that employment in manufacturing industries fell more steeply in Europe than in the United States in the 1970s–1990s.[46]

However, it has to be said that the contraction in manufacturing employment does not allow us to understand the full scale of the changes taking place. It would be more consistent to study in what way and to what degree 'the shift from the Second Wave manufacturing to the new, more advanced Third Wave manufacturing reduces ... the number of workers who actually have to manipulate physical goods'[47] and, consequently, to work out exactly how many people are directly engaged in manufacturing operations.

David Birch of the Massachusetts Institute of Technology (MIT) in the early 1980s worked out that no more than 12 per cent of the American workforce was directly engaged in manufacturing operations.[48] Ten years later, Taichi Sakaiya carried out more detailed research that showed that the number was declining in line with the growth of company size. He wrote: 'The study tells us that in manufacturing enterprises with staffs totalling 100 or more employees … 60.2 percent of employees were engaged in direct production … but among companies with 1,000 or more employees, the number of employees involved in direct production dropped to only 54.9 percent';[49] he calculated that the actual share of the workforce directly engaged in manufacturing operations is less than 10 per cent in the United States and about 12 per cent in Japan.[50] The contraction of the manufacturing workforce in the 1990s may be going relatively slowly in the United States, but in Japan manufacturing employment, which was measured by Peter Drucker at about 30 per cent for the total workforce in the mid-1990s, is expected to halve by the end of the century.[51] Thus less than 5 per cent of the population will be engaged in manufacturing by the year 2000.

There are, however, very strong counter-arguments. Scholars, competing to find the lowest possible share of the workforce that could be engaged directly in manufacturing operations, believe that the category itself is only to be found in the secondary sector. There are workers who are not involved directly in such operations in the secondary sector. But there are also workers in the tertiary sector who are not directly involved in the production of services but who are involved in the production of their material prerequisites. It took scholars until the mid-1990s to understand that only about half of those employed in manufacturing are directly engaged in manufacturing operations. Yet Jonathan Gershuny in the mid-1970s pointed out that 'nearly half of the working population were employed in tertiary industry, less than a quarter of it – 23.1 percent – was involved in providing for the final consumption of services'.[52] There are now twice as many people employed in the tertiary sector as in manufacturing. We shall note here that there is a reverse side to the transition from a manufacturing economy to a service economy that has received much less analysis.

Growth in employment in the production of services and information does not mean that the manufacturing sector is in decline. The opposite, indeed, is true. Technological progress and the development of information technology has penetrated the secondary sector to enable many nations to actually increase production of material goods over recent decades without having to increase consumption of energy and materials[53] or to attract greater workforces. In 1988, just 40 per cent as much blue-collar labour was required to generate the same amount of US industrial output as in 1973. United States Steel provides a good example: in 1980, it 'employed 120,000 people in steel production. Ten years later, it employed 20,000 people in steel production, and yet produced almost the same steel tonnage. Within ten years the productivity of the manual worker engaged in steelmaking had increased seven-fold …

The lion's share of the jump in productivity represents the results of reengineering work flow and tasks'.[54] As a result, 'manufacturing is increasingly becoming uncoupled from labour'.[55]

Drucker said in a different work,

These trends are certain to continue. Unless there is a severe depression, manufacturing production in America is likely to stay at about the same 23 percent of gross national product, which, for the next ten or fifteen years, should mean another near doubling. During the same period, however, employment in manufacturing is likely to fall to 12 percent or less of the total labor force. That would mean a further fairly sharp shrinkage of the total number of people employed in manufacturing work.[56]

Thus the modern economy is a service economy by employment rather than by the share of the tertiary sector in the social product.

There is another significant process to be found behind these figures. Of course, the pace of growth in the service sector is impressive on its own – US gross domestic product has grown by a factor of 11.9 over the last 35 years – but growth in all the sectors of material production (including warehousing and trade) has lagged behind that level. Growth was recorded at factors of 5.4 for agriculture, 6.75 for extractive industries, 7.4 for manufacturing industries, 9.57 for construction and 11.2 for trade. Growth in the service sectors was recorded at factors of 14.1 for government administration, 15.43 for communications, 15.78 for finance and insurance and 24 for personal services.[57] But there is yet another phenomenon, which to a certain extent already pertains to the problem of the new nature of the goods generated in the tertiary sector. Despite higher incomes, high qualifications and generally better job satisfaction, employees in the service and information sectors tend to be less productive than those in the primary and secondary sectors by traditional measures. Service-sector workers in 1960 generated just about 77.5 per cent as much GDP (gross domestic product) as workers in material sectors. By 1992, that figure had fallen to 69.35 per cent. Comparative productivity thus fell by 0.35 per cent a year in the service sector (which includes the production of information and knowledge) over the period. The gap in productivity seems to be widening even more quickly in recent years. The relative decline was as much as 0.37 per cent between 1980 and 1992.[58]

The dynamics of the relationship between material production and the service sector, and primarily the contraction in employment in material production, shows that society is able to use an increasingly large part of its aggregate labour time, not to satisfy the material needs of its members, but to provide for future development and for human needs that until very recently were not considered to be a priority. Thus we can see a salient reduction in the influence of directly material requirements, characteristic of the economic epoch, on modern man.

The second important characteristic of the modern changes is to be found in the growing irreproducibility of goods created in both the secondary and tertiary sectors. Here we find that the two manifestations of the growing sociologizing of production are merged into one. On the one hand, the development of the manufacturing process itself is increasingly dependent on progress in technology and information to cut costs and make products more competitive. On the other hand, the growing significance of demand has to be noted as it becomes increasingly diverse, making so-called 'prestige consumption' one of the most important determinants of economic behaviour.

The unique and irreproducible nature of many material goods and services is one of the characteristics of modern society. Speaking of the irreproducibility of a good or a service, we are trying to define them as not pertaining to mass-production. One of the aspects of this is the individual nature of the goods. Another is the specific nature of the activity of which it is a result. In both cases there are substantial hurdles for the application of traditional economic theory to any appraisal of the corresponding goods. We shall cover this factor in more detail in the next chapter. One way or another, the labour theory of value is faced by the fact that the goods entail neither the cost of reproduction nor labour that could be reduced to the simple labour that lies at the basis of value. Concepts based on interpretations of utility and alternative cost meet difficulties of another kind.

It should be stressed that one of the main factors determining the irreproducibility of goods, services and information is the interpersonal interaction that is manifested during both production and consumption. Firstly, during the creation of a knowledge-intensive product or, to a greater degree, of information, the process of production is to a significant extent identical to the process of communication between the individual creating the given product or information and the creator of other knowledge. Such a dialogue may or may not be made in person, that is of no importance: it is that very consumption of information, received by other scholars, that, with all its subjectivity, is identical to the formation and accumulation of new knowledge. Secondly, the consumption of both information and the products of a number of industries in the tertiary sector, including education and healthcare and, to a greater degree, culture, requires substantial effort from the consumer and the effect of such consumption can depend substantially on the nature of human perception.

Services and products that entail interpersonal interaction are the least reproducible and are the least appropriate for traditional economic appraisal. Yet it is these very sectors that are enjoying the highest growth in terms of GDP. The secondary sector of the US economy grew by a factor of 1.8 between 1980 and 1983 at actual prices. Traditional services, like repairs, hospitality, personal and social services, rose by just 42 per cent. Growth in business services, education and healthcare was more than a factor of 1.8. The growth figure for information, legal services and entertainment was a factor of 2.2.[59]

All this once again goes to show that mass-production under the laws of industrial society is quickly becoming a thing of the past. Thus, without even considering the increasing level of skills in traditional industries, it can be said that 'in 1990, 47.4 percent of the employed population in the United States, 45.8 percent in the United Kingdom, 45.1 percent in France, and 40.0 percent in West Germany were engaged in information-processing activities, whether in the production of goods or in the provision of services, and the proportion continues to rise over time'.[60] Hence the notion that no more than half of the workforce can be engaged in information processing[61] could be disproved within the very near future.

The third fundamental characteristic of the modern economic system is the radical change in organization structures that supplement the general transformation of the industrial economy into the post-industrial production of irreproducible goods and services. Toffler described this restructuring as a shift away from the provision of material needs to the provision of human needs,[62] understood in their full diversity. The very nature of knowledge workers adds a special drama: they are driven by the desire for autonomy and independence, they

> are neither farmers nor labour nor business. They are employees of organizations ... They are not 'proletarians' and do not feel 'exploited' as a class ... It makes absolutely no difference to their economic or social position whether they work for a business, for a hospital, or for a university. Knowledge workers ... are not changing social or economic position. They are changing a job.[63]

It is the very fact that an increasingly large number of people, to use Drucker's words, 'work with a company, for example doing its data processing, but do not work for the company, and are not its employees'[64] that explains the unprecedented boom in small businesses and self-employment. A total of about 20.7 million full-time home-based businesses were set up in 1995 in the United States.[65] Many of those businesses are in high-tech fields. The share of the 500 biggest US companies in gross national product has fallen from 20 per cent in 1970 to just 10 per cent today. In 1996, companies employing 19 or fewer employees accounted for half of all US exports. Companies employing more than 500 people accounted for just 7 per cent of exports.[66]

These figures to a significant degree continue to illustrate the problem of developing the production of unique and irreproducible goods, but they also reflect a new organizational trend with which the modern corporation must contend. Business leaders, prompted by an understanding that companies perform better when they do not separate ownership and participation and activity and supervision and give their employees the chance to manifest their responsibility and undergo self-development,[67] have restructured corporate management away from familiar hierarchical principles to give managers and workers alike a wider role in decision and policy making.[68]

This new trend in management, however, has brought a whole range of consequences for big corporations. Participatory management systems improve efficiency but they also engender a spirit of experimentation and risk that, at least in those nations that have strong traditions of individualism but are not governed by salient paternalist principles, often leads to the emergence of new research and manufacturing structures that frequently set out on their own to pose dangerous competition for the parent company.

The forms and direction of the development of modern production are, one might say, the most distant and indirect prerequisites for the development of creativity. Reflecting the natural evolution of production structures, they nevertheless underline the role and significance of modern types of activity for the further progress of those structures. Representing certain elements of creativity, awakening in people on a massive scale, the new types of activity to an even greater degree become the conditions for their further intensive development. Even at this level of study it can be said that it is impossible to distinguish the material and personal factors of production, which dominated the economized society, in modern economic systems. The erasure of this distinction is a factor of the progress of creative activity, which is fully provided for by the new forms of production.

Making certain conclusions on those trends in the development of the modern economic structure that were noted at the beginning of this section, we highlight the following. Firstly, despite all the existing counter-trends, a significant section of the aggregate workforce is shifting to those sectors of the economy where the main type of activity is merely the delivery of the final product to the consumer rather than a direct interaction of man with the material elements of nature. The share of services in total household consumption in Japan and the United States had reached 50 per cent by the beginning of the 1980s,[69] and is continuing to grow steadily. Without asserting that work in service sub-sectors close to material production are more creative than those directly engaged in material production, we shall note that the corresponding shift in the distribution of the workforce marked the decreasing dependence of man on activity that is directly determined by material necessity. The very fact that society is able to direct an ever-increasing share of its workforce into industries that do not produce material goods and that, according to traditional measures, are clearly less productive than material industries shows that there is a decline in the pressure on man of that necessity which brought about the main institutions of the economic society.

Secondly, the production of irreproducible goods and services expands the opportunities of the individual and requires the development of new abilities in both production and consumption. Toffler's notion of a 'prosumer'[70] is not exhausted merely by the erasure of the distinction between leisure and labour time. A more systemic transformation is taking place in today's world that primarily consists of the emergence of a large sector, in which the production of goods is inseparable from the consumption of the subjectivized conditions of production and the consumption of produced services requires the active participation of the consumer, his independent and far from traditional effort. Thus interpersonal interaction emerges and expands to serve as a crucial prerequisite for creativity on the individual level. The development of the creative powers of the individual, determined, among other factors, by the growing number of goods, the consumption of which is impossible without the creative potential of the individual, is also manifested in the process of production, where the desire of the individual for self-realization and self-development radically transforms traditional forms of economic organizations.

Thirdly, modern trends in the development of industrial production and the new preferences and guidelines of the personalities of the producers themselves have led to a radical shift away from traditional forms of economic organization and an expansion of small-scale production and self-employment in all developed nations. This phenomenon, unlike the change in the structure of employment, which is a distant signal demonstrating the possibility of an expansion of creative activity, and the growth in interpersonal interaction, which is the most obvious form of the materialization of creativity, is to a significant degree the first example of the manifestation of creative activity changing the bases of the modern social structure. Therefore a more detailed analysis of this phenomenon will be given a little later, when we study the very forms of the embodiment of creative activity in the modern world and the nature of their influence on social relations and processes.

Now we turn to an analysis of the second group of prerequisites for the development of creativity, to the processes which have marked the formation of the human personality as a subject of creativity. At the current level of the development of society, the most salient form of this process becomes increasingly high levels of education.

The Growth of Human Opportunities: The Subjective Component of the Prerequisites for Creativity

The development of the modern economy, according to its internal laws, with each year becomes increasingly dependent on human creative activity. Such activity becomes absolutely essential both for the development of production itself and for the consistent consumption of its results. Therefore the second aspect of the problem of the formation of the prerequisites for creative activity is the provision of conditions that facilitate the adequate satisfaction of this demand for creative activity. The latter may be regarded as the formation of a series of prerequisites for creative activity on the subjective individual level rather than on the objective economic level. In this connection we would like to emphasize a number of far from unimportant factors.

Firstly, although there were precedents of creative activity at all stages of the progress of humanity, and history is full of such inspiring examples, the formation of creativity as an activity capable of contradicting economic laws in the whole of society is only possible when society itself and the majority of its members reach a level of material well-being high enough to form new values that determine a new system of priorities and aims for individuals.

Secondly, society must be ready not only to recognize the desire of individuals to develop their abilities but to provide the degree of freedom consistent with creative activity and perceived as the basic value of the modern society. As Toffler wrote: 'The people of both past and present are still locked into relatively choiceless life ways. The people of the future, whose number increases daily, face not choice but overchoice. For them there comes an explosive extension of freedom ... The new society ... now beginning to take form, will encourage a crazy-quilt pattern of evanescent life styles.'[71]

Thirdly, an important component of the life of an increasing number of modern people should become the constant consumption and generation of information. The society taking form today is not one of information technology and professionals (Frank Webster is right to say that 'there is no inherent reason why increases in professionals, even striking ones, should lead one to conclude that a new age is upon us'[72] but a society of knowledge and innovators. Moreover, knowledge is distinguished from the collection of facts because it is information that has been subjectified. This third factor is today, in our view, becoming the most fundamental and the development of the processes connected with the formation of a new stratum focused on the consumption and production of knowledge is having a significant influence on processes at both the psychological and social levels.

Initiating our analysis with an appraisal of material well-being as a factor preparing man for the assimilation of a new motivational structure of activity, we shall make a number of important preliminary remarks. It has to be stressed that there is no direct relation between the degree of well-being and the level of creativity. Creative activity is a phenomenon much more complex than the simple reaction of man to the achievement of a certain level of material well-being. The latter, undoubtedly, facilitates the conception of non-economic values,[73] but it cannot become the only or even the main reason for creativity. A certain correlation may, however, be made between economic success of a nation and the relatively abstract notion of life satisfaction. In some works this correlation is made to appear very close indeed.[74] However, this does not directly pertain to the problem of creativity.

It is more correct to study the problem from the point of view of the primarily material or the primarily immaterial nature of the motivation for activity. Such an approach demonstrates that there is no direct link between the level of well-being and the prevalence of post-materialist values. Indeed, there appear to be stronger materialist values among the better-off than among other social groups.[75] Meanwhile, applied sociological research shows that those with post-materialist values are mostly young and began their independent adult lives in the 1970s or 1980s. They are distinguished more by a high degree of education and desire for social recognition than by their material well-being. The main conclusion derived from this fact may sound unexpected but we believe it is absolutely right: 'In the very nature of things, Postmaterialists tend to be those who start life with all the advantages; to a considerable extent, that is why they are Postmaterialists.'[76] The fact that post-materialist, creative values are not cultivated at a mature age but are built up from an early age, in a very special way ties the formation of creative stereotypes of behaviour to the general level of material well-being. Moreover, the widespread expansion of the new trends will only become possible as and when the new generation replaces the old. Inglehart, referring to the 1980s, said: 'Postmaterialism rose substantially, but virtually all of this change *was due to intergenerational population replacement*'[77] (emphasis added). Those who from a young age strive to achieve economic success are much less likely eventually to assimilate creative models of behaviour and bear post-materialist values.[78] Therefore material well-being, which without doubt facilitates the expansion of post-economic imperatives, cannot be strictly defined as one of its causes and is merely an (albeit important) prerequisite for following such imperatives. Two other factors to be considered below we believe to be of much greater significance.

We must therefore once again stress that economic and social freedom, which is not merely permitted, but even welcomed and cultivated, is a major factor for the progress of modern society. As a manifestation of the 'sociologising' mentioned above, the freedom of the individual is both the cause and the consequence of economic progress. In our view it is impossible to draw a clear line of cause and effect between the development of new social institutions, the formation of new types of social values and economic progress: these processes are profoundly intertwined and today it increasingly seems as if it is the very development of the personality that is the main motor of economic evolution. Touraine in this respect characteristically defined economic progress without freedom as modernization and not development.[79]

The significance of freedom is enormous. It best embodies the desire 'for the fulfillment and enhancement of the self'[80] that is one of the fundamental signs of the post-industrial society. It is freedom that best constitutes the main characteristics of modern society since without freedom it is impossible to create and distribute the knowledge and information that become, as Toffler described them, not only 'the most democratic source of power'[81] today but the main productive resource of modern society. Toffler wrote:

> All economic systems sit upon a 'knowledge base'. All business enterprises depend on the preexistence of this socially constructed resource. Unlike capital, labor, and land, it is usually neglected by economists and business executives when calculating the 'inputs' needed for production. Yet this resource – partly paid for, partly exploited free of charge – is now the most important of all.[82]

The greater the significance of knowledge for modern society, the clearer we understand that it is based on individual creative activity, an activity built on freedom, expressed in freedom and developing freedom. The development of modern technologies is destroying the old barriers and traditional forms of community. Man is becoming free from his familiar forms of communication, overcoming at the same time familiar limitations in space and time.[83] This peculiar destruction of previous forms of human community must not be regarded, as it often is, as a negative phenomenon since it provides an opportunity for the swift advancement and development of the most complex and important individual skills and abilities for modern society. Peter Drucker pointed out that 'innovation cannot be done by committee ... Successful innovators build teams, but they do not work in a team. They work alone and by themselves'.[84] This means that 'the new responsibility of society is to reward the initiative of the individual'[85] and that society must value and respect 'the individual entrepreneur who starts a business on his own, rather than give all approval to the organization man'.[86]

Knowledge always emancipated man and the progress of science is one of the few processes that was never suspended during all the stages and epochs of the history of civilization. However, changes introduced in the modern world by the information revolution, the formation of a new man and significant achievements in material production today allow us to apply knowledge primarily to knowledge itself, as to the main and self-sufficient production factor, rather than to the improvement of tools of production, which engendered the industrial revolution, or to work itself and its organization, which led to the productivity revolution.[87] A whole new social reality has emerged when knowledge has become a force in itself, when science has fully proved its power to transform nature and when the possession of information has become a recognized condition for a worthy place in society.

G.K.Chesterton, discussing the traditions of European philosophy, noted that a certain continuity was lost when modern society came into being: 'It was there, if anywhere, that there was lost or impatiently snapped the long thin delicate thread that had descended from distant antiquity; the thread of that unusual human hobby; the habit *of thinking*' (emphasis added).[88] The desire for thinking was replaced by the desire to know typical of a European science of the 18th and 19th centuries that was experimental and prone to generalizations. Today's transition, in our view, marks the shift from the desire to know to the desire to experience. Only when knowledge became, not merely a source of understanding the world, but a self-sufficient condition for its change in the course of everyday activity, did the giant educational revolution begin. By bringing into being such an important prerequisite for creative activity as education or learnedness, it has radically changed the face of the modern world.

The desire for education and knowledge as the main social priorities was most clearly manifested straight after the end of the Second World War.[89] In the United States there were just three college graduates for every 100 workers before the Great Depression. But by the middle of the 1950s there were already 18 college graduates for every 100 workers.[90] The share of management in the staff of companies rose from 4 per cent in 1940 to 14 per cent in 1990.[91] The number of scientists and research workers increased by more than a factor of 10 between the beginning of the 1930s and the middle of the 1960s.[92]

The immediate postwar period brought the highest figures for the advance of education and research. All post-industrial scholars describe this educational boom as one of the main signs of the birth of a new social structure. This can be shown by the fact that practically a quarter of Bell's best-known work[93] was devoted exclusively to a detailed analysis of the expansion of knowledge and information in American society and the corresponding social processes. As a result, many rushed to say that Marx's fundamental conflict between the bourgeoisie and the proletariat had been overcome and that it could be said that 'the working class as it appears in Marx's *Capital* no longer exists'.[94] Differences between formulas used by various scholars[95] do not change the fundamental thrust of their interpretation. Regarding knowledge as the key production resource of modern society and believing that its economic utilization was embodied in the economics of symbols and signs, Toffler introduces the notion of the 'cognitariat' as a new social group capable of replacing the proletariat: 'as the super-symbolic economy unfolds, the proletariat becomes a cognitariat'.[96]

However, in our view the problems that would necessarily emerge as the result of such a transformation should not be underestimated. Firstly, as practice shows, the swift growth of education and the advancement of the workforce have their limits. Today most nations – both developed post-industrial powers and the fast-developing nations at their heels – still have significant populations untouched by the educational revolution (in addition, the pace of the development of education in them does not satisfy the economic needs), despite severe shortages of qualified personnel. In the United States in the mid-1990s there were 12.5 million students 'in institutions of higher learning beyond secondary school',[97] yet about 20 per cent of the population has just four to six years of schooling, about the same proportion as at the beginning of the century.[98] Similar processes are under way in the 'tiger economies' of Asia, where there are still not enough graduates to meet fast-growing production[99] and a substantial portion of the population has nothing but the most primitive education, despite the fact that the number of students grows by 15–20 per cent every five years.

Secondly, new social stratification emerges, which today can be best seen in the contrast between the developed industrialized nations and the Third World. Usually, when the growing divide between the rich and poor nations of the world is being underlined, it is said that developing nations account for three-quarters of world population but just 25–30 per cent of world industrial output. Yet that divide is not nearly as frightful as the fact that developing nations have just 3 per cent of the world's scientific potential.[100] The swift economic and social progress of the post-industrial nations could bring significant negative processes on a global scale.

Thirdly, the growing isolation of strata and social groups that have access to knowledge and information is becoming increasingly salient within the advanced societies themselves. In recent years it has become increasingly regularly pointed out that, together with the development of the personality and the expansion of creative activity, the swift growth of the intellectual potential of a nation and the conversion of the proletariat into a cognitariat prompts a new kind of social conflict: 'Noneconomic issues,' wrote Ronald Inglehart, 'take an increasingly important place on the national agenda, giving rise to a new axis of political polarization, [based on materialist/post-materialist dimension], reflecting the contrast between two fundamentally different worldviews'.[101] Drucker said the same thing, only in a different way. Recognising that the problems caused by the accumulation of information and the educational revolution were not of a purely economic nature, he stressed that that did not make them of any less importance:

> The centre of gravity in production, and especially in manufacturing, then shifts from manual workers to knowledge workers. Far more middle-class jobs are being created by this process than old blue-collar jobs are being lost. Overall the process enriches as much as did the creation of well-paid blue-collar jobs in the last hundred years. We do not, in other words, face an economic problem; nor is there much danger of 'alienation' and of creating a new 'class war'... [but] that a substantial and growing number of people with working-class backgrounds sit long enough in schools to become knowledge workers will only make things worse for those who don't. The less schooled will increasingly be seen by their more successful fellows ... as 'failures', as 'dropouts', as somehow 'deficient', as 'second-class citizens', as 'problems', and altogether as 'inferior'. The problem is not money. It is *dignity*.[102]

Thus the educational revolution provides enormous opportunities for the expansion of creativity, preparing whole social strata to accept creative values and people to realize themselves as creative individuals. That is beyond doubt. The three fundamental processes – the heightened well-being of most members of society and the conditions for young people to accept post-materialist values and non-economic motivation; the development of social and political systems that provide increasing freedom for self-expression and the allowance of non-traditional behaviour as a necessary condition for the development of the individual; and the ever-wider proliferation of information, the unfolding of the educational revolution – prepare the modern individual for creative activity and form him as a man of the post-economic society.

This process inevitably entails a whole range of contradictions, some of which we have tried to note. The very conditions of the formation of post-materialist values and the inertia of human consciousness could not but prompt a conflict between generations of a greater or lesser degree and hardly surmountable during the transitional period. The desire to maximize the manifestations of the human personality under democracy cannot but be accompanied by the activization of various destructive movements, groups and communities, whose activities are at a severe dissonance with the main trends of social evolution. The proliferation of knowledge and the increasingly clear formation of a class of knowledge workers will undoubtedly be accompanied by new social conflicts and reproduce the stratification of society, with the only difference being that the boundaries of those strata and the principles of their distinction will be very different from those familiar to traditional sociology.

This does not show, in our view, that recent decades have uncovered counter-trends that could act as a barrier to the formation of a post-economic society. Indeed, such phenomena should serve to dispel dangerous illusions of the possibility of forming a totally new organization of humanity unlike any other.

It should again be said that, in discussing *post-oekonomische Gesellschaft* we are talking about a form of *Gesellschaft* that retains and will retain all the qualities of a society or *Gesellschaft*: the division of society into social groups, conflicts between those groups, a centralized organizational structure serving as a sort of pivot for a society, and also a conflict of interests, although this latter conflict should not depend so unswervingly on material interests as its equivalent in the economic society.

We regard creativity as the main type of activity in the post-economic society. Creativity is not the kind of unmotivated activity that is asocial because it contradicts the main principles of the construction of *Gesellschaft*, but is an activity motivated in a non-traditional way typical of the new society. Meanwhile, any type of motivation for activity in the framework of society reflects its social nature and therefore creative activity, which is internally free in terms of its prerequisites and motives, cannot be free externally in forms that represent a danger for the *Gesellschaft* as a whole. Maintaining a balance between the freedom concealed in creative activity as its source and the freedom which it embodies in its manifestation, in forms which optimize the advancement of the social whole, is one of the key tasks facing the social institutions of the post-economic society.

An analysis of the prerequisites for the formation of creative activity to a certain degree, as shown above, coincides with an analysis of its development and even its influence upon the main social institutions and the individual himself. At the same time the study of the main forms of human activity and, primarily, creativity, requires a more detailed and complex analysis of those processes and phenomena which are to a greater extent the result of the development of the trends we have noted rather than their prerequisites. Therefore we begin our analysis with the manifestations of creative activity in modern conditions at the level of the individual producer, before moving on to a more detailed appraisal of the influence of these manifestations upon economic organizations in modern society; in conclusion, we consider the formation of a new system of values and preferences in the framework of society as a whole.

How Creativity Is Manifested in Modern Society

Creativity in modern society is not contrasted with labour in the way that, say, services contrast with material products. Today, as never before, creativity and labour are highly unified in work, and in the real world it is impossible to disengage the two. Therefore we are trying to focus attention on the formation of certain characteristics of creativity within the framework of the notion of work. However, since work is nothing more than a process carried out by specific individuals, their communities and society as a whole, creativity must be analysed through its objective manifestations in the social structure.

We will base our considerations of the forms of manifestation of creative activity on the fact that, although the prerequisites for such activity were primarily conditioned by the development of the social whole, the actual realization of such activity begins with a change in the aims and nature of the behaviour of the individuals that make up the social whole. In any sphere of human activity, creativity is primarily an individual process that, prompted by the desire of the individual for self-realization, fosters the development of a more advanced personality through the individual effort of that personality. This autonomous nature of the creative individual is not absolute: existing within organizations and society, the individual is constantly entering into corresponding relations with counter-agents and the interpersonal nature of creativity is as characteristic of the activity as of its internal prerequisites. Nevertheless, creative activity is formed as a mere reflection of social process in a specific individual.

Therefore below we will try to reconstruct the process of the formation of creative activity on the level of an individual and appraise the influence of that process on the modern economy; later we will turn to creative activity on the level of the modern economic organization – the production firm or corporation; and, lastly, we will consider the question of the realization of the elements of creativity at the level of society as a whole and the formation of new social relations and institutions.

Elements of Creativity and Individual Behaviour

When we said very recently that the basic factor of the economic process was the individual, we meant that the individual is regarded as one of the main elements of the production system, as the embodiment of knowledge and skills that are often called 'professionalism'. In modern conditions the individual remains the main factor of progress, but now as a creative individual with qualities that until very recently were thought to bear no relation to economic laws.

Recognizing information and knowledge as the key resources of production, scholars in recent years have increasingly come to the conclusion that the expansion of the knowledge economy, which is determining the face of a changing society, is conditioned by a whole range of human qualities fairly fully developed by the eve of the millennium.[103] The development of creative activity which, based on internal non-economic motivation, is of a highly interpersonal nature, means that the economic progress is affected as much by the way in which an individual perceives himself and his world and how he relates to himself, his peers and his environment as by information and knowledge.[104] Imagination and not information becomes pre-eminent[105] and, as Habermas wrote, 'money and power can neither buy nor compel solidarity and meaning'.[106] This cannot be overstated. The formation of belief systems at the levels of the corporation, community and society is becoming no less important than the system of economic administration.[107]

The interaction of people as integral personalities and not simple elements of the system of production is becoming the basis of the formation for the formation of the social whole. James Robertson was quite right when he wrote that 'the 21st century economy ... must systematically foster self-reliance and the capacity for self-development. Self-reliance does not mean self-sufficiency or selfish isolation. It requires the capacity to co-operate freely with others. Self-development includes the development of the capacity for co-operative self-reliance'.[108] As a result, the situation arises when new products and services are created by new information and new employees rather than by the development of new technology and production processes, as was the case a few decades ago. When we say today that 'products and technologies ... are increasingly "new" we primarily mean that employees are also new: new to the system; new to each other; new to their tasks'.[109]

Creativity, as we have already noted, is primarily an individual process. Triggered by internal motives, the desire of the individual for self-development and self-realization, creativity is social by nature and individual in character. Undoubtedly, this distinction is highly conditional, since any manifestation of creativity inevitably affects social relations and institutions in the same way that any development in those relations and institutions in one way or another affects the opportunities for and perspectives of creative activity. However, we believe that in our theoretical analysis the distinction of the personal and social aspects of creativity is perfectly allowable and expedient.

The principal manifestations of creative activity are to be seen in the emergence of new behaviour stereotypes, the development of inner motivation as the main factor determining human actions, the greater independence and autonomy enjoyed by modern workers that often manifest themselves in individualism and, perhaps as a counter-trend to the latter, the formation of new kinds of collectives and communities that facilitate the development of the abilities and talents to unite creative individuals in a way that does not entail their uniformity.

The overcoming of traditional values characteristic of the industrial or modern society and the formation of a new system of stimuli and motives for activity is the most salient factor introduced by the development of creativity into contemporary interpersonal relations and, as a consequence, into economic relations.[110] This process is to a significant degree conditioned by the progress of material production. Today, when 'an unprecedentedly large portion of Western populations have been raised under conditions of exceptional economic security'[111] and are as a result free of direct pressure from material requirements, there are vast opportunities for the manifestation of creative activity. Creativity is formed as a result of practically any development in modern production that leads to 'the shift from an economy geared to the provision of a few basic "gut" needs to one that concerns itself with supplying the endlessly diverse needs of the "psyche" as well'.[112]

Some scholars believe that creativity, which is connected with the growing role of inner stimuli and is partially subconscious, is primarily prompted by technical factors.[113] Others tend to stress the importance of a changing social environment, when work primarily entails 'working for yourself and even by yourself'.[114] Each of these scholars is right in his own way because creative activity is as much prepared for by the aspects of the progress of production as it is manifested in them. This serves to further affirm the notion that economic self-interest is an important motive for human actions in an industrial society to explain the simplest economic processes but that it is necessary to appeal to largely non-economic interests and motives in the analysis of complex social interaction.[115]

There has been much debate over the terminology for the new value system. Most Western scholars in the 1970s and 1980s followed Inglehart[116] in calling it 'post-materialist', by which they wished to stress the dominant role of interpersonal relations and solving general problems over high wages and social security. Later another term emerged, 'expressivism',[117] that included certain other characteristics of the value system.

Toffler was closest to the approach that we propose. He regarded the main principles of motivation as primarily a completed post-economic value system.[118] This system thus replaced rather than changed the economic system of values. Yet it was understood even before the Second World War that there was an economic and a non-economic side to any system of beliefs. Peter Drucker, in 1946, was one of the first to study non-economic needs as part of a management theory. He said that 'wants are as much an expression of non-economic needs and desires as of economic ones'.[119] Non-economic human goals were comprehensively analysed in the 1970s and 1980s, too.[120] Yet it was Toffler that first identified non-material aims and motives for individuals today as post-economic rather than non-economic, as the overcoming of the previous economic system of motivation.

All the above-mentioned notions amount to various terms for roughly the same thing: the shift from largely external motives to largely internal ones. Toffler said such a shift could take place in work that 'is "meaningful", "fulfilling", or socially "useful"'.[121] Others believe that the new system of motivation includes 'values like creativity, autonomy, rejection of authority, placing self-expression ahead of status, pleasure-seeking, the hunger for new experiences, the quest for community, participation in decision-making, the desire for adventure, closeness to nature, cultivation of self, and inner growth'.[122] As a rule, this all results in 'moving beyond the "work ethic" to a "life ethic", in which educational opportunity provides the base at any age to switch jobs ... allowing people to use their energies either in employment or community service'.[123]

Active research into changing human values began in the United States and Western Europe soon after the end of the Second World War, but it was not until the end of the 1950s and beginning of the 1960s, when the economy had fully adapted to peace, that more and more doubt was cast on the dominating role of economic and material factors in the system of motivation. There were several reasons for this.

Firstly, in industrial society itself and similar productive operations in the tertiary sector, the material requirements of the majority of workers were satisfied to a level that met most of their main desires and a simple pay rise now meant less than increasing leisure time or a greater diversity of tasks. Abraham Maslow summed up these new desires in his well known maxim: 'What a man can be, he must be. He must be true to his own nature.'[124] This, on the one hand, presupposes man's desire to maximize the satisfaction of his interests as a consumer and as a free individual. The rise in the significance of leisure time and the opportunities for self-realization beyond the process of production first emerged in the 1960s. By the beginning of the 1990s, more than 55 per cent of Americans said they would rather turn down promotion if it entailed less free time that they could spend with their families. Almost all employees were ready to accept a 5 per cent cut in wages if it entailed more leisure time.[175] On the other hand, self-realization in leisure rather than work is always limited since it is the professional activity of a person – whether an industrial worker, knowledge worker or academic – that remains the main substance of his life and it is this professional activity that should primarily be improved in line with his changing values.

Secondly, as a consequence, internally motivated activity began to appear in production processes. During the transition from industrial society to post-industrial society in the 1960s and 1970s, self-realization could not yet dominate production processes. So it was social or collective recognition of various achievements of the workers that was to be of prime importance on the scale of values. Such recognition does not necessarily have to entail a pay rise or promotion. The growing authority of the worker and his influence on the processes taking place in his organization ran parallel, as a rule, with the simplification of organization structures and the reduction in the number of management layers. Michael Hammer said that 'organizations of professionals use very few titles ... people who work in them are likely to go through their whole careers with only a single title or two. Moreover, the titles that people have will describe their professions rather than their ranks in some pecking order'.[126] In the early 1980s during the information revolution production processes shed their routine operations and turned into a field for the application of the creative abilities of workers. It was then that the expansion of non-economic motivation took place in the whole of society.

Thirdly, the knowledge sector is both expanding under the influence of creativity and providing opportunities for the expansion of creativity itself. The sharp rise in the prestige of education after the

Second World War and the formation of knowledge workers as the new class of modern society were initially based on economic motives. But, by the 1970s and 1980s, education became an end in its own right. Earlier the economic appraisal of knowledge prevailed. Knowledge, although it was more than a mere commodity, was nevertheless included in the system of commodity exchange. As a result, to quote Jean-François Lyotard, 'knowledge in the form of an informational commodity indispensable to productive power is already, and will continue to be, a major – perhaps the major – stake in the worldwide competition for power'.[127] Successes achieved by workers in the most advanced information sectors brought a desire for knowledge to open the way to the prospect of earning high wages and a high social status. Workers were ready to waive the immediate satisfaction of their material requirements and invest substantial sums in training, supposing that a college education, that, in the United States during the early post-World II years, seldom cost more than $20 000, would add 'on average some $200,000 to a man's earning power during the thirty years after graduation' and that 'there is no other investment that promises a tenfold return, an average yield of 30 per cent per year, and a thirty-year life'.[128] Now, as forecast by Drucker, the 'motivation for knowledge work must come from within the worker himself. The traditional "motivators", that is, external rewards – pay, for instance – do not motivate him'.[129]

It is workers in the information sector, in science, education, healthcare, politics and culture that are most ready to accept the new motivational factors. J.K. Galbraith said: 'Identification with the goals of the nation, state or community, and adaptation expressed as a desire "to make something of the office" are the only acceptable motives ... The motivation of lawyers, physicians, artists or scientists is assumed to be similar.'[130] Management experts in recent years have with increasing confidence asserted that the means that traditionally provided the greatest results of labour are no longer useful as motives. The prevalence of non-economic aims among knowledge workers is so high that they 'have to be managed as if they were volunteers'.[131] They should be talked with as equal partners in the company. That shows how important non-economic motives are for knowledge workers.

The expansion of creative activity and the forms in which it is manifested radically change human behaviour, as is shown particularly clearly in the desire of people for autonomy. This fact plays an extremely important role today, for two reasons. Firstly, the creative potential of employees is being mobilized to bring swift changes in productive technologies and improves the goods and services produced. Secondly, the creative desires will sooner or later reach some kind of limit within the corporation, resulting in the departure of employees, especially knowledge workers, from traditional economic structures.

It should be noted that the greater the proportion of employees that aim for self-realization and self-development, the smaller the possibility of the old system of centralized management.[132] Hence, 'the further we move into the global knowledge society, not just more, but also more frequent, restructuring is to be expected'.[133] Thus the modern corporation increasingly resembles a community rather than a productive unit. Below we shall give a more detailed consideration of the shift from purely economic unit to sociologized institution.

The creative desire of the modern employee is particularly salient in his wish to 'work with a company, for example, doing its data processing, but ... not work for the company, and [be] its employees'.[134] Ikujiro Nonaka and Hirotaka Takeuchi are quite right when they say that 'at the individual level, all members of an organization should be allowed to act autonomously as far as circumstances permit. By allowing them to act autonomously, the organization may increase the chance of introducing unexpected opportunities. Autonomy also increases the possibility that individuals will motivate themselves to create new knowledge'.[135] Making intellect and information the main resources of the production process brings not only greater autonomy for employees in manufacturing production, but the destruction of the whole system. Toffler stressed that, 'as we move from a machine-intensive to an information-intensive economy, ... as more and more of the important work comes to hinge on personal service and symbol manipulation, the vast industrial concentrations are likely to break up'.[136]

This process unfolded most in the early 1970s, when post-industrial trends started to grow markedly in Western countries. The last thrust of the industrial society that followed the Great Depression was marked by a significant decline in self-employment: from 20 per cent to 10 per cent in the United States between 1940 and 1973; from 29 per cent to 17 per cent in Germany between 1939 and 1970; and from 38 per cent to 21 per cent in France between 1946 and 1970.[137] Self-employment slumped until the early 1970s. A growth in self-employment was noted by several scholars from 1970[138] or 1972.[139] But there were differences between scholars over how intensive the growth was: from 15 and 20 per cent between 1970 and 1984,[140] to more than 25 per cent between 1972 and 1983.[141]

The early 1970s were also marked by a growth in the qualifications and mobility of the workforce. The vast majority of workers that are not employed by major corporations are engaged in the information or service sectors. In Britain no more than 13 per cent of self-employed workers are engaged in manufacturing.[142] The information sector can operate autonomously of major corporations as it is linked with the rest of the world through computer networks and mostly produces and consumes information products. Despite its apparent contradiction with the main trends of economic progress,[143] the growth of self-employment is having an obvious economic effect that fully conforms to current trends. Firstly, it does away with the necessity of huge expense on the physical movement of people. In just one year between March 1967 and March 1968, a total of 36.6 million Americans relocated, mostly to find work, according to Toffler.[144] That figure is now subsiding. Secondly, the dispersion of employees and the creation of nuclear production units increases demand for services that used to be carried out by specialized divisions of major corporations. So the wave of self-employment inevitably serves as a multiplier that is increasingly destroying the monopoly of major corporations over mass-production. The trend led to the forecast that about 20.7 million full-time home-based businesses would be created in 1995,[145] most of them in high-tech industries.

Creativity, prompting the unfolding of such processes, thus provides wide opportunities for further progress. This is reflected in the fact not only that production and consumption are intertwined in the concept of prosumption,[146] but that a whole new work ethic is emerging under which the product carries the imprint of the personality of its creator and under which irreproducible goods, accounting for an increasing share of production, radically undermine the existing economic laws of society. How very right Toffler was when he wrote that 'this step-by-step development, from handcraft to mass production to a new, higher form of handcraft, is one of the keys to understanding the Super-Industrial economy'.[147]

All the factors noted above confirm the growing role of the essential, creative force of humans in providing for the progress of production. The desire to express oneself, not only in leisure time, not only as a consumer, but primarily as a creator of new processes, goods and products, is one of the most important manifestations of creative activity in the modern world. The desire to realize one's individuality through autonomous activity should not be understood, as it often is, as confirmation of the growth of the individualism of modern man. Increasing autonomy is undoubtedly expressed when modern workers reject 'the values of hierarchy, statism and corporatism'.[148] But even admitting that such individualization is not only a factor in the rejection of the old forms of materialist relations[149] but a central element in the whole social transformation,[150] we do not believe that it can be said that modern society will definitely lead to individualism as one of the main characteristics of the new employee.

Individualism and autonomy are not synonymous. The modern creative individual is moved primarily by a desire for self-realization that is unthinkable outside the social whole. His searches, as a producer and consumer and in other forms of human activity, not only do not rule out his adherence to the aspirations of the collective and society but, more likely, presuppose such adherence as their fundamental element. It is far from coincidental that the first manifestations of non-economic behaviour were recorded by sociologists and management experts during the Second World War. Drucker wrote in 1946 that 'the war brought the industrial worker a satisfaction, a feeling of importance and achievement, a certainty of citizenship, self-respect and pride which he had never known before'.[151] In 1944, the 400 000 employees of General Motors made more than 115 000 suggestions for improving production. That is not a manifestation of individualism. That is a desire to make a contribution to the war effort. The Soviet Union achieved much greater economic success during the war than before, despite the first slackening of communist repression.

We believe that the desire for autonomy and self-realization being manifested today does not represent a growth in individualism. Even the departure of employees from their companies which, given a few assumptions, could be regarded as a desire to move more successfully to achieve profoundly individual aims, is embodied, as a rule, in the creation of a new economic community. Working more efficiently than the old, the new community facilitates the development of social production as a whole, reproducing within itself not less but, more often, more developed forms of teamwork than those that existed in the parent structure. Fukuyama wrote:

> The tendency of Americans to leave the companies they work for and start their own businesses is often taken as another example of American individualism ... But those new entrepreneurs seldom act purely as individuals; they often leave with others or else quickly establish new organizations with new hierarchies and lines of authority. These new organizations require the same degree of cooperativeness and discipline as the old ones, and if they are economically successful, they can grow to giant size and become very durable.

He quite correctly concluded that 'American democracy and the American economy were successful not because of individualism or communitarianism alone but because of the interaction of these two opposing tendencies.'[152]

Touching on the coordination of the interests and efficiency of production, we find ourselves among the problems of the structure and trends of the development of the modern corporation. One of the main social institutions of industrial society, the corporation today retains its significance as the main link between the interests of the individual and society. The processes currently unfolding in the modern corporation are no less dependent on the evolution of the system of values and preferences of the individuals that make it up and the nature of their activity than those processes that are discussed above. Therefore the next main group of issues that we wish to explore is connected with the manifestation of creative activity at the level of modern production structures and, in particular, corporations.

Creativity and the Modern Corporation

The production of material goods and services has invariably been of a collective nature throughout the various periods of the development of humanity. People were forced to pool their efforts in order to carry out their aim of transforming their environment. However, such associations were rarely voluntary until the coming of the industrial epoch.

In the political freedom provided by the bourgeois society the main economic system was a new form of production organization, the company or corporation, which had developed as a free association of individuals for many centuries of feudalism. There may be arguments over whether the capitalist type of coercion to labour is a synonym for freedom or is what the Marxists call capitalist slavery. One thing is sure: the corporation of bourgeois society is primarily formed because of the mutual interest of its members.

The corporation is the fundamental element of the industrial society. Having emerged in the industries where the bourgeois order was conceived – commerce and manufacturing – the corporation always included an element of innovation in contrast to the dominance of tradition. In the 19th and 20th centuries, it was the sector of the economy represented by corporations that was identified with the industrial system. Galbraith said it would be 'convenient, even in advance of more exact formulation, to have a name for the part of the economy which is characterized by the large corporations ... I shall refer to it as to [sic] Industrial System'.[153]

It is easy to assume, therefore, that the transition from an industrial to a post-industrial system, from a modern to a postmodern economy cannot be made without radical changes in the corporate world. The modernization of structures and a reappraisal of the role of the corporation in society is the key to the understanding of modern economic processes. 'The modern world is the world of organizations'[154] and in this respect the industrial and post-industrial societies are similar. The distinction between the current and the previous economic order is to be found, not in the rejection of organizations or in their overcoming, but in their acquisition of new qualities previously not characteristic of an industrial corporation. These changes under 'the new reality whose essence is the break-up of the old rules'[155] apply primarily to the nature of coordination and interaction of the interests of corporations and society, the corporation and its employees; the new and, to a significant degree, non-economic aims of production structures; the organization of joint activity in the framework of companies and the interaction of the renovated corporation with its environment.

Unlike the industrial corporation, which Ralf Dahrendorf called an 'imperatively coordinated association',[156] the modern corporation, having become to a significant degree post-economic both in its aims and the methods it applies to achieve those aims, 'is no longer regarded as a concrete expression of capitalism ... It is best defined in terms of the management of markets and technologies rather than in terms of rationalization or class rule'.[157] In industrial society the corporation served, thought Marx, to carry out the aims of the capitalist mode of uniting the worker with the means of production. Today, when information and knowledge are becoming the key resources of production, there is no need to do so. In the former social forms the corporation provided an opportunity to make massive increases in productivity by opening the way to mass-production for which today there is only a conditional requirement. In the capitalist order the production company, as the only source of income for hired workers, was able to dictate the price of labour. Today the situation is quite the opposite. What is the corporation worth today? What can it offer society as its key resource? What justifies its existence? There can only be one answer to these questions: the modern corporation combines into a single social organism people that have both an ability to work and the means of production.

The modernization of the corporation is a natural process that is 'part of the larger transformation of the socio-sphere as a whole, and this in turn parallels the dramatic changes in the techno-sphere and info-sphere'.[158] However, given the factors mentioned above, the movement of the corporation into what Bell called the sociologizing mode[159] is not just about providing employees with maximum social guarantees and job security. It amounts to integrating the employee into the new 'Gemeinschaft' that the modern corporation is. Hammer wrote that

a corporation is more than a collection of processes, more than a set of products and services, even more than an association of people at work. It is also a human society and, like all societies, it nourishes

particular forms of culture – 'corporate cultures'... Every company has
its own language, its own version of its history (its myths), and its own
heroes and villains (its legends), both historical and contemporary. The
whole flourishing tangle serves to confirm old-timers and to induct
newcomers in the corporation's distinctive identity and its particular
norms of behaviour.[160]

Today's corporation unites people, not as simple sources of
physical energy or the appendages of machines and mechanisms, but
primarily as creative individuals. Therefore today's corporation can
be distinguished from the corporations of the capitalist epoch
primarily by its sociologized nature. Its main task is not the primitive
notion of putting an employee to work, but 'to move hundreds of
thousands of human beings into what is, for many of them, an
entirely new culture, with its own tacit assumptions about time,
beauty, etc.'.[161] That is a task of enormous complexity because the
relations between a corporation and its new members is an example
of interpersonal interaction, the mutual penetration of culture and of
a process that is to a high degree creative and irrepeatable.

The modern corporation, based on the maximum utilization of the
creative potential of its employees, applies principles of management
that are cardinally different from those of an industrial-epoch
corporation. Scholars, describing the methods of management in a
post modern society, focus on various aspects and characteristics. But
all such works invariably reveal the contrast of the new methods with
the old and the negation of the old by the new. John Naisbitt and
Alvin Toffler, and T. Cannon and D. Harvey,[162] and dozens of other
modern scholars have found more and more contrasts between old
and new, marking shifts from welfare to workfare, from minimizing
risks from change to maximizing opportunities from change, from
adversarial management to collaborative management, from a high
degree of job specialization to elimination of job demarcation and
from vertical labour organization to more horizontal labour
organization.

Characteristically, however, the majority of scholars avoid
generalizations regarding the true essence of the changes that are
taking place. We would like to note that all the impressive
transformations taking place inside corporations have their basis in
the changes of the basic characteristics of those active individuals
represented at all levels of the corporate structure. The essence of the
phenomenon that is concealed in the evolution of the modern
corporation and that is practically never stated as clearly as it might
be is that labour management is being replaced by creativity
management, that the management of labouring individuals is being
superseded by the management of creative individuals. It is this very

factor that most fully explains the radical and obvious changes in the system of work organization that sociologists are observing today.

When knowledge is the key resource of production and 'workers with skills requiring long formal education, skills rather more esoteric and abstract than the manual and clerical skills organized and even imparted by management in the past'[163] are of strategic importance for corporations, the task of the manager is not so much the direct or indirect pressure on workers to carry out the technological tasks they have been set as the formation of conditions under which the worker is able independently to synthesize and bring into being new ends. The main task of a manager, as Drucker has correctly pointed out, is to maintain the optimal parity between the comprehensive activization of the creative potential of the worker and the ability of leaders of corporations or their divisions to make decisions regarding the principal aims and directions of development.[164]

The employees and managers of modern businesses are characterized by two parallel processes, each of which deserves attentive consideration. On the one hand, the creative activity of knowledge workers is fairly easily arranged in their own circle. Highly qualified specialists engaged in specific tasks or the management of specific processes show such a high ability to manage themselves that even the autonomy or independence of individual employees required for the manifestation of the creative characteristics of their personalities does the corporation no harm. In that connection there is a much lower requirement for managers per se. Forecasts for Britain provide a good example here. The number of professional managers is expected to decline from three million in 1985 to no more than 2 million by the end of the century.[165] Moreover, this forecast decline of more than 50 per cent comes against a background of higher employment in the service and information sectors. And that confirms the growing independence of creative individuals and their ability to create mobile and effective communities that do not require the traditional hierarchical management. The relative decline in the role of managers as an individual social group is to be observed in all the developed nations and the pace of this decline accelerates in line with the development of new forms of the organization of production processes. Hammer described the resulting dominant ethos as management as 'a necessary evil, and the less of it that is needed, the better'.[166]

On the other hand, effective management of a community of creative individuals requires managers that have very different qualities from those of their predecessors. This is chiefly because the executive decision making in structures that presuppose a high degree of decentralization and autonomy depends on the manager enjoying unshakeable moral authority among employees rather than mere qualification, as in the industrial type of corporation. In organizations where employees were moved by economic motives, the mere fact that the manager represented the will of the owner or the owners of the company was enough for him or her to be obeyed. That is not enough in companies where employees wish to be regarded as volunteers. Professor Cannon is very wrong when he says that the most successful companies are managed by their owners and not by hired managers.[167] Cannon, citing companies headed by entrepreneurs like Bill Gates, Anita Roddick and Richard Branson, neglected the factor that such entrepreneurs are successful as managers, not because they own the bulk of the capital of their companies, but because they, as founders of their own businesses, the highest manifestation of their creativity, bear the highest responsibility; because they represent the living history of their companies and embody unshakeable authority in the eyes of their employees and partners. It is such people that 'hold the key knowledge of the organization, maintain its philosophy, pass on its myths, and will be the cultivators of long-term relationships with employees and partners'.[168] The very fact that modern entrepreneurs regard their businesses as their art rather than their property prompts enormous adherence to the missions of the companies among their employees and serves as yet another confirmation that creativity is the main source of development for the modern corporation.

The organizational principles of a corporation, taking optimal account of both the specific nature of its employees and the aims set before it, have been developing throughout the 20th century and can, in our view, be divided into four stages that, overall, reflect the stages of the formation of creative activity of the people united in a corporation. The first stage covered the period up to the end of the Second World War and was totally dominated by the principles of the industrial organization based on the mass-production of reproducible goods and by the economic aims of both the employees and managers of the corporation. The natural embodiment of such a system was Fordism and other such methods of organization geared to achieve maximum productivity and maximum economic benefit.

During the second stage creativity was mostly manifested beyond the process of production. When it was manifested in production it did not have any tangible influence on the motives of the worker. It was at this stage that the growing requirement of people for self-realization was manifested in consumption, which started the process of rejecting mass-production as the ideal type of organization of the economic structure. That in its turn required the diversification of the productive functions of workers, the result of which was the expansion and improvement of the forms of productive motives. Higher productivity was achieved not so much by the relationship of wages and the result of labour as by the creation of good relations that provided the worker with the opportunity to feel his significance for the organization. This shift is usually regarded as a dichotomy of Fordism and post-Fordism.[169]

The next stage is connected with the growth of the de-centralization, demassification and fragmentation of production.[170] That growth was accompanied by the increasingly salient expansion of autonomy and individualism of workers.[171] These changes marked the shift to flexible specialization that was designed to allow companies to react quickly to changes in the market and included such elements as flexibility in output volume,[172] flexible employment,[173] flexible machinery,[174] flexible working practices and flexible organizational forms.[175] Such changes, by bringing into being 'decentralized and dehierarchized management systems',[176] prepared the way for the devolution of decision making lower levels and corresponded to the growing creative potential and the growing organizational abilities of employees. Bell, appraising such situations in their whole, talked of a participation revolution unfolding, first in the factory, trade unions or social organizations, but soon capable of spreading to organizations as well.[177] The result of this, according to Lester C. Thurow, is that '"employees" have a lot more freedom to make business decisions than occurs in a traditional hierarchical industrial firm'.[178]

The three stages mentioned above prepared the way for a shift to the fourth stage, which most closely corresponds to the requirements of the development of the creative individual. This period was witnessed in the 1980s and was marked by the expansion of a productive principle dubbed 'modular specialization'. From the point of view of work itself, modular specialization shifts the stress from individual productive operations to a process of the creation of a good as a whole. Under the new conditions, process-centred work is becoming the field for the application of the coordinated efforts of workers, whose main task now is not the modification of the finished product but the maximum improvement of the processes – from manufacturing itself to innovation decisions – leading to its production, but bearing a very distant relationship to the very formation of the end product.[179] Correspondingly, the creative individual is not set the direction of his search, but is provided with a wide range of possibilities for manifesting his abilities. At the same time the individualized nature of creative activity is balanced by its collective nature. This kind of work today appears to be the optimal type of organization of creativity within a corporation. Hammer said

the time of process has come. No longer can processes be the orphans of business, toiling away without recognition, attention and respect.

They now must occupy center stage in our organizations. Processes must be at the heart, rather than the periphery, of companies' organization and management. They must influence structure and systems. They must shape how people think and the attitudes they have.

He further commented: 'process centering starts a chain reaction that affects everyone from the frontline performer to the CEO [chief executive officers]. Not only are old roles either eliminated or transformed beyond recognition, but entirely new ones ... come into being'.[180]

From the point of view of work organization, such a system marks a shift from centralized management to modular organization based on the idea of 'small components linked together in temporary configurations'.[181] The destruction of the old economic system and its replacement by the new form is such a significant sign of modern production that Toffler believes that the super-industrial society can be defined as 'based on the idea of a semi-permanent "framework" and less durable "modular" pieces'.[182] As a result there emerges a whole new type of organizational activity that has in recent years acquired the name 'teamwork'.[183] Teamwork has two principal advantages that distinguish it from the previous forms of the organization of production. On the one hand, it enables companies to best utilize the desire of creative workers for innovation and initiative and bring down decision making to the lowest possible rung: 'Effective decisions today must be taken at lower and lower levels within the organization. Demands for participation thus do not flow from political ideology, but from a recognition that the system, as structured today, cannot respond efficiently to the fast-shifting environment.'[184] On the other hand, a small mobile group provides the best opportunity for the interpersonal interaction of creative individuals,[185] and it is within this group that feelings of collective action develop that balance individualized desire; specific motives and values are quick to emerge, resulting in what Fukuyama called 'prior moral consensus' that 'gives members of the group a basis for mutual trust'.[186]

It is hard to overemphasize the importance of the result of modular specialization. The corporation that used to be divided in a vertical and hierarchical way is now an aggregate of collectives, each of which is effectively a complete organization with its own aims, values, motives and leaders.[187] A hierarchical structure of management is impossible within these collectives. That in its turn unavoidably means that it is increasingly difficult to apply the hierarchical model in the corporation as a whole. Thus 'fragmentation and dif-ferentiation ... give way to homogenization and possibly create the foundations for building the "planet's first global civilization"'.[188] The very existence of the modern corporation could be at threat if the aims of the individuals and collectives that make it up come to contradict each other or the aims of the corporation as a whole.

In our view this trend in the development of the modern production corporation is conditioned primarily by the development of the personalities of its employees. And this is a factor that is often overlooked by sociologists and economists. The four main areas of pressure on the corporation distinguished by Toffler in the early 1980s – bio-sphere, social environment, info-sphere and politics, or the power-sphere[189] – do not take in the evolution of the economic individual himself, or the growth in his creative abilities and needs. But the corporation development is a certain projection of the general vector of the progress of human activity, a projection which enables us to observe how the awakening of the creative potential of selected personalities leads to the emergence of a new type of society, permeated by post-economic principles. By initiating the system of modular organization, the corporation provides the conditions for its own destruction, for its disintegration into new structures and communities capable of sustaining their own existence and becoming powerful competitors with the parent company not only in production but also in improving the principles of internal organization and the fuller use of the creative potential of the individual. As Naisbitt wrote:

> Working for a big company no longer carries the prestige it once did. It is exciting and satisfying to work for a small company, where a person has more responsibility and control, and is much more engaged in the mission of organization. The small company can more easily comply with all the personnel regulations without tying itself in knots, and it is exempted from some. The very best people are increasingly signing up with small companies – or starting their own businesses.[190]

The satisfaction gained by workers in the new conditions has arisen primarily because they are not employees so much as partners in their own organization, which makes it possible to display the abilities of all of its members to the full.[191]

Modern researchers, as mentioned, often interpret one-sidedly the external factors of pressure on the corporation as being the main ones in today's conditions. No less unilateral is the very widespread interpretation of challenge, posed by new forms of economic organizations before traditional companies, as confrontation and the struggle between small businesses and large industrial structures.

The growth of self-employment, of small businesses, of the number of individual producers of information and knowledge, and the spread of small service providers are plain to see. The share of the 500 biggest US companies in gross national product fell by nearly half between the mid-1970s and the early 1990s[192] and continues to fall; today companies with 19 or fewer employees account for half of American exports, while the big corporations which employ in excess of 500 people export just 7 per cent of all goods and services.[193] However, the expansion of small businesses, sometimes seen as one of the main trends today, may in the future run up against the same objective limits as have the concentration and centralization of industry in the last few decades. Therefore another factor is more important.

Over the last 40 years the very composition of the list of the 500 biggest American enterprises has altered. More than a third of these, representing the elite of the national business, have ceased to exist for one reason or another; another third have been eliminated from the list; moreover, many of them fall within the second or even the third thousand leading businesses. Only 30 per cent of them have retained their positions.[194] This indicates that the new structures, formed as a result of the departure beyond the realms of traditional corporations of their more mobile sub-divisions, which possessed the personnel who were creative to the highest degree, personnel capable of innovation and risk, are not only occupying more and more space on the periphery of contemporary business, but are radically altering the configuration of its main links. The successes of those companies which were formed quite recently but which are becoming leaders in their sectors and countries must be considered, besides the frequently reported successes of small businesses. But since non-traditional forms of production which do not require substantial investment are often the most advanced and achieve the most success, the overall result achieved by companies built on creative potential and the mobility of their leaders is far greater than can be assumed by studying merely correlations of production at large and small enterprises. But that the successes of the new intellectual corporations are no longer limited to small businesses is confirmed by the fact that 15 of the 20 wealthiest people in the United States represent companies that appeared during the last one or two decades in high-tech sectors: Microsoft, Metromedia, Intel, Oracle, Viacom, New World Communications and others.[195]

The rapid spread of non-economic aims pursued by the new business leaders to the emerging high-tech corporations and to society as a whole ensues from such expansion. If previously the social orientation of a company was very secondary, contradicting the objective of maximizing profits, and created primarily no more than the corresponding image for its owners,[196] today social orientation is becoming one of the main forms of a corporation's activity. The modern economic structure belongs to the full extent to those organizations which 'collectively are society',[197] among other reasons because it incorporates social goals in the system of its basic values, and is becoming more socially responsible in its activity, thereby achieving a greater degree of sociologizing, and proving itself to be a social structure even to a greater extent than an economic one.

But it is not the status of an organization that makes the corporation an important element of the social whole. In today's conditions

> the corporation can only function as the representative social institution of our society if it can fulfill its social functions in a manner which strengthens it as an efficient producer, and vice versa. But as the representative social institution of our society the corporation in addition to being an economic tool is a political and social body; its social function as a community is as important as its economic function as an efficient producer.[198]

These non-economic goals of the corporation are linked primarily with a whole range of areas of its activity.

Firstly, corporations, which possess creative individuals as the main source of their development, are at the same time a vital instrument of the formation of knowledge workers and other highly-qualified and independent persons, the main system-formative element of post-economic society. By taking on new workers, the corporations provide continuous education, which all leading sociologists stress is needed by modern society.

Secondly, corporations, by improving their inner structure, not only raise their performance, but also become sources of the emergence and development of new forms of production which, frequently outside the company itself, bring additional dynamism to social production; they not only guarantee growth in productive activity, but also create additional requirements for creative workers.

Thirdly, corporations are the most mobile section of social structures. To be convinced of this it is enough to analyse the rise and fall of modern companies, their capability for restructuring, their reaction to both external and inner challenges. Corporations, in response to changes in trends and motivation, at the same time perform the function of destabilizing society itself, mobilizing other social institutions and giving them the necessary dynamism.

Fourthly, corporations play a key role at the junction of the community of organizations and of society as a single whole. The scale of the activity of modern production companies, especially those acting at an international level, is commensurable with the scale of national economies, on the strength of which society strives to monitor corporations more closely than other organizations and institutions. The intervention of society and the state in the activity of corporations makes their performance more responsive to the principles of social responsibility than the activity of any other social institutions.

The modern corporation, which implies not only industrial manufacturers of goods and institutional providers of services but also scientific research institutes and other knowledge-producing establishments, is one of the main centres of gravity for various forms of creative activity. Moreover, the growth of self-employment noted by many scholars, the separation from industrial companies of selected divisions, the emergence of new production structures and the success of small businesses are only one form of the external manifestation of that creativity which has penetrated the inner fundamentals of the corporation.

In today's conditions, creative activity is still very dependent on economic factors, developing within structures, the general aims of which retain an economic character. The type of behaviour of both company managers and their employees can definitely be regarded as post-materialist in the sense described by Inglehart, but this does not rule out the presence of an essential economic element. We view this development as being entirely natural, since creativity as a profoundly individual process can only manifest itself initially at an individual level, spreading gradually to society as a whole.

It ought to be stressed that modern creative activity stems firstly from scientific institutes and corporations. Moreover, the results of creative activity, the product of individual labours, are assimilated at an individual level, at best at team-level, but not at the level of society as such. Society and the social groups that make up society assimilate not so much theories as ideologies, and the difference between them corresponds to the different characteristics of individual and so-called 'social' creativity.

But a wealth of publications focuses attention on the rapid development of processes which are presented as the clearest and most coherent forms of the manifestation of creative activity. At issue are organizations without economic goals. These organizations, usually referred to as non-profit organizations and classified as 'the third sector', are used to illustrate the fact that creative activity influences social institutions not in a mediatory but in a completely direct manner. However, structures like these cannot serve as an example of the most adequate display of creative activity in the modern world, although they do, of course, represent one of the forms of the manifestation of the creative activity of the people that make up these structures.

The Non-profit Sector: Too Much or Too Little Creativity?

Creative activity is manifested in the most diverse forms. As the desire by man to achieve self-improvement, resulting in the alteration of the personality of the creative person, creative activity cannot be sub-divided into the productive and non-productive. Creativity erases the division of the time spent by a person engaged in creative activity into working and leisure time, and eliminates the customary distinction between labour and leisure.

Therefore, when speaking of the manifestations of creativity within non-profit organizations, we are unable and ought not to view this phenomenon as one taking place beyond the limits of production; simply, in this case, creativity is accomplished outside structures with 'economic' goals. The creativity of profit-making and non-profit organizations differs neither in its goals, nor in its premises, nor in its results; the differences are merely that in the first case the results of creative activity are socialized by imparting to them an external form of economic goods and, in the second, society and its members are faced by the prospect of the direct assimilation of the results of creative activity. Moreover, the characteristics of the activity we use to describe it as creative do not as a rule surpass the corresponding parameters in material production or the service sector.

Creative activity, when viewed at the level of society as a whole, is a complex phenomenon, the future of which is by no means as clear as is often thought. The importance of the development of the third sector as a factor in the formation and expansion of creative activity has been overestimated, for the following two reasons: on the one hand, the lack of understanding of the dual nature of this sphere, consisting both of non-profit organizations, the inner structure of which to a considerable extent reproduces the principles and mechanisms of the functioning of the corporation, and of voluntary organizations, which in fact represent a qualitatively new, 'post-economic' phenomenon; and, on the other hand, the underestimation of the factor we term the 'inner self-sufficiency of creativity', as a result of which the very reasons for the proliferation and development of voluntary organizations prove not to have been fully understood. We will discuss each of these circumstances in turn.

The non-profit sector is being distinguished according to principles which can hardly be considered fully appropriate. It is often believed that the sector exists only because of the division of economic goods into individual and social goods. Moreover, in contrast to the former, which 'are "divisible" ... [and] each person buys the goods or services he wants ... on the basis of free consumer choice', the latter 'are not "divisible" into individual items of possession, but are a communal service – national defense, police and fire protection, public parks, water resources, highways, and the like'.[199] It should also be mentioned that the given sector also incorporates other social services: free education and healthcare, the preservation of cultural wealth, large-scale government construction projects, and so on. The importance of this sector has increased, most of all after the Second World War. As Bell wrote,

> In 1929 … the non-profit sector accounted for 12.5 percent of all goods and services purchased. By 1963 it stood above 27 percent, and it is still rising. In 1929, 4,465,000 persons were employed by government and non-profit institutions, or about 9.7 percent of the labor force. By 1960, 13,583,000, or 20 percent of everyone employed, were in the non-profit sector … [being] the major area of net new jobs, i.e. actual expansion as against replacement. From 1950 to 1960, the non-profit sector accounted for more than 50 percent of new jobs.[200]

However, the fact that this sector produces social goods does not at all mean that its workers belong to the non-profit sector which is an alternative to the traditional economy. This approach can be argued from the following two viewpoints. Firstly, the public sector to a considerable degree represents the same management of supplies that is widespread in the big corporations. It is very difficult to draw a major distinction between the activity of clerks in a defence establishment who place and control orders in industry, and the managers of a corporation, who place orders via their sub-contractors. This thesis is equally applicable in virtually all spheres of consumption by the state; it is also important to point out that state funds are spent on the acquisition of goods and services, the production of which is not profitable by any means for their producers. In this respect the growth of the number of bureaucrats is a phenomenon fully identical to the growth in the administrative staff of large companies.

Secondly, although social goods are a specific type of wealth, the market value of which (in contrast to their production costs) is very hard to estimate, and although reproduction differs markedly from the corresponding processes within the traditional economy, the activity of the non-profit sector does not differ in this respect from activity in the corporate sector. Traditional economically motivated activity is present both in government and municipal administration and in other spheres which produce goods not directly subject to market valuation; moreover, in the public and social sectors, organizations act, as a rule, as more bureaucratized and tightly controlled vertical structures than do those in modern business.

It is these circumstances which formed the basis for distinguishing the phenomenon that is usually described as the 'third sector'.

Belonging to the non-profit sector, the third sector can with much justification be viewed as an alternative system of economy, characterized as socio-economic and opposed both to commercial (or 'private') sector and to government (or 'public') sector.[201] In recent years its development has attracted the attention of a large number of researchers, and many are inclined to view it as one of the factors that determine the future of the modern developed countries. However, although the development of communitarian action can be explained and understood in full, and although it is present in society now because the latter is not only a society of organizations but also a community of communities,[202] the expansion of such activity must be interpreted in the context of its causes and with account taken of its natural limits; and given such an analysis, its tendencies no longer appear so obvious.

As Rifkin, one of the firmer advocates of the conception of the development of the given sector as a fundamental tendency which defines the face of modern society, wrote:

> Third-sector organizations serve many functions. They are incubators of new ideas and forums to air social grievances. Community associations integrate streams of immigrants into the American experience. They are places where the poor and the helpless can find a helping hand. Nonprofit organizations like museums, libraries, and historical societies help preserve traditions and open up doors to new kinds of intellectual experiences. The third sector is where many people first learn how to practice the art of democratic participation. It is where companionship is sought and friendships are formed. The independent sector provides a place and time for exploring the spiritual dimension. Religious and therapeutic organizations allow millions of Americans to leave behind the secular concerns of daily life. Finally, the third sector is where people relax and play, and more fully experience the pleasures of life and nature.[203]

He is echoed by Etzioni, who believed that the inclination of people to 'have a moral responsibility to help themselves as best as they can'[204] is embodied to the full extent by voluntary social organizations. Drucker notes similar processes: 'America's Third Sector institutions are rapidly becoming creators of new bonds of community... In the Third Sector institution new bonds of community are being forged.'[205]

Advocates of this conception, in justification of their attention to the processes resulting in the growth of the third sector, and to its inner laws, make most mention of the huge growth in the number of non-profit organizations. According to Rifkin, there were more than 1.4 million non-profit organizations in the United States in the mid-1990s, compared with 350 000 in Britain, and in Germany there were more than 300 000 in the late 1980s.[206] Even more striking are statistics about how much free time members devote to these organizations. Drucker has said that more than 90 million Americans contributed to the activity of voluntary organizations in the early 1990s,[207] and that 'by the year 2000 or 2010, the number of such unpaid staff people should have risen to 120 million, and their average hours of work to five per week'.[208] But Rifkin paints the fullest picture:

> In 1991 more than 94.2 million adult Americans, or 51 percent of the population, gave their time to various causes and organizations. The average volunteer gave 4.2 hours of his or her time per week. Collectively, the American people gave more than 20.5 billion hours in volunteering. More than 15.7 billion of those hours were in the form of formal volunteering – that is, regular work for a voluntary organization or association. These hours represent the equivalent economic contribution of 9 million full-time employees and, if measured in dollar terms, would be worth $176 billion.[209]

The expansion of voluntary organizations is often viewed as a manifestation of the overcoming of the individualism and the desocializing of society described by most authors of the 1970s and 1980s. As Etzioni put it: 'The eighties was a decade in which "I" was writ large, in which the celebration of the self became a virtue. Now is the time to push back the pendulum. The times call for an age of reconstruction, in which we put a new emphasis on "we", on values we share, on the spirit of community.'[210] Besides this, the growth of the sector is often associated with increased creative activity, with the ever more pronounced desire by man to realize himself in as many types of activity as possible, to overcome the certain aloofness in the customary circle of people and of actions so characteristic both of industrial society and of the industrial type of social behaviour.

But the questions whether the development of contemporary voluntary organizations is an indicator of the real manifestation of the tendency towards socialization, how radically the motives for activity in these associations differ from those in the organizations which have inherited industrial tendencies and whether there is a fundamental difference between the inner structures of these organizations must be approached very cautiously.

Firstly, it must be noted that voluntary organizations are very inclined, if not to the hierarchical system of management, then to the ramification of status structure. This is a very important factor, as it testifies to the desire by the founders and members of associations like these to assert themselves in the collective by acquisition of a certain status. In contrast to modern production, where 'organizations of professionals use very few titles',[211] modern voluntary associations present the opposite picture; Etzioni's statement that 'social movements are the source of the needed political energy'[212] confirms that most of them are built on the principle of political organizations, dominated by a hierarchy and formed with the goal of achieving domineering social positions.

Secondly, the inner structure of voluntary organizations frequently involves remuneration for its executives, and considerable expenses on the upkeep of headquarters and so on. So it happens that social organizations like these perform quite traditional economic activity or are sustained by contributions and donations; moreover, their managers and staff are fully economically motivated executives and employees. These organizations could even be described as a type of corporation operating in the non-profit sector and differing from the traditional corporation more through the main areas of its activity than by inner structure and the motives of a large number of its members.

Thirdly, we consider the very widespread position emphasized by Drucker to be rather one-sided: 'What characterizes these so-called nonprofit institutions of the social sector is their purpose. A government demands compliance. A business sells goods or services. The social sector institutions aim at changing a human being.'[213] To agree with such a claim it is necessary, on the one hand, to acknowledge that the true self-realization of a human being and the true development of that human being's personality take place today outside professional and related activity. On the other hand, all of the changes that have taken place in the organization of production and in the nature of labour activity in the last few decades must be abstracted. But it can hardly be claimed that the development of the personality progresses most successfully in new hierarchic organizations without direct relation to the basic activity of a human being, and not in scientific institutes, industrial and service companies, where people spend most of their life, where all opportunities for the development of creativity are used actively and where most status differences are eliminated.

Therefore it would be more accurate to describe the role of voluntary organizations as structures which reduce some modern social contradictions rather than structures which are capable of determining some new tendency in social progress. In this respect another statement by Drucker, to which he does not draw such special attention and in which he acknowledges that 'the Third Sector institutions are ... a bridge across the widening gap between knowledge workers and the other half' of society,[214] would be nearer the mark; we would add to this the fact that the backbone of such organizations is formed by those very strata of the population which become more and more socially isolated from knowledge workers. Creative activity is definitely manifested in the formation and development of social organizations, but this form of its manifestation cannot become a main trend in the development of creativity. If the desire by one person to communicate with others spiritually close to him is embodied in his incorporation within the framework of the voluntary organization, and if this desire is tied in with the desire thereby to raise his true or illusory social status, we have more of a reaction to relative dissatisfaction with his main activity, a reaction which arises especially strongly among workers not categorized as knowledge workers or administrative personnel.

So, in assessing the manifestations of creative activity at a social level, we must bear in mind the fact that those manifestations may be linked with a lack of opportunities for the corresponding manifestations at a professional level; voluntary organizations are in modern society less a higher form of the realization of creative principles, as is sometimes assumed, than the reaction of certain social groups to the non-creative nature of activity in other spheres.

In their bid to stress the role of voluntary organizations in the contemporary world, researchers often neglect clearly visible contra-tendencies and some of the key phenomena which have brought the traditional and the third sectors closer together. In the modern United States, as the number of voluntary organizations and volunteers has increased, membership of highly socialized social associations has declined. As a result,

> since the 1950s, membership in voluntary associations has dropped. Although America remains far more religious than other industrialized countries, net church attendance has fallen by approximately one-sixth; union membership has declined from 32.5 to 15.8 percent; participation in parent–teacher associations has plummeted from 12 million in 1964 to 7 million today; fraternal organizations like the Lions, Elks, Masons and Jaycees have lost from an eighth to nearly half of their memberships in the past twenty years. Similar declines are reported in organizations from the Boy Scouts to the American Red Cross.[215]

The reasons for this lie, on the one hand, in that many associations like these have turned, in the course of their development, into types of corporative structures and, on the other hand, in that modern companies have evolved towards principles of organization similar to the principles which originally defined the functioning of voluntary associations. So we are able to note, not the usual growth, but the bridging of the gap between traditional structures, on the one hand, and the third sector on the other; moreover, this is taking place because of a change in the nature of profit-making organizations. We have discussed the influence of modern trends in the development of intellectual and creative activity on profit-making companies. As a result the possibility arises of spreading to the social whole the principles of the organization of activity, developed and applied within the framework of the corporation and, in particular, the stimulation of its creative character. But the assimilation and improvement by the corporations themselves of the principles of relating to their staff as volunteers do not, of course, end. Andrew Sayer and Richard Walker stressed the following in this respect: 'As the dichotomy of firm and market breaks down, it becomes possible to see that the world outside the firm needs to be managed and the world inside the firm needs to be regulated in light of external conditions.'[216]

Voluntary organizations are a phenomenon well known to industrial society. It is here that they have put up resistance to the bureaucratically organized production units and played a significant role in the socialization of people, in whom the industrial system inculcated only individualistic values, which were economic by nature. Although voluntary organizations have multiplied in number, their rapid and radical stratification is noticeable today.

On the one hand, associations like scientific organizations, communities of managers, professionals and cultural figures, and associations and unions designed to popularize and affirm values established as general social values are also multiplying. The latter include environmental and human rights organizations, anti-war lobbies, associations of pacifists and the like. For example, '10,000 members of the Environmental Coalition on Nuclear Power, founded in 1970, seek a wider justice, the implementation of a safe, nonnuclear energy policy in the United States. Women Against Pornography seeks to change public opinion about pornography, ending "the degradation, objectivication and brutalization of women"',[217] and so on. These associations can and must be viewed as a manifestation of the creative essence of a human being, that which is determined by a feeling of social responsibility bred as a result of the assimilation of the values of collectivism that are under formation.

On the other hand, many organizations represent not so much those without such a great will to improve themselves within the broader context of their professional activity or to attract the attention of society to certain general social problems, as those who wish to assert themselves within the context of a certain collective or social group. This desire often stems from the lack of opportunity or from the reluctance regarding self-development in a person's main activity. Kuhn and Shriver give the following examples of such associations: 'In the late 1970s, Hurst, Texas, was the headquarters of "The Enough is Enough Club", with a membership of 1,213 fans of national televised "Monday Night Football" who believed "the program would be more enjoyable without ABC sports broadcaster Howard

Cosell"'; they add, 'the members may have found other causes to support after Cosell left the ABC position'.[218] By involving people in collective actions, these organizations do not set about improving the creative potential of a nation as much as express the aforementioned need to ease possible rivalry between new social groups of the modern society, a rivalry viewed by many scholars as a main source of the social conflicts of the future.

A very special place is occupied by organizations setting out to contradict the main values of society, the activity of which is capable of assuming uncontrolled forms and brings results that are hard to predict. There are also numerous examples of these results. The world media have made several reports about these in the last few months, such as the mass-suicide of 39 members of a sect headed by M.H. Applewhite[219] and confrontation between the police and a group intending to proclaim a Republic of Texas. However, we will not discuss these and similar organizations in our study.

The understanding by society of the role and place of voluntary organizations is displayed in the formation of a radically new approach to the evaluation of their activity. We today see attempts to unify approaches to organizations representing both the profit-making and the non-profit sectors. This unification is based on the application of the dynamics of their available intellectual capital as the main parameter for their comparison. In this situation both industrial and service companies and non-profit sector organizations are treated not as ones that create qualitatively different goods from each other but as ones that form and apply specific human capabilities all embraced by the term, 'intellectual capital'.[220] And so modern sociology started to understand that the creative activity of people can be carried out at various levels and in different forms; moreover, the nature of these forms do not determine one interpretation of this activity, whether we acknowledge it as being creative or not.

We by no means want to play down the role of social organizations and social movements as manifestations of the creative activity of the modern person, but we will say that neither at today's stage of development nor in the foreseeable future will man become a universal personality capable of being an expert in all areas. The very choice of profession is a creative act, and a person consciously devotes his life to one specific activity or another. Creativity and its development embody the desire by people to fill their selected activity with a more profound sense and content. This does not exclude self-expression in consumption, in culture or in personal life, although a surge of activity in organizations of the third sector – if these bear no direct relation to the professional activity of a person – can be regarded as confirmation of the fact that the activity is not sufficiently creative, rather than as the embodiment of the aspiration towards additional forms of the development of a person's creativity. As a result, while serving as an example of the direct manifestation of creativity in modern conditions, the effect on society of creative activity performed within voluntary organizations remains incommensurable for civilization. The main area of the expansion of creativity, we believe, is via the production of material and non-material goods.

Notes

1 See, for example, H. Glaser, *Das Verschwinden der Arbeit. Die Chancen der neuen Taetigkeitsgesellschaft*, Düsseldorf, 1988; J. Rifkin, *The End of Work*, New York, 1996.
2 J.K. Galbraith, *The Good Society. The Humane Agenda*, Boston, New York, 1996, pp.90–91.
3 E. Jaques, *Creativity and Work*, Madison, Wis., 1990, p.49.
4 Ibid., pp.vii–viii.
5 K. Marx and F. Engels, *Gesamtausgabe* (MEGA), Abteilung 2, Bd. 5, Berlin, 1983, ch. 3, 1), 16–18 ('a process in which both man and Nature participate, and in which man of his own accord starts, regulates, and controls the material reactions between himself and Nature' (Karl Marx, *Capital*, Vol. I, Moscow, 1987, p.173).)
6 K. Marx and F. Engels, *Gesamtausgabe* (MEGA), Abteilung 2, Bd. 7, Berlin, 1989, Troisième section, Ch. VII, I, 18–20. ('Labour is, in the first place, a process in which both man and Nature participate. He opposes himself to Nature as one of her own forces' (Karl Marx, *Capital*, Vol. I, p.173).)
7 See J.K. Galbraith, *The Good Society*, p.91.
8 Adam Smith, 'An Inquiry into the Nature and Causes of the Wealth of Nations', in *Great Books of the Western World*, Encyclopaedia Britannica Publishers, Vol. 36, 1994, p.1.
9 A. Marshall, *Principles of Economics*, Vol. I, London, 1961, p.65.
10 See H. Arendt, *The Human Condition*, New York, 1959, p.85.
11 F. Fukuyama, *The End of History and the Last Man*, London, New York, 1992, p.225.
12 Ibid., p.376, n. 6.
13 C. Casey, *Work, Self and Society. After Industrialism*, London, New York, 1995, p.26.
14 Karl Marx, *Capital*, Vol. I, p.179.
15 Karl Marx and Friedrich Engels, *Collected Works*, Vol. 4, Moscow, pp.278–9.
16 See Karl Marx and Friedrich Engels, *Collected Works*, Vol. 3, pp.274–5.
17 Karl Marx and Friedrich Engels, *The German Ideology*, Moscow, 1968, p.87.
18 A. Marshall, *Principles of Economics*, Vol. I, p.138.
19 See D. Bell, *The Cultural Contradictions of Capitalism*, New York, 1978, pp.146–7.
20 F. Best, 'Technology and the Changing World of Work', *The Futurist*, April 1984, **XVIII** (2), p.64.
21 J. Ellul, *The Technological Society*, New York, 1964, p.320.
22 R.L. Heilbroner, *Behind the Veil of Economics. Essays in the Worldly Philosophy*, New York, London, 1988, pp.81, 82.
23 A. Gorz, *Paths to Paradise: On the Liberation from Work*, London, 1985, p.67.
24 R.L. Heilbroner, *Behind the Veil*, p.101.

25   Ibid., p.100.
26   Ibid., p.102.
27   See E. Jaques, *Work, Creativity and Social Justice*, New York, 1970, pp.64–8.
28   See S. Bailin, *Achieving Extraordinary Ends. An Essay on Creativity*, Dordrecht, 1988, pp.106, 118, 121.
29   See H. Glaser, *Das Verschwinden der Arbeit*, p.196.
30   See J. Rifkin, *La fin du travail*, Paris, 1996.
31   See, for example, D. Schnapper, *Contre la fin du travail*, Paris, 1997; J.-Y. Calvez, *Nécessité du travail. Disparition d'une valeur ou redéfinition?*, Paris, 1997.
32   Selected elements of this approach were first published in W.A.Faunce, *Problems of an Industrial Society*, San Francisco, 1968, p.170. A first version of the table, complete with additional notes, can be found in V.L. Inozemtsev, 'On the Limitations of the Marxian Theory of Value: Some Methodological Aspects of the Problem', *Social Sciences*, 1992, **XXIII** (4), pp.110–25.
33   P. Nuernberger, 'Mastering the Creative Process', *The Futurist*, August 1984, **XVIII** (4), p.36.
34   A. Touraine, *Critique de la modernité*, Paris, 1992, p.354. ('No experience is more central than the relationship with the other which constitutes both I and other as subjects. Yet it would be artificial to contrast this private relationship with public life. All individuals are caught up in a network of roles. They exist for others, and the encounter with the other never takes place on open ground, as in films where two characters meet face to face on an empty set' (Alain Touraine, *Critique of Modernity*, translated by David Macey, Oxford, England, Cambridge, USA, 1995, p.276).)
35   A. Touraine, *Critique de la modernité*, pp.269–70. ('the antithesis of the individual's surrender to transcendental values. Man once projected himself onto God; in the modern world, man becomes the basic value. The central ethical principle now becomes freedom. Freedom is a creativity which is its own end and which resists all forms of dependency' (Alain Touraine, *Critique of Modernity*, p.209).)
36   A. Toffler, *Future Shock*, New York, 1971, p.302.
37   V.M. Mezhuyev, 'Culture as an Object of Knowledge', in *The Philosophical Problems of Culture*, Moscow, 1984, p.63 (in Russian).
38   G.S. Batishchev, *The Dialectics of Creativity*, Moscow, 1984, manuscript No. 18609 at INION (Institute for Information on Social Sciences) of the USSR Academy of Sciences, p.443 (in Russian); 'The Dialectic Character of the Creative Relationship of Man to the World', PhD dissertation, Institute of Philosophy, USSR Academy of Sciences, Moscow, 1989, p.25 (in Russian).
39   A. Toffler, *The Third Wave*, New York, 1980, p.243.
40   D. Bell, *The Coming of Post-Industrial Society*, New York, 1976, p.288.
41   Ibid., p.283.
42   Ibid., p.127.
43   J. Rifkin, *The End of Work*, p.110.
44   See V. Perlo, *Superprofits and Crises: Modern U.S. Capitalism*, New York, 1988, p.290.
45   See *Statistical Abstract of the United States*, 1982–83, p.394; *Statistical Abstract of the United States*, 1986, p.410; *Statistical Abstract of the United States*, 1992, p.403; *Statistical Abstract of the United States*, 1995, p.424.
46   See M. Forse and S. Langlois (eds), *Tendances comparées des sociétés post-industrielles*, Paris, 1995, pp.72, 73.
47   A. Toffler, *The Third Wave*, p.195.
48   See J. Naisbitt, *Megatrends. Ten New Directions, Transforming Our Lives*, New York, 1984, p.5.
49   T. Sakaiya, *The Knowledge-Value Revolution, or a History of the Future*, New York, Tokyo, 1991, p.239.

50   See ibid., p.240.
51   See *Drucker on Asia. A Dialogue Between Peter Drucker and Isao Nakauchi*, Oxford, 1997, pp.29–30.
52   J. Gershuny, 'Post-Industrial Society: The Myth of the Service Economy', *Futures*, 1977, **9** (2), p.110.
53   See P. Drucker, *The New Realities*, Oxford, 1996, p.116.
54   P.F. Drucker, *Post-Capitalist Society*, New York, 1993, p.72.
55   P.F. Drucker, *The New Realities*, p.117.
56   P.F. Drucker, *Post-Capitalist Society*, p.69.
57   See *Statistical Abstract of the United States*, 1980, p.441; *Statistical Abstract of the United States*, 1986, p.433; *Statistical Abstract of the United States*, 1989, p.422; *Statistical Abstract of the United States*, 1994, p.447; *Statistical Abstract of the United States*, 1995, p.452.
58   See *Statistical Abstract of the United States*, 1980, p.441; *Statistical Abstract of the United States*, 1982–83, p.394; *Statistical Abstract of the United States*, 1986, pp.410, 433; *Statistical Abstract of the United States*, 1989, p.422; *Statistical Abstract of the United States*, 1992, p.403; *Statistical Abstract of the United States*, 1994, p.447; *Statistical Abstract of the United States*, 1995, pp.424, 452.
59   See *Statistical Abstract of the United States*, 1991, p.766; *Statistical Abstract of the United States*, 1994, p.783; *Statistical Abstract of the United States*, 1995, p.779.
60   M. Castells, 'The Information Economy and the New International Division of Labor', in M. Carnoy, M. Castells, S. Cohen and F.H. Cardoso, *The New Global Economy in the Information Age: Reflections on Our Changing World*, University Park, Pa., 1993, p.17.
61   See H.S. Dordick and G. Wang, *The Information Society: A Retrospective View*, Newbury Park, Cal., London, 1993, p.90.
62   See A. Toffler, *Future Shock*, pp.220–21.
63   P.F. Drucker, *The New Realities*, pp.22–3.
64   *Drucker on Asia. A Dialogue Between Peter Drucker and Isao Nakauchi*, p.x.
65   See J. Naisbitt and P. Aburdene, *Megatrends 2000. Ten New Directions for the 1990's*, New York, 1990, p.331.
66   See J. Naisbitt, 'From Nation States to Networks', in R. Gibson (ed.), *Rethinking the Future*, London, 1997, pp.214, 215.
67   See J. Naisbitt, *Global Paradox*, New York, 1995, pp.16–17.
68   See L.C. Thurow, *The Future of Capitalism. How Today's Economic Forces Shape Tomorrow's World*, London, 1996, p.279.
69   See J. Nusbaumer, *The Services Economy: Lever to Growth*, Boston, 1987, p.7.
70   See A. Toffler, *The Third Wave*, pp.37–45, 265–88.
71   A. Toffler, *Future Shock*, pp.301, 302.
72   F. Webster, *Theories of the Information Society*, London, New York, 1995, p.38.
73   See R.L. Heilbroner, *Behind The Veil*, p.94.
74   See R. Inglehart, *Culture Shift in Advanced Industrial Society*, Princeton, NJ, 1990, pp.31–2.
75   See ibid., p.173.
76   Ibid., p.171.
77   Ibid., p.100.
78   Here we believe it is necessary to make a significant clarification. This formulation, which as a rule is fair, requires correction in those cases where the social system lays down an imperative under which post-materialist values must be assimilated as a condition for the achievement of material well-being (such was the case in the former Soviet Union, where education was accessible to the vast majority of the population and was one of the most reliable ways of achieving material wealth in a society where there was no free enterprise).
79   See A. Touraine, *Qu'est-ce que la démocratie?*, Paris, 1994, p.221.

80 D. Bell, *The Coming of Post-Industrial Society*, p.12.
81 A. Toffler, *Powershift. Knowledge, Wealth and Violence at the Edge of the 21st Century*, New York, 1990, p.19.
82 Ibid., pp.81–2.
83 See F. Fukuyama, *Trust*, New York, 1996, pp.316–17.
84 *Drucker on Asia. A Dialogue Between Peter Drucker and Isao Nakauchi*, p.80.
85 J. Naisbitt and P. Aburdene, *Megatrends 2000*, p.334.
86 *Drucker on Asia. A Dialogue Between Peter Drucker and Isao Nakauchi*, p.80.
87 See P.F. Drucker, *Post-Capitalist Society*, p.20.
88 G.K. Chesterton, *St. Thomas Aquinas*, New York, 1933, p.87.
89 See R. Nisbet, 'The Future of the University', in S.M. Lipset (ed.), *The Third Century. America as a Post-Industrial Society*, Chicago, 1979, p.312.
90 See P.F. Drucker, *Landmarks of Tomorrow*, New Brunswick, London, 1996, p.117.
91 See J.I. Nelson, *Post-Industrial Capitalism. Exploring Economic Inequality in America*, Thousand Oaks, Cal., London, 1995, p.22.
92 See D. Bell, *The Coming of Post-Industrial Society*, p.216.
93 See ibid., pp.165–266.
94 K. Renner, 'The Service Class', in T.B. Bottomore and P. Goode (eds), *Austro-Marxism*, Oxford, 1978, p.252.
95 See S. Crook, J. Pakulski and M. Waters, *Postmodernization. Change in Advanced Society*, London/Newbury Park, Ca, 1993, p.112; J. Pakulski and M. Waters, *The Death of Class*, Thousand Oaks, London, 1996, pp.57–8.
96 A. Toffler and H. Toffler, *Creating a New Civilization: The Politics of the Third Wave*, Atlanta, 1994, p.55.
97 *Drucker on Asia. A Dialogue Between Peter Drucker and Isao Nakauchi*, p.9.
98 See E.E. Gordon, R.R. Morgan and J.A. Ponticell, *Futurework. The Revolution Reshaping American Business*, Westport, Conn., London, 1994, pp.27, 196.
99 See J. Naisbitt, *Megatrends Asia*, London, 1996, p.180.
100 See A. Toffler, *The Third Wave*, p.153.
101 R. Inglehart, *Culture Shift*, pp.285–6, 161.
102 P.F. Drucker, *The New Realities*, pp.183, 184.
103 See T. Forester, *High-Tech Society. The Story of the Information Technology Revolution*, Cambridge, Mass., 1988, p.79.
104 See H.W. Opaschowski, *Wie leben wir nach dem Jahre 2000? Szenarien ueber die Zukunft von Arbeit und Freizeit*, Hamburg, 1987, S.15ff.
105 See A. Toffler, *The Third Wave*, p.351.
106 J. Habermas, *The Philosophical Discourse of Modernity*, Cambridge, 1995, p.363.
107 See A. Toffler, *The Adaptive Corporation*, Aldershot, 1985, p.31.
108 J. Robertson, *Future Wealth. A New Economics for the 21st Century*, London, New York, 1990, p.13.
109 A. Toffler, *The Adaptive Corporation*, p.75.
110 For more detail, see W.A. Faunce, *Problems*, p.148.
111 R. Inglehart, *Culture Shift*, p.5.
112 A. Toffler, *The Adaptive Corporation*, p.61.
113 See J. Ellul, *The Technological Society*, pp.403–4.
114 C. Handy, 'Finding Sense in Uncertainty', in R. Gibson (ed.), *Rethinking the Future*, London, 1997, p.21.
115 See J.W. Kuhn and D.W. Shriver, Jr., *Beyond Success. Corporations and Their Critics in the 1990s*, New York, Oxford, 1991, pp.14–15.
116 See R. Inglehart, *The Silent Revolution: Changing Values and Political Styles Among Western Publics*, Princeton, 1977, pp.54–5; *Culture Shift*, p.253.
117 See, for example, C. Bezold, R. Carlson and J. Peck, *The Future of Work and Health*, Dover, London, 1986, pp.60–61.
118 See A. Toffler, *The Adaptive Corporation*, p.100.

119 P.F. Drucker, *Concept of the Corporation*, New Brunswick, London, 1993, p.248.
120 See, for example, R. Bahro, *The Alternative*, London, 1978; B. Frankel, *The Post-Industrial Utopians*, Madison, Wis., 1987.
121 A. Toffler, *The Adaptive Corporation*, p.100.
122 C. Bezold, R. Carlson and J. Peck, *The Future of Work and Health*.
123 D. Lyon, *The Informational Society: Issues and Illusions*, Cambridge, 1996, p.135.
124 A.H. Maslow, *Motivation and Personality*, New York, 1970, p.46.
125 See J. Rifkin, *The End of Work*, p.233.
126 M. Hammer, *Beyond Reengineering. How the Process-Centered Organization is Changing Our Work and Our Lives*, New York, 1996, p.61.
127 J.-F. Lyotard, *The Postmodern Condition: A Report on Knowledge*, Manchester, 1984, p.5.
128 P.F. Drucker, *Landmarks of Tomorrow*, pp.127–8, 128.
129 P.F. Drucker, *The Age of Discontinuity: Guidelines to Our Changing Society*, New Brunswick, London, 1994, p.288; see also his *Post-Capitalist Society*, p.174.
130 J.K. Galbraith, *The New Industrial State*, 2nd edn, London, 1991, p.156.
131 *Drucker on Asia. A Dialogue Between Peter Drucker and Isao Nakauchi*, p.148.
132 See F. Fukuyama, *The End of History and the Last Man*, p.92.
133 H.A. Linstone and I.I. Mitroff, *The Challenge of the 21st Century. Managing Technology and Ourselves in a Shrinking World*, Albany, NY, 1994, p.212.
134 *Drucker on Asia. A Dialogue Between Peter Drucker and Isao Nakauchi*, p.x.
135 I. Nonaka and H. Takeuchi, *The Knowledge-Creating Company*, New York, Oxford, 1995, pp.75–6.
136 A. Toffler, *The Adaptive Corporation*, pp.95, 96.
137 See G. Steinmetz and E.O. Wright, 'The Fall and Rise of the Petty Bourgeoisie: Changing Patterns of Self-Employment in the Postwar United States', *American Journal of Sociology*, 1994, **5**, pp.975–85.
138 See D. Harvey, *The Condition of Post-Modernity. An Inquiry into the Origins of Cultural Change*, Cambridge, Mass., Oxford, 1995, p.158.
139 See S. Crook, *et al.*, *Postmodernization*, p.177.
140 See ibid.
141 See D. Harvey, *The Condition of Post-Modernity*.
142 See D. Lyon, *The Informational Society*, p.82.
143 See J. Robertson, *Future Wealth*, pp.35–6.
144 See A. Toffler, *Future Shock*, p.78.
145 See J. Naisbitt and P. Aburdene, *Megatrends 2000*, p.331.
146 See A. Toffler, *The Third Wave*, p.388.
147 A. Toffler, *The Adaptive Corporation*, p.63.
148 S. Lash, *Sociology of Postmodernism*, London, New York, 1990, p.28.
149 See A. Giddens, *The Constitution of Society. Outline of the Theory of Structuration*, Cambridge, 1997, pp.205–6.
150 See, for example, C. Castoriadis, *Gesellschaft als imaginaere Institution. Entwurf einer politischen Philosophie*, Frankfurt-am-Main, 1984, S.129ff.
151 P.F. Drucker, *Concept of the Corporation*, p.157.
152 F. Fukuyama, *Trust*, pp.273, 280.
153 J.K. Galbraith, *The New Industrial State*, p.29.
154 A. Giddens, *Social Theory and Modern Sociology*, Cambridge, 1987, p.155.
155 A. Toffler, *The Adaptive Corporation*, p.89.
156 R. Dahrendorf, *Class and Class Conflict in Industrial Society*, Stanford, 1959, p.242.
157 A. Touraine, *Critique of Modernity*, p.141.
158 A. Toffler, *The Third Wave*, p.243.
159 See D. Bell, *The Coming of Post-Industrial Society*, pp.288–9.
160 M. Hammer, *Beyond Reengineering*, p.153.
161 A. Toffler, *The Adaptive Corporation*, p.77.

162 See J. Naisbitt and P. Aburdene, *Megatrends 2000*, p.183; A. Toffler, *The Adaptive Corporation*, p.119; T. Cannon, *Welcome to the Revolution. Managing Paradox in the 21st Century*, London, 1996, p.18; D. Harvey, *The Condition of Post-Modernity*, pp.177–9.

163 E. Freidson, *Professionalism Reborn. Theory, Prophecy and Policy*, Cambridge, 1994, p.101.

164 See P.F. Drucker, *Landmarks of Tomorrow*, p.86.

165 See T. Cannon, *Welcome to the Revolution*, p.292.

166 M. Hammer, *Beyond Reengineering*, p.92.

167 See T. Cannon, *Welcome to the Revolution*, p.179.

168 L. Edvinsson and M.S. Malone, *Intellectual Capital. Realizing Your Company's True Value by Finding its Hidden Roots*, New York, 1997, p.130.

169 See W. Bonefeld and J. Holloway (eds), *Post-Fordism and Social Forms*, Houndmills, London, 1991; B. Jessop, 'Fordism and Post-Fordism: Critique and Reformulation', in M. Storper and A.J. Scott (eds), *Pathways to Industrialisation and Regional Development*, London, 1992; D. Harvey, *The Condition of Post-Modernity*; A. Lipietz, *Towards a New Economic Order; Post-Fordism, Ecology and Democracy*, Oxford, 1992; M. Piore and C. Sable, *The Second Industrial Divide: Possibilities for Prosperity*, New York, 1984; A. Sayer and R. Walker, *The New Social Economy: Reworking the Division of Labour*, Oxford, 1992.

170 See A. Toffler, *The Third Wave*, pp.57–9, 255–61, 336–42; *Powershift*, pp.179–83, 220–21, 331–43; also U. Beck, *Risk Society: Towards a New Modernity*, London, 1992, pp.142–9, 191–2; F. Block, *Postindustrial Possibilities: A Critique of Economic Discourse*, Berkeley, 1990, p.47; R.H. Hall, *Sociology of Work: Perspectives, Analyses and Issues*, Thousand Oaks, London, 1994, p.18; S. Lash and J. Urry, *Economies of Signs and Space*, Thousand Oaks, Cal., London, 1994, pp.18–28; A.L. Norman, *Informational Society. An Economic Theory of Discovery, Invention and Innovation*, Boston, Dordrecht, 1993, p.97.

171 See S. Crook, *et al.*, *Postmodernization*, p.177; A. Giddens, *The Constitution of Society. Outline of the Theory of Structuration*, pp.205–6; D. Harvey, *The Condition of Post-Modernity*, p.158; S. Lash, *Sociology of Postmodernism*, p.28.

172 See M. Piore and C. Sable, *Second Industrial Divide*.

173 See R. Boyer (ed.), *The Search for Labour Market Flexibility*, Oxford, 1986.

174 See R. Kaplinsky, *Automation*, London, New York, 1984.

175 See A. Scott, *Metropolis. From the Division of Labour to Urban Form*, Berkeley, Los Angeles, 1988.

176 S. Crook, *et al.*, *Postmodernization*, p.223.

177 See D. Bell, *Cultural Contradictions*, p.204.

178 L.C. Thurow, *The Future of Capitalism*, p.279.

179 See L. Edvinsson and M.S. Malone, *Intellectual Capital*, p.101.

180 M. Hammer, *Beyond Reengineering*, pp.13, 92.

181 A. Toffler, *The Third Wave*, p.263.

182 A. Toffler, *The Adaptive Corporation*, p.130.

183 See P.F. Drucker, *Landmarks of Tomorrow*, p.68.

184 A. Toffler, *The Adaptive Corporation*, p.122.

185 See A. Furnham, *Personality at Work. The Role of Individual Differences in the Workplace*, London, New York, 1995, p.367.

186 F. Fukuyama, *Trust*, p.26.

187 See P.F. Drucker, *The Age of Discontinuity*, p.176.

188 N. Stehr, *Knowledge Societies*, London, 1994, p.248.

189 See A. Toffler, *The Third Wave*, pp.235–7.

190 J. Naisbitt, *Global Paradox*, pp.16–17.

191 See T. Sakaiya, *Knowledge-Value Revolution*, p.275.

192 See J. Pakulski and M. Waters, *The Death of Class*, p.75.

193 See J. Naisbitt, 'From Nation States to Networks'.
194 See *Drucker on Asia. A Dialogue Between Peter Drucker and Isao Nakauchi*, p.126. The same can be said about the number of companies founded and surviving two decades in high-tech industry. As Tom Forester wrote, of the 250 firms founded in the 1960s in the Silicon Valley, around 31 per cent achieved steady growth, while the rest went bankrupt, merged or were taken over (T. Forester, *High-Tech Society*, p.57).
195 See T. Cannon, *Welcome to the Revolution*, p.269.
196 Galbraith wrote that 'seventy years ago the corporation was the instrument of its owners and a projection of their personalities. The names of these principals – Carnegie, Rockefeller, Harriman, Mellon, Guggenheim, Ford – were known across the land. They are still known, but for the art galleries and philanthropic foundations they established' (J.K. Galbraith, *The New Industrial State*, pp.21–2).
197 P.F. Drucker, *Post-Capitalist Society*, p.101.
198 P.F. Drucker, *Concept of the Corporation*, p.140.
199 D. Bell, *The Coming of Post-Industrial Society*, p.283.
200 Ibid., p.147.
201 See J. Robertson, *Future Wealth*, p.47.
202 See A. Etzioni, *The Spirit of Community*, New York, 1993, p.147.
203 J. Rifkin, *The End of Work*, p.245.
204 A. Etzioni, *The Spirit of Community*, p.144.
205 P.F. Drucker, *The New Realities*, p.198.
206 See J. Rifkin, *The End of Work*, pp.274–5, 241.
207 See P.F. Drucker, *The New Realities*, p.198; *Post-Capitalist Society*, pp.62–3.
208 P.F. Drucker, *Post-Capitalist Society*, p.176.
209 J. Rifkin, *The End of Work*, p.241.
210 A. Etzioni, *The Spirit of Community*, p.25.
211 M. Hammer, *Beyond Reengineering*, p.61.
212 A. Etzioni, *The Spirit of Community*, p.230.
213 *Drucker on Asia. A Dialogue Between Peter Drucker and Isao Nakauchi*, p.144.
214 P.F. Drucker, *The New Realities*, p.198.
215 F. Fukuyama, *Trust*, p.309.
216 A. Sayer and R. Walker, *The New Social Economy*, p.128.
217 J.W. Kuhn and D.W. Shriver, Jr., *Beyond Success*, p.86.
218 Ibid., pp.81–2.
219 See *Time*, **149** (14), 7 April 1997; *Newsweek*, **129** (13), 7 April 1997.
220 See L. Edvinsson and M.S. Malone, *Intellectual Capital*, p.174.

6 The Main Aspects of Post-economic Revolution

It ought to be stressed that the concept 'post-economic society' cannot be used to describe any of the societies that exist today. It is only a scientific abstraction, denoting a set of principles which, as follows from the course of history, have to become the main principles in the social organization that is coming to replace modernity. Even so, the term can and must be used in modern sociological and economic theories.

When a century and a half ago the founders of Marxism observed what seemed to them to be the insurmountable crisis of bourgeois society, they quite rightly assumed that the basis of the new social organization was by natural means being prepared by the whole course of the evolution of the preceding social order. At the beginning of their theoretical journey they described communism, not as a goal which must be established, and not as an ideal to which reality must conform, but as real progress which eliminates the existing state of things.[1]

In the late 1960s, when the theorists of the post-industrial order introduced this new term, they stressed many times that 'the concept of a post-industrial society is not a picture of a complete social order',[2] that the concept was an abstraction which reflected the trends and the framework of contemporary social development. Today we speak of the post-economic condition or state, in the same vein as Marx and Engels spoke of communism and the theorists of the 1960s spoke of post-industrial society. Such a society still does not exist as an integral phenomenon, as a real structure, but is created by natural means by all the changes occurring before our eyes. To paraphrase Marx and Engels, it can be asserted that post-economic society is not a goal that should be established, and it is not an ideal to which reality must conform; it is a real movement which eradicates the contemporary condition or state.

Viewing post-economic society as a society under true formation,

211

we are defining the changes of today as a post-economic revolution. The Marxian theory of social revolutions which act as a watershed between the *Gesellschaftsformationen* serves as direct grounds for this. By this approach we try to stress that it is methodologically consistent and justifiable to set the relations under formation today not only against the laws of the industrial society and even the capitalist society but also against the laws of earlier social forms based on commodity exchange, private ownership and the exploitation of man by man.

The post-economic revolution is the beginning rather than the culmination of the formation of the bases of post-economic society. Take the conventional historical parallel between the post-economic revolution and the industrial revolution. Researchers rightly date the industrial revolution to the second half of the 18th and early 19th centuries. This era of leading technical achievement, the development of new forms of production and the emergence of the class of *industriels* as a key element of the social structure was not, however, marked by the acquisition by the industrial sector of the dominating role in social production. As we know, the agrarian sector accounted for more than a half of gross national product in most European countries and the United States in the middle and even in the second half of the 19th century, about a hundred years after the main events of the industrial revolution unfolded. However, the industrial revolution demonstrated the emergence of a new tendency. It showed that a sector as an alternative to the traditional sector began a rapid and self-sufficient development, one that left the traditional economy no hope of survival. In this respect the post-economic revolution is already in its most distinctive phase, demonstrating to the world perfectly the prospects that are emerging and not leaving any opportunities for the now retrograde industrial economy and economic laws.

The conclusion of the previous chapter set down three main aspects to the overcoming of economic laws: the undermining of market economy relations as the most developed form of commodity exchange, characteristic of the highest phases of *oekonomische Gesellschaftsformation*; the radical alteration of the forms and very nature of private ownership, and its subsequent replacement by personal property; and the change in the essence of the main social conflict, consisting of reducing the role of the exploitation of man by man as the foundation of class conflict and the shift of the main elements of confrontation to the other planes of social life. A separate and unique problem, one with which this chapter does not deal, but which merits a thorough analysis, is the *self-sufficiency of the post-economic transformation*, the problem of correlating the new society with its predominantly industrial, and sometimes even agrarian environment.

All three processes representing the elements of the post-economic revolution determine the content of the development of modern post-industrial societies. Moreover, it must be acknowledged that the problem that gives rise to the most heated debates concerns the historical fates of the market economy, the possibilities for overcoming this economy and the consequences that ensue from this. This is the most general problem as it touches issues associated with the nature of commodity production – one of the most essential characteristics of the economic society – and therefore merits first consideration.

The Destruction of the Market Economy

In all the time that bourgeois society has existed, both its opponents and its advocates have spoken continually about the challenges facing that order: the danger of the proletarian revolution has given way to global problems; the crises of overproduction have given way to the problems of the development of the information sector; and so on. But the bourgeois order cannot be overcome or destroyed by anything other than the destruction of the very model that brought it to life. That model, or premise, was the formation and expansion of the market economy – a complete production system geared towards the production and appropriation of value as common wealth, distinct from and opposing the use value of goods.

It is on the strength of this that capitalist society is based on the principles of the universal commodity economy, and the only truly radical challenge for it may be the destruction of the bases of the market. And if the concepts of *post-industrial* or *information* capitalism bear no inner logical contradiction (although they are a little provocative), then the idea of *post-market* capitalism is nonsense. By overcoming the market as a system, the post-industrial revolution overcomes also the capitalist form of the organization of production as the embodiment of the highest form of the development of the market economy.

In economic and sociological theory the market economy and commodity production are often viewed as identical phenomena. Therefore the more frequent desire to distinguish the notion of the conception of the market economy from theses on the theory of the production and consumption of high-tech and information products is, as a rule, embodied only in calls to replace the economic theory of commodities with a new economic theory of products.[3] This approach brings to the theory of the market and of commodity production the term 'products', besides the concepts of market goods and commodities – a term with such a broad meaning that it cannot be used productively within any applied conception. We are proposing another, more consistent path, based on the theoretical distinction of the terms 'market *economy*' and 'commodity *production*'. These terms are related to but not identical with each other.

Commodity production implies an extremely wide range of phenomena which can be expressed in the following assumption: in society there is a distinct division of labour, and the commodities created by various manufacturers and characterized primarily by their *use value* both for the manufacturers themselves and for other members of society, can be exchanged for other goods which satisfy the manufacturer's needs. Commodity production has been characteristic of all periods of the development of the economic epoch, from the time the elements of the economic order coexisted with the laws of the ancient society right up to the culmination of the formation of the whole complex of laws and relations of the post-economic order. The aim of exchange here is to maximize the appropriable use values and by doing this to reorient the value system of society; this reorientation to the fullest extent responds to the desire of the manufacturer; the principles of the quantitative commensuration of commodities may vary as greatly as from calculating labour costs to a subjective evaluation of the goods' utility.

The *market economy*, on the contrary, is a system in which goods' production appeared to be the production of some kind of common value, and the goods themselves serve as the embodiment of a universal equivalent usually called *value*. The condition for the formation of the market economy is the spread of the principles of commodity exchange not only to the majority of consumer goods but also to all of the main conditions and resources of production. It is for this reason that the market economy arises at the stage when economic society reaches maturity, when the epoch of the progression of *oekonomische Gesellschafstformation* is close to its culmination. We have already quoted Marx, who suggested that 'dans le mouvement historique de l'Europe occidentale, ancienne et moderne, la période de la commune agricole apparaît comme période de transition de la propriété commune à la propriété privée, comme période de transition de la formation primaire à la formation secondaire',[4] and thereby considered that the emergence of *oekonomische Gesellschaftsformation* in its complete form had not been accomplished even in the 19th century. The position of Marx is extremely radical today, and we hold the view that the essential elements of the market economy have been encountered in the economies of European countries only since the 15th or 16th centuries. In contrast to commodity production, the goal of the market economy is to maximize the appropriation of value as the embodiment of wealth; the principles of exchange are strictly equivalent and based on the commensuration of the value of exchangeable goods.

So the transformation of developing commodity production into the market economy over the centuries was one of the main elements of the revolution which has eliminated all non-economic features of the social economy and has resulted in the total domination of the principles of *oekonomische Gesellschaftsformation*. The elimination of the elements of the market economy and the reconstruction of the system of commodity production relations as an instrument for the redistribution of use values, for its part, is a vital characteristic of post-economic transformation.

The market economy differs principally from commodity production in that it must always contain a universal equivalent commensurating the value of the goods to be produced, and the growing rate of appropriation of that equivalent by various manufacturers reflects the growing wealth of the latter. The goal of commodity production, as noted above, consists of the growth of the appropriation of concrete use values; therefore in this case there is no acute need for the equivalent, one which commensurates goods. We suggest that *the main difference between commodity production and the market economy lies in the absence or presence of the basis for the commensuration of goods* which gives exchange its equivalent nature.

This is why the overcoming of the market economy does not require the elimination of the exchange of material and non-material goods and products; the latter would be absurd as information and knowledge acquire genuine value only when consumed as widely as possible by all members of society. The main issue lies in freeing exchange from the equivalent *value* characteristic that prevails over it, in overcoming the supremacy of exchange value over use value.

By exchanging information and knowledge, people are exchanging their own products as commodities. Jean-François Lyotard, for one, wrote: 'Knowledge is and will be produced in order to be sold, it is and will be consumed in order to be valorized in a new production: in both cases, the goal is exchange.'[5] This exchange frequently adopts forms as similar to the forms of market exchange as the products of creativity are outwardly similar to the products of labour. However in today's conditions there arises the exclusively important phenomenon that information products, social goods, cultural values and all other products to the extent that they are the products of creativity *cannot be reproduced* and for that reason cannot be set against each other in any equivalent value exchange. Created by activity which cannot be reduced to abstract labour in the Marxian sense, and embodying the factors of production without being subjected to objective evaluation, these goods depart from the traditional forms of market exchange.

The proportions of exchange of products like these for other goods or money are based on the real or imagined social or individual utility they incorporate. This utility is not subject to objective valuation, therefore exchange assumes forms essentially similar to the exchange in advance – the primitive form of commodity transaction which was widespread during the emergence of the economic epoch. As in those times the alienation of goods was initiated in anticipation of the reciprocal alienation of products, implicitly and in advance acknowledged to have a value equivalent to that of the alienated goods, so today the producers of information and knowledge anticipate how their activity will be valued by its consumers or by society as a whole. In contrast with the economic epoch, characterized by the cumulative development of commodity relations and the complication of their structure, the post-economic epoch is based primarily on the return to commodity exchange of its former goals and purposes, on the overcoming of that *market* character that had been assumed by *commodity* relations.

Turning to the consideration of the formation of the principally new qualities of contemporary goods, which makes their commodity exchange possible, but which departs from the realms of market economy, we must dwell on two problems which one way or another concern the quantitative measurement of value: on the changes taking place in the structure and main characteristics of the economy, and on modifications of nature and the character of reproduction processes.

In the traditional market economy the three main conditions and factors of production were land, capital and labour, to be more precise elements of matter as a primary resource, the social form of the organization of production as a secondary resource and the reproductive activity of man as the main element of the process of production. The situation today has altered radically. The primary matter is being replaced by a primary ideal resource, namely *information*, understood in its broadest sense. The place of capital as an instrument of the organization of production is being occupied by knowledge in the form of *intellectual capital* which enables real use to be made of information as the premise for the production of new knowledge. And labour is being replaced by *creativity*, the motives, methods and results of which cannot be reproduced on a broad scale. In the traditional economy all three factors of production have to a great extent been subjected to objectification and reproduction, but in the new conditions this becomes practically impossible.

The problem of reproduction is also being seriously modified. The non-reproducibility of a product is no longer the simple consequence of the inability of the factors of production to be reproduced; valuations of the goods created change constantly, not only as a result of the improvement of production, but also on the strength of the continuous modifications of public opinion concerning those goods.

The subjective nature of such valuations increases constantly, and this begins to determine the features and proportion of contemporary reproduction processes. However paradoxical these statements may seem, today, when it would appear that the potential of the capitalist mode of production has not yet been fully exhausted, life brings the researchers a wealth of examples to illustrate the notions formulated.

As a result the goods to be produced lose, as in an avalanche, the real basis for their commensuration. But the loss by the products of contemporary production of their commensurability is nothing other than the overcoming of the evaluation of goods through value; that is, the destruction of value. Since the appropriation of value as the embodiment of wealth was the main goal of manufacturers in the market economy, the elimination of value is inevitable and leads to the destruction of the very production system. And, finally, to carry the subject further, it is the destruction of value that heralds the twilight of the development of the economic epoch, the beginning of that process which we will describe as the post-economic revolution.

The Factors of Contemporary Production

The majority of economists and sociologists in the 1960s and 1970s regarded post-industrial society as a system in which material production assigns the role of the main economic sector to the production of services and information. But as we have already noted, the share of the primary and secondary sectors in the gross national product of most countries has not fallen during the last few decades; the information revolution, and this is becoming more obvious, is not developing in one specific sector of the economy, but is penetrating all spheres of social production. Its main consequence is not so much an increase in the share of information products in the overall volume of products as growth in the importance of information in any production process and, correspondingly, the growth of the contribution of information to social wealth. As a result, not only the tertiary, quaternary and quintary sectors become the focus of new economic phenomena, but also traditional sectors of production, sometimes to a greater extent than the services sphere, prove to be affected by the changed economic reality. The basis of these changes is the new character of those factors of production which make it impossible to reproduce a finished product and calculate its value. What precisely do we have in mind?

Firstly, the changed conditions of production have greatly reduced demand for raw materials, energy and labour expenditures themselves. Since the mid-1970s, the industries of all leading powers have been consuming fewer traditional materials, mainly coal, oil and metals, replacing these with new advanced but cheaper products. In the second half of the 1970s, when the United States experienced industrial growth, the country started to consume less of all types of energy, and this trend has been sustained almost entirely since 1979.[6] We have already mentioned an absolute drop in employment in industry since the late 1970s, a drop which in the following decade also started to affect construction and transport. The industrial growth of the 1980s and 1990s occurred in most Western countries not only without increased consumption of energy, raw and other materials,[7] but also without the hiring of additional workers: in 1988, former levels of industrial output in America were sustained by just 40 per cent of the blue-collar labour employed 15 years before.[8] The result was a situation where 'manufacturing is increasingly becoming uncoupled from labour'.[9]

All of this is altering the face of contemporary production in a big way. The first difficulties in contemporary economic theory arise. If for many decades the dominating view has been that the cost of a product is formed by the factors of production, and that each of those factors enters the production process possessing a certain social value,[10] today this approach no longer explains either the laws of production or the proportions of the exchange of the goods produced.

Secondly, information becomes a vital production factor now to be understood not as knowledge embodied in machines but as the immediately productive force.[11] While not even being treated as the basis of intellectual capital, information has in the last few decades become the most desirable element of the economy, so spurring the rapid growth of its production, circulation and consumption. The first sectors to experience this were the sectors which broadcast and distributed information. The world telecommunications equipment market grew by more than 50 per cent between 1986 and 1990,[12] and continues to grow. The American market for telecommunications and facsimile communications grew from $63 billion to $185 billion between 1991 and 1996 alone, while the Asia–Pacific region's market is expected to be worth as much as $200 billion by the year 2000.[13] However, since information and high-tech products are most subject to continual and rapid depreciation (the cost of international telephone calls across the Atlantic has contracted by more than 700 times in the last 50 years[14] the growth projections for this market are far from reflecting the real growth of production in the corresponding sectors.

Even more radical changes are taking place in the production of computer software. Every year sees the broader and broader application of computer technology. In more than 15 years between the mid-1970s and early 1990s, the number of computer data base users has risen by more than 50 times.[15] The list of similar examples goes on and on.

We have become witnesses to a radical shift in production towards the information sector. Its quantitative estimation varies greatly: some sources say that information sector workers earn more than half of a country's entire income,[16] that more than 65 per cent of the workforce of the United States[17] and nearly 65 per cent of the workforce of Britain[18] are employed in this sector. We think a more realistic estimation is contained in the following statement:

> The value added of information products and services to the United States Gross National Product is, today, slightly greater than 45%, and for Europe and Japan somewhat more than 40%. The world information industry, even if narrowly defined ... will be greater than $500 billion before the end of the decade. The production, processing and distribution of information is a major industry throughout the world. By the year 2000, it will account for about 40% of the world's industrial production.[19]

But even these estimations make it possible to agree with the fact that 'unlike the Agricultural Revolution, the Information Revolution will not take a millennia to do its work. Unlike the Industrial Revolution, its impact will not be spread over centuries. The Information Revolution will happen within a lifetime'.[20]

The importance of information and knowledge in modern production is defined not by the number of jobs provided by the 'information sector' and not by the share of gross national product that information constitutes. The real importance of the economic revolution taking place today lies in the fact that information as a new and totally unusual factor of production is present in each act of production as a vital element, by the strength of which each product created by society one way or another becomes similar to the information product. It becomes a commodity, and the real expenditures of labour and of production factors required for its reproduction and, consequently, its value, turn out to be incalculable. To understand the full scale of the change taking place, we will look at the parameters by which information and knowledge are distinguished from a number of traditional economic forms.

Information is a unique factor of production, distinguished from all previous ones in that it is not measured in finite terms, is inexhaustible and has such a broad scope for consumption. Once produced, information is distributed among any number of members of a society; moreover, the unlimited distribution of information does not contradict its inner nature. Of course, in a society dominated by commodity relations, information is produced as a commodity, and it must be exchanged for the use values required by the producer. This is turned into the desire to consolidate the right of intellectual ownership in patents, licences and copyright, in other words to monopolize the knowledge created. However, such a monopoly, as a rule, is only transient, and it relates usually to the sphere in which specific scientific achievements are technologically applicable. It does not limit the opportunities for access to the information for researchers and knowledge workers that becomes a source to generate new knowledge.[21] Besides, such barriers are not insurmountable for the distribution of information. Moreover, information resources are becoming more accessible and cheaper by the year[22] (for example the cost of a computer, calculated per megabyte of hard disc memory, fell by more than 2100 times in the period from 1983 to 1996 alone[23]) and patenting laws are unable to protect information from distribution. Software suppliers suffered annual losses of about $1 billion from unsanctioned copying and distribution in the United States in the mid-1990s, and over $3.5 billion in Asia and Europe.[24] So to prevent and even to duly sanction the distribution of information is impossible in today's conditions. Some economists prefer to consider this phenomenon by using the concept of 'non-rival information'.[25]

Information and knowledge do not have the distinguishing quality of *scarcity*: to be more precise, information might have this quality, but this is a very special type of phenomenon which we will discuss below. Usually it is quite possible in practice to assert that

> knowledge is expandable and self-generating. The raw goods of an industrial economy are finite resources; iron ore is used up as steel is manufactured. Unlike iron ore, however, knowledge increases as it is used. In using my knowledge to perform a task, I improve my knowledge and expand my understanding of the task. A surgeon who has performed an operation ten times has more knowledge and understanding of the operation than a surgeon who has performed it once. Thus in a knowledge economy, a scarcity of resources is replaced by an expansion of resources.[26]

Information self-generates more rapidly if a person works in a collective: the emerging system of permanent training and constant creative activity is becoming one of the main conditions for the development of the company, conditions that do not require major material expenditures. A typical feature of the present-day information society is the fact that the information *distribution* sector tends to grow faster than the information *production* sector; in Japan in the early 1980s, up to 13 per cent of the total workforce were engaged in the production of information, compared with over 20 per cent in the distribution of information.[27]

Finally, information lacks the *consumer* characteristic as it is understood in the traditional sense. Information is consumed by a researcher or knowledge worker firstly to develop new information and knowledge, and secondly without limiting the opportunities for other members of society to use the same information for their own needs. As Nicholson pointed out,

> most information is durable and retains value after it has been used. Unlike a hot dog, which is consumed only once, knowledge ... can be used not only by the person who discovers it, but also by any friends with whom the information is shared ... in a special case of this situation, information has the characteristic of a pure public good ... That is, the information is both nonrival in that others may use it at the zero cost and nonexclusive in that no individual can prevent others from using the information. The classic example of these properties is a new scientific discovery.[28]

Thus we find in information hardly any of the features that effected the traditional form of involving the main economic resources in the process of market reproduction. Therefore it would be logical to presume that the value characteristics of information products also must differ markedly from the characteristics of the products of mass production.

Regarding the evaluation of information, we will single out one more feature of information and knowledge – one that relates to neither finiteness, nor exhaustibility nor consumption in their traditional sense, but which can impose a very tight limitation on the spread of information goods: *Information and knowledge may possess the highest degree of scarcity, which we will call 'selectivity'*. The specific nature of human perception, a person's attitudes, the conditions for a person's development, psychological characteristics, the ability to generalize, memory and so on are all defined as *intellect*, and this is the main limiting factor of the spread of information and knowledge. It is on account of this that meaningful knowledge is assimilated by a select few people who become the genuine owners of this knowledge, however protected it may be by patents of one kind or another. This knowledge turns these people's intellect into *intellectual capital* – the second vital factor of production – and the power that these people receive over social goals into power of the highest level and non-economic nature. *For the first time in history, a condition for ownership turns out not to be the right to dispose of a good but the ability to use that good.*

The meaning of information as a primary economic resource is associated with the gigantic growth in the role of the organization of the production process. Moreover, this organization does not so much resolve the technical purposes of mass-production as stimulate the assimilation of information and the development of new knowledge, and provides the conditions in which the creative opportunities of a worker may be opened up to the greatest degree. All of this is so important that sociologists and economic theorists have for more than 20 years now been busily researching 'human capital', which today occupies no lesser a position than financial capital.

These studies have enriched science with the concept of intellectual capital, and it is in this that many have sought explanation of the new economic realities. It is becoming clearer and clearer that this phenomenon is complex and has many aspects. The opinion that 'what is meant by intellectual capital is the combination of four factors: your genetic inheritance, your education, your experience, and your attitudes about life and business' was the dominant one back in the early 1990s; moreover, most of the attention has been paid to the fact that every person 'has a unique combination of these four factors. Whatever total intellectual capital you have is in fact singular; its structure is unique. Intellectual capital cannot be mass produced'.[29] All that was said here was that the environment in which a person works has a marked effect on the formation of his intellectual capital. However, a few years later this phenomenon has come to be viewed primarily in its social aspect, through the prism of its effect on the guarantee of competitiveness and development of the collective and of the company as a whole. To quote Lief Edvinsson and Michael Malone, 'intellectual capital is the possession of the knowledge, applied experience, organizational technology, customer rela- tionships and professional skills that provide [a company] with a competitive edge in the market'.[30] Moreover, they describe intellectual capital as a production resource belonging to a specific industrial company.[31]

This change of stance is of course explained by the *practical meaning* which intellectual capital gains in contemporary circumstances. Just as in the industrial epoch the value of a finished product and the profits from its sale depended not so much on the sum of the cost of the factors of its production as on the nature of their combination, in the post-economic revolution the type of information used and the methods of its application exert a huge influence on the results of the production process. And if in the early 1990s William Hudson tended to use the hypothetical style, when he wrote: 'I hope to draw the reader's attention away from the extrasomatic concept of monetary capital to the mental source of wealth, which is surely our intelligence and the ability to use it fully. I submit that just as a business has a "capital assets sheet", it should also have a recognition of its "intellectual capital"', and continued: 'In the coming decade, banking capital will not be of greater importance to the firm than intellectual capital',[32] then just a few years later the fact that intellectual capital must be manifested in monetary values and the fact that their adequate definition is absolutely vital for an industrial company was no longer subject to serious doubt.[33]

We think it useful to make two remarks regarding the nature of research into intellectual capital. Firstly, the widespread understanding of intellectual capital today testifies to the desire to use the results of research in practice rather than to conceptualize the essence of this new phenomenon. The original definition of intellectual capital is more consistent and productive than the desire to use this term to denote new factors with no direct relation to the material conditions of production. Secondly, no actual method for evaluating the intellectual capital of a company has yet been proposed. We will demonstrate below that the growing discrepancies between the book value of a firm's assets and their market value, often presented as a fine demonstration of the intellectual capital within a firm, in fact mean neither that the value of such an asset is subject to measurement nor that it exists at all.

The understanding of the role and meaning of intellectual capital began to form in the 1970s, when the notion of scientific knowledge as an immediately productive force was widespread, and unprecedented successes by a number of companies from the high-technology sector without considerable material assets were noted. This became typical throughout the world in the 1980s. Acer, until recently a little-known Taiwanese firm with a start-up capital of $25 000 and 11 employees, in 1994 had '8,200 employees worldwide, 70 offices in 27 countries, and revenue ... of almost $3 billion';[34] the invention and constant improvement by a group of specialists of the original model of the portable computer resulted in the fact that 'in 1986 Compaq officially became the fastest-growing US corporation ever, when it entered the *Fortune 500* more quickly and at a higher position than even Apple had achieved'.[35]

Scholars point to the obvious fact that

> with the advent of 'high technology', the markets' ideas of value can be seen to be changing. The stock market appears to be fully aware of the potential value of intellectual capital. If a ratio is taken, for instance, between the 'book value' (or 'physical replacement value') of a company and its 'stock market value' (i.e., its stock price times the number of shares outstanding), this ratio will generally be much higher for companies like Microsoft than for companies like Emerson Electric. The ratio for Microsoft in 1990 was 8 to 1, for Emerson Electric, 2 to 1.[36]

But these figures are far from telling the whole story. Microsoft, with the mere announcement that it would introduce its Windows 95 programme, gave its shares such a boost that the company's market value topped that of Boeing within a few days. Also in 1995, IBM, after a long fight, acquired the Lotus corporation, which occupied seventh or eighth place on the American software market; moreover, a company reckoned to be worth about $230 million was bought for $3.5 billion, and became an example of the biggest takeover in the American computer industry. Another record-breaker was Netscape, also a software producer, which at the beginning of 1997 possessed assets worth $17 million and employed a little more than 50 people, but had a market value of more than $3 billion.[37]

These examples only demonstrate the massive scale now acquired by the difference between the book value and the market value of a company's assets. Taking the American economy as a whole, we see that 'over the past twenty years there has been a significant widening of the gap between the values of enterprises state in corporate balance sheets and investors assessment of those values. [The median market-to-book value ratio for US public corporations over a 20-year period between 1973 and 1993 increased from 0.82 to 1.692.] The gap in 1992 indicates that roughly forty percent of market value of the median U.S. public corporation was missing from the balance sheet.'[38]

However, while acknowledging the important role of information as a factor of modern production, we cannot agree with the view that the phenomena discussed were conditioned by including in the market value of companies or their products the value of intellectual capital or the information applied. The very concept of value loses its effect when the number of value-source factors continually multiplies, as in many modern conceptions. We think that *value* as a category of mass market production is today not only becoming immeasurable but *is even ceasing to exist altogether* under the influence of many factors, from the selectivity of information to the transformation of labour as an economically motivated activity into creativity, indefinable in terms of value. Losing the role of an equivalent of exchangeable goods, value presents the possibility for utility valuations, which to a great extent prevail even today. The excess market value of the leading companies demonstrates only that their product, their possibilities and their potential contribution to the growth of production are given an exclusively high evaluation, as a result of which, on the one hand, society is prepared to invest in such production and, on the other, financial companies, confident of elevating the social meaning of this production, achieve local financial goals by investing money in it.

We now go on to discuss the modification of the structure and dynamics of the *reproduction processes* of the last few decades and the main trends in the destruction of value relations.

Reproduction Processes and the Destruction of Value Relations

It ought to be mentioned that the value problem has always been discussed, and is discussed today, in the context of the market economy, and value itself is interpreted as the basis of the exchange of the products of mass-production, which assume a commodity form. It is the constant nature of the process of creating relatively unified goods that enables the market economy to function; it is the possibility of their unlimited reproduction that determines the everyday character of commodity transactions, a vital condition for the preservation and growth of market infrastructure. To quote Scott Lash, 'the process of commodification is probably more complex in the sphere of *reproduction* than it is either in that of production or exchange'.[39] Therefore at the root of the modern economy development lie the processes of reproduction – both of elements of material wealth, and of social relations; their growth also sets the historical prospects of the category of value.

Marx, as we know, adhered to the labour theory of value and suggested that value is determined not by the amount of labour time expended directly on the production of a good but on the amount of labour time required to reproduce a given good,[40] moreover 'in a given state of society, with a given social average intensity, and average skill of the labour employed'.[41] This definition supposes that a commodity, as the subject of exchange, is reproducible and the costs of reproduction are measurable. This approach is the cornerstone of the whole Marxian theory of capitalism, which acknowledges that 'the value of the labour power ... is determined by the quantity of labour required for its reproduction'.[42] Correspondingly, if the value of labour power cannot be measured in the proposed manner, and if the factors which guarantee its reproduction should contain products which cannot be assessed in terms of value, the Marxian theory of surplus value becomes inapplicable. Pursuing the issue, we inevitably conclude that the production system, which does not entail the exchange of goods based on measurable values and in accordance with these, cannot be termed capitalist in the strict sense of the word.

The marginalists, adherents to the theoretical conception alternative to Marxism, are also unable to ignore discussion of the reproduction processes. They discuss a market where buyers and sellers compete; moreover, consumers define their preferences on the basis of the commensuration of price and utility, and the producers on the basis of the commensuration of price and costs. The movement of prices as a result of the change in demand and supply denotes the certain presence in this theoretical model of the concept of reproduction.

Both Marxism and marginalism account for a huge number of

factors which affect the quantifying of value assessments. Both the Marxists and the marginalists, acting within the framework of their own terminological schemes, one way or another return to the assessment of the problem of reproduction, although they approach it from different angles. The Marx and Engels definition that 'value is the relation of production costs to utility'[43] contradicts to a much lesser extent than it is customary to think the widespread thesis of marginalists that 'value relates relative scarcity to utilities',[44] since production costs and the scarcity of a good are only two differing aspects of the singular reproduction process. And if in Marxism the factor of the limitation of goods is viewed primarily in the sense of the influence on the cost of production via fluctuations of demand and supply, which cause cost to deviate from value, then in modern economics this factor is viewed in the sense of the immediate influence on demand and via this on an equilibrious market price. However, both the influence of demand and supply and the factor of scarcity relate mainly to the value and price of goods which can be reproduced en masse; the theory of economics is, incidentally, a little more suited to the present situation as it gives natural scarcity more meaning than does the Marxian conception.

But the reproduction processes are currently undergoing significant changes that may, we think, become the basis for a radical review of the role of the value characteristics of social production. Three processes undermine the nature of value most of all. The first and most obvious is the acquisition of more and more uniqueness and irreproducibility by the traditional forms of market goods; that is, goods representing the output of a fully identifiable manufacturer and intended for individual consumption. The development of this tendency is based, on the one hand, on a more noticeable progression from mass consumption to specialized consumption. This process is not accidental or episodic, and is one of the essential components of the now unfolding postmodernist changes. As present-day sociologists remark, 'postmodernist culture ... encourages the consumption of goods as "sign-values" rather than use-values; if the consumption of use-values implies that there is at some point coherent limits to the level of consumer demands, the consumption of sign-values does not'.[45] In this case the situation arises in which human needs are far less predictable, thereby making it less possible to apply traditional economic theory both to analyse the formation of demand and to determine the value of the goods consumed. Moreover, any accumulation of so-called 'prestige consumption' requires the maximum diversity of products, and the very factor of the uniqueness and individual nature of goods causes their price to soar, even though production costs may rise completely dis-proportionately.

On the other hand, the tendency described is based on the fact that, as the information revolution unfolds, the irreproducibility of goods becomes not only possible but also necessary on an ever-increasing scale. When the traditional factors of production and the organizational functions of capital are replaced by information products, knowledge and the ability of workers, the process of reproduction changes radically,[46] as a result of which the production of individual goods and goods with a small run begins to prevail. Furthermore, it must be noted that reproduction, the costs of which lie at the basis of value assessments, is not the same as copying; the mass-*copying* of computer programs, data bases, videocassettes and so on is not identical to *reproduction*, and the price of such products is not a reflection of their value. Given how much of the market is filled by goods which are copied rather than reproduced, it is possible to make deductions about the extent to which the outward appearance of value estimations today replaces their real manifestation.

As Martin wrote:

> This question of value becomes even more complex when it is considered in relation to information. Economics is founded on the concept of scarcity. Value relates relative scarcity to utilities, yet information is almost never scarce in this sense. Moreover, traditional views which perceive information and communication as being somehow separate from the world of commodity production and exchange still retain a good deal of force. This essential *difference* of information in an economic sense is very evident in the context of production functions, where the inputs of labour, capital and raw material which combine to make up any good or service are subdivided into constituent elements, each of which can be mapped along continuous cost curves. So far as information is concerned, there are few stable production functions and no easy subdivisions.[47]

Although many scholars today comment on the change of the structure of demand and on the progress of information technologies, responsible for the growing diversity of consumer goods, this process is to a considerable extent only a potential source of the undermining of value relations. Their mass-reproduction becomes *unnecessary*, rather than *impossible*. The expenditures of the factors of production and labour on the creation of individualized and unique goods are difficult to measure, but they exist as an entity and can, if required, be determined with sufficient accuracy. Thus laws of value are being undermined at this level only on the scale in which mass-production is being overcome and the measurement of the value of labour power is being made more complicated.

The second process which is undermining the nature of value is associated with the production of two categories of goods: goods which do not have a mass individual consumer and goods which are consumed only by social groups or society as a whole. The first category consists of products with a high degree of uniqueness, which to a large extent represent items of exchange in the 'sign economy' which is referred to more and more frequently today. These products are not homogeneous, but most of them are related to culture and may be classed as knowledge irreducible to information. Entering an area in which most interactions are of a clearly expressed interpersonal nature, we find ourselves totally unable to quantify value indicators. As Nico Stehr writes,

> attempts to quantify knowledge are difficult to justify because knowledge is less as well as more than a conventional commodity and its value. In a strictly economic account, the value of a commodity can only be determined on the basis of the price it generates in market context. But knowledge rarely acquires such an exchange value; ... the value of knowledge is by no means self-evident.[48]

This understanding may be fully applied to the whole sphere of the exchange and consumption of works of art and cultural values,[49] a sphere in which the irreproducibility and uniqueness of the product itself are combined with the individual and therefore wholly specific nature of that product's consumption and assimilation. Here the monetary evaluation of the corresponding goods has no value basis whatsoever and is grounded only on the correlation between demand and supply and, to a relatively lesser extent, on the historically established methods of correlating them with mass-produced goods.[50]

The second category consists of goods which do not have a specific individual consumer. Services intended for the consumption of selected communities or society as a whole have also not been subjected to traditional value assessments. This issue was raised for the first time back in the 1960s, when it became obvious that the traditional System of National Accounts did not reflect many elements of economic growth or many aspects of the well-being of citizens. Bell commented on the importance of this fact when he wrote that 'in assessing *public* services we do not have a means of estimating actual benefits or values'.[51] A commission was set up in the United States, one which worked out the principles of the System of Social Accounts, in an effort to assess the public services.[52] The System consisted of several sections, the indicators of which were designed to define the 'quality of life' and its growth. The analysis yielded only one result, a conception of 'social opportunity costs', which defines how much society spends on the 'quality of life', based on factors like personal income growth, the growth of government costs on education and healthcare, the creation of jobs for categories of people who had been discriminated against in the past, and so on. It is quite clear that all the merits of these approaches and their meaning for the assessment of various social policy measures are combined with the recognition of the fact that the very value of social goods cannot be assessed adequately. Despite all the attempts to create a system for such an assessment, Bell had to acknowledge that 'for technical and conceptual reasons one cannot measure the value of such goods in market terms'.[53] We think that this statement, made a quarter of a century ago, is no less valid today.

In the context of our analysis it is important to stress that, when humanity is departing from the framework of the industrial economy, when the prevalent system of values and motivation changes, and the needs of people are no longer unified, relations between members of society and the collective become not only a first-degree economic resource, but also one of the principal products of contemporary production. The problem, which lies in the lack of possibilities for 'reflecting an economic value for them'[54] must be recognized as one of exclusive importance. In this connection it is possible to mention that the overvaluation of companies which apply considerable intellectual capital, as described above, was to a great extent conditioned also by the confidence of investors in the creative abilities and the well coordinated activity of the collectives they comprised. The value of social and collective unity, communicative conduct and other factors to be observed only on the level of interpersonal interaction is very high today; however, this sector of *values* also lies beyond the realms of value assessments.

The third process which undermines the very nature of value is related to the expansion of individual activity, which is becoming more and more self-sufficient. Its importance in the destruction of value relations depends on two factors. Firstly, the quantitative growth of atomized producers results in the growth of the market share of individualized goods and the contraction of the sphere of mass-production; in this respect the consequences of individual activity are similar to the consequences of the general demassification of production, of which this individual activity is a factor. Secondly, the phenomenon of the 'prosumer', mentioned by Toffler, arises. This phenomenon no longer affects the abstract–theoretical category of value as one of the foundations of the market system, but the market system itself, based on value. Here we encounter not the difficulty of measurement or the indefinability of value as one of the most important premises of demarketisation, but the very process of demarketisation as such. As Toffler wrote: 'The market ... is a direct, inescapable consequence of the divorce of producer from consumer. Wherever this divorce occurs the market arises. And wherever the gap between producer and consumer narrows, the entire function, role and power of the market is brought into question.'[55]

This book is too short to examine households in detail, but we will mention that modern man expends a very large amount of effort on improving the conditions and forms of his everyday life; by some estimates, if these efforts could be converted into total labour time expended on social production, the share of products and services produced for household consumption would equal from 10 to 15 per cent of gross domestic product. These products and services do not acquire market form and, correspondingly, they do not acquire value assessment; moreover, with the growth of 'prosumerism' this sector has a clear tendency to expand.

All three processes of the destruction of value relations are conditioned primarily by the changing nature of social interaction. The classical forms of the manifestation of the market economy are present where mass-producers conflict with mass-consumers, and all of them together are guided by intrinsically economic motives. When this order is destroyed the value character of exchange, too, is destroyed, and the destruction of the bases of the market economy begins. In the first case we encountered the simplest situation, in which mass-production and the mass-consumer are replaced by individualized production and the individualized consumer. This to a large extent preserves the value characteristics of the economy, and only their quantitative measurement is made difficult. In the second case, consumers represented by communities or society as a whole conflict with the individual producer. Now value becomes impossible to quantify, rather than difficult to measure. In the third case, the rift with the traditional principles is more decisive. As the household, 'prosumerism' and the relatively closed production collectives develop, the value characteristics are eliminated from selected sectors of the economy no longer as a premise but as a consequence of the overcoming of market tendencies.

Thus the value regulators of social production are no longer as valid as they were for industrial society. Now we will look at a problem which we will conventionally term 'the problem of productivity'. We will examine how the results of production today are evaluated in monetary form, and the extent to which monetary estimations, which are close to value indicators in mass-production, can be regarded as such in our era. By analysing these issues we will reveal further proof that value relations are being undermined – proof that is more global and all-embracing than that commented on above.

The modern economy is clearly separated into the service and material production sectors. All of the economic and sociological studies of recent decades confirm the tendency for employment to increase in the service sector and the information branches of the economy. As we have mentioned, not more than 12 per cent of America's total workforce were employed in manufacturing operations in the early 1980s;[56] the indicator had fallen to 10 per cent in the United States in the early 1990s, and was about 12 per cent in Japan.[57] The number of employees in Japanese industry, which attained 30 per cent of the total workforce in the mid-1990s, should, by the year 2000, contract by nearly half.[58] The list of similar examples could be continued.

Branches which produce high-technology services and information products and, first and foremost, healthcare, education, insurance, consulting and financial services, use only highly qualified employees, who receive a far higher wage than the average. Costs on scientific and technical designs are measured in hundreds of billions of dollars in the world in general. All of this, under the prevalence of traditional economic laws, should inevitably result in the high final value of the product, and its evaluation per employee should also prove very high; thus productivity as it is traditionally understood should be above average. However, this is not true in practice. The services and information sectors, which contain the companies with the highest market capitalization, do not yield higher productivity than the industrial sector. Moreover, there is the inexplicable (from the point of view of the theory of value) fact that *productivity in these sectors is declining compared with productivity in the more traditional sectors*. And although many researchers argue that, with the transition to the development of the knowledge sector, evaluations of the goods produced become less defined than in material production, something that must be reflected in the productivity (as Harold Linstone and Ian Mitroff write, 'productivity is a well-established industrial manufacturing measure of worker output for a given level of input. In an information-technology era, the traditional means of measuring productivity become inappropriate'[59]) we believe that this does not solve the whole problem, and that the 'immeasurability' of productivity conceals one of the most vital aspects of the process of the overcoming of value relations.

Statistics testify that in practically all developed countries the share of the tertiary sector and of information production in gross national product grows solely on account of the shift in workforce and inputs to the new sectors of the economy. The situation in which the relatively small change in this correlation requires the mobilization of huge labour and material resources is becoming more widespread. Between 1958 and 1980, the knowledge industry or knowledge production in the United States grew from 28.6 per cent to 34.3 per cent of GNP, or by nearly one-fifth.[60] However, that was achieved by engaging twice as many employees in the production of information and knowledge as at the end of the 1950s. Specialists calculate that the productivity of employees in the production of information, in constant prices, was the same in the early 1990s as it had been 30 years before.[61] But

> manufacturing production in America is likely to stay at about the same 23 percent of gross national product, which, for the next ten or fifteen years, should mean another near doubling. During the same period, however, employment in manufacturing is likely to fall to 12 percent or less of the total labour force. That would mean a further fairly sharp shrinkage to the total number of people employed in manufacturing work.[62]

As we have mentioned, if in 1960 the amount of GDP produced per employee in the tertiary sector was about 77.5 per cent of that produced per employee in the manufacturing sector, the indicator had fallen to 69.35 per cent in 1992, and has fallen more rapidly in the last few years. Do these figures prove that highly qualified employees in the more advanced sectors are creating less and less national wealth? We think that such a state of affairs is inconceivable.

So what does the situation that is emerging mean? In our view there is only one answer: *value assessments in their traditional sense are not applicable in the modern economy.* The shift of the workforce to the service sector is taking place under the influence both of the informatization and atomization of material production, and of the high degree of satisfaction with activity in the information sectors. The desire to obtain long-term or momentary benefit from this process is causing unjustified demand for intellectual capital and the assets of information companies; the more rapidly the spread of creativity eliminates any objective ideas about the value of the products of these sectors, the more rapidly the price of these assets rises. In the midst of all this, the major expenditures on information and technological inputs, coupled with the conservatism of social ideas and preferences, sustain the relatively high level of prices for material goods; and it is here that the unnatural disbalance in the productivity of labour in the different sectors arises. All of this to some extent testifies to the inadequacy of the traditional value characteristics of social production.

The science of economics is seeking two ways out of this situation. Firstly, some theorists are uncovering the desire for some palliative solution. Understanding that value is formed by many factors of production, it is logical to treat all of the new production processes and phenomena – from information as a primary economic resource to intellectual capital as a new form of the organization of the production process – as additional sources of value, besides the traditional ones. Moreover, since it is virtually impossible to measure the value of these conditions of production, all monetary evaluations both of contemporary products and of the production companies themselves can be explained by an appeal to those conditions.

But another, directly opposite, solution would seem more preferable. Attempts to determine the value of goods by the cost of factors of production should be abandoned if, firstly, the sheer number and complexity of the factors of production *prevent* the expenditure of social efforts on the creation of goods from being quantified, and, secondly, such a measurement *is not essential* since the pressure on a person of the material conditions of life has been overcome and the activity of people to an ever-increasing extent is motivated by non-economic factors. It must be acknowledged that the period of exchange on the basis of these value categories is virtually ended, and the proportions and laws of exchange, which are formed within the approaching post-economic epoch, ought to be studied as closely as possible.

The current period is somewhat reminiscent of the epoch of the emergence of the market economy. Value relations formed in such distant times against the background of the radical negation of the very idea of value, and the personal wealth that later became the basis of industrial capitalism was acquired in international commerce. And to the same extent that the prices of the goods which entered Europe did not depend on the costs of their acquisition and delivery, assessments both of the contemporary production of information and of its products are not determined by the expenditure of labour and factors of production. Moreover, to the same extent that the capitals that formed in the commercial transactions of the late Middle Ages laid the basis of the new society and of industrial production, the current quasi-value investments in the new branches of production are enabling an information economy to emerge and the foundations of post-economic society to be formed.

The Diffusion of Value and the Future of the Market Economy

The heated debate on the definition of value arose not so much from the theoretical topicality of the issue as such as from the fact that the solution of the more important and more general issue of the fate of the market economy depends on the nature of the responses to the questions surrounding the future of value exchange. And the very fact that, as Robert Heilbroner rightly points out, 'general problematic of value … is the effort to tie the surface phenomena of economic life to some inner structure or order'[63] makes these problems indivisible.

For centuries value has been associated with equivalent exchange, the latter with freedom of entrepreneurship and the capitalist type of economy which, in turn, are the fundamental values of contemporary developed societies. Not least because of tradition is the theoretical acknowledgement of the possibility for overcoming, and the more so the actual overcoming, of the value nature of exchange a matter of extreme complexity for the researcher. It is for this reason that, the more developed the non-market sectors of the economy become, and the more challenges against value are recorded by economists and sociologists, the more aggressive the apologetics of value become, the more severe the statements by those inclined to treat value as a category virtually distanced from history. Interestingly, the authors of works in which the advantages of the post-industrial order and irreversibility of the information revolution are demonstrated with the most conviction sometimes take this approach.

The evolution of modern views on the problem of value can in a sense be compared with the development of the assessment by economists of the problem of the productive and non-productive nature of labour. As is well-known, the division of labour within social production into the productive and non-productive dates back to the creators of political economy as a science, people who in the 16th–17th centuries attempted by this to justify the prevalent importance of the primary sector for a country's economy. This approach began to be undermined with the development of the industrial economy and had fully outlived its time by the beginning of the 20th century. J.S. Mill, one of the first to begin to study the issue, considered that all labour that created utility was productive, and that

> utilities produced by labor are of three kinds. They are, first, utilities fixed and embodied in outward objects; by labor employed in investing external material things with properties which render them serviceable to human beings ... Secondly, utilities fixed and embodied in human beings; the labor being in this case employed in conferring on human beings qualities which render them serviceable to themselves and others ... Thirdly and lastly, utilities not fixed or embodied in any object, but consisting in a mere service rendered.[64]

The theory that only activity embodied in material and non-material goods having no actual utility is to be regarded as non-productive was introduced by Garnier,[65] then formulated far more fully by Jevons[66] and gained its most coherent rendition in the works of Marshall.[67] Thus the debate unfolded towards the acknowledging new, and new types of, labour as productive, to such an extent that the very concept of productive labour became virtually unnecessary.

Many modern researchers attempt to give debates on the sources of value a similar character. In their latest book, Alvin Toffler and Heidi Toffler write: 'In the new economy the receptionist and the investment banker who assembles the capital, the key punch operator and the salesperson, as well as the systems designer and tele-communications specialist all add value. Even more significantly, so does the customer. Value results from a total effort rather than from one isolated step in the process.'[68] One can agree also with this idea, as *productive activity* has become exceptionally diverse today. However, theories about the formation of value by the very application of information alone, about its creation even in production processes which are fully automatic and do not require human participation, are becoming much more widespread today. Some suggest that the value of goods and assets must be assessed in real time, as assessments may alter radically, not only with every change in technology or trends, but also with the change in the way society or selected social groups relate to the production of various goods. Therefore they propose a new theoretical instrument, 'one that shows the changing values in real time'.[69] There is a willingness to prove that not only human activity, not only values made material in the factors of production, but also information itself as such, automatic technological processes, the forces of nature – in other words all elements which one way or another influence the production process – create value.

In a whole host of modern studies the accent shifts to the role of new factors of production in the process of creating value. It stands to reason here that information and knowledge are the most meaningful factors of the production process. Such approaches to the definition of value started to form virtually simultaneously with the conception of the 'information society', that is in the late 1970s. If at the beginning this was not manifested entirely clearly (Masuda spoke in the first place of the fact that 'information values' in the new society replace 'material values' as the main component of social wealth and the central element of the economic organization,[70] afterwards the concept 'information value' started to be used more rigorously and in a more defined context).

In the mid-1980s, the understanding of information and knowledge as a source of value alternative to labour became widespread in literature. Notably, some authors, particularly Stonier, tried to attach virtually the same qualities to information as Marx and his followers attached to labour; Stonier, for one, formulated the idea of the growth and self-growth of information value.[71] Other scholars supposed that value is created by a specific combination of the factors of production, including during the fully automatized or informationalized economic process. The appeal to the so-called 'value-added networks' became an element of this approach.[72] This appeal is limited in the context of the emerging understanding of contemporary society as a network society that had become fully decentralized.[73] One way or another, the point of view that 'central to the character of knowledge societies is a knowledge theory of value rather than a labour theory of value'[74] is currently very widespread. Moreover, few are confused by the fact that the knowledge theory of value, unlike the labour theory of value, is a sum of theoretical hypotheses rather than a scientific conception which has been substantiated and tried in practice.

However, there is an opposite approach, although this is far less widespread. Its adherents to some extent realize that the changes of today can be characterized more as the elimination of value than as its modification. In many cases researchers acknowledge this factor, but reluctantly, and concentrate instead on other elements of their conceptions. One example is Sakaiya's work on knowledge-value. While attempting to prove and substantiate the meaning of knowledge for the formation of value assessments, the author in his work was forced to emphasize the fact that current value characteristics are subjectivized in the highest degree. He wrote, for example, that

> knowledge-value is generated by *subjective* perceptions ... knowledge-value is like a shooting star that burns brightly only for the instant it passes through the particular 'field' or atmosphere of social circumstances and subjectivities that make it catch fire in the first place. Recognizing that it is created out of such a combustible set of variables is vital to understanding why knowledge-value has no necessary or absolute relationship to the cost of creating it.[75]

This duality can be traced throughout the work, in which attempts to analyse the value of information goods alternate with the acknowledgement of growing demand for products with 'non-quantifiable values'.[76]

On the whole, the understanding that in the modern economy value characteristics are highly subjectivized and that value itself is immeasurable has become reinforced of late. The strengthening of the role of social factors in economic development, the diversification of preferences and values of individuals are leading researchers to deduce that it is necessary 'to return to a broader concept of economics, in which social relations and cultural values are given equal weight with exchange values'.[77] The following conclusion is becoming a fact not only of scientific but also of social awareness:

> if information and knowledge are to be exploited as sources of value, the business environment has to exhibit a complex mix of access and creativity on the one hand and the tight appropriation of economic

benefits on the other. For all commodities, moreover, there is a cultural dimension; they exist within spaces of interconnected social differences and distinction, where individual utility and identity are inseparable from those of other individuals.[78]

We also agree that today the consumption of goods and the consumption of services are becoming inseparable, on the strength of which the consumer expends considerable efforts on the dis-objectification and consumption of high-tech products; and that the value of goods amid the headlong technological and social changes may be preserved at a certain level only fleetingly; however, *none* of these factors can be proof that the category of value today is as widespread and total as in the past. During the consumption of a product, the consumer does not create value, as the latter is *a category of social production*, and consumption takes place after all acts of social interaction related to the production, exchange and distribution of goods.[79] When social preferences or predilections alter the evaluation of a good, process or company, they change their monetary value, but the scale of activity expended on the creation, support and development of the goods is unchanged. The same applies to the use of nature, automatic technological processes and inexhaustible natural sources of energy.

We are deeply convinced that the reasons for the non-acceptance by the majority of modern economists and sociologists of the possibility of overcoming value are similar to those discussed when analysing the limitations of *economic* society. The exclusively broad sense given by the English language to the concept 'economy' and which enables it to be applied even to phenomena in which no *oekonomische* laws can be discovered is present also in many other concepts, including the term 'value'. Its indefinite character is explained by the fact that, firstly, the concept 'value' in itself has very many meanings and does not possess as many complementary terms, just as the concept 'economy' is not contrasted in the English language with a term similar to the notion 'Wirtschaft'. English does not distinguish the concepts of value as an economic category which reflects the basis of the commensuration of goods, and value as the meaningfulness of various material or non-material goods for individuals and for society. In contrast with English, the Russian language does make a distinction in terms of sense with the words *stoimost'* and *tsennost'*. The first is used to describe the processes and phenomena with a clearly *oekonomische* connotation. But the second is used to denote the meaningfulness of a good which is not the subject of an *oekonomische* transaction, and to describe completely different phenomena, like standards of ethics, works of art and cultural heritage. In English, the term 'value' can be used to denote very many things, from economic assessments to social preferences and human qualities; in Russian, this is impossible, and the formula 'cultural values' may be translated only as *kulturnye tsennosti*, but not under any circumstances as *kulturnye stoimosti*. Further confirmation of the exceedingly widespread use of the term 'value' can be the concepts of the same root; the single fact that the value of any process, object or quality can be denoted by the verb 'to evaluate' says a lot.

Secondly, other concepts used to denote values, primarily 'wealth', do more in English to set off the meaning of the term 'value' than can be set against it in the context of theoretical doctrine. To prove this we will once again use the earlier quotation from the work by Alvin and Heidi Toffler: 'In the new economy the receptionist and the investment banker who assembles the capital, the key punch operator and the salesperson, as well as the systems designer and telecommunications specialist all add value. Even more significantly, so does the customer. Value results from a total effort rather than from one isolated step in the process.'[80] But this quotation has a follow-up: 'The rising importance of mind-work will not go away, no matter how many scare stories are published warning about the dire consequences of a "vanishing" manufacturing base or deriding the concept of "informational economy". Neither will the new conception of how wealth is created'.[81] Is it not strange that within the framework of scientific analysis remarks that, in the opinion of researchers, ought to have shown that all new factors serve as elements of the formation of *value*, in the end relate to the process of the production of *wealth*? So what must be eliminated – the 'new conception of how *wealth* is created', or the 'new conception of how *value* is created'? We can find the answer not only in the book by Alvin and Heidi Toffler, but also in the works of most contemporary scholars.

We think that it is hardly possible to improve the terminology that has been established. German, French and Russian terms are hardly catching on with English-speaking scholars. However, we can achieve more definition and demonstrate the change in the system of modern economy at issue even with the not fully correct and not always adequate distinction of the concepts of 'value' and 'wealth'.

In the modern economy, man's achievement is that a wealth previously created to a large extent by his own labour is now created as a result of technological processes which virtually do not require his participation. Every year more and more factors contribute to the formation of wealth; with the development of automatic processes, the production of material goods requires less and less intervention by man; with the development of the industrial application of inexhaustible sources of energy, like the sun, the forces of nature themselves become the source of wealth. However, only in this aspect can it be asserted that today not only human labour but also information and the forces of nature contribute to the formation of social wealth.

It transpires that information wealth and highly qualified activity affect the price of goods not to the same extent as could have happened in traditional circumstances. Goods created largely thanks to information, born of automated production processes or inexhaustible sources of energy, are offered on the market as a combination of three components of value: the traditional value of the material factors of production, the value of information which is embodied in the technologies that created them, and society's ideas of the value of material goods, the traditional articles of mass-consumption. Thus sectors that consume and do not produce information are creating a product constituting less social wealth but possessing more value than a product of the information sector. The latter also explains, on the one hand, the fact that the price of a finished information product is low, for it is the only condition for competitiveness and increasing the share of such goods in overall consumption and, on the other hand, the overvaluation of information companies, as industrial capital, which appropriates considerable values, is capable of investing them in the sectors that create real wealth.

Such processes reflect the emergence of the bases of the post-economic epoch. The fundamental transformation of the whole system of social production consists of the fact that all people, who for the whole of their history have created wealth, expending their labour and overcoming the forces of nature, are today departing from the realms of the process of material production for a process in which wealth may be produced without their immediate participation. The satisfaction of material requirements without increasing labour expenditures serves as a key premise for overcoming the underlying role of material interests and eliminating labour itself as an activity caused by material requirements. Thus the issue of the existence or overcoming of value loses its own meaning and is discussed now in the context of the overcoming of market production and the emergence of post-economic society.

This approach is also justified, in our view, by the nature of modern conceptions of the development of the market economy. Despite the fact that in most studies the category of value is presented as virtually eternal, an analysis of the prospects of the development of civilization in the framework of these very studies produces clear-cut conclusions about the inevitability of the overcoming of market tendencies and the system of commodity production as a whole. We view such facts only as additional proof that value in its traditional understanding is no longer a meaningful category of the current economy.

The market economy has developed throughout the whole epoch of the existence of economic society. Being a natural consequence of the division of labour, the exchange of its products became the first form of equal relations within class societies, and became the sphere in which the economic interests of individuals gained the space for their own realization. As commodity transactions became more regular and an inseparable element of economic ties, personal material interests became more strongly linked with the results of such exchange. As a result the market system, when it reached maturity, became fully subordinate to the goals of selected individuals and guided by individual desires and motives. In the system, as Bell writes, 'the ends of production are not common but individual';[82] it is for this reason that the system is capable of satisfying the interests of groups of people and selected communities only to the extent that this is necessary for the more effective achievement of the goals of selected market subjects; these features of its inner nature are impossible to change, as 'it is the definition of the market that it is directed to and by the individual consumer'.[83]

The whole development of the economic epoch may be viewed as the emergence of the market system, the achievement of its maturity and its inevitable collapse.[84] During the *progression* of the economic epoch, commodity economy was not the most notable but the most important source of the evolution of production systems, which in some way possessed traits of self-development and self-sufficiency, a relation that slowly but surely destroyed the foundations of the prevalent non-economic system. As Toffler wrote: 'Just as the earliest division of labor had encouraged commerce in the first place, now the very existence of a market or switchboard encouraged a further division of labor and led to sharply increased productivity. A self-amplifying process had been set in motion.'[85] The main landmark in the development of commodity production at this first stage was the involvement in the process of the overwhelming majority of members of society. Developing from the bazaars at which goods were traded in the East to the structural commodity economy of mature antiquity and onwards to the systemic commodity production of mediaeval Europe, commodity relations have become more and more the main stimulus of the progress of production. They have more and more rigidly linked the economic interest of maximizing consumption with the production of goods considered to be a social use value.

During the *emergence of the mature form* of the economic epoch the quantitative expansion of commodity relations acquired the features of a qualitatively new phenomenon. The most important change was the rapid expansion of the range of goods at issue; proliferating first to the means and tools of production, then, in the epoch prior to the political disintegration of the feudal orders, to land, commodity relations swallowed up labour power, the very ability to work. It was then that *the market economy arose as the highest form of commodity production*, and the original aims of commodity exchange were replaced by the desire to maximize value as a universal equivalent; for example, workers began to identify their own economic interests with the appropriation of greater value. The interest in this of the entrepreneur formed even earlier; thus two main social groups began to act within the framework of market behaviour. This resulted in the rapid spread of *market* principles to those spheres of activity in which *commodity* relations once prevailed; the emergence of the market system culminated in the capitalist organization of agriculture. As Toffler comments, 'the market expanded ... through the increasing "commoditization" of life. Not only were larger populations enmeshed in the market but more and more goods and services were designed for the market'.[86]

However, the functioning of economic principles in their most complete forms prepared also the conditions for the *crisis and collapse* of this system. The rapid development of productive forces resulted, on the one hand, in the satisfaction of the basic material requirements of a considerable section of society and, on the other, lifted the status of knowledge and turned this also into a productive force. This required the expansion of the limits of the inner potential of the person, and ultimately enabled the person to look beyond the confines of traditional motivation.

The critical point in the development of the market economy came in the middle of the 20th century. To quote Toffler again, 'Today all ... forms of market expansion are reaching their outer limits.'[87] Moreover, technical progress assumed forms which suggested that the unification and the mass reproduction on which the market structure has been based are impossible. Simultaneously, the system of motives and values of people who had attained a high degree of material well-being and intellectual growth changed. They were reoriented from the incrementing of material wealth to self-realization within only a few decades. In the new conditions the market, identifiable with individual freedom, and hailed as 'indeed a wholly new means of social orchestration'[88] started to turn into a radical means of restraining the self-realization of the individual.

It was in the 1960s and 1970s that critical assessments of the market system became widespread. Moreover, very importantly, the forms of organization which supplemented market relations with new principles and methods of production regulation were considered as alternatives to the market economy, rather than planned or state-run forms of the economy as envisaged by the Marxists. Toffler, speaking of trans-market civilization as a short-term development, commented that civilization at any level of its development would depend on the growth of the infrastructure of exchange. Therefore he does not call for the curtailment of exchange relations, but stresses that the information economy enables the spontaneity of exchange to be eliminated and human and information resources currently used to support exchange networks to be utilized for other purposes directly related to the development of individuals and society as a whole.[89] Theses like this are based on the deeper understanding of the fact that 'by itself a free market does not guarantee either a free or a functioning society and economy. ... Its presence is a necessary cause of both a functioning society and economy, but, by itself, is not sufficient';[90] and that understanding in recent years, after the collapse of the communist regimes, did not weaken but, on the contrary, strengthened considerably as it became perfectly obvious that the socialist economies, the real basis of which was the conservation of production structures and of the reform of distribution relations, cannot be competitive with societies based on rapid technological progress.

However, even highlighting the overcoming of *market* relations, by no means all interpret this process as being an integral part of the formation of post-economic society. As a rule the new character of the coming society and new systems of values which guide the behaviour of individuals are treated as factors which complement rather than replace traditional self-interest as an embodiment of the economic motives and material desires[91] of producers. Arguments that the emergence of new post-material values radically alters the structure of economic systems and gives their development a new direction which differs from that of industrial society[92] are also embodied primarily in the dichotomy of the industrial and post-industrial epochs, in rivalry between the material and information systems of economy, but nothing more. Even the well-known formula of Bell which associates the more radical changes in today's society with the 'introduction of non-economic values'[93] is no basis for the formulation of an integral theory of post-economic transformation.

A few more remarks on the essence of current transformation are needed to round off this analysis of the development of commodity relations and the emergence of the foundations of post-economic society. We think that the development of the commodity economy must be treated in the context of the changing interaction between the system-formative factors and the external environment. This approach makes it possible to grasp the nature of its evolution in the past and comment on the marked features of development in the near future. In accordance with this approach, the whole history of commodity production is divided into two stages of development – the progressive and the regressive.

During the first stage commodity relations played the role of a system-formative element that developed within an alien social environment. Overcoming the self-sufficiency of the communal economy, the closed nature of the economic order based on barter, they facilitated the emergence of the first stages of the economic epoch. Confirming producers as independent manufacturers, and enabling them to act with an ever-increasing degree of freedom in conditions where the economic structure was based on overt coercion, they laid the path towards the achievement by the economic type of society of its mature and complete forms. The apotheosis of this process was the formation of the system of universal commodity production and the assertion of the principles of the *market economy* on a social scale.

From that moment, as the latter emerged as the dominating social institution, the situation altered sharply. After penetrating the social whole, commodity production itself became an environment in which new system-formative elements began to emerge. The market structure turned out to be a complex of relations which was able to progress and spread its principles only until such a time as they acquired a universal nature; in the last few decades the principles of the organization of a society based on the supremacy of non-economic, non-material values have been busily asserting themselves. The sphere of the supremacy of commodity relations has been narrowing more and more, the principles of this system are becoming more and more diffuse and cloudy, and the indicators of its universality are declining notably. This process is associated with another measurement of social evolution, to a considerable extent highlighting the division of the history of mankind into three epochs of social development.

In Marxism these three big epochs are the archaic, the economic and communist *Gesellschaftsformationen*, and in post-industrialism they are game against nature, game against fabricated nature and game between persons, or pre-economic, economic and post-economic stages, to use the terminology of our study. But whatever these epochs are called, civilization progresses on the path the main landmarks of which are determined by *the nature, reasons and degree of the subjugation of people*.

In the first stage of social evolution (archaic, game against nature, pre-economic), the main factor that restricted a person in his actions and desires was his *dependence on nature*. In this situation the limitation of material resources made the struggle between man and nature the very essence of the existence of man; primitive forms of social community did not know large-scale inner conflicts, for each of them was able to bring about the ruin of a whole community easily with external natural forces and factors.

During the second stage, when the most rigid forms of man's dependence on nature had been overcome, man started to depend directly on a new type of social organization. Moreover, societies based on coercion did not provide freedom even for their own masters; the goal of survival of the whole socium now became the goal of survival for the ruling classes, while the representatives of the oppressed classes became merely a tool. This condition or state, characteristic of all class societies, can be treated as an example of the *subjugation of 'man by man'*. The global changes introduced to the system of social organization by the proliferation of commodity relations and even the formation of the system of market economy did not alter the situation. While eliminating the ancient forms of coercion and modernizing the system of social organization, the market economy from the very beginning was based on the most obvious form of the dependence of 'man on man', when both were parties to commodity production and exchange, and depended on each other as producer and consumer.

The emergence of the fundamentals of post-economic society is based on the acquisition by humankind of a new quality. At issue is the situation where the material needs which gave rise to human subjugation in the first and second global stages of the evolution of civilization do not dominate over the system of human values and the motives for the activity of people. The need for people's own development, for the satisfaction of their needs for self-realization, social status, social and collective recognition and so on became the dominant factor. Trapped by the needs born of the very course of the betterment of his personality, man becomes *bonded to himself*.

Thus today's world is characterized by two processes: from the social point of view, the main tendency is the emancipation of people from the pressure of the social whole, the acquisition by them of a higher degree of inner freedom; from the economic point of view, the tendency to overcome the economic principles of exchange and to form a new type of production, freed from elements of the market economy, is becoming more and more distinct. But throughout the economic epoch there has existed a category which has embodied the dependence of man on others and on society and has fixed the solitary nature of producers, a condition of the commodity-based economy. This relation, as typical of the economic epoch as commodity exchange, is ownership. Even today, after the development of economic society has passed its peak, this relation and its evolution presents another key problem, one which determines the content of the gigantic social transformation under discussion.

The Displacement of Private Property

For centuries the problem of property has lain at the heart of most social theories. The role of property in any analysis of the laws of the development of society can be seen alone from the fact that many thinkers believe it to be directly linked to the emergence of the social order. 'Le premier qui ayant enclos un terrain s'avisa de dire: Ceci est à moi, et trouva des gens assez simples pour le croire ... fut le vrai fondateur de la société civile', wrote J.-J. Rousseau.[94] Having entered into European sociological theory as part of the philosophical conceptualization of the basis of the organization of society, the notion of property has kept the broad definition that it obtained in the past. Yet in our view the phenomenon of property is embodied in strictly defined economic relations and has fairly clear boundaries within social space and time. The phenomenon of property, as it was formed by the time industrial production came to dominance, was the result of a lengthy process of evolution of a dual nature

Property during the formation of the economic epoch emerged as communities split into individual economic units. We will not seek to assert that this marked the formation of private property as opposed to tribal or communal property. In our view the very idea of *communal* property is more of a logical construct than a real reflection of the state of affairs in the archaic epoch. The idea probably emerged in response to the concept of the division of history into three main evolutionary epochs that preached that *private* property would eventually be replaced by *social* property. Correspondingly, something analogous to social property was required that could serve, even in its most primitive form, as an attribute of the early stages of social progress. We do not believe this construct to have been entirely successful.

It is true that people in the pre-economic epoch worked in communal economic units. But these units were not based on communal property. Such a notion could only be applied to the circumstance that the possessions of one community were regarded as different from the possessions of another. On the contrary, it is probably more true to talk about the *personal* ownership of the community members over vital primitive property and the primitive means of production – from weapons to agricultural tools – that they used in their everyday activity. It was almost impossible to accumulate either such tools or finished products: there were limits to the use tools could be put to and the amount of time finished products could be stored. Our view is that this period was the epoch of *personal* property.

However paradoxical it may sound, the development of property during the formation of the first class societies and the assertion of the bases of the economic epoch was a continuation and development of the process of the formation of personal property. Violence brought the first class inequalities and secured all the wealth of a nation as the personal property of its ruler. This is true not only of the classic case when all the vital possessions of the slave belong to his master but of Asiatic societies, where the ruling class, using a monopoly on land ownership, the surplus product and much of the necessary product, was able to secure the complete suppression of all subservient classes and the personal ownership of their possessions. It was only with the wider unfolding of the principles of the economic epoch that property of a new kind began to appear that we can call *private* property in the full sense of the expression.

Private property emerged when and where individual productive activity not only began to prove its social significance through free commodity transactions but began to focus on the appropriation of universal value equivalent. To clarify this notion, it might be said that the property of an ancient aristocrat, including his latifundia, buildings, agricultural tools, the slaves that made up his *familia rustica* and *familia urbana*, his town house and vehicles, remained personal property by their economic nature and significance as long as the products produced in such an economic unit were consumed within its limits and did not interrelate with other components of social wealth. Moreover, it is also impossible to assign as private the property of a small craftsman or peasant, who enters the market in order to exchange his products for the goods which he lacks in his own household. But, on the contrary, the property of a villa owner who aims at high production and sells his products in the market in order to receive a monetary income may be described as being *private* because it establishes relationships between the owner and his counter-agents that are characteristic of the free subjects of a market economy.

Private property developed alongside the economic society on the basis of both the developing and growing personal property of individual producers and the gradual inclusion of the personal property of the ruling class in the market. As a result the distinction between private and personal property was lost and the notion 'private property' started to be applied to all forms of property, regardless of their nature and purpose, which, in our view, amounts to a deficiency in overall modern sociology.

A kind of synthesis of personal and private property began to occur in feudal society, when commodity relations began to penetrate all social strata. On the one hand, the personal property of craftsmen and peasants turned into private property, used to create a product supplied to the market and exchanged for the universal equivalent that was used to meet feudal duties and wages for apprentices and for the purchase of the products of other craftsmen. On the other hand, the personal property of the aristocracy and, primarily, feudal ownership over land and other irreproducible conditions of production began to be commercialized, began to become private. Eventually, these two types of property became intertwined and representatives of the third estate started to acquire land for capitalist development and aristocrats started to invest in commerce and industry. Thus, in the period marked by the crisis of the feudal order, private and personal property became practically indistinguishable. As much as possible of the personal property of the third estate and the aristocracy was turned into private property. The only point of such a conversion was to increase the opportunities for this property to grow. Much is revealed by the fact that this process came to an end just as commodity relations came to total domination and the market economy formed as a whole system.

Thus we believe that the pre-economic epoch was characterized by personal property as the only form of property that could have existed at that time. The economic epoch was marked as it developed by the emergence and growth of private property, often blended with personal property, as the basis of the economic independence of motivated producers. The differences between personal and private property became less and less clear as commodity relations advanced. Finally, the mature forms of economic society practically know just one form of property, usually called private property, in the same way as they know only one form of commodity production, habitually called the market economy.

However, the differences between personal and private property can be traced even within the framework of the mature condition of the economic society. The personal property of individuals is made up of that part of their personal wealth that does not determine their social status as economic agents. To a certain degree it is correct to assert that personal property determines the freedom of the individual from society, his ability to withstand the dictates of the economic laws that rule society. On the contrary, private property directly reflects the dependence of the individual on the economic system, since it only exists in the constant process of interaction with other economic agents, as an element of the market economy. Undoubtedly, private property dominates in the mature economic society. This is as true as the notion that such a society is dominated by exchange value, the growth and development of which explain the main laws of this kind of economy. However, in the same way that the utility of the corresponding good serves as the condition for the existence and manifestation of exchange value, so private property, which is a form of social cohesion in industrial society, is rooted in personal property, which contradicts the total dominance of the principles of the market economy.

Private property became the basis for social organization when it extended to cover those means and conditions of production without which most members of society would have failed to ensure their survival and reproduction. The logical conclusion of this process was the transformation of labour power into private property. Here the overcoming of the alienation of the means of production from direct producers serves as a condition for the overcoming of the economic nature of society. However, in this case, the formation of social property may not solve the problem because the individual does not regard social property as his own nor as the private property of some other individual; he therefore remains in contradiction, albeit not alien to, his own means of production, interaction with which, as before, is a condition for the appropriation by him of material goods. Such a solution does not do away with the economic nature of society, it merely exacerbates a whole range of characteristic contradictions and frustrates most of the potential for self-development within the market mechanism. The collapse of communist regimes confirms this.

In our view the elimination of this alienation is possible only by transforming the main means and conditions of production into the *personal* property of the economic agent. This will allow the immediate producer to carry out his activities depending *not on the exchange value of his labour power but on the use value of the goods he has produced*. This change is of fundamental significance for an understanding of the prospects for the development and the evolutionary trends of economic society. The displacement of private property will develop as and when society sheds its economic nature and will to a significant degree determine this process. However, in the same way that free-market production cannot be replaced by planned production, so private property cannot be replaced by social property. Equally, the redistribution of goods will lead to nothing but an impasse in social reforms because it does not provide for an improvement in the production system. Equally redistributed property, because it remains in essence private, cannot serve as a condition for the formation of the laws of the post-economic society. In the same way that the market economy in the declining stage of the economic epoch is replaced by renewed forms of *commodity* production, so *private* property will only be displaced on the path to the formation of a new system based on the domination of *personal* property as a factor neither determined by nor determinant of the market economy.

In the modern world the problem of the development of property relations is particularly acute. The greatest social movements have to a greater or lesser degree been associated with one way or another of overcoming this problem. Therefore it is all the more important to look at ways of ameliorating the contradictions and conflicts that are generated by modern forms of private property and to regard the displacement of private property as the second component part of the post-economic revolution, and to also analyse its influence on the main characteristics of the modern social structures.

Private versus Private: Palliative Solutions

Social philosophers for decades and even centuries believed that the main way of displacing private property was to create social or collective forms of ownership over the means of production. However, an attempt to do exactly this in communist nations provided clear proof that social and collective ownership leads to the maximum alienation of property from the producer, a sharp reduction in the amount of freedom for the majority of society and the disorganization of the system of motives and stimuli that correspond to the tasks of modern production. State industries functioned more successfully, but state ownership had, firstly, to reflect a real degree of centralization of production in the respective industries and their significance for the development of the nation and, secondly, to interact with other productive agents according to the laws of commodity production. We will give this matter more consideration during our analysis of the phenomenon and significance of state ownership.

Three processes are usually noted in today's post-industrial societies that represent many elements of the subversion and displacement of private property. The first process is the dilution of the monopoly of the capitalist class over the ownership of the means of production as the middle classes and hired employees actively invest in shares and other securities of manufacturing and service companies. Secondly, employees are acquiring stakes and shares in their own companies. Moreover, corporate stakes are being transferred to workers in order for them to form more united teams and overcome the conflict between employee and employer. And thirdly, there is an increasing number of companies whose capital is totally controlled by its workers.

Yet in our view not one of these three processes can be regarded as a challenge to the existing system of property. Unfolding deep within the market system, these changes have led to a redistribution of property rights, but they have not altered the aim of using property, or the motivation of the individuals that own property, or their social behaviour and, consequently, amount to the modernization of the system of private property and not an attempt to go beyond its bounds. The first of the processes mentioned, the diffusion of property rights among a maximally wide number of owners, cannot today be ignored even by the most superficial observer, since it has taken place on a most significance scale over recent decades and is regarded by many as a serious challenge to the capitalist system. This process reflects a whole range of trends existing within the modern economic system. On the one hand, it is designed to smooth over conflicts between employees and employers. The transfer of a certain number of shares to workers in a company can solve a multitude of problems simultaneously: create an impression of a partnership between employees and employers as corporate co-owners; inculcate workers with extra stimuli for highly professional and intensive work since the payment of dividends becomes something of a supplement to the traditional system of bonuses and concessions; and provide workers with a greater sense of security. The social effect of such a transformation should also not be underestimated: it is often seen as a way of maintaining social justice. On the other hand, a clear economic aim is met: by demonstrating to workers the possibility of earning more by receiving dividends on shares and making capital gains on their market value, the state and companies encourage private investment in production. Often middle-class workers do not invest in the companies which employ them. But the task has not been formulated that rigorously. It is highly characteristic that the first aim, of overcoming certain forms of social conflict, has still to be met. But the second, of generating increased private investment, has been successfully accomplished.

The clearest examples of the fast proliferation of property rights have been provided by nations that have carried out mass radical privatization. Britain and France in the 1980s transferred a huge number of companies into the private sector to bring an immediate increase in the number of small private shareholders. No more than two million people owned shares in Britain in 1983, about 5 per cent of the adult population. That figure had grown to 9.4 million or 23 per cent of the adult population by 1988.[95] This process, however, was tightly regulated by the state, which offered companies to the public on certain conditions, one of which was the transfer of shares to employees. Naturally, the employee stake could not be too big – that would have put potential investors off purchasing the asset. As a result, employees in Britain got an average of more than 10 per cent of shares in their companies. Figures ranged from 6.5 to 31.9 per cent.[96]

It is quite clear that such a process did not provide shareholders with rights other than those to collect dividends and sell their shares: they still could not take part in corporate decision making. In the end this form of redistribution was little more than a form of ameliorating social problems. Within three to four years, most employees sold their shares either on the market or to the issuer itself and the total share of small shareholders in equity fell by 40–70 per cent. And the workers of such companies accounted for a very small share of small investors. It should be pointed out that a similar situation, albeit altered to take account of economic illiteracy and low living standards, took place in the republics of the former Soviet Union and East European states in the first half of the 1990s. Here major capitalists were able to accumulate ownership even more quickly and the effect for employee shareholders was even smaller.

Today small shareholdings are regarded by their owners as a form of saving rather than investment or an opportunity to realize their functions as owners. This explains the fact that most small investors do not try to buy shares themselves, since they understand that their actions cannot be as professional as they need to be. Thus the most effective form of such investment is to buy shares in mutual funds, pension funds and insurance companies.

The scale of such investments is highly impressive. In the early 1960s, more than 87 per cent of all US shares were held by households. Private and state pension and mutual funds held just over 7 per cent.[97] The situation has now radically changed. By the beginning of the 1980s, households and various funds held, respectively, 66 and 28 per cent of shares. And by 1992 households and funds held, respectively, 50 and 44 per cent. In Britain the process moved even faster. In 1982, households and funds held, respectively, 28 and 52 per cent of shares. In 1992, the figures were 19 and 55 per cent, respectively. There has been a dramatic rise in the number of mutual and pension funds and the size of the assets under their management. The number of mutual funds in the United States rose from 1241 in 1984 to 4500 in 1994, and the amount of assets under their management has grown from $400 billion to $2 trillion.[98] In the second half of the 1980s, half of US households that owned shares did so via mutual funds. The development of pension funds was no less impressive. Their assets grew from $548 billion in 1970 to $1.7 trillion in 1989 and are now thought to have topped $2 trillion.[99] This process has brought much more influence over the markets to such funds. Starting in the mid-1980s, transactions carried out by pension and mutual funds accounted for more than half of total volume on the New York Stock Exchange.[100]

Thus private investors are making massive investment in the economy. The personal wealth of even the most famous businessmen cannot be compared to the aggregate financial resources that regular savers put into the economies of the developed nations. Arithmetic shows that 'at the turn of the millennium, in the United States, more than 100 million private individuals own enough shares in stocks, options, mutual funds and indices to make them the majority owners over institutional investors'.[101] Such institutional investors are becoming 'large corporations, with professional staffs whose expertise is in efficient management of diversified portfolios, that is, wide selections of various stocks'.[102] Similar processes are taking place in other developed nations, although not on such an impressive scale. For example, between 1982 and 1992, the relative shares of the equity markets between households and mutual funds changed from 25 and 11 per cent to 17 and 11 per cent in Japan; and from 28 and 4 per cent to 19 and 7 per cent in Germany.[103]

Some observers believe the redistribution of property rights and the growth of the influence of institutional investors marks the beginning of a wholly new phase in the development of capitalism or even the development of something beyond the capitalist mode of production altogether. Drucker writes: 'In pension fund capitalism, the wage earners finance their own employment by deferring part of their wages. Wage earners are the main beneficiaries of the earnings of capital and of capital gains. We have no social, political or economic theory that fits what has already become reality.'[104]

Yet we do not believe that the development of mutual funds marks any kind of qualitatively new phenomenon. We are talking primarily about the desire of workers to increase their incomes and ensure reliable investments for their money. Fundholders like private investors are unable to have any kind of substantial influence over the policies of the funds in which they own far from substantial stock. They remain mere observers of corporate decisions. Moreover, the small investor is even further from the corporation in which he invests than ever since a powerful counter-agent with its own economic interests, which by no means always coincide with the interests of the small investor, lies between him and the corporation. Mutual funds are to a much greater degree an instrument for the 'control of the supply of savings',[105] vital to the balanced development of the market economy than a means by which the small investor may acquire real ownership of the means of production and industrial corporations. And the very fact that control over industrial corporations is shifting from banks to financial organizations and mutual funds may not serve as grounds for substantial advances in the organization of capitalist production. The dissimilation of property has been brought about by purely economic considerations, the motives of small investors fully correspond to the stereotypes of market behaviour and the ownership of such shares is no less private than the ownership of corporations themselves. Therefore, in our view, the significance of this phenomenon as a factor in the change of the nature of modern *private* property should not be exaggerated.

The second process that has a claim to a big role in the displacement of private property really is more radical than the first and, despite superficial similarities, is of a quite different nature. Here we are talking about the controlled and often substantial distribution of shares among employees. This can be done in various ways: wages and bonuses may be paid in shares or employees may be offered shares at concessionary rates. Various such options are carried out in the United States, Canada, Japan and several nations in Western and Eastern Europe.[106] However, the real owners of such corporations try to limit the use employees may make of their shares: usually, employees are unable to sell them on the open market and have to settle for making use of the financial benefits derived from the ownership of such stock; they may use dividends to buy more shares or cash in their stakes upon retirement or leaving the company. There are very few cases of employees gaining any real control over their companies, and they are usually associated with an acute financial crisis at the company concerned.

In the 1970s and 1980s the United States, surmounting the economic problems of the 1970s, developed a special government programme, the Employee Stock Ownership Plan (ESOP). Some parts of this programme were adopted in other nations too. The programme had some positive results, but it is far from representing a major new trend in private property. It is usually only put into action when a company has come upon such hard times that employees closely identify with its survival. One example of the ESOP system in use was at McLouth Steel Products of Trenton, Michigan. In 1986, a group of creditors in the bankrupt company secured a claim on the previous owner's shares. That stake was reduced from 65 per cent to 10 per cent and an 85 per cent stake transferred to employees on condition that they accept a 10 per cent layoff and 10 per cent cut in wages. Within six months production noticeably improved, the company once again became solvent, and soon productivity was up 50 per cent. However, this should not be regarded as a real success of an employee-owned company because, firstly, there was a massive cut in costs and, secondly, the transfer of shares to employees served as a way of delaying payments on previous commitments. Even the continued success of McLouth Steel Products in our view does not provide grounds for asserting that 'employee ownership and participation in managing is one of the new frontiers of American business history'.[107]

Within its first 15 years ESOP achieved fairly serious results, although they were far from big enough to change the general economic environment. ESOP programmes were carried out at 1601 firms employing 248 000 in 1975, and 10 237 firms with employees more than 11.5 million people in 1989. Employees received fairly significant share packets, which averaged at about $7000 per employee in the mid-1980s. The whole programme overall shifted shares worth about $60 billion into employee hands,[108] just 2 per cent of the total assets under the management of mutual funds. It is quite clear that ESOP has not had any radical effect on the process of the redistribution of property. The system, which in the early 1990s embraced about 12 per cent of the US workforce,[109] accounted for only a small share of all the equity held by small private investors.

The relatively modest scale of the ESOP system, we believe, can be attributed to the fact that it was organized 'from the top' primarily in order to solve some of the problems of inefficient firms. It is practically unknown for ESOP to be applied in high-tech companies where knowledge workers make up any significant share of the workforce. Only at a stretch can ESOP be regarded as a method of extending the control of workers over corporate capital. Often the increase in equity held by employees amounts to an alternative to increased wages. This means that the income of the worker is dependent on the performance of the company and the personal property of the employee starts to depend on the well-being of the company.

Such a stimulus undoubtedly bears fruit. It does not so much correspond to the above-mentioned trends, when a company regards its employee more as a volunteer, as diametrically oppose them. Here it is not the firm that becomes dependent on the worker, but the worker that becomes dependent on the firm. Employee ownership limits the diffusion of property only in a few and very unimportant aspects. Under ESOP, employees who receive shares, as a rule, transfer them to the trust controlled by the company managers. This trust is not controlled by employees and in most cases they do not even use the voting rights their shares provide. Thus it appears that, on the one hand, workers merely receive the right of access to an extra part of their company, which, it has to be said, often has a negative impact on the market efficiency of the company. On the other hand, the acquisition of shares amounts for employees to an indirect deduction from their wages: part of their income is forcibly mobilized to accumulate capital for the company itself, overall control over which is retained by management.

These factors have brought substantial criticism for ESOP in the United States.[110] They also explain the cool reception such ideas have received in other nations. In Germany in the early 1990s, just 1.5 per cent of employees hold what are usually highly limited shares in their companies.[111]

The third process which is usually cited when discussing the displacement of private property is the formation of complete worker ownership of the capital of their companies. Sometimes this process is interpreted as an embodiment of a radical mechanism for the overcoming of the capitalist type of property altogether. However, such schemes may only be applied on a very limited scale and primarily at small enterprises in the service sector, agriculture and elsewhere. Such organizations usually serve a propaganda role rather than recruit any kind of significant number of followers.

Worker-owned firms are more common in Europe than in the United States. However, so-called 'workers' cooperatives' are the most widespread form of such firms, both in the United States and Europe. They are, however, usually only capable of solving local problems. Cooperatives advanced most in the crisis years of the 1970s and 1980s. In Britain, the number of manufacturing cooperatives rose from 36 to 1600 between 1976 and 1988. In France, the number of such organizations rose, if we include non-capitalist cooperatives of craftsmen, from 537 to 3000 in the same period. The number of cooperatives in Italy rose from 6500 in 1973 to 20 000 in 1981. However, the cooperative movement ran out of steam by the end of the 1980s and the number of cooperatives and collective enterprises has been falling ever since.

The situation, albeit on a different scale, is very similar in the United States. Workers owned a majority interest in only 1500 of the 10 000 firms officially registered as owned by their workers in 1989. Workers had complete ownership of just 500 firms. But even in the latter cases substantial property rights were surrendered to managers. According to figures from F. Adams and G. Hansen, only 304 cooperatives and joint-stock companies in the United States were really controlled by just 100 000 worker-owners,[112] a mere 0.09 per cent of the American workforce.

The only example of a fairly successful large cooperative company is the Mondragon Cooperative Corporation (MCC), which, founded in the middle of the 1940s as something of a technical college, has developed over more than half a century into a diverse body that, by the late 1980s, included 166 cooperatives, 86 of them industrial and 46 educational. The corporation is a unique combination of industrial and agricultural cooperatives supplemented by a range of bodies that train and retrain personnel. MCC in 1988 was educating 48 000 people from primary school to university level and including training and retraining, yet it has just 18 000 workers.[113] In 1987, one of the MCC groups, Fagor 2010, alone spent $2.7 million on professional training for its staff and other community education programmes.

In conclusion, stress should be put upon the forms of the direct participation of workers in the ownership of their enterprises: from the transfer of equity under privatization programmes to ESOP and the functioning of small cooperatives. None of these forms of participation provides and none of these forms could provide any kind of serious grounds for talking about the overcoming of private property in our understanding of the term. There are several reasons for this. Firstly, all these forms of direct worker participation in ownership have been brought about, not by the successful development of the corresponding productive businesses and their high potential, but, on the contrary, by their disastrous economic condition. Industries in which such enterprises exist are usually the most backward in the economy. Correspondingly, the workers in these industries are far from being the most qualified section of the workforce and cannot, even by controlling the fixed assets of their enterprises, ensure their success.

Secondly, such production firms have never provided new products, technology or market breakthrough in any country or any industry. They are merely a natural reaction to real economic problems and their dynamics hinges on cyclical crises. The tougher the economic problems, the more common are such palliative forms of property and the more actively is ownership transferred to workers in practically hopeless enterprises. And thirdly, over the last few decades that have so radically changed the modern economy, no such business has achieved the kind of significant role in the production of social wealth or in the structure of employment that would have justified its description as a factor with the potential to flower in the coming years. On the contrary, everything shows that such forms of business will continue to occupy modest economic niches and will in no way determine economic trends.

Growing private capital and equity investment in manufacturing and service companies is also a phenomenon deserving of attention. The fast development of such investment over recent decades has seriously changed several principles of modern management, but, like the phenomena discussed above, this in no way changes the nature of private ownership. The main activity of both cooperative members and small private investors remains labour motivated by the receipt of income and directed at the satisfaction, immediate or postponed, of their material interests. Even the most significant investment from the point of view of the small investor into mutual or pension funds does not change his initial status as a hired labourer employed by an enterprise that he does not own. However, the principal point here is that a worker, even owning an income-generating equity stake in a company, may not be regarded as the equal partner of the company and may not enter into a dialogue with the company within the framework of commodity production. Remaining a person who is only capable of offering a company his labour, he remains a hired labourer, whose social situation is determined only by his own labour power.

Meanwhile, the technological changes that have taken place over recent decades provide a more radical challenge to private property by contrasting it with personal property, and it is in this very contrast that the growing post-economic trends are manifested.

Personal versus Private: a Radical Challenge

As we have shown, not one of the traditional transformations of private property is capable of bringing substantial changes in the property and social status of the majority of the population and determining radical changes in the capitalist system of production. Nico Stehr has said,

> The institution of property itself is undergoing an essential correction in modern society. Traditionally, property rights have been the economic basis and symbolic correlate of the rise of individualism. Moreover, these rights constituted relationships between individuals. Today ... they are not closely linked to individuals any more and have therefore become more and more 'invisible'. They do not confer status and command social deference in any immediate sense as did traditional wealth. Many invisible property rights cannot be sold, given away or inherited. There is further change in the nature of property and the rights the individual may derive from property. This change is connected to the shift in the norms which apply to ownership. While ownership once conferred almost unlimited rights to employ and dispose of property in any way the owner saw fit, today such rights are increasingly restricted on the basis of a variety of norms considered to be superior collective goals.[114]

Today we have an opportunity to affirm the truth of Bell's comment that, during the development of the information economy, 'ownership is simply a legal fiction'.[115] And the more obvious this factor becomes, the more topical the whole issue of what is determining such radical change becomes.

We believe that, during the information revolution and the era of intellectual capital, the main factor dissimilating traditional *private* property is a qualitatively new form of *personal* property. For centuries this form of ownership has not played any kind of salient role in the economy. Now principal grounds have appeared for its active development and proliferation. These grounds are the growing role of knowledge as a direct productive resource and the accessibility to any knowledge worker in modern society of the means of accumulation, transmission and processing of information. Today personal ownership of the means of production is used, not for the production of primitive goods, but for the creation of information products, technology, software, new theoretical knowledge in an environment of advanced information and technology.

It is the changing status of knowledge workers that is the reason for the transformation of modern property relations. At first glance, and this is acknowledged by all modern management specialists, this new category of workers differs from all others primarily in the principles under which they are managed, the partially non-material motives, the new attitude that they demand from their employer and the high level of wages. There is a well-known theory that knowledge workers are just a modification of the traditional workforce engaged in capitalist production: the cost of this labour rises in line with spending on its training and qualifications. This theory is marked in red throughout economic theory from Karl Marx, who was one of the first to formulate it, through to Peter Drucker, who regards education as a form of investment in oneself that enables the worker to sell his labour at a higher price.[116] Only a few scholars note that such an investment today has a far from direct economic benefit and is based on motives radically different from the traditional logic of capitalism.[117] In our view, the reason for the profound change in the basic characteristics of the modern workers can be explained only as a consequence of the information revolution.

The information revolution has qualitatively changed the technological basis for social production. The clearest illustration of this is provided by the progress of modern information technology. Over a period of 15 years alone, from 1980 to 1995, the memory volume of computer hard disks grew by a factor of more than 250.[118] Microprocessors are advancing every year: the capacity of a microchip doubles every 18 months.[119] There has been no such progress in any other sphere of production over recent years. The development of the computer industry is being accompanied by active advances in associated technology: information transmission and recording, telecommunications lines, local and global networks, and so on.

Parallel with the fantastic growth of the technical parameters of the information industry there has been an equally impressive drop in the cost of its products. Drucker, comparing living standards of workers on the basis of the cost of a car and the wages of car workers, said:

> Henry Ford brought out the first cheap automobile, the Model T, in 1907. It was 'cheap', however, only by comparison with all other automobiles on the market, which, in terms of average incomes, cost as much as a twin-engine private plane costs today. At $750, Henry Ford's Model T cost what a fully employed industrial worker in the United States earned in three to four years – for 80 cents was then a good day's wage, and of course there were no 'benefits.' Even an American physician in those years rarely earned more than $500 a year. Today, a unionized automobile worker in the United States, Japan, or Germany, working only forty hours a week, earns $50,000 in wages and benefits – 45,000 after taxes – which is roughly eight times what a cheap new car costs today.[120]

Yet such a drop in the price of a car over 90 years pales compared with the speed at which the cost of information products drops over just a few months. If the car industry over the last 30 years had succeeded in reducing the costs in the way that the computer industry has, an executive model like the Lexus would now cost just $2[121] and a Rolls-Royce would only be able to fetch a price of $2.5 if it could burn a gallon of fuel for every two million kilometres.[122]

New technology reduces the cost of production and the cost of the information products themselves and the conditions for their creation. We have already said that, over the postwar years, the cost of international telephone calls has dropped by more than 700 times.[123] But telecommunications is not the industry in which the cost of services and produce have been reduced the most. Here the leader is computer technology. Bill Gates wrote:

> In the spring of 1983 IBM released its PC/XT, the company's first personal computer with an internal hard disk. The disk served as a built-in storage device and held 10 megabytes, or 'megs', of information ... Customers who wanted to add this 10 megs to their original computers could, for a price. IBM offered a $3,000 kit, complete with separate power supply, for expanding the computer's storage. That's $300 per megabyte. ... By the summer of 1996 personal computer hard drives that could hold 1.6 gigabytes ... were priced at $225. That's $0.14 per megabyte![124]

Thus over a period of 13 years the constant price of a single unit of memory fell by a factor of more than 2100. However, computer technology is designed not so much to store information as to transfer it to users, exchange it and copy it. Photocopiers and fax machines and such technology can never compete with modern computer networks as a means of exchanging information. It is today 250 times cheaper to download a megabyte of information from the Internet than to photocopy it.[125] The modern information revolution has not only made knowledge the main productive force. *It has formed the prerequisites under which the means required for the creation, proliferation and reproduction of information products are accessible to every knowledge worker*. And that has changed everything.

A substantial share of the workforce today realistically possesses the means of production but not in the same sense that it is usually used in modern literature. We cannot agree with Drucker, who said that 'collectively the knowledge workers, the employed educated middle class of today's society, own the means of production through pension funds, investment trusts, and so on'.[126] We have only just shown that such a system of ownership of the means of production has no significant affect on the position of workers, their stimuli and social status. Drucker himself admits that '*these* funds are the true "capitalists" of modern society' (emphasis added), and a knowledge worker, this 'true "capitalist"', 'is dependent on his job'.[127] Drucker leaves a lot unsaid when he writes that modern intellectual production units, like the industrial units of the past, require substantial capital investment that could prove 'unproductive unless the knowledge employee brings to bear on it the knowledge which he or she owns and which cannot be taken away'.[128] In other words, Drucker recognizes that the knowledge worker only *owns* his own ability to produce an intellectual product in the same way that an industrial-era worker only owned his own labour power and his ability to create value and surplus value.

Meanwhile, in reality the case is quite different. The nature of the modern knowledge worker is such that it is not merely determined by the fact that such a worker *has the ability* to generate knowledge; investment in his education is not analogous to expenditure on the professional training of a factory worker in the 19th century. The main characteristic of the intellectual worker is, on the one hand, his *uniqueness*, since, as we have already underlined, information, given its current complexity, is far from being accessible to everyone, and the circle of people capable of transforming the information received into finished information products and new knowledge is far from infinite. Therefore, even if we regard the expenditure on the education of a worker as a kind of investment, we see that the real result of such an investment is not growing wages, but something quite different, that cannot be subjected to a qualitative evaluation but is to be found in the nature of the goods created.[129] On the other hand, the modern knowledge worker, and this provides the principal distinction between such a worker and the hired labourer of the capitalist epoch, is in a position to own all *the means of production* required: computer, access to information networks and systems, copiers and data transfer equipment. The information revolution has to a significant degree denied the ruling class of the bourgeois society its traditional monopoly over the means of production upon which its economic might was based. It is characteristic that this monopoly is collapsing primarily in those industries in which technological progress is the fastest and upon the results and accessibility of which other sectors of the economy, with the possible exception of traditional crafts industries, are dependent.

The main factor that deserves to be mentioned in this connection is the change in the attitude of the knowledge worker not only to the means of production but to the product of his activity. In the past a capitalist-era hired labourer possessed a formal monopoly on nothing more than his own labour power; however, given the lack of a deficit of labour in the market, the bourgeois class neither observed nor sensed this monopoly. Knowledge workers in the period of their formation as a social group also made up a certain sector of the working class. The monopoly of the representatives of this class over their labour was more salient. But until the information revolution they sold the entrepreneur their labour power to place themselves in the same situation as all other proletarians. However, the more salient monopoly of the knowledge worker over his knowledge limited supply in the market for the corresponding services and raised the price of his labour power. Today, having acquired access to the means of production as if they were his own, the knowledge worker is departing from the working class. The commodity which the worker offers the entrepreneur is no longer his labour power but a *finished product* created by the worker with his own means of production: information technology, inventions, and so on. The knowledge worker, with the means of production, becomes both the owner of such means of production which appear now in the form of *personal property* and a commodity producer standing outside traditional market laws and exchanging his product for other goods in line with the individual utility of the goods that have been offered in exchange for his product and the social utility of the product he has created. Such a transformation, which is already clear today to an alert observer, amounts, in our view, to the greatest challenge to the modern economy to emerge in recent decades. The desire of knowledge workers for autonomy, manifested in relatively mass-production and coordinated production processes, today has every chance of being fulfilled on an unprecedented scale. In this case all social production will be divided into two such distinct camps – the traditional capitalist and the non-market – that the previous distinctions between sectors, even those between the primary and quintary sectors, will appear to be a mere formality not worthy of any serious attention.

Sociologists started to identify such changes in the early 1990s, although with a mass of reservations. The authors of *Post-modernization* said that the 'control of the means of production is also tightly circumscribed by the extent to which the means of production in a particular context are informational rather than physical in character. Where there is a high informatic content control of the means of production is relatively dispersed among workers'.[130] Similar theses were put forward by a whole range of academics, but the one which deserves the most attention is that of Sakaiya, whom we have already cited. For a more comprehensive commentary we shall quote Sakaiya at length:

A unique facet of the knowledge-value society is its tendency to unite labor and the means of production ... What are the means of production or tools employed by those engaged in the ongoing pursuit of supplanting and increasing knowledge-value? A designer needs a desk and the pencils, triangles, and other tools to draft blue-prints. Cameramen and photographers need their cameras. Most computer software designers require only a small-scale computer to carry out their designs. The tools needed to carry out any of these functions are not that prohibitively expensive. Acquiring them involves costs that are more than reasonably manageable for individuals ... In the end, the most important means of production for creating knowledge-value is the individual mind, and those who are charged with generating it must strive to bring to bear as much knowledge, experience and perception as they can. Creating knowledge-value is a pursuit in which labor and the means of production become inseparably wedded.[131]

As a result of this, 'in a knowledge-value society, the trend toward the separation of capital and labor will be reversed; henceforth they will tend to fuse'.[132]

We are in the main in agreement with these thoughts. But Sakaiya does not provide as acute a contrast between the new worker and the traditional hired labourer as we do in our study. What is more important is that Sakaiya, talking about knowledge-value, stresses that the new worker does not produce *value* as such, not *exchange value* indissolubly connected with the universal market equivalent, but a certain kind of *tsennost'*, to use the Russian, based on knowledge, a specific kind of use value. This conclusion we regard as being exceptionally important for understanding the changing realities of the modern economy.

Thus we find that *personal* property is coming to replace *private* property only to the degree that knowledge work is spreading in the social economy. This leads to the fact that a group of workers, substantial in numbers and even more substantial in influence over modern society, is offering for exchange not its labour power but an individual and unique *product* characterized by a high degree of social utility and is having the opportunity to act on the basis of non-economic motives and to advance and develop its creative abilities.[133] Despite the fact that the production of such products is a mere intermediate stage on the path to the creation by knowledge workers of their own companies and corporations that will start to act within the framework of a market type of behaviour, it can be said with confidence that the *private* ownership of fixed assets and the other material elements of social wealth no longer provides the kind of economic power that it did in bourgeois society. One of the main elements of the overcoming of the basis of the capitalist order is the method of uniting workers with their means of production that is developing before our eyes. And this emerges in those industries upon which social production depends the most.

Such a global transformation could not but be accompanied by serious changes in the behaviour of the owners and managers of industrial companies. Drucker, admitting that workers possess knowledge, wrote that 'technicians, professionals and managers found that they had the "capital" – their knowledge; they owned the *means* of production. Somebody else, the organization, had the *tools* of production. The two needed each other. By itself, neither was capable of producing. Neither, in other words, is "dependent" or "independent". They are interdependent'.[134] Without entering into polemics about the distinction between the means of production and the tools of production, we would agree with Drucker's main idea: at the current stage the most serious *property* of the managers and owners of companies is the organization they have created and nurtured. Moreover, this term conceals an exceptionally multifaceted and complex phenomenon that includes not only internal production technology but personal management and a concept of the behaviour of the enterprise in the external competitive environment.

The problem even today seems to be fairly underdeveloped. We believe Hammer made the most serious step in developing this issue. Considering the changes brought by what he calls 'process centring', Hammer said that the manager was turning into a *process owner*.[135] Hammer himself writes that process ownership is merely a relatively abstract category that reflects the changing social role of the manager rather than the emergence of a new type of property. ('Process centering starts a chain reaction that affects everyone from the frontline performer to the CEO. Not only are old *roles* [emphasis added] either eliminated or transformed beyond recognition, but entirely new ones, like process owner, come into being.'[136]) We, however, believe that the modern manager really is turning into a process owner enjoying full rights whose property is the very organization process itself.

Thus the information revolution is today acting as something of a foundation of the modernization of property relations. A significant share of knowledge workers become owners of the means of production. But only sometimes may this be connected with their ownership of knowledge and abilities. In an increasingly full sense of the word they are becoming owners of all the means of production required to offer major companies and corporations, not their labour, but its outcome, not their labour power but use value embodied in an information product or a new production technology. On the other hand, managers, today very rarely the formal owners of the corresponding enterprise or company, are becoming the owners of the production process to the extent that they control it and the owners of the technology and principles of the survival of the company in the tough market battle with their competitors.

The contrast between the capitalist and the hired labourer as the owners of the values of the means of production and labour power that characterized industrial society is thus being replaced by the relationship between independent knowledge workers capable of developing their own production and the managers of large industrial and service companies as the owners of use values which are different but nevertheless essential for the existence and advancement of the economic process. Moreover, the ownership of knowledge workers over knowledge and the means of production and the ownership of the manager class over the tools of production cannot be understood as *private* property in the traditional sense of the term. In essence, both knowledge workers and managers are able to offer the market an intellectual product, the result of their individual production, rather than an activity or an ability. We believe that these two forms of property represent types of personal property over the means and tools of production that have yet to take their final form and that will eventually undermine traditional economic forms. It is on the basis of these new types of property that new forms of relations are being created under which the social utility of goods will become the main and only regulator of exchange.

Naturally, the institution of private property born of market principles cannot be removed until these principles to a significant degree determine the mechanism of exchange. The market and value nature of commodity transactions will only be surmounted when non-economic motives and stimuli clearly dominate the behaviour of individuals. It is quite clear that such a process cannot by any means be described as complete today. This, however, is not of the most importance. Modified by a multitude of factors, property relations have lost the dominance they had in the industrial society with the formation of the information society. Therefore we believe it is possible to assert that the continued existence of these relations is no longer a significant barrier to the development of the post-economic transformation that interests us.

Truly private property in its 'disintegrated' forms acts more as a symbol of the possession of the means of production and the condition for the receipt of certain incomes than as the embodiment of the ability to act as a manager who enjoys real power. Small property owners are not in a position to enjoy most of the rights that private property provided in the framework of the economic society. They merely help process owners consolidate, to the same degree moreover, that the development of the mechanism of trust transfer multiplies the number of processes. Today it could be said that real ownership is being concentrated in the hands of property managers, whether of major companies or pension funds, insurance companies or some other financial institution, who have become the main shareholders of industrial corporations. But this ownership in the epoch of the information revolution appears to be to a great degree conditional. Handy wrote:

> In the age of intellectual capital, who owns the capital? It's not the shareholders. It can't be, in any real sense. The people who own the intellect are the core workers of the company. In other words, it's the assets who own the assets. Because we can't in any real sense own other people. They can always walk out on us. Nor does it seem right to own another person.[137]

Consequently, we once again come to the conclusion that it is the process owners who are the real owners of companies, one of the most complex of tasks within which is internal organization.

On the other hand, the richest people in the world today are those who founded organizations that provide them with fabulous wealth. Moreover, this does not just pertain to the owners of successful information consortia. T. Walton, one of the richest men in America, owns a controlling stake in retailer Wal-Mart, which he founded himself and which he has managed for more than 20 years. Such property can in a certain sense be regarded as based on personal participation. It can be considered to embody and develop ownership of knowledge and to manifest process ownership. It is characteristic that a significant share of such property is not materialized in monetary wealth or consumed by the owner, but is practically always embodied in the company itself. It is unlikely that Bill Gates, whose personal wealth grows in line with the share price of Microsoft, in which he has a 24 per cent stake, will ever want to sell up to adopt a life of leisure. Modern large private property primarily reflects the success of companies founded by its owners and today with greater confidence than ever before it can be asserted that it will serve as the goal for the self-affirmation of its founders in the development of production and the successful battle with competitive producers.

That is why so much corporate expansion is self-financed. Bell wrote that

> only a minor proportion of corporate capital today is raised through the sale of equity capital. A more significant portion of capital comes through self-financing, by the success of the enterprise itself. In the last decade, more than 60 percent of the capital investment of the nation's 1,000 largest manufacturing firms was financed internally.[138]

Such companies not only see their task as the coordination of their aims with those of society as enthusiastically stated by famous business leaders quoted by Toffler;[139] they also serve as forms of self-expression and self-affirmation for their founders. Responsibility and self-realization is much more important for the owners of such companies than ownership. Drucker was quite right to say that 'the problems to be solved are not problems of ownership or of political control. They are problems of social organisation of modern technology'.[140] All this convincingly shows that economic motives are far from being the only factor of the progress of production and private property is far being from the only condition for its effective functioning.

Thus two new classes – independent knowledge workers and managers who own the means of production and those who have created companies using their own talents and knowledge – are forming under the influence of phenomena that we have interpreted as the formation of a qualitatively new kind of *personal* property. It is characteristic that the first class is made up of those who have more chance of joining the second than of entering the industrial proletariat. However, in the evolution of property relations, it is impossible to avoid contradictions that arise as a result of such relations. Here we are talking about the contradiction between that part of society that is the carrier of modern knowledge and that part of society that forms the basis of the modern middle class. Small *private* ownership does not change the nature of hired labourers, nor does it give them any property rights, apart from the additional income of shareholders in a certain mutual fund or the holders of shares in a financial company.

The expansion of personal property has been manifested over the last decade increasingly clearly, acquiring a general character and no longer limited to the information sector. The notion of the 'electronic cottage' that Toffler introduced in the early 1980s[141] associated individual production with intellectual characteristics and the informational nature of the good produced. But Naisbitt, noting that the 'revolution in telecommunications is simultaneously creating the huge, global, single-market economy, while making the parts smaller and more powerful',[142] was referring to a more general phenomenon. His forecast, made in the early 1990s, that, by 1995, there would be about 20.7 million full-time home-based businesses in the United States[143] has proved to be a major underestimate. Statistics show that 'as many as 30 million persons worked alone in their own firms'.[144] This trend, however, does not represent a movement to individualism or self-isolation. On the contrary, a person in such circumstances is forced to communicate with a greater number of counter-agents than ever before and to absorb and process a much greater amount of information. But – and this is much more significant – this trend entails the fast expansion of the circle of people living and working fully independently, relating to their fellow citizens as complete equals, assimilating a new type of behaviour to a significant degree not determined by traditional economic values and not presupposing the dominance of private property.

The contrast of private and personal property, which today does not entail any sign of antagonism, does not amount merely to the formation of social groups and classes, the representatives of which are the owners of the means of production they personally use, process owners and individual producers of information or material goods. This dichotomy, which exists throughout the entire society, cannot develop without a corresponding reaction from social institutions, governments and state authorities. In this respect the function of the state as an economic unit and the production of social goods is of particular interest. We believe that every year it becomes increasingly clear that state property can be regarded as a specific form of hypertrophied form of personal property and that the state sector is a sphere for the fast development of non-economic principles.

State Property: Between Private and Personal

State property has a special place in the economic structure of modern society. All the changes in property relations that we have identified are particularly salient in the state sector. State property clearly contrasts corporate property and the personal property of citizens. It has economic sources and develops within the system of coordinates of the economic society. On these grounds we can talk with confidence of state property as a form of private property. It embodies the diffusion that is typical of modern private property. There is no other economic unit whose formal ownership is as widely distributed and there is no company whose leadership is as detached from its formal owners. In no other sector do those who manage property but are not its formal owners, that is process owners, have as much power to dispose of the property as they wish. This authority goes beyond the framework of the determination of economic strategies and behaviour and may even become power over the lives of the formal owners of state property. In this case process ownership reaches its fullest embodiment. Possession of this property does not envisage any opportunities for real appropriation and is very like modern private property, which is owned by the founders and managers of major information corporations. And, lastly, despite all the above, state property is designed to serve the interests of all the members of society. It does not serve as the instrument for the dominance of one person over another in the market environment. In this respect it is similar to personal property as we have defined it. Thus state property embodies various elements of all the kinds and forms of modern property and is of a clearly transitional nature. It is clear this form of property cannot last unchanged in a quickly changing society that has taken the first step on the path to post-economic transformation.

State property existed in one form or another throughout the history of class societies. It was often used to achieve the political goals of the ruling class. But its very presence was always dictated by social needs that individuals were not able to satisfy themselves: 'The public household (as against the market, which seeks to serve diverse private wants) has always existed to meet common needs, to provide goods and services which individuals cannot purchase for themselves.'[145] The state, moreover, always acted as an economic manager since the state reflected the interests of individual social groups and classes, interests that during the formation and development of the economic society were of an *economic* nature and content. The state took one of the main roles at all stages in the development of the economic structure. State consumption, removed from the natural commodity turnover, and the incredible expenditure that the state could allow itself, even at the cost of upsetting monetary circulation, were among the main reasons for the destruction of the economic system of the Roman Empire. In contrast, even the first modest signs of its inclusion in market relations that manifested themselves in the early mediaeval period and the new retributory nature of state consumption led to the growth of mediaeval cities around royal courts, the main source of solvent demand for craft products; the systemization of tax collection; the switch to money rents; the appearance in Europe of the first stage budgets in the 14th century and soon the market for government debt instruments, all of which made the government a permanent and indisputable participant in market processes.

The economic functions of the state differed according to the circumstances and state property served to provide for a whole range of various goals, the most important of which, however, remained the maintenance of social stability by eliminating the most acute social conflicts and their causes. After the formation of the industrial society, the main means for achieving such goals become the active intervention of the state in economic life. Such intervention became a priority of government activity in the 20th century.

The toughest test for the capitalist state as an economic manager came with the catastrophic crisis that broke out in the late 1920s and early 1930s. The state, lacking tried and tested tools for tackling such a crisis, used all the opportunities it had in order to ameliorate the consequences of the crisis: public works were financed, citizens were provided with material support, the economy was decisively restricted and an active monetary and credit policy was carried out. With the exception of the most extraordinary tasks, like public works and direct material support for the needy, most of the others were within the field of view of the authorities even in the first years after the crisis had been overcome. During the Second World War, a trend emerged that was to become established in the first postwar years and to play an exceptionally important role for technological progress: science and education became the main recipients of state investment because to fall behind in science and education amounted to a threat to national security. The most impressive breakthroughs, which heralded the coming of the information era, were brought about by state investment, both in the West and in the former Soviet bloc. It is in this decisive area that state property manifested itself as the antithesis of private property, opening the way for the solution of economic problems that were so sharp and complex that they were beyond the reach of private or corporate investors.

In the 1960s and 1970s, when the information revolution become a reality, companies appeared that were capable of developing by using their internal potential. At the same time, however, the bases of political stability were shaken by powerful social movements from both within and outside the most developed post-industrial nations. So much of the state's attention was focused on the development of the social sphere, the easing of class conflicts, the solution of problems associated with unemployment and migration and the provision of healthcare and other social programmes. Thus, with each new stage, state property penetrated an increasing number of spheres that had previously been closed to it.[146]

At present state property occurs in two main forms serving a single group of goals but distinguished by their component parts. Firstly, private property is made up of an aggregate of resources, which the government possesses on the basis of the legislation that exists within the society, as a system of institutions of power and control. In order to balance the development of the social whole, the government redistributes financial flows with the help of taxes, uses the labour of citizens in the framework of certain laws of obligation and controls the natural resources it owns. All these elements of wealth make up the basis of the power which the state may mobilize if a threat emerges to the nation or individual citizens, be it military, political or economic. Moreover, it can also spend these resources on current needs: to strengthen the national currency, to encourage production and exports, to provide grants and subsidies, to provide aid for friendly nations, to finance scientific development and to carry out social programmes. Possessing giant resources, the state today is both the biggest consumer of industrial products and the single biggest institutional investor.

Secondly, the state has property rights over enormous assets, including enterprises and companies in strategic sectors of the economy. Moreover, the state seldom surrenders an important position in an industry once it has occupied it. The only exception is the sale of inefficient enterprises and enterprises created by the government but no longer requiring state management. The best known example of such transfers is the privatization programme carried out in Britain by the Conservative government after it took power in 1979 and the privatization of parts of French industry after the victory of a right-wing coalition in the parliamentary elections of 1986. Yet the real scale of these processes was less significant than their resonance. In France between 1986 and 1989, privatizations were carried out at 138 companies employing about 300 000 people, less than 1 per cent of the workforce.[147]

The overall trend remains the growth in the role of the state with regard to the economy determined by progress itself and the increasingly complex nature of modern production systems. Galbraith rightly says that 'with economic advance and accompanying social responsibility, the problems facing government increase in both complexity and diversity, perhaps not arithmetically but geometrically'.[148] Even when neo-conservative economic policies predominated, the influence of the state not so much diminished as diversified and changed the main superficial forms of its manifestation. The complexity of today's economic and social problems prompts state intervention and the realization of the state's property rights every day and every hour and there is no evidence to show that this trend will change in the future.

Possessing enormous economic abilities, exceeding those of even the most successful corporation or conglomerate, the state can direct the resources it has concentrated into those spheres of the economy and those social reforms that it regards as the most necessary at the given time. State property, like private or personal property, is not something stagnant, a mere statement of ownership of one value or another. And the key problem that today stands before the managers of state property is, in our view, that they do not manage their property in the way that the non-economically motivated owners of personal property manage theirs, despite the fact that the structure of state property is close to that of personal property.

In both economic and sociological literature, discussions have being going on for decades over the degree to which the state should intervene in the economy. Most participants in this discussion came to a conclusion in the early 1970s which is hard to contest. On the one hand, it was recognized that 'with economic development, social action and regulation become more important even as socialism in the classical sense becomes irrelevant',[149] and on the other hand that the 'extension of planning into every corner of economic life'[150] was not a panacea capable of leading to the formation of a more efficient economy.[151] Thus, it would seem, a highly balanced point of view was developed. But the discussions did not come to an end. They continued, according to some impressions, to increase from year to year. At the same time a proposal for a non-economic, or rather, a non-market role for the state was made. This proposal recalled a defensive strategy and was designed to minimize all the possible negative consequences of social or natural phenomena. As Harold Perkin wrote: 'The welfare state in professional society is not optional. It is the essential foundation of every community, an insurance against poverty, crime, violence and anarchy, and the reserve maintainer and improver of human capital on which everything else depends.'[152] A similar position was formulated in regard to the problems that emerged as a result of the disruption of the ecological balance and the exploitation of the environment.[153]

As a result, the view that came to dominate was that the state should primarily react to various symptoms of social deprivation. The use of state property throughout the world is based on this position. It is characteristic that in such an issue as the regulation of economic crises the actions of the authorities can to a certain degree be of a preventative nature, since the laws of the development of such crises are fairly well known. However, the development of technology, the progress of information production and, finally, new scientific research could have consequences that are not only unforeseeable but which could be much harder to overcome than to prevent. We do not know what man may create in the future having received the latest scientific knowledge, armed with modern technology and not motivated by traditional material requirements. Even without having conscious asocial aims, a modern researcher may get results in his scientific work that could present a serious threat to all of humanity.

The power of the state (we are not talking here of its military or police machinery) is in its power of economic resources or, to be more specific, over monetary wealth. It is this power that can temporarily lower unemployment, support the national currency, help painlessly to survive a deficit in the balance of payments and service the giant financial obligations of the government. However, all of this shows that state property is mostly managed on the basis of cause and effect typical of traditional industrial society and that the state has the means most akin to the principles and goals of the economic epoch. Meanwhile, as we have noted, in essence state property is closer to personal property than to private. The state can know today how to tackle the coming economic crisis, how to provide a higher standard of living in an individual region or how to protect the interests of its citizens in a remote corner of the world. But, though wielding administrative and economic levers, it can prove helpless in the face of the desire of individual owners of information and knowledge for self-affirmation in the most dangerous forms for society. Even an attempt to ban certain areas of scientific research and development will fail if the government cannot financially limit such work or even discover that such work is being carried out.

Today it is not known how state property will be used on the basis of those principles and in line with those motives that characterize the activity of those who have personal ownership over the means of production. Stuck in its intermediate position, state property risks becoming the last remnant of private property, an institute that does not correspond to the requirements of a changing situation. Yet surely only centralized social institutions are capable of standing up to the prospect of social disintegration as classes and mass groupings break up and society diffuses into an infinite number of producing individuals, whose aims lose that single basis that they had in the economic order.

These issues bear no direct relevance to the development of property. They are, however, of enormous importance since they reflect the lack of a single unifying principle in post-economic society to replace the material interests that formed the basis of economic society. Therefore we shall examine the *social* changes taking place in modern society as the third main component of the post-economic revolution.

The Elimination of Exploitation and the New Social Conflict

The post-economic society forms as and when individual preferences, personal development and internal spiritual progress determine ever new characteristics of the social whole. In these circumstances, 'l'unité de la vie sociale ne découle plus de l'idée de société. Au contraire, ce qu'on nomme société est plutôt considéré désormais comme un ensemble de règles, de coutumes et de privilèges contre lesquels les efforts créateurs, individuels et collectifs, ont toujours à lutter. Selon cette conception, tous les principes métasociaux d'unité de la vie sociale sont remplacés ... par la *liberté*'.[154] Yet even in the most advanced society there must be some limits on freedom: any desire or interest expressed in individual or collective action inevitably conflicts with the interests of other members of society realized using other methods. It is for this reason that all philosophers and sociologists have stressed and continue to stress that 'the relationship between the self-interest of the citizen and the interest of society is the most fundamental question of a free society'.[155]

The central issues in social philosophy have always been how the individual regards himself, to which social group he ascribes himself, whether he considers his place in society to be free or dependent and whether he believes his activity to be motivated by goals he has set himself or by coercion. The issue of the overcoming of exploitation – understood by the most varied scholars as the oppression of one person by another for material benefit – has always kept its significance both as a matter of theoretical interest and as a prerequisite and an instrument for the transformation of social forms and institutions. Therefore the overcoming of exploitation today is a real expression of social progress that is based on the destruction of value relations and the modernization of the property system. And, if the post-economic order is really to raise the social organization to a higher plane, it will be the ability of this order to overcome the exploitation that leads to the irreconcilable contradictions within industrial society that will serve as the main criterion for verifying such an assertion.

At the beginning of our analysis we will formulate two important postulates that will determine its context. Firstly, the post-economic society cannot eliminate the competitive distribution of goods between its members or make this distribution equal. *The new social organization asserts the principle of freedom, not equality*, and in this differs from the traditional ideal of the communists. Secondly, the new society will not become classless, as presupposed by many utopians. On the contrary, it may become even more divided into separate social groups than its predecessor. But the criteria for social division will not be external characteristics, like ownership of material goods, but personal characteristics, primarily the ability to produce information and to convert it into knowledge. Both these postulates require substantial elucidation that will precede a more detailed consideration of the corresponding issues.

It should be remembered that social contradictions are *replaced* by new forms of conflict rather than simply *overcome* during the course of evolution. Here we are not talking about contradictions as the source of development as they are often understood in Hegelian dialectics. We are referring to real social confrontations that are appearing and that cannot but appear to replace the conflicts of the industrial epoch. The main problems that will face humanity in the near future will be *the overcoming of exploitation, the change in the nature of class conflict and growing inequality in the distribution of material goods.* These problems may be regarded as different aspects of what is essentially a single change. But they are not necessarily identical.

A trend for exploitation to be overcome can already be traced fairly clearly today. This is because the cause of the conflict that lies at the root of exploitation is concealed in the motives that determine the actions of people in the economic society. Exploitation is born of the conflict of the material interests of people, when the need of one cannot be satisfied without injuring the need of another. This injury often takes the form of the seizure of part of the direct output of one individual by another. Since we are here referring to an economic society, it is easy to understand that both sides regard the acquisition of material wealth as their goal. Therefore one of the sides, unable to realize its material interest, becomes the irreconcilable antagonist of the other during the course of the conflict. This is how one of the contradictions of the economic order arises given a shortage of material goods, contradictions that are most dangerous for social order.

Socialists and assorted utopians believed that this contradiction would be overcome by the development of production to satisfy completely the growing requirements of society. Yet this approach is based on so many assumptions that it cannot serve as the basis for determining the real prospects of humanity. On the one hand, production can never satisfy *all* the requirements of society. On the other hand, even if all the requirements of *society* are satisfied it is not obvious that this would entail the satisfaction of all the requirements of the *individuals* of which society is composed. The aggregate of goals and desires of individuals is much wider than the goals and desires of society. Therefore the requirements of all members of society can neither be satisfied nor even determined by the common effort of the social whole. Moreover, in the communist doctrine the notion of the development of the individual radically contradicted the notion of equality. Current activity leaves no room for doubt that every new step on the path to the formation of creativity as the main element of a system of social activity becomes a step on the path to overcoming the highly relative property equality that existed within the framework of the industrial epoch.

By virtue of this, the only real way of overcoming exploitation is to surmount it as a *sociopsychological phenomenon*. This assertion is far less paradoxical than it might appear at first glance if the appropriation of the product of an individual's labour (and we can have no doubt that such appropriation will take place for as long as humans live in communities) *is not perceived* by the individual as against his goals and interests. This is possible if the main goals and interests of the individual are not of a primarily material nature but are instead geared to self-realization. Such interests come to dominate not when all material requirements are hypothetically fully satisfied but at that saturation point when the individual starts to prefer his own personal development to the growth in his material requirement. This explains our interpretation of the overcoming of exploitation and the nature of the new social contradiction.

The class relations of the post-economic society will be a far cry from the harmonious intercourse envisaged in utopian concepts.

Unlike the economic epoch, when an individual was assigned to one class or another according to whether he owned the means and results of production, individuals will be classed according to their ability to process information and knowledge, create new information products and make use of those products that have already been created. During the formative stage of the post-economic society (we touched on this issue in our analysis of the changes in property relations) there is a transitional class division that contradictorily encompasses both the individual's relation to property and his ability to innovate. In some studies this new division is regarded as a stable system that the capitalist society has progressed towards since its very inception. Jan Pakulski and Malcolm Waters said that 'no sooner had capitalist society been established than it began to evolve into a new form in which property declined as the critical factor in economic group formation relative to the development of hierarchically ordered systems of domination, i.e. bureaucracies'.[156] It is well known that the first post-industrial theorists assigned a particularly important role to the study of the new emergent ruling classes, such as the meritocracy and the 'ad-hocracy'.

We, however, believe that such a system, based on the domination of a meritocracy or 'ad-hocracy', cannot be sustained. As post-economic trends develop the main class division will quickly switch from distinguishing the managing from the managed to distinguishing between the creators of a product (primarily intellectual) and the consumers and between those who are capable of producing and consuming such products and those who are not. Even today, when with increasing frequency it can be heard from writers like Drucker, Bell, Toffler and Naisbitt – who have got to the very essence of modern problems – that creative workers cannot be managed on the basis of either economic principles or organizational coercion; when Inglehart and Dahrendorf admit that the main conflict of the future society will be between the adherents of materialist and non-materialist value systems; and when the decision-making stratum of society (or rather the stratum of society that is capable of making decisions) is seen as increasingly alienated from the rest of society, it can be said that there is no doubt that the rule of the bureaucratic elite is coming to an end.

The old elite is to be replaced by a new social system stratified according to the intellect and ability of the individual. In this case it can once again be said that property serves as the basis of class division. But this time it is not alienated property rights over the means and conditions of production but the inalienable rights over one's own abilities; not a sum of material goods that may be used by all with access to it but a system of informational codes that is accessible only to the elect. Thus there emerges a trend which, unlike the trend for the overcoming of exploitation, is not yet clear-cut today. However, it should be admitted that the likelihood of this trend being secured and developed in the future is very high, though with far from clear consequences. In any case, the first clear manifestations of this trend do not give cause for complacency.

Many thinkers considered inequality in the distribution of material goods to be as ancient as humanity itself. Yet economists and sociologists confidently assert that economic progress is capable of eliminating, if not the evil itself, then at least those of its manifestations that pose the greatest danger for social stability.[157] And it is impossible not to admit that they are right. All statistical studies and economic tracts devoted to social policy and social problems in the advanced nations show that a trend towards a reduction in the inequality of the distribution of material wealth did have a place in the developed democracies and that it can be fairly clearly traced throughout the 20th century. However, the picture has changed by the end of the 20th century and today ever-increasing numbers of new theorists have started – some with reluctance, others with concern and still others with unconcealed malicious delight – to note the growing divide between the richest and the poorest sectors of the population. Indeed, the gap between the rich and the poor seems to be widening at the end of the century as quickly as it narrowed at the beginning. Moreover, it is far from difficult to identify the period when superficially positive social changes were reversed. It is again that magic instant in the mid-1970s when the first clear manifestations of the post-economic transformation made themselves felt.

All these manifestations are completely explainable and we have considered some of their aspects in our analysis of the prospects of the development of market relations and modern forms of property. We are talking about that special condition in which the producers of information and knowledge – the main productive resources of modern society – and associated social groups find themselves today. The new class division not only erects an increasingly strong borderline between those that have access to information technology and the ability to make effective use of it and those who do not, it also brings an increasingly disproportionate distribution of social wealth. As mass-production is driven to the periphery of economic life or even driven beyond the borders of post-industrial nations, its workers become stripped of their class status, *déclassés*; their redundancy is not merely temporary unemployment but a complete separation from socially useful activity. Society, its values increasingly formed by the intellectual elite, is providing people with rewards that decreasingly correspond if not to their actual role in society then to what they regard as their role in society, which, under present conditions, amounts to one and the same thing.

This has come as a surprise for optimists who predicted an evolutionary transition to an order of social harmony and who believed that the capitalist society would gradually find a solution to all the contradictions of the industrial epoch. Yet such a turn of events was quite easy to predict, given the obvious irreconcilability of liberty and equality where the discussion pertains to more than merely the freedom to work at primitive manufacturing facilities and the equality of a pauper's lunch. Society, having developed beyond the framework of industrial logic, has today started to recognize that preaching equality of property is just as much a castoff from an idealistic past as the belief that everyone is born with equal abilities. Yet social development is even more dynamic than the consciousness of individual members of society. Inglehart has convincingly shown that the individual's motives and value system practically remain unchanged throughout his life,[158] and we can scarcely expect society to quickly adapt to the notion that one of its most alluring illusions has collapsed. This last point means that humanity at the beginning of the coming millennium may once again find itself on the threshold of new social upheavals.

Stonier wrote, some 15 years ago, that 'the major problem confronting Western governments in the 1980s is the need to devise ... a smooth transition from an industrial to an information economy'.[159] This is more topical now than ever, since over recent years all of the concealed negative potential of the changes that are under way has been revealed to us. In order to make a smooth transition to the post-economic condition we must coordinate the type and pace of development to ensure that the proliferation of non-material values as dominant goes ahead faster than radical disintegration of the system on which they are based under the destructive influence from those who still do not perceive such values as fundamental. Such a task is extremely difficult for even the most advanced nations. We can sense the difficulties of the current situation, the scale of the post-economic transformation and the far from certain prospects of its completion if we bear in mind that the peoples of many regions of our planet have still to taste all the fruits of industrialism.

Having previewed our analysis with these introductory remarks, we can turn to the first of the issues raised.

Exploitation: Objective or Perceived?

In order to determine the conditions for the overcoming of exploitation, it is necessary to turn to the issue that we considered above regarding the main type of activity within the framework of the economic epoch, namely the notion of labour as the main type of activity characteristic of the economic epoch that provides us with the opportunity to analyse consistently the prospects for the development of the relation that has been called exploitation.

Traditionally, the majority of scholars associated exploitation with the oppression of one individual by another and the creation within society of unequal conditions for various social groups. The conflict that determines the phenomenon of exploitation is regarded as a class conflict or its manifestation. We do not share this approach to this issue. The class division of society is in itself born of a long process to find the optimal organization for a social structure that aims to achieve economic ends. As Karl Marx correctly said, 'in grossen Umrissen koennen asiatische, antike, feudale und modern buergerliche Produktionsweisen als progressive Epochen der oekonomischen Gesellschaftsformation bezeichnet werden'.[160] It is the forms of class societies that marked the stages of the economic epoch and not the other way round. *So the economic society is not a manifestation of the class type of social division; on the contrary, the existence of classes and other antagonistic groups is a consequence of the internal contradictions that developed within the economic society.* Therefore the phenomenon of exploitation is a cause rather than a consequence of the class nature of society.

Putting the question this way fundamentally alters our attitude to exploitation as a subject of analysis, although it leaves unchanged one important aspect of the issue: the definition of the phenomenon within the category of the contradictions of the material interests of individual members of society. It may be said that the modern understanding of exploitation to a certain degree returns to the point at which study of the phenomenon began. Adam Smith, considering the relationship between the bourgeois and the hired labourer, stressed that their interests 'are by no means the same. The workmen desire to get as much, the masters to give as little as possible'.[161] Smith precisely identified the essence of the main conflict of the economic epoch: the conflict arises around the distribution of scarce goods when their consumption is seen by the absolute majority of the members of society as the goal of conscious activity.

Labour, as an activity born of the desire to satisfy material interests, leaves an imprint on all aspects of social life and the contradictions that arise in connection with the phenomenon of exploitation most clearly show its unfree nature. In the economic epoch, the interests of most people are within the plane of material interests. Interests associated with the self-realization of the individual, the acquisition of social status and inner self-advancement, also determine the actions of many people. But it can still be said that they do not have any substantial influence on the formation of the resulting social interests and do not set the direction of social evolution. In this respect the economic society is a fully independent system. J.K. Galbraith wrote:

> the relationship between the society at large and an organization must be consistent with the relation of the organization to the individual; there must be consistency in the goals of the society, the organization and the individual; and there must be consistency in the motives which induce organizations and individuals to pursue these goals.[162]

But such a point of view is, in one respect, totally utopian. It also contains an obvious tautology. The interests of the individual, organization and society in the economic condition are always consistent by virtue of the existence and functioning of the economic organism. Moreover, no efforts can and never will be able to make them harmonious and non-contradictory in the sense that the great sociologist has in mind.

The economic society is based on labour, establishes a corresponding system of subordination of material interests and at the same time entails the alienation of part of the result of the individual's labour. This alienation can have several forms: from the complete appropriation of even the most necessary goods with the consequent return of a share by the ruling class (as in despotic Asiatic regimes and, in a certain sense, in the communist world); through the alienation of surplus product by means of the acquisition of the labour of legally free citizens that forms the basis of bourgeois society; to the redirection of part of the product of labour that is sanctioned by the society to meet profoundly social needs (even Marx, talking of the socialist society, noted that in the new conditions it would not merely be that part of the product required to ensure expanded reproduction that would be alienated but 'First, the general costs of administration not directly appertaining to production. Secondly, that which is intended for the common satisfaction of needs, such as schools, health services, etc. Thirdly, funds for those unable to work.'[163] It is wrong to imagine that the first two forms of appropriation amount to exploitation but that the third does not because it takes place within the framework of a society free from exploitation.

In all these cases a single important aspect of the issue should not be allowed to escape our attention: which system of interests determines one society or another. Usually, scholars looking at the possibility of overcoming exploitation talk about the liberation of the individual from labour, which they regard as an unfree activity. This approach is to a large extent taken from Marx, who believed, not in the liberation of labour, but in the liberation from labour. Modern authors, especially those of a socialist persuasion, have to a certain degree perfected this position. André Gorz, talking in his famous work about the mistakes of preceding socialists, said that 'the abolition of work and the abolition of wage labour were goals between which no distinction was made'.[164] He came close to understanding the need to change the inner conditions for human activity, its motives, as well as the external ones. He wrote, 'For both wage earners and employers, work is only a means of earning money and not an activity that is an end in itself. Therefore work is not freedom ... This is why ... it is necessary to free ourselves *in* our work as well as *from* work, and *from* work as well as *in* our work',[165] stressing that 'the abolition of work is neither acceptable nor desirable for people who identify with their work, define themselves through it and do or hope to realise themselves in their work'.[166]

The formation of the post-economic society for several decades remained a process reflected in sociological literature by, at best, an analysis of its objective components: the development of the material manufacturing base, changes in the characteristics of the workforce, the new organization of labour, and so on. It was seldom regarded as a complex sociopsychological phenomenon, as a transformation that concerns not merely the living and working conditions of the individual, but his inner essence that changes his interests and goals, values and desires. Only in the 1990s, when the scale and directions of the changes that had taken place over the last 20 years became quite obvious, did active conceptualization begin of the new trends that could not but lead to the paradoxical conclusion that the real changes taking place in the modern world were of less significance for the new transformations than concepts of their origins, course and directions and that the real place of the individual in society and the real motives of his actions were subordinated to his perception of them.

The public in the late 1980s was shocked by the assertions that

le passage d'un type sociétal à un autre peut s'opérer ... par des transformations internes opérées à la base de la vie sociale ... dans le modèle occidental de devéloppement, c'est donc la culture qui se transforme d'abord: de nouvelles connaissances et de nouvelles techniques apparaissent, associées à une modification des moeurs et des forces de production. Ensuite se constituent de nouveaux acteurs sociaux, avec leur mode d'action; plus tard encore se réorganise le système politique et se mettent en place de nouvelles formes d'organisation; enfin se cristallisent des idéologies qui correspondent aux intérêts des acteurs désormais constitués.[167]

Today comprehension is maturing that such notions are only partly correct and that we have to go further, that in the modern world the definitive role is played by phenomena and processes *opérées à la base de la vie individuelle*, and that social sciences will have to build elements of psychology and sociopsychology into their theoretical constructs in order to conceptualize these phenomena and processes.

At the beginning of the 1990s post-industrial sociology was far from concerned with sociopsychological problems. Toffler said, 'the most important powershift of all, therefore, is not from one person, party, institution or nation to another. It is the hidden shift in the relationships between violence, wealth and knowledge as societies speed toward their collision with tomorrow',[168] and this, if not new, still fully reflected the dominating trend. Today the situation has changed and there is the increasingly wide proliferation of an understanding that the subjective impressions of an individual, no longer subject to social control and clear forecasting, are becoming the determinant of social progress. Manuel Castells in a recent work said, 'the new power lies in the codes of information and in the images of representation around which societies organize their institutions, and people build their lives, and decide their behaviour. The sites of this power are people's minds'.[169] It is the development of the impressions of the individual of his own activity that contains, in our view, the opportunity to overcome exploitation.

Exploitation, therefore, is the alienation by violent means or according to accepted legal norms of a certain share of the product of the individual's labour in the interest of other individuals, organizations or the society as a whole when that product is regarded as the goal of activity. This phenomenon is immanent in the economic society since it is born of every aspect of the manifestation of economic laws. Moreover, the notion that exploitation played merely a negative role in history is very far from the truth. On the contrary, it was exploitation that in the final analysis provided the concentration of material resources and efforts of people where they were most needed. Exploitation provided new and more advanced kinds of production that formed the basis for further progress. As Robert Heilbroner pointed out, 'exploitation ... is the dark netherworld of civilization [but] it is also, of course, the necessary condition for the achievement of civilization, at least so far as its material triumphs are concerned'.[170]

Our definition of exploitation means that the phenomenon cannot be overcome simply by developing production, as believed under all the socialist doctrines. And it cannot be overcome simply by the reform of distribution relations that had such an important place in the arsenal of communist ideas. The only real change that can eliminate exploitation is the change in the internal organization of human activity itself. As long as the individual is focused on the production and appropriation of as much material use value as possible any barrier put in the way of achieving such an aim will be regarded as exploitation. Changing the structure of requirements to ensure that material motives are no longer dominant could completely transform all human activity: an individual, having achieved a certain level of material consumption that he regards as sufficient and normal, will start to associate his main goals primarily with the development of his own personality.

There are two options for carrying out such changes. Both entail increasing inner liberty, but they lead to very different results. To a certain degree it can be asserted that it is here that the new social contradictions of the modern epoch originate. One of the options envisages a fairly artificial self-limitation when the individual determines one or another level of material well-being to be satisfactory and sufficient to allow non-material values and desires to dominate his activity. In such a case the inner satisfaction is derived from activity in which the individual is engaged during his leisure time. This is now seen as one of the main characteristics of Western lifestyles. People, having achieved a high level of well-being by their own standards, are active in a wide range of spheres which widen their horizons, develop their abilities and raise their esteem both in their own eyes and in those of others. However, in this case we are likely talking about an illusory overcoming of the individual's dependence on material goals. Now not only the property conditions of his life but his opportunities for self-realization, which modern man values particularly highly, are in the final analysis dependent on the scale of his remuneration. The conflict that lies at the heart of exploitation is merely camouflaged. The individual sees himself as unexploited until he encounters a direct infringement of his material (!) interests. Moreover, if the main stimulus for labour is defined as material reward, the threat of a reduction in the level of well-being is an important but usually quantitative factor. In the situation that we have analysed, the individual, if he loses his status as a worker, will not only face a reduction in his own material consumption but will lose his opportunity to realize himself beyond the production process. And this could cause an even more serious social conflict than that described by Adam Smith. The potential consequences of such a conflict are today still to be studied. Many people, moreover, are capable of being satisfied with a not very high level of material well-being and channelling all their creative abilities in exotic ways that will in no way serve to improve society as a whole.

The second option envisages that the development of the abilities of the individual and the inner satisfaction that he receives are connected with his main professional activity. In this case there is a much greater satisfaction to be derived by reaching a certain level of material well-being. When sociologists first tried to define this phenomenon, there appeared a not quite correct but indicative term, 'knowledge worker', which has united various characteristics of the new type of worker: firstly, his innate focus on the use of information and knowledge; secondly, his practical independence from external factors of ownership over the means and conditions of production; thirdly, his extremely high mobility; fourthly, his preference for engaging in activity that provides wide opportunities for self-realization and self-expression, even if that impairs his material well-being. The opportunity for autonomous creative activity is of principal importance for such a worker. In this case we are encountering the real transformation of labour into creativity and the subject of labour into a personality motivated by the principles of the post-economic epoch. Drucker stresses that modern knowledge workers *'do not feel* "exploited" as a class' (emphasis added)[171] and we cannot but agree with such an assertion. Moreover, such activity is much more productive since it is internally free. Of course, people always depend on circumstances and nobody is free of the society in which they live, its institutions and principles, but if they primarily act in correspondence with their own inner interests and priorities, and do not aim at increasing their material well-being, the alienation of one or another part of the product they have created and the receipt of one or another level of profit from their activity will not be perceived as a factor that cardinally influences their sense of the world and their actions. In this respect they are beyond the framework of exploitation, and the growth in the number and influence of those who are motivated in this way is one of the main factors that are providing for the new pace and quality of growth in the developed nations in the 1990s.

The overcoming of exploitation is therefore the reverse side of the substitution of creativity for labour. In this connection we should dwell on the changing mechanism for the subordination of material interests. Studying instinctive pre-labour activity, labour and creativity in Chapter 5, we did not touch on the subordination of individual interests in the framework of each of the kinds of activity. However, it is this that allows us to understand why activity that is not motivated by utility cannot be the object of exploitation.

The very notion of interest loses much of its content when applied to conditions dominated by the primitive instinctive activity. However, it can be said that the biological requirements of people could only vary quantitatively and not qualitatively. The dominant desire to satisfy the most immediate material requirements was absolute. The simplest geometrical example will suffice to show that everybody's interests could be shown as parallel vectors on a single plane, varying only by module. The resulting interest, therefore, can be calculated as a simple sum and there was no *social* conflict over the distribution of material goods. In the epoch when labour was the dominant form of activity, the whole picture looked profoundly different. The vectors of individual interests, as before, were still on the plane of material requirements and desires, but they differed not only by scale but in direction, and the resulting vector of social interest could not, except by chance, coincide with that of any given individual. The social state under such a model amounts to the mutual interaction of individuals defined by the contradictions between their material interests. Any individual who wishes to realize his own interest will inevitably clash with the interests of others. The phenomenon of exploitation thus merely reflects the fact that the class structure of society facilitates the redistribution of social wealth to the benefit of the property-holding, capitalist class. It is impossible to surmount such a situation, as we noted above, simply by increasing consumption (that would change the size and not the direction of the vectors) or by modifying distribution relations (since even though it is possible to imagine a society with *standard consumption*, it is hard to conceive of a society whose members have absolutely identical *interests*), and exploitation, we shall stress yet again, is not just an objective economic phenomenon but a subjective psychological one.

Thus the only way to overcome exploitation is to raise interests off the plane of material requirements. Moreover, as soon as people start to recognize that the vector of their main interest is shifting from the plane of material interests to the plane of non-material interests, the entire social whole begins to move because (and this is clearly illustrated in our model) it requires just one vector to leave the plane to remove the resulting vector from the plane too. Obviously, a change in the way a small group of people is motivated and perceives its place in the world will not bring cardinal changes in social guidelines, yet the first stage of the post-economic revolution is characterized by this superficially unclear process. However, in the future, when a substantial sector of the population will be subject to non-economic motivation, it will become the main factor of social evolution.

This transformation, albeit so far latent and far from always salient, is already freeing from exploitation those people who *recognize* non-material interests as most significant. (In this case we understand exploitation, not as the appropriation of the material product from the producer, but as a phenomenon that gives rise to social conflicts over the distribution of material goods.) The individual, by moving beyond this conflict, becomes the subject of non-economic relations and acquires an internal freedom that it would be impossible to achieve within the framework of the economic society. Society, remaining superficially at one, is internally divided, since a new class of people no longer subject to the old system of motives and management arises within a social organism still formally governed by economic laws. The economically motivated part of society, still dominant, retains within itself all the old conflicts but simultaneously enters into a serious confrontation with the non-economic component of society. Moreover, it seems that the elimination of exploitation that all the best minds of humanity had been aiming for is taking place as a new complex of dangerous social contradictions appears.

The formation of the new system of interests and motives has freed people from being the limited instruments of the natural laws of the economic epoch. The last few decades have been richer than ever before in terms of new scientific discoveries and their unprecedented application in real life and in terms of the fast development of companies created in order to realize the intellectual potential of their founders. The free self-realization of members of society is becoming the main resource of industry and the main base for progress and information and knowledge are mere conditions. It was in this way that in the 1970s to 1990s Western civilization proved the hopelessness of the communist experiment to reconstruct the world, as practically all the main sources of progress claimed to be monopolized by the communists (although more in theory than in practice, since in reality they were neglected) turned out to be mobilized within the post-economic transformation. The realities of today show that it is the post-economic form of development that leads to the formation of a society closest to the ideal that the founders of Marxism called communism. However, this development, firstly, is evolutionary and, secondly, envisages the overcoming of a whole range of contradictions, some of which could not even have been imagined just a few decades ago.

The elimination of exploitation, which can be regarded as the greatest achievement of modern progress, is an extremely complicated phenomenon. Talking of going beyond the bounds of exploitation in a sociopsychological sense, we have stressed the concept that this is possible only for people who are really moved by post-economic and non-material interests, motives and stimuli. It is quite clear that such people are even now still in a small minority. They therefore form, if not a special social institution then, de facto, a separate social group, which, on the one hand, determines – and serves as the source of – the development of society and, on the other hand, is separated from most members of society and confronts them as something totally alien.

A whole new social division emerges that separates those who have gone beyond the relations of exploitation from those who remain conscious of themselves as members of an economic society. The real criterion that superficially manifests itself, however, is whether people are capable of creative activity or not. This is the only thing that makes it possible for them to overcome exploitation in its sociopsychological sense. As a result, it appears that strictly psychological measures, the way in which an individual perceives himself and defines his own goals, his thinking style and the maximum level of his creative abilities, determine the new class division of the post-economic society. The new classes will be divided, not by social status or property, but by the individual's immanent qualities and the degree to which he is gifted by nature. The a priori impossibility of breaching the emerging social barrier for the majority of the population to enjoy social recognition and the wealth and power that accompany it could give rise to kinds of class conflict that history has never known.

Class Conflict in the Post-economic Society

The formation of the post-industrial society and, to a greater degree, the beginning of a shift to a post-economic condition have not only changed the relations between the sectors of social production and the mentality and psychology of the worker but have made the previous class divisions anachronistic by eroding the traditional social confrontation between the bourgeois and the proletariat. Today we can hardly talk about the working class or the bourgeois class of parasites as social strata with any kind of influence. Like the freemen and slaves of antiquity and the feudal lords and serfs of the Middle Ages, the proletarians and bourgeoisie are leaving the historical stage, along with the order that characterized their confrontation. In the same way that the slaves did not become the ruling class during the destruction of the ancient world and serfs had nothing to gain from the collapse of the feudal system, so the proletariat did not and could not take over the management of the economy and society. As before the mutual death of struggling classes marked a change in historical epochs, so now it will be new social groups that determine the face of modern society.

The transformation that leads to the formation of the post-economic order does not entail any kind of political coups or revolutions. Its evolutionary nature makes the process of change in the social consciousness slower than it is in reality. Now, when the traditional proletariat is limited to just a few workers in the industrial sector, people often tend to identify themselves as proletarians: 44.9 per cent of Americans in a public opinion poll conducted in 1993 described themselves as working-class, only a fraction fewer than the 45.3 per cent[172] of Americans who regarded themselves as middle-class. Yet the notion of the proletarian is being used less and less often in sociological literature, which is quite understandable since it has become very difficult to define the term. On the one hand, the proletariat can be understood as an aggregate of all hired labour, yet in this case the working class would make up the fast majority of the economically active population, including salaried managers at major corporations. On the other hand, the term is sometimes applied to all workers that generate surplus value, yet this would appear to be exactly the same as our first definition. Discussion of the term[173] is increasingly shifting from mainstream sociology to the pages of socialist and Marxist works and is having an increasingly small influence on the formation of concepts of modern social changes.

Most Western scholars regard the working class or proletariat in its Marxist sense: manufacturing workers engaged in the production of industrial goods. In this respect there is no doubt that society is quickly 'deproletarianizing' in a whole range of ways. The industrial sector of the economy is shrinking and traditional industrial labour is leaving major companies, which now have much greater need for knowledge workers, to small-scale manufacturing and the service sector. Workers employed in these sectors are alienated from each other and form a mass of diverse educational levels, races, nationalities and interests. As the service sector develops, there is increasing demand for routine labour that requires, however, substantial training. Typically, hired labourers employed in the service sector differ quite naturally from the working class as it is traditionally perceived.[174]

Thus change has split the traditional working class into two groups. One of those groups is made up of qualified workers in the industrial sector, who by income and social status could be assigned to the middle class; the second belongs to the stratum described by Gorz as a 'non-class of non-workers' and the 'neoproletariat'. We regard the first of these definitions to be overly disparaging. Yet the sense that Gorz and other Western scholars put into the notion of a 'neoproletariat' seems to us to be quite clear: 'It is composed of those categories of people who either become permanently unemployed, or whose intellectual abilities are rendered irrelevant by the technical organization of labour.'[175] As a result, the proletariat has practically left the historical stage both as a homogeneous oppressed stratum and as a class of people employed in adanced (for its time) industrial production. As Renner said in the late 1970s: 'The working class as it appears in Marx's *Capital* no longer exists.'[176] And this is all the more true at the end of the 1990s.

Most scholars have now turned their attention to a new social group that is gradually forming the main class of modern society, namely, 'a third force between the capitalist and working class of traditional Marxism: the "professional–managerial class"'.[177] This new social group is currently a fairly diverse association, but it is quickly consolidating and acquiring new and clear class interests. Drucker described it as

> a new class which is neither capitalist nor worker but which is rapidly becoming dominant in all industrially developed countries: the employed middle class of professional managers and professional specialists. This class rather than the capitalists has power and control. The capitalist, that is the man who has property title to productive resources, must, to be effective, behave as a manager. And progressively the ownership titles are being held by this new middle class rather than by the capitalists. In the United States today the important capitalists are the institutional trustees for the savings, pension-claims and investments of the little people: insurance companies, pension funds and investment trusts. At the same time this new class is absorbing the worker – socially, economically and culturally. Instead of becoming a proletarian, today's worker joins the middle class of employed professionals – in his tastes, his way of life, his aspirations.[178]

We believe such an interpretation to be basically correct. We do, however, have reservations over the use of the somewhat amorphous term 'middle class' to encompass the new class of professionals and managers. The middle class here is made up of some very diverse components.[179] The term 'professional class' also has unclear boundary lines. Some, like Touraine, have described the class as oppressed by the ruling technocratic elite.[180] But this is a bad fit. Members of the class seldom regard themselves as being oppressed.

The class structure of post-economic society is still at a fairly early stage in its development and it is too soon to talk about an established system. Under these conditions, in our view, particular attention should be given not so much to the terminological definition of individual social groups and classes as to the study of principal boundaries capable of dividing the post-economic world into confronting social groups. But, before we move on to discuss this issue, we will consider the third component part of modern society: the technocratic elite.

Efforts to study the essence of the new ruling class and provide it with a terminological definition began soon after the Second World War, when there were the first signs of a shift from traditional forms of industrial production to an economy based on knowledge and information. Considering the dissimilation of the power of capital as such, Dahrendorf, in the late 1950s, was one of the first to analyse the role of the managing class, the bureaucracy and senior executives as the new elite of the future society. He asked, 'Who, then, constitutes the ruling class of post-capitalist society?', and answered: 'Obviously, we have to look for the ruling class in those positions that constitute the head of bureaucratic hierarchies, among those persons who are authorized to give directives to the administrative staff.'[181]

But in the 1960s and 1970s, most scholars came to the conclusion that the coming society was controlled not so much by the bureaucracy as by the new class that possessed knowledge and information both of production processes and of the mechanism of social progress as a whole. When 'the post-industrial society is becoming a "technetronic" society: a society that is shaped culturally, psychologically, socially and economically by the impact of technology and electronics – particularly in the area of computers and communications – and the industrial process is no longer the principal determinant of social change, altering the modes, the social structure and the values of society',[182] the new elite must primarily have the ability to manage and control these new processes. 'If the dominant figures of the last hundred years have been the entrepreneur, the businessman and the industrial executive,' wrote Bell, 'the "new men" are the scientists, the mathematicians, the economists and the new engineers of the new intellectual technology.'[183] As a result, by the middle of the 1970s, the new ruling class was dubbed 'technocrats', who had possession of knowledge and information and the ability to manipulate them on three main fronts: the national (where the government bureaucracy operates), industrial (professional and academic experts) and corporate.[184] Alain Touraine, however, also described the technocratic class as the dominant class in post-industrial society, which oppressed all other social strata and groups.[185] At about the same time another term emerged: 'the meritocracy'. It was first used in Young's story about the future of humanity, *The Rise of Meritocracy*.[186] The term had a slightly different connotation from 'technocracy' since it marked not only the *objective* place of the meritocracy in the social whole but the *subjective* appraisal of it by society being an important source of its dominant position, which is of particular importance given the quick growth of the significance of subjectivism in social development.

In the second half of the 1970s, a whole new range of terms were offered to label the new ruling elite, but they were of little significance since they were not used beyond very general sociological doctrines. It was called the 'new class' by Gouldner, the 'dominant class' by Althusser, the 'ruling class' by Conell and the 'upper class' by Scott.[187] In the context of our analysis it is important that for the previous 20 years there had been an active erosion and criticism of those positions that placed particular emphasis on the bureaucratic nature of the ruling class of the new society. The assertion that it was not the formal status of an individual within an organization but his real ability in creative activity and the absorption, processing and production of information and knowledge that brought the main power in the new society became increasingly clear. Toffler in this respect was characteristic when he not only said that 'in the Super-Industrial society, however, bureaucracy will increasingly be replaced by *adhocracy*, a frame-like holding company that coordinates the work of numerous temporary work units, each phasing in and out of existence in accordance with the rate of change in the environment surrounding the organization',[188] but made it quite clear that the bureaucratic form of organization was typical of the industrial society and was not born, but, on the contrary, destroyed within the post-industrial social system.

Thus the modern concept of the class division of post-industrial society comprises three main groups: a ruling class (usually interpreted as the technocracy); a middle class of qualified workers and low-grade managers in traditional industry and the service sector, described as a class of professionals; and a lower class made up of physical labourers who could not fit into high-tech processes, representatives of dying occupations, substantial numbers of immigrants from the Third World, ethnic minorities and several other groups that found themselves on the wrong side of post-economic change. So what kind of problems will these three classes create for the society under formation? Firstly, modern economic trends are facilitating the growth of the third and lowest class as industry requires labour of an increasingly high quality. This process is fraught with the possibility of social conflict on a larger scale than ever before seen. Secondly, the role of the dominant class hinges on control of information and knowledge while real power still primarily rests with old structures that act according to the old economic laws, including the state, which is still to reflect fully the interests of the technocracy. Finally, the middle class of professionals, which it is traditional to describe as the basis for stable social progress, is in reality far too diverse to be so, and will likely be split into two by a new social division that now appears inevitable.

The issue of a new class conflict, which was first studied as long ago as the 1950s, is still one of the most topical issues in modern sociology. Attitudes to the issue have evolved in three stages that reflect the evolution of social confrontation in Western societies. The first stage was dominated by the optimistic view that the intensity of class conflict would diminish as the industrial order was overcome. Naturally, scholars did not assert that the new society would avoid any kind of social confrontation, but they did think that one of the most dangerous forms of confrontation would be overcome. Dahrendorf wrote that 'the concept of class should not be applied to the analysis of conflicts in post-capitalist societies', and appealed primarily to the fact that the class model of social interaction would shed its significance as the role of industrial conflict, which was caused by the localization and limitation of the industrial sector itself, was reduced:

> In the post-capitalist society industry and society have, by contrast to capitalist society, been dissociated. Increasingly, the social relations of industry, including industrial conflict, do not dominate the whole of society but remain confined in their patterns and problems to the sphere of industry. Industry and industrial conflict are, in post-capitalist society, institutionally isolated, i.e., confined within the borders of their proper realm and robbed of their influence on other spheres of society.[189]

But this was not the only viewpoint at that time. Jacques Ellul did not believe that the decline in the role of material production would bring less class conflict. He believed that even replacing labour with leisure would merely *transfer the conflict to the subhuman level*.[190] This view was analysed by many eminent sociologists and it is this view that we believe provides the best opportunity for properly reflecting what is happening in Western societies today.

The second stage took place in the 1970s and 1980s, when post-industrial theory became one of the main achievements of sociological thought. This stage brought the concept that class conflicts were far from being connected only with economic problems. In 1990, Inglehart wrote that

> according to the Marxist model, the key political conflict of industrial society is economic, centering on ownership of the means of production and the distribution of income ... With the emergence of advanced industrial society, the impact of economic factors reaches a point of diminishing returns. Noneconomic issues take an increasingly important place on the national agenda, giving rise to a new axis of political polarization.[191]

Touraine noted the same aspects of the issue a little later.[192] Scholars to an ever greater degree focused on problems of status, including issues of the self-definition and self-identification of various strata within a middle class, and the motivation of the actions of representatives of one group or another. The best known version of this problem was formulated by Turner, who wrote that 'the simple divisions between classes have been replaced by a much more complicated and complex social structure involving ... the endless struggle of status communities and status blocs for access to the welfare cake under the auspices of the state'.[193] By the beginning of the 1990s, scholars recognized that society was divided into strata based, not on an individual's relation to property as before, but on the way an individual identifies himself with a social group identical to some social function. The new society, which was even dubbed 'post-class capitalism', 'defies all the predictions of class theory, socialist criticism and liberal apologia. It is neither class divided nor egalitarian and harmonious'.[194]

The third stage in the development of the concept began in the second half of the 1980s, when Western nations began to emerge from recession. It became quite clear that the bourgeoisie and the proletariat only confronted each other within the narrow confines of the industrial sector and that they could hardly be defined as classes at all.[195] On the other hand, the first indications of the future social conflict began to make themselves felt. The greatest figures in Western sociology pointed out that the coming post-industrial society would face a confrontation between those who had developed new ways of thinking and behaving and those who had not; between people, to use Toffler's term, of the Second and Third Wave, between materialists and non-materialists and between industrialists and post-industrialists. Inglehart said: 'rooted in the distinct experiences produced by major historical changes, the Materialist/Postmaterialist dimension is a central axis of polarization among Western publics, reflecting the contrast between two fundamentally different worldviews'.[196] Moreover, the new conflict is so acute and so hard to cure because the social preferences and value systems of an individual barely change during the course of his life, which makes the confrontation between materialists and post-materialists particularly enduring. Toffler put things rather similarly:

> The conflict between Second and Third Wave groupings is, in fact the central political tension cutting through our society today. The more basic political question, as we shall see, is not who controls the last days of industrial society but who shapes the new civilization rapidly rising to replace it. On one side are the partisans of the industrial past; on the other, growing millions who recognize that the most urgent problems of the world can no longer be resolved within the framework of an industrial order. This conflict is the 'super struggle' for tomorrow.[197]

However, in our view such formulations far from exhaust the real situation. Sociologists, talking of people as of adherents of materialist and post-materialist values, are in one way or another considering a subjective factor (such as values and preferences) as a criterion for the new social division. Yet real class confrontation today is not based on the way an individual member of society *regards* himself or to which social group he assigns himself. In the modern world the desires of an individual to realize himself as an adherent of post-materialist values, to join the ranks of the knowledge workers and become an active producer of knowledge and information are limited, not just by subjective factors, but *completely objective ones*, the main one being limitations on access to information, education and knowledge. The intellectual stratification of a nation, having reached an unprecedented scale,[198] forms the basis for any social division.

The problems born of the information revolution are not mere technological problems. They have a clear social measure. Drucker wrote,

> The centre of gravity in production, and especially in manufacturing, then shifts from manual workers to knowledge workers. Far more middle-class jobs are being created by this process than old blue-collar jobs are being lost. Overall the process enriches as much as did the creation of well-paid blue-collar jobs in the last hundred years. We do not, in other words, face an *economic* problem; nor is there much danger of 'alienation' and of creating a new 'class war'... [but] that a substantial and growing number of people with working-class backgrounds sit long enough in schools to become knowledge workers will only make things worse for those who don't. The less schooled will increasingly be seen by their more successful fellows ... as 'failures', as 'dropouts', as somehow 'deficient', as 'second-class citizens', as 'problems', and altogether as 'inferior'. The problem is not money. It is *dignity*.[199]

Thus it is the possession of knowledge and the degree of education that forms the basis for the class divisions in modern society. We should agree with Fukuyama, who asserted:

> in the developed world social status is determined to a very large degree by one's level of educational achievement. *The class differences that exist in the contemporary United States, for example, are due primarily to differences in education.* There are few obstacles to the advancement of a person with the proper educational credentials. Inequality creeps into the system as a result of unequal access to education; lack of education is the surest condemnation to second-class citizenship [emphasis added].[200]

It is this very phenomenon that is both the most characteristic of modern societies and the most dangerous. All previous principles of social division known to us – from those based on property to those based on professional activity or place in the bureaucratic hierarchy – were far less tough and far less dependent on natural and unchangeable factors. The right of birth provided the feudal lord with power over his serfs. Property rights gave the capitalist his place in society. Political or economic power provided the bureaucrat or official with his status. Moreover, the feudal lord could be expelled from his lands, the capitalist could go bankrupt and forfeit his fortune, the bureaucrat could lose his job and his social status at once. And practically any other member of society, finding himself in the place of a feudal lord, capitalist or bureaucrat, could have performed their functions just as well. That is why, during the economic epoch, class struggle could provide the oppressed with the results they desired.

But the situation has changed cardinally with the shift to the post-economic society. Intellectual workers, who today make up the elite of society, regardless of what it is called – the new class, the technocracy or the meritocracy – possess qualities that are not determined by the external social factors. Today neither society nor social relations are able to assign an individual to the ruling class and thus give him power over others. The individual forms himself as the vessel of those qualities that make him a representative of the upper class. It is well known that information is the most democratic source of power since all have access to information, over which it is impossible to have a monopoly. But information is also the least democratic factor of production, since to have access to information is far from being the same thing as possessing information. Information, unlike all other resources, cannot be exhausted or consumed in the traditional sense like other resources. Yet it is marked by the *electiveness, the scarcity of that high level that gives the possessor power of the greatest quality*. It is the specific nature of the individual, his world sense, the conditions of his development, his psychological characteristics, his ability to generalize and, finally, his memory – everything that makes up intellect, the very form in which information and knowledge exist – that serve as the main factor that limits the opportunity to associate with these resources. Thus real knowledge is held by just a small circle of people, true possessors of information, whose social role today cannot be disputed under any circumstances. *For the first time in history, membership of a ruling class is determined not by the right to own some good but by the ability to make use of it.*

Hence it follows that in the modern world it is the people who are able to engender for society the most dynamism and provide the fastest progress that are of the greatest significance. Here we can see the basis for the assertion that, within the next few decades, post-economic values, which already motivate most representatives of the new ruling class, will dominate all of society and economic motives will stop playing any kind of significant role.

It also follows from this that the new social division is capable of generating new problems. Until now, when economic values functioned in society, there was a certain consensus over how desired results might be achieved. Harder work, successful competition in the market, lower costs and other economic methods brought achievement of the economic goals of higher profits and living standards. Employees were to a greater or lesser degree interested in the economic success of their enterprises. Today examples of economic success show that the greatest achievements are made by those entrepreneurs that focus on the maximum utilization of high-tech processes and systems, hire the best educated specialists and, as a rule, themselves possess exceptional abilities to innovate in the technology or business they have chosen. Setting themselves partially non-economic aims – to realize themselves in business, to achieve social recognition for the technology or innovation they have developed, and to found and develop a new corporation that is a reflection of their individual selves – such entrepreneurs nevertheless achieve impressive economic results. On the other hand, materially motivated individuals often fail to achieve their goal of rising to the level of the new elite. The situation is further dramatized by the fact that practically they have no chance of joining the elite because the optimal opportunities for education are made available in childhood and not when an individual realizes that he is undereducated. Moreover, intellectual ability is often determined by an inheritance developed over several generations.

Thus modern class division is born of profound differences between the internal potentials of various members of society. Over the coming decades this class division threatens to become even more rigid than all previous forms of social inequality. It could drive a schism through the middle class that has been seen as the guarantor of stability in Western societies and form one of the biggest barriers on the path to the new society. This is particularly dangerous because the goals and results of the activity of the social groups under formation are diametrically opposed.

Post-economic Causes and Economic Effects

All the changes that we have considered up to now, however ambiguous they may have been, in one way or another demonstrate the progress of society and provide the basis for forming more or less optimistic appraisals of its prospects. Nevertheless, over the last few decades phenomena of a different nature have begun attracting increasing attention. The first response of scholars to such phenomena amounts to a search for ways of overcoming them. But a closer consideration reveals that they are determined by the most fundamental direction of the modern transition and by virtue of this are insurmountable, at least within the framework of established trends.

We are primarily talking about the inequality of the distribution of wealth. This problem has always existed and at all times it has been this problem and not more abstract issues of exploitation or property that has concerned the people and prompted active social movements designed to achieve justice. However, neither history nor modernity have known effective mechanisms for providing equal property relations. Sometimes organized violence has enforced equality, but such organized violence has never proved to be viable or economically efficient and has always failed ultimately.

The growth in the gap between the rich and the poor has traditionally been at the centre of social attention. This gap in most Western nations has narrowed over years since the Second World War as a result of more active social programmes, and a fairly confident growth in real wages and living standards for the middle class weakened social interest in the profits of corporations and the salaries of their executives. Then the situation changed. These changes are today so obvious that even leading economists and sociologists are forced to respond to them, often in contradiction with their own theories. Galbraith said:

> the good society does not seek equality in the distribution of income. Equality is not consistent with either human nature or the character and motivation of the modern economic system. As all know, people differ radically in their commitment to making money and also in their competence in doing so. And some of the energy and initiative on which the modern economy depends comes not only from the desire for money but also from the urge to excel in its acquisition.

Yet this strict and quite correct thought was left behind on the very next page. Here Galbraith, citing the fact that the rich had much increased their share in national income *over recent years* at the cost of the poor, said that 'this, the good society cannot accept. Nor can it accept … the justification … that defends this inequality'.[201] Such changes are least of all coincidental. On the contrary, in our view they inevitably accompany the formation of the post-economic society.

Let us consider the real state of affairs over recent years. The process of the concentration of wealth in the hands of a narrow stratum of people always accompanied the development of a bourgeois society, although this process was far from occurring in a single direction and far from being always dynamic. We cannot but recall that the greatest disproportion in the distribution of wealth was seen during the feudal period, when the entrepreneurial part of the third estate aimed to achieve equality, which it understood as the expropriation of the aristocracy. In societies where there was no property-owning aristocracy, like the United States, and where economic development began with a clean sheet, the concentration of wealth was even greater. In 1828, just 4 per cent of the population of

New York controlled 62 per cent of the city's wealth. By 1845, the top 4 per cent held 81 per cent of New York's wealth. The top decile of the American population in 1860 owned 40 per cent of national wealth. By 1890, the top 12 per cent owned 86 per cent.[202] This, as we can see, represented an impressive growth in the concentration of wealth in the United States in the second half of the 19th century. In Britain, this growth was no less impressive. McRae has shown that income distribution inequality in Britain at the end of the 20th century is greater than at the beginning: he calculated that the top 10 per cent of the population actually enjoyed proportionately 4 per cent more income than the bottom 10 per cent in 1990 than in 1906.[203]

Thus it would be logical to suppose that inequality in distribution of incomes does not have a linear dynamic: disproportion has periods of growth and decline. This presupposition is confirmed by statistics. Figures show that there was a marked decline in the wealth held by the top decile or percentile of the populations of most advanced Western nations, starting at the beginning of the 20th century and ending in the mid-1970s. The share of overall household wealth held by the top 1 per cent of the American population dropped from 30 per cent in 1930 to less than 18 per cent in the mid-1970s. In Britain, the downward trend was even clearer: from more than 60 per cent to 29 per cent for the top 1 per cent and from 90 per cent to 65 per cent for the top 10 per cent. In Sweden, figures for the share of the national wealth held by the top percentile and top decile fell from 49 per cent to 26 per cent and from 90 per cent to 63 per cent, respectively.[204] Robert Heilbroner cited similar figures and added that 'the trend over the last century has been gradually in the direction of a more equitable division of income and wealth: for example, the share of total after-tax income going to the topmost 5 percent of American families fell from one third in 1929 to one sixth in the early 1980s, and the concentration of wealth also declined, although not so sharply, from the end of the nineteenth century until the 1970s'.[205] By 1976, the top percentile of the American population held just 17.6 per cent of national wealth, the lowest figure of its kind in US history.[206] Against this background, the United States saw the unrestrained enrichment of executives in major corporations, whose salaries rose out of all comparison with those of other hired employees. In 1960, the chief executive officers (CEOs) of America's top 100 corporations earned an average of $190 000, a ratio of 40:1 to the average wage before tax and 12:1 after. By the end of the 1980s, the average CEO salary had topped $2 million, a ratio against the average wage of 93:1 and 70:1 before and after tax, respectively.[207] Yet it has to be admitted that there is no necessity for proportional wage awards for executives and regular employees.

Thus events were recognized as developing very successfully

within the framework of the humanization and socialization of the industrial economy towards which Western nations aspired throughout the 20th century. However, after the 1970s, new and quite different trends began to emerge, at first weakly and then more clearly. First came economic recovery and then tax reforms and then the consequential economic boom and fast advances of practically all industrial and service equities. These were the new trends which began at the end of the 1970s and first reached their peak at the beginning of the 1980s. The top percentile of the American population that had held 19 per cent of national wealth in 1977 had already acquired 24 per cent by 1981 and more than 30 per cent by the time Ronald Reagan ended his first term, in 1984. The pace of the growth in the concentration of wealth tailed off in the second half of the 1980s, but by the 1990s the top percentile of Americans owned 39 per cent of national wealth, more than double the figure in 1976.[208] The gap between the top 5 per cent of society and the bottom rose from a factor of 15 to a factor of 22.5 during the 1980s alone.[209]

The trend towards the greater concentration of wealth was bolstered during the late 1980s and early 1990s by a whole range of factors, especially the technological leap of the late 1980s. This period marked the peak in the growth of the market value of new high-tech companies and the wealth of their owners and founders. All this started to change traditional notions of the way rich Americans got richer. Bill Gates, founder and main shareholder in software company Microsoft, is alone thought to be worth $36 billion, which shows that innovation had started to generate individual wealth within just a few years. Such wealth had previously only been accumulated by years of hard work by financial or industrial dynasties. Not only the executives of major corporations but the founder-managers of high-tech companies and even individual specialists in high-tech fields could achieve incomes beyond all comparison with those of average Americans. As early as 1988, more than 1.3 million Americans reported annual incomes in excess of $1 million.[210] There are now more than three million such people.

Yet the widening of the gap in incomes would never have been of such a scale and its consequences would never have comprised such a danger had it not been for the real reduction in the income of the most needy. This process, which began in the mid-1980s and which took place despite economic growth, had never occurred before in the history of the industrial society. The income of those who earned more than $1 million a year rose by 2184 per cent during the 1980s and the income of those who earned between $20 000 and $50 000 a year rose by 44 per cent. But the income of the bottom 25 per cent of Americans actually fell by 6 per cent.[211] The drop in income for the bottom 20 per cent of families was even more dramatic, at 24 per cent.[212] The share of that 20 per cent of national income, which had risen to 7 per cent by the early 1970s, had plunged to just 4.6 per cent by the mid-1980s.[213] The figure for the poorest two-fifths of the population fell from 16.7 per cent to 15.4 per cent in the same period.[214]

As Robert Kuttner wrote,

> The widening of inequality, beginning in the mid-1970s and accelerating in the 1980s, is one of the best-documented recent economic trends. No matter how you measure it, the income distribution in the United States has become more extreme. During the quarter-century between 1947 and 1973, the economy both grew faster than in our own era, and produced an earnings distribution that gradually became more equal. Median family income, adjusted for inflation, slightly more than doubled. The bottom 20 percent of households, however, realized income gains of 138 percent, while the top 20 percent gained 99 percent. These trends reversed after 1973. In the period between 1979 and 1993, the top 20 percent gained 18 percent, while the bottom 60 percent actually lost real income. And the poorest 20 percent lost the most income of all – an average of 15 percent of an already inadequate wage. Wealth, far more concentrated than income, has now reached its point of greatest concentration since the 1920s. All of the gains to equality of the postwar boom have been wiped out.[215]

Thus the first stage of the post-economic transformation – when fundamental changes in the motivation of activity, new information technologies and the growth in the role of knowledge began to be embodied in the substitution of creative activity for labour; when the first prospects of overcoming exploitation appeared; and when human activity became freer than it ever had been before – was also marked by sharp growth in property inequality, which should have declined, one would have thought, under the formation of a more humanitarian society.

As a rule Western theorists do not provide a detailed analysis of the reasons for this phenomenon. They try to uncover its roots in current economic trends, the weakening of the role of the state and reduced taxation for the best paid groups and biggest corporations. Such factors are, no doubt, of much significance. But any attempt to explain changes of a post-economic nature with economic factors is bound to fail in principle. Yes, the tax policies of the early 1980s did lead to a recovery in output and modernization, but in the 1990s growth was powered by other trends. Tax reforms undoubtedly prompted the growing disproportion of incomes and wealth, but they do not determine this phenomenon today, almost 20 years after Western economies started to pull out of the crisis of the 1970s.

Sometimes scholars stress discrimination on grounds of race, gender, educational level and so on. They point out the reduction in state aid for the poor, especially Afro-Americans and Latinos, single mothers and a whole range of other groups. They also point to the reduction in incomes for high-school graduates and high-school drop-outs as a sign of the imperfection of the current system. Reich, for example, noted that between 1973 and 1987 the average wage of a man who had not graduated from college had fallen by 12 per cent and that the average wage of a man who had dropped out of high school had fallen by 18 per cent. Moreover, the income of non-graduate Black Americans had fallen by 44 per cent. He compared these figures with those of Japan, where high-school graduates increased their average wages by 13 per cent over the same period.[216] This comparison, however, on closer inspection may say more about the achievements of the United States than about those of Japan.

Wage differentials between people with different levels of education are today becoming the subject of increasing, if not adequate, attention. In the 1950s and 1960s, education was regarded by many Americans as a very profitable investment that would enable them not only to advance their career more quickly but to increase their earning power. Drucker said that spending on education of around $20 000 would add 'an average of $200,000 to a man's earning power during the thirty years after graduation', and 'there is no other investment that promises a tenfold return, an average yield of 30 per cent per year over a thirty-year life'.[217] In the 1970s and 1980s, a breakthrough occurred in the United States as a result of which spending on education is today five times greater than all other spending, including clothing, food and housing, carried out before a worker reaches maturity. This spending, about $100 000, actually exceed, average investment in manufacturing capacity, about $80 000, upon which the worker will labour.[218] Thus today investment in people has become the most important investment and education has become the single most important factor that determines the productivity of a worker and his level of remuneration.

Only in recent years has an understanding of this phenomenon as extremely significant – and of this trend as important and sustained – become widespread among economists and sociologists. Charles Winslow and William Bramer, for example, said that a

> great educational divide is already in evidence. Consider one study that compared increases in real income of workers before and after the dawning of the information age. For 1968 to 1977 in the United States, real (inflation adjusted) income grew 20%, an increase that did not depend on the education of workers. High school dropouts gained 20%, college graduates 21%. But during the next decade, educational

differences were crucial. From 1978 to 1987, overall income increased 17%, but high school dropouts actually declined 4% while college graduates grew 48%. The number of low-skilled jobs is declining dramatically, *and there will be no turning back from that trend* [emphasis added].[219]

In our view the growing inequality in the distribution of social wealth is one of the most characteristic trends of the late 20th century. Its development is not just caused by political factors, the weakening of government economic regulation and the growing differentials in education. The fundamental reason for the changes in the proportion of distribution is the change in the role and significance of certain factors within the production process. All the trends we have considered above for undermining the economic society are of direct significance to the phenomenon. We shall dwell on this point in more detail.

Firstly, with the development of production, which increasingly depends on the use of information and knowledge and the ability of the worker to respond quickly with decisions in unforeseen circumstances, to utilize received knowledge to increase his own knowledge, processes and technological innovations, it emerges that the objective appraisal of such subjects of production is practically impossible. In conditions where such workers may be managed only as volunteers – since they not only do not recognize control and pressure above them as possible, but are extremely mobile and the subject of considerable interest from their corporations – they ought to be regarded as partners. Thus their remuneration grows. Moreover, each new year carried out in such a form of activity does not lower the abilities of an individual, as happens at a steel mill or behind a burger counter. On the contrary, it makes a worker more valuable, his abilities more advanced and his income bigger. This kind of worker appeared in the very period that followed the formation of the basic characteristics of the post-industrial society, when the basis of competition became not price but quality, its new attributes and the openness of production to the future.

Secondly, the formation of production aimed at the creation of irreproducible goods, information and knowledge provided for a boom in the most high-tech industries. In such industries not only do the workers possess unique and irreproducible information but the results of their activity are also to a significant degree unique and irreproducible. High-tech production, having turned out to be one of the main conditions for further economic progress, is of great value and, despite the relatively low price of its mass-distributed goods, provides enormous incomes for its creators. It has been often noted that the 1980s and especially the 1990s were a period when the new industries posted records for output and profits and financial performance. The main income from this business did not go to the factory workers that churned out the electronic equipment on semi-automated production lines or mass-distributed the information product, but to the creators and owners of the corresponding technology. Weizsaecker calculated that in Germany gross national product rose over 20 per cent in the 1980s, while real wages remained unchanged and returns on capital doubled.[220] High-tech firms as a rule have the highest market capitalization, which provides their owners (usually their founders) with an additional and high-power instrument for augmenting their personal wealth. In 1996–97 Bill Gates increased his personal wealth by $14 billion, thanks to a reappraisal of his stake in the capital of Microsoft.

Thirdly, a serious factor that led to increased incomes for the most highly educated part of the population was the possibility of moving beyond the traditional organization of production. Now it is not rare for specialists in programming and new information products, designers, architects, artists and a whole range of other professions able to create unique and irreproducible goods – and having the ability to acquire as personal property their means of production – to act as individual producers of such goods, which have a high market value and bring substantial incomes. It is characteristic to note that, on the one hand, creative workers really are capable of earning more by selling goods which they have created completely autonomously and, on the other hand, that their potential for autonomous activity raises their value to the managers of companies in which they may work, and that their ability to leave the company makes the manager dependent on the worker rather than the worker on the manager and, correspondingly, raises the income which they may command.

There is a radical dissonance with the situation of the unskilled worker. The market for unskilled labour is currently very competitive when there is substantial migration and the level of income that is considered to be satisfactory in, say, Southeast Asia, is much lower than that of, say, Europeans or Americans. Most people on the market for unskilled labour have no qualities that would mark them out from the crowd. There can be no talk here of the factor of exclusivity and irreproducibility that characterizes the knowledge worker. Industrial and service companies when hiring low-skill labour, as a rule, provide mass-produced and primitive goods and services. Consequently, incomes are fairly modest and survival depends on price competition and quantitative rather than qualitative performance. Thus increasing wages is hardly a method to be employed to raise competitiveness. And, what is most significant in this case, workers find themselves in a situation where they are completely dependent on the policy of managers because they have no basis upon which to achieve a better position since they may be easily replaced by other job seekers and because they are not able to conduct independent activity as the vendors of labour rather than the producers of a finished product.

The breakthrough into the post-economic condition is combined with social polarization, both in terms of a new class confrontation developing between people with differing value systems and intellectual levels and in terms of a property division that is reaching a degree that could be dangerous for society. It appears that attempts to smooth out these contradictions or to redistribute incomes will inevitably lead to a lower pace of economic development, which will worsen the position of any given nation on the international stage that is the scene of active competition between various post-industrial economies, not to mention the newly industrialized nations. As a result, Western powers will shortly once again face a stark choice between technological and economic progress and social stability. This problem will be particularly tough, since the traditional economic instruments that governments are used to will no longer provide any solutions.

The post-economic revolution currently under way is having undoubtedly progressive consequences, but it is also starting processes that could seriously destabilize functioning social institutions. One of those processes pertains to the new class division and the new social inequality. This division would be no more dangerous than, say, the split in capitalist society between bourgeois and proletarians, if it were not for certain circumstances.

Firstly, the central conflict of industrial society, which arose around the distribution of material wealth, had clearer positions than in today's collision. A conflict based on the possession or lack of property can be resolved through redistribution or ameliorated by raising the well-being of the poorest groups in society: that is, practically by transferring more property to them. Today the main resource that provides the growing well-being of the non-economically motivated section of society is knowledge and abilities which can neither be alienated nor redistributed. Moreover, it is quite clear, looking at the larger picture, that economic support for the most needy is completely ineffective. In the past, it may have given individuals greater opportunities to achieve some kind of success in their lives. Today this is more than unlikely. Educational support is extremely difficult and would take, at best, decades – or, as is more likely, generations – to have any effect. Therefore the social division that is emerging and the conflict that accompanies it could prove to be more dangerous and, at least, harder to cure, than those of bourgeois society.

The second factor is completely unstudied. It is obvious that over recent decades an increasing share of social wealth is being redistributed in favour of the highly educated who are either engaged in high-tech companies or are engaged in independent activity based on information and knowledge. Characteristically, they either started their life fairly well-off or achieved a high level of well-being thanks to their own efforts. But, one way or another, material factors are of secondary, subordinate importance. We have examined this phenomenon as a prerequisite for the elimination of exploitation and this substitution of value systems really is one of the greatest achievements of the post-economic transformation. At the same time, the oppressed class of society has still to absorb and has still to have the opportunity to absorb post-materialist values. Representatives of this class are aiming to achieve only material goals and (partly by virtue of this) are subject to exploitation in the 'best tradition' of the industrial epoch. Thus, on a purely psychological level, we have a phenomenon that seriously distinguishes the current class division from that of capitalist society. In the industrial epoch, the biggest share of social wealth went to the bourgeoisie, whose *economic* interests were beyond doubt. Yet today the bulk of the social wealth goes to a technocratic class that does not see material values as having such a degree of importance. Thus the desire to achieve material wealth is the fate of those who cannot achieve it and, on the contrary, those who achieve material wealth do not set out to do so. This spiral, if developed, could inspire a strong backlash from the economically motivated section of society.

Thirdly, class confrontation was at its worse when the capitalist society was in its formative stage. It was the accumulation of capital and the formation of the technical means of production that brought the most ruthless exploitation of the proletariat, which in turn provoked the most radical protests of the oppressed class. The conditions of the working class improved throughout the rest of the development of capitalist society, from the middle of the 19th century right through to the last decades of the 20th century, with the possible exception of the years of the Great Depression, in 1929–32. Therefore it can be said with some grounds that at least since the beginning of the 1930s the class factor has not posed a threat to the industrial order in most Western powers. Now a new trend has emerged. The post-economic society under formation is moved by other, non-material, desires of those who have moved beyond the framework of economic motivation. Therefore its development will become increasingly dynamic in line with the share of non-economically motivated individuals within society. Thus a condition for the success of the new order is the fastest possible development of a new class with non-economic values. This will simultaneously worsen the material condition and raise the awareness of an especially alienated class. So today we can see no way of pre-empting social conflict within the economic society.

Moreover, and this may be regarded as a fourth important factor, the post-economic upper class under formation still retains loyalty to the authorities but by its nature is hostile to the institutions of the modern state, which embody those methods of social management and economic regulation that are characteristic of the economic society. This factor is also capable of frustrating the formation of the basis of the new civilization because, on the one hand, it is quite clear that under current conditions it will be impossible to reduce the role of the state and, on the other hand, it is still far from clear what the organizational principles of the new system of governing and the methods of regulating classes and groups moved by new motives will be.

Thus the social problems of modern Western societies, which are on the threshold of post-economic civilization, are much more serious than might appear at first glance. Having undergone several decades of relative social harmony, having secured a convincing victory over the communist system and making use of the benefits of confident economic growth, the modern Western world is in all respects unready to face a marked escalation of social confrontation. At the same time – and this is no less important – the division of society into materialists and post-materialists is a characteristic not only of developed Western democracies: the whole world is divided primarily on this count. The main battle, economic and political, that will take place over the first half of the 21st century, in our view, will be between nations to join the ranks of the post-economic world. Thus the new society has sprouted into a hostile world both in the developed nations and, possible more so, in the wider world. The progress of humanity will depend on the way these first sprouts of post-economic society develop.

Conclusion

Obviously we cannot claim to have analysed in this chapter all the main aspects of the modern post-economic transformation. Yet even this limited analysis shows that the transformation entails a complex social change, defines the limitations of the economic epoch and opens the way for the new social system that will replace the economic society. Our reader has had the opportunity to be convinced that the social transformation that began a few decades ago is moved by internal sources and is in this sense completely self-contained. We believe it is possible to identify five component parts of this process and have outlined these below in line with the logic of the comprehension of nature and the essence of the transformations under way.

The first of these components is undoubtedly the technological revolution of the 1960s–1990s. It is from this revolution that all scholars began their analysis of the modern post-industrial society and it is technological progress that they described as being the main criterion for the declaration of a post-industrial, technetronic, information or other society. Technological progress over recent years has provided for an unprecedented development of society that is primarily reflected, not in traditional indicators of productivity, but in the growth of the real power of humans over nature. Throughout the developed world, starting in the 1980s, trends advanced that showed that there were all the prerequisites – economic and environmental – for the sustainable development of humanity and the unrestricted development of human personalities. Thus the technological progress that began about 30 years ago and which is now gathering increasing dynamism, can be regarded as *the main material component of the post-economic revolution.*

The second component, which has also been noted by most scholars studying modern economic changes, was the active destruction of value relations and the undermining of the role of market laws. The radical change in the nature and form of the organization of the productive forces led traditional reproducible and countable factors of production to lose their leading role. Economic success began to be determined by information resources, which cannot be given a value and which depend not so much on the nature of the information as on the ability of the people working with it to derive new knowledge from it to move one production process or another forward. The pursuit of new knowledge became characteristic of the modern economy. The proportion of the exchange of goods in the post-economic society is to a great extent determined by such indicators as the scarcity of a product, the scarcity of the ability to process information, the scarcity of knowledge and the scarcity of the optimum combination of traditional and new factors of production, because such knowledge resources have a very specific nature of irreproducibility and may by no means be successfully utilized by all workers. Under such circumstances, the price of such a product cannot be based on the expenditure of labour, land or capital and is increasingly determined by the individual preferences of consumers. The price of a company is determined partly by the expected preferences and the expected nature of development. As a result, market relations conceal some new kind of basis and, with the passing of time, the correspondence of the previous form to the new content of these relations will be restored; so far, however, it is not clear what social consequences such a process will bring. The destruction of the previous basis of value relations could be described as *the first main direction of the post-economic transformation*.

The third component of the transformation is the dissimilation of property which leads, among other things, to the practical elimination of the traditional class of capitalists from the stage of social confrontation and to the emergence of a new force, the managers that control all the aspects of a company's business rather than enjoying ownership of its assets. A new form of property develops, personal property over the means of production. As a result, potential representatives of the class of hired labourers capable of producing information and knowledge and appropriately acting in the new economic condition become increasingly less dependent on the traditional institutions of industrial society. The greatest success is enjoyed by information consortia and corporations that have been able to combine not only property and management but property and creativity, since such successes are to a significant degree determined by the talent and energetic activity of their founders and owners. As a result, the conflict between labour and capital that is characteristic of industrial society is overcome both by the depersonifying of capital and by giving employees greater room for manoeuvre when their freedom amounted to no more than optimizing the sale of their labour power. Thus the change in the forms and relations of property lead to the overcoming of the traditional class conflict of the economic society. We call this phenomenon *the second main direction of the post-economic transformation*.

The fourth component is the change in the principles of social stratification. Society is starting to be divided into groups that could be called the ruling and the alienated classes. Moreover, all modern trends show that the middle class that for the whole of the last century served as the guarantor of social stability is to be split in two under pressure from the changes under way in society and that its representatives will come to fill the ranks of the upper and the lower classes, which will become increasingly alienated and separated from each other. The danger of this new confrontation is not only that the main criterion for assigning an individual to one class or another will be his ability to absorb and process information and create new knowledge, which practically amounts to the predetermination of occupying by an individual one or another social niche, probably for his entire life. The danger is also that, under the new conditions, an unprecedented disproportion will develop between the aims of people and their real opportunities. The social elite, which is focused now, not on the acquisition of material goods, but on the receipt of new knowledge, striving for inner self-satisfaction from its own activity, will nevertheless enjoy the main share of social wealth. The lower classes, striving to ensure a decent quality of life by appropriating material goods, will be denied the opportunity to achieve the level of well-being which they desire. The nature of such a confrontation entails the danger of serious social cataclysms. Unfortunately, today there are no trends under consideration that promise the possibility of the natural overcoming of this contradiction. This phenomenon we call *the third main direction of the post-economic transformation*.

Finally, the fifth component of the post-economic transformation is the global sociopsychological change, the likes of which humanity has never faced before. When material needs are satisfied and when the real role of knowledge is understood, man is motivated by his inner need to become more than what he is, to widen his horizons and opportunities, to know and to know how, to discover that which he did not know before. Such aims over several decades have become dominant for a significant proportion of society and it is hard to overestimate the consequences of this. This transition, which we call the shift from labour as an economically motivated activity to creativity, the aim of which is the self-realization of the individual, has provided an unprecedented degree of subjective freedom for those who are engaged in creative activity. Not presupposing material aims, they are not subject to exploitation, and the dependence of society upon such people and the results of their activity is such that it is these very people who receive all the material advantages generated by modern civilization. The unrestricted expansion of creativity lies at the root of technological progress which we have observed over the last few decades. These two processes are taking place in parallel and are supplementing one another, upon which we shall dwell further below. Thus the transition from labour to creativity that takes place at the psychological level today provides a greater influence on all the aspects of the life of the social whole than those changes that take place within the scope of economists and sociologists. The formation of creativity as the most proliferative form of human activity is *the main non-material component of the post-economic revolution*.

Such are the five main components of the post-economic transformation. It is quite clear that the role of the motive force of this social change is played by a rather contradictory unity of the first and fifth factors. The development of forms of human activity and the progress of material production presuppose and supplement each other. During the period of the dominance of purely economic laws and the absolute dominance of material interests and aims, such technological progress as can be seen today would have been impossible. Yet the opposite is equally just: the formation of creativity on the scale and in the forms that determine it as a general social phenomenon was also not fated to take place before the bulk of society reached a relatively high level of material well-being and had a real opportunity to acquire and make use of the information and knowledge provided by the technological revolution. Thus it can be asserted without doubt that technological and sociopsychological progress, changes in the material component of modern society and the transformation of the consciousness of those who are most responsible for the corresponding changes are currently taking place on a parallel basis, supplement each other and provide each other as a source for future development. Their combination serves to provide the post-economic transformation with its continuity and dynamics.

The second, third and fourth components are more likely a background against which the main changes take place and an aggregate of their consequences than relatively independent phenomena of social life. Yet it is within these components that are reflected the inner contradictions without which such a major social change would have been unthinkable. This is why the main problems which the new society will inevitably face will be connected with (a) moves to bring the still common market methods of regulation of social production in line with modern non-value appraisals of the goods produced; (b) the inevitable unification of property forms and relations; and (c) the elimination of the potential threat to social stability that arises from the polarization of the two main social groups that make up the post-economic society. Moreover, certain individual measures aimed at the amelioration of the most acute manifestations of the conflict will not produce the desired results. They are capable, on the contrary, of merely slowing the formation of the post-economic system and drawing out the period during which society is in a state of social uncertainty, which, in our view, would be an undoubtedly negative consequence of such measures. Meanwhile, the move forward cannot be continued at the former pace without looking back at the emerging contradictions.

Studying the process of the formation of the post-economic society, we have not tried to seek a way of overcoming the contradictions which the process entails. It should be said that the three problems listed above, despite their single nature, have a whole range of peculiarities that determine different approaches to their solution. The first and second of these are connected with the modification of market relations and changes in the traditional forms of property, and need gradual and controlled amelioration that presupposes primarily the unacceptance of the situations in which their sharp and unmanageable solution proves capable of paralysing the economic mechanism of modern society. The third problem is much tougher because it cannot in principle be solved naturally within the next decade. An increase in living standards of the alienated class, its attraction into the post-economic economy and the elimination of the acuteness of social contradictions is possible only after the new society starts to develop fully on its own basis. Without wishing to make any dubious analogies, we will clarify this thought by giving the example of the formation of industrial economy, when the first centuries of the capitalist development saw a quick and bloody conflict between the representatives of the new ruling class and the oppressed majority and only subsequently, at the end of the 19th century, started to show a trend towards the increase in the well-being of practically all members of society and the amelioration of class conflict. Today we are once again on the threshold of a global social change. Once again, as before, a new class is being formed, this time bereft of the desire to exploit the lower classes. Meanwhile, the society that has been established over centuries is impossible to destroy and the fact that there is an enormous number of people unready for change cannot be removed from the list of factors that are determining the nature of the post-industrial revolution. Therefore the only option that we believe can be implemented and accepted is connected with measures designed, not so much to include the representatives of the lower classes in post-economic forms of economic management as to support acceptable living standards for them and avoid open social conflict in advanced post-industrial nations so long as their development has not been completely grounded on post-economic principles. Only after the completion of such a transformation can we once again return to the problem of the formation of a homogeneous social organism, and in the new conditions the problem will be effectively solved.

Thus in the most developed economies the post-economic transformation is today limited by certain spheres of the economy and certain social strata. At the same time, this transformation is taking place in a very specific environment, whose influence on its course should not be underestimated. The reality is such that, for the absolute majority of humanity, the post-industrial nations with all their inner conflicts and contradictions appear as a single, albeit alien, phenomenon, as a herald of values that are totally unknown to them and therefore also alien. The analysis that we have undertaken would remain one-sided if we did not touch on the relationship between the post-economic world under formation and its environment.

Notes

1 See Karl Marx and Friedrich Engels, *Collected Works*, Vol. 5, Moscow, p.49.
2 D. Bell, *The Coming of Post-Industrial Society*, New York, 1976, p.119.
3 See P.F. Drucker, *The Age of Discontinuity*, New Brunswick, London, 1994, p.164.
4 K. Marx, 'Premier projet de la lettre à Vera Zassoulitsch', in K. Marx and F. Engels, *Gesamtausgabe* (MEGA), Erste Abteilung, Bd. 25, Berlin, 1985, S.224. ('in the historical development of Western Europe, ancient and modern, the period of the agricultural commune appears as a period of transition from communal property to private property, as a period of transition from the primary form to the secondary one' (Karl Marx and Friedrich Engels, *Collected Works*, Vol. 24, p.352).)
5 J.-F. Lyotard, *The Postmodern Condition: A Report on Knowledge*, Manchester, 1994, p.4.
6 See J. Naisbitt and P. Aburdene, *Megatrends 2000. Ten New Directions for the 1990's*, New York, 1990, p.7.
7 See P.F. Drucker, *The New Realities*, Oxford, 1996, p.116.
8 See P.F. Drucker, *Post-Capitalist Society*, New York, 1993, p.72.
9 P.F. Drucker, *The New Realities*, p.117.
10 See L. Edvinsson and M.S. Malone, *Intellectual Capital*, New York, 1997, pp.23–4.
11 See N. Stehr, *Knowledge Societies*, London, Thousand Oaks, 1994, p.101.
12 See H.S. Dordick and G. Wang, *The Information Society*, Newbury Park, London, 1993, p.69.
13 See J. Naisbitt, *Global Paradox*, New York, 1995, pp.122–3.
14 See J.D. Davidson and Lord William Rees-Mogg, *The Sovereign Individual*, New York, 1997, p.185.
15 See W.J. Martin, *The Global Information Society*, New York, 1995, p.151.
16 See T. Stonier, *The Wealth of Information: A Profile of Post-Industrial Economy*, London, 1983, p.24.
17 See J. Naisbitt, *Megatrends. The New Directions, Transforming Our Lives*, New York, 1984, p.4.
18 See I. Barron and R. Curnow, *The Future with Microelectronics: Forecasting the Effects of Information Technology*, London, 1979, p.19.
19 H.S. Dordick and G. Wang, *The Information Society*, p.2.
20 J.D. Davidson and Lord William Rees-Mogg, *The Sovereign Individual*, p.14.
21 See G.J. Mulgan, *Communication and Control: Networks and the New Economies*, New York, 1989, p.46.
22 See H.A. Linstone and I.I. Mitroff, *The Challenge of the 21st Century*, Albany, NY, 1994, pp.284–5.
23 See B. Gates, *The Road Ahead*, New York, London, 1996, pp.34–6.
24 See H.R. Variah, *Intermediate Microeconomics. A Modern Approach*, 4th edn, London, 1996, p.598.
25 See K. Arrow, 'The Production and Distribution of Knowledge', in G. Silverberg and L. Soete (eds), *The Economics of Growth and Technical Change: Technology, Nations, Agents*, Brookfield, Vt., 1994, p.12.
26 R. Crawford, *In the Era of Human Capital. The Emergence of Talent, Intelligence and Knowledge as the Worldwide Economic Force and What it Means to Managers and Investors*, London, New York, 1991, p.11.
27 See T. Morris-Suzuki, *Beyond Computopia: Information, Automation and Democracy in Japan*, London, New York, 1988, p.131.
28 W. Nicholson, *Microeconomic Theory: Basic Principles and Extensions*, 6th edn, Fort Worth, 1995, p.286.
29 W.J. Hudson, *Intellectual Capital. How to Build It, Enhance It, Use It*, New York, 1993, p.16.

30   L. Edvinsson and M.S. Malone, *Intellectual Capital*, p.44.
31   See ibid., pp.19–20.
32   W.J. Hudson, *Intellectual Capital. How to Build It*, p.7.
33   See L. Edvinsson and M.S. Malone, *Intellectual Capital*, p.76.
34   J. Naisbitt, *Megatrends Asia. The Eight Asian Megatrends that are Changing the World*, London, 1996, p.18.
35   T. Forester, *High-Tech Society*, Cambridge, Mass., 1988, p.141.
36   W.J. Hudson, *Intellectual Capital. How to Build It*, p.37.
37   See L. Edvinsson and M.S. Malone, *Intellectual Capital*, pp.2–3, 34.
38   Ibid., p.5.
39   S. Lash, *Sociology of Postmodernism*, London, 1990, p.49.
40   See Karl Marx, *Capital*, Vol. I, pp.199–200.
41   Karl Marx and Friedrich Engels, *Collected Works*, Vol. 20, p.124.
42   Karl Marx, *Capital*, Vol. II, p.384.
43   See Karl Marx and Friedrich Engels, *Collected Works*, Vol. 3, p.426.
44   G.J. Mulgan, *Communication and Control*, p.174.
45   S. Lash, *Sociology of Postmodernism*, p.40.
46   For more detail, see A. Giddens, *The Constitution of Society. Outline of the Theory of Structuration*, Cambridge, 1997, p.302.
47   W.J. Martin, *Global Information Society*, p.91.
48   N. Stehr, *Knowledge Societies*, pp.109, 117.
49   See S. Lash, *Sociology of Postmodernism*, p.46.
50   See T. Sakaiya, *The Knowledge-Value Revolution*, New York, 1991, pp.63–4.
51   D. Bell, *The Coming of Post-Industrial Society*, 1976, p.281; for more detail, see J. Nusbaumer, *The Services Economy: Lever to Growth*, Boston, Dordrecht, 1987, p.49.
52   See D. Bell, 'Notes on the Post-Industrial Society', *The Public Interest*, 1967, 7, pp.116–18; 'The Idea of a Social Report', *The Public Interest*, 1969, 15, pp.72–84; *The Coming of Post-Industrial Society*, 1973, pp.324–37.
53   D. Bell, *The Coming of Post-Industrial Society*, 1976, p.118.
54   R. Miller and G. Wurzburg, 'Investing in Human Capital', *The OECD Observer*, April–May 1995, p.16; quoted from L. Edvinsson and M.S. Malone, *Intellectual Capital*, p.125.
55   A. Toffler, *The Third Wave*, New York, 1981, p.278.
56   See J. Naisbitt, *Megatrends. The New Directions, Transforming Our Lives*, p.5.
57   See T. Sakaiya, *Knowledge-Value Revolution*, p.240.
58   See *Drucker on Asia. A Dialogue Between Peter Drucker and Isao Nakauchi*, Oxford, 1997, pp.29–30.
59   H.A. Linstone and I.I. Mitroff, *Challenge*, p.193.
60   See B. Smart, *Modern Conditions, Postmodern Controversies*, London, New York, 1992, p.39.
61   See H.S. Dordick and G. Wang, *The Information Society*, pp.4–5.
62   P. Drucker, *Post-Capitalist Society*, p.69.
63   R.L. Heilbroner, *Behind the Veil of Economics*, New York, 1988, p.105.
64   J.S. Mill, *Principles of Political Economy*, Vol. I, New York, n.d., pp.45–6.
65   See J. Garnier, *Traité d'économie politique*, 5th edn, Paris, 1863, p.25.
66   See W.S. Jevons, *The Principles of Economics*, London, 1905, p.88.
67   See A. Marshall, *Principles of Economics*, Vol. I, London, 1961, p.65.
68   A. Toffler and H. Toffler, *Creating a New Civilization. The Politics of the Third Wave*, Atlanta, 1995, p.61.
69   L. Edvinsson and M.S. Malone, *Intellectual Capital*, p.72.
70   See Y. Masuda, 'Computopia', in T. Forester (ed.), *The Information Technology Revolution*, Oxford, 1985, p.623.
71   See T. Stonier, *The Wealth of Information: A Profile of a Post-Industrial Economy*, London, 1983.

72 See H.A. Linstone and I.I. Mitroff, *Challenge*, p.162.
73 See M. Castells, *The Rise of the Network Society*, Malden, Mass., Oxford, 1997.
74 N. Stehr, *Knowledge Societies*, p.160.
75 T. Sakaiya, *Knowledge-Value Revolution*, pp.252–4.
76 See ibid., p.219.
77 V. Mosco, 'The Political Economy of Communication', in R.E. Babe (ed.), *Information and Communication in Economics*, Boston, 1994, p.109.
78 W.J. Martin, *Global Information Society*, p.92.
79 As one example of the spread of 'prosumerism', Alvin Toffler cites the system of self-service, for instance at filling stations (see A. Toffler, *The Third Wave*, p.270). But what is being overlooked is that the rapid spread of automatic filling stations is linked not so much to the increasing demand of drivers to become 'prosumers' as to the lower cost of petrol, which owners are able to establish by reducing costs on personnel. Moreover, the efforts of the consumer have not increased, but decreased the price of the fuel. As a result the real labour expenditures have not decreased (the labour of the attendant is replaced by the labour of the driver), but the price of petrol, a measurement of social efforts on its production and delivery to the consumer, has decreased. The labour of the 'prosumer' does not increase the value of a good, but is expended outside the boundaries of that circle of relations in which the very concept of value exists.
80 A. Toffler and H. Toffler, *Creating a New Civilization*, p.61.
81 Ibid.
82 D. Bell, *The Cultural Contradictions of Capitalism. Twentieth Anniversary Edition*, New York, 1996, p.223.
83 P.F. Drucker, *Concept of the Corporation*, New Brunswick, London, 1993, p.253.
84 See V.L. Inozemtsev, *Ocherki istorii ekonomicheskoi obschestvennol formatsii (Essays on the History of Economic Formation of Society)*, Moscow, 1996 (in Russian).
85 A. Toffler, *The Third Wave*, p.40.
86 Ibid., p.284.
87 Ibid., p.285.
88 R.L. Heilbroner, *Behind the Veil*, p.23.
89 See A. Toffler, *The Third Wave*, p.287.
90 *Drucker on Asia. A Dialogue Between Peter Drucker and Isao Nakauchi*, pp.161–2.
91 See J. Robertson, *Future Wealth. A New Economics for the 21st Century*, London, New York, 1990, p.25.
92 See B. Smart, *Modern Conditions*, p.37.
93 D. Bell, *The Coming of Post-Industrial Society*, 1976, p.43.
94 J.-J. Rousseau, L'inégalité parmi les hommes, Paris, 1965, p.108. ('The first man who, having enclosed a piece of ground, bethought himself of saying *This is mine*, and found people simple enough to believe him, was the real founder of civil society' (J.-J. Rousseau, 'On the Origin of Inequality', *Great Books of the Western World*, Vol. 35, Encyclopaedia Britannica Publishers, 1994, p.348).)
95 See M. Bishop and J. Kay, *Does Privatization Work? Lessons from the UK*, London, 1988, p.33.
96 Ibid.
97 See J.R. Blasi and D.L. Kruse, *The New Owners: The Mass Emergence of Employee Ownership in Public Companies and What it Means to American Business*, New York, 1991, p.54.
98 See J. Pakulski and M. Waters, *The Death of Class*, London, Thousand Oaks, 1996, p.76.
99 See J.W. Kuhn and D.W. Shriver, Jr., *Beyond Success: Corporations and Their Critics in the 1990s*, New York, Oxford, 1991, p.150.
100 See ibid., p.151.
101 L. Edvinsson and M.S. Malone, *Intellectual Capital*, p.200.

102 J.W. Kuhn and D.W. Shriver, Jr., *Beyond Success*, p.150.
103 See J. Pakulski and M. Waters, *The Death of Class*, p.76.
104 P.F. Drucker, *Post-Capitalist Society*, p.78.
105 J.K. Galbraith, *The New Industrial State*, 2nd edn, London, 1991, p.55.
106 See G. Durso and R. Rothblatt, 'Stock Ownership Plans Abroad', in C. Rosen and K.M. Young (eds), *Understanding Employee Ownership*, New York, 1991, pp.169–96.
107 J.W. Kuhn and D.W. Shriver, Jr., *Beyond Success*, p.310.
108 See C. Rosen, 'Employee Ownership: Performance, Prospects and Promise', in C. Rosen and K.M. Young (eds), *Understanding Employee Ownership*, p.3.
109 See F.T. Adams and G.B. Hansen, *Putting Democracy to Work: A Practical Guide for Starting and Managing Worker-Owned Businesses*, San Francisco, 1992, p.171.
110 See, for instance, J. Vanek, *Crisis and Reform: East and West. Essays in Social Economy*, Ithaca, NY, 1989, pp.115–37.
111 See G. Durso and R. Rothblatt, 'Stock Ownership', p.182.
112 See F.T. Adams and G.B. Hansen, *Putting Democracy to Work*, pp.20, 171–2.
113 See R. Morrison, *We Build the Road as We Travel*, Philadelphia, 1991, p.9.
114 N. Stehr, *Knowledge Societies*, pp.84–5.
115 D. Bell, *The Coming of Post-Industrial Society*, New York, 1976, p.294.
116 See P.F. Drucker, *Landmarks of Tomorrow*, New Brunswick, London, 1996, p.125.
117 See L.C. Thurow, *The Future of Capitalism. How Today's Economic Forces Shape Tomorrow's World*, London, 1996, p.281.
118 See T. Forester, *High-Tech Society*, p.2.
119 See B. Gates, *The Road Ahead*, p.34.
120 P.F. Drucker, *Post-Capitalist Society*, pp.38–9.
121 See J. Naisbitt, *Global Paradox*, p.99.
122 See A. Toffler, *The Third Wave*, p.140.
123 See J.D. Davidson and Lord William Rees-Mogg, *The Sovereign Individual*, p.185.
124 B. Gates, *The Road Ahead*, p.36.
125 Ibid.
126 P.F. Drucker, *The Age of Discontinuity*, p.276.
127 Ibid.
128. P.F. Drucker, *Post-Capitalist Society*, p.64.
129 See A.W. Branscomb, *Who Owns Information? From Privacy to Public Access*, New York, 1994, pp.7–8.
130 S. Crook, J. Pakulski and M. Waters, *Postmodernization. Change in Advanced Society*, London/Newbury Park, Ca, 1993, pp.114–15.
131 T. Sakaiya, *Knowledge-Value Revolution*, pp.66–9.
132 Ibid., p.270.
133 See M. Hammer, *Beyond Reengineering: How the Process-Centered Organization is Changing Our Work and Our Lives*, New York, 1996, p.77.
134 P.F. Drucker, *Post-Capitalist Society*, p.66.
135 See M. Hammer, *Beyond Reengineering*, p.73.
136 Ibid., p.92.
137 C. Handy, 'Finding Sense in Uncertainty', in R. Gibson (ed.), *Rethinking the Future*, London, 1997, p.30; for more detail, see C. Handy, *Beyond Certainty. The Changing World of Organizations*, London, 1996, pp.183–202.
138 D. Bell, *The Coming of Post-Industrial Society*, New York, 1976, p.294.
139 See A. Toffler, *The Adaptive Corporation*, Aldershot, 1985, pp.156–7.
140 P.F. Drucker, *Concept of the Corporation*, p.232
141 See A. Toffler, *The Third Wave*, pp.204–5.
142 J. Naisbitt, 'From Nation States to Networks', in R. Gibson (ed.), *Rethinking the Future*, p.216.
143 See J. Naisbitt and P. Aburdene, *Megatrends 2000*, p.331.

144 J.D. Davidson and Lord William Rees-Mogg, *The Sovereign Individual*, p.154.
145 D. Bell, *The Cultural Contradictions of Capitalism*, p.224.
146 For more detail see ibid., pp.225–6.
147 See J. Naisbitt and P. Aburdene, *Megatrends 2000*, pp.164–5.
148 J.K. Galbraith, *The Good Society. The Humane Agenda*, Boston, New York, 1996, p.71.
149 Ibid.
150 R.L. Heilbroner, *Business Civilization in Decline*, New York, London, 1976, p.111.
151 For more detail, see A. Toffler, *Future Shock*, New York, 1971, p.449.
152 H. Perkin, *The Third Revolution. Professional Elites in the Modern World*, London, New York, 1996, p.215.
153 See J. Robertson, *Future Wealth*, p.16.
154 A. Touraine, *Le retour de l'acteur. Essai de sociologie*, Paris, 1988, p.96. ('the unity of social life is no longer derived from the idea of society. To the contrary, what is called society is considered henceforth more as a set of rules, customs and privileges against which individual and collective efforts at creation must always struggle. In this view, all metasocial principles of the unity of social life are replaced ... by freedom' (A. Touraine, *Return of the Actor. Social Theory in Postindustrial Society*, Minneapolis, 1988, p.39).)
155 P.F. Drucker, *Concept of the Corporation*, p.262.
156 J. Pakulski and M. Waters, *The Death of Class*, p.70.
157 See, for example, F. Fukuyama, *The End of History and the Last Man*, London, New York, 1992, p.102.
158 See R. Inglehart, *Culture Shift in Advanced Industrial Society*, Princeton, NJ, 1990, p.100.
159 Quoted in D. Lyon, *The Information Society: Issues and Illusions*, Cambridge, 1996, p.56.
160 Marx and Engels, *Werke*, Bd. 13, S.9. ('in broad outline the Asiatic, ancient, feudal and modern bourgeois modes of production may be designated as epochs marking progress in the economic development of society' (Karl Marx and Friedrich Engels, *Collected Works*, Vol. 29, p.263).)
161 Adam Smith, *An Inquiry Into the Nature and Causes of the Wealth of Nations*, Chicago, 1952, p.28.
162 J.K. Galbraith, *The New Industrial State*, p.168.
163 Karl Marx and Friedrich Engels, *Collected Works*, Vol. 24, p.85.
164 A. Gorz, *Farewell to the Working Class. An Essay on Post-Industrial Socialism*, London, 1997, p.2.
165 Ibid.
166 Ibid., p.6.
167 A. Touraine, *Le retour de l'acteur*, p.339. ('The passage from one type of society to another can be accomplished ... through internal transformations happening at the base of social life ... In the Western model of development, culture is always first to change: new knowledge and new techniques emerge, and they are associated with changes in mores and in forces of production. Then, new social actors come into being with their mode of action; later yet, the political system is reorganized and new forms of organization are put into place; finally, ideologies solidify, which correspond to the interests of the newly constituted actors' (A. Touraine, *Return of the Actor*, p.159).)
168 A. Toffler, *Powershift. Knowledge, Wealth and Violence at the Edge of the 21st Century*, New York, 1991, p.464.
169 M. Castells, *The Power of Identity*, Oxford, 1997, p.359.
170 R.L. Heilbroner, *Behind the Veil*, p.87.
171 P.F. Drucker, *The New Realities*, p.23.
172 See W. Greider, *One World, Ready or Not. The Manic Logic of Global Capitalism*, New York, 1997, p.382.

173 See A. Sayer and R. Walker, *The New Social Economy: Reworking the Division of Labor*, Cambridge, Mass., Oxford, 1994, pp.25–6.
174 See J. Pakulski and M. Waters, *The Death of Class*, pp.57–8.
175 A. Giddens, *Social Theory and Modern Sociology*, Cambridge, 1993, p.279.
176 K. Renner, 'The Service Class', in T.B. Bottomore and P. Goode (eds), *Austro-Marxism*, Oxford, 1978, p.252.
177 D. Lyon, *The Information Society*, p.61.
178 P.F. Drucker, *Landmarks of Tomorrow*, pp.98–9.
179 See D. Harvey, *The Condition of Postmodernity*, Cambridge, Mass., London, 1995, p.347.
180 See A. Touraine, *The Post-Industrial Society. Tomorrow's Social History: Classes, Conflicts and Culture in the Programmed Society*, London, 1974, p.70.
181 R. Dahrendorf, *Class and Class Conflict in Industrial Society*, Stanford, 1959, p.301.
182 Z. Brzezinski, *Between Two Ages*, New York, 1970, p.9.
183 D. Bell, *The Coming of Post-Industrial Society*, New York, 1976, p.344.
184 See B.S. Kleinberg, *American Society in the Postindustrial Age: Technocracy, Power and the End of Ideology*, Columbus, Oh., 1973, pp.51–2.
185 See A. Touraine, *The Post-Industrial Society*, p.70.
186 See T. Young, *The Rise of Meritocracy*, London, 1958.
187 For more detail, see A. Giddens, *Social Theory*, pp.263–4; J. Pakulski and M. Waters, *The Death of Class*, p.55.
188 A. Toffler, *The Adaptive Corporation*, p.87.
189 R. Dahrendorf, *Class and Class Conflict*, pp.201, 268.
190 See J. Ellul, *The Technological Society*, New York, 1964, p.400.
191 R. Inglehart, *Culture Shift*, pp.285–6.
192 See A. Touraine, *Critique de la modernité*, Paris, 1992, pp.308–9.
193 Quoted in J. Pakulski and M. Waters, *The Death of Class*, p.65.
194 Ibid., p.147.
195 See A. Touraine, *Le retour de l'acteur*, p.133.
196 R. Inglehart, *Culture Shift*, p.161.
197 A. Toffler and H. Toffler, *Creating a New Civilization*, p.25.
198 See E.E. Gordon, R.R. Morgan and J.A. Ponticell, *Futurework. The Revolution Reshaping American Business*, Westport, Conn., London, 1994, p.205.
199 P.F. Drucker, *The New Realities*, pp.183–4.
200 F. Fukuyama, *The End of History*, p.116.
201 J.K. Galbraith, *The Good Society*, pp.59, 60.
202 See J.D. Davidson and Lord William Rees-Mogg, *The Sovereign Individual*, p.208.
203 See H. McRae, *The World in 2020*, London, 1995, p.110.
204 See J. Pakulski and M. Waters, *The Death of Class*, p.78.
205 R. Heilbroner, *Visions of the Future. The Distant Past, Yesterday, Today, Tomorrow*, New York, Oxford, 1995, p.88.
206 See H.A. Linstone and I.I. Mitroff, *Challenge*, p.228.
207 See R.B. Reich, *The Work of Nations. Preparing Ourselves for 21st Century Capitalism*, New York, 1992, p.169.
208 See J.I. Nelson, *Post-Industrial Capitalism. Exploring Economic Inequality in America*, London, Thousand Oaks, 1995, pp.8–9.
209 See H.A. Linstone and I.U. Mitroff, *Challenge*, p.8.
210 See J. Rifkin, *The End of Work*, New York, 1996, p.174.
211 See H.A. Linstone and I.U. Mitroff, *Challenge*, pp.228.
212 See R.B. Reich, *The Work of Nations*, p.169.
213 See D. Harvey, *The Condition of Postmodernity*, pp.330–31.
214 See J.I. Nelson, *Post-Industrial Capitalism*, p.9.
215 R. Kuttner, *Everything for Sale. The Virtues and Limits of Markets*, New York, 1997, p.86.

216 See R.B. Reich, *The Work of Nations*, pp.205–6.
217 P.F. Drucker, *Landmarks of Tomorrow*, pp.127–8.
218 See L. Thurow, *Head to Head*, New York, 1993, p.206.
219 C.D. Winslow and W.L. Bramer, *FutureWork. Putting Knowledge to Work in the Knowledge Economy*, New York, 1994, p.250.
220 See E.V. von Weizsaecker, A.B. Lovins and L.H. Lovins, *Factor Four: Doubling Wealth – Halving Resource Use. The New Report to the Club of Rome*, London, 1997, p.279.

7 The Post-economic Transformation and the Modern World

On the eve of the 21st century, humanity is ready to enter the post-economic epoch. We can see a large-scale social transformation before our eyes that inevitably affects people in both the most advanced nations and the most remote corners of the world. It is for that reason that, despite the primarily theoretical and often even methodological nature of our study, we cannot limit ourselves to a mere appraisal of the main factors of social progress which, however important they be, merely determine the direction of the development of the modern world; they do not explain its external characteristics. To create a complex picture of the switch from the economic society to the post-economic society, a study should be made of the phenomena that are the direct consequence of the profound and cardinal changes that are taking place within the whole society.

The technological successes of the last decades have undoubtedly played a vital role in the post-economic transformation. The embodiment of the achievements of human reason in the new production systems to provide for the satisfaction of the main material needs has paved the way for the self-perfection of the personality and thus has opened up for humanity an inexhaustible source of progress, the main mover of the current transformations. By bringing information and knowledge – truly inexhaustible resources – to the foremost position among the factors of production, the technological revolution has pushed aside the limits imposed by the exhaustion of natural resources and energy, not least because it overcomes the previous requirement for the unrestrained growth in their consumption. The revolution determines radical changes in employment and its structure, and provides for fast economic growth and the expansion of new sectors of the economy without causing any of the social upheavals that appeared likely only a few decades ago. Thus the post-economic transformation possesses a serious internal basis, formed by the interrelation and interdependency of

319

technological and personal progress, ensuring the stable development and resilience of the system that is coming into being in the face of practically any external factor.

As a result, as we approach the end of the second millennium, a situation has developed that can be described according to its internal characteristics as the most stable for several hundred years. The formation of the post-economic system of preferences provides a changing world with the very non-market mechanisms of development that it needs. The current stage of the post-industrial technological revolution is synchronized in the developed nations with the first precedents of the successful overcoming of environmental danger and the significant easing of the influence of the exhaustibility of natural resources. Lastly, the political defeat of communism has brought to an end the global conflict that has lasted the entire century and has minimized the threat of global war. For the first time in history, humanity has the productive potential to meet the material needs of all of Earth's people and the globalization of the economy has provided a strong basis for the mutual toleration of nations. The background to all these processes is the humanization of social life, which is connected with the expansion of the post-economic system of values at the centre of which lies the individual and his desire for self-improvement.

However, stability does not mean the modern world is free from all the conflicts that inevitably arise during the course of social progress. It is these conflicts we would like to review in the concluding chapter of this book. Conflicts that pose a threat to the sustainable development of civilization originate in two main groups of problems. First, we need to be aware of the equivocal nature of several processes going on in states that are moving more rapidly than others along the path of post-economic transformation. These factors can be called 'internal', since they are created by the specific features of the changes in system within the framework of the developed countries. They are all related in one way or another to the discrepancy between the post-economic essence of the changes going on and that primarily economic form with which many economic processes and phenomena are currently invested. Second, conflicts are also extremely important in relations between countries that are heading in the post-economic direction and states that are still at the industrial, or even the pre-industrial, stage of development. These problems can be called 'external', since they are created by the nature of interaction between the emerging, more or less integrated post-economic system and the conditions of its development represented by the South and countries of the former Eastern bloc. Jumping ahead for a moment, we will note that, over the past 25 years, post-industrial states have displayed such obvious dominance over the rest of the world that intra-system discrepancies in post-economic structures are currently much more important for the destiny of civilization than the problem of how this part of the world interrelates with the other parts.

When communist regimes were suffering economic collapse, and several countries, which only yesterday seemed hopelessly behind the leaders, manifested sustainable and dynamic economic development, ideas about the various kinds of borders that divide the modern world also underwent serious changes. Whereas, several decades ago, the main dividing line was between the Western and Eastern blocs, which were fighting for influence among the non-industrialized countries, today the most obvious dividing line in the world is that between those countries that are developing in the direction of the post-economic society and those that have still not resolved their basic economic problems, have not achieved a sufficient level of industrialization and do not possess the necessary intellectual potential to join the post-economic states. At present, when it is obvious that the impressive achievements made by the United States and other post-industrial powers in the 1900s 'are only the beginning of a prolonged period of economic expansion for the entire developed industrialised world',[1] it is a given fact that the huge abyss separating the emerging post-economic world from the other regions of the planet will continue to widen and must be taken into account to sufficiently understand modern global problems.

The borders of the emerging post-economic world are quite precisely defined, and it is easy to surmise which countries will belong to the world elite by the end of the first quarter of the next century. In so doing, we are not announcing the arrival of Pax Americana, as Zbigniew Brzezinski, for example, does when he notes that 'American power ... is unlikely to be challenged in the foreseeable future by any of its potential rivals'.[2] We prefer to talk about the rise in influence of the G-7 and the countries bordering on them in this case (we do not mean Russia, which has been accepted into the G-7 primarily for short-term economic reasons), rather than the achievements of the United States alone. We must understand that, in the 21st century, having reached a post-economic state, these countries, which as before represent the minority of the world's population and territory, will be quite capable of taking firm and effective control over the functioning of the rest of the planet, which at the beginning of the approaching century will be firmly managed by the powers that have entered the post-economic era.

The process of development of the post-economic revolution[3] has, in our opinion, two characteristic features which are largely determined by the conflicts mentioned above. We believe the source of post-economic transformation can be considered the point at which the internal conflicts in post-industrial countries become the only real determinant of the development of civilization. In so doing, we emphasize that this underlines the fact that, in order to undergo sustainable post-economic changes, leaders need to make social and economic progress in internal self-sufficiency which will allow them to advance along the designated path regardless of external factors. The first stage of this journey, which got off to a dynamic start in the mid-1970s when Western countries began to reorient their production towards the use of information technology, thus overcoming many of the social conflicts within the post-industrial states, leading to their absolute economic domination over the communist world and a decrease in their dependence on the developing countries as raw material suppliers and sales markets, ended when prerequisites were created for a sustainable economic boom during the 1990s, the Soviet bloc collapsed and most of the developing countries showed they were incapable of independently overcoming the economic problems facing them. As a result, the dynamism of civilization is currently determined exclusively by the post-industrialized system.

Resolution of the structural discrepancy in developed countries between the new trends and the traditional forms of economic system, public organization and political life will provide evidence that the post-economic transition period has reached its end. Today, as paradoxical as it may seem, we are seeing an acute conflict between these aspects of society as a whole. Each step along the path of post-economic development is threatened by a catastrophic upsetting of the balance between the forms and relations that have developed, which cannot be viewed purely as a theoretical construction. Overcoming the value regulators of public production will inevitably cause serious upsets on the stock markets and financial markets, the indices of which are already extremely far from the real state of economic indicators. Property relations cannot be successfully modified until there is a radical change in the situation with state debt, as well as corporate and private debts. Exploitation and many other social problems cannot be resolved while there is such a fantastic difference in the level of education and information of the social strata and groups that constitute developed societies. Such contradictions can and should be resolved during the evolution of modern social systems; however, it will be impossible to talk about the maturity of the post-economic society until this extremely difficult process shows signs of genuinely coming to an end.

Owing to the exclusive position that the countries which have largely assimilated into their social structure the elements of post-economic condition are occupying on the threshold of the next century, we begin this part of our study with a review of the current state of affairs in the post-industrial world and an evaluation of the conflicts that still exist within the societies of which that world is made up.

The Roots of Sustainability in the Post-economic Society

At the present stage of development of the post-economic society, the most important factor is technological progress. Although a change in human priorities and values, an expansion in creativity and the replacement of traditional forms of labour are of fundamental significance during this period, they usually do not yet have a direct effect on social development. People's self-realization is manifested in their search for technical and social knowledge, and in the creation of production and management systems which will make it possible to advance further along the path of post-industrial progress; however, the most noticeable influence on world economic processes during the 1970s to 1990s is not creative activity as such, but its manifested results and consequences.

The technological development of Western countries during the past few decades has resolved three fundamental problems. The first of them can be considered the formation of the modern economy as a global economy that ensures the maximum efficiency of production and draws a significant number of countries into the post-industrial world's sphere of influence. This process is of great significance for the formation of mankind as a community of tolerant and patient individuals, and for resolution of national, racial and religious hostility. It has made it impossible for uncivilized forms of large-scale conflict to arise in the post-industrial countries and those close to them in level of development. The second of these problems is associated with maintaining harmonious interaction between man and nature. The 1980s were an epic turning point in the dissemination of new technology capable of drastically reducing both environmental pollution and demands for non-renewable resources. And although this process has still not become sufficiently widespread across the planet as a whole, the trends that have developed in post-industrial countries inspire great optimism. The third significant factor concerns the fact that the Western world has succeeded in passing through the first stage of post-economic transformation without allowing widespread social conflicts, an increase in unemployment, or a rise in social tension. The resolution of these three problems has in turn laid the foundation of the stability of developed societies; given the importance of the factors mentioned, we are compelled to give consideration to each one of them. Global technological changes have in the last few decades become the main source of social progress: the globalization of economic life itself, being one of the most characteristic traits of the present day, is to a large degree dependent on the expansion of information as a basic resource for production,[4] and this fosters to the fullest extent possible the capacity to surmount each and every barrier to the development of post-industrial business firms.

So global technological changes have become the source of progress during the past few decades. Throughout the entire postwar period, a definite tendency has been traced in developed countries towards the rapid development of scientific and technological potential. Whereas, during the extremely favourable times before the Great Depression, there were only three college graduates in the United States for every hundred workers, in the mid-1950s, their number increased to 18.[5] The number of scientists employed in scientific research institutions increased more than tenfold from the beginning of the 1930s to the middle of the 1960s alone,[6] and the percentage of management personnel in enterprises increased from 4 per cent in 1940 to 14 per cent in 1990.[7] In parallel, spending on education between 1958 and 1972 increased from 11.8 per cent to 14.8 per cent of the gross national product (GNP), and the production of information services increased from 4.9 per cent to 6.7 per cent.[8] The situation also developed in the same way in European countries. Approaching the end of the 1970s with enough scientific and technological potential to create an information revolution, the Western powers proved capable of carrying out several measures for rapidly incorporating these achievements into the economy. The coming to power of neo-conservative governments in the United States, Britain and the Federal Republic of Germany (FRG), and the subsequent changes in tax policy, ensured an active increase in investment in the most advanced branches of the economy. For example, the reduction in taxes initiated by the Reagan administration in 1981 released funds equivalent to 58 per cent of all the expenditures on the technical rearmament of American industry during the first half of the 1980s,[9] which resulted in an economic boom that determined the United States' position in the world for the entire decade.

As a result, the G-7 member states, that entered the 1970s under conditions of relative uncertainty and inconsistency, arrived at the beginning of the 1990s more influential in economic relations than they had ever been previously. In 1990, the members of the G-7 possessed 80.4 per cent of the world computer technology and provided 90.5 per cent of high-tech manufacture. The United States and Canada alone accounted for 42.8 per cent of all the world's expenditures on research, while Latin America and Africa together provided less than 1 per cent of such research. Whereas the average global number of scientific and technical workers amounted to 23 400 per million people, in North America this index reached 126 200.[10] The developed countries controlled 87 per cent of the 3.9 million patents registered in the world as of the end of 1993.[11] In this way, technological progress closed the gap between the economic levels of the most advanced post-industrial countries and ensured mutual penetration of their economies, while widening the gap between them and the rest of the world.

The laying of the foundations of post-economic societies became a time of rapid growth of interdependence between national economic systems, which is usually called 'the globalization of the modern economy'. According to several researchers, increased global economic interdependence made the success of modern Western countries possible, ensured economic growth in several regions of the Third World and assisted in the fall of communist regimes.[12] Today this phenomenon is the aggregate of complex and contradictory processes, the distinguishing features of which are the greater interdependence of industries themselves, the activization of commercial flows, the new nature of financial ties and active migration of the workforce.

The development of industry beyond the framework of national states is largely associated with the expansion of transnational companies which represent the high-tech industries. Taking advantage of the potential differences to be found on the labour, capital and technology markets of each country, they not only raise their own economic indicators (for example, the ratio of sales volumes of 50 of the largest multinationals to the American GNP increased from 28 per cent to 39 per cent between 1975 and 1989),[13] but they also make the principle of global activity itself a universal one, preparing the way for an understanding of the fact that 'the local company can soon become the uncompetitive company'.[14] Today 500 of the largest multinationals provide more than one-quarter of the world's manufacture of goods and services.[15] In addition, these companies provide one-third of the export of industrial goods, and four-fifths of the trade in technology and management services.[16] The 300 largest corporations own 25 per cent of the capital invested in the world economy and involved in foreign direct investments.[17]

The development of contemporary companies that proclaim the principle of globalism will naturally expand the framework of economic interaction between certain countries. As John K. Galbraith notes, 'the good society cannot allow itself to be identified with the nation-state alone; it must recognize and support the larger international forces to which the individual country is subject. And this is not a matter of choice; it is the modern imperative'.[18] Futhermore, it should always be borne in mind that this mutual penetration is currently an extremely important factor, not so much in the large-scale opening of national borders all over the world as in the rapprochement of states that are acquiring post-economic features. In the process, the external borders of the post-economic world are becoming increasingly transparent.

For example, the high indices in export ratios to the GNP in the EU countries (47 per cent in Holland, 27 per cent in Switzerland, 25 per cent in Germany and 18 per cent each in France and Britain)[19] are primarily associated with the commodity turnover within the Community. US imports also mainly fall on developed countries, or the rising economies of Southeast Asia (between 1981 and 1986, economic growth in South Korea and Taiwan, by 42 per cent and 74 per cent, respectively, was caused by the United States importing the products manufactured by these countries).[20] And despite the fact that, for every dollar the American family spent on domestic goods in the mid-1980s, 45 cents was spent on imported goods and services,[21] the number of importing countries was still quite limited. At the same time, we should not forget that one-third of the economic growth in the United States itself was provided by an increase in deliveries abroad, and the country is still one of the world's biggest exporters.[22]

Globalization of financial flows assumed much greater proportions at the end of the 20th century. The main index of the internationalization of capital, the ratio of cross-border operations in shares and obligations to GNP, which did not even reach 10 per cent in developed countries in 1980, constituted 72.2 per cent in Japan, 109.3 per cent in the United States, and 122.2 per cent in France by 1992.[23] During the second half of the 1980s and the first half of the 1990s, turnover on the stock markets increased throughout the world more than eightfold. The currency market became another important direction in the activation of financial flows. As early as the end of the 1980s, researchers noted that this was the only sector in which turnover doubled between 1979 and 1984,[24] a period of relatively slow economic growth. The financial flows that passed daily through the US-based Clearing House Interbank Payments System reached values, beginning in 1993, which exceeded $1 trillion.[25] At the same time, the main world financial centres are even more noticeably concentrated in the leading post-industrial states, and their turnovers only emphasize the level of the control those states exercise over the rest of the world.

The migration of the workforce is much less inclined to develop activity than the movement of goods or financial transactions. This is also more of an indication of the achievements of the post-industrial society than of its failures. Noting that globalization has moved very much further in the realm of financial operations and organizational structures than it has in the realm of changes in the labour market,[26] M. Waters points out that the drop in immigration to the developed countries became a reality starting from the middle of the 1970s,[27] when the principles of post-industrialism began to dominate. Today, with a high level of education and qualified manpower, companies prefer to take on local employees, instead of sending their own staff to the country; jobs not calling for qualifications and offering very low wages are the only area where immigrant labour is used, as a result of which those who come from other regions tend to fill the ranks of the lowest classes of society.[28]

For example, within the EU, where there is essentially no restriction on movement and work within the Community, only 2 per cent of the workforce is employed outside the national borders, and this index exceeds 10 per cent only for relatively backward Portugal.[29] In Japan, the percentage of foreigners does not exceed 0.5 per cent of the population.[30] All this shows the degree to which the developed world, within which there is a massive absence of economic stimuli for population migration, is trying to protect itself from resettlements occasioned by the former material motives.

Internationalization of the present-day economy, which is primarily widespread within developed post-industrial states, shows the increasing self-sufficiency of the post-economic world. This also confirms the policy conducted in the use of natural resources and environmental protection. The achievements in this area are extremely impressive. Although active restructuring of industry is frequently associated with the oil crisis of the mid-1970s, we think that its deeper reason lies in the base of the information economy, which can develop more efficiently when not only information itself, but most other resources, are not limited. Advancing along this path, modern technological development led to the fact that 'we live today in a world of effectively unlimited resources – a world of unlimited wealth'.[31] It is important to emphasize that this effect was not at all achieved by drawing genuinely unlimited resources into the economic turnover, but by means of major renovation of the methods for using those resources which have always been considered finite and exhaustible.

For example, mankind has not succeeded in learning how to make efficient use of solar energy, 16 000 times more of which reaches the earth than is produced by the combined capacity of all present-day sources of energy. The cost of its use decreased more than 30-fold between 1970 and 1990, but it has to become even cheaper before it can become a real alternative to energy used at coal-burning plants.[32] The main effect, however, was achieved by actively reducing the use of traditional types of natural resources, which greatly delayed the exhaustion of those resources whose final depletion used to seem very near at hand.[33]

The increase in production is currently outdistancing the increase in use of energy and mineral resources, and this is an important characteristic feature of a society whose progress is based on the use of the latest technological achievements. From 1973 to 1985, GNP of the main developed countries increased by 32 per cent, whereas energy use rose by only 5 per cent.[34] In the second half of the 1980s and the 1990s, a further economic rise occurred against the background of an absolute reduction in energy use. With an increase by a factor of 2.5 in the GNP, the United States is using less ferrous metal today than in 1960.[35] Agriculture, one of the highest energy consumers, reduced by a factor of 1.5 its direct use of energy between 1975 and 1987, and its total energy use (including indirect) by a factor of 1.65;[36] the list of such examples is endless.

During the last decades great achievements have been made in the applying information and knowledge to the material components of end products. For example, whereas immediately after the Second World War the cost of material and energy represented 80 per cent of total expenditure on the manufacture of copper wire used in telephones, the introduction of the optical-fibre communication system reduced this figure to 0.1 per cent.[37] Between 1973 and 1986, the average new American car decreased its gasoline consumption from 17.8 to 8.7 litres per 100 km.[38] Large industrial companies are increasingly refusing to use materials that are rare and associated with widespread interference in nature. The photography method created by the Kodak Corporation that does not require the use of silver drastically reduced the market for this material. The same happened when Ford announced the manufacture of catalysers based on a platinum substitute and the manufacturers of microsystems stopped using gold contacts and leads.[39] As a result, in recent years, the markets for most mineral resources manifested stable trends in price reduction, which at times assumed scales that were catastrophic to the manufacturer. Suffice it to say that, in the United States, 'for the first half of 1997, U.S. energy prices were down to a 16% annual rate'.[40]

The developing countries responded by increasing the excavation and export of raw materials as a way of maintaining their relative prosperity. However, the results were largely unexpected for the exporters. On the one hand, the rise in production which encountered reduced consumer demand caused a dramatic decrease in prices for most mineral resources. Throughout the 1980s, the actual prices of export goods from the countries of the South fell by 40 per cent, those of oil and other fuels by 50 per cent,[41] while 'the World Monetary Fund price index for 30 basic commodities fell by not less than 74%'.[42] And, on the other hand, in the mid-1970s additional efforts were made throughout the world to discover new deposits of mineral resources. The increase in volume of prospected reserves of natural resources was the greatest in the last hundred years. Whereas on the eve of the 'energy crisis' oil reserves were estimated at 700 billion barrels, in 1987, instead of decreasing to 500 billion barrels, they increased to 900 billion, with expected additional deposits being capable of increasing the known reserves in the next few decades to 2 trillion barrels. Between 1970 and 1987, estimates of gas reserves increased from 1500 to 4000 trillion cubic feet, copper from 279 million to 570 million tons, silver from 6.7 billion to 10.8 billion troy ounces, and gold from 1 to 1.52 billion troy ounces.[43] 'Between 1970 and 1990,' wrote Donella H. Meadows and Dennis L. Meadows, 'the world economy burned 450 billion barrels of oil, 90 billion tons of coal, and 1,100 trillion cubic metres of natural gas. Over that same twenty-year period, however, new deposits of oil, coal, and gas were discovered … Therefore, although fossil fuel consumption rates are now higher than they were in 1970 … the ratio of known reserves to production … has gone up for both oil and gas',[44] from 31 to 41 years and from 38 to 60 years, respectively.

The most important characteristic feature of post-economic development today is that the new techniques of resource use are spreading throughout the world, regardless of the falling prices of fuels and minerals. Despite the close relationship which has been forming over the past decades between the price of resources and the level of their use, resource-saving techniques are not developing fastest in the countries with high prices for energy carriers, but in those where the spread of the information revolution is creating the necessary prerequisites for their introduction. At present, the United States is the leading developer of resource-saving techniques, setting a new level of car engine economy for the first decade of the next century within the range of 1.2 and 2.1 litres per 100 km, radically lowering the standards of water consumption over the last ten years, and creating techniques which make it possible to eliminate 99 per cent of the heating, 90 per cent of the electricity and 50 per cent of the water supply expenses to offices. The EU countries are also in the avant-garde: in Holland, for example, methods are being used which make it possible to save up to 92 per cent of the energy used in the home, while, in Germany, the demand of paper plants for water has decreased almost 30-fold in the last 20 years.[45]

It should also be noted that the development of this sector of the market is extremely promising, since, first, most environment-protection systems do not lead to an increase in the price of the end product, but greatly economise on materials, raw material and energy, and second, demand for them is far from satisfied. For it is typical that, in Europe, approximately 80 per cent of all ecological techniques are fighting pollution by utilizing and rendering harmless wastes and discharge, and only 20 per cent are directed at changing the production process to minimize such wastes.[46] Therefore the creation and use of techniques which make it possible to improve the very nature of the production process and not merely overcome its negative consequences have great prospects; Drucker is absolutely right when he refers to this sector as a market whose growth potential under present-day conditions is second only to that of communications and information products.[47]

At the same time, developed countries have significantly reduced the level of environmental pollution. The National Environmental Policy Act was adopted in the United States in 1969, followed by the Clean Air Act in 1970 and the Clean Water Act in 1972, as well as more than 13 000 other laws which currently constitute US ecological legislation. In Germany, corresponding measures began with a law on air quality approved in 1963 by the regional parliament of North Rhein-Westfalia federal state and supplemented by the Waste Disposal Act of 1972 and the Federal Emission Act of 1974.[48] The significant improvement in the ecological situation in Europe and the United States in the 1980s was the first phenomenon of this kind since the laying of the foundations of the industrial system, and one of the most outstanding achievements of post-industrialism.[49] In the current situation, ecological danger is associated primarily with the development of the underdeveloped countries.

The stable development of modern post-industrial societies is also being manifested in social problems and employment. During the second half of this century, Western countries have carried out the most universal transformation of the structure of the labour force of any known throughout history. Within two generations, gigantic population masses have left primitive manual and monotonous labour and been drawn into the manufacture of complex technological goods and services. We think that two important components should be noted in this process.

On the one hand, there has been a release of manpower from agricultural production and its partial incorporation into industry, but it has been incorporated to a much greater degree into the service sphere. In the United States, the number of those employed in this sphere exceeded the number employed in industry as early as the end of the Second World War,[50] and the percentage of farm workers decreased from more than 60 per cent of the working population in 1850 to less than 2.7 per cent at the beginning of the 1990s.[51] Correspondingly, whereas in 1900, approximately 13 million people worked in the material production sphere in the United States, and no more than 5 million in the service sphere, by the end of the 1980s, these indices constituted 35 million and 65 million people, respectively.[52] Similar processes emerged from the 1950s onward in European countries as well: in Germany and France, from 1960 to

1991, the proportion of agricultural workers fell from 14 per cent to 3.4 per cent and from 23.2 per cent to 5.8 per cent;[53] in the mining industries, whose share of GNP of EU countries today does not exceed 3 per cent,[54] the employment rate has gone down by more than 12 per cent in the five years since 1991.[55] This has been paralleled by a process of growth in the services sector of the national economies of all the leading industrial countries. Whereas the tertiary sector accounted for over half the GNP of the United States in the mid-1950s, it today represents more then 73 per cent;[56] in the EU, this sector accounts for about 63 per cent of GNP and 62 per cent of the number of employed workers, while for Japan the corresponding figures are 59 per cent and 56 per cent.[57] This example provides the best possible illustration of the process of unification of the structure of production in the most developed countries of the modern world.[58]

On the other hand, beginning in the 1950s and 1960s, despite the sustained growth in the number of employees in the service sphere, employment began to reorient towards the information sector. Evidence of this was polarization of segments of the economy, whereby the fastest development was achieved in the high-tech branches of industry and those branches of the service sector in which elements of subject–subject interaction were manifested more, which is characteristic of the post-economic society. Employment in the information sector increased from 30.6 per cent in 1950 to 48.3 per cent in 1991, and its ratio to employment in the manufacture of industrial goods from 0.44 to 0.93.[59] If the dynamics of the corresponding changes manifested in the 1980s are maintained, the number of information employees should exceed the number of manufacturers of industrial goods and services in 1996–7.

The essentially smooth redistribution of employees and the active policy to create new jobs are great achievements. The results of these processes were particularly noticeable in the 1980s and 1990s. For example, the forecasts that predominated in the second half of the 1970s, which declared that unemployment in the United States could reach 15 per cent[60] to 20 per cent[61] of the working population in the following decade proved to be completely unjustified.[62] By the beginning of the 1990s, the level of unemployment in the United States, France, Germany and Britain constituted between 6.6 and 7.8 per cent of the working population. For the first time in the postwar period, the dynamics of this vital index were encouraging (for example, J. Rifkin, who describes the horrors of unemployment, admits that, whereas in the 1950s its average level in the United States was 4.5 per cent, in the 1960s, 1970s and 1980s, it had definitely increased to 4.8 per cent, 6.2 per cent and 7.3 per cent, respectively, at the beginning of the 1990s it had decreased to 6.6 per cent[63]). In this respect, it should also be noted that the achievements made can largely be associated with the end of the formation of the post-industrial structure. For example, while its foundations were being laid, from the beginning of the 1970s to the beginning of the 1980s, the level of unemployment in all the main Western economies increased; when the fruits of economic restructuring became sufficiently obvious, its dynamics shifted in the opposite direction.[64]

In the meantime, the trends in the United States and the EU countries differed from each other. By July 1997, in the former, a country that most fully embodies the main advantages of information technology, unemployment had fallen to an all-time low for the previous 24 years of 4.8 per cent,[65] while in Germany and France it reached 12.4 per cent and 13.1 per cent, respectively.[66] The only element of similarity between patterns of employment growth in these two segments of the post-industrial world lies in the fact that, both in the United States and in the main European countries, the unemployment level among university graduates was constantly three times lower than among those who had incomplete high school education.[67] The widely held impression of the relative backwardness of Europe is not entirely correct and requires special explanation. In our view, it has subjective as well as quite objective origins. On the one hand, there is a radical difference between the American and the European ways of thinking: whereas European thinkers are convinced that 'each country possesses some kind of historical predestination, which to a large degree determines its features and characteristics',[68] American sociologists today make the over-confident assumption that 'power and culture as a rule go hand in hand' and that the Europeans are 'misguided in thinking that their continent will remain at the centre of culture, even if their political influence wanes'.[69] On the other hand, in providing their citizens with a high standard of material well-being and a high quality of life, and by sharply reducing the backwardness compared to the United States that existed in the 1960s according to the given indicators,[70] the European countries have put themselves in the complicated position of extremely high production costs (with labour costs in the forefront) and the disproportionately high taxes needed to maintain the achieved level of social welfare. This being so, the latter is not an insuperable obstacle to economic progress; high-tech companies are thriving well enough, the continent enjoys the most highly qualified workforce and the most educated population, while the foreign direct investments of European companies are growing faster than those of their American competitors.[71]

We are inclined to believe that Europe today is a community that offers the United States and the other post-industrial regions an image of their future, rather than of their past. Now that they have achieved a high quality of life, the European countries are today enjoying the fruits of post-economic development in the form of a lessening of mobility of people, the prevalence of values of self-fulfilment over those of material success, and so on. At the same time, this sort of transformation under present-day conditions is not endangering the internal stability of European societies. The only serious conflict to which they are fully exposed in such a situation is the conflict between the different strata of society, which are at once admitted and yet left out of this post-economic structure. European unemployment, which has become an extremely acute problem, is to a considerable extent caused, not only by falling demand for industrial labour, but also by the changing preferences and values of the population of the continental countries.

At the same time, the United States' achievements in providing high employment indices are primarily associated with the mobility of the workforce equivalent to the range of changes fostering the formation of the post-economic society. Between 1990 and 1999 alone, a reduction by 10 million (!) of the 20.5 million jobs is expected in the United States in the industrial sector, whereby more than 9 million of them will be recreated in changed form at other production facilities, and the net loss in industrial production will constitute a total of 834 000 jobs.[72] It is expected that the overall employment indices will increase by 25 per cent with a population increase of only 15 per cent. According to the forecasts, between 1992 and 2005, more than 26 million jobs will be created in the United States, which will exceed the increase in this index for the period between 1979 and 1992.[73] Such forecasts look extremely realistic: in July 1997 alone, 316 000 jobs were created in the American economy,[74] which essentially exceeded the predicted level twofold. During the 1990s, the tendency towards an increase in the percentage of citizens from the home country in the overall number of employees at the largest multinationals was also more characteristic of the United States than of the other developed countries. Statistics show that multinationals also prefer to organize their own production in the developed countries, which today accounts for two-thirds of their foreign personnel,[75] whereas in the developing countries they are only buying the raw material and parts they need manufactured at officially independent enterprises.

The increase in self-employment and the number of jobs in the small business sphere, which is natural in periods of radical social change, is an important resource for resolving the problem of employment under the conditions of post-economic transformation. We have already noted that by 1995 approximately 20.7 million full-time home-based businesses had been created in the United States,[76] and this process is only one of the elements of the development of alternative employment. According to the calculations of David Birch, large corporations cut 2 236 000 jobs between 1987 and 1992, largely because technologically routine operations were transferred to third countries; but during the same period, small businesses created 2 296 000 jobs, most of which were more highly paid.[77] Of course, the shifts in employment take their toll: at present, 8.1 million Americans have temporary jobs, 2 million work 'on call', 8.3 million are self-employed 'independent contractors'. Their overall number has reached 14 per cent of the workforce[78] and could increase to as much as one-third by the beginning of the 21st century.[79] But we believe that this phenomenon does not demonstrate the irreparability of the problem, but, on the contrary, that it can be and is being resolved. In the meantime, we have to agree with Alvin and Heidi Toffler, who think: 'yet it is no longer possible to reduce joblessness simply by increasing the number of jobs because the problem is no longer merely numbers. Unemployment has gone from quantitative to qualitative'.[80] Unemployment today is in fact more 'qualitative' than 'quantitative'. This gives rise to a great many problems (some of which we will discuss below); however, the experience of the last few years provides more justification for optimistic than for pessimistic forecasts. The current state of affairs in this area shows that one of the most difficult stages of post-economic transformation did not cause any serious social cataclysms. Under conditions where society could permit itself the expenditures necessary for further restructuring the manpower market, or creating demand for highly qualified personnel and support of released workers, the process of forming a structure equivalent to the new employment tasks will be one of the natural aspects of the processes going on and will not present a potential threat to the overall direction of present-day transformations.

The next important problem, which is impossible to miss during an analysis of the state of the modern post-industrial world, is associated with an evaluation of its economic power and influence on the eve of the 21st century. By analysing it, we will also be able to determine how realistic is the challenge to Western civilization that it is currently thought could be posed by the countries of Asia, Latin America and the Persian Gulf.

By the end of the 1980s, three distinct centres of economic power had developed, all of them represented by countries that can be considered members of post-industrial civilization. If the amount of value added is viewed as an indicator of the significance of a particular economy, it turns out that the United States is in first place, providing 25.8 per cent of the world index, followed by the EU with 19.4 per cent, and the Pacific Ocean region bringing up the rear, with Japan, China and the ASEAN countries together providing 16.2 per cent of the world value added. The position of the EU, which is the highest capacity market in the world, even looks a little better than the US position in this respect, since the European community has a good trading position which ensures more than 40 per cent of the world trade turnover, and in so doing does not have a large aggregate negative trade balance in operations with other large economic centres. On the contrary, the United States has a significant trade deficit both with the EU and with Southeast Asia, which is turning into the world's only net exporter.[81]

The antagonism between these three centres, which is given so much attention today in economic and political literature, should not be evaluated from a negative point of view. In recent decades, post-industrial civilization, that includes the United States, Western Europe and Japan, as well as to a certain extent some of the members of the British Commonwealth (Canada, Australia and New Zealand) is not only quite strictly separate from those who are trying to become full members of this club (the countries of Southeast Asia, the Persian Gulf, some countries of South America and Mexico, South Africa, and others) but also reveals indices of economic development which shed no doubt on the stability of the balance of forces that has formed. Although, over the period since the Second World War, the percentage of old industrial countries in the volume of world production of goods and services has constantly decreased, it is not worth overrating either the degree of its decrease or the significance of the dynamics of corresponding processes. It is well known, for example, that by the middle of the 1980s the United States' share of world industrial production had decreased to 33 per cent, from 58 per cent in 1955,[82] while the same index for the entire Western world decreased from 74.6 per cent to 57.8 per cent between 1953 and 1980.[83] However, this picture reflects an artificial separation of Japan from the other developed countries, and, when its potential is taken into account, the reduction seems much less abrupt – from 77.5 per cent to 67.0 per cent.

Economic growth in Japan does not seem to be a destabilizing factor for the development of the post-industrial world, but, on the contrary, provides it with a genuine global nature and self-sufficiency. Although Japan is not an offshoot of the whole of Western civilization to the extent that the United States is, for all its achievements,[84] the redistribution of the centres of power among the developed countries that is happening today has a primarily positive value. This redistribution is not regarded by us as a violation of certain optimal proportions; on the contrary, the latter acquire their final form. And everyone knows that the second half of the 1970s and beginning of the 1980s was a time of impressive Japanese achievements which made the United States doubt for a while the reliability of its leading position. Whereas in 1971, 280 of the 500 largest multinationals were American, by 1991, there were only 157.[85] By that time, Japan had essentially caught up with the United States in the number of companies in the World Top 1000, having 345 top companies as opposed to 353 for the United States.[86] At the end of the 1980s, it had 24 of the largest banks at its disposal, whereas the EU countries had 17 such banks, and North America only five; nine of the ten largest service companies also belonged to Japan.[87]

Moreover, these statistics reflect only one side of the economic processes going on, and for a fuller understanding of the changes occurring, we need to turn to additional facts. First, an analysis of the ratio of the gross national product of the three centres of the post-industrial world shows that the changes are much less global than they may seem at first glance. For example, between 1973 and 1986, the United States' share in the world production of goods and services decreased only from 23.1 per cent to 21.4 per cent, the EC's share from 25.7 per cent to 22.9 per cent, and Japan's share increased from 7.2 per cent to 7.7 per cent.[88] Under conditions in which Japan increased its GNP from 27 per cent to 38 per cent of the US index, the United States itself kept its GNP ratio in strict correspondence with the European countries: with Germany at a level of 16 per cent, with France at a level of 13–14 per cent, and with Britain at 11–12 per cent; as a result, over 15 years, between 1975 and 1990, the ratio of the sum GNP of the European countries, members of the OECD and Japan to the US GNP increased from 107 per cent to 112 per cent,[89] which constitutes an increase of only 0.29 per cent per year.

Second, we should not forget the important characteristics of the Japanese economy. The country began advancing along the path of accelerated industrialization relatively recently, and the growth of its share in the world economy is quite understandable, particularly against the background of European countries and the United States, which, being the richest regions of the world, manifest a tendency towards a maximum reduction in saving rates and low economic growth. Moreover, Japanese industry today is largely oriented towards an increase in mass-production and serial production industries; for example, Asian companies are most successful on both the American and European markets in the sale of household electronics, office equipment, cars and motorcycles, cellular telephones, computers and so on. At the same time, although in 1991 the EC had a trade deficit with Japan of $35 billion in electronics alone, and the United States in 1990 had a deficit of $22.3 billion,[90] these figures do not indicate Japan's technological supremacy over Europe and the United States. Much more important is the scale on which new technologies are being used in the economies of different countries. The fact is that today 80 per cent of American homes are linked by cable networks, as opposed to 12 per cent of Japanese homes; in the United States there are 233 personal computers (PCs) per 1000 of the population, in Germany and England about 150, whereas in Japan there are only 80; 64 per cent of Americans regularly send email, with between 31 per cent and 38 per cent of the inhabitants of the continent of Europe doing so, while only 21 per cent of Japanese do,[91] and one could give many more similar examples.

It should also be noted that the Japanese version of industrialization is based on the maximum use of the potential of extensive growth and is largely oriented towards the development of large enterprises and industrial groups, which artificially support the number of Japanese companies in the ratings of world business leaders. The United States, on the contrary, largely bases its economic progress on intensive methods and is oriented towards the development of small and medium-size businesses, which are assuming increasingly greater proportions as the transfer to an information economy is carried out. This is also confirmed by the fact that, in 1992, ten of Japan's largest companies produced 15.1 per cent of GNP, while in the United States this index did not exceed 12.5 per cent.[92]

Third, it should be noted that, since the beginning of the 1990s, this frightening trend for the Western world has been overcome to a certain extent. Whereas, in the middle of the 1980s, Japanese industry achieved its maximum success, providing 82 per cent of the world's manufacture of motorcycles, 80.7 per cent of the manufacture of domestic video systems and approximately 66 per cent of the photocopying equipment,[93] in recent years the situation has changed drastically. Relying on the turbulent development of high technology, the prerequisites for which were laid in the 1980s, the United States entered a period of stable and rapid economic growth, while the growth rates of the Japanese economy slowed perceptibly, and there was a drastic and prolonged decrease in growth on the stock markets.[94] 1991 was a year of great success for European and Japanese producers in the Top 500. At that time, they included 168 European companies, 157 American and 119 Japanese,[95] which, on the whole, adequately reflected the economic potential of Europe, the United States, and Japan. By the beginning of 1997, the situation had changed: the number of American companies on the list increased to 203 (up 29 per cent), the number of European companies decreased to 126 (down 25 per cent) and the number of Japanese companies fell to 110 (down 7.5 per cent). Moreover, the market capitalization of the first, which constituted $4.25 trillion, was only a little inferior to the European and Japanese taken together, which had a corresponding index of $4.3 trillion.[96] We will note that the US population was half that of the total population of the EC and Japan.

And finally, when comparing the potentials of the various centres of economic power on the threshold of the 21st century, the openness of particular trends to the future should be taken into account. Japanese industry has made great strides, particularly in the manufacture of electronic systems. For example, by the end of the 1970s, it had successfully ousted American manufacturers from the microchip market, outdistancing the United States in 1985, and maintaining a gap of 16 percentage points in 1989. However, having allowed such a situation in a branch characterized by mass-production, the United States never yielded its leading position either in the creation of new data processing systems or in software development. At the beginning of the 1990s, 57 per cent of the world software market was in the hands of American companies.[97] In 1995, total sales of computer and data processing services amounted to 95 billion dollars,[98] of which three-quarters were taken up by the United States.[99] As a result, equilibrium on the microchip manufacturing market, which was destroyed in the early 1980s, was restored in the mid-1990s, with the shares of the United States and Japan evening out. By the end of the 1980s, the Japanese economic miracle had shown us how far a country that preaches the industrial paradigm could go, when surrounded by neighbours that belong to the post-industrial world. The shares of the industrial giants were quoted on the Tokyo stock exchange at prices that brought shareholders a dividend of less than 1 per cent per annum on their capital investment; the country held the world's largest financial reserves.[100] Even so, today little is left of that former greatness: many enterprises are working at 70 per cent of their productive capacity,[101] growth rates are close to zero, the fund index slipped, between mid-1996 and November 1997, from a level of nearly 23 000 to less than 14 000 points, and the securities of many major finance houses, including the biggest on the market, Yamaguchi Securities, have fallen more than tenfold (!).[102] It is easy to understand why, in recent years, 40 per cent of the leaders of Japanese firms have reached the conclusion that the United States will stand alone as world leader in the 21st century, a confident assessment shared by only 32 per cent of their colleagues in the United States,[103] however. This last point seems to us to be evidence of a gradually dawning realization that quantitative indicators of the vigour of production do not determine economic progress in an era of qualitative changes.

All this convinces us that an optimal balance is being established before our eyes among the three centres of the post-industrial world. Its current state is extremely stable, and the rivalry among the growing centres of post-economic civilization is only helping all three regions to achieve greater economic success. The United States still occupies the leading position in the world economy and politics, which is an important guarantee of the stability of post-industrial civilization. During the last 25 years, it would seem that the United

States has accomplished the impossible: at moderate rates of economic growth, an exclusively high level of well-being of the population, and an extremely low, recessive, tendency of economic entities to economize,[104] it has ensured unprecedented investment in the most advanced industrial branches, and improved the sphere of high-tech production, the education system and the scientific infrastructure, which has made it the unconditional leader on the threshold of the 21st century.

Today, the United States is at the peak of its success, and in a position which is distinguished by unprecedented external stability. Its contribution to world industrial production exceeds the country's percentage of the Earth's population more than fivefold,[105] and direct foreign investments do not go beyond the limits permitted by the dimension of its economy.[106] American producers control 40 per cent of the world communications market, about 75 per cent of the trade in computer services and four-fifths of the software market.[107] Stable economic growth is accompanied by a strengthening of partnership relations within the society. With the most satisfactory employment pattern, using only 2.7 per cent of the workforce in agriculture,[108] and not more than 1.4 per cent in the mining industry,[109] the United States today can offer 156 jobs for every 100 on offer in 1975, whereas the European equivalent stands at a mere 96.[110] The very low levels of unemployment over the last few decades, and of expenditure on defence and the Federal budget deficit achieved in the mid-90s,[111] have been directly responsible for the stabilization of, and even the fall in, the indicators for all kinds of asocial phenomena with which the United States is moving forward into the next century.[112] The purchase of American companies by foreign investors, which is frequently viewed as a threat to the United States' national interests on the part of Japan and Asian countries, is actually not one. The point here is not even that the main investors in the US economy are countries belonging to the post-industrial world – Britain, Germany and France, with Japan lagging seven times behind investing only a seventh of Britain's investment – there is a more important fact. In 1986, American investors held securities in foreign countries of a value less than one-third the total of American shares in the possession of foreigners.[113] By 1995, for the first time in the 20th century, Americans had gained control over a greater volume of shares issued abroad than those held by foreign investors in the United States itself. Typically, 70 per cent of these acquisitions were made by American corporations during the first half of the 1990s alone, and the total amounts that US corporations are potentially able to invest in the economies of foreign countries are today estimated at $325 billion for the period up to the year 2000 alone.[114]

Three characteristic circumstances should be noted here. First, an increase in foreign investment not only does not deprive the recipient country of any opportunities, but actually ensures additional conditions for its development. According to Robert Reich, labour secretary in the Clinton administration, 'when foreign money and strategic brokerage are added to American problem solving and identifying, the result may be better for Americans than before',[115] since most of this investment is not directed at the sectors characterized by mass-production and using low-qualified but, under the conditions of developed countries, extremely expensive manpower, but rather at new industries that have made positive changes in the employment structure and increased their demand for personnel with high qualifications.

Second, despite all their significance, these processes cannot be the source of a real threat to the technological potential of Europe and the United States from the new industrialized countries. If we take a look at the American and European industries in which Japan and Southeast Asia are making the most of their investments, it is easy to note that banking transactions, operations on the real estate market and several service spheres take the lead. Moreover, European and American investors are the most active agents on the high-tech market, where more than 80 per cent of German investment is directed, approximately 63 per cent of American, and only 57 per cent of Japanese. In addition, European and American companies are penetrating most resolutely and with the greatest success into Japan and other regions of Asia. For example, from 1986 to 1987 alone, American companies increased their expenditures on the scientific research and innovative projects they implement in Japan by 33 per cent, while the same index for the United States itself amounted to only 6 per cent. One of the consequences of this was the transformation of IBM, which employs 18 000 workers in Japan and has an annual sales volume of $6 billion, into one of the leading Japanese exporters of computer technology.[116] The fact that traditional industrial centres are in no real danger of losing their technological supremacy is also confirmed by the fact that the percentage of resources directed by Asian investors to manufacturing industries decreases as the potential of the recipient country increases, constituting only 16 per cent for the EU.[117]

Third, the increase in investment in the United States (from 11.2 per cent to 29.0 per cent of the world volume of direct foreign investments between 1975 and 1985) is occurring against the background of a decrease in Europe's percentage (from 40.8 per cent to 28.9 per cent).[118] Thus, while a particular region is reaching post-industrial maturity, it becomes a less active recipient of investment, since its potential is limited by its reduced industrial potential, and high-tech branches require the inflow of intellectual rather than financial resources.

It can be maintained with certainty that the traditional industrial centres, Europe and particularly the United States, are currently manifesting stable and dynamic development in laying the foundations of a post-economic society. At present, the United States leads in production growth and the dynamics of basic stock indices, has had the lowest unemployment rate over the past few decades and one of the highest investment levels in education and science. It also tops the list of richest countries in terms of per capita well-being, and this list is very similar to the list of states that are the biggest investors in the American economy. As of 1991, only Switzerland and Luxembourg, the main European financial centres, had indices close to the United States', calculated in terms of the purchasing power of the national currencies. A GNP level between $17 000 and $20 000 per capita per year was provided only by (in descending order) Germany, Canada, Japan, France, Belgium, Austria, Denmark and Sweden.[119] It should be noted that all the indices reviewed can serve as confirmation of the unity of post-industrial civilization in its opposition to the rest of the world. With each passing year, it becomes more distinguished from its less fortunate neighbours on the planet, being not only the source of 97 per cent of all transnational investment,[120] but also a recipient of more than three-quarters of this investment, while the share of the Third World countries, which constituted two-thirds on the eve of the Second World War, has currently decreased to one-quarter.[121]

During the past few years, there has been a great deal of talk about the economic achievements of the Asian countries. Are they capable of creating serious competition for the Western world? Without ruling out this prospect entirely, it is necessary to make a sober assessment of their potentialities in conditions based on information and the kinds of knowledge of present-day economies. After all, the real basis for the relative wealth and prosperity of these states is still their occupation of a certain niche in the world's industrial economy. Having set up assembly shops, where mass industrial production is actively going on, they base their success on imported technology and cheap manpower.[122] The degree of such prosperity will never be as high as in the countries of the post-industrial bloc, or its stability as sustainable and long-term. Yes, the calculations show that, if China sustains the rate of growth it achieved at the end of the 1980s, by 2008 it will have a higher GNP than the United States, or if this rate slows by half, it will reach this same level by 2014. It is a well-known fact that Hong Kong, with its population of five million, which became part of the People's Republic of China on 1 July 1997, as the special Administrative Region of Siangan, has the second-largest airport in the world in terms of passenger flow,[123] is the eighth largest trading centre in the world,[124] and since 1992 has consumed more luxury items – cognac, expensive wines, cars and prestige furniture – than the 60 million inhabitants of aristocratic Britain, whose colony it was until recent times.[125] But what reflects the absolute magnitude of China's GNP, if by the beginning of the 1990s the per capita consumption of the country's main consumer products was less than or, at best, coincided with the same indices achieved by Taiwan as early as the end of the 1960s?[126] It must not be forgotten that, even when the People's Republic of China catches up with the United States in terms of GNP, its indicators per capita of the population will still be six times lower than the American ones. What is Hong Kong, apart from a financial centre needed by the West to conduct transactions in all the time zones simultaneously, and a place for concentrating the immigrant workforce from all over Asia which manufactures cheap commodities for the American and European middle class?

We frequently hear about the magnificent achievements of Asian companies, of their entry into new markets, and their incredibly high growth rates. In this respect, the situation is even more obvious. For example, as of the beginning of 1997, there were only 30 companies from Hong Kong, Singapore, Malaysia, Taiwan, Indonesia, South Korea, Thailand and the Philippines among the world's 500 largest companies. Their total market value amounted to approximately $412 billion, and it is characteristic that a similar index for the companies of Switzerland and Holland on this same list (not counting jointly owned Dutch–British and Swiss–Swedish companies) amounted to $470 billion, and counting those joint companies reached $691 billion.[127] We will note that the population of Switzerland and Holland is twenty times less than the population of the above-mentioned Asian countries.[128] All of this emphasizes once again the limited potential of economies that are oriented towards industrial manufacture rather than the creation of technology, information and knowledge, and makes it more obvious that the richest states of the modern world are limited only to post-industrial countries.[129]

Concluding this section, we would like to note that today, in an era of rapid formation of the border between the post-economic part of the world and the rest of its territory, the only way to achieve recognition in the world elite is to achieve successful development in keeping with the laws governing post-industrial society. Countries wishing to join this group on the basis of extensive development and the import of technology will not be allowed into the cherished circle until they begin developing on their own basis, until they provide new technological solutions and developments, until they create a new post-industrial worker, who can disseminate post-economic values.[130] This is not easy, but we cannot exclude the possibility of a 'late bloomer'. However, it should be understood that a country that makes this journey will not be able to embody elements of opposition to the Western world since, by the time it becomes a part of it, it will become its natural component, perhaps not in its cultural traditions, but in its methods of production, level of education, moral principles and vital reference points of the population. For this reason, a real challenge to the Western world is impossible today, and the front-running countries can only be caught up with by entering their ranks on the basis of their principles, and this process will naturally be controlled by the post-economic community itself. Thus a rigid, but still surmountable, border arises between the post-industrial world and the rest of mankind. Transfers across it in the foreseeable future, about which we will go into more detail below, will apparently be possible for a considerable number of countries, although with each new decade the post-economic landmarks will become increasingly inaccessible for most of the world.[131]

At the same time, it should be kept in mind that the semblance of prosperity, which has been 'spilled' over the entire post-industrial world, may disappear if in the next few decades due attention is not paid to the contradictions ripening along with the formation of those stable trends which are leading to the formation of post-economic elements of social organization. Today, as the world's most developed countries are entering the second stage of post-economic transformation, conflicts and contradictions characteristic of the corresponding period are quite dangerous and require, not only in-depth study, but also social and political wisdom, measured decisions and considered actions capable of ensuring their evolutionary and non-catastrophic resolution.

The Inner Contradictions of Post-economic Society

All who write about the developed countries of the West inevitably mention their external prosperity. These are not superficial evaluations which conceal the deep-rooted disparities of con-temporary society. The deep foundations of this prosperity are also fully self-sustaining, and the evolutionary tendency is witness to its openness to the future. But many of the current changes, which are for the most part positive, contain significant contradictions, capable on a certain level of becoming dangerous for the evolutionary development of post-economic societies.

In the preceding chapters we did not probe deeply into how acceptable is the pace of the social changes caused by the technological advances of the last few decades for a social structure characterized by a certain degree of inertia and historical stereotypes. This issue is of extreme importance. Amid the radical changes in production, the rapid revision of the technological and theoretical schemes and conceptions, it becomes important to preserve the conformity between the essence of the processes in the making and their external forms. To attain that compatibility is necessary first of all because the changes that are initiating and provoking the post-economic revolution may be noticed primarily on an individual level, and sometimes even on a sociopsychological level. As a consequence, many economic conformities and relations, which have in many cases already acquired a new content, continue to be treated as typical economic ones, owing to their evaluation from a purely formal point of view. This is illustrated by a whole number of examples: suffice it to say that essential nature conservation technologies, in purely economic terms, appear to be loss-making; growth of gross domestic product may not reflect the real wealth and economic influence of a nation at all, and evaluations of various products or companies may not concur with their production costs or book-values.

Today, when Western societies are immersed in the peripeteia of the revolution which we call post-economic, the gap not only between the unfolding processes of renewal and notions about these, but also – and more dangerously – between the state of the economic whole and the imperatives of the most diverse spheres of human activity becomes clearer and clearer. The result is the situation where people attempting to control the social processes at work in society by interpreting traditional indicators are like pilots who carry out difficult manoeuvres aided by instruments but are unable to see the real situation. With each new step towards the post-economic state, the possibility of mistakes increases since, as it emerges, former indicators can to a lesser extent be regarded as an adequate reflection of the changes taking place today.

This situation would be highly dangerous even if such inadequate information was to be used only to interpret the processes that are taking shape independently and outside the people's will. But the changes of the said indicators become the reason for the movement of a huge mass of material goods and financial resources, the disorganization of which may have a direct bearing on the lives of tens, even hundreds, of millions of people. The growing disparity between these indicators and the reality they purport to describe is fraught with grave dangers, which may well push back the prospect of establishing a post-economic society, and have unpredictable consequences for the world as a whole since, if the normal course of economic development is disrupted in only one of its main industrial centres, this would cause a chain reaction which leads to world destabilization. Moreover, the source and premise of such a process may be a banking crisis or exchange crash which does not even have any immediate relation to economic development as such.

Today, when the main resources that determine economic progress are to an unprecedented degree concentrated in the main post-industrial regions, no external factors can determine their loss of the prevalent position. But it is precisely because of this concentration that any incorrect decision, the likelihood of which increases with the growth of the inaccuracy of all types of economic information, may turn out to be very harmful, if not even fatal, for developed countries. Therefore it can be stated that precisely the inner incompatibility of the post-economic nature of contemporary societies of the West with the economic form of the manifestation of the processes in those societies is a greater threat to mankind than a challenge from developing countries, environmental disbalance, growing nationalism, problems related to the disintegration of the Eastern bloc or the activity of militarized regimes and international terrorism. And specifically, the inner lack of conformity between the economic form in which the processes going on inside modern Western societies manifest themselves and the post-economic nature of those societies constitutes a source of the greatest possible dangers for humanity as a whole.

Our analysis concentrates mainly on economic relations, so we will leave aside other problems which may be caused by new social conflicts in developed societies, the contemporary understanding of freedom and the new opportunities for the self-realization of the personality. We will dwell primarily on those elements of the emerging post-economic civilization which are associated with changes in cost correlations and in the system of ownership.

The proliferation of unlimited but at the same time non-reproducible goods, the strengthening of the role of information and of other unique resources in the manufacturing of finished goods in any industry and in the service sector, the reduction of the cost of raw materials and labour in the cost of the end product, not to speak of non-materially motivated activity, which has become a key factor of the manufacturing process – all of this makes the traditional characteristics of economic processes more and more conventional. We will discuss three, most dangerous in our view, deviations of ideas about economic processes from their real essence.

As the first example we will take the macroeconomic indicators of the modern economy. The most important of these is still gross national product. Inadequacies were already well known: GNP does not only involve repeated itemizations of one and the same expenditure of inputs and labour as value is added to a product, but also reflects, as a positive factor, the growth of any social efforts, including those that cannot be seen as indicative of the increased prosperity of a nation.[132] In today's conditions it is hard to apply the indicators for a number of new reasons.

Firstly, it accounts only for direct production costs and is unable to account for the damage caused to society and the environment through their use: 'By taking account only of naturally occurring production costs or those that can be scientifically demonstrated … [such instruments as this] … are not capable of "internalising" long-term costs and other less measurable losses.'[133] However, calculations show that the US automotive industry alone – from pollution and the use of land for building roads to loss because of accidents and the deterioration of the nation's health – has incurred external losses of up to $1 trillion annually, a seventh of the country's GNP.[134] Al Gore writes: 'In calculating GNP, natural resources are not depreciated as they are used up. Buildings and factories are depreciated; so are machinery and equipment, cars and trucks. So why, for instance, isn't the topsoil in Iowa depreciated when it washes down the Mississippi River after careless agricultural methods have lessened its ability to resist wind and rain?' And he concludes: 'Our failure to measure environmental externalities is a kind of economic blindness, and its consequences can be staggering.'[135] Secondly, in the information revolution, the movement of cost indicators, one of which is GNP, no longer reflects the real correlation between goods which are produced and goods which are consumed, as the continuing reduction of costs in the production of the more high-tech products inevitably results in the artificial understatement of growth rates in the post-industrial economies. Is this not why officially published statistics show that the rate of economic growth in developed countries has dropped from 5 per cent in the 1960s and 3.6 per cent and 2.8 per cent in the 1970s and 1980s, respectively, to 2.0 per cent in the 1990s,[136] although this slowdown was recorded amid a most significant leap in technology in the Western world over the last few decades? Thirdly, GNP as an indicator is unable to reflect adequately the meaning and role of intangible assets, something of clear importance today. To a considerable extent, it is for this reason that the impression of audacious economic breakthroughs achieved by countries geared towards mass-production based exclusively on secondary technologies is created. Fourthly and finally, GNP does not retain the qualitative characteristics of a product, yet these characteristics are the most important in modern production. It is therefore no accident that the patterns of GNP and alternative indicators[137] like, for example, the Index of Sustainable Economic Welfare (ISEW), introduced by Daly and Cobb in 1989,[138] or the Genuine Progress Indicator[139] become varied in their purpose.

Thus the disparity between the cost characteristic of the main macroeconomic indicators and the clear shift in social preferences towards quality characteristics of goods is one of the most important, but not the only proof of the disorientation of the development of contemporary post-industrial societies.

Many believe that national income as an indicator and its derivatives do not possess the same flaws as GNP. However, these are unable to reflect adequately the real state of affairs either. Take, for example, the new phenomenon in the United States and in Europe, which consists of the loss of relative proportionality in the growth of the incomes of workers and capital profits. In the United States in the 1980s, productivity in the manufacturing sector grew 35 per cent, but growth in real wages did not ensue; similarly, corporate profits throughout the 1990s have reached new record highs virtually every year.[140] In Germany in the 1980s the wage index was constant, but profits posted by industrial companies doubled,[141] and the process is gathering momentum. However, we do not believe that these figures testify to increased social injustice. This is largely because the dividing line between the proletariat and knowledge workers today is very narrow, and the profits of corporations can in many cases be treated as the result of the labour of their owners and managers. The immeasurability of knowledge, today the main product of most companies and corporations, and their monopoly over their own information technologies are resulting in higher profits for corporations in general, leaving the earnings of unqualified workers unchanged. The reflection of the incomes of knowledge workers as profits is yet again proof of the unacceptability of cost indicators in today's conditions, demonstrated most clearly in individual industries and enterprises.

It is important to mention that the growth pattern of the previously similar macroeconomic indicators like GNP and the ISEW, worker incomes and corporation profits changed radically between 1973[142] and 1979,[143] just when the Western world was entering the first stage of post-economic transformation.

The second example of the inadequacy of traditional indicators is the growth of the non-material and intangible (according to economic principles) assets of contemporary corporations and the related consequences. With the spread of modern technologies, the main indicator of the activity of a company becomes not its book-value but its ability to increase its share of the market and to introduce new highly competitive products. The latter is based only partially on objective factors. For example, when Microsoft in 1995 introduced Windows 95, its share prices soared within a few days to top those of Boeing, the United States' biggest exporter;[144] however, it must not be forgotten that the introduction of the new product was in this case accompanied by the most expensive advertising campaign in the computer industry, which cost the company $250 million,[145] and that Microsoft is clearly the US company about which most legends are spun.

Meanwhile three very alarming factors can be observed today. One is associated with the fact that the share of non-material and intangible assets of modern companies and corporations is growing, yet not always in line with the traditional understanding of the growth of their real economic potential. Netscape, a widely-known firm founded at the beginning of 1994, with assets worth $17 million and little more than 50 employees, now has a market value of more than $3 billion.[146] However, the company does not make profits, and the owners of its shares, which in 1995 alone rose in price from $28 to $130,[147] cannot expect any dividends in the foreseeable future.

Looking at the US economy as a whole, we see that

> over the past twenty years there has been a significant widening of the gap between the values of enterprises stated in corporate balance sheets and investors' assessments of their values. [The average market-to-book value ratio for US public corporations over a twenty-year period between 1973 and 1993 increased from 0.82 to 1.692.] The gap in 1992 indicates that roughly forty per cent of market value of the average US public corporation was reduced in the balance sheet by about 40 per cent.[148]

This rule is applicable to various sectors of the economy to differing degrees. The book-value of companies averages at about one-third of their market value in such areas as healthcare, personal services, radio broadcasting and publishing, electronics and data processing; it is 80 per cent or more in the automotive industry.[149] This being so, it is evident that within each branch of industry the capitalization of a company will depend on the level of qualification of staff and management,[150] although, on the whole, the trend can be clearly seen whereby new and aggressive companies possess more intangible assets than those which have worked on the market for a longer period of time: the corresponding ratios are 0.45:1 for IBM, 1.35:1 for Hewlett-Packard, 2.8:1 for Intel, 9.5:1 for Microsoft, 10.2:1 for Reuters and 13:1 for Oracle.[151] Netscape's ratio is a staggering 60:1.

These processes also have a marked effect on all aspects of economic life. On the one hand, stock indexes grow irrespective of the true development of the production of goods and services. If in the United States industrial output rose by not more than 50 per cent between 1977 and 1987, the market value of shares quoted on all American stock exchanges increased almost fivefold,[152] while the volume traded on the New York Stock Exchange (NYSE) and the combined capital of all the finance houses operating on the exchange grew more than tenfold.[153] Moreover,

> in the entire year of 1960, a total of 776 million shares of stock were traded on the New York Stock Exchange – about 12 per cent being securities of the companies concerned – and each of those shares had

been held, on average, about eight years. By 1987, at the height of the boom, 900 million shares were exchanging hands each week, with the result that 97 percent of the outstanding shares were traded during the year.[154]

At the height of the stock market crisis of late October 1987, an absolute record was set on the NYSE: 1.196 billion shares were traded in the space of one single trading session;[155] and on that same day the sum total of trading on the five leading world stock exchanges exceeded 9 billion shares.[156] On the other hand, it has to be said that overall financial assets are becoming more and more distanced from real output. As a result of the process, which began in the second half of the 1980s, 'by 1992 financial assets from the advanced nations of the Organization for Economic Cooperation and Development totaled $35 trillion, double the economic output of those countries ... [It is predicted] that the total financial stock will reach $53 trillion, in constant dollars, by the year 2000 – that is, triple the economic output of those economies'.[157]

The third alarming factor is associated with the rapid growth of shares leading to an unprecedented cleavage between the financial and stock markets, and real economic growth, especially noticeable in the last few decades, when 'money, instead of being a measure of value as it had been, became in every developed country just so many cards in political, social, or economic games'.[158] Given the fivefold growth in the market value of shares in American companies between 1977 and 1987, which we have already noted, the correction that occurred in 1987 amounted to not more than 25 per cent. During the following decade, economic growth was lower than in the 1980s, but even so the previous achievement on the stock exchange was repeated, and by August 1997 the Dow Jones Index was up 4.75 times, representing a twofold increase since the beginning of 1996 alone. Such a situation is bound to lead us to the conclusion that 'today, shares are over-valued to a much greater degree, and yet, on Wall Street, no attention is paid to this factor', largely because those who hedged against excessive overvaluation one or two years ago have to a large degree been discredited by the successes achieved by the market since that time;[159] the gap between indicators that reflect growth in real production and the successes of the stock market continue to widen. Evidence of this was provided, much less than ten years ago, by the corrections to the stock indexes of October 1997, when only peripheral overvaluations and, to an even greater extent, those markets subject to the influence of foreign investors, such as Hong Kong, South Korea, Russia, Brazil, Hungary and a few others, found themselves faced with a fall in quotations comparable to that experienced by the developed countries in 1987; similarly, during the

October 1987 crisis, indexes on the NYSE fell by 6.7 per cent, those in London by 7.6 per cent, in Paris by 11.2 per cent and in Frankfurt by 14.5 per cent; in the last two cases the reverse shifts were both swift and radical.[160]

It should be admitted that the emerging trends cannot be surmounted within the foreseeable future, not so much because the dangers arising from them have not been adequately assessed, but rather because they are entirely in line with the main thrust of the undermining traditional value-based relationships. The subjectivization of the valuations that have occurred on the stock market has today become a self-perpetuating process. On the one hand, this is caused by the activity of traders, which is increasing at an even more rapid rate than the growth rate of stock indexes. All financial experts today are convinced that this process will assume yet more active forms in the very near future. Despite the fact that the 1 billion share deals per day mark was passed only once on the NYSE, its present capacity allows the processing of deals involving 3 billion shares a day; on a NASDAQ computerised system with half the turnover towards the end of 1997, the capacity was available for trading in 1.5 billion shares daily,[161] and a similar trend is observable on stock market-places worldwide. The growth in trading and the specifics of the groups of the traders give rise to additional factors of indeterminacy; thus it is not at all easy to explain by traditional logic the fall in American stock indexes in the wake of the collapse of the Southeast Asian markets which has in the first place hit the most dangerous competitors of American producers.

On the other hand, we observe less and less of a link between share prices and such traditional factors as corporate profits and percentage levels. The movement of stock indexes today runs counter to the usual rules rather than in obedience to them: thus the boom of the first half of the 1990s happened under conditions where real yield for US Treasury Bond holders was 8.2 per cent annually;[162] the period from July 1996 to August 1997 was no less extraordinary, being marked by growth in all the basic American stock indexes (DLJ, DJ US Market, S&P 500, NYSE Corporate, NASDAQ Composite and Value Line), ranging from 31.2 per cent to 37.8 per cent,[163] at the same time as a rise in the dollar exchange rate against the major world currencies, which was bound to worsen the position of American producers. If in the 1970s dividends on shares totalled between 7 per cent and 11 per cent annually, the indicator today is no greater than 2 per cent for the highly liquid shares.

Meanwhile, we must not overlook another important problem clearly evident in any analysis of the movement of the present-day stock market. While, for example, in the course of economic crises right up to 1973 it was impossible not to detect a close correlation between stock market movements and reactions in the production sector, in recent years that correlation has been on the decline. In 1986–9, US GNP revealed a persistent upward trend, rising on average by 3.3 per cent per annum (and notably by 3.1 per cent in 1987),[164] while the drop in the stock index in 1987 was slightly less than the collapse that marked the beginning of the crisis and the stagnation of the late 1920s and early 1930s, during which the country saw a 24 per cent fall in GNP. Analysing the situation in late October 1987, J. Baudrillard writes: 'if anything can be gleaned from this situation, it is the degree of difference between the economy as we think it to be and the economy as it is really; and it is precisely this difference that protects us against a real collapse of the production economy'.[165] This absolutely sound thesis has a reverse side to it, however. Indeed, stock market catastrophes may be capable of making less impact on the real dynamics of the economy, but those real dynamics must no longer be seen in their positive aspects as a sufficient condition for the absence of such catastrophes; the high level of competitiveness of American industry and encouraging macroeconomic indicators did not prevent an almost 10 per cent correction in the stock market index in Autumn 1997. At the same time, trends clearly discernible in the modern economy mean that a sector which is linked to the movement of the said illusory indicators is becoming an important place for the concentration of efforts and an important source of livelihood for an ever-growing number of people, and a collapse of the financial sector in and of itself, even without entailing a concomitant collapse of production, may lead to no fewer social upheavals than a crisis in industry. Today's subjective economy is losing the former link with the real objective economy, but, in losing that link, it is itself becoming a given element determining the economic growth of modern society.

Therefore the view that 'the first priority is to reregulate finance capital. Governments will have to reimpose some of the control measures that they discarded during the last generation, both to stabilise financial markets and to make capital owners more responsive to the general needs of the producing economies'[166] is correct. Meanwhile, the majority of developed countries, including the United States, regarded themselves as suffering to a greater extent not from an excessive freedom of their economic subjects, but rather from active interference by government in economic life; according to J.E. Garten's calculations during 1991–94 state regulation cost the average American family 7000 dollars a year, whereas direct taxes paid by that family did not exceed 6000 dollars;[167] consequently, it is abundantly clear that there will be no more of such measures. By the same token, the danger is that today's stock market, which already virtually ignores the conformities of real production, is still being controlled under the influence of the change in traditional economic indicators and is retained as a substantial factor in the development of modern post-industrial countries.

Lastly, a third example to illustrate the gap between the real movement of material values, services and information, on the one hand, and financial flows on the other, is the expansion of operations with national currencies and new financial instruments. Their volume is growing more and more compared with other segments of the stock market, and they are naturally capable of influencing the state and development of national economies in the most radical way. Amid the globalization of the economy this phenomenon does not cause surprise, but the rates of its growth are greater than would appear to be safe in terms of economic stability. Daily trading on the currency market in 1992 averaged about $1.2 trillion, nearly double the 1989 level; just as significantly, this growth did not comply either with the scale of the real assets of countries represented on the market or with the volume of their national bank reserves. In 1983, when the currency markets of the United States, West Germany, Japan, Britain and Switzerland sustained a daily turnover of $39 billion, the foreign exchange reserves of the US FRS and central banks of the four other countries reached $139 billion; in 1992, when reserves grew to $278 billion, trading volume rose 16 times to $623 billion.[168] In the 1980s, there was also a no less active increase, at the rate of 20 per cent per annum, in the volume of foreign direct capital investment. Between 1983 and 1989 alone, the volume of government securities and promissory notes traded on the stock markets of the leading industrial centres more than tripled.[169] In the first half of the 1990s, the growth rates of these indicators were up by nearly 35 per cent.

All of these examples show that 'the financial system has achieved a degree of autonomy from real production unprecedented in capitalism's history, carrying capitalism into an era of equally unprecedented financial dangers'.[170] And this situation is not the simple result of increased activity by market speculators, capable of making a few financial companies and banks go bust; it is the result of profound changes in the economic structure, changes which have not received adequate expression on the surface level today. The world economy, developing largely under the influence of essentially non-market factors, is now achieving more complete market forms which one day will inevitably enter into an irreconcilable variance with the new post-economic conditions. In that situation a serious financial crisis, like that of Autumn 1997, would be a lesser evil; however, it has every chance of acquiring proportions far greater than an ordinary exchange crash. The fact is that the separation of financial flows from real economic development is merely one manifestation of the preservation by the post-economic society of its economic form;

the other aspect of this phenomenon is concerned with the credit sector and government finances.

The emergence of the post-economic society and new relations around cost evaluations exerts a very marked influence on economic life in another way, for two important reasons which, from the point of view of their own form, relate more to property, although they too emerge in the process of surmounting value proportions. One of these factors is linked to the acquisition by information and knowledge of the status of factors of production. This is making the main form of investment in new processes and technologies ability and knowledge, rather than money. As a result, as the share of knowledge workers grows in the able-bodied population, the volume of investments in money form is decreasing without creating economic decline. On the contrary, the process is parallel with the intensive development of the scientific and high-tech sectors both in industry and in the services. The accumulation of resources is embodied in people themselves and in their abilities; it is the latter that provide economic growth, which cannot in effect be explained in terms of traditional economic theory. The US economy has been on the up since the start of the 1990s, but this may seem irrational if it is remembered that, in 1989, US citizens tended to be the biggest spenders among the populations of all developed countries, and savings constituted not more than 4.6 per cent of disposable income.[171] However, the government, as we have mentioned, is guided mainly by economic categories and needs free monetary resources to deliver social, military and political pro- grammes. The consequence of this disproportion is the growth in budget deficit and the internal government debt.

The other factor is caused by the fact that with the development of the information economy the productivity of new branches, expressed in traditional cost indicators, is falling. Between 1958 and 1980, the knowledge industry, or knowledge production, rose by 20 per cent as a share of US GNP.[172] The cost of this increase was to double the number of workers involved in the production of information and knowledge compared with the late 1950s; if, in 1960, GNP produced by each worker in the tertiary sector came to more than 77 per cent of that produced by each industrial worker, the indicator in 1992 had fallen to 70 per cent, and in recent years the process has been speeding up. This does not only reflect the unreal nature of cost indicators; these in today's conditions make an information product artificially undervalued, while the results of traditional manufacturing are overvalued. Therefore the important adjustments to the trade balances of the leading powers are fully comprehensible. Where about a quarter of all American exports consists of commodities which virtually represent intellectual property rights,[173] and exports by the countries of Southeast Asia consists primarily of consumer goods, the problem of the uneven evaluation of various goods then becomes a problem of international accounting. In our view, this factor plays an important least role in determining the foreign trade deficit of developed countries; we will mention also that the most dangerous trade balance discrepancies are to be seen in the United States, the country that has advanced more than others towards the post-economic state, while the situation is entirely favourable in Japan, which currently combines the advantages of industrial production with some elements of the post-economic structure.

Thus it would appear that the rapid progress towards the emergence of the post-economic society is causing negative factors to arise in the countries where it reveals itself, and governments are having to try and rectify the situation. Moreover, this is an extremely difficult, if not impossible, task. The best example is the United States. Even if account is taken of the deficit reduction achieved under the Clinton administration (and this seems to be a matter of fact: in 1996/7 the Federal budget deficit amounted to only $22.6 billion, or 0.3 per cent of GNP, representing a reduction over the previous five years from a level of $290 billion, or 5 per cent of GNP),[174] the statistics for growth of the national debt continue to be alarming; moreover, they reveal a clear division in post war history between the periods up to and after the mid-1970s which accompanies the pattern of all main macroeconomic indicators for Western countries. If during the 20 years up to that period the debt rose from $274.4 billion to $483.9 billion, or by 76.35 per cent, in the next period the debt rose to $4.67 trillion, an increase of 9.65 times.[175]

It costs so much to service this debt that the growth of this indicator as a result of the government's efforts to reduce the deficit can neither be altered nor slowed down. Between 1992 and 1994 alone, when the deficit was reduced by nearly 20 per cent, the debt grew by 17 per cent. As William Greider mentioned,

> despite this budget discipline the debt costs continued to escalate. In practical reality, the US government had to borrow more money every year – $200 billion or more – simply to pay the interest due on its old debt. ... Paying the rentiers has become a major function of national governments. In the United States, interest costs had swollen from $52.5 billion in 1980 to $184 in 1990. By 1996, debt payments would reach $257 billion – despite deficit-reduction campaigns by Clinton and his predecessor, George Bush. US spending devoted to debt was roughly equal to national defense or Medicare and Medicaid combined.[176]

It is worth stressing that the debt problem exists not only on the federal budget level. Moreover, here we see only the tip of the iceberg, and we are unable to estimate the scale of the process. In the first half of the 1990s, the US government, in addition to the purely federal debt of about $4 trillion, had also issued budgeted guarantees for a whole host of programmes, from the development of agriculture to aid for students, totalling $6 trillion. Also, from the second half of the 1980s, the practice of local government (state and county) loans was introduced. These also grew in size in the 1990s in connection with reduced federal subsidies. There was also consumer credit, and the debt of private individuals approached the federal debt in size. Companies also acted as borrowers, so much so that more than 90 per cent of their profits after tax went on paying off bank interest.[177] As a result, the accumulation of debt reached unprecedented proportions, and totalled 180 per cent of GNP.[178] If present trends continue, the volume of national and municipal debt in 30 years from now will amount in the United States to 250 per cent of GNP, twice the debt ceiling attained in the years immediately following the Second World War.[179]

The same happened in other countries (although not in Japan). However, the given indicator is lower in countries where the level of employment and the structure of GNP are closer to the standards of industrial society. Among members of the European Union, in which gross debt in most countries is greater than gross national product, the indicator is lower in Sweden and Germany, at 95 per cent and 60 per cent, respectively;[180] however, it is known that in these countries the industrial sector generates more GNP than in other members of the EU. The only country not to close 1996 with an internal debt or to exceed budget revenues with spending was, as before, the Vatican.[181]

Germany's example illustrates how the problem of deficit and growth of government debt in Europe is escalating. Between 1980 and 1991, the federal government's external debt rose from 38.05 billion to 243.21 billion Deutschmarks: the debt as a share of exports rose from 10.9 per cent in 1980 to 75.3 per cent in 1993; as a share of GNP from 2.6 per cent to 16.6 per cent; and as a share of foreign exchange reserves from 43.1 per cent to 368.4 per cent.[182] Such huge adverse changes can be explained largely by the need to support the unified Germany, although Germany today is the main advocate of the speedy formation of a new European currency system, and its own economic processes may throw up major obstacles to this. Most other European countries are facing the same problems. And it is becoming more and more commonplace to increase the government debt and deficit in order to take the edge off the most serious social problems. Measures like these were the core of the programme of the Labour Party, which won the British elections, and the French Socialists, who won elections in France, in 1997. The conservatives in Germany are also likely to lose their majority in the next elections to the German parliament in 1998.

Escalating indebtedness is one of the most acute problems of modern economies. We agree entirely with Zbigniew Brzezinski, who regards national indebtedness and trade deficit as the two most dangerous phenomena which threaten the stability of the United States.[183] Present-day doctrines about reducing the balance of payments, which include plans in the United States to achieve a balanced budget by 2004 and the proposed switch to a single European currency (one of the requirements for which is to reduce debt to 60 per cent of GNP), are unlikely to be fully implemented; trends in recent years, despite a whole string of optimistic figures, especially for the United States, do not suggest that the goals set can be achieved.

Many other questions regarding the regulation of trade balances both in individual developed countries and in the post-industrial world as a whole remain to be solved. Attention has usually been focused on the emergence of Japanese capital in Europe and the United States (in the 1980s alone, Japanese investments in their economies rose from just a few hundred million dollars to $54 billion,[184] and the greater disequilibrium of commodity flows between the main centres of the post-industrial world (Japan's trade surplus, which between 1980 and 1995 rose by 27 times, from $5 billion to $135 billion, was more than half accounted for by visible exports to the United States).[185] However, these tendencies to a certain extent are compensated by the interaction of the economic systems of individual post-industrial countries. As we have mentioned, Japanese car manufacturers may be producing a large number of cars in the United States and in Europe, but, on the other hand, IBM is one of the biggest exporters of computers from Japan. Between 1969 and 1983, American companies boosted output of their products abroad by more than 12 times,[186] and the trend is becoming stronger. Therefore the main process should be recognized as one of the escalation of trade disproportions on the fringes of the post-industrial world.

Japan became a net exporter virtually before it was recognized as a member of the group of the world's leading industrial nations. Many comment that today, having failed to match the technological level of the United States or its level of productivity, Japan has ceded first place in trade with the United States to China and other rapidly developing countries from the region. If, in 1988, China accumulated a surplus of $3.5 billion for the year in trade with the United States, seven years later the indicator had risen nearly tenfold, to reach $33.8 billion; from June 1996 the US deficit in trade with China exceeded its deficit in trade with Japan ($3.3 billion, compared with $3.2 billion, a month). Meanwhile, Chinese exports to the United States are four times greater than imports from America, while the corresponding figure for Japan is just 1.6 times.[187] These assessments, incidentally, are substantially overstated, and real figures look far more correct. (As van Kemenade wrote, 'the US figures for Chinese trade surpluses were approximately \$22.8 billion in 1993, \$29.5 billion in 1994 and \$33.8 billion in 1995. Chinese statistics, however, show much lower figures: approximately \$6.3 billion in 1993, \$7.5 billion in 1994 and \$8.6 billion in 1995. There are two main reasons for the discrepancies: one is that the US figures include the entrepot trade via Hong Kong and Singapore, and the other is the difficulty of determining which part of the processing was done where, and to whose trading balance it should be credited'.[188] Nevertheless, the disparities, linked, on the one hand, with the active import both of overvalued mass-produced goods from the new post-industrial countries, and of the relatively undervalued primary commodities from the Persian Gulf and other Third World regions and, on the other hand, with the export of information and technology outside the post-industrial community, require a very careful approach indeed. This is because in today's conditions the methods of organizing such interaction also condition the prospects for the accession by developing countries to the club of post-industrial powers, and the nature of the approach by the European Union, the United States and Japan to poorer countries, which will be discussed below.

Regarding exports and imports of products and technology, it is necessary once more to mention that here we are witnessing the supremacy of the post-industrial nations in the modern world economy. The less developed states of Africa and Latin America, and the Persian Gulf states, are geared towards exporting their natural wealth – resources that cannot be replenished and the limitations of which are clear. The newly industrialized powers are exporting more and more consumer goods, manufactured by industrial methods from limited resources. The post-industrial countries, for their part, are investing in each other and are exporting to other countries mainly knowledge and information. Yet

> knowledge and information are a very peculiar economic resource. When moved from the United States to Europe, it is a net import to Europe and a net addition to the European stock of capital. But there is no corresponding decrease in the American stock of capital. We have conveyed knowledge, and we get paid for it. But we have not 'exported' it. Indeed we have probably enriched our own knowledge resources and made them more productive. This is not possible with any other resource. No other resource can be conveyed from one man to another in such a way that the process of transfer enriches both.[189]

Moreover, since it is 'much easier to transfer knowledge between regions at a comparable level of development than it is to transfer knowledge to countries where there are few people ready to receive it',[190] investments by developing countries are becoming more and more confined within the framework of the post-industrial world itself.

To round off our assessment of the inner disparities of the post-industrial civilization, we will mention that these contradictions are far from a final solution. The emergence of the fundamentals of the post-economic society in Europe, the United States and Japan today is synchronized with the process of change of the location of each of the centres in the structure of the world economy. This highlights the quantitative aspects of several of the processes in the making, rather than their content. Instead of radically reviewing the methods and forms of regulating the financial sector, most governments are trying to alter their balances of trade and payments, which are of secondary importance from the point of view of the development of post-economic society as a whole. Instead of making more use of new methods to assess economic successes, attempts are being made to provide growth in GNP and other indicators which are far from reflecting the changing reality.

It looks like all centres of the post-economic world will at some stage achieve relatively similar macroeconomic characteristics. Just as the United States 30 years ago was a net investor in Europe, Japan today is a net investor in the United States. The European Union and the United States both export and import roughly equal amounts of capital, while Japan's ratio of exported/imported capital to/from the US is nearly eight times greater. This, in our view, proves merely that preserving relative stability in the post-industrial world, at least while post-economic transformations are taking place, presupposes close interaction between the post-industrialized countries and the less developed territories. The status of net creditor held today by Japan may tomorrow shift to other, so far less industrialized countries, and such disproportions will be observed until the post-economic world begins to develop fully on its own basis. The most important factors for this possibility are, on the one hand, overcoming the inner disparities that arise on the path towards post-economic transformation and, on the other, providing, if not the most ideal, then the most acceptable type of cooperation between developed countries and the rest of the world, a cooperation capable of eliminating the danger both of a global ecological catastrophe and of the uncontrolled development of political processes in the poorest regions of the planet.

The Post-industrial World and the External Environment: The likely scenario for the interaction

In the initial period of the transition from the industrial to post-industrial society, discussion of the economic confrontation and potential political confrontations between developed states and the rest of the world has led many researchers to deduce that these problems may be the main ones in the 21st century. But the last 20 years have changed a lot in the alignment of economic and political forces and in the assessment of the prospects for the development of post-economic civilization.

We think that relations between the developed countries and the rest of the world in their economic aspect can be seen from several points of view. Firstly, the growing struggle by some developing countries for the right to join the community of post-industrial nations is of great interest; this attempt is already today raising many of the economic problems experienced by the West. Secondly, the post-industrial world is clearly becoming anxious about the primitive methods of industrialization being used elsewhere, which are worsening the environmental problems. Thirdly, it is already clear which countries for the coming decades will not only be unable to join the group of developed countries but will not even be able to provide their people with acceptable levels of consumption, something that will inevitably result in political problems with which mankind will have to contend in the next century.

As we have mentioned, the current type of cooperation between the developed world and the developing countries differs radically from that which prevailed before the beginning of active post-economic transformation. In the new conditions, countries of the South are no longer the 'Third World', a position which has to a considerable extent determined the results of the political confrontation between the 'first' and the 'second' worlds. Having lost the status of Third World countries, they also lost a considerable amount of the resources which they would have received from outside. Today, most of the countries that have not in the past been part of the 'first world' are counting on being its 'reserve' on the understanding that dynamic development outside the post-industrial perspective is impossible. Therefore the post-economic community can and must dictate its own conditions to these countries in the confidence that those conditions will be accepted.

We are not saying that the time has come to announce a new Monroe Doctrine, but we are stressing that developing countries today do not even possess the right to choose that they held in the 1960s and 1970s, not even on a very limited scale. They represent the rearguard of the post-economic world, and the only question is what position they will adopt in this rearguard and how much it will cost the great powers to make this wagon and bring it into organized motion.

The Economic Aspects of Confrontation

The current post-industrial world lives side-by-side with a number of countries representing already fully identifiable 'zones of growth'. Their economic development is capable of altering the general picture of the globe at the start of the 21st century. A sufficient understanding of relations between these countries and traditional centres of economic might today requires, as never before, a radical review of the ideas and prejudices that have formed over the decades.

About 15 years ago, Alain Touraine wrote that 'aujourd'hui, la sociologie doit étudier les trois mondes: le premier, celui des sociétés industrielles avancées d'Occident; le deuxième, qui correspond aux pays communistes; et le Tiers-Monde'.[191] These traditional terms are unacceptable today, as the most important factor for assigning countries and regions to one group or another is no longer their political or ideological characteristics, but the level of their economic development. Dismissing the possibility of dividing the world into 'first', 'second' and 'third', of placing North against South, Donella and Dennis Meadows, from a slightly technicized but nonetheless generally correct point of view, write: 'the distinction we think is most accurate for our purposes is between cultures that are industrialized and less-industrialized'. In these terms they go on to suggest:

> the degree to which different parts of the world (including whole nations and also subsets of populations within nations) have undergone the Industrial Revolution: the degree to which their economies have shifted from agriculture-based to industry- and service-based, the degree to which their main energy sources are fossil and nuclear fuels, the degree to which they have absorbed the labor patterns, family sizes, consumption habits, and mindset of the modern technological culture.[192]

However, the less industrialized countries should not be viewed as a single entity. They are a number of highly diverse groups and conglomerates, according to both their contemporary slot in the world economy and the prospects that are opening up.

Countries which do not belong to the post-industrial group are often subdivided into several groups by criteria which appear superficial and which do not give a full idea of their opportunities and prospects. According to World Bank classification, developing countries are subdivided into states with low-income, lower-middle income and upper-middle income groups, while all of these together are in contrast to the developed powers, who are classed as high-income countries. Criteria include life expectancy, average per capita consumption of basic items, access to education and healthcare, and so on. Obviously, on this basis countries like Hong Kong, Singapore and West Asia fall into the high-income group, putting them on the same footing as societies in the post-industrial world. States with a low level of development are those with a per capita income of $290 a year, that is, with a population that lives below the absolute poverty line.[193] As a result, this approach assigns most developing countries to the lower-middle and upper-middle income groups and, in our view, cannot serve as a serious instrument to analyse the prospects for their development.

We believe that a more productive approach is one based on an assessment of the role which this or that country or territory is capable of playing in the economic development of mankind in the decades to come. From this point of view, it is necessary to distinguish four regions capable of becoming important catalysts for change. The first is definitely the countries of Southeast Asia and China. Leadership here is gradually shifting from Japan, which is being incorporated into a group of post-industrial powers – with a new quality of economic growth stemming from its emerging post-industrial status and where unbridled expansion has been halted – to China, which is establishing an economic hegemony in Asia. The second place is held by certain industrial regions of South America which, for all their poverty and major social problems, possess considerable technological and intellectual potential which is capable of playing a role in their development. The third group is West Asia, where countries have to a degree crossed the boundary of post-economic development and will remain in the next century among the most developed, but at the same time least dynamic, regions of the world. The fourth region consists of Russia and the European members of the Commonwealth of Independent States, which possess high technological potential but which may gradually become a secondary and subordinate, but nevertheless integral, part of the European economic organism. For this they must develop sectors capable of filling the consumer market with goods, even if this is achieved with imported technologies and capital, and breed workers able to appreciate Western values and standards of conduct.

These countries, the majority of which will remain incapable of influencing the world economic situation to a great extent, are juxtaposed with a group of clear outsiders, the most obvious being countries of Africa, which have only a minimum of technological potential and a very low level of industrial development, and which are constantly plagued by ethnic conflicts. The situation in some Latin

American states, with their serious social problems and low standard of living, appears to be as yet undefined. And economic progress is unlikely to be achieved in countries of Southern Asia – from India and Bangladesh to Cambodia and Laos – which are overpopulated and also dogged by religious and cultural confrontation. As a result, the world's population is divided into three parts: about one-fifth lives in post-economic and nearly post-economic countries; two-fifths in countries which in the first half of the next century are likely to achieve considerable economic growth; and two-fifths in countries which at best will eradicate poverty.

Concerning the influence of developing countries on the economic situation in post-industrial societies, it is necessary in our view firstly to focus on the Asian countries, as only they are capable of posing serious competition during the first decade of the 21st century. Widespread beliefs that these countries are a combined entity confronting the United States and European Union are far from true. Even so, the economic progress in the countries of Asia is providing the major part of the overall rise in the economic indicators of the developing countries, which has reduced the share of industrial powers in world output from 72 per cent in 1953 to 64 per cent in 1985.[194] In the first half of the 1990s, rates of growth also remained very high: from 1991 to 1995, eight out of ten economies showing growth rates above 50 per cent were concentrated in the Atlantic–Pacific region, while for China and Indonesia the given indicators were 136 per cent and 124 per cent, respectively; on 1996 results, growth of more that 7.5 per cent was shown only by the economic systems of Vietnam, China, Malaysia, Singapore and Thailand.[195]

The Asian economies, from Japan to Vietnam, have a number of similar features, many of which stem from the nature of the values prevailing in those societies and from behavioural stereotypes. Even the relatively superficial view of the personal and societal preferences of Americans and Asians indicates a high degree of disparity between them. In contrast to Europe and the United States, where the driving motives are personal values, and the main social guidelines freedom of expression and personal freedom, the Asian states are inclined to communitarianism and self-discipline, and workers there would prefer to work hard in strictly organized collectives.[196]

Both traditional values and the desire to preserve and increase well-being that has been achieved over the last decades are inclining the populations of the latter countries towards accumulation and investment; for example, personal savings in these countries typically account for more than one-third of GNP, and according to 1996 results they attained 48 per cent in Singapore, 40.5 per cent in China, 38.7 per cent in Indonesia and 35.1 per cent in South Korea,[197] whereas the corresponding indicators for the 1990s have not risen above 17 per cent in the United States, 19 per cent in Britain and 21 per cent in Germany and France.[198] However, devotion to labour values and high degree of organization leads to the more effective, although to a certain degree extensive, use of human resources. As we know, 'Japanese workers or "salarymen" work on average 2,150 hours per year and rarely take more than about 10 days' holiday per year, being at work on average some 224 hours (or nearly six weeks) more per year than their American counterparts and a staggering 545 hours (or nearly 14 weeks) more per year than the French and the Germans!' Moreover non-productive costs do not attain the scale characteristic of the United States and Europe, which can be confirmed by the fact of 'the astonishing disparity in CEO pay between the US – where the average compensation package for a CEO in one of the top 30 companies was $3,200,000 in 1992 – and Japan – where the same executive would have got just $525,000'.[199]

So we have an ideal blend of factors for rapid industrial progress and the development that goes with it in any country – from 18th century England to 19th century Germany to the Soviet Union of the 20th century. On this point we should notice that the corresponding stage is marked primarily by phenomenal external indicators of productivity and relatively low overall results. In the same way as in the USSR the industrial development of the 1920s–1940s led to overstrain for all the forces of the nation rather than to a substantial improvement in their material well-being vis-à-vis the rest of the world, so too, today, 'a reduction in the gap between the industrial potentials of countries should not be identified with their coming closer to one another in the realm of providing social prosperity'.[200] In the course of the 1980s, the per capita GNP indicator in Thailand, Malaysia and Indonesia fell by 7 per cent, 23 per cent and 34 per cent, respectively, compared with similar indicators calculated for the G-7 countries.[201] Therefore, looking at the economic development of the Asian 'tigers', it is necessary, to an ever-increasing extent, to take account of the fact that, in those societies, at their present stage of development at least, no real process of establishment of a post-industrial social structure is under way.

At the same time, among Asian states we must single out those countries which have for some time now been embarked upon the path of creating the technological bases of a modern economic system, and those that only recently started out on that road. The first group consists of Japan, South Korea, Singapore and Thailand. It can be said that they are increasingly – and, of course, on account of their specific features – being brought into post-economic transformations with all their ensuing consequences, although their economic development today suggests that they are not moving in this direction entirely on their own. However, Japanese corporations which specialize mainly in reproducible goods do not share the same traits as American companies, which develop according to their own designs, produce more information than material wealth and trade in patents throughout the world, and are demonstrating a phenomenal discrepancy between their market value and the real value of their assets. Japanese companies, involved primarily in mass-production of material goods, do not show this tendency. On the contrary, if the Dow Jones Index in recent years has grown by more than 2.5 times, the composite Nikkei Index from 1989 to 1995 fell proportionally even more.[202] Moreover, average daily turnover on the Tokyo exchange has fallen by nearly 40 times, and the average five-year growth rate of Japan's GNP between 1970 and 1994 fell from 11.5 per cent to 2 per cent,[203] whereas the results for the first half of 1997 showed signs of economic decline. These are quite natural processes. Having accumulated huge manufacturing and financial potential as an industrial power among post-industrial powers, Japan today combines elements of both systems; as an industrial power it is pressured by its neighbours, and as a post-industrial power it cannot compete on equal terms with the United States and Europe.

The second type of economy is represented by China and countries which are coming more and more into the sphere of its influence. China is the only country which, for a period of 17 years (1979–95), has sustained GNP growth of nearly 10 per cent annually; moreover, this growth of late has not slowed down but has increased; it was higher than during the 1980s at 12.8 per cent in 1992, 13.5 per cent in 1993, 11.8 per cent in 1994 and 10.2 per cent in 1995.[204] In terms of GNP, China, taking into account the recent return of Hong Kong and the incorporation of Macao, which should take place in 1999, may outstrip the United States only ten years from now. Countries nearby are quickly falling under Chinese influence, both through investments and through the activities of ethnic Chinese. By the middle of 1994, these ethnic Chinese owned controlling interests in 517 of the 1000 biggest industrial companies that top the listings on stock exchanges in Seoul, Taipei, Shanghai, Zhenjiang, Hong Kong, Bangkok, Kuala Lumpur, Singapore, Jakarta and Manila.[205] Furthermore, in Thailand and Singapore they had taken over ownership of more than 80 per cent of the leading companies, and in Malaysia and Indonesia, where the Chinese population does not constitute more than a third of the overall population,[206] 62 per cent and 73 per cent, respectively. In this connection it is quite easy to explain the entry into circulation of the term 'non-communist Chinese societies'[207] which is used more and more frequently to refer to Hong Kong, Taiwan, Singapore, South Korea, Malaysia and, sometimes, Indonesia. China and its neighbours, geared clearly towards the industrial type of development, use imported technology to saturate both their own markets and, to a greater extent, those of developed countries, and their immediate goal is not membership of the club of post-economic powers. An independent economic policy, supremacy in Asia, an independent position in the world as a political and military power, and leadership on consumer markets with the gradual orientation towards its own intellectual and technological potential are China's main short-term ambitions.

Many have commented on this state of affairs. Acknowledging that the Asia region provides up to 40 per cent of world economic growth on the eve of the new millennium, they point out that the region is clearly divided into two groups of countries: Japan, South Korea, Hong Kong, Singapore and Taiwan, on the one hand, and Malaysia, India, China and Indonesia on the other.[208] The World Bank in 1993 declared the Chinese Economic Area to be the world's 'fourth growth pole', together with the United States, Japan and Germany. Moreover, it forecast that Asia, which already possessed the world's second and third biggest economic empires, will approach the year 2020 with four of the world's five leading economies.[209] According to other forecasts, the new industrial states of the region will account for 57 per cent of the world's production of goods and services, while OECD member states, including Japan, will claim a share not greater than 12 per cent in 2050.[210]

However, we would like to warn the reader against such forecasting. According to calculations by experts of the Rome Club at the beginning of the 1970s, the Earth's resources today should be close to exhaustion, but this is far from being the case. The same may happen also with ideas that promise that China, where industrial development has been achieved only in selected areas, will become the world's leading power in half a century. We do not rule out the possibility that, from an economic point of view, it may turn out so, although the basic problem lies in the fact that today neither the People's Republic of China nor the other countries of the region have made any attempt to go beyond the boundaries of economic considerations,[211] and how weighty their economic advantages will be in the middle of the next century is hard to say.

The economic future of the Asian countries will depend on the solution of four important problems. Firstly, the main condition for their successful development and emergence as equal members of the community of post-economic powers will be to overcome the secondary and somewhat extensive character of economic growth. The traditional values that contributed to the powerful surge by the Asian countries in the 1970s cannot continue to be the basis for successful development in the future. Economic growth, which reached an annual 8.5 per cent in Singapore between 1966 and 1990, was achieved by increasing investments as a share of GNP from 11 per cent to 40 per cent, raising the level of employment from 27 per cent to 51 per cent of the population, and making the working day 50 per cent longer.[212] These factors today have largely outlived themselves, and growth has also slowed down considerably since the end of the 1980s. We have mentioned the intensive work of the Japanese worker; this, however, is rooted not so much in tradition as in the fact that Japan has officially established a working time of 2200 hours a year, compared with 1900 in the USA and 1550 in Germany.[213] But the continued use of extensive factors is possible only if a small part of the population has been involved in economic reform (as in China), or if transformations were launched from a very low initial level (as in Malaysia and Indonesia). In any event, as the standard of living increases, the level of savings and investments, the fundamental reasons for the Asian success story, are beginning to decline.

There are many examples of this in Taiwan, where savings accounted for 35 per cent of GNP in the 1970s, but not more than 25 per cent in the 1990s, and where the government debt rose from 4 per cent to 14 per cent of GNP between 1990 and 1994 alone.[214] What had seemed like an entirely sound South Korean economy, which today occupies the eleventh place in the world, is now in a completely predictable kind of crisis, where growth rates have fallen almost to zero, the external state debt stands at 22 per cent of GNP,[215] the fall in the exchange rate of the national currency exceeded 30 per cent in the third quarter of 1997 alone,[216] and the volume of foreign currency reserves, of which the country was previously so proud, is now unclear,[217] while the government is making desperate efforts to secure IMF loans three times bigger than those granted three years ago to Mexico, which few would be able to place among the developed countries.[218]

Today, taking into account the crisis of Autumn 1997, it becomes clear to what extent the reduction in growth rates has been curbed somewhat by the flow of Western investments: foreign direct investments in the Asian economy totalled $130 billion in 1993, and have tended to rise by about 10 per cent annually since, thereby, even at that period, outstripping industrial output growth in Asian countries.[219] Krugman's general assessment of the current situation in the region is very realistic: 'the newly industrializing countries of Asia, like the Soviet Union in the 1950s, have achieved rapid growth in large part through an astonishing mobilization of resources ... Their growth, like that of the Soviet Union in the high-growth era, seems to have been driven by extraordinary growth in inputs like labour and capital rather than by gains of efficiency'.[220] This formula acquires special meaning if it is remembered how Western experts exaggerated the estimated economic potential of the Soviet Union in the 1970s.

The problem of the extensive character of the economic growth of most Asian economies seriously modifies ideas about the meaningfulness of their achievements over the last few decades. When 'profits derive not from scale and volume but from continuous discovery of new linkages between solutions and needs',[221] then 'growth alone does not make for modernization. To join the rich world means to acquire the ability to grow indefinitely, not by doing more of the same but by moving continuously into ever-higher value-added production'.[222] Therefore a major review of the results and scale of the economic achievements of Southeast Asia can, in our view, be expected in the coming few years.

Secondly, the method by which Asian goods find their way to the European and American markets bears a serious incongruity. If in Germany a worker at a BMW factory receives up to $30 an hour, and in the United States workers at textile factories or in the metals industry receive respectively $10 and $24, then in Singapore a highly-qualified specialist receives not more than $4, in Mexico $2, in China and India the given indicator stands at 25 cents; and in Vietnam, where BMW set up an assembly plant in 1994, the wage is $1 per day.[223] Bearing in mind that a worker of medium qualification in the countries of Southeast Asia using Western technology is capable of achieving 85 per cent of the labour productivity of the average for post-industrial societies,[224] it should be emphasized that more than four-fifths of all the added value in this region of the world is absorbed practically without compensation[225] by consumers in the developed countries, where the goods produced are sold at low prices. So the standard of living is still low. Demand for the product is still negligible compared with that in a post-industrial state. To follow one criterion of consumer standards close to those in post-industrial states, annual income per household is $25 000, so, of the 181 million such households in the world, 79 per cent are in developed countries: 36 per cent in North America, 32 per cent in Western Europe, and 11 per cent in Japan. In the five leading Asian 'tiger' states – China, South Korea, Taiwan, Indonesia and Thailand – there were no more than 12 million families with such a high standard of living in 1990,[226] and, by the most optimistic of estimations, not more than 50 million such households will exist in the whole of Asia by the year 2000.[227] This constitutes just two-thirds of the number of such households in the United States and less than half of all households of this sort of income in the European Union, which has without doubt been the biggest single market in the world since 1993. Undoubtedly, in the countries of Asia over the last decade there has been a growth in consumption of the main industrial goods, including high-tech products; meanwhile, noting the development of the car industry, for example,[228] and the growing volume of sales in China and India of computer and communications technology, it is impossible not to take into account the fact that the rates of such growth are conditioned not so much by large absolute magnitudes as by the phenomenally low starting level, when in China there was one car per 400 people, and India, with her almost one billion population, had fewer telephones than London.[229]

This is explained by the fact that the developing countries of Asia and Latin America have concentrated their most advanced and competitive industries in so-called export-processing zones, which rose in number from two before the 1973 crisis to 116 in the late 1980s. Most of these were located in Singapore, Hong Kong, South Korea, Malaysia and Taiwan.[230] Caused by the low level of domestic demand, the policy which promoted Asian goods on the markets of post-industrial nations still did not make these new economies homogeneous. The Asian countries today cannot afford to abandon foreign markets, on which they depend. In contrast with the post-economic world, they are not self-sufficient and are able to preserve today's rate of growth thanks only to gigantic demand for their products.

Thirdly, the fastest-developing Asian countries depend on the post-industrial states in the sphere of technology and education; moreover, there is no sign that this dependence is being overcome. We have already mentioned the extent to which the post-industrial nations dominate where the sale of patents, information technology and intellectual property as a whole is concerned. They also possess the bulk of the intellectual and technological potential. The Asian countries are making their first attempts to break free of this kind of dependency; it is no accident that, over the last 20 years, Singapore has been channelling 20 per cent of all state resources into the development of education.[231] However, at the present time only post-industrial Japan boasts educational statistics which can almost rival those of Europe and the United States: some 53 per cent of Japanese school-leavers enter higher education, compared with 44 per cent in France and 65 per cent in the United States.[232] But young people from the less-developed countries prefer to study abroad. It is also calculated that the development level of higher education in South Korea and Taiwan is fully geared to present demand.[233] The number of students from these countries in foreign universities is constantly on the increase, and many of them do not return home after graduation; and even if the percentage of such students fell in the period from 1980 to 1991, in the case of South Korea from 41 per cent to 23 per cent and of Taiwan from 53 per cent to 32 per cent. Although only 23 per cent of all Koreans studying abroad remained there after graduation in 1991, compared with 41 per cent in 1980, and 32 per cent of Taiwanese students compared with 53 per cent, the figure for China remains very high, at 95 per cent.[234] And countries able to finance education sufficiently well are having to pay special attention to vocational training in order to sustain the potential of their industries. For example, there are more graduates of engineering in South Korea than in Britain, Germany and Sweden combined,[235] yet this cannot serve as a means of joining the post-industrial order, as illustrated by the record-breaking number of engineers produced by the former USSR. This problem is more acute still in China, Thailand, Malaysia and other countries in the region.[236]

Fourthly, the economic progress of the Asian nations depends radically on the scale and areas of foreign investment. The breakthrough to the level of industrialized nations achieved in recent decades by Taiwan, South Korea, Malaysia and other 'tigers' has been caused largely by a heavy flow of capital from Japan and the West.[237] Per capita foreign direct investment in Malaysia in the mid-1990s was more than $1100, and even more in South Korea and Taiwan, not to speak of Hong Kong and Singapore, where the indicator has been higher still. If in China, between 1979 and 1995, GNP grew almost fivefold, one of the most important contributors to this situation was a massive 4000 times increase in the amount of foreign investment, from $51 million to $200 billion. The need for investment in China today is greater than ever, because its per capita foreign direct investment ($105) reaches only 10 per cent of this figure for Malaysia. In the coming decade, China intends to attract some $500 billion of investments just to bring its industrial infrastructure up to date. This figure, especially in view of the volumes of investments in the Russian economy, appears grandiose, and yet, according to the assessments of Western experts, it will take 30 years and a total of $55 trillion to turn China into a fully developed country, which even then will fall short of the United States.[238] Clearly, money like this cannot be raised on international financial markets.

Therefore the economic growth of the Asian states, for all of its dynamism, and for all the changes that it brings to the alignment of forces in the contemporary world, is, on the one hand, based on secondary factors (to quote Ian Morrison, 'the tigers are extremely successful, but have not as yet broken through into the consciousness of the world as part of the first-curve mainstream'[239] and, on the other hand, is not self-sufficient, because it remains highly dependent on the reaction of the markets of the post-industrial powers.

Nor must it be forgotten, firstly, that even the quantitative indicators of the development of the Asian economies are not as striking as they would sometimes appear. China, for example, began its industrialization when average yearly per capita income was $490, above the United Nations accepted absolute poverty line of $370. As of 1993, China's GNP was $580 billion, as much as in the state of New York and far behind that of California. As William Greider commented,

> by extrapolating from the relative purchasing power of China's 1.2 billion citizens, some economists have excitedly proclaimed that China is actually the third or fourth largest economy in the world and can even catch the United States in ten to fifteen years. Measured in hard currency, the only measure that matters in global commerce, this claim is nonsense.[240]

This formula, for all of its polemic nature, is truer than many of those discussed above. Secondly, those who comment on the rapid growth of the Asian countries sometimes fail to notice that 'America also does not suffer from lack of dynamism', showing an immense capacity for renewal, and that 'the combination in America of the market and freedom, despite the existence of profound inequality and division, though aggravated through the impact of many global trends, still gives her the capability ... to generate opportunities and ideas for the whole world'.[241] The economic and social situation in the United States, characterized by high economic growth, reduced unemployment, low inflation and busy efforts in the field of scientific and technological research and design,[242] is a very stable basis for the country to mark new achievements at the start of the next millennium.

Naturally, the post-industrial powers must not underestimate the challenge to their economic stability. Tom Cannon draws the right parallel between the current situation and the alignment of forces at the start of this century. Noting the growing achievements of the Asian economies and pointing out that 'North American and European corporations cannot afford to ignore these markets,' he says: 'The UK's failure to compete effectively in North America, Germany and other growth markets at the start of the 20th century was a key point in its decline as a major industrial power.'[243] Therefore the Western world tries to monitor closely the potential for the expansion of these markets and their exploitation. In this connection, attempts to assess the progress of Asian countries from the point of view of fatal consequences for Western civilization and to seek political ways of resolving the arising economic conflicts can hardly be considered constructive.

Today's changes in the influence of the world economic centres are fully objective: as at the start of the 20th century, an island state with a paltry population on a world scale lost control in a natural way over regions with a population that ran to billions, now the industrial nations are unable to sustain a material output high enough to satisfy the needs of the whole of civilization. However, quantity indicators are not as important as they used to be; world supremacy is provided nowadays by the capability of countries and regions of swift changes, radical innovations, and technical and intellectual progress. The main task of the developed countries today is to retain their unique leadership in the information and technology spheres, and in this respect even the smallest regions in terms of population and natural resources can find themselves at the forefront of progress as long as they wish, determining the direction in which mankind will progress. It is precisely this that contains the main condition for the domination of post-industrial powers over the rest of the world, and its loss would have far more serious consequences than imbalances of trade and of flows of labour power and capital.

A survey of the economic rivalry between the Western post-industrial nations and Southeast Asia gives a sufficient idea of the economic aspects of relations between developed countries and the developing world. At issue are not problems that may arise through the hypothetical expansion, for example, of the Latin American states – they could be genuinely topical only if the Asian newcomers actually entered the group of post-industrial powers. Only in this situation will new territories become 'candidates', and to them will shift the centre of the most dynamic changes. If in the highly likely event that China and its neighbours do not succeed in becoming members of the select few, the issue of supplementing the ranks of the post-industrial nations can be considered closed. In this event the economic and technological domination of the relative minority of mankind over its majority may be preserved for many long decades, which will be fraught with new problems, the scale of which and the methods of resolving which can hardly be determined with sufficient accuracy today.

At the same time the economic disparities which in the past often took the form of economic wars and serious political conflicts can be fully resolved on the civilized level achieved by mankind. Becoming even more complex is another problem, linked to the attempt by new industrial nations to present an economic challenge to the traditional leaders. Applying in the economic struggle economic methods based on the expansion of material production, they stimulate growth in both the expenditure of raw and other materials and of energy, and the harmful impact on the environment, which puts the normal functioning of the planetary biosphere under threat. Therefore the environment is becoming one of the most important factors of that instability which mankind can expect in the next century.

Civilization on the threshold of the 21st century is facing a real threat to its own existence, based, not on political factors, as has been the case in the latter half of the 20th century, but on the discrepancies between the level of economic development so far achieved and the provision of the standards of material well-being. Post-economic transformation, the first stage of which began, in the most developed countries of the West, in the mid-1970s, is the natural response to such a state of affairs. At the same time, a whole range of problems, in particular, environmental ones, cannot be solved as a direct result of economic progress. This requires coordinated efforts by all national governments and international organizations to protect the environment and to make the 'ecological movement one of the most important driving forces on the path to a new era'.[244]

The Ecology and the Making of a Post-economic System

From the 19th century the economies of nations traditionally viewed as part of the Third World were oriented towards supplying the advanced Western economies with raw materials largely for objective reasons, but also under Europe's pressure to steer them that way. However, objective reasons behind this pattern of development probably outweighed all others. In the second half of the 20th century most former colonies won their independence, and the countries whose economies were of a close character were drawn into the global system of international division of labour primarily as exporters of fuel and other resources. The opposite roles of the industrialized and developing countries as producers of industrial goods and suppliers of material and components for their manufacturing became the chief economic factor determining ecological problems of the whole of mankind.

It is important in this context that, first, the scenario being played out in the developing countries, in which they act as raw material suppliers, pushes to the limit their natural environments and dramatically undercuts the benefits of resource-saving technologies in the industrialized world. Second, Third World nations seeking access to external markets and economic vibrancy through developing their industrial potential make the most of every available means, to the detriment of the ecology. And third, the countries which fail to maintain even the meagre standards of living of their populations slip into abject poverty and are no longer capable of dealing with devastating natural disasters. This also has a very negative effect on the whole biosphere. All these factors are compelling governments and international organizations to address the ecological aspects of the North–South divide in earnest.

The modern world is divided, as never before, into two parts, which reveal markedly different, if not opposite, trends in their development. On the one side are the European countries, the United

States and Japan, which are clearly aiming for post-economic benefits and want to leave behind the characteristic problems of industrial civilization; on the other side are the other areas where, despite the uneven economic potentials, the dominant trend is towards industrialization, whether it be pursued in genuine actions or merely proclaimed. While on the economic front this opposition is moderated and obscured to a degree by the fact that the post-industrial nations inevitably retain the production of material values as the basis for further progress, in the ecology the divergent trends come to the fore.

As we have pointed out, for close to 25 years the industrialized powers have been moving forward, devoting more and more attention and committing more and more funds to ecological conservation and restoration of the environment, cutting down hazardous waste and the use of non-renewable resources, as well as minimizing the environmental impact of production. The turnaround from previous attitudes to environmental matters was not so much motivated by growing prices for raw materials, or any other economic factors, as by the truly sweeping character of the post-industrial transformation which shifted the focus from material production onto the 'production' of information and knowledge. When Ernst U. von Weizsaecker makes the point that countries with the highest prices for natural resources enjoyed the most dynamic growth (he states, in particular, that 'there was a clear energy price "hierarchy" among the four biggest economic powers between 1975 and 1990: Japan, the EC, the USA and the USSR. It is well known which of these economies flourished and which stagnated during this period')[245] he fails to factor in a variety of other interconnected reasons which brought about the collapse and break-up of the Soviet Union, and how limited Japan's success story turned out to be compared with US economic development. Furthermore, it is precisely the United States that leads the world in R&D, including conservation technology. Let it be emphasized once again that, in our view, the radical change of attitude with regard to natural resources did not occur in the past few decades because the economic conditions in which these resources were used had changed, but as a direct consequence of inevitable expansion of the sector in which information is produced and consumed, replacing material output as the key factor of production. That is why the orientation of modern post-economic society towards ecological matters is just as natural as the information basis on which this society rests.

But not a even post-economic condition can bring man into full harmony with his natural environment. For all their significance information and knowledge are no substitutes for material resources still being used by most industries. In limiting agricultural land use, man can do little but go for far more intensive farming techniques and spread more fertilizer and pest control chemicals to cultivate the soil on the remaining acreage. Even though modern-age technology helps clear industrial waste and gas emissions of up to two-thirds of NO_2 and three-quarters of SO_2, it cannot be reasonably expected that all toxic chemicals will be removed from waste, as the high cost of treating it – at least in this day and age – would render unprofitable and impracticable any production from which such waste results.[246] The use of new energy sources, including nuclear energy, also involves the danger of radioactive contamination and inevitably creates additional problems in storing, utilizing and dumping nuclear waste, and so on.

In the meantime, we have sufficient grounds to say that the post-industrial powers currently account for far less environmental pollution per GNP unit than the developing countries and former members of the Eastern bloc. For 1994–5, the share of the United States in global production stood at 26 per cent, while accounting for 23 per cent of total carbon emissions. Germany did even better, with a ratio of 8 per cent to 4 per cent, not to speak of Japan's record 17 per cent to 5 per cent production/carbon emission ratio. As for the developing countries, Indonesia, with its 0.7 per cent share in global production, accounted for 1 per cent of carbon dioxide emissions; Russia had a ratio of 2 per cent to 7 per cent; and China, with an equivalent production share, had over 13 per cent.[247] In determining the real extent of this problem one needs to take into account continuing industrial growth in a number of Asian and Latin American countries.

Thus it will be seen that, at the turn of the 21st century, the dominant ecological problems are rooted in the steadily growing pace of natural resource utilization by the less industrialized nations, which goes hand-in-hand with a steep increase in water, air and soil pollution and the erosion of the existing ecosystems, deforestation and soil destruction across vast territories throughout the world.

While the industrialized countries are cutting down their exploitation of resources to maintain their ecosystems, the newly industrialized nations go in the opposite direction, with the consequence that, for the present, there is no global tendency towards more frugal use of resources.[248] What is more, measurements of carbon dioxide in the atmosphere, carried out at the Mauna Loa laboratory in Hawaii since the end of the Second World War, not only showed an increase of about 13 per cent between 1960 and 1995,[249] but also highlighted the conspicuous absence of any changes in the dynamics of this process; all efforts by the post-industrial world to control hazardous emissions into the atmosphere and optimize the exploitation of resources have failed to put an end to their linear growth.[250]

At a time when the post-industrial countries are taking more and more steps to maintain their ecosystems, other trends are dominant in the developing states. Europe takes pride in its massive and successful reforestation projects which have brought back to life formerly primaeval areas, and cleaned up the Rhine, and the United States has almost doubled the area of its forest and wildlife preserves and specially protected territories over the last two decades; but elsewhere, throughout a far greater part of the world, a very different and more ominous change is taking place. Since 1850, 7.7 million square kilometres of forest have been cut down,[251] and, although the modern world still has 40 million square kilometres out of the 60 million that existed on the Earth in the time before the beginning of human economic activity, it is significant that half of the losses have occurred in the last four decades. The United States lost one-third of its forested areas during the 20th century, while it took China only the last 30 years to lay waste three-quarters of its forests.[252] Half the world away, the Amazon area, which is the site of active timber cutting, was until recently the 'lungs of the planet'. The outlook appears extremely uncertain.

The situation is not any better in other areas either: drylands make up 18 per cent of all the territory of the developing countries; unrestrained overcropping and overexploitation pose an all too real threat of turning them into lifeless deserts beyond any hope of restoring them for farming. Albert Gore notes that, 'according to a joint study by the World Resources Institute, the International Institute for Environment and Development, and the United Nations Environment Programme, the dryland regions of the Third World are approaching a state of acute crisis: an estimated 60 percent of the dry croplands and 80 percent of the dry rangelands are now spiraling downward in productivity as a result of overexploitation.'[253] Since 1970, the deserts in Africa, Asia and the Americas have advanced by 120 million hectares, which is a larger area than land in agricultural use in the whole of China. Farmers the world over lost more than 480 billion tons of fertile black soil – an equivalent of all the rich black soil in the Indian subcontinent – in just 20 years. In the same space of time, over two-thirds of arable lands in Central Africa deteriorated to an extent that the soil became virtually barren and unsuitable for modern agriculture; the unique Aral Sea ecosystem is now a thing of the past; and soil condition in Brazil and other Latin American countries is worse than ever. Now it is perfectly clear that the centre of environmental deterioration from human activity has shifted to the developing world; industrialized nations still account for most air pollution, but their share in air, soil and water pollution is nonetheless diminishing, while ninety per cent of the damage in terms of extinction of species, soil erosion, the destruction of forests and wildlife, and also desertification can be ascribed to the developing countries of the Third World, bearing in mind that Russia and the CIS countries are among them, especially in respect of the sacrifice of nature to the interests of world trade. The most alarming cases of local water and air pollution today are to be found in the developing and new industrially developed countries, such as Mexico, Wuhan, Taipeh and Cairo; by comparison, the Ruhr and Pittsburgh look almost like spas.[254]

On the basis of all indications, the damage done to the environment by Third World countries, as well as its root causes, constitute a trend that is likely to continue even decades from now. Newly industrialized countries, and above all the Southeast Asian 'dragon economies', are linking their future, despite the good and justified underlying reasons, perhaps too directly, with 'making the grade' among the advanced industrialized countries, and will use every available means to catch up. The scale of the changes is noticeable even at a superficial glance. Whereas in the past the Asian countries were in the position of energy suppliers to the world market, the situation is now radically different. Up to 1993, China was a net exporter of oil; today she imports over 600 000 barrels a day and it is anticipated that the figure will reach 2.7 million barrels a day by the year 2010.[255] Uncontrolled environmental pollution is also growing at comparable rates. On the other hand, the resource-saving potential of Western nations which have actively and consciously tapped it for the last 20 years is now more or less exhausted. A long-awaited technological breakthrough in this area may take many years or decades to materialize.

According to the most optimistic estimates, toxic emissions – carbon dioxide, sulphur oxides and nitrogen oxides – into the atmosphere alone, which lend themselves more easily to strict control and to a certain extent reflect the levels of industrial development in specific geographical areas, will not exceed the stable average of 2.8 billion tons per year for the period from 1980 to 2010. A drop in these emissions cannot be expected until the year 2010, when it will be possible to employ radically new purification technology. Newly industrialized economies, most notably Southeast Asian countries, will increase their emissions of hazardous chemicals by a factor of 2.96 by that time, from 249 million to 738 million tons. But even the growth in pollution in those nations, which stems from their high rate of development, would then be outpaced by other developing economies (excluding Eastern Europe and the republics of the former USSR) which will be releasing more pollutants into the atmosphere. These countries will be responsible for 3.84 times more pollutants, and by 2015 they will leave far behind all the industrialized countries taken together, as far as air pollution is concerned.[256]

This and other forecasts indicate a very unwelcome trend towards less and less efficient economics; the current growth rates for harmful waste in newly industrialized economies are tending to go down, whereas the picture in the less developed regions is nowhere near as rosy: pollution is on the rise, full stop. Thus, for example, China, which is developing its national industry vigorously, is making extensive use of coal mined in its own coalfields for fuel. In the meantime, 'calculations by the East–West Center in Hawaii suggest that the coal China burns adds more sulphur dioxide and nitrogen oxides to the atmosphere each year than is being cut by the improved environmental controls of all the OECD countries combined'.[257] China, which already accounts for 13 per cent of the world's CO_2 emissions into the atmosphere, does not only balk at taking any serious environmental measures but also recently approved a programme to expand its grid of coal-burning power stations and other energy-producing facilities,[258] in the course of which coal consumption in the country will amount to three-quarters of world volume.[259] As a whole, by 2025, CO_2 emissions into the atmosphere by the developing countries will increase fourfold compared with the present-day level.[260]

Even more illustrative in this respect is the production and use of 'ozone-killer' substances. As is well known, this problem has had wide international repercussions and led to the signing of a Montreal Protocol on chemicals in common use which deplete the planet's protective ozone layer. The document required all countries to completely phase out their production of such chemicals by 1998. Ten years ago the major producers of ozone-depleting chemicals were the United States, the EC, Japan and Russia. Their aggregate output was 971 000 metric tons of active hazardous chemicals per volume. In 1994, all these countries produced a total of only 90 000 tons, ten times less than prior to their signing of that document. The United States was the only country to eventually stop production of these chemicals, but where are we now? China has emerged as the sole leader, producing 90 900 tons, that is, more than the whole industrialized world and Russia taken together. As if this were not enough, other newly industrialized economies as well have cranked up production of such substances: South Korea by 15 per cent, Mexico by 21 per cent, Malaysia by 24 per cent, Indonesia by 69 per cent, China by 95 per cent, the Philippines by 109 per cent and India by 193 per cent.[261]

In our view, in the decades to come the Third World is unlikely to be in shape to take any real steps to carry out vital environmental protection measures. The one serious source of funds for conservation projects could be revenue from selling their natural resources and fuel, but, in the medium term, 'traditional raw-material suppliers in the Third World will find ever-smaller markets for their ever-cheaper resources',[262] and export will only bring the majority of resource-mining countries and areas just enough returns to keep up their current levels of domestic consumption and payments to service outstanding liabilities in foreign debts. Although newly industrialized economies – above all those in Asia – possess considerable financial resources, they are primarily interested in effective investment of them in the productive sector of the economy, where environmental protection is a long way from the top of their list of priorities.

Maintaining an ecological balance requires huge financial and material input. The major problem, as we noted above, is that, while being profitable in most cases, and providing full return on the investment after a certain period in industrialized countries, environmental protection in other geographical areas cannot bring about any positive economic effect in the foreseeable future. Therefore at present the solution to environmental problems is a good economic indicator of whether or not the post-economic societies are capable of acting globally to maintain the stability of the Earth's ecosystem and, as a result, maintain the pace of their own development.

The situation concerning environmental protection, which is taking shape in the modern world, gives grounds only for guarded and limited optimism. According to minimum estimates, $125 billion annually for no less than 20 years are needed to finance programmes which can only slow down the negative processes in the 'South', let alone restore the mutilated and lost ecosystems. The true magnitude of the required input comes out in bold relief in comparison with funds provided by the industrialized nations in various assistance programmes for Third World countries: $55 billion a year in the early 1990s,[263] and the clear trend is towards less and less aid. Between 1992 and 1995, the United States cut back aid through official channels for developing countries from $11.7 billion to $7.3 billion. Despite the efforts of Japan, which provided twice as much assistance as the United States, in 1995 'overall assistance levels have been brought down to their lowest level since 1973 and now average just 0.3 percent of GNP'[264] of the leading industrialized nations.

Many economists, sociologists and politicians proposed different plans for emergency assistance to the Southern regions of the planet. Lately, following the 1992 Rio de Janeiro Earth Summit, the idea of widescale aid to the Third World has come into the focus of international debates. Put to good use, this amount of aid (about $100 billion a year) could well help address the most pressing ecological problems. Efforts are being made to bring home to the public in industrialized countries not only that it is imperative that aid be provided now, but also that these payments would not be too heavy a burden for the post-industrial world to bear in the face of the mounting crisis. Thus the authors of a recent special report compiled for the Rome Club emphasized that the cost was no more than 0.7 per cent of the GNP of the leading industrialized nations.[265] Albert Gore stressed that the United States alone is capable of coping with this task, never mind that the cost would then soar to 2 per cent of GNP.[266] At the same time, the author points out that the United States provided an equivalent share of its GNP after the end of the Second World War as part of the Marshall Plan, which for decades provided stability on the European continent.

According to this scenario the launching of a global 'Marshall Plan' of active economic aid to the Third World, and thereby significant improvement in the environmental situation in developing countries, would lead to 'the establishment, especially in the developing world, of the social and political conditions most conducive to the emergence of sustainable societies'.[267] Whether one likes it or not, such a plan is bound to run into serious difficulties. One difficulty is allocating so considerable a percentage of funds from the operating budget turnover of the industrialized nations. Now that the United States is faced with the need to gear up the modernization of production to keep US-made products competitive with Asian imports on its domestic and foreign markets, and the European Union is pulling out all the stops to bring down unemployment and deal with the challenges of creating a close European confederation, the several per cent of GNP that advocates of a global Marshall Plan say are needed would come in handy in developing their own national economies. Albert Gore's stand on that issue is also typical: as a high-profile campaigner for environmental protection in 1992, he called for broader support for the Third World; however, US foreign assistance programmes were pared down between 1992 and 1995, precisely during his term as Vice-President of the United States, running for a second term and winning the 1996 election.

Another, and equally important, problem has to do with the way in which not only hypothetical but also very real money, channelled to developing countries in the framework of environmental programmes, is spent. Countries which for many decades have provided ample proof, not only of their economic inefficiency, but also of their management which more often than not fails to put to good and effective use the financial resources flowing into their economies. This determines to a certain extent the failed negotiations and meetings in the past few years, which never fulfilled the promise of new packages of international agreements and documents regulating the next environmental measures.

We do not believe that developing countries can be regarded as a monolithic group. There is enough diversity to make each of them unique. Later we will consider the perfectly justified division of these countries into the 'Third' and 'Fourth' Worlds, proposed by some scholars. In our view, this division can also determine specific and constructive ways of solving environmental problems as well as economic ones.

One has to admit that, given the situation in Asian countries and a part of Latin America (excluding the Amazon area), any real and effective Western involvement in ecological policies of new industrially developing countries is virtually impossible. At the same time, the history of economic progress demonstrates that, in individual countries achieving higher standards of living, concern for safe ecological conditions gradually comes to the top of their agenda. Some Asian countries only recently found successful solutions to the problem of food self-sufficiency; enormous proportions of their populations have yet to be involved in the system of modern production; they have poor technology and low levels of education. That is why environmental protection is not and cannot become their natural priority any time soon. Nevertheless, it is obvious that, as soon as these countries achieve levels of development comparable with one at which the governments and citizens of Western nations recognized these same problems as their most important priority, they will give ecology very high prominence. By the time this happens they will also appreciate the purely economic benefits of up-to-date environmental protection schemes and technology, which will speed up their spreading throughout the world. Japan provides a fine example of this pattern of development: after a huge industrial leap forward in the 1960s and 1980s, it now boasts one of the world's highest indicators of appropriations for ecological needs, while accounting for the lowest pollution per GNP unit. Similar processes can be expected to unfold in the next few decades in other newly industrialized countries of Asia; two or three decades from now, that region's largest economy – mainland China – will follow suit.

Regrettably, this scenario does not ring true for the poorest countries. There the ecological problems lie chiefly in the crisis of the natural environment: forest decay, shrinking animal population, deterioration of fertile soil and so on. The most appropriate option in their case is programmes of direct aid from the international community, including the identification of some countries and regions as ecological disaster areas and control over these areas by international organizations which will carry out the necessary projects on the ground, as well as subsequent international supervision of the environmental conservation systems put in place through these projects. This brings us very close to identifying the poorest countries as a 'Fourth World' requiring more and more unconventional and competent approaches as the problems and dangers associated with such areas are woven into a very complex and unusual web.

The Problems and Outlook for the World's Poorest Regions

When tens of newly independent states were emerging in Africa and Asia during the 1960s and 1970s, many sociologists in the West and socialist East contended that statehood and political freedom of these nations would secure their speedy economic development. That never happened, dashing the hopes for sustainable growth. As R. Heilbroner remarks, calculations show that between 1750 and 1990 the gap in average standard of living between citizens of the countries of Europe and those of the developing world grew eightfold,[268] and that more than two-thirds of these imbalances have been due to the technological changes of the last few decades. Consequently, the most important mission of the post-industrial world is to minimize the impact of political, ecological and humanitarian threats, rather than establishing equal partnerships with them.

On the one hand, in the last few decades independent countries of Africa and Asia have proved to be largely incapable of efficiently using industrial technology. Worse still, they lack the necessary drive to build up their agricultural sector. Agricultural and mining techniques brought there by colonizers were from the beginning oriented towards supplying European countries with typical colonial goods and some natural resources needed by the colonizing states; for the overwhelming majority of locals in the colonies, the economic ways of primitive survival had never changed. A relatively efficient system of management created by colonists, and their effort to develop education and healthcare, had both positive and negative results: hard-won independence from foreign masters brought about a spiralling polarization of property in all developing countries and a growing gap between rich and poor, caused by the restoration of communal social structures and semi-tribal organization. Steeply declining mortality rates led to a demographic explosion, increasing the strain on the environment manifold despite very low levels of consumption, with disastrous consequences. The environment began to deteriorate at a fast rate without any rational use of land and other natural resources, or technology to offset the loss.

On the other hand, in the wake of independence from colonial rule came violent conflicts inside and between the new nations, triggered by a variety of contradictions, whether political, religious, ethnic or racial. Some of these contradictions were rooted in the policy of colonial authorities who had demarcated the borders between those countries with questionable logic. For example, Pakistan's claims on Indian territory after repeated hostilities between those two countries remain a major destabilizing factor in Asia. However, the problems of the poorest nations are determined to a far greater degree by their purely internal contradictions, ranging from a tug-of-war between various clans and factions for power in a given country to ethnic conflicts sweeping whole regions. Civil wars in Somalia, Ethiopia, Sri Lanka, Afghanistan, Mozambique and Angola have continued unabated for decades; the social clashes in Pakistan, Burma, Eastern Timore, Zaire, Guatemala and Nicaragua have gone on for just as long. About 1.75 million people were wiped out during six years of Maoist rule in Cambodia. The ethnic conflict unfolding in Rwanda and neighbouring countries before the eyes of the whole civilized world is even more tragic: one million people fell victim in less than a year (this number is higher than the death toll among soldiers and civilians during the Second World War on the Western front in 1944–5, from the allied landing in Normandy to Germany's capitulation).

As a result, the Third World divided in two even before the economic and political bankruptcy of the Second World became evident and finally brought it down. Areas enjoying relative advantages for a number of reasons – for example, the Persian Gulf countries with their oil, and small Southeast Asian countries which Japan included in its sphere of interest – have achieved significant success through high levels of investment in their national economies, moderate foreign debt and, with the exception of the Persian Gulf nations, reasonably low military spending. A majority of other countries which chose a different course of development by running up a high foreign debt, opting for economic isolationism and bloated military programmes, and in some cases indulging in essentially socialistic experiments, have drifted into the 'Fourth World' and ever-deepening poverty. Despite efforts in the last few decades to eradicate poverty in those countries, its grip became stronger and stronger. Even such relatively successful economies as India, with its burgeoning industry, and Nigeria, the most populous country in Africa and the major oil exporter on the African continent, had respective annual per capita incomes of $360 and $278, respectively, which put the standard of living of 90 per cent of their combined population of just under a billion people below the UN-defined poverty line.[269] In this situation one cannot but agree with the very uncomforting view that 'this "Fourth World" has become a concern of the world system not as a ... partner in future growth but as an object of poor relief and riot control'.[270] Meanwhile, as each year goes by, it becomes increasingly evident that 'no one among the futurologists and specialists on post-industrial society knows what should be done to deal with the problem of crying poverty and exploitation in the countries of the South'.[271]

The economic development of that part of the world in the last 30 years, even if we exclude the impact of military and ethnic conflicts, suggests a clear pattern of the demise of vast geographical areas. Uncontrollable population growth has been a defining factor in the development of these regions since the middle of the 20th century. While mortality dropped by more than 2.5 times around the world between the mid-1950s and the mid-1990s, more through eliminating mass hunger and improving nutrition than through healthcare achievements,[272] the corresponding birth rate fell by only 30 per cent;[273] the gap between these indicators was even wider for developing countries. As a result, with adjustments for active migration, from 1950 to 1985 the population of highly industrialized countries grew by a modest 41 per cent, whereas in the world's least developed regions the figure was 119 per cent. As a consequence, 'in aggregate the citizens of today's industrial democracies would account for a progressively diminishing share of the world's population. Whereas they comprised not more than a fifth of the Earth's inhabitants in 1950',[274] by the year 2025 that share will not exceed 14 per cent.[275]

It should be noted that the population growth rate is now lower in those regions of the developing world which have a marked tendency towards economic progress. Higher levels of education, increasing involvement of broad sections of population in the economy, a higher percentage of working women, and a variety of other factors make for lower birthrates, coupled with rising standards of living. By contrast, the outlook for Africa is bleak. According to current projections, by 2025 the population of the least industrialized African countries will grow by more than three times and will number 1.58 billion people; the continent's share in the world's population will soar from 12 per cent to 15 per cent and upwards.[276] By the end of the first quarter of the 21st century, Nigeria will have a population of 301 million, Zaire, 99 million and Tanzania, 84 million, meanwhile, in these countries the forecast is for the maintenance of the former level only, or even a fall, in volumes of production of the main types of product.[277]

Demographic problems not only provoke greater resource shortages and breed poverty, but also have an impact on other aspects of modern life. Until recently, urbanization in the developing countries did not attract very much attention for the simple reason that the world's most densely populated urban areas were concentrated in industrialized countries, as well as Latin America, China and India, where the governments, with varying success, could keep the situation under control.[278] A very dramatic change could occur in the near future. As early as the mid-1970s, the urban population of the developing countries had exceeded that of OECD. In 1990, it was already close to 1.4 billion; by the year 2010, it is entirely probable that it will reach 2.7 billion, that is, more than two-and-a-half times more than the number of urban dwellers in the developed regions of the planet.[279] The different directions of the trends is also underlined by the fact that, among all the biggest megalopolises, the number of inhabitants in the period between 1985 and 2000 will fall only in London.[280] The concentration of huge masses of people in vast agglomerations in the Third World, not to mention the population of African cities, who in conditions where there is a virtually complete absence of industrial production represent 'pure consumers', only heightens the risk of social conflicts and epidemics raging out of control. It is not accidental that in African cities with a population over 200 000 the number of HIV-infected people has reached one-third of the population.[281] This problem is by no means confined to the 'Fourth World'.

Now, more than ever, all odds are against any closing of the gap between the poorest African, Asian and Latin American nations and the industrialized North. Post-economic transformation, which began in the 1970s, has done more than strengthen the positions of post-industrial powers and reduce to a minimum the influence on their policy by the countries of the South. A far more painful blow has been dealt by new trends towards sharp reductions in consumption of natural resources, falling prices for these resources, and more and more attractive Western financial markets for potential investors. This spells lower revenue for developing countries, petering-out investment in their economies and worse lending terms on credit markets. In 1985, the share of investment by the post-industrial world in less developed countries was three times lower than capital the post-industrial countries invested in each other's economies. At the same time, in ten years the share of African countries, which had received 6.7 per cent of all direct foreign investment in 1975, fell to a mere 3.5 per cent.[282] Falling prices for raw materials starved their production and put many national companies out of business. The share of sub-Saharan Africa in world trade in primary goods diminished from 7.2 per cent in 1970 to 5.5 per cent in 1980, and to 3.7 per cent in 1989. By that time the national industries had come to a virtual standstill as investment, the lifeblood of industry, had been cut off. The drop in production considerably reduced the share of those countries in corresponding world indicators for the same period: from 1.2 per cent to 0.5 per cent and down to 0.4 per cent, respectively.[283]

Poor as they are, these showings are not the worst danger that exists in the current situation. Even bigger problems are being caused by a drop in production of the most basic goods, both in absolute terms for individual countries and, to an even greater extent, in per capita terms. A new trend took shape in the 1970s towards increasingly more pronounced reorientation of world production from quantitative to qualitative indicators, that is, from; manufacturing to services and information processing. Against the backdrop of the demographic shifts this takes the form of virtually zero growth in per capita volume of industrial production (no more than 10 per cent between 1973 and 1990).[284] If that is true for the 'haves', it is easy to see the implications for the regions that are the 'have-nots' of the world. As the basic needs of post-industrial countries are being satisfied more and more fully, the rate of growth of the production of the most essential agricultural crops is slowing down. (Thus wheat yields growth in the United States in the 1960s was 45 per cent of that in the 1950s, going down to 10 per cent in the 1980s in comparison with the 1970s).[285] Consumers are far more concerned about quality and the biological safety of food and other products than about price and availability.

Under present-day conditions, it is more and more apparent that the huge gap between rich and poor regions is largely caused by deficiencies in resource utilization, outdated production methods and technology, and people's inability to innovate and renovate, rather than a lack of resources. In the poorest Southeast Asian countries, about 40 per cent of fertilizer used on rice paddies 'are wasted because of inefficient application, while poor crop management, storage and handling wastes up to 20 percent of rice grown'.[286] Primitive tools keep an African farmer from growing any more than an average of 600 kilograms of grain, in stark contrast to his American counterpart, who grows no less than 80 tons. That is why, even in countries perceived as relatively prosperous in colonial times, the economies are slipping a cog. For instance, in Côte d'Ivoire, 'on a per capita basis ... GDP regressed at a rate of –4.6% per year during the 1980s'.[287] Attempts to gather no matter how meagre a harvest with the help of primitive equipment deteriorate the soil in 'Fourth World' countries on an unprecedented scale. To date, according to the information of the Food and Agriculture Organisation of the United Nations, in sub-Saharan Africa, where 42 per cent of soil in uncultivated areas has low natural fertility, two-thirds of crop land have degraded so badly that they are unusable for agriculture.[288]

Thus the countries of the Fourth World will hardly find, by the beginning of the 21st century, the ways decisively to reduce the gap separating them from post-economic civilization. In all likelihood it will be a time of interim steps to ensure the survival of the populations of the poor nations. As previously noted, the post-industrial community sets the pace and determines the trends in lowering the growth rate of agriculture and industry, which cannot be avoided in transition to a new post-economic stage. The prospects of the 'Fourth World' are changing very dramatically in the process. While world grain production grew by 182 per cent in the period between 1950 and 1990, the growth decreased to a mere 3 per cent between 1990 and 1996. That means that the per capita production of grain the world over spiralled down from the 1984 record volume of 346kg to 336kg in 1990, and 313kg in 1996, at a rate of about 0.9 per cent a year.[289] Understandably, these global trends have had the most negative effect on African, South Asian and Latin American countries. Decreased grain production only lends emphasis to the general tendency throughout agriculture in developing states (from 1985 to 1989, per capita food production fell in as many as 94 countries) and the entire economies of the 'Fourth World' (per capita income fell in 40 countries in the 1980s).[290] In 13 countries, including Nicaragua, Kenya, Zaire, Kampuchea, Ethiopia, Afghanistan, less food is produced and consumed per capita than 30 years ago.[291] Close to one-quarter of the world's population now lives in areas where production has steeply declined and continues to fall. The reach and power of this trend is seen in the fact that there were only seven countries in 1990 where average per capita income was lower than it had been in 1960, but by 1996 the number had nearly tripled, to 19.[292]

An analysis of the economic policies of 'Fourth World' nations points to another regular pattern: those countries which directed their policy towards deriving all possible advantages to their economies from economic contacts with the outside world showed growth in production volumes and other macroeconomic indicators. That upswing flowed directly from the extent to which their economies were open to foreign business. Equally important is that the countries pursuing such a policy have avoided negative per capita GNP and continue to stay in the black as far as these indicators are concerned. By contrast, countries that reduced contacts with the outside world to a minimum, which up to the 1970s had relatively satisfactory growth rates, have in the last 20 years found themselves in an economic backwater: half of the states 'moderately' directed towards minimal contacts with the outside world have started to admit a fall-off in the average per capita GNP indicator, while in the group of countries that have significantly limited their contacts with their neighbours this trend was observed in four-fifths of the overall number.[293] This goes to demonstrate the enormous complexity and contradictory character of the situation now existing in the 'Fourth World'. On the one hand, it cannot sustain the current consumption levels, let alone make any economic headway without closely cooperating with the West. On the other hand, in today's world such cooperation will not translate into an equal partnership.

One only needs to look at the directions in which the West proceeds in its relations with the 'Fourth World' and Southeast Asia's 'tiger economies' to see immediately that they are directly opposite: the West imports artificially overvalued mass-produced industrial goods from the Asian countries, while exporting artificially undervalued information and technology, but brings industrial goods into the poorest countries, while chiefly importing from them raw materials and other resources. Shrinking demand for such imports has tipped the scale to an unprecedented imbalance of trade with the 'South'. As the price index for goods from the 'Fourth World' devalued by a factor of almost 3.5 between 1974 and 1991, developing countries had no choice but more and more actively to solicit loans from Western governments, private banks and international financial organizations to maintain acceptable levels of industrial goods imports.[294] If in 1974 the foreign debt of the developing countries totalled $135 billion, by 1981 it had reached $751 billion, to skyrocket to $1.935 trillion in the early 1990s.[295] The countries of Central Africa ran up huge debts at the fastest rate; their hope for sustainable economic development now looks illusory.[296] By 1992, the ratio of foreign debt to GNP in comparison with the same figures for 1980 was 67 per cent as compared with 29 per cent for Indonesia, 77 per cent (53 per cent) for Morocco, 153 per cent (29 per cent) for Jamaica, and 768 per cent (147 per cent for Guyana, with very similar figures for other countries in that group.[297] It is sufficiently evident that for the overwhelming majority of developing countries any real recovery from their outstanding debt as achieved, for example, by South Korea, is an ever-elusive and unrealistic prospect, given today's circumstances. With very few exceptions, the majority of them cannot do any better than to pay interest on foreign liabilities by incurring fresh debts.

Such a variant of 'globalization' of the economy, leading to a situation where the share of world trade of the poorest states, in which 20 per cent of the world population lives, fell from 4 per cent to less than 1 per cent from 1960 to 1990, gives rise to two serious consequences.[298] First, 'Fourth World' countries are turning into net suppliers of products and, in recent years, also of capital, for the post-industrial regions. Reaching $167.8 billion in 1994, the sum of current debt of the developing countries for the first time lagged behind the interest of $169.5 billion, paid on foreign loans. The West collected more than $1.7 billion in a net money transfer from the debtor countries.[299] In reality that was only a fraction of the real sum, as the disadvantaged position of the poor countries leaves a lot of room for the North to manipulate the prices and dictate their own terms regarding where the loans will go to and how they will be used, perpetuating the cycle of poverty in the South. As we noted above, therein lies the danger of ecological cataclysms, ethnic and military upheavals and even catastrophic epidemics which may affect most people on the planet.

Second, the accumulation of irrecoverable debt jeopardizes the financial stability of post-industrial nations themselves. Injections of funds into the 'Fourth World' economies still pay a dividend in the shape of interest paid from new loans, but the odds are that they will end up no differently from loans to a bankrupt person: the creditor is bound to be landed with 'assets' of questionable worth, from which he cannot derive any use or profit, and additional expense for maintaining them. If this is so, the gradual and strictly controlled writing-off or serious restructuring of debts suggested by some developing countries is not a bad solution to the debt crisis after all. However, it leaves wide open the question of the actual use of the loans, as well as the money that could be saved under the debt write-off programme.

It can be assumed that the stability of mankind's development in every sphere of life in the first half of the 21st century, or lack of it, will be determined by whether or not the problems plaguing the 'Fourth World' can be successfully solved. In the decades to come, three regions – Northern and Central Africa, some South Asian and the least developed Latin American countries – will be receiving more than four-fifths of all economic aid to underdeveloped countries.[300] We may reasonably expect in this situation that, in shaping their relations with regard to such regions, the industrialized nations will pursue the principles of what may be termed 'remodelled colonialism'. Today, unlike in the past, there is little reason to press the point that 'the dominant flow of historical forces in the 21st century could well be this: economic development leads to demands for democracy and individual ... autonomy; instant worldwide communications reduce the power of oppressive governments; the spread of democratic states diminishes the potential for conflict'.[301] Western values are not going to spread as widely as many people would like them to, precisely because they are post-economic values and cannot be assimilated in areas and societies which have yet to go through an economic stage of progress from beginning to end.

This obviously raises the issue of a number of emergency measures that need to be taken with regard to countries clearly belonging to the 'Fourth World'. Awakening to the dangers posed by problems in those nations, the post-economic powers will probably act in their best interests to abandon their demand that those countries meet all their debt obligations; they could write off outstanding debts and accumulated interest, and provide sizable financial packages to ensure ecological safety and sustained social development in 'Fourth World' countries. The authors of the *State of the World* report put forward similar, albeit not fully consistent, proposals:

It is time for lenders to cancel the bulk of the debts owed by the governments ... of the 32 most severely indebted countries ... – some $200 billion – in exchange for a human security conditionality: commitments by the debtors to reduce their military expenditures and armed forces, and to invest resources that otherwise would have gone into debt servicing in areas of social and environmental need.[302]

We do not believe that a 'bailout' programme implemented along these lines can bring about any positive and tangible change, so long as money saved that way is not used for satisfying the most essential needs, and it will by no means ease the military and political tensions.

Apparently, the only viable solution is concerted and well coordinated action in the framework of the international community to eliminate the ecological and humanitarian threats posed by the problems in underdeveloped regions around the world. Humanity now recognizes the potential of the United Nations as a means for preventing organized violence and ethnic conflicts. In the very near future, a clear understanding should emerge in the public consciousness of the need for solidarity in responding with positive action to the diminishing ability of some countries to provide their population with the most basic means of sustenance, and their failure to protect the environment. That response needs to be ruthlessly effective: economic aid begins to flow in with the proviso that the national governments relinquish their sovereignty over areas hard-hit by economic and environmental crises, and step aside for international organizations or foreign countries to take control in the framework of an international body vested with greater powers than the council for trust territories, disbanded by the United Nations.

In the existing situation any calls for equal relations between the post-industrial regions and developing countries are no more than wishful thinking. The modern Western model has provided compelling proof that not even relatively advanced and industrialized economies (such as the former USSR and Eastern bloc countries) can hold fast under pressure from a system whose main resources are information and cutting-edge technology, which cannot be produced, replicated or adequately used by 'Fourth World' countries. Material consumption is no longer the major motive force behind human activity in a post-industrial world; in such an environment, progress takes on a post-economic character, opening new prospects for reprioritizing the areas of investment of the material resources. Lending support to the poorest countries for sustained development of the whole of humanity then becomes one of the most important priorities, and perhaps the most important goal. At present, the West has not enough resources to accomplish this. Even so, there is a growing understanding of the need to do everything humanly possible to prevent the degradation of both nations and the environment in Africa, Asia and parts of Latin America. To this end one may have to sacrifice the rising levels of consumer consumption and the high rate of economic progress in the post-industrial part of the world, for the destiny of the whole of civilization is in the balance.

In summing up this part of our study, we first point out that the emergence of the post-economic order of civilization is a gradual and even-paced evolutionary process that admits of no leaps or breakthroughs. Although perceived in all the continents as a form of economic, political and social revolution, the changes occurring over the last 30 years are in reality a logical result of core processes going deep to the heart of Western civilization and evolving throughout the close of the industrial era.

As this millennium is drawing to a close, the emerging first stage of post-economic transformation coming hard on the heels of industrialization can be traced. The change, which began to take place in the most advanced post-industrial countries, left the rest of mankind virtually untouched; yet it brought about a whole new understanding of the immediate prospects for civilization and the modern geopolitical reality that overturned the analytical constructs of 30 years ago.

First, the economic systems, serving the purpose of undoing the economic-type social organization through uncompromising denial of the superficial manifestations of economic processes, have run aground. Western countries, whose progress is propelled by man's creative potential, the formation of new motivations and preferences, and the enhanced role of sociopsychological factors, represent the sole viable way for mankind to transcend the constricting boundaries of economic society. The creation of conditions conducive to one's human growth, resting on the solid foundation of a new type of self-evolving economic mechanism, has hewn into shape a world where the modern post-industrial societies do not so much stand as three conflicting 'centres of power', but appear rather as one single 'pole' which genuinely determines the situation throughout the world.

Second, it is more or less clear from what we are seeing today that the emerging post-economic system is self-sufficient. In the modern world, the personal development of an individual is a source of technological progress; the reorientation of production primarily towards information and the creation of knowledge reduces the consumption of material resources and energy, giving a new impetus to economic development by lessening the dependence of industrialized countries on other, less developed, regions. An analysis of the maelstrom of processes at the heart of post-industrial civilization shows that old economic relations are being superseded more and more actively and irreversibly.

Third, the post-economic world has gone a very long way towards establishing economic control over the rest of humanity. With a growing share of information and knowledge in exports from post-industrial countries replacing conventional goods, these countries are finding themselves in a good position to eat one's cake and have it by buying both raw materials and manufactured goods from third countries, while keeping their national resources virtually intact. The transfer of production and technology to the outside world by most advanced countries in exchange for finished products does not imply any economic 'freeloading' on their part. On the contrary, their production continues to grow, not only in the information and services sectors, but also in industry, even as that is shifting into the high-technology area. Despite obvious contradictions observed in post-industrial society, the economic balance of the post-economic world, still expressed in macroeconomic terms, also demonstrates remarkable stability and easily lends itself to control: the flow of relatively overvalued industrial imports from newly industrialized nations is offset by the post-economic powers through their use of resources brought in from developing countries and devalued in a no less dramatic proportion in the course of the current transition.

Thus it will be seen that the evolution of post-economic principles reinforces the largely positive trends, well attuned to the future, that are having a noticeable impact on the development of countries which did not shut the door on them. The leaders of post-economic change are today beginning to reap the benefits of their efforts, the beginning of which goes back to the 1970s and 1980s, when the stage was set for this change. As a result, the industrialized Western countries enjoy quite robust economic health and dynamic growth that are immune to any adverse economic factors.

We now have plenty of reasons to say that the initial stage of a post-economic revolution is basically over: not only has the post-industrial world reached a state guaranteeing it continued and relatively stable development, made important steps towards forming a set of motivations adequate to maintaining that state, and achieved some major breakthroughs in technology, it has also drawn a clear line between itself and the rest of the world, thereby ushering in a new age of civilization, which in our view will be characterized by the two processes. On the one hand, the countries set on course for post-economic development face the need to find adequate forms of this development, consistent with the new trends. We have thoroughly analysed this problem, which is by no means confined to the creation of a system of non-economic growth indicators or a search for regular laws and patterns, replacing the law of value. The situation is far more complex than this, and it may take many decades for people, whose activity is already motivated in many cases by factors other than economic ones, to instil these principles in their workgroups, corporate structures and local and central governments. One cannot expect so far-reaching a change to be easy. The existing disproportions in values and property distribution may or may not make citizens of industrialized countries any better off than they really are, but they do produce quite a convincing illusion of wealth. Paradoxically, those people are rich in that they have access to information and an incredible range of knowledge, while that wealth is not adequately represented by a sum total of the material values they own. Maintaining parallel, non-contradictory growth and the strengthening of the post-economic constituent of public interest, as well as the formation of a system of new ways to evaluate economic processes, is the essence of the new stage of current post-economic change.

On the other hand, for all the self-sufficiency of this post-economic community, post-industrial countries cannot but take into account the trends in the rest of the world, which are perceived as being dangerous for the evolutionary pace of present-day transformations. To a greater or lesser extent, the problems they encounter spring from the fact that the industrialized countries, drifting father and farther away from the rest of humanity, are too small a part of this world to have sufficient economic, natural and even human resources to exercise effective and efficient control over the whole of civilization. It is not in the nature of post-economic society for one post-economic country or another to perform any policing functions. Very much to the contrary, the emerging society is introversive, and precisely the concentration of post-industrial countries only in particular geographical areas is fraught with the danger of the developments in other parts of the world getting out of control.

From this point of view, the coming new age will probably mean for the post-economic powers a long period of rethinking and trying to comprehend their changed place in the world. It seems that the future holds two alternative scenarios. The first, and the one we would prefer to follow, is that some developing countries successfully moving towards industrialism, and adopting Western-type social values, are going to jump on the bandwagon of post-economic civilization, assuring its dominance throughout the world; at the same time, the post-economic countries will seek (and will ultimately find) ways to provide precisely directed and therefore effective aid to the population of the 'Fourth World'. That will put an end to its slide towards absolute poverty and increased risk of environmental disasters in the Southern part of the globe. In the second, worst-case scenario, the newly industrialized economies will not be able to become a part of the community of post-economic powers, which will have speeded their progress. In that far less favourable setting, the most economically advanced countries will have to put forth a massive effort to support the 'Fourth World', but the newly industrialized countries would be their potential enemy whose political and environmental policy they are virtually unable to steer in the desired direction, and whose actions they cannot control. One could also predict extreme situations, in which some countries outside the community of post-industrial nations may team up to oppose it. (However, given strong dependence of civilization on the economies and technology of the leading industrial countries, there is little likelihood of this course of events.)

We are convinced that, in the world we are entering, a policy assuring the loyalty of newly industrialized nations to the post-economic world opens a straight and direct road to this new society. For post-industrial countries there is no escaping from the fact that, among the alternatives lying before them, only the creation of a beneficial environment for an expansion of the community of post-economic powers can lessen existing ecological and social problems. Such a policy must also be directed against ecological and political dangers from the 'Fourth World'. It should also ensure that the Third World flows with the wave of change towards the one, clear goal – that of joining the post-economic world – without being pushed from behind by countries it could otherwise lead in an altogether different direction. The principle of 'divide and rule', which must be applied by the post-economic countries, no matter what scenario materializes in the first half of the 21st century, no longer means an attempt to dominate the rest of humanity, but eases the transition of nations around the world to a new social level, to which, as we now know, there is no other viable alternative. That principle gives humanity a chance to go through the most profound and global change in its history without leaving a bloody trail of violence and war in its wake. Basically, revolutionary change through non-revolutionary forms of that change must become humanity's main goal and guiding principle in this new stage of the making of a post-economic world.

Notes

1   P.Z. Pilzer, *Unlimited Wealth. The Theory and Practice of Economic Alchemy*, New York, 1990, p.14.
2   Z. Brzezinski, *Out of Control. Global Turmoil on the Eve of the Twenty-First Century*, New York, 1993, p.xiii.
3   For more details, see V.L. Inozemtsev, 'Posteconomic Revolution: A Theoretical Construct or a Historical Reality?', *Herald of the Russian Academy of Sciences*, Birmingham, Al., **67** (4).

4   See M. Waters, *Globalization*, London, New York, 1995, p.156.
5   See P.F. Drucker, *Landmarks of Tomorrow*, New Brunswick, London, 1996, p.117.
6   D. Bell, *The Coming of Post-Industrial Society*, New York, 1973, p.216.
7   See J.I. Nelson, *Post-Industrial Capitalism. Exploring Economic Inequality in America*, Thousand Oaks, Cal., London, 1995, p.22.
8   See M.R. Rubin and M.T. Huber, *The Knowledge Industry in the United States, 1960–1980*, Princeton, N.J., 1986, p.19.
9   See P.Z. Pilzer, *Unlimited Wealth*, p.14.
10   See M. Castells, *The Information Age: Economy, Society and Culture. Vol. 1: The Rise of the Network Society*, Malden, Mass., Oxford, 1996, p.108.
11   See C.-F. von Braun, *The Innovation War. Industrial R&D... the Arms Race of the 90s*, Upper Saddle River, N.J., 1997, p.57.
12   See J.P. Kotter, *The New Rules*, New York, 1995, p.42.
13   See M. Carnoy, 'Multinationals in a Changing World Economy: Whither the Nation-State?', in M. Carnoy, M. Castells, S.S. Cohen and F.H. Cardoso (eds), *The New Global Economy in the Information Age: Reflections on Our Changing World*, University Park, Pa., 1993, p.49.
14   T. Cannon, *Welcome to the Revolution*, London, 1996, p.261.
15   See P. Dicken, *Global Shift: The Internationalization of Economic Activity*, London, 1992, p.48.
16   See W. Greider, *One World, Ready or Not. The Manic Logic of Global Capitalism*, New York, 1997, p.21.
17   See J. Dunning, *Multinational Enterprises in a Global Economy*, Wokingham, 1993, p.15.
18   J.K. Galbraith, *The Good Society*, Boston, New York, 1996, p.120.
19   See H. McRae, *The World in 2020*, London, 1995, p.47.
20 ` See L. Thurow, *Head to Head. The Coming Economic Battle Among Japan, Europe and America*, New York, 1993, p.62.
21   See J. Rifkin, *The End of Work*, New York, 1996, p.90.
22   See E.E. Gordon, R.R. Morgan and J.A. Ponticell, *Futurework*, Westport, Conn., London, 1994, p.200.
23   See M. Castells, *The Rise of the Network Society*, p.85.
24   See J. Kolko, *Restructuring the World Economy*, New York, 1988, p.193.
25   See F. Webster, *Theories of the Information Society*, London, New York, 1995, p.144.
26   See M. Waters, *Globalization*, p.93.
27   See ibid., p.90.
28   See J.K. Galbraith, *The Culture of Contentment*, London, 1992, pp.34–7.
29   See H. McRae, *The World in 2020*, p.271.
30   See A. Etzioni, *The Spirit of Community. The Reinvention of American Society*, New York, 1993, p.159.
31   See P.Z. Pilzer, *Unlimited Wealth*, pp.1–2.
32   See D.H. Meadows, D.L. Meadows and J. Randers, *Beyond the Limits: Global Collapse or a Sustainable Future?*, London, 1992, p.76.
33   See A. Gore, *Earth in the Balance: Forging a New Common Purpose*, London, 1992, p.331.
34   See H. McRae, *The World in 2020*, p.132.
35   See L. Thurow, *Head to Head*, p.41.
36   See C.J. Cleveland, 'Natural Resource Scarcity and Economic Growth Revisited: Economic and Biophysical Perspectives', in R. Costanza (ed.), *Ecological Economics. The Science and Management of Sustainability*, New York, 1991, pp.308–9.
37   See P.F. Drucker, *The New Realities*, Oxford, 1996, p.116.
38   See E.U. von Weizsaecker, A.B. Lovins and L.H. Lovins, *Factor Four: Doubling Wealth – Halving Resource Use. The New Report to the Club of Rome*, London, 1997, pp.4–5.

39 See P.Z. Pilzer, *Unlimited Wealth*, p.5.
40 *Wall Street Journal Europe*, 14 July 1997, p.2.
41 G. Arrighi, *The Long Twentieth Century. Money, Power and the Origins of Our Times*, London, New York, 1994, p.323.
42 P.Z. Pilzer, *Unlimited Wealth*, p.25.
43 See P.Z. Pilzer, *Unlimited Wealth*, p.25.
44 D.H. Meadows, D.L. Meadows and J. Randers, *Beyond the Limits*, pp.67–8.
45 See E.U. von Weizsaecker, A.B. Lovins and L.H. Lovins, *Factor Four*, pp.4–5, 8, 11, 13, 28, 80, 83.
46 D.H. Meadows, D.L. Meadows and J. Randers, *Beyond the Limits*, p.97.
47 See P.F. Drucker, *Managing in a Time of Great Change*, Oxford, 1995, pp.150–51.
48 See E.U. von Weizsaecker, *Earth Politics*, London, Atlantic Highlands, NJ, 1994, pp.14, 17.
49 See T. Cannon, *Corporate Responsibility*, London, 1992, p.188.
50 See M. Castells, *The Rise of the Network Society*, p.296.
51 See J. Rifkin, *The End of Work*, p.110.
52 See V. Perlo, *Superprofits and Crises: Modern U.S. Capitalism*, New York, 1988, p.290.
53 See N. Stehr, *Knowledge Societies*, London, Thousand Oaks, Cal., 1994, p.75.
54 See *Panorama of EU Industry*, Brussels, Luxembourg, 1997, Vol. 1, pp.1.2–1.6; 2.2–2.3.
55 See *Panorama of EU Industry*, Vol. 1, p.2.3.
56 See *Handbook of International Trade and Development Statistics*, United Nations Conference on Trade and Development, 1993, p.446.
57 See *L'Europe en chiffres*, Paris, 1995, p.318.
58 See T. Copeland, T. Koller and J. Murrin, *Valuation. Measuring and Managing the Value of Companies*, New York, 1996, p.11.
59 See M. Castells, *The Rise of the Network Society*, p.296.
60 See I. Barrom and R. Curnow, *The Future with Microelectronics*, London, 1979, p.201.
61 See C. Jenkins and B. Sherman, *The Collapse of Work*, London, 1979, p.115.
62 See T. Morris-Suzuki, *Beyond Computopia*, London, New York, 1988, pp.102–4; M. Castells, *The Informational City*, Oxford, 1989, pp.180–88.
63 See J. Rifkin, *The End of Work*, p.10.
64 See P. Dicken, *Global Shift*, p.425.
65 See *International Herald Tribune*, 2–3 August 1997, p.1.
66 See *International Herald Tribune*, 10 July 1997, p.2.
67 See *Statistical Abstract of the United States, 1994*, Washington, 1994, p.861.
68 J. Baudrillard, *America*, London, New York, 1988, p.73.
69 I. Kristol, 'The Emerging American Imperium', *Wall Street Journal Europe*, 19 August 1997, p.6.
70 See T. Copeland, T. Koller and J. Murrin, *Valuation*, pp.9–10.
71 G. Arrighi, *The Long Twentieth Century*, p.304.
72 See P.Z. Pilzer, *Unlimited Wealth*, p.102.
73 See M. Castells, *The Rise of the Network Society*, p.222.
74 See *International Herald Tribune*, 2–3 August 1997, p.1.
75 See P. Dicken, *Global Shift*, p.401.
76 See J. Naisbitt and P. Aburdene, *Megatrends 2000. Ten New Directions For the 1990's*, New York, 1990, p.331.
77 See J.P. Kotter, *The New Rules*, p.78, note.
78 See L.C. Thurow, *The Future of Capitalism*, London, 1996, p.165.
79 See M. Castells, *The Rise of the Network Society*, p.266.
80 A. Toffler and H. Toffler, *Creating a New Civilization. The Politics of the Third Wave*, Atlanta, 1995, p.53.

81 See P. Dicken, *Global Shift*, p.45.
82 See H. McRae, *The World in 2020*, p.7.
83 See S.P. Huntington, *The Clash of Civilizations and the Remaking of World Order*, New York, 1996, p.86.
84 See J. Baudrillard, *America*, p.76.
85 See W. Greider, *One World, Ready or Not*, p.22.
86 See A. Sayer and R. Walker, *The New Social Economy: Reworking the Division of Labor*, Cambridge, Mass., Oxford, 1994, p.154.
87 See L. Thurow, *Head to Head*, p.30.
88 See M. Castells, 'The Informational Economy and the New International Division of Labor', in M. Carnoy, M. Castells, S.S. Cohen and F.H. Cardoso (eds), *The New Global Economy in the Information Age*, p.25.
89 See *Statistical Abstract of the United States, 1994*, Washington, 1994, p.863.
90 See T. Forester, *Silicon Samurai. How Japan Conquered the World's IT Industry*, Cambridge, Mass., Oxford, 1993, pp.7, 8.
91 See D.C. Moschella, *Waves of Power. Dynamics of Global Technological Leadership 1964–2010*, New York, 1997, pp.204, 207–8.
92 See F. Fukuyama, *Trust. The Social Virtues and the Creation of Prosperity*, New York, 1996, p.327.
93 See T. Forester, *Silicon Samurai*, p.147.
94 See J. Naisbitt, *Megatrends Asia. The Eight Asian Megatrends that are Changing the World*, London, 1996, pp.20–26.
95 See W. Greider, *One World, Ready or Not*, p.22.
96 See *Financial Times FT 500 1997*, London, 1997, p.88.
97 See T. Forester, *Silicon Samurai*, pp.44–5, 85, 96.
98 See *World Economic and Social Survey*, 1996, p.283.
99 See J. Barksdale, 'Washington May Crash the Internet Economy', *Wall Street Journal Europe*, 2 October 1997, p.8.
100 See P.F. Drucker, *Managing in a Time of Great Change*, p.166.
101 See H. De Santis, *Beyond Progress. An Interpretive Odyssey to the Future*, Chicago, London, 1996, p.8.
102 See J. Tett, 'Yamaichi Looks Close to Collapse', *Financial Times*, 22–3 November 1997, p.1.
103 See M.J. Mandel, *High-Risk Society*, New York, 1996, p.99.
104 See C. Offe, *Contradictions of the Welfare State*, Cambridge, Mass., 1993, p.48.
105 See J. Naisbitt and P. Aburdene, *Megatrends 2000*, pp.16–17, 21.
106 See *OECD Communications Outlook 1995*, Paris, 1995, p.22.
107 See J. Barksdale, 'Washington May Crash the Internet Economy', p.8.
108 See J. Rifkin, *The End of Work*, p.110.
109 See T.A. Stewart, *Intellectual Capital. The New Wealth of Organizations*, New York, 1997, p.8–9.
110 See C. Handy, *The Hungry Spirit*, London, 1997, p.26.
111 See H. De Santis, *Beyond Progress*, p.15.
112 See A. Etzioni, *The New Golden Rule*, New York, 1996, pp.70, 76.
113 See S. Lash and J. Urry, *Economies of Signs and Space*, Thousand Oaks, Cal., London, 1994, p.20.
114 See J.E. Garten, *The Big Ten. The Big Emerging Markets and How They Will Change Our Lives*, New York, 1997, p.37.
115 R.B. Reich, *The Work of Nations*, New York, 1992, p.150.
116 See ibid., pp.120, 123.
117 See P. Dicken, *Global Shift*, p.78.
118 See ibid., p.54.
119 See H. McRae, *The World in 2020*, p.26.
120 See D.C. Moschella, *Waves of Power*, p.214.

121 See P. Dicken, *Global Shift*, p.54.
122 D. Bell, 'The World and the United States in 2013', *Daedalus*, **116** (3), p.8.
123 See J. Dimbleby, *The Last Governor. Chris Patten and the Handover of Hong Kong*, London, 1997, p. 366.
124 Ibid.
125 See H. McRae, *The World in 2020*, pp.7, 20.
126 See J. Rohwer, *Asia Rising. How History's Biggest Middle Class Will Change the World*, London, 1996, p.123.
127 See *Financial Times FT 500 1997*, p.88.
128 See *Statistical Abstract of the United States 1994*, Washington, 1994, p.850–52.
129 See A. Callinicos, *Against Postmodernism*, Cambridge, 1994, p.137.
130 J.E. Garten, *The Big Ten*, p.22.
131 See H. Bertens, *The Idea of the Postmodern: A History*, London, New York, 1995, pp.232–4.
132 See E.U. von Weizsaecker, A.B. Lovins and L.H. Lovins, *Factor Four*, p.271.
133 See E.U. von Weizsaecker, *Earth Politics*, p.127.
134 See E.U. von Weizsaecker, A.B. Lovins and L.H. Lovins, *Factor Four*, p.189.
135 A. Gore, *Earth in the Balance*, pp.183–4, 189.
136 See L.C. Thurow, *The Future of Capitalism*, p.1.
137 See T. Jackson and N. Marks, *Measuring Sustainable Economic Welfare*, Stockholm, 1994.
138 See H.E. Daly and J.B. Cobb, Jr., *For the Common Good*, Boston, 1989.
139 See C. Cobb, T. Halstead and J. Rowe, *Redefining Progress: The Genuine Progress Indicator, Summary of Data and Methodology*, San Francisco, 1995.
140 See W. Greider, *One World, Ready or Not*, pp.74, 197.
141 See H. Afheldt, *Wohlstand fuer niemand?*, Munich, 1994, S.30–31.
142 See R. Kuttner, *Everything for Sale: The Virtues and Limits of Markets*, New York, 1997, p.86.
143 See E.U. von Weizsaecker, A.B. Lovins and L.H. Lovins, *Factor Four*, p.279.
144 See W. Greider, *One World, Ready or Not*, p.22.
145 See K.E. Sveiby, *The New Organizational Wealth. Managing and Measuring Knowledge-Based Assets*, San Francisco, 1997, p.116.
146 See L. Edvinsson and M.S. Malone, *Intellectual Capital*, New York, 1997, pp.2–3, 34.
147 See I. Morrison, *The Second Curve. Managing the Velocity of Change*, London, 1996, p.62.
148 L. Edvinsson and M.S. Malone, *Intellectual Capital*, p.5.
149 See K.E. Sveiby, *The New Organizational Wealth*, p.6.
150 See J.M. McTaggart, P.W. Kontes and M.C. Mankins, *The Value Imperative. Managing for Superior Shareholder Returns*, New York, 1994, pp.26–9.
151 See K.E. Sveiby, *The New Organizational Wealth*, p.7.
152 See *Statistical Abstract of the United States 1994*, Washington, 1994, p.528.
153 See D. Harvey, *The Condition of Postmodernity*, Cambridge, Mass., Oxford, 1995, p.335.
154 R.B. Reich, *The Work of Nations*, p.193.
155 See *Wall Street Journal Europe*, 29 October 1997, p.16.
156 See *Wall Street Journal Europe*, 3 November 1997, p.9.
157 See W. Greider, *One World, Ready or Not*, p.232.
158 P.F. Drucker, *Managing in Turbulent Times*, Oxford, 1993, p.155.
159 F. Norris, '10 Years On, Lessons Of a "One-Day Sale"', *International Herald Tribune*, 18–19 October 1997, p.16.
160 'Wall Street Claws Its Way Back', *International Herald Tribune*, 29 October 1997, p.1.
161 See D. Kadlec, 'Wall Street's Doomsday Scenario', *Time*, 11 August 1997, p.28.

162 See W. Greider, *One World, Ready or Not*, p.232.
163 See G. Ip, 'Smaller Shares Loom Larger on Wall Street', *Wall Street Journal Europe*, 2 October 1997, p.16.
164 See *Statistical Abstract of the United States 1995*, Washington, 1995, p.451.
165 J. Baudrillard, *The Transparency of Evil*, London, New York, 1993, p.26.
166 W. Greider, *One World, Ready or Not*, p.317.
167 See J.E. Garten, *The Big Ten*, p.131.
168 See W. Greider, *One World, Ready or Not*, p.23, 245.
169 See S. Lash and J. Urry, *Economies of Signs and Space*, p.2.
170 D. Harvey, *The Condition of Postmodernity*, p.194.
171 See L. Thurow, *Head to Head*, p.160.
172 See B. Smart, *Modern Conditions, Postmodern Controversies*, London, New York, 1992, p.39.
173 See J. Boyle, *Shamans, Software and Spleens: Law and the Construction of the Information Society*, Cambridge, Mass., London, 1996, p.3.
174 See G. Baker, 'Clinton Holds Out Vision of a "New Economy" for US', *Financial Times*, 28 October 1997, p.1.
175 See *Statistical Abstract of the United States 1994*, Washington, 1994, p.330.
176 W. Greider, *One World, Ready or Not*, p.308.
177 See P. Kennedy, *Preparing for the Twenty-First Century*, London, 1994, p.297.
178 See G.P. Brockway, *The End of Economic Man*, New York/London, p.213.
179 See C. Handy, *The Hungry Spirit*, p.236.
180 See W. Greider, *One World, Ready or Not*, p.285.
181 See A. Englisch, 'Der Papst will den Euro und sein eigenes Gelt', *Welt am Sonntag*, 6 July 1997, S.47.
182 See M. Castells, *The Information Age: Economy, Society and Culture. Vol. 2: The Power of Identity*, Malden, Mass., Oxford, 1997, p.366.
183 See Z. Brzezinski, *Out of Control*, p.104.
184 See T. Forester, *Silicon Samurai*, pp.15–16.
185 See W. Greider, *One World, Ready or Not*, p.297.
186 See R.B. Reich, *The Work of Nations*, p.73.
187 See R. Bernstein and R.H. Munro, *The Coming Conflict with China*, New York, 1997, pp.131–2.
188 W. van Kemenade, *China, Hong Kong, Taiwan, Inc.*, New York, 1997, p.33.
189 P.F. Drucker, *The Age of Discontinuity. Guidelines to Our Changing Society*, New Brunswick, London, 1994, p.158.
190 Ibid., p.158.
191 A. Touraine, *Le retour de l'acteur. Essai de sociologie*, Paris, 1984, p.88.
192 D.H. Meadows, D.L. Meadows and J. Randers, *Beyond the Limits*, p.xix.
193 See P. Dicken, *Global Shift*, pp.441–2.
194 See ibid., p.20.
195 See C. Hampden-Turner and F. Trompenaars, *Mastering the Infinite Game. How East Asian Values are Transforming Business Practices*, Oxford, 1997, pp.2, 3.
196 See J. Naisbitt, *Megatrends Asia*, p.73.
197 See C. Hampden-Turner and F. Trompenaars, *Mastering the Infinite Game*, p.113.
198 See H. McRae, *The World in 2020*, p.76.
199 T. Forester, *Silicon Samurai*, pp.199–200, 206.
200 G. Arrighi, *The Long Twentieth Century*, p.334.
201 See R.A. Dalat (ed.), *Pacific-Asia and the Future of the World System*, Westport, Conn., 1993, pp.77–8.
202 See J. Naisbitt, *Megatrends Asia*, p.23.
203 See J. Rohwer, *Asia Rising*, p.83.
204 See W. van Kemenade, *China, Hong Kong, Taiwan, Inc.*, pp.4, 6.
205 See J. Naisbitt, *Megatrends Asia*, p.3.

206 See *Drucker on Asia. A Dialogue Between Peter Drucker and Isao Nakauchi*, Oxford, 1997, p.7.
207 P.F. Drucker, *Managing in Turbulent Times*, p.136.
208 See T. Cannon, *Welcome to the Revolution*, p.26.
209 See S.P. Huntington, *The Clash of Civilizations and the Remaking of World Order*, p.103.
210 See J. Naisbitt, *Global Paradox*, New York, 1995, p.339.
211 See C. Handy, *Beyond Certainty*, London, 1996, p.181.
212 See P. Krugman, 'The Myth of Asia's Miracle', *Foreign Affairs*, 1994, 6, p.70.
213 See P. Smith, *Japan: A Reinterpretation*, New York, 1997, p.124.
214 See J. Rohwer, *Asia Rising*, p.16.
215 See F. Gibney, 'Stumbling Giants', *Time*, 24 November 1997, p.55.
216 See *Financial Times*, 21 November 1997, p.1.
217 See M. Schuman, N. Cho, 'Korea Moves to Tackle Economic Woes', *The Wall Street Journal Europe*, 20 November 1997, p.28.
218 See N.D. Kristof, 'Crisis Shakes Faith In the "Asian Miracle"', *International Herald Tribune*, 22–3 November 1997, p.1.
219 See J. Rohwer, *Asia Rising*, p.211.
220 P. Krugman, *The Myth of Asia's Miracle*, p.70.
221 R.B. Reich, *The Work of Nations*, p.85.
222 J. Rohwer, *Asia Rising*, p.79.
223 See J.H. Boyett and J.T. Boyett, *Behind Workplace 2000. Essential Strategies for the New American Corporation*, New York, 1996, p.xv; J. Garten, *The Big Ten*, p.45; J. Naisbitt, *Megatrends Asia*, p.110.
224 See J. Garten, *The Big Ten*, p.45.
225 See G.P. Brockway, *The End of Economic Man*, p.245.
226 See I. Morrison, *The Second Curve*, p.122–3, 167.
227 See W. Greider, *One World, Ready or Not*, p.19.
228 See P.W. Daniels, *Service Industries in the World Economy*, Oxford, Cambridge, Mass., 1993, p.31.
229 See J. Garten, *The Big Ten*, p.39.
230 See P. Dicken, *Global Shift*, pp.181, 183.
231 See E. de Bono, *Serious Creativity*, New York, 1995, p.18.
232 See H. McRae, *The World in 2020*, p.77.
233 See C. Handy, *The Age of Unreason*, London, 1995, p.27.
234 See I. Morrison, *The Second Curve*, pp.16, 17.
235 See P. Kennedy, *Preparing for the Twenty-First Century*, p.198.
236 See J. Naisbitt, *Megatrends Asia*, p.180; *Drucker on Asia*, p.9.
237 See D. Kantor, *Understanding Capitalism*, London, New York, 1995, p.88.
238 See W. van Kemenade, *China, Hong Kong, Taiwan, Inc.*, pp.4, 6–7, 37.
239 I. Morrison, *The Second Curve*, p.99.
240 W. Greider, *One World, Ready or Not*, p.32.
241 I. Morrison, *The Second Curve*, pp.138–9.
242 See R. Farley (ed.), *State of the Union. America in the 1990s*. Vol. II, New York, 1995, p.85.
243 T. Cannon, *Welcome to the Revolution*, p.26.
244 M. Castells, *The Power of Identity*, p.124.
245 E.U. von Weizsaecker, *Earth Politics*, p.61.
246 See D.H. Meadows, D.L. Meadows and J. Randers, *Beyond the Limits*, p.181.
247 See L.R. Brown, C. Flavin, H. French *et al.*, *State of the World 1997. A Worldwatch Institute Report on Progress Toward a Sustainable Society*, New York, London, 1997, p.8.
248 See E.U. von Weizsaecker, A.B. Lovins and L.H. Lovins, *Factor Four*, p.199.
249 See E.U. von Weizsaecker, A.B. Lovins and L.H. Lovins, *Factor Four*, p.225.

250 See T. Cannon, *Corporate Responsibility*, p.182.
251 See M. Waters, *Globalization*, p.106.
252 See D.H. Meadows, D.L. Meadows and J. Randers, *Beyond the Limits*, p.181.
253 A. Gore, *Earth in the Balance*, p.123.
254 E.U. von Weizsaecker, *Earth Politics*, p.91.
255 See J. Garten, *The Big Ten*, p.72.
256 See F. Duchin, G.-M. Lange *et al.*, *The Future of the Environment. Ecological Economics and Technological Change*, New York, Oxford, 1994, p.33.
257 H. McRae, *The World in 2020*, p.135.
258 See E.U. von Weizsaecker, *Earth Politics*, p.166.
259 See J. Garten, *The Big Ten*, p.97.
260 See H. de Santis, *Beyond Progress*, p.157.
261 See L.R. Brown, C. Flavin, H. French *et al.*, *State of the World 1997*, p.166.
262 L. Thurow, *Head to Head*, p.41.
263 See P. Kennedy, *Preparing for the Twenty-First Century*, p.121.
264 See L.R. Brown, C. Flavin, H. French et al., *State of the World 1997*, p.6.
265 See E.U. von Weizsaecker, A.B. Lovins and L.H. Lovins, *Factor Four*, p.219.
266 See A. Gore, *Earth in the Balance*, p.304.
267 Ibid., p.307.
268 See R. Heilbroner, *21st Century Capitalism*, New York, London, 1993, p.55.
269 See W.J. Martin, *The Global Information Society*, New York, 1995, p.200.
270 R.W. Cox and T.I. Sinclair, *Approaches to World Order*, Cambridge, 1996, p.193.
271 See B. Frankel, *The Post-Industrial Utopians*, Madison, Wis., 1987, p.144.
272 See D.C. North, *Structure and Change in Economic History*, New York, London, 1981, p.15.
273 See D.H. Meadows, D.L. Meadows and J. Randers, *Beyond the Limits*, p.25.
274 N. Eberstadt, 'Population Change and National Security', *Foreign Affairs*, 1991, p.128.
275 See T. Cannon, *Corporate Responsibility*, p.183.
276 See H. McRae, *The World in 2020*, p.99.
277 See P. Kennedy, *Preparing for the Twenty-First Century*, p.25.
278 See M. Castells, *The Rise of the Network Society*, p.404.
279 See Z. Brzezinsky, *Out of Control*, p.51.
280 See T. Cannon, *Corporate Responsibility*, p.216.
281 See H. McRae, *The World in 2020*, p.99.
282 See P. Dicken, *Global Shift*, p.56.
283 See M. Castells, *The Rise of the Network Society*, p.134.
284 See D.H. Meadows, D.L. Meadows and J. Randers, *Beyond the Limits*, p.5.
285 See L.R. Brown, C. Flavin, H. French *et al.*, *State of the World 1997*, p.34.
286 See P. Kennedy, *Preparing for the Twenty-First Century*, p.69.
287 M. Castells, *The Rise of the Network Society*, p.134.
288 See L.R. Brown, C. Flavin, H. French *et al.*, *State of the World 1997*, pp.55, 119.
289 Ibid., pp.24–5.
290 See D.H. Meadows, D.L. Meadows and J. Randers, *Beyond the Limits*, p.5.
291 See C. Caufield, *Masters of Illusion. The World Bank and the Poverty of Nations*, New York, 1997, p.332.
292 Ibid., p.331.
293 See P. Dicken, *Global Shift*, p.179.
294 See E.U. von Weizsaecker, *Earth Politics*, p.97.
295 See W. Greider, *One World, Ready or Not*, p.282.
296 See G.P. Brockway, *The End of Economic Man*, pp.202–3.
297 See C. Caufield, *Masters of Illusion*, p.165.
298 M.-F. Baud, 'Market Globalization', *UNESCO Courier*, 1996, 11, p.34.
299 See C. Caufield, *Masters of Illusion*, p.335.

300 See F. Duchin, G.-M. Lange *et al.*, *The Future of the Environment*, p.21.
301 R.L. Bartley, 'The Case for Optimism', *Foreign Affairs*, 1993, 4, p.17.
302 L.R. Brown, C. Flavin, H. French *et al.*, *State of the World 1997*, p.131.

Conclusion

After beginning this book with a discussion of the theories of history created by philosophers throughout the centuries, we went on to stress that the two key elements of each historical doctrine are the way the author interprets the facts and his personal methodological position, largely conditioned by the subjective aspects of his perception of the world. This duality is characteristic of any theory but, while the natural sciences have progressed far into the objectification of knowledge, abandoned speculative schemes and provide substantiation for most of their postulates, the dependence of historical conceptions on the general outlook and social orientation of their authors has not undergone radical change throughout the centuries. We will stress here one such subjective aspect which recurs again and again, however perfect the latest interpretation of progress turns out to be.

Social theories differ from scientific theories not only in that they are concerned with the constantly changing subject of research; social theories themselves are an important factor of the transformation of that subject itself. Therefore the subjective nuances of an author's position are of primary importance in social science, and the most important prejudice, which is manifested to some extent in any conception of history, is the discussion of the author's own times as an important turning point in history. It stands to reason that none of the historians represents the development of civilization as a linear process, but any complex and contradictory movement towards a certain goal always contains turning points. This factor gives rise to many problems, some of which are no longer purely theoretical, although this is the price of surmounting the narrow frameworks of the conceptions of the global rotation, free from this prejudice and at the same time unable to explain either the genuine nature of history or most of the conformities of the development of civilization.

However diverse the theories of St Augustine and Marx, Hegel and the current postmodernists, they are absolutely identical in their attitude to their own times which they regard as the most important for the history of mankind. So in this respect progress is far slower than in scientific interpretation of the conformities of historical

403

development. The idea of St Augustine of contrasting the epoch stretching from the birth of Christ to the Day of Judgement, with the many preceding stages that reflected the chronology of the biblical events, was misguided. However, this mistake was present in the theory that practically gave birth to the current view: it was committed less than four centuries after the beginning of the extensive spread of Christianity, when this was indeed seen as the last step towards the redemption of earthly sins, and the thought of the perishability of the earthly city should have occurred to the author, who died just a few months before the seizure and destruction by the Vandals of his native Hippo. Such prejudices have a totally different value in our times. Born again with the formation of the fundamentals of modern society, they have become unprecedentedly widespread. Flouting the foundations of their own conceptions, destroying their inner logic and ignoring the arguments they themselves have only just used, philosophers of all ideological trends attempted and are attempting to surpass each other in overemphasizing the meaningfulness of their own epoch for the progress of the human race. Moreover, if the fathers of Christianity at the dawn of its spread sincerely wanted to improve the world through the betterment of man, the theorists of our age believe that it is beneath their dignity and calling to reform the beginnings of the earthly world order, imbedded by the Lord in the human soul. They believe only the whole material *civitas terrestris* to be a worthy object of the application of such noble efforts. And so, for over two hundred years, man has been struggling to overcome every new wave of such reformism.

In the middle of the 18th century, Europe entered the Age of Reason, after overcoming what would appear to have been one of the most terrible periods of its history, leaving behind an epoch of sharp contradictions – the latter Middle Ages – when Europeans perished in colonial wars on other continents and destroyed each other in religious infighting, when the Curia patronized the arts and sanctioned the unseen sweep of inquisition, and the economic progress of protestant countries was, perhaps, no more noticeable than the crisis of the major European monarchies was felt. In these conditions, the desire to rationalize the existing order, to establish just social relations, to fully realize the potential of the sciences and the arts, to make humanity better than it was, became more widespread than ever before in world history. The coming of a new epoch seemed absolutely inevitable; such ideas were not put forward, by some thinkers or by a group of plotters, but were favoured by all. Philosophers and historians, economists and politicians were convinced of the need for renewal; they were listened to by the powers that be, they were close to the authorities, some of them were even admitted to the authorities, and most of them were treated with affection by autocrats in all parts of the continent. What did these people preach and what was the basis of their theories?

Assuming that the progress of reason, understood in most cases to be the development of the sciences, the arts and technology, had become so advanced that the path towards the establishment of a just world order was already open, the ideologists of the Enlightenment confidently stated that all previous epochs – the period of the formation of the social economy of Ferguson and Smith or the stages of the progress of human reason of de Condorcet – could be consigned to the past, opening the way to a truly new civilization. To achieve this it was necessary once and for all to break free from formal inequality, from the shackles of subjugation; it was necessary to emancipate the human soul, give space for the development of industry, the sciences and the arts and to provide people with the equal rights granted them by God's will – the visions of the 18th century, which today seems to us to be one of the most majestic pages of European history, were limited to this. There was relative consensus on ways of attaining these goals: almost all philosophers believed that the will of the enlightened monarchs to implement reforms was capable of establishing a kingdom of freedom, equality and fraternity on a world scale in the near future and without any catastrophic eruptions.

The goals defined by the philosophers were noble and the means by which the future changes would be achieved were clear. But the rulers did not want to hear their words about equality and justice, words which today might seem very naive. However, these words were heard by people who, after grasping the elements of the new outlook, would not reconcile themselves to the fact that they would not live to see the triumph of the new order, a triumph which seemed so obvious and so close. The result is common knowledge. Instead of long-awaited freedom, the revolutionaries imposed bloody repressions on the people. The civil war that gripped France took place amid the incessant mutual destruction of revolutionary cliques, who acted in the tradition of Hobbes' notorious idea of war fought by all against all. For nearly 30 years, Europe was locked in unending war. As a result, in all warring nations hundreds and thousands of people died and economic processes slowed down, but the problems that revolution was designed to resolve were the same. Did the revolutionaries want an enlightened monarchy? They got Talleyrand and Fouché, who took the place of Turgot and Colonne. Did they strive for economic freedom and prosperity? In 1815, France was in a more lamentable state than in 1789. Did the idea of freedom, equality and fraternity come to life? These words remained only on placards and coins, while poor peasants in rural areas were supplemented by impoverished factory workers in the cities.

Here we will mention the following interesting fact. The European powers won victory over the army of the usurper, the dynasty was restored to the throne, and France entered the longest period of peace in its history. The economy began to grow in the early 1820s, the monarchy was overthrown in 1848 and, as a result of curbing subsequent attempts to perform radical social experiments, France today is one of the most developed post-industrial states. But do not many of the French idolize the name of Napoleon, who brought their homeland nothing but misery? Are not many historians unwilling to reject the interpretation of the Holy Alliance as a reactionary organization which attempted to slow down the development of the European states? This gives much food for thought.

A hundred years had passed since the participants in the Enlightenment proclaimed the coming of the reign of Reason. The inequality in that period became even more pronounced, and exploitation even more intolerable. The old privileges of the nobility gave way to the power of money. Naturally, the idea of equality and justice did not become less popular for this reason. And new philosophers conceived a new idea.

This time the conception was a truly scientific interpretation of history. Like many preceding theories, only far more consistently and scrupulously, the new conception viewed economic progress as one of the fundamentals of the evolution of the social organism. Turning to the past, it mentioned the period of the birth of humanity, untouched by economic conformities, an epoch of very slow progress and very undeveloped social ties. Evaluating the present, the conception showed how and when that period was displaced by the era of the domination of economic relations; it demonstrated their inner potential and opened up a mechanism for their self-development, a mechanism that guaranteed the progressive movement of the entire society. Anticipating the future, Marxist theory was the first to argue convincingly for the inevitability of the emergence of a society which its founders called 'communist', supposing it to be the third fundamental phase of social progress; and the theory noted that the arrival of the hypothetical 'realm of freedom' was impossible without radical economic restructuring which would stem inevitably from the achievement by humanity of a qualitatively new level of development of the productive forces.

This picture was naturally more complete than that drawn by the Enlightenment. It described the real course of historical progress and revealed its true source. What should have been the natural conclusion from this understanding of history? The collapse of economic society is just as indisputable as the economic progress provided by this society. The development of the productive forces inevitably gives rise to the reformation of the relations of production in such a way that the upset balance will be restored and from that period there will begin the formation of a new, communist system.

But the process of productive forces development is gradual and does not take place in a flash; meanwhile, *oekonomische Gesellschaftsformation* has already reached its peak. Was a period of its descent really necessary? Would it not have been simpler to use some radical means and immediately alter the fundamentals of the social order? As a result, the practical recommendations of the Marxists fundamentally contradicted their theoretical postulates. Describing the emergence of *oekonomische Gesellschaftsformation*, which in history took more than one millennium, the revolutionaries believed that it could be overcome in a few years. Stressing that their contemporary means of production were unable to provide the communist principles of production and distribution, they stated that the productive forces had already entered into the final contradiction with the relations of production which could be resolved only by revolution, one that would violently overthrow the bourgeois order. And, finally, in the perfect understanding that never before had any of the opposing classes of the Asiatic, the ancient and feudal society achieved supremacy in a new order, the Marxists confidently named the proletariat, the best organized but, in the middle of the last century, also the most impoverished class alienated from the achievements of progress, as the main driving force of the proposed transformations.

It seems that even the dose of poison that enabled de Condorcet to avoid the guillotine contradicted his ideas of the triumph of reason less than the theory of the proletarian revolution contradicted the humanistic and scientific foundation of Marxist teaching. But the calls of the revolutionaries of the early 20th century were as distanced from the fundamental ideas of social evolution laid down in the theory of *Gesellschaftsformation* as were the invocations of the *ami du peuple* from the philosophical quests of Voltaire and Shaftesbury. However, the simplification of the theory served successfully to proliferate it this time also; moreover, everything was repeated, in virtually the same manner, with the only exception that the new confrontation had spread beyond Europe to the whole world.

The Russian Revolution of 1917 showed that, with every new century, social experiments became more dangerous, and the desire to benefit the human race proclaimed by the revolutionaries ended where it always had in the past, that is with their coming to power. Again there was civil war, again terror and violence were directed not only against the real enemies of the new regime but also at those who might display disloyalty to it. Having vanquished and strengthened their positions, the revolutionaries began their inner conflict, spilling as much blood as it would have taken to ensure victory in the world revolution. The extreme contradictions between the new and the traditional systems gave rise to new world confrontation, then the Cold War, in which the aims of the two opposite blocs led to conflicts on all continents. However, the realities of the twentieth century made a military victory over the Soviet bloc impossible; the Western world would have to wait nearly half a century for its natural destruction. Moreover, the decisive advantages in the economic rivalry with the Eastern bloc enabled the West only to withdraw from the boundaries of industrial production; the defeat of so-called 'socialism' became obvious between the mid-1970s and the beginning of the 1990s, when with all clarity it revealed its inability to create and reproduce post-industrial structures. In 1989, the process of the destruction of the Soviet bloc assumed very distinct features, and by the mid-1990s the post-Soviet states had virtually ceased to exist as a meaningful force in world economics and politics. The forces which from the point of view of previous logic can be described as reactionary conducted the second world restoration at a cost of tens of millions of lives and unbelievable consumption of energy to improve and develop arms, and brought the planet to the verge of environmental catastrophe; the latest revolutionary idea has been conquered, and the natural course of economic and social development has been restored.

The new restoration seriously changed humanity's attitude to revolutionary doctrines. The military and economic alliance of the Western nations, which for half a century enabled them to effectively counter the spread of the socialist model of development to all corners of the planet, is not in itself similar to the Holy Alliance, although its role was exactly the same. And this does not diminish the importance of the North Atlantic alliance or other political associations of Western countries; on the contrary, it affords a more rational view of the past historical transformations.

The French Revolution and the events that followed, on the one hand, and the Russian Revolution and the world confrontation of the 20th century, on the other, are very similar phenomena. In both cases the beginning of the revolutionary processes was laid by new social doctrines, distinguished by the fact that from a certain moment the study of society becomes an instrument for its modernization, and the tasks of a truly scientific analysis can be fully replaced by the desire to change society in the interests of certain social groups. In both cases on the wave of the real revolutionary process there appeared people who least of all understood the profound essence of the doctrine they had adopted and who strove to use merely its slogans in the struggle for their own goals and interests. In both cases successful political revolution led to a gigantic wave of violence, directed both outside and inside the revolutionary camp itself, towards precluding the possibility of normal evolutionary development in a given country or countries, towards confrontation with the rest of the world and, ultimately, to the inglorious conclusion of an experiment which left their peoples on the wayside of economic progress.

But the ideals of freedom, equality and fraternity, the idea of the 'realm of Reason' did not become less attractive after 1815. The understanding of a future society free from prejudice and class difference had not become less desirable because the best representatives of the nobility destroyed each other and the worst came close to the throne. Surely the ideas of communism in their positive aspects cannot be considered to have become exhausted. Surely with account taken of today's experience we cannot say that the conception of a new, non-economic society proved itself bankrupt, which makes us think about the global lesson taught by the two biggest revolutionary movements of recent centuries.

Both revolutions were caused by the desire to create a more just order. Neither the band of revolutionaries in 1789 nor the group of political émigrés in 1917 could have come to power if they had not cleverly used the will of the people to change the existing state of affairs. At issue in the first case was the formation of the fundamentals of a society which offered the freedom of entrepreneurship and the development of capitalist tendencies, and in the second of a socium free of all exploitation and which would be non-economic by nature. At the start of the 19th century, monarchic Britain and Prussia aligned against the revolutionary, advanced France. But just a few decades later these 'reactionary' countries taught France very useful lessons on developing capitalism, the creation of which the French revolutionaries wanted to expedite. Likewise the contemporary Western world really prevailed over the USSR in economic rivalry by the formation of a post-economic society which the Communists had been building for decades in words alone. The most important lesson that humanity ought to draw from the cataclysms of the past centuries is that real progress can only be evolutionary, that to speed up artificially processes which have their own objective dynamics and their own inner laws leads to the destruction, in a most radical way, of the inner logic of the development of civilization. Whereas an understanding of the actual meaning of the French Revolution has not finally matured today, two hundred years on, the illusions about the nature of the Russian Revolution had been dissipated before the end of the communist experiment, and that inspires great hope.

At the end of the 20th century, humanity has begun to realize the danger and harm of radical revolutionary bursts; there has arisen a dim but increasingly more coherent understanding that evolutionary development is the guarantee of constant social progress. Yet today, when the countries of the free world are only just beginning to feel fully the results of their victory in global rivalry, words about revolution can be heard more frequently than ever before. This may reflect the unfulfilled desire to reform society, after making its understanding as some kind of transitory order generally accepted.

Of course such an interpretation today will be rejected outright, for all are convinced that modern revolution, be it technological or informational, is neither similar to a proletarian uprising nor a prelude to anything like it, and they should not even be compared. However, it must not be forgotten that the gigantic social unrest of the past was kindled not only by the visions of political philosophers but also by major upheavals in technology and economics. After all, the replacement of artisan workshops by factories caused the eruptions of the late 18th and mid-19th centuries. And it was the contradictions of the factory system that caused the proletarian movement at the beginning of the 20th century. In our view researchers who proclaim the emergence of the 'technetronic', information or network society are merely exciting the reader with such definitions, neglecting the obvious fact that the feudal society was not one of ploughs and hammers, just as the capitalist society is not one of the steam-powered machine and internal combustion engine. Neither in the past nor in the future can society be adequately defined without addressing its inner, deeply *social* ties and relations; for a profound understanding of the direction of the development of civilization it is insufficient to describe, even in full detail, the foundations of its technological progress. The information revolution being proclaimed today will definitely have as its main consequences social changes of no smaller scale and no less contradictory nature than those experienced by previous generations.

The optimists may say that today there are no conditions able to enact the radical social transformations of the past. There is no revolutionary class groaning under the burden of unjust exploitation and waiting just for a signal to rock the foundations of the existing order. There is no socially widespread theory to advocate revolutionary change. And there are former contradictions capable of spurring a popular movement for the overthrowing of the unjust order. The optimists are right; however, they forget one vital factor which has made itself more and more evident in the last few decades. The 'demassification' often limited to the spread of individual and small-scale production, on the one hand, and the modernization of contemporary consumption, on the other, consist in reality mainly of cardinal changes in the sphere of human awareness, motivation and behaviour.

In this context the role and meaning of the current technological revolution is modified in a big way. Even without creating a class capable of struggling for the overthrow of the existing order, it awakens in each person desires which are fundamentally in conflict with trends characteristic of the economic epoch. Even without formulating a new theory or ideology, it brings to human awareness new values which modify the pattern of activity motivation more strongly than the decades of communist propaganda. Finally, by eliminating former contradictions, contemporary changes inevitably give birth to new ones, contradictions, moreover, not between classes but between individuals. We become witnesses to social disintegration, the potential for which does not subside because it takes place in forms which do not clearly manifest themselves. In his *Cours de philosophie positive*, August Comte wrote that sociology – the science of society – is one of the most complex systems of man's knowledge about the world at his disposal; later, he changed this attitude, indicating quite rightly that psychology – the science of man himself, his feelings and emotions, actions and deeds – is even more complex. Today we are crossing from a society whose main laws lie in the sociological system of coordinates to a socium in which deeply personal, *psychological* ties and relations prevail. And it stands to reason that this new condition, or state, is more complex not only as an object of awareness but also as an object to be governed.

For a fuller picture, we will return to the problems already discussed. The Utopians, who dreamed of a just society without money and markets, believed this could be achieved by virtually turning the entire population into slaves. The Marxists, who strove to overcome market laws, spent several decades creating a system for the planned production and distribution of products. The results are well known: the utopian illusions remained illusions, and their liberal variations disintegrated with the bankruptcy of Owen's system of fair exchange; the socialist planned economy existed a little longer, but the consequences of its end were greater and more destructive. Today value exchange is actively being overcome with the loss of measurement of value itself, with the loss by material production of its underlying role, with the supremacy of the production of information and knowledge evaluated primarily from the point of view of their social utility. The most weighty factor in the given process becomes the change of the very nature of human activity, the spread of non-material motivation, the overcoming of the process of labour and its replacement by creative activity.

Advocates of the theory of Fourier attempted to socialize in a phalanx even the most insignificant household items, exclusively in order to rid themselves of the very concept of private ownership that they so disliked. In Eastern Europe, the communists only rarely attempted in practice to attain a similar ideal in real life, but they succeeded in creating an economic system that had never existed before, one in which all means of production were owned by the government and used in the interests of the ruling bureaucracy. The authors of more profound and original theories could not imagine that the economic meaning of private ownership could be overcome, not by socializing production, but by its global and all-round individualization. Today private ownership, formed within the economic epoch as a mechanism for appropriating material benefits by representatives of the wealthy classes is quickly transformed under the influence of a number of factors which differ radically from those which, in the view of revolutionaries, should have put an end to private ownership. The development of new technologies leads to a point where the main factor of production is the ability and knowledge of workers, that is their inalienable attributes; and the technological process presents the real possibility for the personal ownership of the means of creating modern information products. The owners of the giants of material production, which a few decades ago still prevailed in society, are today beginning to depend on the owners of information and knowledge, which are so overvalued that it becomes easier for new entrepreneurs to establish control over industrial empires. And once again it must not be forgotten that the desired independence of the intellectual worker from the owners of the means of material production has become a reality only in Western countries, whereas in the countries where until recently communists used to rule, the overwhelming majority of people remain rigidly dependent on the owners of production facilities and natural resources.

For centuries all social reformers believed that exploitation could be overcome only by means of eliminating the class of exploiters. Both the seekers of justice in the 18th century and the revolutionaries of the 20th century gained success in this field more than in any other. However, it transpired that the elimination of the class of exploiters was unable to free the peasants, forced to work in their previous conditions, or the workers, who are closely tied to their means of production whether owned by the class of alien capitalists or by their own proletarian state. War with exploitation was waged without understanding of the nature of the phenomenon, which did not consist of the alienation of part of the products, but depended on the extent to which such alienation contradicted the fundamental interests of the producer. But as a result of the modernization of the system of values brought about by the information progress and knowledge becoming the main factor of production, of primary importance today is the desire, not to increase to the maximum one's own material wealth, but to better oneself, to become something greater than one already is. This change does not eliminate the very phenomenon of the alienation of part of a product but the features of that product which made it a source of exploitation. And again it is necessary to stress unconditionally that, in the distribution of wealth in the developed post-industrial countries, exploitation in its former, classical sense no longer exerts a decisive influence on social relations. At the same time, in the former communist states, where the standard of living, which was not high as it was, has dramatically declined over recent years, the wave of revengeful conservatism is gaining force precisely with calls for a fairer distribution of the national wealth.

All of the processes mentioned have the same deep roots: the transformation of the nature of human activity. The current technological revolution has caused two fundamental changes: on the one hand, for the first time in history, it has satisfied the main material needs of most members of society and, on the other, it has made the improvement of individuals not just a matter of their choice but also the main condition for their social recognition. Today, when the improvement of the individual is still not as self-sufficient as was recently the attainment of a new level of well-being, a mechanism is at work in society which stimulates constant development of a person's intellectual potential. This mechanism creates a competition of knowledge, at times no less fierce than the competition of property. In the course of time, the process of self-improvement of the personality will become without doubt the prevalent aspect of human development. Then creative activity motivated by a desire for maximum self-realization will cast labour, born of the need to satisfy material requirements, aside entirely. The new social structure, at first sight, cannot but be fairer and more humane than the previous one: after all, the objective of the reformers of all times was humanity's departure from the confines of 'purely material production' and the creation of conditions for the all-round development of people's personality. But it cannot go unnoticed that traditional forms of social interaction must give way to new ones, the nature of which is today totally unclear. Located as if on different planes, the interests of creative people do not conflict like the interests of individual members of the economic society; they do not create the same contradictions which penetrate this socium, but at the same time they do not form a single resultant vector which determines the direction of social progress. But can it be said with confidence that the problems caused by the latter factor would not outweigh the advantages born of the former?

In our view, there is today nothing more unreasonable than to present the coming society as a model of social harmony. In surmounting the mature forms of *oekonomische Gesellschaftsformation*, humanity is entering a period of its descent, of the overcoming and destruction of its conformities. But the phase of the decline of any social structure, however simple, has never been a peaceful period in its evolution. The decline of the feudal system, which by way of evolution had reduced to a minimum the economic influence of the aristocracy, did not happen peacefully, but for nearly three centuries gave rise to major European cataclysms. And the decline of traditional industrial capitalism and the transition to post-industrial society was not entirely smooth either, and if it had not been for the titanic efforts of governments to implement anti-crisis regulation in the prewar years and to finance scientific and technological research in the postwar years, the global confrontation of the 20th century might have ended in serious upheavals. Today we are entering a phase of transition on a broader scale, and it would be very dangerous to underestimate the potential hazards and contradictory nature of that transformation.

Furthermore, the special nature of today's era is determined by the circumstance that practically nothing is known about a new society that will replace the existing one. Whereas when the feudal order was being destroyed the structures that replaced it had already practically emerged and were waiting only for their political recognition and for new opportunities for their development, and whereas in the period of late capitalism it was relatively clear what social problems were fraught with the most danger and by what means they could be overcome, today the situation is radically different. There are no new *social structures*; only new *individual* systems of values and preferences are emerging, and the forms and directions of their evolution are still unclear. Moreover, the social institutions that are being preserved possess in their arsenals only those instruments for regulating social conflicts and contradictions that have been used in the previous, economic era. It is reasonable to suppose that in certain circumstances these instruments may become not only ineffective, but even dangerous.

Therefore it must be remembered that humanity is capable in the next decades of achieving, not only a qualitatively new level of technical and intellectual progress, but also a hitherto unseen intensification of social contradictions and conflicts. This time there are unlikely to be any clashes between political clans, parties or classes. The conflicts of the new period may arise from some complex interlacing of contradictions arising between individuals or between their communities, united by factors of an inherently subjective nature.

Today we can see how the fundamentals of the traditional market economy are being overcome. A huge number of goods is being exchanged for others without the slightest consideration for the costs which still form the price of the goods of many branches of social production. The overvaluation of some goods and of whole branches coexists with the undervaluation of others; the productivity, measured in indicators which can still be used for measurement, is, on the contrary, far greater in the traditional sector than in the new, promising areas of production. Meanwhile, market institutions continue to function, the majority of the population of all developed countries has already been involved in the movement of fictitious symbols of ownership, and the decline in the significance of material interests, linked with the emergence of the foundations of the new society, is supported today only by the stability of the irrational system, which sustains a high level of social well-being, undermined from within by the same circumstances which it itself brought to life.

The borderline between knowledge workers, who have gained access to the means of production and are able to counterbalance the owners of the fixed assets of industrial companies as equal partners, and hired workers, who, as previously, have to sell their labour power to entrepreneurs, is becoming more and more obvious. The forms in which ownership rights are being exercised are becoming more and more complex, and the factors that restrict such rights more and more numerous. In this context the owners of private property receive such opportunities to improve their knowledge and technology that, in the absence of public control, could become potentially dangerous for society as a whole.

Exploitation has been overcome nowadays in the consciousness only of those members of society who have access to knowledge, not too scarce a resource these days, but a highly conditional resource, one which demands of a person qualities for its assimilation which cannot be acquired as easily as property was acquired in the era of the initial accumulation of capital. Orientation to the creation of information products increasingly shapes the circle of people who cannot be their creators, not because they do not possess the opportunity to acquire the necessary technical means, but because they are incapable of assimilating information and acquiring new knowledge, since that is how their life has turned out, how they were brought up and educated. The idea of equality, stemming from the Age of Enlightenment, from the naive Cartesian understanding of human awareness and reason as a kind of tabula rasa, is being consigned to the past, and the bitterness of parting with this illusion may outweigh all of the virtues of a society which has overcome market production, ownership and exploitation.

Considerable problems are also associated with the need constantly to manoeuvre between completely diverse issues. On the one hand, the vital task is the maximum use of new, post-economic methods of regulating economic and social problems inside developed countries; but, on the other, the character of relations with the outside world remains wholly economic, since in most regions of the planet industrial production, and sometimes even farm production, prevails, rather than the creation of high-tech and information products. The problem of interaction between the post-economic and economic sectors on a global scale becomes especially acute as any programmes of cooperation and aid designed to support the Third World can bring only purely economic results. But just as in the developed countries people capable of generating knowledge and creating information products do not look for work as labourers or fast-food servers, but join the relatively closed community of knowledge workers which is opposed to the majority of society members, in the developing countries most talented specialists and scholars try to enter this group, not in their homeland, where the group as such is virtually absent, but in developed countries. It is for this reason that the share of intellectual potential concentrated in the Third World does not exceed 5 per cent of the overall intellectual potential of humanity, and continues to decline. Thus the emergence of a boundary between knowledge workers and the rest of society begins to take place not only within the framework of individual countries but also on a world scale, and that contradiction cannot be resolved by economic methods alone.

So the formation of the foundations of the new society can hardly take place smoothly and without hitches. On the contrary, social cataclysms that mediate it can turn out to be extremely dangerous. This can happen in any field – be it the development of market tendencies, the evolution of property relations or the modernization of the class structure – *a new, non-economic content of deep-rooted economic and social processes enters into sharp and insurmountable contradiction with the economic forms of their manifestation.* The emergence of such an acute incompatibility and the ensuing destruction of a given economic form may have extremely grave consequences for the entire society, since such destruction will signify the disintegration of the whole economic order in the absence of both principles that actually unite society and the unifying tendencies obviously present in the economic era.

Is it possible to avoid such scenarios? Can the transition to the post-economic state be relatively painless at all? Of course it is impossible to give a definite answer today, but some very general deductions can be made from all that has been said. First, the current technological revolution should be distinguished from the social revolution; it should be stressed that they develop separately and in parallel, and are not directly interdependent. To a certain extent it can even be asserted that one of the tasks facing modern society is to slow down somewhat a whole number of economic and social processes which most clearly broaden the gap between the foundations of the social set-up and the economized form of their manifestation. Such measures may hold up the onset of a radical conflict capable of destroying the social equilibrium.

Second, since such measures may create a highly conventional, if not altogether illusory effect, it is worth assessing the possibility of improving present-day economic structures by means of ridding them of the most fetishistic yet fictitious symbols; and, perhaps most importantly, at issue are the current forms of financial capital, the overvaluation of selected companies and branches, the extravagant spread of the symbols of ownership, which represent no real elements of social wealth, and so on. The abnormally rapid growth of money value of shares in industrial companies with relation to the growth in output – a growth sustained for two decades and which has assumed massive proportions – itself partly reflects the destruction of the value principles of exchange. However, the consequences of a possible crash on exchanges, which would affect the overwhelming majority of the population, may eclipse the historical optimism of sociologists who anticipate the emergence of a non-market economy.

Third, it is necessary to mention the new systems able to influence the behaviour of individuals for whom economic values have lost their former meaning. The formation of new systems of social relations, which enable the central institutions of society effectively to govern its non-materially motivated members, is today the most important condition for social stability over the next few decades without which the new society cannot emerge.

Fourth, it is necessary to start creating an effective system to counter the growing new confrontation provoked by the division of society into its materially-motivated and non-materially motivated members, into those who possess knowledge and information technologies and those who do not. For this it is necessary to combine for a prolonged historical period the economic methods of influencing non-economically motivated people both within post-industrialist nations and on a world scale.

In conclusion, we must stress that tendencies which have arisen from the development of social processes in the last few decades will not necessarily persist in the near future. We are unable to determine precisely the future that awaits humanity. But we are able to assert that the transition to the new civilization which is beginning today with the triumph of knowledge and on a wave of unprecedented historical optimism, will not be easy. New hopes and expectations will be intertwined with the destruction of previous ideas, values and priorities; today this seems impossible, but did the Romans who glorified Marcus Aurelius, the philosopher on the throne, expect that their empire had only two hundred years to live? Opening a new page of history, the difficulties of parting with the past, with a gigantic epoch which was harsh and unjust, yet glorious and great, an epoch which represented a single and unique path that had been trodden by humanity, must not be underestimated. In this epoch creativity was a rarity, but it produced great cultural monuments revered by humankind; nobleness was also the lot of few, but it will be recalled by the whole human race as an inherent feature of the past epoch; the irreparable tragedy of the revolutionaries lay in the inability of their ideas to give society real progress, but the seekers of a better future did not diminish in number.

Not one attempt at the revolutionary transformation of the world has ended in long-term success, although the tasks proclaimed by the trailblazers were fairly local. Today humanity is departing from the realm of the economic era, overcoming the material interests that used to rule the world; not even the Lord was able to prophesy this, when He proclaimed that man will be doomed to grow his own bread by his own sweat. But all attempts by humankind to radically change this world have been held back by the deep-rooted laws of social evolution, which returned civilization to the natural path of its development; we hope that this will be repeated tomorrow. This is the main and, perhaps, the only ground for optimism, with which we continue to look into the future.

> Say not thou, What is the cause that the former days were better than these? for thou dost not inquire wisely concerning this. (Ecclesiastes, 7.10)

Subject Index

ability, social division according to
173–4, 221, 273–7, 285–6, 292–5,
303–4, 307–8, 415
academics 102
Acer 223
'ad-hocracy' 275, 290
'adaptive corporations' 98
Africa 361, 381, 388, 390
agriculture 375, 385
civil wars 382
foreign debt 387
population growth 383
research 324
urbanization 384
Age of Enlightenment 45, 51, 52, 57, 59,
405, 406
Age of Reason 404–5, 406
agrarian society 91–2, 110–11
see also pre-industrial society
agriculture
agrarian society 91–2, 110–11
ancient societies 50
communes 71–2
developing countries 381, 385–6
energy use 328
environmental issues 373–4
feudalism 68
industrial revolution 212
labour changes 330
overexploitation 375
utopianism 33, 35
aid programmes
see also debt
developing countries 378–9, 388
alienation
exploitation 412–13
labour 155, 279
means of production 98–9
post-industrial society 103
Ancient Greek philosophy 17–22, 28–9, 59

archaic/primary society 71–2, 112,
243–4, 245–6, 247
see also pre-economic/pre-industrial
society; primitive society
aristocracy 246, 247, 296
Asia 388, 390
civil wars 382
environmental issues 380
poverty 381
Southeast 361–71
agriculture 385
economic power 334, 335–9, 339,
340, 341–2
environmental issues 376
exports 326, 353–4
Western nations relationship 387
Southern 362
West 361
Asiatic mode of production 67, 72
assets, non-material 346, 347–9
association 43, 44
atomism 21
automobile industry, IT comparison 258–9
autonomy 180–1, 182–3

barbarism 34, 36, 67
BMW 367
bourgeoisie
class conflict 286
means of production 98
revolution 77, 78–9, 85–6
Britain
employment 326
GNP 336
industrial decline of 370
management 187
politics 355
privatization 250, 270
shares 251
wealth distribution 297

bureaucracy 289–90

capital
  intellectual 216, 221–4, 229, 232, 265
  ownership 265, 307
capital-relation 74
capitalism
  class divisions 275, 304
  commodity production 7–8, 35–6, 66,
    213–15, 225, 240–4, 248
  corporations 184, 185
  decline of 414
  emergence of 69–70
  France 409
  labour value 225
  Marxism 71, 74
  ownership 262
  'post-class' 291–2
  post-industrial 127
  productive forces 79–80
  professional-managerial class 288
  social progress 47, 51
carbon dioxide emissions 374, 376,
  377
Chaos theory 18
China 361, 362, 364–5, 369–70
  consumption 368
  deforestation 375
  economic power 334, 341–2
  exports 356–7
  pollution 374, 376, 377
  wages 367
choice, freedom of 168
Christianity
  Aquinas 43
  historical theory 21, 22–8, 37, 404
  methodology 44–5
  Modern Age philosophy comparison
    28–9
CIS *see* Commonwealth of Independent
  States
civil wars, developing countries 382
civilis conversatio 43
class
  see also ruling class; social division
  aristocracy 246, 247, 296
  bourgeoisie 77, 78–9, 85–6, 98,
    286
  'cognitariat' 96, 99, 172, 173
  formation of 49
  French Revolution 54
  industrial society 55
  knowledge workers 173, 174, 260–1
  Marxism 66–7, 113

post-economic/post-industrial society
  273, 274–5, 286–95, 303–5, 307–8,
  309, 310
  exploitation 278
  Marxism comparison 112–13
  professional-managerial 287–8, 290
  service sector 96
  technocractic 101–3, 288–90, 304
proletariat
  definition 286–7
  exploitation of 304
  information-based society 172
  Marxism 407
  revolution 77–8, 83, 85–6, 410
  property 246
  struggle 68, 85
coercion, commodity relations 243, 244
'cognitariat' class 96, 99, 172, 173
collectivism 190, 201–2
colonialism 81, 381–2
commodity production 7–8, 35–6, 66,
  213–15, 225, 240–4, 248
Commonwealth of Independent States
  (CIS) 361, 376
communes 43, 71–2
communication 41–2
  see also telecommunications
communism 36, 110, 112, 406–7, 409
  collective ownership 249
  demise of 87, 105, 108–9, 285, 320, 321,
    325
  Eastern Europe 411–12
  equality 273, 274
  exploitation 281
  labour 150
  natural progression 211
  negativity 126
  revolution 79, 81, 83–4, 113
  social formation 72
communitarianism 362
community
  Aquinas 26
  'phalanx' 34
  St Augustine 25
  state-formation 19–20
  voluntary organizations 197, 198
Compaq 223
complementary economy 100–1
computers 218, 220, 223–4, 258–9, 338,
  340
conflict
  Hobbesian theory 30
  social 272–305, 307–8, 309–10, 322,
    323, 414

consciousness, social 64
consumption 164, 167
  'Fourth World' 386
  information 220–1
  marginalism 225
  prosumerism 229–30
  public services 228–9
  specialized 226
  value 237
cooperatives 255
corporations
  see also multinationals
  'adaptive' 98
  creativity 184–94, 200–1
  employee shares 249–50, 252–4
  executive incomes 297, 298
  investment 251–2
  non-material assets 347–9
  non-profit organizations comparison
    196, 199
  ownership 265
  restructuring 166
  wages 347
creation, Christian concept of 23
creativity 7, 141–3, 147–203, 216
  corporations 184–94, 200–1
  individuals 176–84
  knowledge workers 282
  labour 100
  non-profit organizations 195–203
  objective (material) prerequisites
    159–68
  self-realization 308
  subjective (non-material)
    prerequisites 159, 168–74
  technology relationship 308, 309
  work relationship 147, 148–58
culture, corporate 185–6
currency 326, 352
cyclical development
  Ancient Greece 17–18, 19, 20–1
  Christian opposition to 24, 25
  Old Testament 22–3

debt
  developing countries 387–9
  national 354–6
decentralization 189
deindustrialization 103
democracy, utopianism 33
desertification 375–6
developing countries 320, 322, 358,
  359–93
  economic aspects 359, 360–72

environmental issues 359, 372–81
  knowledge workers 416
  poorest regions 359, 381–90
dialectics, Hegelian 64
discrimination, wealth distribution 300
distribution
  information 219–20
  wealth inequality 273, 276, 295–303,
    304, 413
division of labour
  commodity production 240
  historical transformation 5
  Marxism 65–6
  philosophy of history 49–50
  positivism 53
  slavery 68
  social production 7–8

Earth Summit 1992 378
Eastern Europe 105, 108–9, 251, 411–12
ecology *see* environmental issues
economic society
  see also industrial society; *oekonomische*
    Gesellschaft
  exploitation 273–4, 278, 279, 281
  formation 136–40
  labour 140–1
  Marxism 68–70, 71, 74, 76, 110, 112,
    133
  property 245, 246–7, 248
  state property 268
  value 237
economics
  Asiatic vs ancient modes of
    production 67
  class conflict 291
  corporations 184–5
  creative activity 158–9
  developing countries 359, 360–72,
    378–9, 386–90
  environmental issues 371–2, 373
  Gesellschaftsformation 71
  globalization 320, 323–7, 387–9
  inner contradictions of post-economic
    societies 320, 343–58
  international centres of power 334–42
  labour/work distinction 149–58
  market economy
    decline of 212, 213–44, 306–7, 309,
      414–15
    economic relations 137
    industrialization 69–70
    property 247, 248
  Marxism 64–70

oekonomische Gesellschaftsformation 70,
    72, 73–7
positivism 54
post-industrialism 94–5, 133, 390–1
postmodernism 128
social progress 47–51, 63, 76
social revolution 82
state management 268–72
terminology 134–9, 237–8
economy
    definition 134–5
    formal vs complementary 100–1
    manufacturing industry 94, 161–3,
        164, 218, 232, 233
    planned 67, 411
    primary/secondary/tertiary divisions
        89, 90–1, 159, 217
    service sector 159, 160–7
        information 129, 217
        labour changes 287, 330–1
        post-industrialism 89, 93–4, 96–8,
            105–6
    productivity 230–2
education
    class divisions 293
    creativity 168, 171–2
    income inequality 300–1
    knowledge workers 173, 179–80, 193,
        258, 260
    post-industrial society 93–4, 103, 114
    Southeast Asia 368–9
    state investment in 269
    technological progress 324
Employee Stock Ownership Plan
    (ESOP) 253–4
employees *see* workers
employment
    see also self-employment;
        unemployment; workers
    autonomy 180–3
    corporations 185–6, 187–8
    globalization 326–7
    post-industrial society 94, 96–7
    production stages 188–9
    restructuring 160–3, 165–6, 218, 230–1,
        330–2, 333–4
    United States 339
    worker creativity 179–82
energy resources, environmental issues
    327–9, 373, 374, 376, 377
Enlightenment 45, 51, 52, 57, 59, 405, 406
entrepreneurs 171, 188, 295
environmental issues 104–5, 323, 327–30
    developing countries 359, 371, 372–81

GNP indicators 346
Epicureanism 24
equality
    Christian principle of 23
    communism 36
    exploitation 273, 274
    Hobbesian opposition to 30
    income 296
    primitive societies 48
ESOP *see* Employee Stock Ownership
    Plan
Europe
    debt 355
    economic power 334–5, 336, 337, 340,
        358
    employment figures 330–1
    environmental issues 329–30, 375, 377
    exports 326, 357
    labour 327
    Southeast Asia comparison 362, 363
    Third World aid programmes 379
    United States comparison 332–3
evil, Hobbesian philosophy 30, 31–2
evolution
    creation comparison 23
    Democritus 41–2
    economic formation 76
    labour 65
    positivism 56
    post-industrial society 93
    social 1–3, 409
exchange
    commodity production 7–8, 35–6, 137
    market economy 214, 215–16, 240, 242
    Marxism 66, 69, 74
    value 233–4
exploitation
    commodity relations 74
    economic society 8–9, 54
    Marxism 66
    post-economic revolution 212,
        272–305, 322, 412–13, 415
    Russian Marxism 85
    social transition 72
exports 326, 353–4, 356, 357–8
    see also trade deficits
    developing countries 368, 387
expressivism 178

feudalism 50–1, 56, 58
    decline of 414
    Marxism 68–9
    property 246–7
    wealth distribution 296

financial flows 269, 326, 352
flexible specialization 130, 189
Ford 328
Fordism 188
formal economy 100–1
fossil fuels 328–9, 376, 377
'Fourth World' 381–90, 392–3
France
    education 368
    employment 330–1, 332
    financial flows 326
    GNP 336
    politics 355
    privatization 250, 270
    Revolution 54, 70, 79, 405–6, 408, 409
free individuality 110
freedom
    see also liberty
    corporations 184
    creativity 168, 170
    economic 135–6, 137
    political 135, 138, 140
    post-economic society 272–3
futurology 1–2, 90, 126

G-7 countries 321, 324
General Motors 183
Germany
    employment 330–1, 332
    environmental issues 329, 330, 374
    exports 326
    GNP 336
    income 347
    national debt 355
    wages 367
Gesellschaftsformation (social formations)
    70–7, 81–4, 85, 86, 110–11, 133
globalization 320, 323–7, 387–9
GNP (gross national product) 326, 331,
    336, 341–2, 345–7, 355
    'Fourth World' 386
    Southeast Asia 362–3, 364, 366
    United States 324, 325, 328, 351, 353
God 23–4, 25, 45
government
    Aquinas 44
    Aristotle 20
    financial regulation 351
    Luther/Tertullian comparison 27
    market processes 268
    Plato 19
    resources 269
    utopianism 33
Great Britain *see* Britain

Great Depression (1920s and 1930s)
    268–9
Greek philosophy, Ancient 17–22, 28–9,
    59

Hewlett-Packard 348
historical materialism 64, 113
history 403–5
    Ancient Greek/Roman theories 17–22
    Christian theories 21, 22–8, 37
    coherent theories 16, 41–60, 63–115
    inadequate theories 15, 17–37
    Marxist conception 63–88, 110–14
        periodization 70–7
        revolution 77–84
    perception of 2–3
    periodization 3–4, 13–16
    post-industrialism 88–109, 110–14
    social contract theories 28–32
    utopianism 32–6
Holland 326, 329, 342
home-based businesses 266
Hong Kong 341–2, 361, 365, 368, 369
human nature, Hobbesian conception of
    30, 31
hunter-gatherer communities 48

IBM 223–4, 259, 340, 348, 356
ideas, social progress 57
immigration 326–7
immobility, progress conflict 58
income
    see also wealth
    inequality of 276, 295–303
    international differences 367
    macroeconomic indicators 347
India 81, 362, 365, 382
    consumption 368
    pollution 377
    wages 367
individual
    creativity 175, 176–84, 189
    innovation 171
    self-development 152, 154–5, 156, 167,
        176
    self-realization 175, 183, 241, 274, 281,
        308
    society relationship 6, 47, 136–7, 140,
        272–3, 279
    well-being 282
individualism 182–3, 198, 257
Indonesia 362, 363, 364, 365
    national debt 387
    pollution 374, 377

standard of living 367
Industrial Revolution 137, 212
    developing countries 360
    information revolution comparison
        219
industrial society 89–90, 91–3, 95, 98,
        110–11, 114
    see also capitalism; economic society
    corporations 184, 185
    economics relationship 137
    exploitation 304
    motivated activity 179
    ownership 264
    positivism 54–5, 58
    voluntary organizations 101, 201
    work 151
industry *see* industrial society;
        manufacturing industry
inequality
    ancient mode of production 67
    'information war' 103
    Marxism 66
    property 49
    utopianism 33
    wealth 273, 276, 295–303
information
    see also knowledge
    contemporary production 217, 218–24
    creativity 158
    education 180
    employment 331
    environmental issues 328, 373
    exchange 215
    exporting 357–8
    freedom 170–1
    GNP indicators 346
    intellectual capital 216, 221–4, 229,
        232, 265
    investment 353
    irreproducibility 227
    knowledge workers 260
    market economy 216
    means of production 99
    non-material interests 5–6
    post-economic/post-industrial society
        94, 101–3, 391
    production 164, 168–9, 231–3
    ruling class 288–90
    service sector relationship 96, 97–8
    social division according to 173–4,
        221, 273–7, 285–6, 292–5, 303–4,
        307–8, 415
    value 228, 235–7
    wealth 239

information class 96
information society 90, 97, 108, 128, 129,
        410
    property relations 264
    value 235
information technology 258–9
    see also computers
    developing countries 368
    employment 162
    futurology 1, 2
    Japan 336–7, 338, 340
    post-industrial society 94, 97–8
    Western countries 322
    worker incomes 302
instinctive pre-labour activity 7, 65,
        283–4
instinctive work 153–8
institutionalism 108
Intel 348
intellect
    self-realization 413
    social division according to 173–4,
        221, 273–7, 285–6, 292–5, 303–4,
        307–8, 415
intellectual capital 216, 221–4, 229, 232,
        265
interests
    see also motivation
    material 4–5, 6, 7, 66, 282–5, 304
        exploitation 9, 273–4
        labour 278–9
        market economy 240
        oekonomische Gesellschaft 135, 136,
            138, 139–41
    non-material 4–5, 6, 178, 274, 281, 284
internationalization *see* globalization
interpersonal interaction 164–5, 167
    corporations 186, 190
intervention, state 270–1, 351
investment
    private 251–4, 256
    Southeast Asia 369
    Third World 384
    United States 339–40, 341
irreproducibility 164, 215, 216, 226–7,
        301

Japan 361, 363–4, 365, 366, 373
    aid programmes 378
    economic power 334, 335–8, 339, 340,
        358
    education 368
    employment 162, 327, 331
    environmental issues 373, 374, 377, 380

exports 354, 356
incomes 367
Jesus Christ 23

knowledge
see also information; knowledge
    workers
competition of 413
corporations 187
creativity 158
distribution of 219–20
education 171–2, 173
environmental applications 328
exchange 215
exporting 357–8
freedom 170–1
human development 56–7
intellectual capital 216, 221–4, 229,
    232, 265
investment 353
modern society theories 128–9
non-material interests 5–6
ownership 412
post-economic/post-industrial society
    93, 94, 99, 101–3, 391
production 164, 168–9, 231–2
ruling class 288–90
social division according to 173–4,
    221, 273–7, 285–6, 292–5, 303–4,
    307–8, 415
value 228, 235–7, 306–7
knowledge workers
autonomy 165
class divisions 173, 174, 292–5
corporations 187, 193
developing countries 416
education 179–80
income 301, 302, 347
property relations 257–8, 259–62,
    263–4, 266, 415
self-realization 282
technology 99
well-being 282–3
Kodak Corporation 328

labour
see also employment; work; workers
capitalism 69
creativity 141, 142, 147, 175, 216, 283,
    308
division of
    commodity production 240
    historical transformation 5
    Marxism 65–6

philosophy of history 49–50
positivism 53
slavery 68
social production 7–8
economic society 140–1
globalization 326–7
liberation from 279–80
Marxism 64–6
material interests 7, 278–9, 284
post-industrial society 100, 103
pre-industrial society 92
productive/non-productive 234
proletariat 287
as property 248
service sector 89
unemployment 105–6
unskilled 302–3
wealth production 239
work distinction 149–58
labour theory of value 94, 164, 225
land ownership, beneficiary to feudal
    system 68
Latin America 324, 361–2, 388, 390
laws of nature 42, 45
leisure 100, 154–5, 179, 195, 282
liberty
see also freedom
Hobbesian state 30, 31
linear development 18

McLouth Steel Products 253
Malaysia 362, 363, 364, 365, 368
investment 369
pollution 377
management
class relations 288
corporations 166, 186–7, 190
non-profit organizations 196, 198–9
ownership 263, 264, 266
manufacturing industry 94, 161–3, 164,
    218, 232, 233
marginalism 225–6
market economy
destruction of 212, 213–44, 306–7, 309,
    414–15
economic relations 137
industrialization 69–70
property 247, 248
Marshall Plan 379
Marxism
class 287, 291
historical theory 63–88, 110–14, 406
periodization 70–7
revolutionary doctrine 77–84

Russia 84–8
labour 150
negation 126
new social order 211
oekonomische Gesellschaftsformation 133,
    137, 407
planned economy 67, 411
production 6
social evolution 243
social revolutions 212
value 225–6
mass-production 164–5, 188, 227, 229,
    230
material dependence 110
material interests 4–5, 6, 7, 66, 282–5,
    304
    exploitation 9, 273–4
    labour 278–9
    market economy 240
    oekonomische Gesellschaft 135, 136, 138,
        139–41
material production 110
materialism
    historical 64, 113
    Modern Age historical theories 29, 30,
        32
    post-industrial society 91
    post-materialism conflict 292
MCC *see* Mondragon Cooperative
    Corporation
means of production
    alienation 98–9
    exploitation 8–9
    industrialization 69
    ownership of 248, 249, 257, 259–64,
        307, 411–12
meritocracy 96, 127, 275, 289
methodology
    historical theories 37
    periodization 15
Mexico 367, 377
Microsoft 192, 223, 265, 298, 302, 347,
    348
middle class *see* bourgeoisie;
    professional-managerial class
Modern Age, theories of history 28–37
modification (succession) theories 125,
    130–1, 132
modular specialization 189–90
Mondragon Cooperative Corporation
    (MCC) 255
monopolization of knowledge 219–20
morality, positivism 53
motivation

see also interests; values
non-economic 169, 176–80, 284–5, 295,
    304–5, 308, 417
multinationals 325, 333, 335–6
mutual funds 251, 252

national debt 354–6
developing countries 387–9
natural condition 45, 46
natural law 29, 42, 45–6
nature
    see also environmental issues
    instinctive work 155
    pre-industrial society 92, 243–4
    pre-labour activity 7
    technological progress 323
neo-Marxism 130–1
neo-Platonism 21
neoproletariat 287
Netscape 224, 348
'new historical school' 89, 90–1
Nigeria 382, 383
non-economic motivation 169, 176–80,
    284–5, 295, 304–5, 308, 417
non-material assets, corporations 346,
    347–9
non-material interests 4–5, 6, 178, 274,
    281, 284
    see also non-economic motivation
non-profit organizations 98, 101, 105,
    194, 195–203
North-South divide 105, 372–3, 387

oekonomische Gesellschaft 9, 136, 137, 138,
    139–40
    see also economic society
oekonomische Gesellschaftsformation 70, 72,
    73–7, 85, 113, 114
    market economy 212, 214, 215
    Marxism 133, 137, 407
    revolution 79, 80–1, 82–4
Old Testament 22–3
Oracle 348
organization theories of society 129
ownership
    see also property
    communism 249
    Hume 50–1
    intellectual capital 221
    Marxism 65–6, 74, 75, 137
    means of production 248, 249, 257,
        259–64, 307, 411–12
    personal property 245–7, 248, 257,
        261, 262, 264, 266

positivism 53
post-economic revolution 212, 244
primitive society 48–9, 86
process 263, 264–5
Rousseau 46
ozone gases 377

Pakistan 382
peasantry 69
periodization 3–4
   Aquinas 26, 44
   historical theories 13–16
   Marxism 70–7
   'new historical school' 89
   post-industrial society 95
   St Augustine 25
Persian Gulf 382
personal dependence 110
personal property 212, 245–7, 248, 257,
      261, 262, 264, 266, 307
'phalanx' 34–5
Philippines 377
philosophy
   Ancient Greek 17–22, 28–9, 59
   Enlightenment 405–6
   historical theory 13, 14
   political 28
   positivism 52–8, 59
   Roman 20–1
   social contract theories 28–32
   utopianism 32–6
planned economy 67, 411
political philosophy 28
political revolution 77, 78–9, 84, 85
politics
   see also government; political
      philosophy
   economics relationship 54
   post-economic class conflict 291–2
pollution 329–30, 374, 376–7
population growth 383
Portugal 327
positivism 52–8, 59, 88, 91, 107
'post-class capitalism' 291–2
post-industrialism 88–109, 110–14,
      126–7, 129, 211
   class 291
   conflicts 319–93
      developing countries 359–93
         economic aspects of
            confrontation 359, 360–72
         environmental issues 359, 372–81
         poorest regions 359, 381–90
      employment 323, 330–4

environmental issues 323, 327–30
globalization 320, 323–7
inner contradictions of post-
      economic societies 320, 343–58
international centres of power
      334–42
economics 133, 359, 360–72
as emergence of new society 130, 131
market economy 213
service sector 160, 217
social evolution 243
technology 306
post-materialism 169–70, 178, 194, 242,
      292
post-oekonomische Gesellschaft 9, 135, 138,
      139, 174
postmodernism 127–8, 130, 226, 403
poverty, developing countries 381–90
power
   international economic centres 334–42
   ownership 49
   state 33–4, 271–2
pre-economic/pre-industrial society
      91–3, 95, 110–11, 114, 139, 151, 243–4
   see also archaic/primary society;
      primitive society
pre-labour activity, instinctive 65, 283–4
pre-oekonomische Gemeinschaft 9
predetermination 23
primitive society 5–6, 48–9, 71–2, 86,
      139–41, 151, 243–4
   see also archaic/primary society; pre-
      economic/pre-industrial society
   barbarism 34, 36, 67
   natural condition 45, 46
private property
   see also ownership
   displacement of 245–72
   post-economic revolution 212, 307,
      309, 322
   social division 293–4, 303
   social transition 8, 48–9, 71–2
   unequal distribution of 296
   utopianism 34, 36
privatization 250, 270
process ownership 263, 264–5
production
   Asiatic vs ancient modes of 67
   commodity 7–8, 35–6, 66, 213–15, 225,
      240–4, 248
   contemporary factors 217–24
   creativity 166, 177
   environmental issues 327–30, 371, 373
   feudalism 68–9

Fordism/post-Fordism 188–9
GNP indicators 344–7
information 99
irreproducibility 164, 215, 216, 226–7,
    301
Japan 336
material 110, 158
means of
    alienation 98–9
    exploitation 8–9
    industrialization 69
    ownership 248, 249, 257, 259–64,
        307, 411–12
modes of 67, 70, 71, 73, 74–5, 76–7, 86
periodization 3–4
post-industrial society 127
pre-industrial society 92
productivity 162–3, 230–33
relations of 6–7, 64–5, 79–80, 82, 83,
    84, 406–7
reproduction processes 216–17,
    225–33
social regulation 160
superstructure 86–7
Third World 384–5
value-adding 235
wealth distribution 301–2
Produktionsweisen 70, 71, 74, 80–1, 113,
    114
professional-managerial class 102,
    287–8, 290
progress
    see also social progress
    Asiatic vs ancient modes of
        production 67
    Christian theories of history 26, 27
    communism 36
    cycles relationship 19
    economic 136–7, 170
    historical theories 15
    human activity 142
    immobility conflict 58
    technological 3–4, 56, 306, 319–20,
        323–5, 343–4
    post-industrialism 89, 94, 106, 111
proletariat
    definition 286–7
    exploitation of 304
    information-based society 172
    Marxism 407
    revolution 77–8, 83, 85–6, 410
property
    see also ownership
    displacement of 245–72

personal 212, 245–8, 257, 261–2, 264,
    266, 307
post-economic revolution 212, 307,
    309, 322
social division 293–4, 303
social transition 8, 48–9, 71–2
state 268–72
unequal distribution of 296
utopianism 34, 36
'prosumerism' 167, 182, 229–30
'proto-industrialization' 92
psychology 411
public services 228
public-sphere theory 131

quality of life 228–9

rationalism 138
reason
    see also Age of Reason
    social contract 29
redistribution
    post-economic society 303–4
    property rights 8, 248, 249–52
reforestation 375
Reformation 26
regulation theory 131
religion
    Ancient Greek philosophy 17–18,
        21–2
    Christianity 21, 22–9, 37
    dogmatization 26
    positivism 53
reproduction processes 216–17, 225–33
research
    intellectual capital 223
    social evolution 1–2
resources
    environmental issues 327–30, 373, 374,
        378
    state ownership 269
Reuters 348
revolution
    France 405–6, 408, 409
    Gesellschaftsformation 70
    Marxism 77–84, 111
    post-industrialism 95, 111
    Russia 85, 86, 407–8, 409
rights, property 249, 257
Roman Empire
    destruction of 268
    philosophy 20–1
ruling class
    see also aristocracy; technocracy

intellect 294
  personal property 246
  post-industrial society 102
rural communities, disintegration of
  136, 137
Russia
  see also Soviet Union
  economic development of 361
  environmental issues 376
  Marxism 84–8
  pollution 374, 377
  Revolution 407–8, 409
Rwanda 382

scarcity, information/knowledge 220,
  221, 226, 227, 306
science, state investment in 269
sects 202
selectivity 221
self-development 152, 154–5, 156, 167,
  176, 181, 201
self-employment 165, 167, 181–2, 194,
  333
self-realization 183, 199, 241
  creativity 155, 175, 177, 179
  non-material interests 274, 278–9, 282,
    308, 413
  technological progress 323
  workers 181, 188
self-sufficiency 322, 327, 390–1
service sector 159, 160–7
  information 129, 217
  labour changes 287, 330–1
  post-industrialism 89, 93–4, 96–8,
    105–6
  productivity 230–2
shares
  see also financial flows
  employee 249–51, 252–4
  United States 339, 348–50
'sign economy' 228
Singapore 361, 362, 363–4, 365–6
  education 368
  wages 367
slavery 31, 48–9, 56
  Engels 67–8
  Stalin 85
  utopianism 33–4
small businesses 165–6, 167, 191–2, 194,
  333–4
  see also home-based businesses
social associations 200, 201–2
social conflict 272–305, 307–8, 309–10,
  322, 323, 414

social contract 28–32, 44–5
  Ancient Greek philosophy 20
  Christian theories of history 27
  critique of 47–8
  positivism 55
social division
  Christian theories 24
  information classes 102
  knowledge/ability criteria 173–4, 221,
    273–7, 285–6, 292–5, 303–5, 307–8,
    415
  utopianism 34–5
social formation 70–7, 81–4, 85, 86,
  110–11, 133
social goods 195–6
social institutions
  see also corporations
  post-industrial society 98, 100–1
  voluntary organizations 98, 101, 105,
    194, 195–203
social mobility 96
social progress
  see also Gesellschaftsformation
  Aquinas 42–4
  Christian theories of history 26, 27, 37
  coherent historical theories 59
  economic factors 47–51, 63, 76
  inadequate historical theories 15, 37
  market exchange 8
  Marxism 63, 70, 81
  ownership relations 50–1
  positivism 52–5, 56, 57–8
  post-industrial society 89, 95
  utopianism 33, 34, 35
social relations 45, 86, 417
  conflict 272–305, 307–8, 309–10, 322,
    323, 414
social responsibility, corporations 192–4
social revolution 77–8, 79, 80–4, 85, 111,
  139
social values 98, 99, 103
socialism 64, 75, 96
  competitiveness 242
  defeat of 408
  exploitation 274, 281
  labour 279–80
  Russian 86, 87
society
  conflicts 268, 269, 272–305
  cyclical development of 17–18, 19, 20–1
  definitions 129
  Hobbesian 30–1
  Marxism/post-industrialism
    comparison 110–12

material/non-material interests 4–6
organization theories of 129
periodization 4
social progress 51, 55–6
state 18–19
succession vs emergent theories 125,
    130–2
'technetronic' 97, 128–9, 289, 410
Thomism 43–4
utopianism 33–7
socioeconomic formation 85, 86
sociology 55, 411
sociopsychological factors 274, 281, 308
software 338
solar energy 327
South America 361–2
South Korea 326, 362, 363–4, 365, 366
education 368–9
national debt 387
pollution 377
standard of living 367
Southeast Asia 361–71
agriculture 385
economic power 334, 335–9, 339, 340,
    341–2
environmental issues 376
exports 326, 353–4
Western nations relationship 387
Soviet Union 366–7
see also Russia
state
Ancient Greek conception of 18–20
association 44
Christianity 24, 25, 27
financial regulation 351
Hobbesian 30–1
intervention 270–1
Modern Age philosophers 29, 30
ownership 249
post-industrial society 104
property 268–72
social conflict 305
utopianism 33–4
status 198–9, 200, 291
stock market 322, 326, 348–52
Japanese 364
stratification
knowledge/ability 173–4, 221, 273–7,
    285–6, 292–5, 303–5, 307–8, 415
'post-class capitalism' 291–2
subjectivity
historical theory 14
knowledge-value 236
social theories 403

succession (modification) theories 125,
    130–1, 132
superstructure 64, 78, 79, 82, 83, 86–7
Sweden 355
Switzerland 326, 341, 342
'symbolic capital' 101

Taiwan 326, 342, 365, 366
education 368–9
standard of living 367
teamwork 190
'technetronic' society 97, 128–9, 289, 410
technocracy 89, 101–2, 288–90, 304
technology
see also information technology
creative activity 308, 309
environmental issues 327–30, 374
executive incomes 298
GNP indicators 346
hi-tech industries 192, 223–4, 301–2,
    325, 340
information wealth 239
intellectual capital 223
Japan 336–7
Marxism/post-industrialism
    comparison 111
North-South divide 105
ownership 412
periodization 3–4
post-industrial society 89, 91, 94, 97,
    99, 107
productivity 162
progress 3–4, 56, 306, 319–20, 323–5,
    343–4
telecommunications 218, 258, 259, 266
unemployment 105–6
work 151
worker incomes 302
telecommunications 218, 258, 259, 266
terminology
economics 133–9, 237–8
work/labour 148–58
tertiary sector see service sector
Thailand 362, 363–4, 365, 367
'theory saturation' 114
third sector 196–7
see also non-profit organizations
Third Wave of historical change 131
Third World 105, 172–3, 359, 382, 393,
    416
see also developing countries; 'Fourth
    World'
aid programmes 378–9, 388
dryland areas 375

environmental issues 372, 376, 377–8
investment 341
urbanization 383–4
trade deficits 336, 353–4, 356
trade unions 103
transnational companies *see*
multinationals

unemployment 105–6, 331–2, 333, 334
United Nations 389
United States
aid programmes 378, 379
cooperatives 255–6
corporations 348
economic power 334–6, 337, 338–41,
358, 370
education 171–2, 300–1, 324, 368
Employee Stock Ownership Plan
(ESOP) 253–4
employment figures 218, 330–1,
333–4, 339
energy resources 328, 329
environmental issues 330, 373, 374,
375
Europe comparison 332
exports 326, 356, 357
GNP 324, 325, 328, 351, 353
income 347, 367
individualism 183
information sector 219
investments 251
national debt 354–5, 356
post-economic transformation 321
productivity 231–2
service sector 94, 96–7, 161, 162, 165–6
shares 348–9
small businesses 192
Southeast Asia comparison 362, 363
voluntary organizations 197–8, 200
wealth distribution 296–7, 298–9
unity
of action 44
Christian theories of history 23, 26
universal brotherhood 43
universities, Southeast Asia 368–9
unskilled labour 302–3
urbanization, Third World 383–4
utility
exchange value 215–16
labour 234
utopianism 32–6, 273, 274, 411

value
commodity production 214

destruction of 217, 224, 225–39, 306–7,
322, 411, 417
exchange/use conflict 215
intellectual capital 223–4
knowledge 235–6, 262
labour theory of 94, 164, 225
terminological variations 237–8
values
see also interests
Asian 362–3
non-economic/post-materialist
169–70, 178, 242, 284–5, 292, 295,
304–5, 308
social 98, 99, 103
Western 388
Vietnam 362, 367
voluntary organizations 98, 101, 105,
194, 195–203

wages *see* income
war 29, 31, 32, 405
civil 382
wealth
distribution of 276, 295–303, 304, 413
knowledge as 392
value relationship 238–9
welfare state 271
well-being
material 168, 169–70, 282–3
quality of life 228–9
work
see also employment; labour
creativity 147, 148–58, 175
freedom from 280
workers
see also knowledge workers
autonomy 180–3
class 286–7
company ownership 249, 254–6
company shares 249–50, 252–4, 256
corporations 185–6, 187–8
creativity 177
income inequality 301–3
international wage differences 367
motivation 179
personality development 191
productivity 163, 188–9
redundancy 276
standard of living 258
voluntary organization membership
199–200
working class *see* proletariat

Yamaguchi Securities 338

Name Index

Adams, F. 255
Albert the Great 57
Althusser, Louis 289
Antiphon 18
Applewhite, M.H. 202
Aquinas, St Thomas 22, 24, 26, 31–2,
   42–4, 45, 55, 57, 59
Arendt, Hannah 149
Aristotle 19–20, 22, 31, 42, 43
Aron, Raymond 89–90, 110–11
Augustine, St 24–6, 42, 45, 59, 403, 404

Bacon, Francis 14, 44, 45
Bacon, Roger 57
Baudrillard, Jean 351
Bell, Daniel 90, 98, 107, 109, 110, 112, 127
   abstract analysis 130
   class 96
   corporate capital 265
   decentralization 189
   economics 133
   freedom 140
   individuals 240, 275
   interpersonal games 156
   knowledge 172
   non-economic values 242
   non-profit sector 196
   ownership 257
   pre-industrial society 92–3
   public services 228–9
   service sector 97
   'sociologizing' 100, 160, 185
   succession 131, 132
   technocrats 289
   work 151, 152
Bert, F. 151
Birch, David 161, 333–4
Blanqui, A. 35–6
Bonaparte, Napoleon 406
Bramer, William 300–1

Branson, Richard 188
Braudel, F. 91–2, 135
Brzezinski, Zbigniew 90, 97, 109, 128,
   321, 356
Bush, George 354

Campanella, Tommaso 33–4
Cannon, Tom 186, 188, 370
Castells, Manuel 281
Chesterton, G.K. 171
Clark, Colin 89
Clinton, Bill 354
Cobb, J.B. 346
Comte, Auguste 42, 52, 55–7, 59, 88, 411
Condillac, Étienne Bonnot de 64
Condorcet, Jean-Antoine de 52, 64, 88,
   128, 405, 407
Conell 289
Cooper, Anthony Ashley see
   Shaftesbury, Third Earl of
Cumberland, R. 32, 44

Dahrendorf, Ralf 90, 185, 275, 288–9,
   290–1
Daly, H.E. 346
Dante, Aligheri 57
Democritus 18, 21, 41–2
Descartes, René 45
Dopsch, A. 134
Drucker, Peter 90, 99, 171, 258, 266, 275,
   288
   education 300
   environmental issues 330
   investments 252
   knowledge workers 165, 173, 180,
      259–60, 263, 282, 293
   management 187
   manufacturing industry 162, 163
   non-economic needs 178, 183
   third sector organizations 197, 198, 199

Edvinsson, Lief 222
Ellul, Jacques 151, 291
Engels, Frederick 52, 63, 64, 86, 88, 110, 211
    class 66–7
    labour 65, 69
    revolution 77–8, 80–3, 86, 111, 113
    slavery 67–8
    value 226
Epicurus 21
Etzioni 107, 197, 198–9
Eusebius Caesarienus 25

Ferguson, Adam 47, 48, 64, 65, 405
Feuerbach, Ludwig Andreas 64
Ford, Henry 258
Fourastié, Jean 89, 90
Fourier, Charles 34–5, 36, 64, 411
Francis Victoria 27
Fukuyama, Francis 149, 183, 190, 293

Galbraith, John K. 148, 149, 180, 184, 270, 279, 296, 325
Garnier, J. 234
Garten, J.E. 351
Gates, Bill 188, 259, 265, 298, 302
Gershuny, Jonathan 162
Glaser, Hermann 152
Gore, Albert 346, 375, 379
Gorz, André 151, 280, 287
Gouldner 289
Greider, William 354, 370
Grotius, Hugo 29, 44

Habermas, Jürgen 176
Hammer, Michael 179, 185–6, 187, 189–90, 263
Handy, C. 265
Hansen, G. 255
Harvey, D. 186
Hegel, G.W.F. 403
Heilbroner, Robert 90, 151–2, 233, 281, 297, 381
Herder, Johann Gottfried 46, 88
Hesiod 18
Hobbes, Thomas 29–31, 45, 405
Horowitz 112
Hudson, William 222
Hume, David 50–1, 59, 64

Inglehart, Ronald 169, 173, 178, 194, 275, 277, 291, 292

Jacques, Elliott 148, 149, 152

Jevons, W.S. 234

Kahn, H. 90, 112, 133
Katz, R.L. 128
Kautsky, Karl 82
Krugman, P. 366
Kuhn, J.W. 201–2
Kumar, K. 128
Kuttner, Robert 299

Lactantius 24, 42
Lash, Scott 225
Lenin, Vladimir Ilyich 63, 84–5, 87, 88
Lichteim, J. 90
Linstone, Harold 231
Locke, John 44, 45, 59, 149
Lucretius 21
Luther, Martin 26–7
Lyotard, Jean-François 180, 215

Machiavelli, Nicholas 29, 31
Machlup, F. 128
McRae, H. 297
Malone, Michael 222
Marcus Aurelius 417
Marshall, Alfred 140, 150, 234
Martin, W.J. 227
Marx, Karl 52, 63–88, 96, 110–13, 211, 403
    alienation 279
    class 172, 278, 287
    corporations 185
    labour training 258
    oekonomische Gesellschaftsformation 133, 137, 214
    value 225, 226
    work 149, 150
Maslow, Abraham 179
Masuda, Y. 90, 128, 235
Meadows, Dennis L. 329, 360
Meadows, Donella H. 329, 360
Mendels, F.F. 92
Mill, John Stuart 55, 57–8, 88, 234
Mitroff, Ian 231
Montchrestien 136
Montesquieu, Charles Louis de Secondat 45
More, Thomas 33–4
Morrison, Ian 369

Naisbitt, John 90, 150, 186, 191, 266, 275
Nicholson, W. 221
Nonaka, Ikujiro 181
Nuernberger, P. 156

Owen, Robert 64, 411

Pakulski, Jan 275
Penty, A. 126
Perkin, Harold 90, 271
Plato 18–19, 20
Plotinus 21
Polybius 20–1, 29
Ponyatovski, M. 90
Porat, M 128
Proclus 21, 31

Reagan, Ronald 298, 324
Reich, Robert 300, 340
Renner, Karl 287
Riesman, David 90, 126
Rifkin, Jeremy 90, 153, 197, 198, 331
Robertson, James 176
Roddick, Anita 188
Rostow, Walt 90
Rousseau, Jean-Jacques 45–6, 64, 135, 245

St Paul 22
Saint-Simon, Claude-Henri de Rouvroy, comte de 52–5, 59, 64, 88, 128, 138
Sakaiya, Taichi 161–2, 236, 261–2
Sayer, Andrew 201
Scott 289
Seidenberg, R. 90
Servan-Schreiber, J.-J. 90, 111
Shaftesbury, Third Earl of (Anthony Ashley Cooper) 46–7, 64, 407
Shriver, D.W. 201–2
Smith, Adam 47, 48–9, 51, 59, 64, 65, 88, 149, 278, 405
Soboul, A. 92
Spinoza, Benedict de 45
Stagirite 19, 20, 22
Stalin, Josef 85–7, 88
Stehr, Nico 228, 257
Stonier, T. 90, 128, 235, 277

Tacitus 21, 22
Takeuchi, Hirotaka 181
Tertullian 24, 25, 27
Thurow, Lester C. 189
Toffler, Alvin 90, 104, 107, 109, 241–2, 266
 'ad-hocracy' 290
 'cognitariat' 172
 commodity production 241
 company ownership 265
 corporations 186, 191
 division of labour 240
 employment 165, 182
 freedom of choice 168
 individual ability 275
 information economy 181
 knowledge 170
 modular specialization 190
 motivation 178
 pre-industrial society 92
 production 160
 'prosumerism' 167, 229–30
 social processes 281
 society definition 129, 130
 Third Wave 131, 132, 292
 unemployment 334
 value 235, 238
Toffler, Heidi 235, 238, 334
Touraine, Alain 107, 129, 360
 social conflict 291
 technocracy 289
Touraine, Alaine
 creativity 156–7
 freedom 170
 professional class 288
Turgot, J. 47, 48–9, 52, 64
Turner 291

Umesao 128

van Kemenade, W. 357
Varro 136
Veblen, Thorstein 89
Voltaire 407

Walker, Richard 201
Walton, T. 265
Waters, M. 326–7
Waters, Malcolm 275
Weber, Max 138
Webster, Frank 168–9
Weitling, W. 35–6
Weizsaecker, Ernst U. von 302, 373
Wilde, Oscar 10
Winslow, Charles 300–1

Young, M. 96
Young, T. 289

Zasulich, Vera 71, 73, 83, 110